Questions
of Communication

A Practical Introduction to Theory

Questions of Communication

A Practical Introduction to Theory

THIRD EDITION

Rob Anderson
Saint Louis University

Veronica Ross
Greenville College

Bedford/St. Martin's
Boston • New York

For Bedford/St. Martin's

Communication Editor: Jennifer Bartlett
Developmental Editor: Jeannine Thibodeau
Senior Production Editor: Harold Chester
Senior Production Supervisor: Joe Ford
Marketing Manager: Richard Cadman
Art Director: Lucy Krikorian
Text Design: Eriben Graphics
Cover Design: Robin Hoffmann
Composition: Stratford Publishing Services, Inc.
Printing and Binding: R. R. Donnelley & Sons Company

President: Charles H. Christensen
Editorial Director: Joan E. Feinberg
Publisher for History, Political Science, and Communication: Patricia Rossi
Director of Marketing: Karen R. Melton
Director of Editing, Design, and Production: Marcia Cohen
Managing Editor: Erica T. Appel

Library of Congress Control Number: 2001090563

Manufactured in the United States of America.

7 6 5 4 3 2
f e d c b a

For information, write: Bedford/St. Martin's, 75 Arlington Street, Boston, MA 02116 (617-399-4000)

ISBN: 0-312-25080-0

Acknowledgments

Acknowledgments and copyrights appear at the back of the book on page 239, which constitutes an extension of the copyright page.

Preface

Writing, it seems to us, is a mixture of experience, listening, and preparation—to which we add quite a few lonely hours and a great deal of guesswork. We're not just writing for ourselves, but from ourselves for others. But one of the joys of textbook authors is that we receive the kind of feedback that at least reduces the guesswork.

When a book finds its niche, as *Questions of Communication* evidently has done, readers are not reluctant to tell you what works for them and what doesn't. We have invited feedback, and we appreciate the effort that it takes. Going into a third edition, we're still flattered and pleased that so many students and teachers, at so many different kinds of campuses, have found the book's tone and readability appropriate for their needs. We are deeply indebted to them for their support. A new edition gives us the opportunity to explore new ideas and to refine previous ones, to sharpen the writing in some places, and to update examples where necessary. Even with all the changes, however, the philosophy that guided the first edition remains constant. We're convinced that a communication theory course can be inviting and accessible while also being intellectually rigorous.

Assumptions

Our philosophy of accessible rigor is not an oxymoron, but it does depend on certain assumptions about education. One such assumption is the need for integration. Despite the importance of clear distinctions, we assume classes should spend more time tying concepts and process together than pulling them apart. We attempt to support the former kind of teaching and learning, while recognizing that students should enter the disciplinary conversation with reasonably clear definitions of concepts. Otherwise, communication theory courses, if we don't watch out, can devolve into a batch of little theory packets and bullet-point lists that students must memorize in order to get a good grade.

Our second assumption is that both students and teachers are curious about how communication works. Not everyone is. Many are content to ignore why some friends understand them more readily than others, or why some relationships are satisfying when others fall flat. Some people don't particularly care if electronic media might be changing how they perceive the world or why certain messages might be ethically defensible when others are not. However, students majoring in communication are curious about these kinds of issues and, we've found, are willing to exercise their intellectual curiosity when sincerely invited to do so. Although it is important to know the skills of communicating (e.g., public speaking, interpersonal sensitivity, small group decision making, and interviewing), skills alone are not enough for a specialist in communication. At the same time, students may lose their enthusiasm for the field if they encounter too much abstraction all at once. We think students should be introduced to theory in practical contexts that are relevant for their own life stories.

Therefore, we also assume that students look for ways to be active learners, not passive receivers, and that they respond to texts that blend concepts into narratives that serve as foundations for application. This book isn't primarily intended for sophisticated researchers or for theoretically savvy advanced students. New undergraduate communication majors will have plenty of opportunities to probe the intricacies of specific theories in upper-level courses. Here, we want to introduce the theories by respecting and attempting to address students' real questions. Somewhat more streamlined in scope and more conversational in tone than most theory books, this text is appropriate for lower-level nonskills courses in communication theory, which are often among the first courses a student takes in the discipline. The book is also suitable as a main text in courses that introduce and survey the landscape of the discipline.

Our Approach

We believe that a unique approach distinguishes this book from the many excellent communication theory texts on the market:

- We emphasize the role of questioning more than the compulsion for answering or resolving every question. Knowledge is built more by developing the ability to ask and seek answers to intelligent questions than by receiving answers from presumed experts. Focused questioning is the one theme that most consistently cuts across methodological and theoretical camps in studying communication. Although as authors we take broadly interpretive, qualitative, and applied roles in our own scholarly work, we also have a healthy respect for quantitative and behavioral social science research. Genuinely helpful communication theorizing is motivated by systematic approaches to phenomena, whether those approaches are quantitative, qualitative, or (increasingly) both.
- We emphasize that theory and practice are not opposites, but two ways of looking at the same process—the process of learning. Effective theories help communication specialists with such practical tasks as writing, reading, speaking, and listening.
- We emphasize the role of students as learners in the context of higher education. Our explanations include numerous examples and research findings specifically relevant to the campus context.
- We emphasize that communication theory is not a disciplinary possession but an enterprise that unites many scholars in the humanities and social sciences. Therefore, this book supports a broadly based general education or liberal arts philosophy. In other words, we argue that the most practical education is liberalizing and expansive, and that through it, we can improve the dialogue among the disciplines.
- We emphasize the need to clarify and integrate theoretical concepts, rather than enumerate many of the diverse categories, terms, and abstractions that are more appropriately covered in advanced courses. We believe that introductory students should be excited by the possibilities of their subject, not intimidated by elaborate lists of concepts and subconcepts. Of

course some brief lists are inevitable in presenting information in an organized way.

- We emphasize a narrative tone, talking readers through basic ideas and encouraging new and individualized questions. In addition, we occasionally (as in our explanations of cultural theory and persuasion) illustrate ideas through narratives interwoven throughout a chapter; the narrative helps readers relate their learning to real-life problems.

- We emphasize that ethics can be a generalized framework for communication problems and choices. Chapter 10 is devoted to ethical theory and philosophy, but ethical issues are important in all chapters.

- We emphasize the interdependence of many communication theories and concepts by boxed "Links" inserted throughout the text. These are designed to call attention to where various topics are discussed in different ways elsewhere, and to reinforce for students that theorizing is a cooperative venture that cuts across boundaries and traditions. A student's good experience in previous general education core courses (literature, philosophy, history, science, and others) will pay dividends in our brand of communication theory experience.

In addition, three special sections appear at the end of each chapter to help students and teachers refine their questions about relevant concepts:

- "Reviewing Key Theories." This feature, new to this edition, succinctly summarizes how important theories relate to each other. Students can use these sections to double-check how well they understand the big picture of each chapter, and they will be reminded of connections between theories and research traditions as well.

- "Testing the Concepts." We employ a question-and-answer format to focus students' attention on particularly important or interesting topics. We include these questions, which are similar to or nearly identical to those asked by students in our classes, in order to test the implications and practicality of chapter content from a student perspective. The questions and responses should also generate further questions and class dialogue—and maybe an argument or two.

- "You, the Researcher." These sections include a wide range of projects and activities designed to stimulate students' out-of-class investigation and exploration of related topics. Students are asked, for example, to conduct informal research that could stimulate class discussion or personal reflection, or to do more formal studies in which they collect data through interviews, mini-experiments, and observations perhaps for a research paper or report. Each chapter presents several projects from which the student or teacher can select one or more that are appropriate to the course. These activities illustrate the range of communication research, thereby reinforcing the researcher's role in theory building. We hope students realize in this way that theorists don't specialize in armchair noodling, but are also active investigators. In the introduction to "You, the Researcher" in Chapter 1, we include some guidelines for research that involves human participants.

Major Changes for the Third Edition

Although we retain the approach and basic themes of the book, readers of the second edition will notice quite a few differences in this new edition. We want the book to be even more accessible and readable. Specifically, the third edition includes the following major changes:

- A new chapter, "'How Do We Work Together toward Common Goals?': Theorizing Organizational Communication" (Chapter 6), introduces students to the tradition of organizational communication now popular in many curricula. Numerous departments offer stand-alone courses in organizational communication, public relations, training, conflict management, and small group communication that will be supported directly by this introductory theoretical material. The chapter focuses on three broad traditions—management-based, systems-based, and discourse-based theorizing. More specifically, we present scientific management theory, administrative theory, the contributions of the Hawthorne studies, Theory Y, bureaucratic theory, homeostatic theory, structuration theory, conversational autonomy theory, organizational culture theory, workplace democracy theory, and feminist organizational theory.

- A reorganized chapter, "'How and Why Do We Create Relationships?': Theorizing Interpersonal Communication" (Chapter 5), merges the former chapter-length topics of relational interdependence and rules theories. Although we found the previous organization workable, we believe many teachers will appreciate a more unified opportunity to introduce the rich theories of interpersonal life.

- A new feature, "Reviewing Key Theories," helps students understand how ideas build on each other systematically. In effect, each chapter now has two kinds of summaries, serving different functions. While "Testing the Concepts" summarizes especially intriguing points by answering representative student questions, "Reviewing Key Theories" summarizes how important theories relate to each other.

- A greatly expanded "Glossary," revised on the advice of a number of students, helps students keep track of necessary terminology. As teachers, we have been somewhat suspicious over the years about glossaries full of nugget definitions. Do they help students solidify their awareness of concept nuances (a pretty good result), or do they just supply a list of legislated oversimplifications that undercut students' knowledge in the long run (a subversive result)? Here, our goal continues to be to frame these terms as an "access vocabulary" with which students can enter the discipline's conversation about communication, not as the final word on any of these important concepts. No glossary or dictionary can ever adequately contextualize complex ideas, but good glossaries encourage helpful check-backs after which a reader can revisit a longer section with greater clarity.

- A series of important conceptual additions enhances this edition. In addition to the significant new organizational theories presented in Chapter 6, many topics receive fresh or expanded attention in the third edition of *Questions of Communication:* agenda-setting, co-cultural theory, communibiology, compliance-gaining and interpersonal persuasion, coordinated management of meaning, cultural studies, diffusion of innovations, etic and emic research approaches, expectancy-violations, medium theory, online contexts, public journalism, standpoint theory, and symbolic convergence.

Appreciations

Families matter. They are certainly the foundation, and at times the backstop, for all we do. This book is no exception. Again, we want to thank publicly Dona, Eric, and Neil Anderson, and Stephen, Corey, Chris, Jennifer, Alexa, and Andrew Ross.

Many of the earliest reviewers of this text were our questioning and thoughtful students at Saint Louis University, Greenville College, Southern Illinois University Edwardsville, and the University of South Florida. They went beyond remembering concepts to involve themselves in genuine learning. You will meet them indirectly in these pages; their curiosity and respect for ideas actually stimulated our desire to write a theory text years ago. Dr. Rob Drew of Saginaw Valley State University invited a group of his theory students to review the book for us, and they were generous, supportive, and perceptive in their suggestions. Thanks to Anne McDonald, Michael Van Dyke, Mark D. Covel, Kara Fiebke, and Kathryn R. Bremmer for their efforts. People who work closely with committed students will not be surprised to hear that their critiques were as perceptive and helpful as many of the solicited faculty reviews assessing the book over the years.

Colleagues recently have helped us in important ways. For example, Dr. Peggy Bowers and Dr. John Pauly at Saint Louis University have shared their experiences teaching communication theory classes with this book, and the new edition is better because of their feedback.

One colleague who is no longer with us, Bob Hawkins, deserves special recognition, and we would like to dedicate this text to his memory. Years ago, when one of us (R.A.) was a young teacher more or less adrift in academe, Bob exemplified open curiosity in a senior faculty member. Although already successful and comfortable in his profession, Bob reoriented his career by taking on new academic specialties, and new learning. He wasn't afraid to become the rookie or to look foolish, and therefore displayed, it seems, the most extraordinary kind of wisdom. Bob was a teacher who was forever the questioning student, forever the gracious cross-cultural host (or stranger), forever the gentle advocate for other learners who hadn't yet found their voices. Forever the listening friend who would accept you no matter how stupidly you acted, he also was never the put-down artist or showy performer. Few of us are fortunate enough to have known such teachers.

The editors, staff, and reviewers at Bedford/St. Martin's have encouraged us consistently in writing this book. Communication editors Tisha Rossi and Jeannine Thibodeau have provided expert support as the project progressed and, just as important, friendship. Harold Chester, our production editor, was extremely helpful in coordinating dozens of manuscript and design decisions. We are also grateful to the reviewers engaged by Bedford/St. Martin's. They provided helpful feedback to improve this edition, although we remain responsible for goofs, slip-ups, and any generalized short-sightedness that might still mar the book. (Here's a fact of academic life. We took all suggestions seriously, but couldn't take all suggestions. Some reviewers may say, "That's still there? I told them to bag it." Bless them; they may be right. But for each such instance, it seemed, several others told us, "This works well for my class." Bless them, too.) The reviewers we appreciate so much are: David Brenders, DePaul University; Rob Drew, Saginaw Valley State University; Robert Huesca, Trinity University; Charles Pavitt, University of Delaware; Don W. Stacks, University of Miami; Wayne Wanta, University of Oregon; and J. Macgregor Wise, Clemson University.

Rob Anderson
Veronica Ross

Contents

PART TWO: OUTER AND INNER FORMS OF COMMUNICATION

PART THREE: SOCIAL, CULTURAL, AND PUBLIC FORMS OF COMMUNICATION

Chapter 5   **"HOW AND WHY DO WE CREATE RELATIONSHIPS?" 136**
Theorizing Interpersonal Communication

PART FOUR: ISSUES OF ETHICS AND COHERENCE IN COMMUNICATION

Questions
of Communication
A Practical Introduction to Theory

Jean-Claude LeJeune/Stock, Boston

Introduction:
"Why Study Communication?"

Reasons for Learning and Ways of Knowing

Some Direct Talk about How Textbooks Are Written

The Doubting Game and the Believing Game

Stages and Types of Learning
Perry's Harvard Study
Belenky and Colleagues' *Women's Ways of Knowing* Study

Knowledge in an Ethical Framework

Reviewing Key Theories

Testing the Concepts

All thoughtful inquiry, and hence all useful education, starts with questioning.
All usable knowledge, and thus all practical science, starts with the provisional
acceptance of answers. Education is a dialectic in moderation in which probing and
accepting, questioning and answering, must achieve a delicate balance.

BENJAMIN R. BARBER, *An Aristocracy of Everyone* (1992, p. 110)

Some Direct Talk about How Textbooks Are Written

Political scientist Benjamin Barber's comment about education captures the spirit of our book as well as anything we've read. Learning begins with curiosity, with not knowing something that you think you might need. That's the impulse, we think, for a class, a lesson, a training session, or any other situation in which we gather together in order to learn. Anyone who wants to learn can benefit from being with other curious learners, preferably those who can model the process of asking questions and listening alertly for possible answers.

After decades of learning and teaching about communication, we've noticed that sometimes people don't understand our excitement about the behind-the-scenes reasons that make the communication process interesting and involving. Communication students typically enjoy meeting people and look forward to learning how they can speak and listen more effectively in their every-day lives. Learning about communication is a stimulating opportunity to learn about people. Meeting people is an indispensable part of an education in communication.

However, consider another side to the study of communication, one that applies to students who intend to specialize in communication—as managers, trainers, teachers, personnel directors, or public-relations practitioners, for example. If this applies to you, then keep in mind that your co-workers, clients, and fellow students will expect you to function effectively as a resource and, occasionally, as a troubleshooter. Thus, in addition to good communication skills you will need to develop an awareness of communication as a broad area of study. Speaking, listening, writing, and reading skills are not enough. Effective communication specialists are also able to suggest workable alternatives, direct people to helpful readings, and explain interpersonal and public communication topics clearly without being simplistic. Our premise in this book is that communication study is a complex, intellectually exciting, and pragmatic calling. Let's examine this statement claim by claim. First, studying communication is complex because human society is ultimately founded on **communication**, which we will define for now as the development of shared meaning through messages. What human activity, then, is unrelated? Almost everything from solitary contemplation through the most carefully coordinated advertising campaign can be understood by considering its relationship to communication. Specific behaviors such as complimenting a friend or choosing a class to take have communication implications, as do general cultural patterns such as preferences for certain types of art or literature.

Second, communication study is intellectually exciting in part because it poses a paradox, a situation of self-contradiction in which an assertion or a recommendation cannot logically be possible. For example, the request "Be spontaneous!" is paradoxical because if it is followed literally, the listener would not behave spontaneously (Watzlawick, Weakland, & Fisch, 1974, pp. 62–73). Similarly, we inevitably experience paradoxes as we study communication by communicating about it. Although this sounds odd, the problem—which researchers term **reflexivity**—is common and unavoidable. The dilemma it poses is similar to that of a person with poor eyesight trying to see his or her glasses clearly. The person needs the glasses in order to see in the first place, yet he or she wants to see the glasses clearly, too. If you hope to analyze how human language works, can you escape using language to analyze itself?

Curiosity leads us to question our lives; it seems natural to wonder "why?" when we are confronted with our own existence. In his well-known book *The Lives of a Cell* (1974), biologist Lewis Thomas discusses the dilemmas of human personality, mind, and language. For example, you might assume that it would be useful for communicators to strive for precision (and often you'd be right). Yet, paradoxically, according to Thomas, too much precision creates problems:

> *Ambiguity seems to be an essential, indispensable element for the transfer of information from one place to another by words, where matters of real importance are concerned. It is often necessary, for meaning to come through, that there be an almost vague sense of strangeness and askewness. Speechless animals and cells cannot do this. The specifically locked-on antigen at the surface of a lymphocyte does not send the cell off in search of something totally different; when a bee is tracking sugar by polarized light, observing the sun as though consulting his watch, he does not veer away to discover an unimaginable marvel of a flower. Only the human mind is designed to work in this way, programmed to drift away in the presence of locked-on information, straying from each point in a hunt for a better, different point.*
>
> *If it were not for the capacity for ambiguity, for the sensing of strangeness, that words in all languages provide, we would have no way of recognizing the layers of counterpoint in meaning. (pp. 94–95)*

Although we will never see the glasses clearly, we shouldn't become discouraged by the paradox and quit looking. Simply asking questions that yield ambiguous answers creates a condition of learning. It would be tempting to think of a communication theory book as a collection of things that we know for certain. Tempting, but misleading. Actually, this book is closer to an exploration of the questions we believe the discipline is most interested in answering now. If it's a collection of anything, it collects clues to what we don't know but are trying to understand better.

We are doing something essentially human when we explore questions that have no set answers. According to Thomas (1983), the shared ground inhabited by those who study social life is "bewilderment": "What we have been learning in our time is that we really do not understand this place or how it works, and we comprehend our own selves least of all. And the more we learn, the more we are—or ought to be—dumbfounded" (p. 157). In order to learn anything new, we must first learn to respect the mysteries, and then to place ourselves near those who ask the questions that address the mysteries. Saying that you are interested in communication without being curious about, and often bewildered by, the "whys" behind it seems to be a contradiction of terms.

Third, communication study is pragmatic. Later we'll develop an argument for how practical communication theory can be, but you should know that we recognize no distinct boundary between theory and practice. These terms, which suggest emphases or approaches in learning, are interdependent. A theory cannot be taken seriously unless it is linked to concrete experience and put into practice. Conversely, concrete experience, to be useful, has to be evaluated, generalized, and made transferable to new situations. Theory-building is our method for accomplishing this transfer.

Finally, communication study can be thought of as a calling. Scientist-philosopher Michael Polanyi (1962) observed that some personal commitments seem to come from both external and internal sources. A **calling**, as he discussed it, emerges from a situation to which someone must form a response, an external circumstance that the person discovers is relevant to the self and worthy of commitment. Its existence is neither wholly objective and external nor wholly subjective and internal but personal. That is, a calling develops from someone's particular perception of what is important in the world. It's not caused; it just seems to develop gradually. However, people can solidify a calling by the substance of their choices. We've noticed that many of our students choose their majors, and thus their careers, in roughly this way. Although studying communication at first seems to be the "right thing" to do, students are not yet clear about the exact nature of their commitment. They find some classes and assignments more interesting, relevant, or useful than others. To respond to the calling, we suggest that you investigate the full range of commitments it requires. Someone who enjoys meeting people and for whom interpersonal communication is "fun" may, on that basis alone, choose a communication major. But a communication specialist needs to possess much more than basic communication skills or a pleasant disposition. Interactional and intellectual commitments are both essential.

Most readers will encounter *Questions of Communication* in an undergraduate class for communication majors that emphasizes ideas rather than skills. Skills are important, but they're emphasized elsewhere in the curriculum. While reading this book, you'll be able to decide the extent to which you'll join in the intellectual curiosity that supports the calling you've tentatively chosen. We hope that through these chapters you'll come to understand that asking questions about the ambiguities of human communication can be challenging and interesting.

As authors, we will make several assumptions that may seem unusual at first (this is the "direct talk" mentioned in the heading for this section). We hope you'll think carefully about what these assumptions will mean for you:

1. *You— as students— are the primary audience for this book.* That is, when writing, we let the needs of students guide us. Our central "question of communication" was "How can students best merge the intellectual and the interactional facets of their calling?"

2. *You aren't the only audience for this book.* In the text, we also address the concerns of those who teach communication theory courses as a forum for ideas that range across the social sciences and the humanities. These faculty have direct experience in advising students on how to integrate ideas so that the broad shape of liberal arts learning is emphasized. We've tried to provide stimulating raw material for that synthesis, while also covering the range of topics traditionally associated with communication theory. In addition, our audience includes any reader who is interested in learning more about communication.

3. *The chapters are meant to be easy to read.* This is relative, of course. Comic books would be easier to read. So would *People* magazine. Quantum physics and continental postmodern philosophy are likely to be harder. But we understand that the specialized terminology of social science, however necessary, can intimidate readers. The text invites you into that language without drowning you in its detail. Wherever possible, we introduce ideas by discussing examples and practical applications in direct everyday language (not just with technical definitions). You might think of this book as a doorway into communication theory, where you will learn much about the topic but not all the details you may eventually want to know. We provide some brief lists to help you understand the shape of an idea. But generally we avoid long laundry lists of the seven factors of this and the six exceptions to that, and we also bypass most of the ins and outs of academic hairsplitting and infighting. The discipline's many professional journals provide lively forums for discussion and argument. Students who are intrigued by the concepts in this book will be better prepared to investigate the professional literature.

4. *The chapters are also meant to be hard to read.* We don't apologize for this. A simplistic narrative account of a complex concept only trivializes learning. Part of the responsibility for your understanding of the concepts in this book is ours, and the other part is yours. We are guided here by E. F. Schumacher's (1979) explanation of the classical notion of **adaequatio:** In any situation that calls for learning or appreciation (a class or a symphony, a novel or a parlor game), the perceiver must be at least adequate to the demands of the situation or its messages will seem meaningless, the way a foreign language might sound like gibberish and its writing appear to be mere squiggles on paper. For example, it's easy for someone who knows nothing about classical music or the structure of symphonies to listen to Beethoven and then proclaim, "This is boring and too hard to listen to—a bad piece of music." It's easy to say that Picasso is a poor artist if the observer refuses to learn anything about the kind of art that Picasso is attempting. This doesn't mean that criticism is out of bounds or unjustifiable. Rather, it means that critics should be responsible enough to make themselves adequate to comprehend the nuances of messages. Think of a topic in which you are "adequate" in terms of Schumacher's notion of *adaequatio*. If you're a jazz musician, you would wince at hearing someone describe jazz as "all sounding alike." If you're a fan of

science-fiction literature, you would consider it unfair if someone new to the field dismissed Isaac Asimov and Octavia Butler, two very different writers, for the same reasons.

Try to avoid blaming or praising particular communication theories too soon, at least until you've done your best to understand the system of thought to which you're responding. This might require that you reread sections of the book that you find difficult or look up the meaning of unfamiliar words in a dictionary or the text's glossary. Remember, part of your education involves responding to, not just receiving, information and knowledge. This leads us to a valuable distinction between two types of responding that should help you in your studies.

The Doubting Game and the Believing Game

Many people use the noun *intellectual* as a put-down, as a synonym for what used to be called an "egghead." Intellectuals, to some, are people who live only "in the mind," people who are not sufficiently connected to the real world to know the differences between common sense and ivory-tower abstraction. Some intellectuals are probably like that.

When we say that communication theory is an intellectual study, we are using that term in a precise way. To Peter Elbow (1973), an intellectual is "someone who tries to figure out what is true by means of the best processes available, and uses them in a rational, disciplined way to try to avoid deluding himself" (p. 148).[1] If this is what an intellectual does, then Diane Sawyer is an intellectual journalist, Spike Lee's movies are intellectually motivated, and Barbra Streisand manages her career as both an entertainer and an intellectual. In other words, intellectuals do not live entirely in their heads but are grounded in practical experience as they use their full mental potential.

Elbow (1973), a well-known writing teacher, reinforces two attitudes that are central to intellectual life when he refers to the doubting game and the believing game. By "games," Elbow means that we not only hold these attitudes in our heads but also use them to develop rules for acting in the world (much like the rules of board games). The games are described in this introduction to provide a better handle on what you'll be asked to do in your course. Any significant learning, Elbow claims, ultimately depends on the willingness to play both the doubting and the believing games.

The **doubting game** has profoundly influenced modern scientific research. In fact, the meaning of science has in many ways been defined through doubting. When you "play" the doubting game, you look for errors, find faults, and try to pick apart whatever you're looking at so that you can see what's wrong. Doubt, in this sense, emphasizes logic, method, technique, precise control, definition,

---

[1]We use gender-neutral language, and suggest this practice to students out of fairness, accuracy, and a sense of gender equality. However, some otherwise relevant quotations predate this usage, or their authors have made different stylistic decisions. We have chosen to present such statements in their original form, without making the value judgment (by inserting "[sic]" or by other means) that the authors were mistaken.

and analysis. In a doubting game approach, the world is sliced into segments so that its flaws and problems can be noticed more readily. Someone playing the intellectual doubting game responds to a new idea with skepticism: "What's wrong with it? When won't it work? Who can't use it?"

If you play the **believing game**, however, you find out that belief is more than the absence of doubt (Elbow, 1973). The object of the believing game is not to disprove but to support and clarify. Therefore when you are confronted with a surprising, disagreeable, or ambiguous message, a believing-game communicator's first response might be "In what ways is this true?" or "How could this make good sense from the other person's point of view?" The believing game assumes a willingness to suspend doubt, argumentation, and premature conclusions in favor of momentarily accepting the plausibility of another person's position.

Although both approaches are reasonable in different contexts and are often interdependent, the believing game may be more central to such tasks as understanding and building communication theories and doing literary criticism. Moreover, the believing game often sets the stage for the doubting game; we can be realistic in our distrust of a concept only after a sincere attempt has been made to perceive it as valid in the same way and in the same spirit in which it was offered.

Consider an example from a family counseling context. A young boy complains to the counselor that his parents never listen to him. One response (based on the doubting game) might involve doubting the boy's memory or sincerity and correcting his error: "But just the other day your mom and dad sat in this office and listened to you complain for twenty minutes!" Such a strategy might be intended to help the boy understand that his complaint is not reasonable. Another approach (based on the believing game) would focus on tentatively accepting his perception even though the external evidence seems to deny it. Perhaps then the counselor would discover that the boy's meaning for "listening" involves a certain kind of responsiveness that his parents haven't given. Only by establishing the potential believability of the boy's position can that position be disproved, or shown to be valid. Whether he's right or wrong, he feels ignored, and that's his reality. Until he is confirmed at some level, he'll miss the validity of alternative views, and so will the counselor and his parents. In other words, in situations where meanings are uniquely constructed and personally held, the doubting game must be tempered by the believing game.

The study of communication involves much more than memorizing the meaning of terms associated with various theories. Recall is not what developing theoretical appreciation is all about. Instead, *Questions of Communication* will help you become a better critic of communication and, ultimately, a better theorist yourself. You'll still need to master a basic vocabulary if you are to become "adequate" to discuss the theories. But as you read you should be both a believer and a doubter. Believe that these theories made good sense to their originators and followers and in the context of the theorists' assumptions about human behavior. Unless your background knowledge and creativity approximate those of the theorists, the believing game is absolutely essential (although this assumption in no way makes the theories and concepts of others more correct than your own in the long run). Give the theories a chance, and then apply reasoned skepticism consistent with the doubting game. You may ultimately accept or reject the new learnings, but you'll at least have given them a chance.

Stages and Types of Learning

Developing a critical attitude is one of the primary outcomes of higher education. Even so, many first-year college students are unaware of the attitude changes they're likely to experience as a result of their undergraduate education. They believe they've come to college in order to "get" an education, but researchers have found that the most successful students often use their personal experience to "build" an education.

Two particular research studies have contributed significantly to our understanding of how adults learn in college and other educational environments. Both studies can be thought of as providing **developmental theories**, in that they attempt to explain how people progress to more sophisticated forms of learning over time. They also emphasize human communication, but they do not claim overtly to be communication research. Perry's 1970 study focuses on the experiences of male students at Harvard from 1954 to 1963. Belenky, Clinchy, Goldberger, and Tarule's 1986 study, which builds on the Harvard research and on Gilligan's (1982) studies of women's "voice" issues, suggests that women's and men's learning styles differ somewhat in formal and informal settings.

The studies are important because (1) their findings suggest learning choices that are especially appropriate for communication theorizing; (2) they provide **typologies**, or category systems, of communication within the particular context of adult learning; and (3) you can use them to begin to diagnose your own learning perspectives. However, keep in mind that a typology cannot describe precisely the experiences of all individuals progressing through college life or model all potential subgroups within an overall learning population. Both studies examined here are based on in-depth interviews with many people over extended time periods, and as such they are helpful in providing clues and generalizations. But neither study can claim definitely that "this is how it is" with students, with women or men, or with learning. There are too many different kinds of campuses, types of students, and goals for learning.

Perry's Harvard Study

While some students always expect teachers to provide clear-cut and well-defined answers to questions, many others rightly expect to accomplish at least some of their learning by comparing ideas or solutions to problems with others. Perry's (1970) Harvard study attempted to determine whether a four-year college education helps students develop more flexible and contextualized qualities of learning, replacing more simplistic forms in which students try to understand the world "in unqualified polar terms of absolute right-wrong, good-bad" (p. 3). In other words, after four years of communicating in college, can students perceive the world in more of its subtleties and shades of gray?

Perry's findings suggest that many college students progress through stages of learning—from a simplistic either-or or yes-no stage of seeking answers to a more personal learning style based on a pluralistic worldview and a commitment

In Chapter 4 you'll read about *cognitive complexity,* which is the ability to process the subtle implications of perceptions and communication messages. As your cognitive complexity increases, you will become increasingly able to make fine-tuned distinctions that are more discerning rather than seeing the world as "entirely this" or "entirely that."

to making learning more personal and practical. Despite the unique personalities of respondents, the study notes that groups of students tend to define learning in similar ways at certain points in their college careers. Perry calls these attitudes "positions" to indicate how students move from one attitude to the next as they progress toward a college degree. He identifies nine such positions, but to simplify and summarize we can reduce them to five basic categories (see A Theory Extension, below).

Perry's study found that college is a profoundly life-changing experience for most students and that often they are not fully aware of how they change as they progress through the educational experience. In some ways, being in college is

---

A THEORY EXTENSION

PERRY'S POSITIONS OF LEARNING

- **Duality:** Students are both certain about and protective of their long-held ideas; ideas encountered in college either fit a student's current thought (are probably right, they think) or don't fit (and are probably wrong). ("Don't confuse me with facts—I already know what I believe.")

- **Multiplicity:** All reality is fundamentally negotiable, because authorities often can't even agree among themselves; no position is necessarily any better than another. Students begin to respect multiplicity and disagreement. ("I know researchers say attribution theory works that way, but I don't agree; in my family things are different.")

- **Relativism:** There are many possible points of view, but the truth of each one is always relative to context and circumstance; every truth seems "up for grabs." ("Compared to what?" is a typical inquiry from a relativist.)

- **Commitment foreseen:** Going beyond the dilemmas of relativism, many students begin to order their tentative commitments with a stronger sense of identity and more position-taking on issues. ("Although studies in family communication may never be conclusive, I tend to think the social exchange model is the most realistic approach.")

- **Commitment:** Although learning is developed flexibly, it is also guided by the student's personal commitments. The learner realizes that others' views are not only different but also potentially persuasive. Students who take this position have a strong sense of personal identity and are also comfortable with constant change. ("Even though my family and I have always thought of ourselves as staunch conservatives, I learned a lot from the readings on Marxist theory in my political science course.")

Source: Perry, 1970 (pp. 57–176).

very different from the rest of our everyday lives, so much so that we might be tempted to contrast it with the "real world." Nonetheless, college life is a real-world activity. In higher education, students encounter a complex mix of different viewpoints that reflect a pluralistic society. In higher education—as in the workplace or the family—students' appreciation of the role of communication is the crucial factor in determining how they balance authorities, theories, learning styles, and personal commitments.

Harvard's undergraduates progressed through identifiable stages of development as they gradually became committed to personal beliefs and more open to the views of others. Not all of the students experienced their education in this way, but enough did to allow Perry to identify a general pattern.

Belenky and Colleagues' *Women's Ways of Knowing* Study

The Harvard study was based on interview data collected from male Harvard students. Agreeing with the importance of this developmental communication study, another research team set out to explore what the Harvard study did not: the experience of women in various contexts of formal and informal learning. Belenky et al. (1986) wanted to know if women's styles of integrating new experiences might differ from those of men.

In interviews with 135 women learners, conducted over five years and producing thousands of pages of transcript for analysis, Belenky et al. found enough similarities to produce a similar typology. However, they noted several important differences. For example, women tend to elaborate on their experiences differently. In Perry's (1970) study, doubt is a prerequisite to the development of contextual and relativistic thinking that supports personal commitment. Feeling confirmed—which can come from others' recognition, assurance, and social support—follows. But Belenky et al. found that for women confirmation, not doubt, is the more common prerequisite (pp. 193–194). These authors speculate that a different pattern of socialization may lead women to start the learning process with an interest in relational support, rather than with a need to doubt. (Remember, however, that such studies illustrate only the tendencies of certain behaviors to illustrate men's or women's experience; they do not suggest what is "right" for men or women to do. Some men, for example, more closely approximate the Belenky patterns than do many women.)

Belenky et al. also noted that men and women tend to use different metaphors to describe their experiences. (A **metaphor** is a figure of speech that asserts a sameness about different things, as in "That exam was a killer.") Whereas men tend to speak of seeing things in new ways, women more commonly use a metaphor of *voice* to describe their intellectual development. Thus, for example, a man might say, "I see what you mean," "These stories appear to be similar," or "I noticed that you wrote another memo," while a woman might comment, "That speaks to me," "These stories sound similar to me," or "I hear you."

Another difference between the Perry and Belenky studies is that the latter identified "perspectives" instead of a series of sequential "positions" or stages. Belenky and her colleagues weren't surprised that a study of a pluralistic institution with strong traditions such as Harvard would tend to socialize its men toward pluralistic assumptions in a readily identifiable set of stages. Yet studying women

See additional discussions of confirmation in Chapters 5 and 10. If you were a teacher, how could you ensure that your students—male and female—experienced confirmation in your classes? In Chapter 7 you will also read about how different theorists have discussed the extent of differences in male and female language use. Some believe gender differences in language use have been somewhat exaggerated.

in more diverse contexts simply yielded different perspectives that researchers were not as ready to claim as a distinct developmental sequence. Belenky et al. identified five such perspectives (see A Theory Extension, p. 14).

The Belenky et al. study has contributed to how we think about learning in general, as well as to our understanding of the communication styles that seem to be typical of women. Although the researchers do not identify precise developmental stages, there are similarities between their categories and Perry's typology. Effective learning involves constructing answers that are contingent on context and interpretation within a pluralistic society. Learning is itself a "question of communication," in that it evolves not from pronouncements or prescriptions but from learners' participation in a dialogue of differing perspectives.

Communication specialists might draw a simple lesson from these two studies. Readers who approach this book from the perspectives of "commitment" (Perry) and "constructed knowledge" (Belenky et al.) will find their task much more rewarding. In this book, we attempt to engage students in an ongoing conversation about communication, rather than just presenting facts for memorization.

Knowledge in an Ethical Framework

As you read the preceding section on learning perspectives, you may have considered questions such as these: "How much faith do I place in my own ideas and feelings?" "How certain am I that I'm right?" "How willing am I to listen to others' ideas and feelings, and which of these ideas can I trust?" "Am I willing to accept opposing points of view as valid?" "Do I give appropriate credit to people who invest their time and energy in studying human problems, or do I too readily believe or dismiss their notions?" "Do I sometimes defend my ideas simply because they're mine?" "To what extent do I state my views to others in a way that reflects what I think they may want to hear?"

These questions not only reflect potential problems in everyday living but also imply an ethical foundation to theorizing and researching. Theorists are, in a word, learners, and the "texts" they study are usually not the textbooks written by authors but the social practices of everyday communication. Theorists are learners at a more basic level than they are defenders of a particular dogma. Although we like to think of theorists as being committed to learning and as having an open attitude toward knowledge, they too face dilemmas in expressing their theories.

Any investigation has ethical implications. The process of learning always involves decisions about what is right or wrong, good or bad, positive or negative. People with knowledge often have power, but they cannot avoid **ethics**, the study of the criteria on which moral judgments of right and wrong are made. They only avoid ethical awareness. Suppose you believe knowledge is gained only by reception. This seems innocent enough, but it is hardly a benign belief if you insist that your instructors tidily package answers for you at the end of each class session. Other students, of course, will be affected by this event, and their learning expectations might be different. How you express your beliefs will affect the direction your group takes, and this gives you a kind of power.

Although we will discuss ethics in more detail in Chapter 10, we should clarify our ethical perspective for communication education. In general, we believe

A THEORY EXTENSION

BELENKY ET AL.'S PERSPECTIVES OF LEARNING

- **Silence:** Women in this perspective feel as if they have no voice, or that they cannot contribute meaningfully to intellectual or social conversation. They are often dependent on others to think and speak for them. They possess little or no motivation for learning, and they lack confidence when they fear that authorities will contradict them.

- **Received knowledge:** The received knowledge learner collects the wisdom of others and may even pass it on. Although she listens well to voices of authority, she doesn't believe she could be a voice of authority for others. This category is similar to Perry's "dualistic" position, with one important difference: Whereas men who accept a dualistic position become psychologically aligned with the authorities who supply them with answers, women who are received knowledge learners experience authorities as distant and separate from themselves.

- **Subjective knowledge:** These women elevate subjective knowledge and disregard or reject the external answers experts provide. They claim to know things intuitively and experientially, and they often distrust language, rational analysis, and abstraction.

- **Procedural knowledge:** Women in this perspective tend to believe that the answers to important questions can be discovered in the procedures that have guided others in their quest for knowledge. Thus procedural knowledge learners try to attain such "how to" knowledge in order to gain entrance into the game of competence. They seek the formulas necessary for success and are suspicious of teachers who are unwilling to provide them. Researchers found two types of procedural knowledge learners—*separate knowing* and *connected knowing*. Unlike the more objective "knowledge is out there" assumptions of the separate knower, the connected knower shares the subjectivist's distrust of external authority and emphasizes values of sharing, perspective-taking, and cooperative development of ideas.

- **Constructed knowledge:** This perspective involves a process of "integrating the voices." These women share many of Perry's assumptions about personal commitment, including its role in guiding learners through complex choices. For these learners, answers should be neither received nor intuited but constructed by real people on the basis of their firsthand experiences. Self and other are both necessary. An answer can tentatively address a situation, but it does not necessarily persist across situations. These women are flexible; when contexts change, they expect the answers and actions to change as well. As one respondent commented, "Circumstances change. Our way of looking at things change[s]. Time may have given us what we think are right answers, but it also gives us a different set of problems" (p. 138).

Source: Belenky et al., 1986 (pp. 23–152).

that learning and teaching about communication are ethically defensible to the extent that all individuals concerned:

1. Remain open to being persuaded by the statements of others, whether they are experts, peers, neither, or both.

2. Are willing to try new ideas, even those that are viewed by others as "mistakes." Invite others to experiment also. In this spirit, communicators may share insights creatively, without unnecessary defensiveness.

3. Accept that multiple perspectives on reality are held as valid by different people, especially in different cultural contexts. For example, did you read the accounts of the Perry and Belenky et al. research projects with an attitude of dismissing either men's or women's learning styles as deficient? Is it possible to learn the distinctions first as simply different, rather than as better or worse in an overall sense? Remember, too, that scholars often disagree on what counts as evidence or backing for a knowledge claim. Accepting multiple perspectives as valid does not mean that you must agree with all those perspectives. Rather, it means that you are willing to participate in Elbow's *believing game* by attempting to experience the level of commitment that another person has for a particular perspective or point of view.

4. Attempt to test any tentatively held knowledge by applying criteria developed by social consensus. That is, people who are interested in developing new learning should understand the social context in which their learning occurs. A learner who is unaware of the existing research in a field of study—called the field's **literature**—is not sufficiently prepared for further learning. Remember, however, that the consensus of judgment in any area of study at any given time does not represent the only possible judgment or even the best one (see Chapter 1). It simply means that accumulated wisdom should not be ignored.

5. Live with ambiguity, but treat contradiction as a signal to start questioning things. Not everything will be or needs to be explained. However, when two "accepted" facts, ideas, or definitions seem to contradict each other, and it seems they both can't be true, regard that as an invitation or a challenge to further study. You may end up finding a paradox or making a genuine contribution to your understanding of communication—but in either case the ambiguity will be worthwhile.

6. Evaluate knowledge claims against your personal experience and the everyday pragmatism of what works. In other words, when you take a position, hold it tentatively, and, until you learn otherwise, trust your own experience. After all, personal experience is your own accumulated (but usually unsystematic) research. This doesn't mean that you mistrust the experience of others but that your own life forms one basis for evaluating it. In addition, accept the responsibility of introspection; ask yourself questions that test your experience and probe your prejudices, moral assumptions, and beliefs about cause and effect.

Boiled down, this ethic can be summarized as the art of open questioning— an art that is ultimately also scientific. Everything else, in a sense, flows from the questions that we're curious or courageous enough to ask. In words that summarize the premise of this book, biologist Robert McFarlane (1992) explains why education should emphasize not the accumulation of facts but the questioning of previous assumptions:

> *Science, from one perspective, is the art of phrasing questions and identifying their attendant assumptions. Its basic tenet is that nature has no secrets. The obstacles to furthering knowledge lie in formulating the right questions and in circumventing ambiguous answers, never an easy task. The best practitioners know that incisive questions and skillful analysis will ultimately yield their reward. Artful questions may require new technology, often from unrelated disciplines. New questions may require fresh insight, unencumbered by the baggage of past experience, and a probing mind to test old concepts. The importance of the proper question is often overlooked, by experienced observer and novice alike. (p. 31)*

REVIEWING KEY THEORIES

Each chapter will conclude with a brief capstone section in which we will summarize key themes and distinctions of theories presented there. Because we intended this opening essay to be primarily an introduction to the attitude with which successful learners approach communication, we're not labeling it overtly as a chapter, and we don't present specific communication theories, either. At the same time, the two studies of how college students learn are meaningful enough for you to be able to distinguish them—so, at the risk of some oversimplification, let's compare and contrast.

Perry's Harvard study focused on the learning stages men typically experience in college, moving from a faith in dualistic, right/wrong thinking, through a belief in multiplicity and relativism, to a sense in which a flexible personal commitment can guide learning. The effective college student, Perry found, went beyond relativism to establish personal beliefs, but this kind of student appreciated and remained open to a wide variety of alternative perspectives.

Belenky and her colleagues, in their *Women's Ways of Knowing* study, focused instead on women's experiences. They discovered many similar patterns: Women who were relatively ineffective learners did not take particular responsibility for their learning choices, depending, instead, on others' answers. Especially effective learners, Belenky found, were able to not only trust themselves and their own subjective experiences but to integrate the voices of self and others to produce "constructed knowledge."

The two studies were similar in their finding that good learning means building an education that is uniquely your own, not relying on the education of others warmed over. Responsibility, commitment, increasing faith in self, and a willingness to talk over possibilities emerge as positive characteristics in both studies. The studies differ, however, in that Perry was studying students' development in stages, whereas Belenky and her colleagues were not. It is possible to interpret the latter study as implying stages, but the authors were clear in stating that they could only identify "perspectives" that different women exemplified. Another difference between the studies was the Belenky team's willingness to speculate about the interpersonal conditions that might distinguish women's from men's ways of knowing.

TESTING THE CONCEPTS

Each chapter will also contain a brief section in which we "test" concepts by subjecting them to reasonable commonsense scrutiny. We've designed them to summarize particularly troublesome themes in a question-and-answer format that supplements authors' opinions with other voices. Although we have written and streamlined the questions, most of them are adapted from spontaneous questions asked over the years by our students. They will stimulate your thinking about the implications of communication topics and reinforce the practicality of communication theory. The questions may suggest other questions to you. Your instructor is probably hoping you will ask them in class.

"I don't feel a 'calling.' I'm just taking this class to fulfill a requirement. Does this chapter apply to me?"

Although most students who take a communication theory course are communication majors, we realize that many are not. Even for them, a serious discussion of the complexity of communication and its connection to learning should be helpful. What it takes to learn more effectively and what it takes to communicate more effectively are essentially the same thing: Ask relevant questions about reality, be open to others' answers, and find a way to develop a realistic commitment to the answers you build for yourself.

"I've been communicating since I was a baby. Why is it so important to study something I already know how to do and have done naturally for so long?"

Like anything else that's worthwhile in life, solutions to communication problems are not lined up in neat rows. Tentative answers are often puzzled out individually by people who are basically experimenters in their own lives. "Can other people's solutions help me and you, though?" is a valid question. Sometimes the answer is yes, but sometimes it is no. Communication theorists are like consultants—their responsibility is to survey the solutions people reach individually and to note the patterns that, when generalized, could apply to the rest of us.

"When I play the doubting game in the classroom, I come across as argumentative; but if I believe everything the instructor says, I become a robot. Is there a happy medium?"

Yes. The happy medium is to avoid concentrating on either one or the other, emphasizing instead a blend of doubting and believing. In the questioning you do in class and elsewhere, the best clarifications come when you buy into a topic enough to believe that it's important, but not so much that you accept answers without question. Accepting professors' opinions as absolute facts is dangerous for you and your professors. The danger for them is that they will cease to learn and question themselves.

"As a woman, I've often felt that no one listens to me in class, so I practice silence as a defense mechanism. How can I learn to speak up? Is there a theory to explain this?"

(V.R.): Often, women feel less self-assured in college and believe that men will dismiss their comments as "emotional" or "trivial." As an only child, and a daughter at that, I often heard my father (obviously from another generation of communicators) make comments like "You don't know what you're talking about; stay out of this." After years of hearing similar verbal and non-verbal responses from men, silence became a protective buffer for me. Questions that integrate both doubting and believing are an effective first step toward becoming more assertive in class. Use your questions to break the silence, but also to speak up for the things you understand from your reading and your own experience.

"Why the emphasis on ethics? Shouldn't science and the search for knowledge be value-free?"

We emphasize the importance of ethical alertness, here in the Introduction as well as in Part Four, because no social knowledge can be considered seriously apart from potential applications. Ethical theory is a practical way of evaluating the uses to which theories of communication might be put. Asking and answering such questions as "What works?" and "Why does it work?" will take us only so far; they will give us insights into our options in public life. Beyond this, though, asking the ethically oriented "whether" question (whether we should in fact do such things) is the practical ground on which communication options must be evaluated.

Aaron Haupt/Photo Researchers

CHAPTER 1

"How Do We Learn to Think about Communication?"

The Importance of Questioning and Theorizing

The enemy of theory is not practice but hack-work.

Vernon E. Cronen, "Communication Theory for the Twenty-first Century" (1998, p. 30)

There is a continuum of seeing what is to be done and doing it,
and seeing what has been done and reviewing it, reseeing it and redoing it.
Theory and practice are continuous. And by our practice may ye know our theories.

M. C. Richards, *The Crossing Point* (1973, pp. 81–82)

Some years ago, a highly motivated and intelligent student named Ted took a communication theory course taught by one of your authors. Throughout the term, Ted read carefully, wrote creatively and intelligently, and contributed consistently to class discussions. He was hungry for learning—and he fully digested the material. In short, he was a teacher's dream.

Ted also questioned the text, the teacher, and other students. He wouldn't settle for easy answers. "What else?" he would ask. "How do you know?" "Who says so?" "What are some other explanations?" "Why couldn't it be another way?" Such persistent questioning can be a teacher's nightmare because it's not always easy to respond to highly inquisitive students. But Ted questioned so sincerely, persistently, and selflessly that it was obvious that he wasn't showing off. "Put up, or shut up," he seemed to say. He wanted the rest of us to put up our own best ideas. He would not settle for a mere survey course where terms and names were memorized and tested on exams. Ted represented a style of learning that we should remember when deciding how to teach and learn communication theory.

Ted demonstrated the most fundamental attitude of scientific learning: the willingness to ask meaningful questions. He wanted the course to stress ideas and thereby to prepare him to theorize more effectively. He wanted to participate in theory-building rather than to just observe the theories that others have built. We'll consider this process of theorizing in more detail later in the chapter. For now, we can think of theorizing as a way of making an educated guess, as an explanation-in-process, open to change. Throughout this book, we stress the importance of theorizing, of approaching communication from the standpoint of the questions that motivate theorists. This is a practical as well as a challenging introduction to the study of communication. As you read the book, you may notice that it is unlike a traditional textbook in its style of teaching. You will learn about communication through your own questioning and theorizing. Ted wanted to become either a communication specialist in a large organization or a college teacher. He'd declared a major and made a commitment to learning as much as possible about it. He had, in short, found what we termed in the Introduction a *calling*—a decision to submit "to the vast area of information and belief surrounding his selected field of inquiry" (Polanyi, 1967, p. 79). Most professions, and especially academic ones, are described in terms of inquiry, which is just another way of saying that professionals are expected to ask a lot of questions and to be persistent in seeking answers.

While writing this book, we assumed that our readers were responding at least tentatively to a calling. We also assumed that by enrolling in a course that goes beyond basic communication processes, you are hoping for assistance in becoming a better questioner. Although you may have chosen to study communication because of your skill in conversation or public speaking, you should also know that the discipline has a rich intellectual heritage. Effective communication specialists in such areas as management, training, public relations, marketing, journalism, and teaching possess not only good performance skills but also the ability to theorize. As social scientist Kurt Lewin has observed, nothing is as practical as a good theory (1951, p. 169). Theories help us apply what we understand in one situation to new or unexpected experiences. What could be more practical than that?

We cannot assume that you share Ted's learning style or personality. However, because all communicators must make assumptions about their audience, we can assume that you share Ted's curiosity about communication and that you have a calling. Your curiosity and your calling will combine to make your education in communication both personally relevant and professionally valuable. In this chapter we will accomplish several goals. First, we will attempt to demystify the term *theory*. "Oh, that's just fine in theory," people often say, "but it'll never work in practice." By saying this, they imply that theory is lofty, abstract, and, worst of all, impractical. Instead of this dismissive attitude, think of academic theorizing as simply a logical extension of the everyday process of learning. Second, we'll relate theorizing to an attitude of availability to show how crucial this attitude can be. Third, we will explain the more formal theory-building cycle of communication studies, the components of a theory, the research process through which theories are developed, the functions of theory in the academic world, and some criteria for evaluating theories. Finally, we will discuss theory-building goals to show what theorists hope to accomplish in their work.

Theorizing as an Everyday Occurrence

Imagine that you play tennis every Saturday morning with a group of friends. You usually look forward to the event, but on this particular Friday night you feel especially tired and not in the mood to exercise tomorrow morning. You'd rather stay home and do some low-level activity. You seriously consider calling your tennis partners to cancel out.

Just then, your roommate comes in and says, "I hope you aren't planning anything tomorrow morning—that's the only time I can make all those phone calls you promised you'd help with. I'm counting on you." Suddenly, playing tennis tomorrow morning looks like a good idea. You reply, "Hey, I'd like to help, but I play tennis every Saturday morning, remember?" Something interesting has happened here. Even though your roommate has just suggested the exact kind of activity you were considering a moment ago, you object to it. Why? Let's consider several possible reasons:

1. You say no because you want to teach your roommate a lesson about assumptions.

2. You say no because you have compared rationally the consequences of inconveniencing one person versus inconveniencing several people.
3. You say no because you dislike making phone calls and weren't serious when you promised to help.
4. You say no because you are selfish.
5. You say no because you just realized how much you enjoy playing tennis.

Note that each explanation relies on a different implicit **theory** about the situation, a different tentative explanation for what happened. But as our hypothetical example illustrates, analyzing human behavior even in everyday situations is a complex task because many possible explanations can account for a single action. How, then, do we identify the most appropriate explanation(s)?

Studying communication theory offers general clues, criteria, and definitions. Although such clues may not apply to particular individuals, events, or relationships, they can help us make sense of our world. The act of theorizing is more than just guessing, and although it might begin as a kind enlightened guesswork, the best explanations come from sustained attention and curiosity. This leads us to an expanded definition of the concept: *To theorize is to respond to meaningful questions with tentative answers.* Although the term *theory* was originally associated with seeing and vision (Williams, 1976, p. 266), it now refers to the explanations people use to resolve the ambiguities of life. (A word we sometimes use similarly, *speculation,* is also etymologically related to vision.) People speculate and theorize all the time, though at various levels.

A **formal theory**, in a scientific sense, presents a set of tentative answers built in response to focused questions, often phrased as propositions and described systematically. Although it may sound odd to refer to answers as "built" rather than discovered, this is precisely what we intend. The answers are not "out there" waiting to be found; rather, they have to be invented from the intellectual materials at hand—insights, clues, concepts, and data. You have a genuine answer only after you've worked to build one, not when you've passively received it.

One communication theorist working within social psychology has systematically researched the kinds of behavior we hypothesized about earlier. Brehm's (1966) theory of **psychological reactance** cannot claim to describe the motives of all real people caught in similar Saturday morning predicaments, but it can highlight communication patterns that help explain the interaction. Brehm's theory, in short, predicts that people tend to react to situations in ways that protect their range of options. Therefore if your roommate's expectations were perceived as a threat to your freedom of choice about how to spend your Saturday morning, you would most likely react by asserting your right to choose. By expressing your desire to play tennis, you are also telling your roommate that you want choices. Brehm's theory, then, is based on a perceived connection between how people speak and their psychological needs.

Notice the similarities between Brehm's research and what any observer could do on the spot. In both situations, the person theorizes to structure ambiguous events by offering tentative answers in response to focused questions. Although the everyday theorist doesn't have the same capacity to conduct research as the professional theorist, the fundamental process varies only in that the

⬚LINK

Brehm's theorizing about psychological reactance attempts to account for a widespread and persistent tendency in human behavior, not just how individuals may react to others in certain situations. As such, his theory was an example of the search for what theorists call a *covering law* of behavior. See the discussion of covering laws later in this chapter.

professional can be more systematic in finding evidence to support or reject a hunch. We are doing something theoretical when we pay close attention to practice. Dillon (1990) suggests that "practice is not a matter of brute action but conception and reflection. It is knowledge-in-action, an enactment that is informed by an understanding at once theoretical and empirical and practical. Hence the far-off realms of theory...are nearer to practice than we may have guessed. They are not worlds apart. They form the one world of questioning" (p. 1).

Schön's (1983) discussion of **reflection-in-action** shows how closely tied theory and practice should be (see A Theory Extension, below). The most effective practitioners may have developed a storehouse of useful techniques, but more importantly they are willing to revise their behavior in light of ongoing informal theories and are open to change. According to Schön, practitioners who "overlearn their routines...may miss important opportunities to think about what [they are] doing." They may find themselves "drawn into patterns of error [they] cannot correct" and be "selectively inattentive to phenomena that do not fit the categories of [their previous] knowing-in-action" (p. 61). In effect, not just all practice, but all perception of the world becomes theory-dependent (Hanson, 1958). We cannot perceive any new circumstance meaningfully without bringing previously learned generalizations to bear on it. Approaching each situation as if it were brand new is psychologically impossible.

A THEORY EXTENSION

DONALD SCHÖN (1983) ON THEORISTS' "REFLECTION-IN-ACTION"

- "When someone reflects-in-action, he becomes a researcher in the practice context. He is not dependent on the categories of established theory and technique, but constructs a new theory of the unique case.... He does not keep means and ends separate, but defines them interactively as he frames a problematic situation" (p. 68).
- "Many practitioners, locked into a view of themselves as technical experts, find nothing in the world of practice to occasion reflection. They have become too skillful at techniques of selective inattention, junk categories, and situational control, techniques which they use to preserve the constancy of their knowledge-in-practice. For them, uncertainty is a threat; its admission is a sign of weakness" (p. 69).

Clearly, improvisational jazz musicians and good freelance basketball players are skilled in constructing "new theories of the unique case" because they cannot afford to rely on previous techniques. Which of the communication professions do you think depend most on Schön's reflection-in-action type of theorizing? Journalism? Organizational consulting? Teaching? Public relations and advertising? Why?

Source: Schön, 1983 (pp. 68–69).

The Attitude of Availability

You are a theorist of relational negotiation in the workplace when you object to a supervisor loudly criticizing a new employee in front of the entire staff. You are a theorist of family communication when you decide to ease tension by suggesting that more activities be done together with siblings, parents, partner, or children. You are a theorist when you decide that the friend you've written to for five Christmases but who has never responded is no longer interested in maintaining your friendship. In each case, you have asked yourself a question, collected some informal evidence, and formed a tentative conclusion. Your theory about each would include general expectations for relationships and particular expectations for these unique relationships. Although in the last example a letter from your friend might convince you otherwise, your current decision that the friendship is over would remain in place until further data became available.

As the preceding examples illustrate, each insight into communication has to integrate both the general and the particular. Effective theorists learn that generalizations do not mean that the expected outcomes will automatically fall into place. Exceptions or variations will always occur at the level of concrete particulars; if too many exceptions occur, the basic theory must be revised to account for them. At some point in most theory courses a student will "disagree" with a scholarly theory by citing a personal example ("That theory isn't right—my parents were completely different"). Although the student's experience may very well be valid, this may not be a true disagreement with the theory itself but simply an exception to it or a variation on a theme.

At the core of scientific theorizing are the abilities to adjust the generalizations as the particulars change and to develop generalizations that one knows will not contain all possible particulars. This kind of flexibility is also psychologically healthy, as one psychiatrist (Kubie, 1961) reminds us:

> *The measure of health is flexibility, the freedom to learn through experience, the freedom to change with changing internal and external circumstances, to be influenced by reasonable argument, admonitions, exhortation, and the appeal to emotions; the freedom to respond appropriately to the stimulus of reward and punishment, and especially the freedom to cease when sated. The essence of normality is flexibility in all of these vital ways. The essence of illness is the freezing of behavior into unalterable and insatiable patterns. (pp. 20–21)*

Another way to describe this psychological flexibility is to say that the effective communicator—and, therefore, the effective theorist—is available to change. **Availability**, a person's or a group's flexibility or openness to be changed by new messages, is necessary to theorizing in four major ways:

- Curiosity
- Willingness to be surprised
- Adequate knowledge
- Appreciation of multiple perspectives

First, the theorist should be *curious*. Theorizing, in fact, demands curiosity— a willingness to ask "Why?" while also accepting that complete explanations are not possible. Curiosity is intimately related to the process of creativity, another process that can't be taught readily. Curious people tend to be satisfied with neither a situation of ambiguity nor a state of supposedly complete explanation.

Second, the theorist should be *willing to be surprised* and to accept the consequences of surprise (usually the loss of certainty). It may be uncomfortable at times to recognize how limited your own perspective may be. In her essay "Seeing," Pulitzer Prize–winning writer Annie Dillard (1975) tells the true story of a group of cataract sufferers who were born sightless. After surgeons discovered techniques for performing safe operations that would allow them to see the world, these newly gifted people reacted quite differently to their personal miracles. Some described the task of viewing the "dazzle of color-patches" as "tormentingly difficult" (p. 28). A young girl, upon visiting a garden, stood transfixed in front of what she called "the tree with the lights in it" (p. 30). Other patients described their newfound ability to see as intimidating, uncomfortable, even threatening. Some refused to open their eyes or to make sense of the new images before them, preferring instead the comfort of depending on others' interpretations of the visual world. You may have been intimidated by a new area of study or other event that helps you identify with the fears these individuals encountered in their new world of vision. But for theorists and others, learning cannot take place without a willingness to be surprised.

Third, a theorist should be *knowledgeable*. Curiosity doesn't develop in an information vacuum, nor does it develop in an environment in which a single set of assumptions predominates. Anthropologists, who theorize about human variability between cultures, understand this well. According to Gregory Bateson (1980), all knowledge is based on sensing differences (pp. 31–32). Thus, in order to understand where you are or what you are doing, you must also learn about places other than where you live and about the behavior of strangers. Mary Catherine Bateson (1990)—a prominent scholar and the daughter of anthropologists Bateson and Margaret Mead—emphasizes the need to be knowledgeable about things beyond your own most comfortable surroundings. "One of the great steps forward in history," she writes, "was learning to regard those who spoke odd-sounding languages and had different smells and habits as fully human, as similar to oneself. The next step from this realization, the step which we have still not fully made, is the willingness to question and purposefully alter one's own conditions and habits, to learn by observing others" (p. 57). Theorists become knowledgeable, and therefore more effectively curious, when they read and experience widely in seemingly separate areas.

Therefore, fourth, the theorist should *understand and appreciate multiple perspectives on communication,* perspectives that are held both concurrently and provisionally (Littlejohn, 1982). Being curious means that you continue inquiring even after you've developed a perspective on an issue. If you are an expert in the theory of group decision making, for instance, could you ignore new theories of how individuals develop verbal plans for upcoming interactions? Surely not, because the perspectives overlap. You'll continue asking, synthesizing, and asking some more. Abraham Kaplan's (1964) **law of the instrument** refers to the unfortunate tendency of a theorist or a researcher to view all problems in the light of one technique, methodology, or perspective. Just as the child who discovers a hammer will also find many things in need of hammering (to use Kaplan's analogy), the single-minded Marxist theorist might see only exploitation in economic power relations and the experimentalist might be convinced that quantitative laboratory studies are the only valid type of communication research.

Remember Ted, the inquisitive student we told you about at the start of the chapter? One afternoon late in the term, he enlivened a theory discussion with a question that went something like this: "Well, we've studied all these different theories. Systems of this, laws of that, rules, principles, blah, blah, blah. Which one is right?" Although only Ted knew for sure, the instructor's theory was that Ted understood the implications of his question and looked forward to the kind of discussion it would generate. The class eventually concluded that it was not useful to claim that any one theory is supreme or correct. Because theories tend to be developed for different reasons, to explain different phenomena, or to examine similar phenomena in different settings, it is probably unwise to wish for a single theory to unite all communication studies.

The diversity inherent in theorizing enriches the field. Donald Campbell's (1969, 1986) model of scholarly or scientific knowledge as a fish's scales helps us to understand why. Each small scale, which represents a specialty or a theoretical insight, overlaps other small scales until the entire fish is covered. No one scale (specialty) can or should cover the entire fish (discipline), but the coverage is sufficient if we coordinate the overlapping. Such diverse scholars as literary critic Wayne Booth (1990, pp. 325–327) and philosopher of science Michael Polanyi (1967) advocate similar models. Polanyi (1967) calls his notion the **principle of mutual control** in science, and claims that it works well because of the "chains of overlapping neighborhoods" (p. 72).

Communication theory, therefore, is not a horse race in which the various explanations (and explainers) are straining to win, place, or show; it's more like a convention in which the various points of view are given forums and opportunities to be influential. We will discuss the evaluation of theories later in the chapter (some theories, as you might expect, are more useful than others in helping us to understand communication). But by discussing what motivates successful theorists, we have demystified the process of theorizing somewhat. Let's consider what professional communication specialists do when their curiosity motivates them to explain human interaction systematically.

Recall from the Introduction that building theories is remarkably similar to being a successful college student. As good learners progress through college, they tend to become more tolerant of others' opinions, more aware of a wider range of evidence that must be questioned, more comfortable with ambiguity, and more willing to construct personal commitments. In other words, they become effective theorists.

The Theory-Building Cycle in Communication

Science as Methodical Inquiry

Curiosity motivates scientists, but they must be familiar enough with existing knowledge to say, in effect, "We haven't learned enough; this doesn't seem to explain what it needs to explain." Human knowledge is usually advanced when curious people shake their heads and mutter, "I don't know…yet." The "yet" is crucial. Moreover, the scientific method is more open to revision and based more on the subjective, creative arguments of scientists struggling to solve human problems than most people assume (Kuhn, 1970). Most important, perhaps, current knowledge should not breed complacency but cycles of reconsideration.

We've used the word *science* several times without defining it, which is what most people do. But we should examine it more closely. Despite its aura of objective precision and its association with such academic disciplines as chemistry, biology, and physics, *science* is a relatively new word in the English language. From its earliest known usage in the fourteenth century until the middle of the nineteenth century, it typically referred to methodical inquiry, often theoretically based. Literature could be studied "scientifically"; so could religion or political strategy. In the twentieth century, however, *science* generally came to refer to the objective observation of and inquiry into areas where experimentation, specification, and control—rather than personal experience and interpretation—are appropriate (Williams, 1976, pp. 232–235).

Lately, however, we seem to be returning to a broader notion of science in the social sciences (which usually include not only communication but also psychology, sociology, anthropology, and political science). Thus a scientist today is not necessarily someone who conducts precise experiments that measure objective truths (see Fay, 1996). Certainly, experimentation plays an exciting role in the scientific community's attempt to understand human behavior. But the social scientist does not assume that controlled laboratory methods are the only way to do so. As we will use the term in this book, **science** is the systematic attempt, applying various methodologies, to ask and answer meaningful questions while remaining open to alternative answers. Researchers who are careful observers and who employ **qualitative methodologies** (which explore and describe the qualities of phenomena) or **quantitative methodologies** (which focus on isolating, counting, and analyzing units of phenomena) are scientists when they respond to their curiosity with systematic questioning. Let's be even more specific. Qualitative researchers may refer to themselves as *interpretivists* (those who study relatively intangible and subjective patterns of human interpretation) or as *naturalistic researchers* (those who study communication in natural settings). Quantitative researchers, in contrast, tend to be *experimentalists* (those who structure laboratory comparisons of how different groups and individuals communicate in certain ways) or *survey researchers* (those who use questionnaires or precision interviews to collect data and illustrate general trends among social communicators). In practice, however, qualitative researchers are not averse to counting things if it advances their understanding, and quantitative researchers often engage in interpretation and speculation. The distinction is not as clear-cut as a textbook discussion might imply. Still, most researchers, if pressed, will align themselves with one label or the other.

Historically, both quantitative and qualitative scholars have been systematic, thorough, and, considering our previous definition, scientific in their missions. The vast majority of scholars in both areas of research acknowledge the value of quantitative and qualitative studies as well as the many variations within each approach. However, they sometimes disagree about the relative importance of their respective contributions to our knowledge of communication. Quantitative scholars, for example, claim that their methodological precision gives them more control over observations and experiments, allows them to study larger and more varied groups of people, results in better generalizations, and is a more objective means of gathering data than qualitative studies can provide. Quantitative scholars also argue that their methodology delineates cause-effect relationships more precisely and, therefore, produces data that are empirically valid—that is, better able to relate to observable reality.

Qualitative scholars counter that cause-effect attributions of quantitative research far too often assume one-way influence (i.e., a particular cause directly creates a particular effect), and that most quantitative studies are conducted in artificial settings that cannot truly represent real-world situations or take into account complex issues of race, class, gender, and power. Qualitative scholars believe that their method of studying dynamic communicating in natural settings preserves the subjectivity that is essential to learning about communication systematically. While each group understands the reasons that scholars are attracted to the other camp, they tend to disagree about the relative significance of their contributions. Communication researcher Janet Beavin Bavelas (1995) is worried about the folly of methodological narrow-mindedness. Bavelas questions the bases of the distinctions between quantitative and qualitative methods, suggesting that the widely accepted dichotomies (e.g., empirical/nonempirical, statistical/nonstatistical, objective/subjective, deductive/inductive, hypothesis testing/exploratory, artificial/natural, not generalizable/generalizable, and laboratory/real world), when they are applied to distinguish quantitative from qualitative research, are more misleading than instructive. She criticizes the narrow-mindedness of researchers who claim theirs is the only valid way to do things: "A highly restricted choice of methods inevitably stunts the growth of theory.... [I]f we reject polarization we may discover new, previously unexplored combinations of both approaches" (p. 51).

Another important critique has stimulated a deeper understanding of the scientific enterprise. Biophysicist and feminist theorist Evelyn Fox Keller (1985) argues that traditional Western science was long based on a male model of knowing. In this model, a separation between knower and known was assumed, analysis was the tool, and domination of nature by "mankind" was the goal. Keller claims that the male conception of science restricted women's participation; defined as "unscientific," women were excluded because their skepticism of objectivity contradicted the concerns of established scientists. Viewing the traditionally objective model of science as incomplete rather than "wrong," Keller believes science should strive for what she terms **dynamic objectivity**, which "grants to the world around us its independent integrity but does so in a way that

---

REVIEWING KEY IDEAS

SCIENCE INVOLVES:

- Methodical questioning.
- Appropriate suspicion about answers.
- Qualitative and quantitative research methods.
- Dynamic objectivity.
- Linkage with humanistic values and concerns.
- Ethical and rhetorical engagement.

remains cognizant of, indeed relies on, our connectivity with the world" (p. 117). Dynamic objectivity "makes use of subjective experience…in the interests of a more effective objectivity. Premised on continuity, it recognizes difference between self and other as an opportunity for a deeper and more articulated kinship" (p. 117). Keller's suggestion integrates Elbow's doubting and believing games, quantitative and qualitative research methods, and the objective and subjective realms of human knowledge (see Reviewing Key Ideas, p. 30).

As these and other communication scholars suggest, the traditional scientific attitude is helpful, but it should not serve as the only stimulus for theory development. Humanistic thought, sometimes misleadingly presented as opposed to science, actually complements it. Both scientific and humanistic inquiry can be rigorous, sustained, committed, and based on theory. Researchers in the humanities perhaps do emphasize theories of interpretation, valuing, and subjectivity more than the so-called social scientists do. If anything, the subject matter of the humanities is more open to speculation and theorizing, though it may be less open to verification. Qualitative research methods are thus prevalent in the humanities, but this may be seen as complementing social science rather than competing with it. Social science and humanities scholars are, in effect, teammates (Brown, 1987; Farrell, 1987; Montagu, 1962), and this book reflects their interdependence. As one humanities scholar puts it, "In spite of the trappings of objectivity in which we like to drape our psychological, educational, social, and artistic theories, the knowledge they have to offer is always indeterminate in the sense of being relative to the values behind them. When we ask for objective solutions to social or artistic problems, we are asking for brain surgery with a monkey wrench" (Hardison, 1972, p. xx). Researchers in the humanities often search for their answers in different places, asking research questions, but ultimately the overriding goal is the same: "How can we better understand the human animal?"

The theories you will read about in this book were developed by real, flesh-and-blood people who were and are smart, knowledgeable, insightful, and creative in some ways, and—since they're human—probably shortsighted and narrow-minded in others. Science is built on the work of theorists who attempt to be systematic, but it is also marked by a messy collection of arguments and comparisons, mistakes and happy accidents. Science progresses as much by wrong answers as it does by accurate ones. But those wrong (or inappropriate, or unhelpful, or irrelevant) answers have to be identified as such. Doing science isn't just doing the study; it's also fleshing out the implications of the study afterward, in the context of other work by other scholars, in other places, at other times, with other subjects, with other methods, and perhaps with other expectations. Science is less like a sterile laboratory than like a playing field or a town meeting. The playing field metaphor reminds us that scientists play by rules that are commonly accepted and have expectations that are relatively well understood. This is part of the ethical dimension of communication theory that applies even at the early stages of inquiry. For example, investigators should not allow personal biases to affect the results of a study, should not exploit human participants with whom they work, and should not falsify data. They should attempt to share their results with other scientists and describe their methodologies accurately enough to allow comparisons with other studies.

The town meeting metaphor reminds us that science is an arena that is, in some ways, essentially rhetorical. **Rhetoric** is the purposeful process of forming and processing messages to achieve personal and social goals. The scholar presents theories to the scientific community expecting them to be understood, agreed (or disagreed) with, and persuasive. They often aren't. But, as theorist Klaus Krippendorf (1989) points out, "the history of communication research is not so much about communication but about creative scholars, about researchers talking to each other and playing with ideas" (p. 77). In other words, scientists don't just do science; they also argue science. This doesn't imply that they yell and scream at each other (well...maybe some do). Instead, they theorize in public, advertising their own interpretations and, we hope, remaining open to the interpretations of other theorists.

The Cycle

Scientists advance their claims and argue through a process shown in Figure 1-1. Let's examine each of these stages in detail, considering some of the various building blocks of theories. Remember that even though we use the term "theorizing" for one particular step in the cycle, the whole cycle really characterizes the theory-building process, not just that step. Our description is cast as if you, the reader, were the theorist.

1. *Asking.* At this initial stage in the theory-building process, you are confronted with a problem, situation, or phenomenon that you are unable to explain. It may involve a state of ambiguity or, as Dewey (1933) says, a **felt difficulty** (the realization that something is wrong). Perhaps your felt difficulty is simply a curiosity about what else is "out there," and you feel compelled to explore it. Perhaps you're not satisfied with your current understanding of something you consider to be intriguing. Whatever the problem may be, at this stage you begin to ask questions: "What if?" "What else?" "Why is a certain result so regular?" Asking ideally leads to observing, an attempt to gather information that is relevant to your questions.

2. *Observing.* Through observing, you are able to focus your questions in ways that may lead you to possible answers. In a sense, systematic observing surveys the relevant landscape and provides a context for your questions. You read, watch, plan, and notice differences as they arise. Many researchers specialize in **descriptive research**, which charts conceptual territories by gathering information about them. Often the goals of such research are exploratory; for example, linguists use surveys to map speech variations among people in various geographical regions within a culture, and public-opinion pollsters profile the attitudes of the electorate. Although descriptive research is sometimes unfairly regarded as less prestigious than other research traditions, it is a crucial component of the theory-building cycle. Observing is interdependent with the next step we'll consider, theorizing.

3. *Theorizing.* At this stage, you bring your critical and creative powers to bear on the problem you face. You begin to build tentative answers and construct explanations that make sense and are reasonably consistent with your data. You also develop a **research question**, which asks as clearly as possible what

LINKS

❑ Chapter 8 describes how rhetoric works in both public and interpersonal life.

❑ Jurgen Habermas, discussed in Chapter 10, advocates a communicative rationality that ideally governs modern scientific arguments. His approach to dialogue helps to explain how scientists and other communicators find procedures for reaching a consensus.

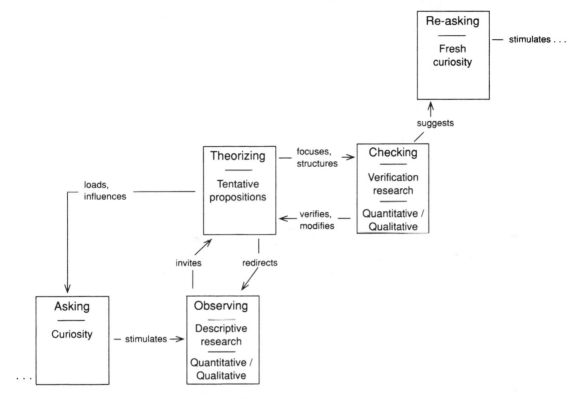

FIGURE 1-1 Stages of the Theory-Building Process

relationship between behaviors can be found in a focused investigation, and a **hypothesis**, which is a tentative statement of truth. Smith (1988) supplies examples: "Do stereotyped portrayals of women in television entertainment programs affect the self-concepts of young female viewers?" is a research question, and "Different value systems of parents and their college-age children are linked to unwanted verbal conflict" is a research hypothesis (p. 24). Although theorists phrase hypotheses as statements rather than as questions, the assumption is that all hypotheses are in effect open questions. If you hypothesize, "Quitting my part-time job will improve my grades," you may be expecting to have twenty or so extra hours per week to spend studying. But whether you will actually devote all twenty hours to studying and improve your grades are open questions.

Theorizing also involves other aspects of clear thinking and communication (see Reviewing Key Ideas, p. 34). Theorists build theories from **concepts**, complex or abstract ideas that are labeled with special terms to aid our understanding and discussion of them. Consider, for example, the highly abstract concept we refer to as "attitude." Without the term, it would be difficult to discuss the concept at all, for it is essentially an abstraction that we have invented to help us understand the tendencies of people to behave consistently in similar circumstances.

The conceptual term **attitude** refers to predispositions to act, choose, or evaluate in certain ways, over time; we might say that LaDonna has a positive attitude about school if we note her perfect attendance and consistent class participation. Concepts are not "things," then, until you name them; they are transitory tendencies that must be inferred from other observations. When we label tendencies as "attitudes," though, we can study them *as if* they were "things." Theories are constructed out of such units.

A concept, in this sense of a theory unit (Dubin, 1969, pp. 27–41), has both attributes and variables. **Attributes** are those properties the theorist claims are present whenever the concept is discussed (e.g., attitudes by definition are usually considered to have cognitive, affective, and behavioral components). **Variables**, particularly important notions to scientists, are properties that may be present in varying degrees, such that "there may be some of the property present or a lot of it" (Dubin, 1969, p. 35). LaDonna's liking of school becomes a variable that can be measured; its levels can be compared over time, or compared with those of other students in her class. Attitudes vary in their direction and intensity, as well as their expression. Theorists therefore could speculate about levels of these variables under different conditions. To be observed, the basic building blocks of theories—concepts—must be assembled into **propositions**, which are the formal claims the theorist wants to assert to the scientific community. They are the academic equivalent to a lawyer's "brief." A proposition differs from a hypothesis in that the theorist has already collected much of the evidence needed to support the claim made in the proposition. Because this book is an introduction to theorizing in communication, we have decided to focus on the concept level of the process, rather than specifying all the propositions scholars have advanced for their theories. This approach should give you enough distinctions and information to allow you to follow up more concretely with individual theories that are especially relevant to your career or personal interests.

4. ***Checking.*** The propositions of any theory cannot be considered apart from the process by which they were developed. Thus at this stage of the theory-building process, verification research (as distinguished from descriptive research) is used to check or verify hypotheses and tentative answers. As you might guess, **verification research** goes beyond a survey of the behavioral landscape to probe for answers in areas where the theorist most expects to find them. As a theorist, you would check on your earlier hunches, often with quantitative experimental or highly focused qualitative methods such as interviewing or participant observation. Of course, you should not strain to verify your theory.

REVIEWING KEY IDEAS

THEORIZING:

- Responds to a problem with *research questions* and *hypotheses*.
- Identifies *concepts,* which have both *attributes* and *variables*.
- Organizes concepts into *propositions* that are backed by evidence.

Confirmation of your theory could result from the checking stage of the cycle, or further testing could refute the theory's propositions. Generally, confirming or refuting a theoretical assertion is not the task of a single study, however sophisticated it may be. Researchers first familiarize themselves with what is called **the literature** of their field—research that has already been conducted and shared through publication—and then look for areas that are in need of further study.

Researchers must be as open to evidence that refutes their hypotheses as they are to evidence that supports them. This is why experimental researchers create **null hypotheses**, which are overt statements that remind the researcher *not* to expect significant differences in a given reasonable direction because of the potential for unintentional self-deception and bias. A null hypothesis says, in effect, "Although the hypothesis that brought me to this point might give me a certain expectation, I will overtly remind myself to expect no difference as I manipulate variables and look for results within this study. Therefore I'll have more confidence in the actual results, knowing that there is this check on the bias of expectation." Sometimes even scholars overlook the connection between theorizing and researching. In the introduction to his influential book on theorizing, Dubin (1969) warns against this oversight. He advocates "bridg[ing] the gap" between theory and research, and he views the "bridge" not as a static connector but as facilitating "traffic" between theory and research (p. 2). In this sense, theorizing is not primarily an armchair activity of speculation, but it actively recognizes interdependent relationships among asking, observing, theorizing, checking, re-theorizing, and re-asking.

5. **Re-asking.** The results of the checking step of theory-building must be fed back into the total system of questioning reality. New questions and new theories develop to reenergize the theory-building cycle. As philosopher of science Karl Popper (1968) notes, "theories are nets cast to catch what we call 'the world': to rationalize, to explain, and to master it. We endeavour to make the mesh ever finer and finer" (p. 59).

Evaluating Theories

Evaluating a theory, whether it is your own underdeveloped and informal hunch or a professional scholar's formal set of propositions, involves asking questions that are based on relevant criteria—the standards by which one can fairly judge the quality or accuracy of a claim. A common set of criteria used in evaluating theories of communication asks questions about the theory's organization, predictiveness, heurism, parsimony, consistency, refutability, and imagination.

The following informal checklist of questions can help you evaluate theoretical explanations in this book and elsewhere. Use the criteria and questions in the checklist in conjunction with the functions of theories discussed in the previous section.

1. *Criterion of organization.* Does the theory clarify a complex process without sacrificing its essential characteristics? Is the theory itself poorly organized? Theories ideally help scholars to organize a field of study for themselves, enabling them to see its relationships more clearly.

2. ***Criterion of predictiveness***. Does the theory give us a reasonably good idea of what to expect in the future? Good theories help us make decisions that may not even have been anticipated before the theories were developed. Theories, even if they do not attempt to account for a linear causality, will still help us to predict others' reactions to the phenomena explained by the theories.

3. ***Criterion of heurism***. Does the theory stimulate further research and speculation? A theory, observed Abraham Kaplan (1964), can serve as "matchmaker, midwife, and godfather all in one" (p. 303), in stimulating others to prove or disprove its validity through further research. If so, it's said to be heuristic. Even if a theory proves to be technically inaccurate or wrong, such as some predictions of general relativity or Freudian psychoanalysis, it can serve society well if it fuels curiosity and stimulates later attempts to correct the errors.

4. ***Criterion of parsimony***. Is the theory sufficiently complex to explain the processes and events it claims to represent, but not overly complicated or repetitious? When a theory organizes and explains many things without leading to a proliferation of unnecessary propositions and concepts, it meets the criterion of parsimony. In applying this criterion, remember that no theory can reproduce reality exactly; therefore a theory should not be criticized for being incomplete just because it isn't congruent with all experience. Einstein once said that good science doesn't try "to give the taste of the soup" (quoted in Rudner, 1966, p. 69), reminding us that no matter how thoroughly we describe the characteristics of soup or the reactions of someone tasting it, we cannot expect the theory to be as satisfying as the experience itself. In other words, theory cannot reproduce reality, but it can help us manage our understanding of it. Note here that parsimony does not necessarily mean that theories should be simple. This criterion only warns about the dangers of unnecessary complexity, and these are not the same things.

5. ***Criterion of consistency***. Does the theory avoid contradicting both itself and known external findings currently accepted as true? Is it, in other words, consistent? This criterion is often the object of intense scientific dispute. You can ask questions like the following to determine whether a theory meets the criterion of consistency: Are basic concepts defined in different ways in different parts of the theory? Are different effects predicted in similar situations or conditions, without adequate explanation? Philosopher of social science Alfred Schutz (1967) discusses what he calls people's "stock of knowledge at hand," which they bring to bear on everyday problems (p. 81; see also Gurwitsch, 1974, pp. 118–124). This expectation is developed by both social and personal experience, and the individual uses it to evaluate new explanations as they are offered. Any new theory should attempt to explain how it is consistent with, or why it deviates from, the "stock of knowledge" developed by ordinary people in ordinary situations.

6. ***Criterion of refutability***. Is the theory open to tests that could potentially refute it? According to Popper (1980), genuinely helpful theories are vulnerable to criticism; they do not make such vague predictions that proponents of the theory could claim that virtually any phenomenon might fit under the theory's umbrella. Rather, theories should be open to being disproved or refuted if warranted by the evidence. As experienced researchers know, to search only for confirmation is to invite confirmation wherever one looks. Popper (1980) notes that

"some genuinely testable theories, when found to be false, are still upheld by their admirers—for example, by introducing ad hoc some auxiliary assumption, or by reinterpreting the theory ad hoc in such a way that it escapes refutation" (pp. 22–23). He cites astrology as an example of an everyday theory that some people use to guide their communication decisions but that does not meet the criterion of refutability:

> *Astrology did not pass the test. Astrologers were greatly impressed, and misled, by what they believed to be confirming evidence—so much so that they were quite unimpressed by any unfavourable evidence. More-over, by making their interpretations and prophecies sufficiently vague they were able to explain away anything that might have been a refutation of the theory had the theory and the prophecies been more precise. In order to escape falsification they destroyed the testability of their theory. It is a typical soothsayer's trick to predict things so vaguely that the predictions can hardly fail: that they become irrefutable. (p. 23)*

7. ***Criterion of imagination***. Is the theory imaginative and interesting? This criterion, more subtle than the others, is also one that many otherwise effective theories do not fully meet. It implies that how a theory is presented rhetorically, not just how it is developed and researched or how precisely it predicts consequences, contributes significantly to its ultimate acceptance. As researcher M. Scott Poole (1990) wrote, "a good theory should be exciting; it should make us enthusiasts. We should be able to have fun applying the theory to different problems and contexts" (p. 237). But what is exciting to one person might spell boredom to another: 0–0 soccer matches? Computer programming? Theorizing about why conversations develop as they do? And, we should note, imagination is ultimately the least useful and most potentially misleading of the seven criteria for evaluating a theory. Clever and attractive explanations may seem imaginative, while failing to meet other criteria and being backed by scant testable research. Successful theories catch our attention with striking metaphors, analogies, and visual models that illustrate the patterns accounted for by the theory. *Metaphor*, a vivid comparison that highlights an important factor or relation, is crucial to both the theory-building process and the evaluation of a theory. Sociologist Richard Brown (1977) argues that "new metaphors not only represent appearances, they change them and even create new ones. New metaphors lie at the heart of new theories" (p. 99).

Consider, for example, how Frank E. X. Dance's (1967) reading in DNA research helped him incorporate both metaphoric and geometric representations into his theoretical description. As shown in Figure 1-2, his model resembles a **helical spiral**. Although the figure doesn't capture much detail about communication, it vividly suggests the central feature of Dance's perspective: Communication might appear to be a clear-cut activity in which messages are exchanged between communicators, but it is actually a circular process that constantly changes over time to different, and constantly new, levels. The helical nature of the image shows that nothing ever stays unchanged as communication occurs; neither people nor their meanings "hold still," and the impact of communication widens. (The implications of this viewpoint are discussed in detail in Chapter 2.)

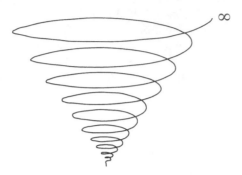

Figure 1-2 Dance's Helical Spiral Model

Source: F. E. X. Dance (Ed.), *Human Communication Theory* (New York: Holt, 1967), pp. 298–309. Reprinted by permission.

Dance's metaphor is intriguing, as it reinforces his idea that communication could be represented in nonlinear and dynamic ways, not just as message-sending from a source to a receiver.

What Do Communication Theorists Hope to Accomplish (Other Than Building Theories)?

One educational theorist claims that most types of learning can be phrased in response to three basic questions: (1) "What?" (2) "So what?" and (3) "Now what?" (Borton, 1970). Effective communication theorists also address these questions. They ask "What?" questions to pinpoint areas that are in need of further study: "What do we not know about…?" They ask, "So what?" (phrased as "Why?" questions) to identify the importance of their tentative answers: "Why is this approach distinctly useful?" or "Why is it important for other people to know about these insights?" And they address "Now what?" questions to set the stage for larger issues of future social planning: "Now that we have this new insight into communicative processes, what social significance might it possess?" So far in this chapter our discussion of communication theory has been focused on the first two questions. In this section we will place communication theorizing in a larger framework by asking, "Now what?"

Covering Laws or Rules?

Theorists need to ask whether their theories and research will eventually add up to anything that's socially significant: "Now what?" (see Reviewing Key Ideas, p. 39). Can we advance far enough to discover some relatively invariant and highly generalizable principles that are applicable across many different types of people and situations? Some theorists think so; they search for **covering laws** that will help to explain and predict human behavior on a macroscopic scale (see Berger, 1977). Our earlier discussion of psychological reactance theory is an example of a theorist's attempt to create a covering law of human behavior: that

REVIEWING KEY IDEAS

TO EVALUATE A THEORY, ASK:

- Does it help clarify complex processes? (*criterion of organizing*)
- Does it help us predict the future? (*criterion of predictiveness*)
- Does it generate further research and questioning? (*criterion of heurism*)
- Does it explain succinctly without being more complicated than it needs to be? (*criterion of parsimony*)
- Does it avoid contradicting itself internally, and avoid unexplained external contradictions? (*criterion of consistency*)
- Does it seem capable of being refuted or tested by gathering persuasive evidence? (*criterion of refutability*, sometimes also called *falsifiability*)
- Does it demonstrate, and stimulate, creativity? (*criterion of imagination*)

people will tend to protect their behavioral options in communication with others (Brehm, 1966).

Covering law theorists want to ask questions like: "What factors of human life tend to apply across contexts and tend to transcend the uniqueness of individual experience?" The studies and methods of the natural sciences are applied to the objective of identifying consistent cause-effect relationships. If the physical law of gravity applies in both New York and New Delhi, laws theorists reason, then perhaps diligent social scientists might likewise discover which characteristics of human behavior would be equally applicable in the United States and India, or in the nineteenth as well as the twenty-first century. These theorists thus tend to ask larger questions about human communication, questions about commonalities in human nature, affiliation, motivation, values, and needs. An example of one type of laws approach in communication is Charles Berger's **uncertainty reduction theory** (Berger & Bradac, 1982; Berger & Calabrese, 1975), which suggests that a basic

REVIEWING KEY IDEAS

LAWS, RULES, OR BOTH?

- *Covering law theorists* attempt to create general or macroscopic explanations that apply widely across social and cultural contexts.
- *Rules theorists* attempt to create specific explanations that demonstrate how behaviors become regularized in specific contexts.
- Many theorists respect and use both approaches.

theme of human interaction is to develop strategies that help predict interactional outcomes by attaining additional interpersonal knowledge. Although the strategies may vary, according to Berger, the impetus toward reducing uncertainty will persist.

Similarly, other forms of human behavior have been explained by law-like generalizations. Cognitive **consistency theory** researchers, for example, study why people's tendency to maintain a state of inner balance, consistency, and congruence seems related to their communication decisions (e.g., Festinger, 1957). Another law-like generalization is found in the work of those who advocate **social exchange theory** (Gergen, 1969; Roloff, 1981). Social exchange theorists say that interaction is guided by people's desire to maximize communication "profits" and "rewards" while minimizing their "losses" and "costs." While each individual's reward structure is somewhat unique (e.g., you might value friendship more than monetary gain), the basic assumption is that people persistently enact economic strategies and judge relationships by what they get out of them relative to what they invest in them.

Not everyone wants to discover grand, overarching laws, however. Some communication researchers have chosen to investigate a different realm of quite specific behaviors-in-context, without trying to assume that they add up to covering law explanations. They want to identify the specific guidelines, or **rules**, that govern people's unique communication choices within particular situations. In this case, the theorist looks not at general human tendencies but inside particular cultures, organizations, and occasions for insight into how people regulate their communication with others (see Pearce & Cronen, 1980; Shimanoff, 1980). In this sense, then, rules refer not to the things people are compelled to do, except in the sense that there might be social pressure if rules were violated. They refer to the regularities, decision patterns, norms, and expectations underlying what people actually do. Rules theorists try to understand the criteria people use, largely unconsciously, when speaking and acting in public. Communication rules are inferred by observing people in action, though no attempt is made to generalize such rules to universal laws. It is this emphasis on specific contexts that is the chief difference between rules approaches and covering laws approaches: "A rule is a followable prescription that indicates what behavior is obligated, preferred, or prohibited in certain contexts" (Shimanoff, 1980, p. 57).

In Chapter 5 we'll discuss *coordinated management of meaning* theory, an influential rules-based approach, and its contributions. Here, though, without swamping you in too much detail, we want to note a historical controversy in the communication field over the relative value of covering laws approaches and rules perspectives. The disagreement raises basic questions: Should we aim high to establish which grand laws regulate human behavior across situations, and perhaps even somewhat deterministically? Or should we aim toward studying more local episodes, establishing which contextual rules regulate the specific communication behaviors of humans within situations, adopting an assumption of more human choice and control? This question has long been debated in the professional journals and conventions. The current status of the controversy is that it seems to be a nonissue, despite the important questions it stimulated. Many scholars today recognize that both approaches can yield fruitful results. In fact, Charles Berger (1998) recently stated that the debates over this kind of "meta-theory" (the theoretical consideration of whether the covering law approach is better than rules, or vice versa) were an "abject waste of time" (p. 13).

Still, the distinction is interesting and implies somewhat distinctive philosophies of human nature. Are human communication behaviors primarily inherently determined? In the **motional view of behavior**, humans are "put in motion" principally by potentially predictable, lawlike forces. Or do humans make choices independently, choices that largely determine their own fate? In the **actional view of behavior**, humans internally choose to initiate, and choose how to initiate, their own actions.

Systems Theory

The motional and actional views of behavior are supplemented (and sometimes informed) by yet another approach to interaction and causality, the systemic view. Many contemporary scholars synthesize scientific assumptions about interaction by applying **general systems theory (GST)** concepts (Bertalanffy, 1968; Ruben & Kim, 1975). Systems theorists argue that change in human relations is neither caused primarily from the outside in nor chosen from within but is a process of mutual adjustment among relationships within a system. GST, perhaps the definitive interdisciplinary effort, was biologist Ludwig von Bertalanffy's (1968) attempt to argue that the same basic principles guide all dynamic systems—including biological, human, environmental, political, and social systems.

General systems theory is not without its critics, however. Some see it as belaboring the obvious, untestable, and not terribly fruitful in generating new research (Phillips, 1976). But since the publication of Watzlawick, Beavin, and Jackson's influential *Pragmatics of Human Communication* (1967), many communication theorists have taken most of the theory's claims for granted. Systems theories assume that it is more fruitful for researchers to study relationships than individuals, behaviors, or things.

Anatol Rapoport thinks of a system as a "bundle of relations" (quoted in Davidson, 1983, p. 26), while Davidson (1983) reminds us that those relations are intangible: "A system is a manifestation of something intangible, but quite real, called organization. A system, like a work of art, is a pattern rather than a pile. Like a piece of music, it's an arrangement rather than an aggregate. Like a marriage, it's a relationship rather than an encounter" (pp. 26–27). Thus, for example, students who gather to try out for a play have established only minimal relationships with one another and, therefore, are an "aggregate" of individuals in Davidson's terms. But the play's cast, once chosen, forms a system of relationships and roles that takes on an organization all its own. That system cannot be analyzed simply by looking at the actors or their individual motives. The entire system must be taken into account. This notion of wholeness influences our more formal definition of a **system** as a unit of analysis in which a change in any part affects all other parts and all relations among the parts.

Fisher (1982, pp. 198–201) describes the basic concepts within systems theories of communication, which we have paraphrased and extended here:

1. ***Holism/nonsummativity.*** Both holism (understanding a whole process or thing) and nonsummativity (the whole will always mean or function as

LINKS

❏ Recall the tentative distinctions we made earlier between quantitative and qualitative research. Quantitative researchers who identify themselves as behaviorists often adopt philosophical positions that are consistent with laws approaches. Qualitative researchers, who tend to rely more on interpretation, often identify with rules approaches. Although there are many exceptions, why do you think this general tendency might have developed?

❏ In Chapter 5, we'll discuss a more detailed approach to distinguishing action and motion, suggested by Kenneth Burke's thought.

more than the sum of its parts) suggest that you won't be able to understand a system by dividing up its components, analyzing them individually, and then adding them up ("summing" them) to try to get a sense of the whole. The whole cannot accurately be predicted by examining its subparts because it is by their interaction that the whole is formed. "The parts of the system are less important than the connectedness of the parts," according to Fisher (1982, p. 199). Theatrical directors and athletic coaches sense this when they refer to the "chemistry" in their casts and teams.

2. ***Openness.*** This term refers to how a system interchanges information with the environment outside its boundaries. In human systems especially, the boundaries are to some extent open, allowing the interchange of information between the system and outside elements. To the extent that the system becomes closed to outside information (perhaps feedback from rehearsal audiences), it begins to exhibit **entropy**—that is, it becomes increasingly disorganized and unpredictable. The system quits learning. An open system exhibits **equifinality**, which suggests that any given state or configuration of the system can be arrived at by various actions of system components. For example, there are many ways for the members of the cast to interact with one another and the director to produce a given outcome, such as favorable reviews of the play.

3. ***Hierarchical organization.*** Each system is simultaneously: (a) its own distinctive organization, (b) a part of a larger system (a subsystem), and (c) a collection of smaller systems (a suprasystem). Systems theorists thus realize that their "unit of analysis," whatever they choose to study, could be studied in vastly different ways just by taking alternative macroscopic or microscopic views. The system under study, then, is known as a **holon** (Koestler, 1967), which could be studied as a system in its own right, as a component of a larger system, or as an environment for a collection of smaller systems. A communication theorist interested in theater, for example, could study a cast as a holon, therefore, or might be more interested in studying a more complex holon made up of the system formed by the cast, the script, the set, the director, the stage crew, the musicians, and the audience—the show. Individual actors could serve as holons, too, if they were studied as system organisms composed of psychological and biological subsystems. So the analysis could go (perhaps infinitely?) in either direction.

4. ***Organized complexity.*** A system provides itself with ever-increasing states of differentiation. In order to survive and thrive, a system must take into account many different kinds of information, especially external *feedback* (see A Theory Extension, p. 43), to create complex internal structures for processing alternatives. Most systems are in a state of dynamic, always-changing complexity in which flexibility of response is a major criterion. Imagine analyzing as a system the mind of an improvisational actor such as Robin Williams or Whoopi Goldberg. The complexity of their talent involves changingness, not complicated stability. Thus the whole issue of **causation**, or the assumed connections between some events and changes in other events ("What caused her to react to that comment that

way?"), becomes problematic and complicated in systems theory. This is why systems theorists are skeptical of single or linear explanations (causes) for phenomena.

5. ***Self-regulation.*** This term refers to how a system regulates itself internally by balancing the relations among its components, or the characteristics or properties of those components. Although the environment always has some effect on a given system (e.g., a theater's acoustics will subtly influence how loudly the actors say their lines), each communication system establishes an internal *homeostasis,* or balance of relations, that allows it to generate its own distinctive kinds of information and to set its own goals.

General systems theory is less a theory of communication than it is a theory about theorizing about communication. Nevertheless, it helps us to organize our ideas about communication theory. If you consider systems approaches as ways to organize your communication thinking, then many of the concepts we describe later in this book can be organized in terms of a systems framework.

Now what? How might such a framework alter your worldview? Systems theory might lead you to any number of discoveries: that everything within a system is connected; that a system's components are all vulnerable to change; and that change is a function of the system itself, and is not just a direct cause-to-effect sequence. For example, consider a systems-oriented response to the question "What's wrong with this office?" A systems theorist would not reply, "The office is managed by an incompetent supervisor," because it cannot be assumed that the

---

A THEORY EXTENSION

FEEDBACK:

In communication theory, **feedback** refers to any message from your environment that can help you assess how effective your previous messages were in accomplishing certain goals. Good feedback serves as a control mechanism by which a system adapts flexibly within its context.

- *Examples:* Grades provide feedback for students, but so can such informal behavior as a teacher's interpersonal responsiveness, attention, friendliness, and perceived annoyance. In addition, students' performance on an exam or assignment provides teachers with feedback on how well they're meeting their goals of helping to create effective learning.

- *Types:* **Positive feedback** enhances or reinforces a tendency within a system. **Negative feedback** inhibits or regulates a system tendency by imposing a predetermined desired level or criterion. How do you think grades might function as positive feedback for students? How might grades function as negative feedback?

boss alone makes the office ineffective. Instead, a systems theorist would first think of the office as a holon, with its own inner and outer ecology, and then ask further questions: "Do any extra-system requirements and information influence the supervisor's behavior?" "Would any other supervisor in the same office be subject to the same influences?" "To what extent have subordinates invited or influenced the supervisor's behavior?" Systems theory, in short, looks beyond easy answers in response to communication questions. In its emphasis on connection and relationship, it constantly asks us to consider "What else?" "Who else?" "How else?" and "Why else?"

REVIEWING KEY THEORIES

This chapter has explained that theorizing is a common, informal, everyday activity, but also one that can be done systematically and formally by scholars who want to define communication more specifically. The work of these scholars is accomplished through what we've termed the theory-building cycle, which integrates research and explanation in a process of asking and re-asking clear questions.

Although we didn't mention specific theories here except as brief examples, we did sketch three basic orientations that can guide theorists (some call them "meta-theories"). The distinctions are not impermeable boundaries but more like philosophical tendencies. First, the goal of *covering law theories* is to develop highly generalizable principles of communication that will apply across situations. People who consider themselves to be covering law theorists tend to think of humans as being subject to these laws whenever they communicate. The goal of *rules theories* is the converse—the explanations these theorists seek are not generalizable across contexts but are closely tied to the particular situations in which they are found. Finally, *systems theories* attempt to show that communication must be examined holistically as the active and interdependent interrelation of its different parts.

REVIEWING KEY IDEAS

CHARACTERISTICS OF HUMAN SYSTEMS:

- *Holism/nonsummativity* (you can't predict the behavior of a system merely by considering the sum of its parts)
- *Openness* (how the system interchanges information with the environment outside its own boundaries)
- *Hierarchy* (how any system can be seen as made up of smaller subsystems, and as components of larger systems)
- *Organized complexity* (how a system becomes differentiated within itself in order to deal with ever-changing tasks)
- *Self-regulation* (how the system regulates itself by establishing an internal balance of relations)

TESTING THE CONCEPTS

"Is Ted real?"

Definitely. He is real in two ways. First, he actually took a theory class with content similar to the one you're enrolled in now. But, more important, Ted's attitude and motivation represent the real-life qualities of successful communication students. Such students expect to be seen as unique individuals. They ask their instructors to explain the implications of issues presented in class, and they insist on having their own voices heard in a group.

"I'm not at all theoretical. I want to study practical things. Why is it important for me to analyze all these theories of the communication process?"

In order to be a practical communicator, you should first understand how you've come to know what you do about communicating. Whether you realize it or not, you theorize about many aspects of life without thinking of it in that way. As you go about your daily activities, you question why something happens or doesn't happen, take your observations into account, then check them out. Ultimately, if your tentative conclusions aren't helpful, you'll question some more. When you do this, you are developing a theory about some everyday process. If you are curious, are willing to be surprised, are experienced at trying things out, and respect others' views, you already have experience in theory-building. By fine-tuning this process and learning from others' theorizing, you become more comfortable and more effective in applying communication skills. What could be more practical?

"Should all theorists become researchers, too?"

In one way, yes. Most scholarly work assumes that theorists work from data. Ideas shouldn't come from thin air, nor should they remain there. That is, theorists are responsible for showing how their theories are, or can be, practical and useful.

But in another sense the answer is no. One type of theorist (who is still a researcher, we would argue) doesn't attempt to demonstrate practicality just by creating data. Instead, this theorist/researcher also synthesizes the work of others into a more coherent larger pattern or whole. In the discipline of communication, many theorists fulfill this role well. We especially recommend the work of Julia Wood (1996), Frank E. X. Dance (1967, 1982), Stephen Littlejohn (1996), and W. Barnett Pearce (1989). This role doesn't suggest a lack of originality; these and other scholars have made many original contributions to communication theory. Skillful synthesis is itself a kind of research.

"You mentioned 'mystery' in relation to communication theory several times. Can't we just let some things be mysterious, without overanalyzing them?"

This question, common in communication classes, uncovers an important problem: As indicated by the experience of some writers, "analysis can become paralysis." Overanalyzing the communication process, or even becoming excessively aware of it while it happens, can disable communicators. But the major reason for studying theories of communication is not to guide your moment-by-moment choices of language and behavior while in conversation with others. Practical theories provide the backdrop against which specific problems, as they arise, can be understood. In the language of *gestalt psychology* (a historical branch of psychological research that focuses on perceptual problems), this is called a **figure/ground relationship**. The ground, the backdrop, surrounds and provides context for the figure, or object of perception on which you wish to focus—and to understand one you need to understand the other. A communication specialist who serves as a resource to others in an organization must be able to provide insight and clues that help people deal with the inevitable dilemmas of communication. The specialist who responds with useful suggestions or explanations based on theories of communication, however tentative they may be, is far more competent than one who says, "I'm sorry, but communication is just too mysterious to be understood."

To understand the nature of mystery is to respect the unknown, the undiscovered, perhaps the undiscoverable. The mysterious demands our attention but makes no promises and often won't yield to our solutions. The world refuses to sit still as a puzzle waits to be solved. Of course, some aspects of communication may always remain a mystery. Some theorists have begun to examine the role of mystery in guiding how human beings relate to each other (Goodall, 1991; Pearce, 1989). This is exciting work. You might want to investigate the topic in a special class project or independently.

"Because theories are really similar to positions taken in arguments, how do we know who can settle the arguments? Who decides?"

No board of appeals governs an academic discipline. There are no elections for choosing the "best" theories, although a journal once ran an article listing and ranking influential communication theorists (Beniger, 1990). Instead, a theory is considered successful if it is used by other theorists and if it helps people organize concepts and ideas better than they could before the theory was developed. Many theoretical arguments are never "decided," because observers inevitably disagree about what constitutes a good account of social phenomena.

Try to think of theoretical arguments not as formal debates but as ongoing conversations within an intellectual arena, where the give-and-take of fact and opinion continually modifies all positions within the dialogue. Thus some positions that once seemed mutually exclusive or even contradictory in this scholarly interchange might later be modified by the conversation into theories that are actually compatible.

"You stress the importance of asking questions, sometimes even more than answering them. Are all questions good?"

Not necessarily. Some contemporary philosophers of communication, notably Gadamer (1982, pp. 325 ff.; Palmer, 1969, pp. 198–201), believe that a genuine or true question always presumes an openness to experience (or a willingness to be surprised, in the language we used earlier in the chapter). Genuine questions therefore address issues about which the questioner does not already know the answer. Ambiguity doesn't just stimulate a question; it is the very presumption by which a question is defined. This is why theorizing is so exciting and far from being the "dry" subject many new students assume it to be.

Gadamer (1982) contrasts true questions, however, with false or distorted questions (p. 327). Although false questions masquerade as true questions, they are actually presuppositions and assertions in disguise. They presume not to discover answers but to know them already. As such, they don't invite new learning as much as they warm over and assert what we already know. As an example, consider how attorneys use cross-examination in a courtroom. Some lawyers are taught in law school that if they have to ask a witness a question to which the lawyer doesn't already know the answer, the case is in deep trouble indeed. The lawyer is an advocate with a case to present and a "side" to represent. Although this may be necessary in the legal field, it is not what Gadamer has in mind as genuine questioning. Nor can it be a model for inquiry in the creative arts and sciences. A sentence that ends with a question mark may not be a true question, then. And a theory to which a theorist is irrevocably committed is not a genuine theory. In both cases, the questions are false.

YOU, THE RESEARCHER

In this and the following chapters, we'll suggest some useful projects for you to try. These suggestions will range from small teasers to tasks involving library research or experience-based excursions that could serve as the basis for term papers. They are designed to give you a taste of what it's like to be a practicing communication scholar. They may also stimulate class discussion and help you see the links between the chapters and possible applications in your own life. Most of the projects can be accomplished effectively in a relatively brief period of time.

Before you begin working on these activities, however, there are a few things you should keep in mind. First, even though the projects involve research they in no way approximate the complexity of the research studies discussed in this book. Most of the theories you will learn about in this course came from scholars devoting years of commitment to studying communication. Therefore, while the activities are designed to be interesting and practical for you, they will not supply results that can verify or refute scholarly theories.

Second, because our focus in this book is on asking questions in order to theorize, many of the end-of-chapter activities have basically descriptive or exploratory research goals. Experimental research, with its emphasis on the precise control of variables, is usually too complicated and intricate to simulate in class activities.

Finally, some of the research projects ask you to collect data from other people, such as other students or faculty members on campus. *A very important point:* Before beginning any activities that require others' cooperation or participation, students and faculty should make themselves aware of any campus guidelines for conducting research with human co-participants or respondents.

Most colleges and universities now require (usually through a clear and succinct policy) prior approval for any studies, formal or informal, that require the willing or unwitting participation of others. Check your institution's regulations, which are usually described in a faculty handbook or in other general campus publications.

1. Carefully read the past week's editions of your local newspaper, or the previous four issues of a national newsmagazine (including the editorial, sports, and cartoon sections). In a notebook, copy all sentences that mention the concept of theory. In addition, note when and how your friends use *theory* and *theoretical* in everyday conversation. Which, if any, of the sentences use the concept in a negative context in your opinion (e.g., a book review that refers to the author's point of view as "merely theoretical")? Which, if any, of the sentences refer to the concept in a positive or neutral context (e.g., a scientific article that cites Einstein's "theory of relativity" to explain a phenomenon)? Discuss how—and how often—our culture tends to employ the concept of theory.

2. Draw a diagram, or construct with any materials at hand a three-dimensional representation, showing how each of the following is a "system." (You may need to talk with friends or other students to learn more about how each system is composed of components, properties, and relationships.)

   - A stereo system (including such audio components as amplifier, preamplifier, tuner, tape deck, CD player, turntable, patch cords, speaker cables, and speakers)
   - A sports team (e.g., softball, baseball, basketball, football, soccer, volleyball)
   - The organization of a restaurant's kitchen
   - Photosynthesis in a plant

   You have just created "a systems model." A good model, which we'll discuss in greater detail in the next chapter, simplifies and represents the basic operation of a complex process without oversimplifying it. In a model, the relationships become clearer, although complexity must be sacrificed.

3. Conduct a series of interviews to determine how the concept of theory is used in other disciplines. Interview three faculty members from departments other than communication, one from each of the following areas:

   - Natural sciences (e.g., chemistry, biology, physics, astronomy)
   - Social sciences (e.g., sociology, anthropology, psychology, political science)
   - Humanities (e.g., literature, philosophy, art, music, languages)

   Begin each interview by introducing yourself and explaining the purpose of your interview. Then ask this question: "How does a new theory in your field get accepted or rejected?" Respond to the professor's answer with whatever follow-up questions or comments you think are appropriate, based on your reading of this chapter. Take careful notes or, if the interviewees agree, tape-record the interviews. Finally, compare your findings with this chapter's discussion of the theory-building cycle. Do the various disciplines have anything in common? If so, what? Are there any significant differences? Do these professors use such terms as *science, research,* and *verification* in ways similar to or different from their colleagues in other fields?

Jeffry Myers/Stock, Boston

CHAPTER 2

"When Have We Communicated?"

Theorizing Communication

> To learn to be human is to develop through the give-and-take of communication
> an effective sense of being an individually distinctive member of a community. . . .
>
> JOHN DEWEY, *The Public and Its Problems* (1927, p. 154)

Communication techniques have become marketable commodities in today's consumer culture. It sometimes seems as if the world were divided into two almost equally large groups—the people who want to be saved by the techniques, and the supposed experts who want to save them. As teachers of communication, we have mixed feelings about this trend. Although it's nice to see that communication is recognized as an important problem, it seems inappropriate to imply that studying it is a technique-centered fad.

Popular culture, at least in North America, is infatuated with the companion concepts of communication and relationship. Television and radio talk shows, advice columns, and everyday talk at parties and offices all seem to point to a "lack of communication" as a root cause of society's maladies. "More" communication and prescriptive techniques are packaged for marriage partners, families, committees, football teams, and organizations, as though communication were a medicine. After we take a prescribed dose, presumably we'll hurt less.

Communication: A Cure?

Two stories in major urban newspapers, which coincidentally appeared on the same day, illustrate our popular preoccupation with "communication." One front-page article reported that a mayor telephoned the owner of a sports franchise and subjected his secretary to obscene name-calling and taunts. The columnist ended the story by wondering if this was a case of too much impulsive anger, "or just not enough communication?" (Koman, 1990, p. 4).

In the other article, the manager of a baseball team that had lost 95 of 162 games the previous year was interviewed about his leadership style. Unidentified players had accused him of being "unfairly critical and uncommunicative." But now, the interviewer discovers, "community" has become a high priority for the manager, who claims that "communication is crucial to managing a ballclub" (O'Neill, 1990, p. 3D). Of course, he's right; communication is indeed crucial. But the team's poor record the previous year was not caused by a *lack* of communication any more than the mayor's bad manners were. Both incidents were examples of particular kinds of communication, not examples of its absence. Communication is crucial because without it there wouldn't even have been a "last season" for the manager, and indeed there wouldn't have been a team.

Academic theories in communication studies tend to treat communication as neither a fad nor a handy self-help tool but the basic process that constitutes human cooperation and conflict in the first place. Recall, from the Introduction, our preliminary definition of *communication* as a process in which people interpret messages in order to coordinate their individual and social meanings. Through communication we cooperate in sharing meanings in order to achieve some sort of coordination in relationships.

You might ask, "If communication becomes a fad now and then, what's wrong with that?" While some fads are trivial, such as the hula hoop, others can be harmful, such as spiked heels on women's shoes or diets that produce rapid weight loss without medical supervision. Still, you might ask, "But what could be detrimental about a preoccupation with communication, a central process of human understanding? Who could fault modern society for trying to improve relationships through more understanding?" Unfortunately, the understanding of communication that often accompanies this goal is subtly dangerous. Communication is trivialized when it is viewed simply as a medicine or a self-help treatment that can be prescribed in greater or smaller doses. People who try "more" communication as a fix-it technique often find that nothing is fixed. An open and honest conversation—presumably "good" communication to many people—may reveal that the speakers actually like each other less than they originally thought they did, or that they feel less motivated to listen to or agree with each other. Venting feelings in an office or a family setting, presumably to add more communication, can increase, not decrease, resentment and conflict.

Studying communication theory provides alternatives to this popularized communication-is-the-answer philosophy, but they are not neat and tidy. Contemporary theorists understand that communication is not so much a single answer to human problems as the central process by which we become human in the first place, and the process by which we can understand the everyday problems we face. Therefore, communication is not itself an answer, but to understand communication more fully is to know more about how life's questions get asked. Theorists have not developed a single unified, sophisticated, and definitive description of communication to replace the simplistic view of it as a fad. Nor are they likely to do so.

Researchers develop alternative explanations for communication and different models of it that attempt to illustrate its processes. Communication theory is necessarily a pluralistic, not a unified, field. Studying these explanations can be frustrating because they often contradict each other. However, studying them can also be eminently realistic and practical. Another way of stating the major theme in this chapter is that communication is the only way we can live, behave, and develop symbolic relationships. It isn't just a therapeutic medicine to be taken when something is wrong with a relationship at home or work.

This chapter describes some basic facets of communication about which most current theorists and researchers agree. First, you'll read about communication as the process through which people use messages to create human environments for relationships. This definition will be contrasted with a more simplistic information-transmission definition. Second, we'll explore the implications of the concept of *process*. Third, we'll discuss the impact of a relational or mutualistic, rather than an individualistic, perspective, using *transaction* as an explanatory key. We'll use the knotty problem of meaning to test the practicality of our vantage point on communication. Finally, we'll consider whether sender/speaker intention is necessary in a helpful specification of communication. This brings us back full circle to where the chapter begins—with the claim that an appreciation of the flow of communication (though more complex and less intuitive than a sender–receiver model) is actually more practical for communicators, researchers, and theorists.

We also have a secondary agenda in this chapter. We hope to show that communication, an interdisciplinary venture, is not owned by any one academic discipline or even by a family of disciplines. We'll cite authorities in communication, psychology, sociology, anthropology, philosophy, economics, literature, biology, management, and other fields while stressing this important point. Practical communication theory comes from all directions, not just from the social sciences, the humanities, experimental studies, or communication scholars. The symbolic nature of human interaction provides a hub for the theorizing of many persuasions and disciplines.

Defining Communication Realistically

Ancient Roman and Greek teachers had a creative explanation for how people communicated. They believed that Mercury (Hermes to the Greeks), the god with wings on his feet and cap, grabbed an idea from one person's head, skewered it on his spear, and then thrust it into another person's head in an unambiguous, irrevocable act of delivering the goods (Thayer, 1968, p. 3). Mercury, "the messenger," also came to be known as the god of commerce; you can still see his image today portrayed in the logo of a prominent national floral-delivery company.

You may be amused by this Mercury "model of communication," assuming that it's too superficial to account for all the complex variables of human interaction. And, of course, it is. Yet contemporary Western culture retains the single most misleading and possibly dangerous concept of the ancient transportation-of-an-idea notion. By believing that Mercury could transfer an idea, the Romans assumed that the idea supposedly delivered to the receiver was *the same idea formerly found only in the brain of the sender.* However, isn't an idea (or an image, intention, or feeling) an intangible, an interpretation, and a personalized, unique meaning? As such, it cannot be transferred as a whole to another person; rather, it can be hinted at or suggested only in fragments, largely because other communicators share in the same cultural stock of ideas. But consider the words used today to oversimplify this amazingly intricate process: *transmitting, conveying, feeding back, exchanging, delivering.*

A classic volume of research findings, influential with social scientists for years, informed readers that communication is "the transmission of information, ideas, emotions, skills, etc., by the use of symbols" (Berelson & Steiner, 1964, p. 527). Similarly, influential philosopher A. J. Ayer (1955) claimed that in typical conceptions of communication, "the connecting thread appears to be the idea of something's being transferred from one thing, or person, to another" (p. 12). Unfortunately, some prominent dictionaries of social science also reinforce this transfer/transmit theme (Corsini, 1984, p. 249; Goldenson, 1984, p. 160; Theodorson & Theodorson, 1969, p. 62; Wolman, 1973, p. 69). Michael Reddy (1979) refers to this preoccupation as the **conduit metaphor** (a conduit is a pathway or a channel through which a substance moves from one place to another). Reddy shows how conduit thinking is deeply embedded in the English language (Reddy, 1979; see also Lakoff & Johnson, 1980). If we think and speak in English, says Reddy, we cannot completely escape conceptualizing communication in conduit terms. Our language makes it seem natural for us to consider ideas, feelings, and intended meanings as objects to place into containers (words, language) for the purpose of sending them to other people. However, reminding ourselves that this metaphor misstates the complexity of the communication process is a step toward a more realistic understanding.

As Lakoff and Johnson (1980) show in the following examples, it's difficult to understand conduit thinking as a metaphor because we are so thoroughly immersed in certain linguistic assumptions. Yet, listening closely, we can hear the metaphor in everyday talk:

It's hard to get that idea *across* to him.

I *gave* you that idea.

Your reasons *came through* to us.

It's difficult to *put* my ideas *into* words.

When you *have* a good idea, try to *capture* it immediately in words.

Try to *pack* more thought *into* fewer words.

You can't simply *stuff* ideas *into* a sentence any old way.

The meaning is right there *in* the words.

Don't *force* your meanings *into* the wrong words.

His words *carry* little meaning.

The introduction *has* a great deal of thought *content*.

Your words seem *hollow*.

The sentence is *without* meaning.

The idea is *buried* in terribly dense paragraphs (p. 11).

W. Charles Redding (1968) reported that in his workshops for middle- and upper-level managers, almost 100 percent of executives agreed with this initial characterization of communication: "When Person X 'communicates' with Person Y, what happens is that he transmits meanings (information, facts, ideas, etc.)... to the mind of Person Y" (p. 101). The rest of Redding's workshop was devoted to encouraging people to change this natural, but fallacious, assumption to a more realistic one.

Another organizational communication specialist (Haney, 1973) wisely doesn't want students to forget completely about transmission. But although something is conveyed from place to place in an act of human speech, it isn't meaning: "Some neural impulses are sent from the brain to the abdominal muscles (for air power), the larynx (for phonation), and the articulatory organs (jaw, teeth, tongue, glottis, lips, and so forth) and A is now *transmitting*. Transmitting what? Words?

Thoughts? Meanings? Ideas? Feelings? The Message? No—vibrations—simply compressions and rarefications of molecules in the air" (p. 183). When we move molecules through speech or create symbols or images in other ways, we create the conditions in which meanings can be partially accessible to others. But the inner state of a communicator never travels from person to person. We take messages as clues that others are somehow attempting to connect with us. Then, as if we were building the same bridge but starting from different shores, we tentatively begin to construct a responsive message. If we want to continue building the bridge, we monitor each other's progress and direction and try to use compatible methods. We acknowledge the inevitability of trial and error. We know the meeting can never be exact. The bridge, admittedly imperfect, only comes into being at the meeting, however. Only then do the two sides meet with something in common. To avoid being misled by yet another metaphor, think of the bridge as people's common access to cooperation and coordination, not as the means by which they share exactly the same thoughts and feelings.

This notion of commonality is at the root of all purposeful communication, in etymology as well as in function. In communication, meaning is created that is common to the participants. *Communication, common, commune, communion*— the similarities among these words are not accidental (Williams, 1976, pp. 62– 63). Shared meaning is not the property of individuals, nor is it transmitted from one to the other; rather, it is pooled between them. The center of two separate beings, the link, becomes their communication. Are they two beings any more? Yes and no. Yes, they remain separate and unique. No, their communication has, in a sense, made them one functioning unit, a system with interdependencies.

Despite the interdependent relationship among communicators, communication is not always pleasant or strategically planned. Some people call every disagreement or conflict a "communication breakdown" and any confrontation of different values a "communication gap." They assume that if the other person just understood them well enough, if they could just "get their idea across" better, the disagreement would disappear. Conflict is seen as evidence of a lack of communication, and a signal to inject more of this magical stuff into the conversation. However, with better understanding comes dual possibilities—we may agree with or appreciate each other more *or* less.

Communication as a process is omnipresent and, therefore, neutral. Although personifying concepts is always somewhat inaccurate, another metaphor might help here. Communication, in a sense, doesn't care what happens through its workings. Of course, people care about communication, but it doesn't return the favor. Communication is much more like a constantly shifting environment than a tool for ensuring the results we individually or collectively want. We don't work with it as much as we work within it. Communication theorist W. Barnett Pearce (1989) provides an insightful summary of this point: "The process of describing forms of communication is made more important because the discovery that we live in communication transmutes communication from a secondary to a primary role in human life. Rather than a means by which 'internal' states are expressed and 'objective' facts represented, communication is that process by which 'persons,' 'institutions,' and 'facts' are constructed" (p. xvi).

Communication: Continually Changing?

What Is a Process?

A realistic definition of communication should not rely on jargon. Still, this chapter has presented a number of common terms in fairly restricted ways. One example is the notion of a process. In everyday talk, the claim that something is a process implies that events occur sequentially. We "use" a process to accomplish a preset goal or to make sure a problem is solved smoothly. In this sense, parliamentary procedure is a good process for running meetings, and one form of rationality could be learned by applying John Dewey's process of reflective thinking. When we speak of "processing paperwork" and "word processing," we imply movement toward a defined end. Such ways of referring to process are reasonable and valid.

The flow of communication, however, is best described by a different notion of process, one developed by prominent philosophers and theorists (Johnson, 1946; Kress, 1970; Whitehead, 1930). In communication theory, process usually doesn't refer to a sequential way of doing things. Rather, when communication is said to be a **process**, theorists are in tune with contemporary scientists, who argue that the world is not composed of discrete and isolated *things* that affect each other in neat packages of cause and effect called *events*. The scientific concept of process is fundamentally ecological; it suggests that everything is interlinked, sometimes even to the point that it's hard to tell where or when one thing begins and another ends. We may choose to simplify our explanations and discuss "events," implying as we do that they have clear-cut beginnings and endings. For example, you might simplify how we talk about people and imply that Professor Jones was the "same" person with the same attitude before and after you complained about your grade. These are compromises of everyday speech, through which we convince ourselves that the world is manageable.

A more realistic idea, though admittedly harder to grasp, is that nothing is static or unchanging. The universe is in constant flux, movement, and adjustment, much of which we can sense only indirectly with our human perceptual apparatus. Thus, for example, Professor Jones's attitude did change after your conversation, but perhaps not in the direction or magnitude you would have liked. Nor was your teacher the same person after your talk, since all people are constantly affected by their surroundings. Communication is, in a fundamental way, neither an accomplishment nor a simple event. It is a process of continual change that is impossible to slow down or stop. There aren't snapshots or instant replays of communication, then, because when it's frozen or analyzed into an event, it ceases to be living communication.

Because human communication is a process in constant creative flux, and one that cannot be stopped or manipulated at will, we have to use artificial verbal concoctions such as "components," "stages," "conclusions," and "causes," among many others, to aid in our understanding of it. But as process theorists remind us, we do not discover these phenomena in external reality. The concepts are manufactured and then layered over the reality we experience in an attempt to make that reality appear more manageable. Philosopher Alan Watts (1975) asks, "Can we think of the heart as separate from the veins, or the branches from the tree? Just what exact delineations distinguish the bee process from the flower process? These distinctions are always somewhat arbitrary and conventional, even when described with very exact language, for the distinctions reside more in the language than in what it describes" (p. 13).

Brenda Dervin (1993) has suggested that if theorists want to remain true to what they profess in their classes and business consultations, they would do more of what she calls "verbing." As Dervin describes it, **verbing** is a way of reminding ourselves that whatever noun labels we use, we are really studying fluid processes, such as "thinkings and emotings, listenings and arguings, positionings and vacillatings, cooperatings and contestings, polarizings and nuancings, categorizings and hierarchizings, nounings and verbings" (p. 51). She admits that such terms sound clumsy, but we still need the reminders. Although the communication discipline earnestly encourages students to adopt a process-centered theoretical perspective, too many researchers still tend to "posit the subject as moving from one state to another. The emphasis is on the states, not the moves" (p. 51). It's a matter of not practicing what we preach: Unfortunately, Dervin claims, we often "focus on entities, not process; on nouns, not verbs" (p. 51). For example, Dervin would advise researchers studying how people get angry with each other to define their task as studying the active *process* of people's "emotings" rather than the *things* we imagine as "emotions."

The Difficulties of a Process Orientation

As Watts (1975) and Dervin (1993) illustrate, the nature of language presents problems to anyone who studies it from a process orientation. The separations and distinctions signified by words are absent in our everyday flow of experiencing. Language, indispensable in human experience, imposes a kind of artificial order on that experience. Therefore theorists and researchers face an especially difficult challenge. To be as precise and clear as possible, they invent more and more specific linguistic category systems—called **taxonomies**—with which to describe a complex world. But if the communicative world exists more as relationships-in-flux than as things, the boundaries described by the words actually belong to the words. Philosopher Alfred North Whitehead (1930) shows how **spatialization** (the cutting of reality artificially into static categories to ignore the world's inherent "fluency") "is the shortest route to a clear-cut philosophy expressed in reasonably familiar language" (p. 319). Unfortunately, the clarity that results from spatialization may be only a false security. As Watts suggested earlier, the bee process is the flower process, and vice versa. By using artificial linguistic divisions (would Dervin remind us to say "dividings"?), students of communication risk removing themselves from the very process they seek to understand.

Scientist Werner Heisenberg (1958) grapples with a similar problem in his **uncertainty principle**. Although his idea is far more complex than we need to describe here, it's relevant to note that many scholars suggest that it has a clear implication for researchers: You cannot study a phenomenon in isolation, because the very methods used to observe and measure nature interfere with and alter natural processes. We end up studying, in other words, what may be happening only because we're studying something (see also Zukav, 1979, pp. 132–136). Researchers can never be completely sure whether some observed effects have been influenced by the observations themselves. Because the world is itself in a process of constant change, research cannot be conducted apart from that process.

Another problem with the process orientation is simply stated, but its implications are complex and frustrating. Process thinking doesn't sound practical at first. It *feels* as if our lives have starts, stops, and turning points, even though conceptually we might agree that processes are ongoing and constantly changing. Our direct experience of communication, therefore, seems to contradict our process understanding of it. Despite all our reminders in this book, you probably still think of your personal relationships as capable of being frozen, stuck, stopped, started anew, and in many ways manipulated like objects. Intellectually, you may agree that communication is always flowing in some new direction and that it's impossible to freeze it long enough to study it precisely (even though we attempt to do just that). "Stop the world! I want to get off," screamed a character in a famous Broadway play. Communication theorists face this dilemma every day. Their theories attempt to explain how people manage events, explanations, and transitions, such as fault finding, leave-taking, and conversational turn-taking, in their lives. They "punctuate" sequences of actions through individual attention and relational redefinitions.

In fact, the term **punctuation** is used by some theorists to describe how people structure their experience in terms of their perceptions of when things start, stop, change, renew, and so forth (Bateson & Jackson, 1964; Watzlawick, 1984). Periods, commas, and other punctuation marks help readers understand how writers structure their messages. In writing, punctuation is an attempt to provide order. (That last sentence "ended" where the period signaled its conclusion.) Analogously, two communicators who blame each other for starting an argument are "punctuating" the disagreement differently. (I might think our argument last night started because we ended up seeing the movie I chose, and that the argument has passed. You might attribute the argument to my prior unwillingness to listen to your suggestions and thus consider the argument still in progress. Sound familiar?) A recognition of the effects of punctuation has saved many relationships; it permits the talk to shift from blaming to discussing the reasons for different punctuations.

A process orientation is practical, therefore, because it helps us stay clearheaded in times of interpersonal crisis and helps us focus on real, rather than illusory, communication problems. Here are some of its reminders for everyday application:

- Something is always happening to change the developing flow of communication. As one communication book suggested, "nothing never happens" (Johnson, Senatore, Liebig, & Minor, 1974). Complacency, despair, and stagnation—despite being experienced as "real" emotions and frustrations—don't adequately describe a world in constant change. The future may or may not be brighter, but it will be different from the present and the past.
- Data are always available. Since relationships don't vanish, interpretive clues remain. For example, your roommate may stop talking to you as punishment for some personal insult. The process of constructing meaning continues, however, and you begin to notice how your roommate looks at

LINK

You will read more about how theorists developed the concept of *punctuation* later, in Chapter 5. It is a vivid demonstration of how the observable behaviors of communication become meaningful primarily as they are interpreted by individuals who may see them differently.

you or how long she stays away from the apartment or how she fidgets while watching television. All of these acts are potential messages, and as Watzlawick, Beavin, and Jackson (1967) point out, once you are in a relationship it's impossible to avoid communication. Although some scholars advance a more restrictive definition of communication based on the intentions of communicators, the reminder is still valid. Potentially helpful data for clarifying an interaction are always available.

• You cannot change only one part of a process or fiddle with only one variable. Although you may hope to do so, you will inevitably be frustrated by what communication theorists call "interdependence" or "wholeness." Changing any single part of the whole will affect the relationships among the other parts of the whole, and thus the other parts will relate to each other in new ways. Thus, for instance, if you work in a small office and change your relationship with the boss (by becoming more competitive, let's say), that is not "just between the two of you" and "nobody else's business." Your co-workers may or may not be tactful, but they are not, technically speaking, mere observers of a process. They are inextricably part of the process, and their experience is affected by all changes in the office. Changing one relationship affects the dynamic of the entire group, perhaps in unpredictable ways. It is practical to be better able to predict such system effects.

Communication can create interdependent well-functioning systems out of accidental collections of individuals, and then it can sustain those systems dynamically. As B. Aubrey Fisher (1978), one influential analyst of human systems, explains:

> *Two adults and three children may constitute a mere "aggregate" or a "heap" (system-theory jargon for a nonsystem). But when they live together as a family and affect each other in the day-by-day living together, they constitute a collective system called family— identifiable as a single unit. The individual identities…become amalgamated into the collectivity…such that what happens to one (for example, an illness, a broken teen-age heart, a loss of job income) affects every other member of the family unit. (p. 197)*

Family systems also comprise neighborhoods, which can themselves be analyzed as systems. The various levels of systems analysis can, of course, stretch in both directions, larger or smaller, from any system upon which you might be focusing (see A Theory Extension, p. 61).

Mutuality and Transaction

Interdependence, ecology, and *system* have become hallmark terms of contemporary culture. No longer is it realistic to think of the United States as being self-sufficient with regard to world resources, as the oil policies of Middle East countries often demonstrate. And decisions made by students in small, sequestered apartments in Beijing, China, some years ago profoundly affected macroeconomic and diplomatic strategies debated in the world's major capitals.

Individualistic Approaches: One to Another?

In the United States especially, a preoccupation with the self still seems to drive our attitudes about communication. When we want to compliment or advise someone, what do we tend to say? Here is a brief list of typical comments that illustrate the individualistic bias in our talk; the list suggests in both obvious and subtle ways a predominant informal *nonprocessual* "theory":

"You're so self-reliant."

"He's an independent thinker."

"She's her own person."

"You've learned to meet your own needs."

"He's self-actualized."

"She's really made something of herself."

"You're a self-starter."

"He's into self-help and self-development."

"She has power over others."

"Be yourself."

"Do what you think is right."

"Decide for yourself."

"Take your future in your own hands."

"Make your own decisions."

"Be the captain of your own fate."

"Look out for number one."

A THEORY EXTENSION

PRACTICAL REMINDERS: PROCESS ORIENTATION OF COMMUNICATION

- Conditions, states, and meanings can't be frozen; tomorrow may not be better or worse than today, but it will not be another today.
- Humans constantly interpret their lives by using messages as data. Instead of assuming that communication is not happening, assume it is, and then ask, "How?"
- Beware of the assumption that "it's nobody else's business." Communication relationships are interdependent on many levels, and observers are inevitably participants, too.

Taken singly and in context, these statements seem reasonable. After all, people do "make personal decisions" and some "have power over others." But as a group such comments emphasize the individual's contributions to communication and largely neglect how others influence communication outcomes. Some social scientists with an interest in communication bemoan this trend, including Bellah, Madsen, Sullivan, Swidler, and Tipton (1986). After conducting extensive interviews, they conclude that the American tendency toward individualism—one that has been helpful in many ways—has now become potentially "cancerous" (p. vii). Similarly, sociologist Charles Derber (1979), in an analysis of conversational narcissism, argues that "America is developing…not toward greater community or cooperation, but toward an intensification of the entrenched individualism" (p. 93). **Conversational narcissism** refers to people who believe they must monopolize conversations to prove they are effective communicators.

The **individualistic orientation** of communication defines communication in terms of what one person does to others by aiming messages that may either hit or miss designated targets. Similar to Reddy's (1979) conduit metaphor discussed earlier in this chapter, communication is assumed to be made up of message manipulations that are controlled by a sender and designed for a receiver. Communication is an "I" process; I communicate *toward* or *at* you. In this sense, then, communication appears to have a well-defined intention, and, if the target is hit with the intended message, it produces predictable effects in the targeted receiver. This set of assumptions about communication implies that a well-chosen message will "work" for the sender, unless there is noise (interference that detracts attention from the message) in the **channel** (the medium through which messages are conveyed).

Mutualistic Approaches: Both Sides Now?

Although the notion that communication moves from individual to individual may seem reasonable, most theorists now recognize a more **mutualistic orientation**, one that focuses on relationships rather than on individuals (Reardon, 1987, pp. 125–158). This approach also incorporates the concept of **transaction** (Dewey & Bentley, 1949), which implies a relationship between system elements in which the definition of each element depends on changes in the other elements within the same system, such that nothing can be defined in isolation. Rosenblatt (1978) adds a slightly different dimension when she says that transaction, in this theoretical sense, is "an ongoing process in which the elements or factors are…aspects of a total situation, each conditioned by and conditioning the other" (p. 17).

Many academic disciplines apply transactional theory in their research. Transactional psychologists have used the concept to probe the processes of human perception (Ames, 1951; Bruner, 1986; Toch & MacLean, 1962). Literary critics have applied transaction and allied concepts to the analysis of poetry and other literature (Clark, 1990; Rosenblatt, 1978). Theorists of media and journalism have stressed the theoretical and practical relevance of transaction (Killenberg & Anderson, 1989; Wenner, 1985). Mainstream communication theorists have used it to emphasize a general state of reciprocity and mutual causality in interpersonal relations (Barnlund, 1970; Hall, 1977; Mortensen, 1972; Rasmussen, 1976; Stewart, 1990; Windahl & Signitzer, with Olson, 1992). Dewey and Bentley (1949, p. 116) point out that the word *transaction* customarily refers to the deals or negotiations that result in agreements, or to the straightforward exchange of goods and services. But since Dewey introduced the concept around 1930, its meaning has become somewhat more specialized.

In order to understand communication transactionally, consider the following scenario: You attempt to establish a new friendship with someone you've noticed in class. You do everything you can think of to be friendly to her—you walk to the water fountain with her at break, you suggest studying together, you even offer to tape a class session you know she'll miss because of a dental appointment. Despite your efforts and good intentions, she seems aloof and noncommittal. Why? One way of explaining the communication situation is to assume that she is just a quiet person. You might call her "shy," if this explanation makes sense to you. But Dewey and Bentley (1949) point out the problem of such an explanation and suggest that the basis of this human difficulty is the activity of naming. We sometimes try to name things and their characteristics as though meaning came directly to us from those things in a linear fashion. They call this kind of understanding *self-actional,* because it assumes that a thing generates its own inherent meaning and all you have to do is "get it."

An alternative way of explaining your predicament would be to assume that your actions in some way made her back off from you. In this case, you would begin to criticize yourself: "That was stupid. I'm too pushy. I caused her to respond to me that way." Or you might think that her quietness caused you to respond with a nurturing or helping attitude. This is a somewhat more sophisticated view of the situation because it assumes a two-way flow of action. Unlike your first explanation, which relies on a single external factor (the student's shyness), the second explanation allows for the possibility that you may have influenced the other person's behavior. Based on this analysis, you may conclude that you and your classmate reacted to each other's actions. This type of understanding, which recognizes the causes and effects of actions and reactions, is what Dewey and Bentley (1949) call *interactional.*

When Dewey and Bentley surveyed the intellectual scene, they thought most science and social science researchers asked the kinds of questions that would generate self-actional answers. Although Newtonian physics and some explanatory systems in psychology had moved toward a more interactional perspective, the relationship between the processes of naming and the named (or between knowing and the known) was not adequately recognized until the publication of Dewey and Bentley's book.

Let's try some hypothetical thinking about our previous example. Suppose that your classmate's quiet behavior wasn't necessarily an unchangeable component of her personality that can be objectified—"thing-ized"—by calling it shyness. At the same time, imagine that you didn't *cause* that behavior, nor did she somehow cause your nurturance or friendliness. What you're supposing here, then, is that the world isn't composed of isolated objects with necessary attributes (self-actional), and it also isn't like a tabletop of billiard balls that move only when they're hit or caused to move by external objects (interactional). So-called

Thinking transactionally, of course, is closely related to other central concepts of this chapter. Through its transactional nature, human communication constitutes our experience. Transactional thinking depends on a process orientation, because it discourages analysis that depends on separate things that exhibit their own properties. It illustrates why interdependence is necessary to systems theory. With transactional thinking, perception is a matter of creativity, not certainty; we don't receive meanings as much as we conceive them. In Chapter 11, you'll read about the evolution of the discipline of communication. Its beginnings can be traced from speaker-centered concerns that are fundamentally individualistic and self-actional to more contemporary trends that are more mutualistic and transactional.

common sense encourages self-actional and interactional explanations; they are simple to provide.

Dewey and Bentley (1949) thought we must think transactionally in order to create explanations that depend not on objects but on the active relationships that connect them. They regard this kind of relational thinking as most consistent with the complex nature of the world. Again, let's be practical. Practicality doesn't mean always adopting the most obvious or the simplest explanation. It's truly practical to take complex factors into account, and in their proper context. Dewey and Bentley (1949) bring a transactional approach to communicating down-to-earth with common terms: "In ordinary everyday behavior, in what sense can we examine a talking unless we bring a hearing along with it into account? Or a writing without a reading? Or a buying without a selling? Or a supply without a demand?... We can, of course, detach any portion of a transaction that we wish, and secure provisional descriptions and partial reports. But all this must be subject to the wider observation of the full process" (p. 134). In other words, we cannot isolate things from each other if we hope to understand them more clearly.

The transactional perspective recognizes that all parties in a communicative relationship are mutually engaged in defining both themselves and each other. Toch and MacLean's (1962) influential article on perception presents several excellent examples. In baseball, for instance, a pitcher is defined as a player who takes the role of throwing the ball toward the plate so that the batter can try to hit it. But the pitcher cannot be defined in terms of his or her activity alone, because without the batter, pitching cannot occur (throwing, maybe, but not pitching). The same is true of the batter, whose role is dependent upon that of the pitcher. Neither can function without the other in a game of baseball. Nor can we define a batter or a pitcher without including both of them in our definition. Furthermore, although competition seems to dominate the two players' relationship, it is the transactional character of the game that allows cooperation and teamwork to exist even among competitors.

The act of speaking, therefore, cannot be analyzed outside the context of listening, for a similar reason. Speaking is *defined* in part by listening. We understand a person's behavior only by placing it in the context of a larger relational process. Neither speaking nor listening could function without the other. Similarly, your classmate's "shyness," if that's the label you choose, may be accounted for transactionally as a function of the context in which it occurs, rather than as a personality trait that belongs to her and for which she is responsible, and not as a simplistic reaction to your behavior. In short, it belongs to the relationship.

Meaning

Some of the most derogatory statements we can make about another person's speech might include "It doesn't mean anything" and "You don't mean what you say." We obviously use the word *meaning* in very different ways. When it is used to refer to the overall significance of something or someone, a message that I understand but consider trivial will seem "meaningless" even though I have interpreted it and attributed my own personalized meaning to it. In another sense, *meaning* refers to the specific socially agreed-upon codes that we call language, as well as to the different abilities of people to share in that code. At the start of an introductory physics course, for instance, you might say that you do not yet know what *quantum* means. The word is semantically meaningless to you, but in a larger sense it is meaningful to your relationship with the professor and the course. Perhaps you also develop hazy associations by connecting the term with other, more familiar concepts of physics.

How can we analyze meaning, then? Obviously, it is a key concept in communication, for without some notion of how meaning develops, we cannot tell whether communication has occurred or whether it has been successful when it does occur. **Meaning** can generally be defined as the conscious pattern humans create out of their interpretation of experience, whether that interpretation is relatively subjective and personalized (Boulding, 1956) or sociocultural and interpersonal in origin (Mead, 1956). However, defining meaning doesn't necessarily make it measurable. As anthropologist Victor Turner (1986) observes: "Obviously, there is much that can be counted, measured, and submitted to statistical analysis. But all human act[s are] impregnated with meaning, and meaning is hard to measure, though it can often be grasped, even if only fleetingly and ambiguously. Meaning arises when we try to put what culture and language have crystallized from the past together with what we feel, wish, and think about our present point in life" (p. 33). This view of meaning has four interconnected implications for communication theorists (see Reviewing Key Ideas, p. 67).

Meaning Is Processual

Meaning is not a constant or a package but a process that changes with the flow of time. It not only has a history, but also tends to persist until it is contradicted. Its forward reach is supported by the images humans construct from previous meaning-making. According to economist and social theorist Kenneth Boulding (1956), the meaning of any new message for an individual is the change it produces in the person's existing image of the world. All communicative action that is meaningful, therefore, is embedded in a historical framework. What something means is largely determined by how it is perceived at any given moment.

Meaning Is Personalized

Describing the meaning *of* a circumstance implies that we attribute meaning *to* the circumstance. The meaning of any word you look up in the dictionary does not exist in the word itself but in the consciousness of those who use the word in speaking or listening. The dictionary, which is really more a public opinion poll than a repository of meanings carried by words, simply reports on how the majority of educated speakers develop interpretations when they use words. Although the conduit metaphor suggests that words can "contain," "carry," or "send" packages of meaning, most contemporary theories support the notion that words and other messages point to meanings that are uniquely personalized.

Meaning Is Co-Constructed

Although meaning has a personalized subjective component, it is not ultimately a product of isolated **intrapersonal** (within-the-person) interpretive acts. In fact, if communication is transactional and mutualistic, how can meaning—the fuel of communication—be wholly an individualistic invention? Rather, the ground rules of communicative meaning are intersubjective. Meaning emerges from relationships because it is in relationships, not in our heads, that our lives are led.

For example, suppose we ask you, "What is your meaning for a B grade?" Obviously, your personal history is involved. What kind of grades have you already received in the class? What's your GPA? Have you previously cared much about the grades you received? Your personal feelings and goals are also uniquely involved. Your goals for this class may be different from those of the student sitting at the next desk, and therefore you're gratified to get a B while she is terribly disappointed with one. But we also need to recognize that our meanings for messages constantly emerge from our real and inferred relationships with others. For instance, your relationship with the professor provides the context for the grade, and you understand that the grade is in part a relational message. Dr. Jones has power, advanced knowledge, and prestige, so perhaps it is fitting that she evaluate you. The grade doesn't come from outer space but instead originates in her reasoned attempt to give you feedback. Your grade for Communication Theory 201 does not really attach directly to the work you turned in but is mediated through the relationship of you and your work to Dr. Jones and her expectations, perceptions, and interpretations.

Martin Buber's (1965b) philosophy of dialogue shows how this kind of meaning exists within the realm of human life he called **the between:** "We tend…to forget that something can happen not merely 'to' us and 'in' us but also, in all reality, between us. Let us consider the most elementary of all facts of our intercourse with one another. The word that is spoken is uttered here and heard there, but its spokenness has its place in 'the between'" (p. 112). The genuine location of meaning, Buber suggested, is not within the psychology of persons, or in an abstract faith in spirit but, instead, in the meeting of persons in their relationship—that is, "between" them. Buber affirms the mutualistic dimensions of meaning while also acknowledging that people do in fact develop personalized meanings that are unique only to them. By walking the "narrow ridge," as Buber put it, between the two extremes of interpretation, he acknowledged the I-nature of unique experience but simultaneously stressed the We-nature of communication and meaning-making.

Meaning Is Multidimensional

Finally, meaning evidently can't be reduced to a single, easily articulated message. It develops in the complex patterns that we use to organize and interpret our world (Blakemore & Greenfield, 1987; Young, 1978). It has multiple facets and dimensions and is, therefore, multidimensional. However, our everyday talk seems to assume the opposite—that meaning is sent to receivers from senders in tidy packages (we hear people say, for example, "I know exactly what you mean!"). A sequence of words may seem to constitute a speaker's single utterance: "I'd like to turn my paper in late." And it seems reasonable for us to ask the student, "What do you mean?" However, by asking that question, we assume that it is possible to state *the* meaning "behind" the statement or *the* meaning that presumably motivates and expresses the intention of the statement. In most communication, however, multiple, complex meanings (many of which the speaker is unable to describe very specifically) stimulate the statement. Although the speaker may have in mind a certain persuasive intent or even what Infante (1980) and others call a "verbal plan," many other meanings are unconsciously and *simultaneously* represented by the comment. In our example, then, the student who says "I'd like to turn my paper in late" may also mean that he or she (1) is overburdened, (2) seeks empathy from the professor, (3) is ashamed to request an extension, (4) wants to remain tentative about the request, (5) hopes the professor will reconsider the policy of weekly papers, or (6) dislikes the professor but expects to mask that feeling (among many other possible meanings). When we speak, we have multiple intentions, many of which we may not be fully aware of or acknowledge consciously.

Some theorists and philosophers use the term **polysemy** to describe the dependence of symbolic communication on the multiple meanings that can arise from interpretation (Condit, 1989; Ricoeur, 1981; Rommetveit, 1987; Ullmann, 1966). Symbolic communication is highly polysemous because whenever we say a word we are laying open all the possible meanings for the word that reside in the language. Puns, tact, sarcasm, spontaneous verbal surprises, and verbal playfulness all emerge from the polysemic possibilities of interaction. A person speaking a word is, in effect, inviting listeners to participate, not just as receivers but also in the construction of mutual meanings. Context, therefore, not simply the word, must be considered in developing meaning. From the transaction, both parties have the opportunity to discover something new about themselves.

When we communicate, we not only express what we already believe, intend, or plan; we also discover new beliefs, intentions, and so on. Anthropologist and conversation analyst Michael Moerman (1988) helps us to understand how the multidimensional nature of meaning affects our informal communication. If meaning were instead one-dimensional, we could assume that, as message senders, we are in charge of expressing our own predetermined beliefs or intentions. We could also evaluate our talk by using this simple criterion: "Did I accomplish my objective?" But are speaker and listener really accomplishing different things, or are they both involved in one coordinated process? Moerman's investigation of **overlaps**—occasions when people find themselves speaking simultaneously—led him to conclude that mutuality in communication is highly pronounced, so much so that "the conscious actor cannot be the author of his or

---

REVIEWING KEY IDEAS

MEANING IS:

- *Processual* (always changing).
- *Personalized* (inevitably varying somewhat among individuals and groups).
- *Co-constructed* (not just inner thought, but intersubjective).
- *Multidimensional* (involving many levels and possible interpretations).

her talk" (p. xi). As a result, we are never completely in charge of our own speech, much less in control of our communication relationships.

Intention and the Definition of *Communication:* A Controversy

The study of communication had a speaker-centered, rhetorical focus for centuries (Stamp & Knapp, 1990). The intent of the speaker was of prime concern, and definitions of *communication* tended to be molded by the communication events (speaker-to-audience) in which scholars were most interested. Later, as our interests broadened to include interpersonal communication, listening claimed our attention as well. We needed to refocus the concept of communication in order to take into account unintended effects, as well as intentions from a listener's point of view. Why is a speaker's intention to form overt messages any more crucial, for example, than a listener's intention to gain new meaning by interpreting messages?

One particular approach was accepted as a truism within communication studies for many years. Watzlawick, Beavin, and Jackson (1967) asserted "the impossibility of not communicating" in interactional situations, presumably where the parties are aware of each other's presence. This was proposed as an **axiom**— a firmly established claim that needs no further support—so they were reasonably confident about their conclusions. Because they identify communication largely with behavior, Watzlawick and his colleagues claim that communication is unavoidable. All behavior has communicative potential. Their contribution, simply put, is that communication can be seen as a constantly occurring environment for human experience. Two people who are together cannot stop communicating because they can't avoid behaving in some way, and any behavior has message value when the other person attributes meaning to it. Silence, absence, lack of eye contact, and other nonverbal behaviors, intended or not, all might constitute communication from the perspective described in Watzlawick, Beavin, and Jackson's *Pragmatics of Human Communication* (1967, pp. 48–51).

Introductory communication texts repeated the axiom often, solidifying its acceptance. Scholars expanded their interest in the unintended effects of messages in interactional environments. Researchers could study almost anything because all types of human action could potentially fit under the conceptual umbrella of communication.

However, some scholars have renewed their interest in a narrower definition of communication. Arguing that if communication is conceived as everything, nothing really is specified, these theorists (Infante, Rancer, & Womack, 1990; Motley, 1990; Scott, 1977) want to distinguish communicative behaviors from other human processes, such as perception and nonsymbolic nonverbal behaviors. According to one approach within this more restricted area of focus, "human communication represents the execution of the individual's most recently adopted communication plan" (Infante, Rancer, & Womack, 1990, p. 11). By placing communication primarily within an individualistic framework, these authors portray it as an outcome of the separate intentions of its participants. Without denying the importance of process-centered views of reality, such theorists advocate restricting the definition of communication to achieve greater conceptual clarity.

Despite their different areas of focus, both of these approaches to the study of communication offer valuable insights. The broader transactional approach can help us understand the complexity of communication, while the narrower individualistic approach can help clarify some communication concepts more precisely. We tend to agree with Stamp and Knapp (1990) on this issue: "For interactional participants, the most important aspect of intentionality may not be what an encoder really intends to accomplish with a particular message or what attributions a decoder makes about the message but how the interactants in the relationship ultimately negotiate the two perspectives" (p. 296). "Communication," therefore, is also a useful label for what happens when participants aren't fully aware of their intentions but are aware of the relationship between them.

Models of Communication

Several times in this chapter we've used the word *model* in different contexts. Although in everyday life a *supermodel* can be someone who displays expensive clothing for potential buyers, a *role model* is someone who supposedly behaves in an exemplary way, and a carefully constructed *model airplane* duplicates the colors and relative dimensions of a full-size plane, a *communication model* serves a somewhat different purpose than advertising, emulation, or copying.

A **model** of communication—or of any other process, object, or event—is a way of simplifying the complex interaction of elements in order to clarify relevant relationships, and perhaps to help predict outcomes (see Reviewing Key Ideas, below). McQuail and Windahl (1993) define a model as "a consciously simplified description in graphic form of a piece of reality. A model seeks to show the main elements of any structure or process and the relationships between

---

◁ L I N K

This controversy surrounding the two main approaches to studying communication reinforces a similar point made in Chapter 1 about theorizing. It is not necessary for theorists to prove that their definitions or concepts are "right" in order to conduct research or make stimulating contributions to scholarly understanding. We believe it is a measure of the strength of a discipline that different theories can test each other, calling forth clearer conceptions while still stimulating distinctive programs of research. It is through this process that knowledge advances.

REVIEWING KEY IDEAS

EFFECTIVE COMMUNICATION MODELS:

- Clarify, explain, and help to predict outcomes of basic processes by skillful simplification.
- Avoid oversimplification by ensuring that essential elements are retained.
- Can be physical, visual, or verbal depictions, although most models of communication combine strong visual elements with written explanations.

these elements" (p. 2). Because not all aspects of a complex process can be modeled, even if they are known, the theorist constructing a model must make a challenging set of choices. Of the many different factors that make up the process, which ones can be omitted without doing a disservice to its essence? What static symbolic or visual elements (words? lines? arrows?) can be appropriately substituted for the dynamic reality of communication? Modelers abstract and generalize the empirical world, hoping for a kind of truth to emerge from their creativity. A model can be physical, visual, or verbal. However, most attempts at communication modeling have been combinations of the visual and the verbal, and have had largely instructional goals

Modeling the next version of the Beetle is a big challenge for Volkswagen's designers, and the thoroughness of the engineers and the extent of their knowledge might surprise you. But they have something tangible to shape and to subject to wind tunnel and other tests. Modeling communication in a way that captures the essence of the process presents very different challenges. Communication is hard to get hold of because it doesn't sit still.

All of us carry models in our heads all the time, whether we know it or not. One scientist (Bross, 1970) notes that "all of us are accustomed to using verbal models in our thinking processes and we do it intuitively" (p. 14). The questions become: Are your verbal models of how communication works sophisticated enough to do you any good? Will they help you predict what kinds of responses are necessary in any given situation? Will they help you decide how to assist another person in mutual cooperation? Will they help you troubleshoot in times of conflict or misunderstanding? In other words, are they practical? We believe that contemporary communication theory has shown individualistic models to be impractical. Such a model seems simple, even elegantly so (see Figure 2-1 for an example).

But what is omitted? The process nature of communication is neglected, as is the recognition that all participants actively contribute to outcomes. Although the changing character of the communication process cannot be fully captured by any static model, we can build in such factors as feedback to suggest that communication is not a one-way phenomenon. Some feedback models of communication attempt to suggest that communication depends on the two-way, cause-effect interactions of message/feedback/response. One example is shown in Figure 2-2.

What became known as **information theory** was based on a similar feedback model (Shannon & Weaver, 1949). Information theory, which developed from research conducted at Bell Laboratories in the 1940s, had a profound effect on the vocabulary of communication theorists at mid-century. It considered senders as sources of information who encoded messages designed to be transmitted through channels for the subsequent decoding of receivers. An intended mes-

◁ L I N K

Review the "You, the Researcher" section of Chapter 1. It asks you to diagram a rudimentary communication model. If you did the exercise earlier, reconsider your diagram to see if it meets the criteria for an effective communication model.

FIGURE 2-1 An Individualistic Model

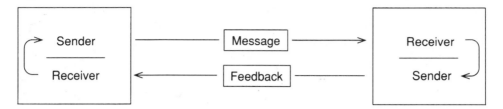

FIGURE 2-2 A Simple Feedback Model

sage becomes a **signal** when it is encoded, and that signal assumes the status of message again when it is successfully decoded by the receiver. Any channel through which a signal moves is considered to have a certain degree of *noise,* which is any interference in the system that reduces the chance that the decoded signal will match the encoded one. **Information** was defined as a message or set of messages that reduce uncertainty for the receiver; its measure was the **bit**, the amount of information necessary to reduce uncertainty roughly by half. Information theory illustrated well the communication problem of *channel capacity* and efficiency (how many messages can be decoded accurately in a given period of time), and helped define how senders and receivers reduce uncertainty in mediated, especially technological, situations. However, because it largely neglected the problems of meaning, mutuality, and process in favor of intentionalistic communication assumptions, it does not shed much light on process and change in communication relationships and doesn't function particularly well as a general model of communication. As Logue and Miller (1996) observe, it is "well known" that "interaction models have largely supplanted transmission-reception models in contemporary studies of communication. Whereas older models had presented communication as a linear flow of information from a 'source' to a 'receiver,' the newer ones depict it as an ongoing process of reciprocity and exchange in which all parties, by influencing and adapting to each other, jointly shape both the sequence of the overall process and its outcomes" (p. 369).

Despite the emphasis on reciprocity or mutuality, some theorists have despaired of ever adequately capturing "process" changes in communication, and have settled for presenting lists of relevant variables as their models. One such attempt, Berlo's (1960) variables model of communication, is shown in Figure 2-3. Any understanding of communication starts with the ability to identify its essential elements. Therefore the primary purposes of the variables model are (1) to clarify the "ingredients" that affect the tasks of encoding and decoding and (2) to show how senders and receivers use similar personal (skills, attitudes, knowledge) and contextual (social system, culture) cues to understand both the code and the content of messages as they are sent through channels.

Unlike these more static models, Dance's (1967) helical spiral model of communication emphasizes the changing nature of the process, though to the exclusion of everything else (see Figure 1-2 in Chapter 1). Still, by following the flow of communication with the spiral, we see clearly that communication is not a linear transmission but one that travels indefinitely in circles, back upon itself—never to the same place from which it started but to a new position that is itself already

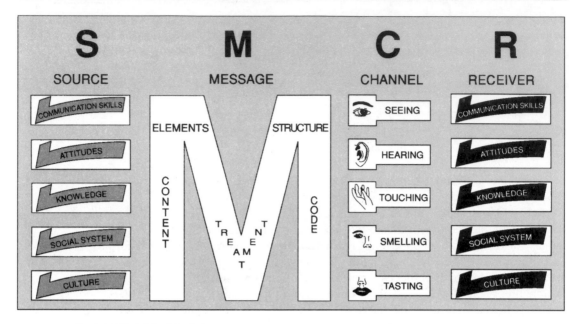

Figure 2-3 Berlo's Variable Model

Source: "A Model of the Ingredients in Communication" from *The Process of Communication: An Introduction to Theory and Practice* by David Berlo, copyright © 1960 by Holt, Rinehart and Winston, Inc. and renewed in 1988 by David K. Berlo. Reproduced by permission of the publisher.

flowing into something yet newer. So, when you reply to me, it is to a changed me, and with a broadened perspective. Dance attempts to illustrate this by a spiral that ever-widens into infinity.

Finally, the transactional perspective of communication, discussed at length earlier in the chapter, differs significantly from those of the self-actional and interactional approaches. Instead of aiming or trading messages, communicators build relationships. A transactional model developed by Barnlund (1970), shown in Figure 2-4, may appear cluttered and complicated at first, but notice how many mutualistic assumptions he acknowledges with some relatively straightforward symbols. The two people (P_1 and P_2) each represent simultaneous encoding (sending) and decoding (receiving) functions enfolded within personal experience. Encoding (E) and decoding (D) are depicted not as alternating subprocesses of communication but as mutually dependent ones. Each contributes to what the communicators are building together. In effect, the persons represented in the model do not "transfer" meaning "across" to each other but agree to "meet in the middle," or, in Buber's terms, in *the between*. Each still has access to his or her private cues (C_{PR}) (e.g., unique feelings, insights, values) in what some psychologists call a **phenomenal field**—the array of cues available for individuals' interpretation at any given time. In addition, both parties share access to a field of public cues (C_{PU}), though the meaning of these will differ for each communicator.

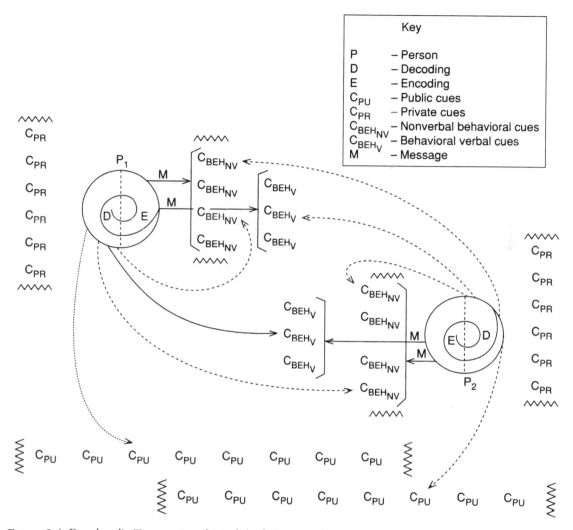

FIGURE 2-4 Barnlund's Transactional Model of Communication

SOURCE: "A Transactional Model of Communication" by D. C. Barnlund. From *Foundations of Communication Theory,* edited by Kenneth K. Sereno and C. David Mortenson. Copyright © 1970 by Harper & Row. Reprinted by permission of Addison Wesley Educational Publishers Inc.

Still, such a model has its deficiencies and compromises; it, too, is an over-simplification. To make it more explanatory, you might imagine that Figure 2-4 has built in, as inherent factors, the variables Berlo mentions. Imagine that the negotiation process illustrated by the "relationship" between communicators is constantly in flux in the way Dance suggests, adjusting to accommodate the messages communicators contribute to it. If your mental model can integrate these ideas, then your understanding of communication will be theoretically more solid and pragmatically more useful.

REVIEWING KEY THEORIES

This chapter focused on defining orientations to defining communicating, and didn't try to survey many theories. Its central idea is to encourage you to define communication as a mutualistic phenomenon, rather than an individualistic transmission of messages back and forth. Within the discussion of communication models, however, we did highlight the *information theory* of Shannon and Weaver as an example of individualistic, conduit-like assumptions, and the *transactional approaches* of Dewey and Bentley, and Barnlund, as examples of mutualistic assumptions.

TESTING THE CONCEPTS

"If people understood each other better, wouldn't there be fewer conflicts? And if so, does this mean that communication and conflict are opposite processes?"

If communication allows people to understand each other better, some conflicts can be resolved. Many conflicts result from misunderstanding and ignorance. Yet many conflicts result from accurate interpretations, too. Therefore improving communication might also improve people's understanding of why they disagree, and, in fact, deepen their disagreement. Communication is a neutral process, not a prescription for a "good" life but the only way that human life can be understood.

"Isn't the conduit definition of communication easier to understand than the mutualistic definition?"

Yes, but its simplicity is misleading. The conduit metaphor makes the problems of communication appear more manageable than they really are; it also encourages people to take simplistic solutions seriously.

"Should I agree with the broad definition of *communication* (all behavior can be communication) or the narrower definition (only intentional messages are communicative)? Which is right?"

Both approaches can be helpful, but neither is necessarily "right." What does *right* mean? There is no holy definition of *communication* hidden somewhere in a golden shrine, so to what can theorists compare their definitions? Definitions should be compared with each other, and with suitably applied criteria of appropriateness (see Chapter 1). Thus if it helps you to define *communication* broadly (or narrowly), do so. However, make yourself aware of the arguments of other perspectives as well.

"Does this chapter mean that no one can ever fully understand me?"

In a sense, yes. Your inner meanings (images, feelings, and so forth) may not even be fully understood by you. And how many people can read your mind? So, no one can ever fully understand you. But the other side of this story is important to remember, too. Meaning is not just an intrapersonal issue (within personal cognition and experience) but an interpersonal one. Buber (1965b) says meaning resides in "the between" of relationships, and in this way communicators can be said to have full access to understanding relational meaning.

"Shouldn't science search for the one Truth? How can communication study be scientifically based if the discipline tolerates conflicting theories and definitions?"

A truly scientific attitude is one that remains open to new and different interpretations. In the scientific world, nothing is fixed or unchanging. That's why textbooks are constantly being revised in the scientific disciplines. Further, conflicting theories encourage science to re-energize itself continually. Communication theorists cannot realistically attempt to identify a single theory that explains all of what we call communication.

"Isn't 'transaction' just a fancy way of saying that communication is two-way?"

No. It is a fancy word to some people, but it implies much more than the two-way trading of messages. It is a theorist's way of noting that communicators simultaneously affect and define each other, and neither party can fully control these effects. You can't change another person without simultaneously being changed. Examples: You can't be persuasive without someone else being persuaded. No one can be a leader without followers. (If they don't define themselves as followers, who are you leading?)

"So what? How can what I've learned in this chapter change how I communicate to my friends?"

It may not. At least, it won't change things directly. But it may change how you think about your talk with others. For example, you might consider why you used the phrase "communicate *to* my friends" in your question, rather than "*with* my friends." If communication is basically mutualistic, an attitude of *with* could mean that you'd be more ready to invite others' reactions, and more able to understand how others' meanings may affect yours in subtle ways. Personal theorizing and personal behavior are intimately related.

"I've always thought meaning was in words. Why don't words mean what they mean?"

To counteract the misleading aspects of the conduit metaphor, try to think of words as stimulating people to create meanings within communication relationships. If the meaning was "in" the word, then the same word would trigger the same reactions in everyone who knows the word (which, of course, is not at all what happens). Although the nature of language as a code ensures that native speakers of the same language generally will not diverge very far from one another's meanings, this results from habit and agreement, not from any inherent meaning in the words themselves.

YOU, THE RESEARCHER

1. Try some speculative, introspective research. Think creatively about objects or events with which communication might be compared.
   - Think in terms of analogies: How is communication like a Frisbee? A rubber band? A key? A sporting event? A lightbulb?

- Questions: How is communication also unlike these analogies? What other analogies can you think of? How are these analogies similar to or different from communication models? Which of the analogies are most similar to the conduit metaphor? Least similar?

2. Simulate on a smaller scale and with a different audience Redding's (1968) informal survey of executives described in this chapter (see p. 55).

   - On a sheet of paper, type the linear and one-way definition he used to stimulate discussion with business executives ("When Person X 'communicates' with Person Y, what happens is that he transmits meanings (information, facts, ideas, etc.)...to the mind of Person Y" (Redding, 1968, p. 101). Make five copies and give them to five friends who are not in your communication class.

   - Below the definition, ask your friends (your studys participants, in terms of research) to write brief reactions to the following questions: (A) Does this definition make sense? (B) Would someone who believes communication works this way be successful in most organizations? (C) If you could change anything about the definition, what would it be?

   - Researchers *hypothesize,* or make educated guesses, about the outcomes of their studies. A *hypothesis* is based on prior research findings but is not meant to bias upcoming results; researchers are willing to be surprised by whatever reactions these participants have. (In fact, as discussed in Chapter 1, quantitative researchers often employ what they call a *null hypothesis*, which states explicitly that no significant differences will be found between, for example, two groups that are compared. This move is intended to counter the natural biases of researchers to expect or desire particular kinds of significance in their findings.) Here, simply make your best educated guesses about the participants' specific responses.

   - Determine how to code your results. For example, of the five respondents, how many believe that Redding's definition (which was a purposely inaccurate statement) captures the essence of communication? What other good questions about the results suggest categories into which you could code the results?

   - After you have compiled results, compare your findings with those of other students. Do most of the participants responding to the surveys seem to agree or disagree with linear, one-way, self-actional perspectives on communication? Do they have confidence in the effectiveness of one-way models? If they believe that an inaccurate conception has practical value in organizations, what does this tell you about contemporary organizations or how we need to prepare people for them?

3. Try some secondary or supportive research on professional versus popular definitions of *communication*. In your school library, find three recent articles about communication in professional journals such as *Communication Theory, Communication Monographs,* or the *Journal of*

Communication; and three articles about communication in popular magazines, such as *Redbook, Reader's Digest,* or *Psychology Today.* Read the articles closely to see whether *communication* is defined explicitly or implicitly. Take notes on what you find. Compare the popularized definitions with the professional ones. What did you discover?

Peter Vandermark/Stock, Boston

CHAPTER 3

"How Do Contexts Affect Our Meaning?"

Theorizing Physical and Social Contexts

> The conceptualization of knowledge of and about a context is often rendered
> in the static language of photography: we are taking pictures of a scene;
> this is what you see in it. But the scene was not the same before the photographer
> entered, and it changes after the picture is taken.... What is even more confounding
> is that a context is given meaning in sentences uttered by the participants who, in turn,
> are influenced by those utterances to "see" the context in their own interpretive ways.
> What one person "sees" as the context is not necessarily what another person "sees"
> (or responds to) in it, even though their roles may be clear to the researcher and to
> them and despite the fact that they share precisely the same physical environment.
>
> H. L. GOODALL, JR., *Living in the Rock 'n' Roll Mystery* (1991, p. 29)

Imagine that you're in a theater audience, and two characters in the play are being married. The actors are simply playing roles, of course, but for the sake of our example, assume that they are both single. After the ceremony onstage, are these two actors legally married in real life? Of course not; presumably, this is because the actor conducting the ceremony is not a minister or a justice of the peace. And, besides, everyone knows this is just a play.

But, humoring us some more for the sake of argument, suppose that the actor playing the minister is actually a minister (some ministers are actors, and vice versa, in real life), that the state requires no formal prior license application, and that the dramatic marriage ceremony performed onstage contains the same words, surrounded by the same kinds of witnesses as other such ceremonies. Now... *why* aren't the two people legally married after such a ceremony? By what definition of marriage can you state with assurance that these two actors pledging their eternal love onstage will in fact remain unmarried? In this example, which we freely adapted from a recent article (Taylor, 1996), we begin to glimpse how our everyday contextual awareness of communication works. Even though the words are the same, even though they are uttered by someone legally entitled to perform marriages, and even though the "lovers" affirm completely their desire to be married, there's something wrong—something that legal definitions of marriage in governmental statutes cannot take into account. There's nothing wrong with the content, but something is very wrong with the context. And the primary meaning of this particular communication event taking place in front of you can be understood only by context awareness. If you understand why this example is meaningful, you're well on your way to understanding the importance of this chapter. Now you're doing contextual analysis in communication.

Although it is tremendously important that we humans speak, doesn't it matter where and when we speak, and what else might surround or accompany the words we address to each other? Although some of our focus in this chapter is on what the popular media call *body language* or what scholars term *nonverbal communication,* we are in fact interested primarily in the impact of broader issues of context. As Cody and McLaughlin (1985) suggest, "We need to know more about how situational applications, interactional constraint, and impinging environmental cues operate in the real world to influence behavior" (p. 303). What is needed, they write, is "ecologically sound understanding" (p. 303).

Context

Context is challenging to define because it refers to everything in a frame of interest except what you're focusing on. Normally, a definition is a way to focus on or specify a concept. Defining *context* becomes a paradox of sorts because in order to define the term the definer has to place in the foreground of perception that which by definition is not foregrounded. Once we analyze context it ceases to be a context for us. Perceptual and Gestalt psychologists talk about the **figure/ground relationship,** in which a figure is the focus (what you are consciously attending to) and the ground is composed of the perceptually deemphasized background stimuli against which the figure is perceived (Bolles, 1991; Koffka, 1935). Context is the ground for communicators.

Context is not a "thing," nor is it an organized collection of things that can be isolated or analyzed precisely. When you read a newspaper article, for instance, the article becomes the figure or text. Its placement on the page (e.g., at the bottom of page 8 next to the obituaries) is an aspect of not only the text but also the *con*-text. Notice that context can be a mixture of both verbal and nonverbal elements in a communication environment. Moreover, context is not just a given in communication; rather, it is achieved and elaborated on by communicators. In face-to-face communication, Nofsinger (1989) explains, context is often created and modified through conversations. Although not all communication is conversation, of course, theorists usually regard context in the same way—as a dynamic and ongoing social process, not as a static variable.

Understanding the influence of context means that it might be significant that a particular **communication cue** (a simple message or interpretable act, such as an oral or a written statement, a gesture, a logo, a picture, or an advertisement):

appears after an earlier one (rather than before it);

is printed in **bold** type in a company newsletter (rather than in standard type);

is uttered in a whisper in church (rather than at normal volume);

is said to one particular person in the presence of others (rather than in private);

is broadcast by a radio station late at night (rather than in prime time);

is presented unknowingly by a person's clothing, such as when certain colors or types of clothing are accidentally associated with urban gangs (rather than intentionally); and

is in the foreground as other events take place in the background (rather than vice versa).

These examples illustrate that context is an ecological concern for communicators. An **ecology** is an environmental system in which everything interrelates and in which organisms are studied in relation to their environment (Hawley, 1986). Changes in any part of the system affect the other parts of the system. Developing contextual awareness is a question of noticing the connections between messages and their social, intellectual, and physical settings. Messages aren't offered one at a time but in complex mosaics that are impossible to take in all at once. Too

⬅️**LINK**

Recent research and theorizing in a perspective called **communibiology** (Heisel, McCroskey, & Richmond, 1999; McCroskey, 1998; McCroskey & Beatty, 2000) suggests that in interpersonal communication (see Chapter 5), the effects of context are not as decisive as some previous theorists claimed. Instead, McCroskey (1998) states, research into genetically set individual "temperaments" or "traits" mitigates environment in important ways: "Environment or 'situation' has only a negligible effect on interpersonal behavior" (p. 10). The communibiology position is controversial, and is currently being debated in academic journals (Beatty & McCroskey, 2000a, 2000b; Condit, 2000a, 2000b). It might be interesting for you to try to decide, as you read this chapter, which aspects of context the communibiological theorists would admit are important, and which they'd think are overrated.

Barker's ecological study provides a practical reminder that is consistent with a systems theory approach. See the section on systems theory in Chapter 1.

much focus on individual elements makes you "miss the forest for the trees," a particularly apt cliché that emphasizes context awareness.

Ecological assumptions guided Barker's (1968) study of a small-town community. He concludes, among other things, that children's actions could often be more accurately predicted by the behavioral patterns expected of the places in which children communicate than by the "behavioral tendencies" or personalities of the children themselves (p. 4). Many communication students are surprised to learn that context can have more impact than personality on how communication develops.

Understanding the context of communication events is therefore practical in several respects. It helps us to distinguish kidding from criticism, sarcasm from sincerity, and silliness from seriousness. Through context we learn that a crowded city bus is not an appropriate setting to discuss a marriage proposal, and that timing is crucial in planning when and where, not just how, to ask your supervisor for a day off. Often it's not just what is said that's crucial but *where* and *when* it's said, *what else* is said in the same situation, and *what else* is expected. A text is often important only because of a certain context. Given the importance of context, then, it is not surprising that some theorists and researchers specialize in the study of communication contexts. In this chapter we'll discuss two major types of contextual communication: (1) the more immediate physical and psychological context surrounding a particular communication episode, and (2) the broader social context or interactional setting in which communication occurs. It is important to note these distinctions if we hope to translate theoretical insights into everyday pragmatics. Can we know what is right or wrong, or good or bad, to say without context awareness? Is it appropriate to tell jokes when meeting someone for the first time? Although you may have a generalized answer for this question based on your personality and previous experience, would that answer change if we stipulated that you'd meet your partner at a dinner party or, alternatively, at a new job on the assembly line, or at the funeral of your friend's father, or at a TV station where you're being interviewed on the air?

Physical and Psychological Context: Nonverbal Life and the Theory of Immediacy

The verbal and nonverbal message systems are not independent or autonomous. They depend on each other for context. Yet it is the nonverbal system that more nearly completes our picture for what *context* means, and for that reason we'll concentrate on it in this first section.

The Nonverbal Message System: How Is It Theoretically Important?

While verbal symbols can serve as contextual cues for other verbal symbols, most analyses of communication context focus on the nonverbal realm. This is understandable if you realize that words are only a tiny fraction of all the stimuli available to us when we interpret situations and ideas. Most of what we learn comes from nonverbal messages or artifacts. Most of our ability to interpret verbal messages depends on nonverbal information.

Thus theorists have developed assumptions about the impact of both intentional and unintentional nonverbal messages (see Reviewing Key Ideas, p. 85):

1. ***The nonverbal system invites contextual analysis.*** Indeed, its contextual nature is one reason that theorists so often refer to **metacommunication**, the ability to communicate *about* communication (*meta* is a prefix that indicates self-reference) (Watzlawick, Beavin, & Jackson, 1967). Metacommunication tends to regulate human interaction. For example, if you put down, or criticize, your friend while also smiling, your smile is a signal to your friend about how to interpret your comment. While we converse, we simultaneously offer nonverbal commentaries on how our verbal offerings should be taken.

2. ***The nonverbal system emphasizes relationship-defining messages,*** rather than the content-specifying, naming messages of the verbal system. Language employs many symbols that stand for aspects of the object world by arbitrary social agreement. Thus, for example, the word *book* and the object you hold in your hands right now relate to each other only because of a social code, or agreement. But once we're participants in that agreement, the letters *b-o-o-k* call to mind the object, even when the object is absent. Language enables us to communicate at a distance. In the nonverbal system, messages assume a more immediate and direct connection to what is being expressed and to the relationship of the communicators. The meaning of a book might be indicated by showing an actual book to a listener. Nonhuman animal communication is based on this relation-defining function, rather than on category-naming (though some people like to think their pets are capable of both): "When I open the refrigerator and the cat comes, rubs against my legs, and mews, this does not mean 'I want milk'—as a human being would express it—but invokes a specific relationship, 'Be mother to me,' because such behavior is only observed in kittens in relation to adult cats, and never between two grown-up animals" (Watzlawick, Beavin, & Jackson, 1967, p. 63).

3. ***The nonverbal system cannot be avoided.*** Linguist Mary Ritchie Key (1980) writes that her "beginning premise is that when human beings interact, language...may or may not occur, but extralinguistic correlates always occur" (p. vii). The nonverbal system can neither be ignored nor turned off as if it were a faucet or a light switch. Nonverbal messages constantly surround us as perceptual or psychic backdrops for whatever else we are doing. Because we seek meaning and closure, it is paradoxical (from an observer's point of view) to perceive literally a "blank look" or a "noncommittal gesture." The gesture or the look is ultimately interpreted in some way. Nonverbal messages can also exist even in the negative—silence or absence, whether intended or unintended, may be interpreted by others as contextual cues.

4. ***The nonverbal system is typically more believable and persuasive than the verbal.*** Listeners presented with a verbal and a nonverbal message that are contradictory tend to assume that the nonverbal cue is more true or genuine than the verbal one, other factors being equal. Thus, for example, a speaker who, while sweating profusely in a cool room, claims,

"I'm not nervous!" will probably be viewed as nervous. Similarly, someone who scowls, turns red, and shouts, "I'm not mad!" will be perceived as angry.

5. ***The nonverbal system is behaviorally complex.*** Despite scholarly debate over what behaviors to study and what terms to use to describe them, a basic vocabulary of nonverbal theory has emerged in recent years. We have borrowed the following typology from Burgoon, Buller, and Woodall (1989) but will describe each technical term briefly in everyday language:

a. *Visual and auditory codes*

Kinesics: The study of the meanings of body movements, macro (major) and micro (minor). (Much of this research is based on the work of anthropologist Ray Birdwhistell, 1970.)

Physical appearance: The study of how variables such as height, weight, and demeanor affect interaction. (For a fascinating discussion of the effects of such factors on male–female relationships, see Nancy Henley's *Body Politics* [1977] and "Body Politics Revisited" [1995].)

Vocalics: The study of how voice can create the context for understanding words (e.g., by its rate, pitch, volume, or tone).

b. *Contact codes*

Haptics: The study of how people develop meanings for touch behaviors.

Proxemics: The study of distance as a communication message.

c. *Place and time codes*

Environment: The study of how meaning is affected by where people interact; the study of environment may be direct and physically based, such as the effects of urban housing design on interaction (Yancey, 1977), or it may be indirect and technology based, such as the effects of electronic media on workplace interactions (Acker, 1989).

Artifacts: The study of the communicative potential of object display; it can involve explicit "object language," such as showing someone the fish you just caught or the ring you just bought, or implicit effects such as the jacket you're wearing being impressive to an observer.

Chronemics: The study of how people communicate different messages through the manipulation of time; it can involve being late, early, and "on time," for instance.

Clearly, theorizing about human relationships must take nonverbal messages into account. It is their implicitness that makes them so important (Douglas, 1975). Nonverbal messages are a crucial component of our study of communication context.

Immediacy

Psychologist Albert Mehrabian (1981) developed his **immediacy theory** of implicit communication while studying nonverbal messages, although its basic concepts can be applied to language use as well. Essentially, by "immediacy" Mehrabian meant those behaviors by which we signal to another person the desire to be closer to them, psychologically and contextually. The theory identifies three levels of emotional response: *attraction, dominance,* and *arousal.* At various times, Mehrabian has also called attraction "liking," "evaluation," or "positiveness"; dominance has been discussed as a "power," "potency," or "status" issue; and arousal has been discussed as "responsiveness." In other words, people can make immediacy decisions on the basis of liking another person, on the basis of power or prestige estimates, and on the basis of the perceived responsiveness of others.

People reveal their *attraction* to another person by body language and movements, by eye contact, by haptic (touching) messages, or by physical proximity (closeness). These signals are what Mehrabian calls "immediacy cues"; they signal a desire by one communication partner to be directly "with" the other as much as possible. We might illustrate *dominance* over others by leaning away from them, or by focusing sustained attempts at eye contact in their direction, for example. Likewise, *emotional arousal* is significantly more apparent with nonverbal behaviors than it is with the spoken word. Words like "I love you" are more meaningful to an intimate partner when they are accompanied by "immediate" activities such as a hug, a kiss, or a gentle touch to the face. Andersen (1999) believes that "immediacy behaviors include any interpersonal behavior that performs the following four functions (pp. 187–189):

- "Immediacy behaviors signal availability and inclusion."
- "Immediacy behaviors communicate approach and involvement."
- "Immediacy behaviors increase sensory stimulation."
- "Immediacy behaviors communicate interpersonal warmth and positive affect."

Mehrabian's immediacy concept is important for understanding context. If much of the meaning in social situations is dependent on nonverbal cues, as Mehrabian and other theorists have shown (estimates range as high as 93 percent, although such guesswork is so imprecise that it seems somewhat ridiculous to attach such a specific number to it!), and if human relationships are largely maintained and defined nonverbally (Weitz, 1974), then we should understand more about the environments that facilitate and impede immediacy. Berger and Luckman (1966) established a philosophical basis for a *here-and-now* contextual focus among communicators. "Here" indicates an immediate spatial dimension; communi-

---

REVIEWING KEY IDEAS

TO UNDERSTAND THE NONVERBAL MESSAGE SYSTEM:

- Analyze context, not just the messages themselves.
- Understand messages within contexts as defining relationships.
- Know that nonverbal communication is always part of your communication experience.
- Realize that when a nonverbal message and a verbal message contradict each other, people tend to trust the nonverbal.
- Acknowledge that the nonverbal message system involves a complex set of visual/auditory codes, contact codes, and place/time codes.

cators often desire direct physical access to each other, traditionally in face-to-face situations. "Now" indicates an immediate temporal dimension; communicators want to know that others are available to them in the present moment, not on some future occasion. To what extent, then, does environmental design affect immediacy?

Physical Settings: Environment and Space

People and Environment. Psychologist Robert Sommer (1969) has devoted much of his career to researching the effects of personal space, environment, and the effects of human-designed physical settings (e.g., architecture) on communication. His view of communication is part of an overall perspective on humanity: As creative creatures, we cannot escape the effects of environment, even insisting on constructing our own. "All people are builders, creators, molders, and shapers of the environment; we are the environment," Sommer says (1969, p. 7). Not only do we select our environments but we begin changing them from the onset of our interactions within them. Human presence changes everything. Students personalize their rooms with flags, posters, stuffed animals, sports equipment, and mementos from the past. Our personalized environmental designs are not always harmonious with other people. A student once told us about an unusual visit to a professor's large office, in which the only visitor's chair in the room was placed just inside the door. When the student arrived for an appointment, she assumed that she should scoot the chair a few feet closer to the large desk separating the two of them. She had just begun to move it when the teacher snapped, "What do you think you're doing? I put the chair there for a reason." Needless to say, she did not stay long. That, perhaps, was the reason for the professor's decor.

In far more pleasant ways, too, human spaces reflect the personalities of those who live within them. One of the authors recalls visiting Levittown, Pennsylvania. Her hosts provided photographs of how it used to be on their street and of the numerous streets that made up this community—identical houses, all in a row, the same facades, the same yards. Now, each individualized dwelling reflected its owners' personalized communication preferences. Places had become homes. Clearly, we construct and change our environments. But Sommer's conclusion—that we *become* the environment—is somewhat more radical.

Consider, for example, how the seating arrangement in a small group setting (such as a classroom) can shape communication patterns. Sommer (1969) conducted such a study, focusing on the seating positions people tend to choose for rectangular and round tables. Students who were asked to make diagrams of themselves and another person at a rectangular table "overwhelmingly chose a corner-to-corner or face-to-face arrangement for casual conversation," but not for other communication tasks. When a cooperative activity was the goal, the students chose a side-by-side arrangement, but for a competitive activity they chose a face-to-face arrangement or, on occasion, a distant seating pattern (p. 62). Thus the seating patterns tended to represent and symbolize visually the cognitive and experiential evaluations of the participants: Side-by-side seating represented a mutual orientation toward a common direction, whereas face-to-face seating permitted a maximal orientation toward the other, simulating confrontation or a mutual exchange of ideas. Similar findings resulted from the study involving round tables. Most pairs who wanted to talk cooperatively used adjacent chairs, whereas "competing pairs chose to sit directly across from one another" (Sommer, 1969, p. 63).

In addition, Sommer (1969) studied small student groups in a natural setting, the college cafeteria. (Recall from Chapter 1 that *naturalistic research* is so termed because the researcher studies a communication phenomenon in its naturally occurring setting or context; Lincoln & Guba, 1985.) He found that the "spacing of individuals…is not random but follows from the personality and cultural backgrounds of the individuals involved, what they are doing, and the nature of the physical setting" (p. 68). In other words, communication outcomes depend not only on people's personalities and tasks but also on their environments.

In many college classes that encourage discussion, the instructor suggests a circular seating arrangement unless the class is so large that it's impractical or the desks are bolted to the floor. In fact, it has become a hallmark of many communication faculty, as distinct from colleagues in some other departments—and annoying to countless maintenance staff on campuses who have to arrange desks in rows at the end of each day. Although this arrangement might seem to be an idiosyncracy, it is actually founded on research that investigates classroom interaction when students are in rows. As shown in Figure 3-1, where students sit in a traditionally set-up classroom has a dramatic effect on how often they contribute to class discussions, and how often teachers note their presence. Students who sit within the smaller triangle tend to contribute significantly more to class discussions than do students who sit outside it but within the larger triangle. And those who sit outside both triangles tend to contribute the least (Hurt, Scott, & McCroskey, 1978, p. 95). A circle can help to balance the contributions and improve the group's attentiveness.

In another study, Sommer (1974) focuses on the negative consequences of what he calls **hard architecture** in human-designed environments. The characteristics of hard architecture include a lack of permeability; a high expense of construction, alteration, or razing; clearly marked status levels; the selection of materials and furnishing based on ease of purchase and maintenance; and uniformity in design and layout (pp. 25–26). Sommer contends that hard architecture can inhibit effective communication because it is planned to resist human imprint. To inhabitants, it seems "impervious, impersonal, and inorganic" (p. 2). He also argues that much of today's architecture cuts us off from one another (or, in Mehrabian's terms, decreases our chances for immediacy in nonverbal relations). Examples include windowless offices in which workers are separated by cubicles and apartment buildings that stack families on top of one another.

Many of our readers are college students and faculty who spend much of their time on campuses that discourage human immediacy. Many of these institutions (although attractive to look at) seem similar to penitentiaries in design and construction. Buildings may resemble large blocks of brick and glass that are multilayered and compartmentalized. Landscaping is often black asphalt and rock with some trees, flowers, and color at the fringes. Some classrooms are windowless cubes. Sommer (1974) writes: "I have never taught in a classroom that had even a single picture on the wall. There were no flowers or green things of any kind and no tropical fish, terraria, or tapestry. The classrooms lacked all of those things that would convert a bare room into something lived in" (p. 95). Although most financially strapped universities are unlikely to invest in an aquarium or an attractive carpet for every classroom, and although university classes are obviously less likely to be "homey" than elementary classrooms, it isn't difficult to read the educational philosophy of architects from the kinds of rooms they design for educational

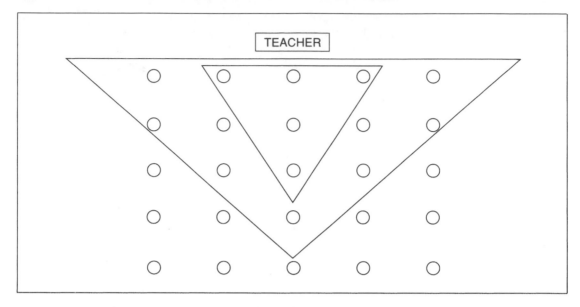

FIGURE 3-1 Contribution Patterns in a Classroom

communication. Generally, the rooms are more hard than soft, more impersonal than personal, more institutional than human, more efficient than inviting or spontaneous. Maybe your classrooms aren't like this. We should not be surprised, though, if the students and faculty within such hard environments sometimes have hard reactions to each other—such as manipulation, objectification, or dismissiveness—when more immediate and responsive attitudes would be the ideal.

Sommer also includes airports in his indictment of hard architecture: These "funnels and tunnels," as he calls them, "rank high in any list of socially destructive buildings" (1974, p. 70). Regarding the impersonal and anticommunicational nature of the waiting areas, Sommer writes: "To see [a family] sitting dumbly side by side in the shiny plastic chairs is heartrending" (p. 75). Because the seating is arranged to discourage conversation, often members of a group will stand in front of those seated so that they can form a social circle and thereby communicate more directly. Although some newly constructed airports may have been designed with "softer" assumptions, other terminals of public transportation, such as bus stations, typically maintain hard design characteristics.

Try to think contextually about other kinds of physical environments. For example, Blair, Jeppeson, and Pucci (1994) analyze the design of the Vietnam Veterans Memorial in Washington, D.C. They show how the structure is purposely nonfunctional and in some ways inefficient for visitors, how it suggests a variety of possible interpretations, and how it invites visitors into certain kinds of communicative experiences that reflect the political nature of the memorial. As an example of so-called *postmodern* architecture, the Vietnam Veterans Memorial doesn't have to be efficient in the traditional ways in order to make a statement about experience. Instead, it "attempt[s] to 'speak' not only to architects about technical architectural matters, but also to viewers and users of buildings about substantive socio-cultural matters. It questions and critiques ideas as well as architectural forms" (p. 359). (See A Theory

Extension, below.) In this sense, architecture is not only a context in which communication occurs; it can also be analyzed as a communication text or message.

When Sommer says that people "become" their environment, whether in a classroom, a home, or an airport, he implies that the social presence of any one person becomes part of the overall context for other people. And if this is so, how do we arrange ourselves with and for each other? This was the research question asked by anthropologist Edward T. Hall, whose work we review next.

People and Space. One of the authors of this book (VR) recently experienced a telling example of contemporary society's concern with "personal space":

> *I was visiting EPCOT Center and Disney World with my family, on a day when temperatures exceeded 100 degrees. In addition to the typical crowds, two large international groups were looking for entertainment. Our family had crammed a two-week vacation into four days. After I had been pushed, shoved, stepped on, and plowed into for the thousandth time, my younger son, ever affectionate, kept walking up to me and placing his arm around my shoulders. In a moment of desperation, what should have been a touching episode became a caustic one. I snapped, "Get out of my space! I need room, and you're invading my personal space." For the next several hours, I walked alone, feeling isolated, and deservedly so.*

A THEORY EXTENSION

POSTMODERN THEORY: A FIRST LOOK

Although the controversies surrounding **postmodern theory** are described in more detail in Chapter 4, it is useful to introduce some defining characteristics of postmodernity here. This way of thinking about the world largely ignores many traditional assumptions of Western civilization, such as rational predictability, concrete meaning, the scientific method, and clear understandings that fit neatly into an overall explanation. "Modernists" have applied these expressions of rational thought since the Enlightenment in the eighteenth century. Modernists offered a coherent type of rationality that would presumably apply to human thought whatever the culture or time. But postmodern thinkers see the world in a different way, arguing that language itself and new forms of media have created an age in which meanings are increasingly harder to pin down and tougher to specify. Whereas modernist theorists work for specification of meaning, postmodern theorists claim that our old ways of being sure about things aren't realistic anymore. We've lost our assurance that we can distinguish the real from the phony, so the former distinctions that seemed so solid just don't help, and may even inhibit our learning. Obviously, ours is a time in which both modernist and postmodernist trends influence us. The implications for communicators are unsettling.

The "you're invading my space" concern is common in contemporary society. We encounter its many variations ("Get out of my face!"; "I need room to move") in television commercials, magazine articles, and everyday speech. But why is space so important to the communication context? Because, as Hall (1959) emphasized, "space speaks." By that he means that people often provide valuable information about themselves and their relationships in the way they choose to place themselves relative to other people and external objects. The study of such spatial messages is called, you'll recall from our earlier section, *proxemics.*

In his research with people in the United States, Hall (1966) also found that communicators tend to make four relatively distinct distance choices. The first category, touching to eighteen inches, is called **intimate distance**. When we become psychologically close with others, we are more ready to allow them into this space. **Personal distance** ranges from eighteen inches to four feet. Students and professors, managers and employees, or new acquaintances might still consider this an uncomfortable distance, especially in most North American cultures, where it connotes close emotional involvement. In the personal distance area, people experience the feeling of being invaded. Nonverbal theorists sometimes refer to this phenomenon as the "protective bubble" of space, within which most people will feel threatened by someone's uninvited advances. **Social distance** ranges from four feet to twelve feet. Many business situations, such as those involving salespeople and customers, fall within the social distance range. Finally, **public distance**—more than twelve feet—is usually reserved for public occasions that are relatively impersonal or performance-oriented, such as public speaking (Hall, 1966).

A good example of the communicative use of physical space can be seen in the movie *War of the Roses*. When the Roses were first married, they couldn't get close enough, a fact especially well symbolized by their interaction at the dining-room table. Previously, they were happy in their small apartment, where they sat corner-to-corner at a small square table, holding hands and enjoying their time together. But at their new residence their dining-room table is larger and longer. At first, they sit next to each other at the larger table, but as their marriage deteriorates they take seats at opposite ends of the table. By the end of the film, their table seems to have grown to about four times its original length, a symbol of the distance between them and, ultimately, of the end of their marriage. They both want a divorce, and the physical distance is both symptom and symbol of their psychic devastation.

Proxemic messages also contribute to Mehrabian's immediacy phenomenon. When Albert Scheflen (1974) researched the developing rapport between psychotherapists and clients, he could discern a clear link between subjective involvement in their relationship and how they sat with each other—their patterns of proxemics and posture. For example, therapists, as they began to feel more rapport, tended to shift from leaning backward with their arms crossed to leaning forward more with their arms and legs uncrossed. Scheflen concludes that "the subjective experience of rapport…occurs in connection with the assumption of a characteristic pattern of postures" (p. 85). He calls this the **rapport constellation**. The therapist thus signals a more immediate involvement not necessarily with words but also by shifting the bodily context in which the words are spoken and heard. Interestingly, in the forty-minute therapy sessions studied by Scheflen, this shift also tended to happen as a "climax" around the twentieth or twenty-fifth minute, after which the sequence of nonimmediate to immediate is repeated (p. 86). Moving toward or away from another person is often experienced as a direct commentary on the relationship, whether or not we mean it as such. It's simply a part of what anthropologist Ray Birdwhistell, a pioneer in nonverbal theory and research, calls "learning to be a human body" (1970).

Part of how we "learn to be a human body" is to develop expectations for others', and our own, nonverbal behaviors. Burgoon's (1983; Burgoon & Jones, 1976; Burgoon & Walther, 1990) **expectancy-violations theory** has attempted to explain this complex process and to give theoretical typologies of nonverbal context, like Edward Hall's, a bit more dimension. Her theory focuses on persuasive situations in which people's expectations about reasonable or proper nonverbal behavior can be known, and she asks a simple question about them: What happens when those expectations are violated? For example, when a highly attractive person performs an immediacy cue, but one that violates norms, will that person be perceived as more persuasive (as the attractiveness might suggest) or less persuasive (as the fact of norm violation might suggest)? Think about a relative stranger from one of your large classes who stops by your library desk to ask you to take notes for him while he and his basketball teammates go to a tournament in Chicago. He touches you on the shoulder familiarly and sits briefly on the desk corner, grazing your arm. Some research in the expectancy-violations literature suggests that if you admire him (for whatever reason), his violation of proxemic norms will actually work to his advantage; you're more likely to be willing to comply with his request. On the other hand, low-attractiveness or low-credibility persuaders will be more effective if they maintain the normal/normative distance associated with conversations in their culture. Again, we can see that the literal content of what is done or said is not inherently meaningful. Instead, what else is happening, socially and psychologically, creates the context in which the "same" behavior can have very different effects.

Social Context: Communicators and Technologies in Situations

In social situations, we interact with other people, taking them into account and coordinating our actions toward them with our own personal goals. While social situations are often contrasted with personal ones, it's difficult to conceive of a social situation without also considering individuals, and vice versa (Stamp, Vangelisti, & Knapp, 1994, pp. 170–171).

In this section we'll review two ways of organizing social context, one that has been useful for decades (Ruesch & Bateson, 1968), and one that is a more recent suggestion (Lievrouw & Finn, 1990). In presenting these ideas we aren't implying that they are the only two ways to analyze social context, only that these alternatives suggest the broad range of conceptual possibilities.

Social Levels of Communication

Ruesch and Bateson (1968) argue that how researchers choose which levels of social communication to examine will influence how much and what kind of detail they're likely to find. In other words, studying social situations is like using a microscope: "As magnification increases, the area of the field must decrease.... Depending upon whether [the researcher] focuses upon large or small entities, he will see the various functions in greater or smaller detail" (p. 274). If you decide to study larger units or levels of social organization, you will find less resolution of detail. Four basic levels of communication are distinguished by Ruesch and Bateson, each with progressively more systemic complexity.

Level I Communication. This is the "within one" level of **intrapersonal** processes, in which inner physiological and psychological messages are perceived by a communicator. The person is considered a system of communication in and of itself. Thus when you contemplate whether to enroll in a class, to complain about your new car, or to go to the library, you're processing inner messages at this level. Although Level I communication is not a context of social interaction, it is the necessary prelude to one. Intrapersonal processes, of course, assume that there will be external social influences, as, for example, in the development of the self-concept.

Level II Communication. This level could be termed the "one-to-one" level or, as the communication literature refers to it, the dyadic situation. In the **dyad**, a two-person system, each communicator observes and participates in the two-way communication that develops, and this presents dilemmas. According to Ruesch and Bateson (1968), individuals tend to specialize in either observation or participation and are not realistically able to do both equally well. Some information inevitably will be overlooked in the dyadic mode. Job interviews, dates, marital arguments, and counseling are examples of Level II communication.

Level III Communication. At this level, communicators engage each other in group situations. The context is marked by an unequal division of functions among the communicators in the group, as in a hierarchical organization or a group with designated leadership roles. The group can be seen as having a *center* and a *periphery,* with messages being sent primarily in a one-way fashion. Ruesch and Bateson (1968) identify two types of message (and therefore two sublevels) at this level: The "one-to-many" message is sent to people at the periphery by someone at the center of the group (e.g., when a corporate chief executive distributes a letter to employees about impending layoffs), whereas the "many-to-one" message is sent to the center by those at the periphery of the group (e.g., when union members request a meeting with the CEO to discuss the layoff policy). Modern businesses at this level are often organized for specialization involving relatively narrow one-way messages and roles rather than for dialogue.

Level IV Communication. At this final level, also known as the "many-to-many" level, *cultural communication* takes place. As Ruesch and Bateson (1968) explain, "In addition to intrapersonal, interpersonal, and organized group networks, which are variously perceived as such by the individuals, there is a host of instances in which the individual is unable to recognize the source and destination of messages, and therefore does not recognize that these messages travel in a network structure" (pp. 281–282). Such cultural networks, therefore, operate invisibly from the standpoint of individual actors within the culture(s)—a point we will make again later in Chapter 7's more complete analysis of cultural communication theorizing. However, these networks are no less important to communication. Rather, the pervasiveness of the sources and destinations of such messages simply makes them hard to pin down because they are so pervasive. Level IV messages may be **space-binding** (bringing people in different places "together" for a time while attending to the same set of messages, such as our culture-wide system of advertising) or **time-binding** (integrating past and present, such as a team of archaeologists publishing a book about an ancient and nearly forgotten culture). Clearly, analysts focusing on this level would have to become very familiar with the media of mass communication in modern societies.

One innovative study in this vein is Donal Carbaugh's (1989) *Talking American: Cultural Discourses on "Donahue."* The author analyzed numerous televised talk shows, fleshing out a number of themes Americans seem to use implicitly in their talk about self, social roles, relationships, and the notion of communication itself. He notes, for example, that talk show guests and audience members talked about "self" as if it were a possession, and as if "self" exists along the three dimensions of "independent–dependent" (in relationships), "aware–unaware" (of self-concept and of others), and "communicative–closed" (about the content of social

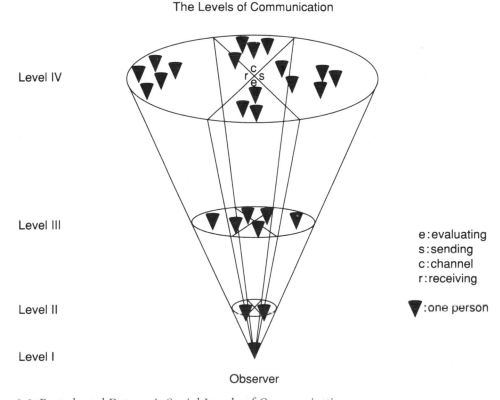

The Levels of Communication

Level IV

Level III

Level II

Level I

e : evaluating
s : sending
c : channel
r : receiving

▼ : one person

Observer

Figure 3-2 Ruesch and Bateson's Social Levels of Communication

Source: *Communication: The Social Matrix of Psychiatry,* by Jurgen Ruesch, M.D., and Gregory Bateson. Copyright © 1987, 1968, 1951 by W. W. Norton & Company, Inc. Reprinted by permission of W. W. Norton & Company, Inc.

Chapter 4, "How Do We Become Ourselves?" will describe several theories that explain our cognitive contexts for communication, what Ruesch and Bateson call Level I ("within one") intrapersonal communication. Think of contexts as being both external and internal; if this chapter concentrates on the outer phenomena of context, the next one will focus on inner context.

choices). A cultural theme inferred by this research was that the optimal American self is independent, aware, and expressive (1989, pp. 61–86). Remember that if themes are truly cultural, they don't just represent the specific shows Carbaugh studied; they don't originate with these interviewees, these expert guests, these audiences, or even from the television medium itself. They can be studied there because they have no real identifiable source. Cultural themes are interwoven throughout the culture; they are for all practical purposes sourceless and pervasive.

Ruesch and Bateson (1968) organize their system in terms of these four levels of communication. However, they also show that each level is composed of four basic communication actions: evaluating, sending, channel choices, and receiving. As shown in Figure 3-2, they illustrate their model as a cone that is subdivided into these basic human activities.

A Communication Systems Model of Social Context

A good example of a recent attempt to conceptualize social contexts in a new way is Lievrouw and Finn's (1990) model emphasizing the role of **mediation** in human interaction. If a process is said to be "mediated," we mean that its success depends in part on some other entity, such as a technology or, in the case of labor–management mediation, a third-party negotiator. Traditionally, communication scholars have viewed some forms of communication as mediated (e.g., television and newspapers) and other forms as nonmediated (e.g., face-to-face dyadic communication). Traces of this traditional distinction are present in Ruesch and Bateson's (1968) model of the social levels of communication. According to Lievrouw and Finn (1990), however, the distinction is misleading because all forms of communication, including face-to-face (FtF) interaction, may be viewed as mediated. Interpersonal situations typically emphasize one or more of the five senses, which are mediated at least by "natural channels" of light and air, they argue. Furthermore, "most scholars of interpersonal communication do not think of FtF communication as mediated because the descriptive phrase itself, 'face-to-face,' dismisses the dimension of space (distance) as important. Yet distance is a relevant variable" (pp. 41–42). The question isn't *whether* communication is mediated, but *how*.

Lievrouw and Finn's (1990) systems model of social contexts suggests that the three fundamental dimensions of any communicative act are temporality, involvement, and control. *Temporality* is how people experience time in their communication relationships. *Involvement* refers to how people bridge both physical and psychological forms of distance. Through involvement, individuals become more engaged with others and with themselves in cognitive, affective (emotionally based), and sensory ways. Finally, *control* refers to the exertion of influence in social settings. Through awareness of the control dimension, communicators understand how much control is inherent in a situation and the balance of control distributed among participants.

Mapping these variables into a three-dimensional model (shown in Figure 3-3), Lievrouw and Finn (1990) create a "space" within which different types of communication systems are described in terms of their mediation and social characteristics. Temporality is represented as a continuum ranging from simultaneous to nonsimultaneous events, while involvement is represented as a range of indi-

---

REVIEWING KEY IDEAS

RUESCH AND BATESON'S SOCIAL LEVELS OF COMMUNICATION

- Level IV: Cultural (many-to-many)
- Level III: Group (one-to-many/many-to-one)
- Level II: Dyadic (one-to-one)
- Level I: Intrapersonal (within one)

---

viduals' low to high involvement in the situation. The control continuum ranges from receiver-oriented through equal control to sender-oriented control.

Figure 3-3 shows Lievrouw and Finn's dimensions model before specific systems and social networks are located within it. Next, the authors place various mediated social contexts in the space to illustrate the extent to which each depends differently on temporality, involvement, and control. Thus, for example, the position of database systems technology (item 14) in Figure 3-4 reflects its (1) high degree of receiver-based control, (2) nonsimultaneous usage (i.e., user and designer are not co-oriented at the same time), and (3) low degree of user involvement. As this example illustrates, Lievrouw and Finn's model invites a rich analysis of communication contexts. Unfortunately, the model appears to be excessively complex unless you decide to trace a particular medium carefully, locating it in the

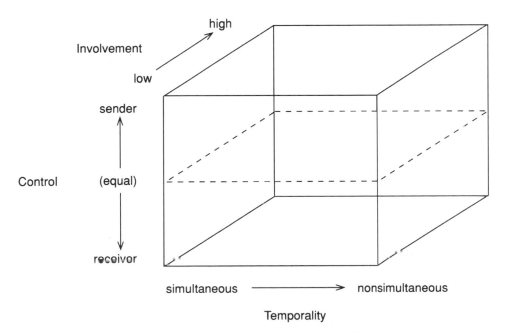

FIGURE 3-3 Lievrouw and Finn's Dimensions of Communication Behavior

SOURCE: L. A. Lievrouw and T. A. Finn, "Identifying the Common Dimensions of Communication," in B. D. Ruben and L. A. Lievrouw (Eds.), *Mediation, Information, and Behavior* (pp. 37–65). Copyright © 1990 by Transaction Publishers. Used with permission.

three-dimensional space described by *temporality, control,* and *involvement.* Check your understanding by looking at e-mail (item 11): Why is it portrayed to be under nearly equal control of sender and receiver? Why is its involvement portrayed as quite low? Why is its time dimension portrayed as generally nonsimultaneous? If you are familiar with "instant messenger" e-mail technology, offered in some online services, decide where to place it in Lievrouw and Finn's model.

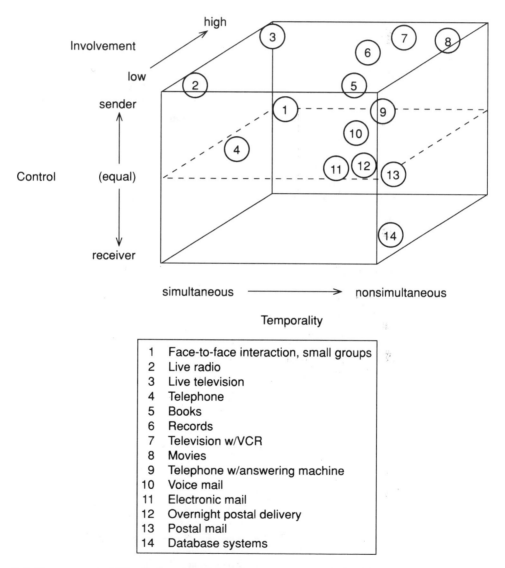

FIGURE 3.4 Lievrouw and Finn's Communication Systems, Arrayed within Dimensions of Communication Behavior

Source: L. A. Lievrouw and T. A. Finn, "Identifying the Common Dimensions of Communication," in B. D. Ruben and L. A. Lievrouw (Eds.), *Mediation, Information, and Behavior* (pp. 37–65). Copyright © 1990 by Transaction Publishers. Used with permission.

The ability of the communication systems model of social context to chart different kinds of mediation provides a valuable clue to an emerging area of theorizing about computer-mediated communication that could be termed **access theory** (Anderson, 1997). Conceiving of a new communication context as based on access to messages rather than on message reception contrasts with our traditional assumptions of how communication works. Older media contexts presumed that senders direct and deliver messages to receivers. Though computer users are still able to transfer messages in this way (and will be able to do so with far more sophistication in the future), much of the new online culture—which is exemplified by databases, Internet surfing, e-mail, chat rooms, and virtual reality—does not depend on senders knowing the physical presence or exact physical placement of receivers (Heim, 1987, 1993; Landow, 1992; Lanham, 1993; Snyder, 1996). In fact, the phenomenon of **hypertext** presumes that access processes of reading and listening are really forms of coauthorship; the reader/listener not only determines when access occurs but also, through a series of self-controlled choices, affects the ultimate and unique shape of the experience. According to language theorist Ilana Snyder (1996):

> *[Hypertext] is an information medium that exists only on-line in a computer. A structure composed of blocks of text connected by electronic links, it offers different pathways to users. Hypertext provides a means of arranging information in a non-linear manner with the computer automating the process of connecting one piece of information to another....*
>
> *A hypertext is constructed partly by the writers who create the links, and partly by readers who decide which threads to follow.... Hypertext differs from printed text by offering readers multiple paths through a body of information: it allows them to make their own connections, to incorporate their own links and to produce their own meanings. (p. ix)*

In contrast to the long-held directedness or conduit theories of communication that have always assumed that audiences were to some extent targets of speakers, writers, and broadcasters, we clearly have entered an era that Gozzi and Haynes (1992) call "distant presence." Communicators contribute messages to databases and virtual forums, for example, and other communicators can subsequently access those messages, but the messages are not actually sent to receivers. Digitally mediated systems are not propelled by producers, and they thereby blur the traditional distinctions between producers and consumers, and between senders and receivers. The listener/reader of a hypertext message chooses how to coproduce the message. This, as a recent commercial said, changes everything. The new psychological and sociological communication contexts of the twenty-first century will also be molded by **virtual reality**, in which seemingly immediate experiences can be digitally packaged to be deferred—at a communicator's choice—to later times and other places.

Still in its relative infancy, online technology is more prominently used by some cultural groups than by others. And, for the moment at least, it seems more like a "lean" medium than a "rich" one in terms of the diversity of cues, senses and presence involved, to use the terminology of some theorists (Morris & Ogan, 1996; Walther, 1992). Yet the future is becoming clearer, and it will include increasing amounts of interactivity, receiver control, coauthorship, and immediacy, as our technological media system increasingly mimics face-to-face presence. Lievrouw and Finn (1990) help us see that all analyses of mediated systems must exist within an overall cultural context, just as FtF communication must. The authors extend their model to show how the cube must itself exist within cultural assumptions about communication. They write: "…communication cannot take place unless culture, relationship, and content have been accounted for. Without these contextual elements, the attempt at communication will be nonsensical. In any given communication situation the context may influence communication and vice versa" (p. 55).

As with any tentative model, Lievrouw and Finn's is incomplete. Yet, considered with the Ruesch and Bateson model, it helps us to clarify how disparate concepts can fit together. Both approaches demonstrate how social contexts influence not only *what* is communicated between people but *how* it is communicated. Applying them to an emerging theoretical terrain of electronic access, we can also glimpse the future.

REVIEWING KEY THEORIES

This chapter has stressed the importance of context, a factor that is easily overlooked by many people who are just starting their study of communication. Although *context* can mean many things, here we stressed the nonverbal messages that make up social and physical contexts.

In considering nonverbal social context we looked specifically at Mehrabian's *immediacy theory,* which suggests that communication depends on cueing others that we are willing to help create a "here-and-now" form of being together; that we are oriented toward them socially, psychologically, and physically. Allied with Mehrabian's theory as it is often applied is the work of Edward T. Hall in *proxemics,* Robert Sommer in *physical environment* and *hard architecture,* and Judee Burgoon in *nonverbal expectancy-violations theory.* Burgoon discovered that communicators who are deemed highly attractive or prestigious can violate others' expectations of nonverbal norms (such as proxemics) and be more persuasive as a result.

Although they are not full-blown theories, two pairs of theorists attempt to model the social spaces in which human communication occurs. First, Ruesch and Bateson's *social levels of communication model* divides our interaction into four types, ranging from inner reflections to the pervasive cultural networks of communication in which it's difficult even to identify where, when, and how powerful messages come into being. Second, Lievrouw and Finn's *communication systems model of social context* demonstrates how our media of communication create very different contexts for our experiences of communication. Allied with this emerging discussion of new media are the assumptions of *access theory,* in which user control of access becomes the prevailing assumption, replacing older assumptions that communication worked by messages being directed toward receivers.

TESTING THE CONCEPTS

"Does a contextual approach to communication mean that I'll never be able to 'pin down' what people mean, or what causes them to act in the ways they do? Will meaning always be contextual?"

In all likelihood, people will continue to be held accountable for their words and actions in most situations. Most philosophies of social science, after all, assume that human beings are actors, not reactors, and that we are for the most part capable of choosing our own destinies. However, learning about the influence of context provides useful reminders: that meanings are not neat and tidy packages but are more like interpretations negotiated under the ground rules of differing contexts. This is why it is extremely hard to pin down such meanings. It is a matter of developing communication tolerance.

In another sense, an ecological approach to context does present some problems for determining causality because it relies on a systems model of communication. Consider, for example, the specific context of family interaction; a systems approach helps to explain the intricate dynamics of relations among parents and children. If all changes in a system are interconnected, as the model suggests, it would be difficult at best at any moment in time to point to X and say with certainty that it "caused" changes in Y. This causal ambiguity is the basis of a feminist critique of systems theory applications in counseling and mental-health disciplines (Cottone, 1992, pp. 262–267; Walters, Carter, Papp, & Silverstein, 1988). In a context of family violence against women, systems approaches seem to come dangerously close to implying that women somehow could share part of the responsibility for male violence! In terms of power, roles, and relational control, the causality, and thus the responsibility, appears more linear and more attributable than an ecological systems approach would indicate. Other feminist theorists are not as ready to sacrifice systemic or ecological assumptions (Goldner, Penn, Sheinberg, & Walker, 1990). Cottone (1992) argues for a middle-ground "contextualist" paradigm that more realistically allows for attributions of somewhat linear causality, without sacrificing the overall transactional insight of systemic-relational theory. In other words, you can still recognize the importance of ecological relations without assuming that victims are partially to blame for conditions of domination. Some things happen because he or she or they decided to make them happen, not because the "context" of a relationship or a social situation "caused" them.

"Sommer sounds as if he's criticizing 'hard architecture.' Is there ever a place for it? Does it serve any useful functions?"

Sommer's value judgments are displayed in his critique of the so-called hard architecture of airports. But it is also possible to argue that for the majority of travelers using public transportation, privacy-oriented waiting areas (e.g., where the seats do not face each other) are more functional than personalized waiting areas (where soft and inviting seating is designed to encourage conversation, even among strangers). In some other contexts, such as a congregation facing forward while sitting on the wooden pews of a country church, inviting more comfortable interaction would defeat the primary purpose of the gathering. Effective planners of organizational meetings, workshops, and group gatherings understand that the psychological, physical, and social components of a situation must be coordinated with the purpose of the particular meeting involved.

"Do people automatically know what kind of communication I intend when I choose, for example, the social distance of four to twelve feet?"

No, not automatically. But because of a variety of social-context expectations, they could probably make an educated guess about what you would not discuss at that distance. For example, marriage proposals and intimate gossip are unlikely in this context because they usually demand more immediacy cues. Remember, too, that Hall's (1966) study is based on a relatively narrow sample—middle-class and mostly white Americans from the Northeast. Many people would not fit this pattern exactly. In two follow-up chapters, Hall presents evidence on distance differences noticed in other cultures (pp. 123–153).

"Do chat rooms and other online contexts fit into the categories of Level II (dyadic), Level III (group), or Level IV (cultural) communication in Ruesch and Bateson's model?"

Here is an example of why traditional communication analyses must adapt to new forms of mediation and presence. Although many online relationships develop in an essentially dyadic way, the phenomenon known as "lurking" complicates that assumption. **Lurking** occurs when a person observes an online "chat" without contributing to the conversation. While most chat rooms identify the screen names of all users logged on to a room, in some cases it may not be possible to know how many lurkers there are. It becomes hard to know where the *center* and the *periphery* might be in any online group. Formerly, the various social means of production were typically centralized in positions of power, while consumers were at the periphery. How does that change when literally anyone can create his or her own Web page on the Internet, becoming a potential information source for millions of other people? Finally, the Internet itself, that formally and informally interlinked worldwide network of computerized users and information, is obviously a many-to-many context, which is how Ruesch and Bateson defined Level IV.

YOU, THE RESEARCHER

1. Keep a small notebook in which you can jot down brief observations and notes throughout the day. Carry the notebook with you for three days, and:

   - Pay especially close attention to any ongoing relationship in which you talk to the same person several times a day.
   - At the end of each day, make a list of the comments that could easily be misunderstood if a hypothetical eavesdropping reporter simply quoted you or the other person accurately but did not specify the verbal or nonverbal contexts in which the statements were made.

   Analyze the statements and incidents. Which were dependent on a physical or psychological context? On a social context? Draw some conclusions about how hard or easy it is to distinguish among the types of context.

2. Visit three different third-grade classrooms. Observe (a) what is displayed on the walls; (b) what objects and materials are prominent in the room; and (c) the arrangement of desks and other furniture. Then consider the following questions:

   • How might these features of context affect student learning?
   • Which contextual features are purposely intended to promote learning? Which are not? In both cases, whose choices do they represent?

   After formulating your research question (see Chapter 2), write a brief paragraph describing a study you could do on the effects of context in elementary classrooms. Discuss your proposal in class.

3. Videotape or audiotape a television program that features political discussion (e.g., *The McLaughlin Group, Hardball,* or *Meet the Press*). Identify *episodes* (sequences of talk that seem to have identifiable beginnings and endings) in which the literal meaning of a person's words is in your opinion clearly the opposite of what that speaker intends. For example:

   • Are the speakers using irony, sarcasm, or another speech strategy that depends on contextual awareness?
   • What contextual factors signal the "proper" ways in which the words should be taken?

   Play the excerpts for four friends whose political orientations differ (e.g., two Democrats and two Republicans). Later, interview them to discover if there were any striking differences of interpretation that might be attributed in part to the political affiliation of the observer. Then ask yourself, "What are the limitations of such an investigation, considering the small sample size?" Research communication or social psychology journals to find at least one study that is basically an expanded version of your informal investigation. How did the researcher(s) deal with the problem of sample size?

4. Visit the waiting area of an airport or a bus terminal, and take notes on its design. Note how the seats are arranged and what materials they are made of. How do these features encourage or discourage communication among travelers? What assumptions about communication in this context might have guided the designers? In answering these questions, try to apply as many concepts from this chapter as possible. Discuss your findings in class.

5. Conduct an analysis of your classroom. First, compile a comprehensive list of its features. Describe the features in neutral terms (e.g., not as having "ugly green walls" or as being "too small" but as "light green" and "14 by 23 feet"). Then write a brief essay about what the room's features reasonably allow you to infer about the educational philosophy of its designers or architects.

Erich Hartmann/Magnum Photos

"How Do We Become Ourselves?"

Theorizing Personal Experiences

> The formulation of experience which is contained within the intellectual horizon of an age and a society is determined, I believe, not so much by events and desires, as by the *basic concepts* at people's disposal for analyzing and describing their adventures to their own understanding. Of course, such concepts arise as they are needed, to deal with political or domestic experience; but the same experiences could be seen in many different lights, so the light in which they do appear depends on the genius of a people as well as on the demands of the external occasion. Different minds will take the same events in very different ways.... Every society meets a new idea with its own concepts, its own tacit, fundamental way of seeing things; that is to say, *with its own questions*, its peculiar curiosity.
>
> SUSANNE K. LANGER, *Philosophy in a New Key* (1951, p. 17)

Susanne Langer, one of the most prominent intellectuals of the twentieth century, consistently stressed the importance of asking good questions about human symbolizing. She describes why personal experience depends on concepts that, in fact, aren't entirely personal or private at all. Personal questions are necessarily social questions. Our personal concepts develop in our social climate; in this way, they are contextual. Symbolic communication supplies us with these concepts, and we assume that thinking with them is natural, normal, and real. Therefore what people assume to be true about their personal experience shapes the kind of communication that develops between them and other people. These assumptions do not determine the communication, of course. But it is helpful to have a general understanding of how the human mind processes information, solves linguistic problems, develops a sense of self, and applies its assumptions to others' messages. Why is this knowledge practical for communicators?

The Assumptions of Experience

A friend of ours once traveled to Japan, where he taught interpersonal and intercultural communication to Japanese students. Bob thought he had prepared himself carefully for the many cultural differences he would find in Japanese classrooms. Instead, he was surprised by the extent to which the classroom behavior of many students differed from his expectations. He was forced to test his assumptions about student interest and learning in lectures and classroom discussions. Some of the students seemed so passive and unexpressive, so ready to write down his every jest and offhand remark. Were they bored? Were they grade-hungry robots who were uninvolved in participative learning (as he might have assumed in an American classroom)? Or were they simply demonstrating a different style of involvement, a different type of personal experience? He soon discovered that most of his students were interested and involved, but that their involvement was experienced and demonstrated differently. The exterior is not a particularly reliable indicator of the interior unless you understand the nature of the exterior-interior linkage.

Bob carried to Japan a certain mental model of expected student behaviors, despite being intellectually aware that Japanese and American interpersonal styles differ. He was therefore surprised when actions that violated his model could still be considered good student behaviors by others. We're not referring here to an inexperienced person but to a bright, scholarly, sensitive, and worldly educator who had been teaching for decades, even in culturally diverse classrooms. If he could be surprised by the extent of the cultural differences he encountered, there's a lesson here for the rest of us. As Langer suggests in the chapter-opening quotation, all humans build inner models naturally and normally to structure the world, making the unmanageably complex dither of stimuli more comprehensible. We rarely consider how unique and idiosyncratic our models or expectations may be, and how easily they can contradict those of other people and groups.

Surprise

It would be easy to assume that Bob simply increased his knowledge about Japanese students and then naturally improved his communication with them. But the process was more complicated than that. He realized that in order to learn about the students he would have to learn something about his own cognitive patterns as well.

Cognition refers to those processes of mind through which people come to know, perceive, understand, remember, and evaluate aspects of their world. If our friend had assumed that the Japanese students' cognitive styles were basically similar to his own, he would have cut off his chances to learn about them as well as to learn about himself. He had to recognize not just that the styles differ but also how they differ. By doing so, he gained a better understanding of his own experience as well, recognizing that his response to this situation was not the only possible human response. He was, in a word, surprised.

As we noted in Chapter 1 on theory construction, surprise is a vital element in the process of explaining or understanding anything. Jerome Bruner (1986), a prominent contemporary researcher of the human mind, claims that surprise is an "extraordinarily useful phenomenon to students of mind" because it provides a "window on presupposition" (p. 46). In other words, it shows us what has been taken for granted. When you are surprised by something or someone, you are learning. You are forced to abandon the model of mind on which you had been relying and to imagine new possibilities. Bruner's career shows this, as his interests have ranged from his early narrowly cognitive notions of the human psyche to his more recent concerns with the interpersonal and transactional dimensions of communication (Bruner, 1979, 1986, 1990).

Sensing Self from "Who You Aren't"

Any cross-cultural experience reminds us, if we're alert, how little we understand about our own ways of thinking and feeling. Again, surprise is a key. Anthropologist Edward T. Hall (1977) suggests that this social phenomenon can be explained by a systems approach to communication: When the mechanisms of the human nervous system work smoothly, they utilize *positive feedback*—that is, feedback that tends to support or reinforce the directions being taken by previous perceptions, assumptions, and expectations. The organism remains essentially unaware of its own patterns of processing information. To use a computer analogy, the program is functioning smoothly. Cognitive processes become so integrated and seem

LINK

In the terms of cultural theorists, our friend was a sojourner or stranger in Japan. He gradually discovered more effective ways to adjust, creating an identity that was not quite either an American way of being a teacher or a Japanese way but a third way, a blended kind of cross-cultural teaching style. To balance this example, Chapter 7 will describe the story of another sojourner, a Japanese student attending a U.S. university.

Hall's distinctions may make more sense if you review the definitions of *feedback* and *system* in Chapter 1.

so natural that they are taken for granted and, in a sense, become invisible. Hall (1977) puts it this way: "People's nervous systems are organized according to the principles of *negative feedback;* that is, the whole thing works so smoothly and automatically that the only time the control system is consciously brought into play is when the input signals deviate from the norm. Therefore, people individually and collectively are for the most part unaware of the patterns and reference signals governing behavior" (p. 54; emphasis added). The "great gift" we can give each other, Hall says, is not a direct knowledge of otherness but a knowledge of self that comes through contact with others who are sufficiently different (operating as negative feedback that contrasts with an individual's own assumptions).

You find out *who you are* by meeting *who you aren't*. A clear sense of self doesn't simply emerge from a stable cultural experience. Instability plays a role as well. You have to be shaken somewhat by communicating with people whose personal experiences test your own—or, as Hall (1977) says, people who are "members of the opposite sex, different age groups, different ethnic groups, and different cultures" (p. 44). Intercultural communication becomes a valuable proving ground for trying out our cognitive assumptions.

Whatever our social contacts, we can develop perspective by looking inward at the ways in which human beings make, or avoid making, decisions and interpretations about messages. Studying this process should increase tolerance for the distinctive behaviors that are alien to us but seem so natural or normal to others. By now you've noticed that this chapter on personal experience is not primarily concerned with the brain and its physiology. It's not just about psychology either, though psychologists have long explored this territory. Rather, our focus is on where inner private experience and outer social experience intersect. You'll learn about theories that try to explain:

1. human *perception,* the process of translating messages or input from the senses into awareness
2. human *language,* the system of symbols with which we make sense of and express that awareness
3. human *cognitive organizing systems,* which connect our personal experiences into a patterned whole

Although it may seem as if this chapter's main topics—perception, language, cognitive organization—have been arranged from simple to complex, the arrangement we chose for them is actually arbitrary. We could have arranged the topics in nearly any order because each is as complex as the others and each contributes equally to our understanding of how the others work. Perception is influenced by language, for example, and vice versa. A particular person's sense of self influences how she or he mentally organizes the world, and vice versa.

Perception, Not Reception

Perception and Activity

Perception is usually defined as the process by which an organism assimilates, makes sense out of, and uses sensory data. In normal human perception, for example, we use our senses of sight, sound, smell, taste, and touch to provide clues to what goes on around us. This seems simple enough, but let's consider a few examples:

- Juan, a new college student, is a little late for class on the first day of the semester. He parks his car and quickly walks to Bryce Hall. He's grateful to see that the professor has not yet arrived, and that there's time to choose a seat toward the back of the room, relax a bit, catch his breath, and look around. What does he see?

- Jill, a first grader on a field trip to the zoo, steps off the school bus, holding hands with her teacher, Mr. Jones, and her best friend, Kate. She's excited because this is her first visit to a zoo. But she's a little scared, too, because the animals she'll see here are real. She wonders if any animals might bite or escape from their cages. As she walks through the front gate with other excited children and some parents, she hesitates, and Mr. Jones and Kate gently tug her hands. Jill's eyes open very wide, as she tries to take it all in at once. What does she see?

- Sarita might look calm to others sitting in the doctor's waiting room, but they don't notice the constant flexing and unflexing of the muscles just above her knees. They have no idea that she's worried about missing the rest of the high school soccer season just because of this stupid strain or twist or whatever it is. Sarita's mind is racing: "Where's that nurse, anyway? Who has all day to sit here?" She absently picks up a *Newsweek* and leafs through it. What does she see?

Although these examples focus on only one sensory capacity, they illustrate that perception is more complex than is commonly assumed. The commonsense answer to the question "What does he or she see?" would be that this person sees what is in the setting to be seen: Juan, we might assume, sees students fidgeting nervously, maps hanging on the wall, and paint chipping off old radiators, among many other physical features of the room. Jill could see the reassuring smiles of zoo attendants as well as the bars safely separating the kids from the hippos. And Sarita might see an interesting article on high-definition television, an advertisement for the new Volvo, and a column suggesting that it's more common to sue a lawyer than one might think. All of these assumptions might be safe if human perception were an objective process in which our brains receive data through our senses and record what is available to perceive. But it's not. Perception helps us make sense of outside information, but human beings aren't simply sponges for soaking up stimuli. Juan, Jill, and Sarita might not see any of these things at all, due to their cognitive and emotional preoccupations.

The commonsense view of perception is represented by the simple diagram shown in Figure 4-1. Do we simply receive stimuli (S) and store them as internal representations of the outer world? Or is the process more dynamic, fluctuating, creative, and active than such a model indicates? Although it is still an oversimplification, Figure 4-2 better illustrates the usual pattern of human perception. In this model of selective perception, we are active in the process, in that we "reach toward" and select some stimuli and systematically ignore (or filter out) others. Nor are our inner representations necessarily "close" in form or function to an objective outer reality of stimuli. The unique experience of each of us appears to become immediately a part of the experience of perception. The external stimuli (e.g., S_1 in Figure 4-2) enter our consciousness in a form modified somewhat by our previous experience—our expectations, values, attitudes, beliefs, and other cultural assumptions. Of course, some types of stimuli, such as an unexpected loud noise or turning a corner and bumping into someone, can be thought of as incoming and inevitable (e.g., S_3). However, most perceptual activities aren't explained well by the commonsense assumptions that we see what's there to be seen, hear what's creating sound in our immediate environment, and so forth.

Selectivity

Research on selective perception has shown that we miss much of what can be perceived in our environments and that what we do notice is selectively perceived, interpreted, and retained (Toch & Smith, 1968). Some scholars even contend that if we were to attempt to attend to and process all available stimuli at any one time, the result might be madness. Birdwhistell (1970), for instance, estimates that, at any given point in time, as many as ten thousand bits of "minimally discernible" sensory information are available to us per second (p. 3). Processing all of this information at once would be impossible. Instead, the human mind compensates by pre-

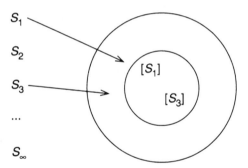

FIGURE 4.1 A Commonsense View of Perception

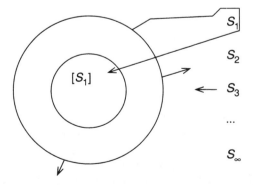

FIGURE 4.2 Perception as an Active Process

deciding, on the basis of **perceptual salience** (perceived importance to the self), what is most important to it. It monitors the environment, scanning for stimuli that, at that moment, are most relevant, dangerous, interesting, or applicable to the self.

When considering selective perception, keep in mind three things: (1) selectivity is built into our sensory experience, (2) selectivity is not total, and (3) selectivity seems to support an internal strain toward consistency (see Reviewing Key Ideas, below).

First, selective perception is not a matter of perceiving worldly objects accurately and subsequently dismissing, distorting, or deselecting them internally. Instead, the evidence suggests the counterintuitive conclusion that expectations and selection habits become integrated with our sensory apparatus directly. As Boulding (1956) observes:

> *Even at the level of simple or supposedly simple sense perception we are increasingly discovering that the message which comes through the senses is itself mediated through a value system. We do not perceive our sense data raw; they are mediated through a highly learned process of interpretation and acceptance. When an object apparently increases in size on the retina of the eye, we interpret this not as an increase in size but as movement. Indeed, we only get along in the world because we consistently and persistently disbelieve the plain evidence of our senses. The stick in water is not bent; the movie is a succession of still pictures; and so on. What this means is that for any individual organism or organization, there are no such things as "facts." There are only messages filtered through a changeable value system. (pp. 13–14)*

For example, consider the experience of a medical school student. As reported by Llinas (1987), the medical student had a thorough understanding of the physiology and functional anatomy of the visual system. He technically understood that the retina, the motor neurons, and the other parts of the eye all contribute to sight. But he confided to his professor (with some courage, we imagine), "I still

---

REVIEWING KEY IDEAS

PERCEPTION: ACTIVE SELECTION OF STIMULI

- Perceptual expectations are built into experience itself. We see and hear, for example, as much with our personal values as we do with our eyes and ears.
- Selectivity in perception does not mean that perception is completely arbitrary or idiosyncratic. Different people can and do agree about many perceptions.
- Perceptions are often selected to support an inner consistency among a person's beliefs, attitudes, and values.

⬕LINK

Our perception of the world is intimately linked to the hypotheses we make about the world. This leads to a disturbing suspicion: Does a culture provide subtle lenses through which we think we observe "facts," but actually we find what we expect to find? Chapter 7 will revisit this issue. For now, consider some social implications of this fact, as summarized by Bolles (1991): "When perception is the issue, prejudice often turns up under the guise of science. As recently as the 1960s, scholarly journals published articles about perceptual differences between men and women in which the authors took for granted a woman's 'natural' subordination to men. Researchers in South Africa published articles supporting the policy of apartheid by reporting that cultural differences between the local races are so profound that education cannot change perception. (p. 108).

do not understand...how I see" (p. 351). Llinas (1987) analyzes why knowing the anatomy is not the same thing as understanding perception:

> *This problem arises because we forget to tell our students that seeing is reconstructing the external world, based not on the reflecting properties of light on external objects but, rather, on the transformation of such visual sensory input (a vector) into perception vectors in* other sets of coordinate systems. *Indeed, we should have reminded our students that in order to see one requires first to have moved within the world and to have established, via the use of natural coordinates, the properties of objects with respect to our own physical attributes (the weight of each object, its size with respect to that of our body, etc.). It would be clear then that it is only through the ability that our brain has to transform measurements in one set of coordinates (the visual system) into comparable sets of measurements (visually guided motor execution) provided by other sensory inputs (for example, touch from fingertips) that one can truly develop the necessary semantics to be able to understand what one sees.... It is easy to demonstrate that in order to see we must interact with the external world by means of movement. In adult man, visual reversal following the wearing of inverting prism goggles can occur only if the subject is allowed to move about while wearing the goggles.* In short, then, we are able to measure and recreate universals on the basis of our own physical properties because, through interactions between our brain and the rest of our body, a set of natural coordinates has been embedded in our central nervous system. *(pp. 351–352)*

In other words, neither the anatomy of sight nor any of the other senses can by itself explain "seeing" or perception. Instead, understanding perception involves recognizing that there is a **semantics** (an organized structure of meanings) for how mind and body work together to create our links with the world. The senses don't simply deliver information for the mind to process. Instead, mind, brain, and the senses are all part of the same system. This is why we see, hear, and feel with our hypotheses as much as we do with our eyes, ears, and skin.

Cognitive psychologist Jerome Bruner (1983) concludes that because hypotheses guide our perceptions, we are "never indifferent, always tuned, ever readier for some events than for others" (p. 95). And, in a striking thought, another neuropsychologist asserts that perhaps babies would never learn to see if they were not allowed to roam through an environment, touching things while experimenting with hypotheses (Gregory & Miller, 1983, p. 62).

In one study of children's sensory perception that gained the attention of the news media, Bruner and a colleague asked children to describe the relative size of coins (Bruner & Goodman, 1947). The estimates the children gave were consistent only when their economic background was factored into the analysis (i.e., children from low-income families tended to perceive the coins as larger, whereas children from high-income families perceived them as smaller). Somehow a perceptual crossover developed, in which "perceived value" and "perceived physical size" were merged (Bruner, 1983, pp. 69–70; Bruner & Goodman, 1947).

These types of studies help us understand the phenomenon known as the **self-fulfilling prophecy**, in which we seem to see and hear what we've already preordained for ourselves (Rosenthal & Jacobson, 1968). This may set up the conditions in which an outcome becomes literally real primarily because we have expected it into existence. For example, if you expect to dislike your new roommate before you even meet her, you might accentuate the negatives in your initial impressions of her and act defensively toward her. Then, in the self-fulfilling part, her behavior, in turn, may be modified when she perceives (correctly) that your reaction to her is negative and doesn't seem fair. Finally, when you notice her negativity, you conclude that it confirms your initial expectations.

The second characteristic of selective perception is that it is not total. Just because you desperately want your team to play well, your perceptual system will not normally distort the final result of a lost game. Selectivity operates within certain boundaries of experience. We do not necessarily filter out new information because it conflicts with what we already know; many other variables can intervene. If, for example, a teacher requests that you follow certain study habits that contradict those you've used successfully over the years, you might choose not to ignore, neglect, or distort this new information. The information might appeal to you, in which case you may try to integrate it with what you already know about studying. Recognizing the gap between what you already know or expect to happen and what is new or surprising is called *learning.*

Bruner (1960) described learning as involving three "almost simultaneous" processes: acquisition, transformation, and evaluation (pp. 48–49). *Acquisition* is how a person perceives something that's different from what was known before, explicitly or implicitly. *Transformation* is how the mind can change newly acquired information to make it fit unanticipated situations. *Evaluation* is the process of checking whether the information can be successfully applied in new situations. In recent years, Bruner has emphasized communication more in his explanations of learning (1983, 1986, 1990). His newer work emphasizes that learning is fundamentally "collaborative" and, in many ways, an interpersonal phenomenon (1983, pp. 127–133; see also Vygotsky, 1962). In essence, he argues, humans learn by comparing their inner experiences with new external information in the context of immediate (e.g., face-to-face) or imagined and indirect (e.g., reading) human interaction.

The third characteristic of selective perception is that it appears to maintain an inner consistency among attitudes. Traditionally, social psychologists and most quantitative researchers in communication have treated attitude as a key cognitive variable. An attitude was presumed to be an inner disposition to behave in certain ways that are preferred to other behaviors. Thus an attitude is defined in terms of external behaviors and is based on an external metaphor (the "attitude" of a boat is its tendency to lean or list to one side). Of course, an attitude is an inferred or hypothetical construct within the mind.

Researchers who have contributed to **consistency theory** believe that **homeostasis**, or system balance, is a preferred state of being for humans, although this can never be achieved in a static way. People's minds are too complex and the stimuli of experience too changeable. Simply stated, individuals' attitudes do not always fit neatly with each other within personal experience. They might clash with, diverge from, or contradict previously believed or taken-for-granted perceptions. What happens then? Let's consider how you might react to these two conflicting bits

⊟**LINK**

Review the discussion of theory-building in Chapter 1. Could scholarly research be affected by self-fulfilling prophecies? What safeguards would help to prevent this problem?

of information: (1) that Professor Samily is your nicest and most effective teacher, and (2) that you've just heard she's been charged with plagiarism by the university. You attach a positive value to her, and also to the university. Yet the university, at least in this instance, negatively values the professor. These facts, when considered side by side, seem to create a kind of psychological tension or discomfort, which has been researched by different scholars as *cognitive dissonance* (Festinger, 1957), *incongruity* (Osgood & Tannenbaum, 1955), and *imbalance* (Heider, 1958).

In order to restore internal harmony or minimize disharmony, you might engage in one or more cognitive tactics, such as *denial* (a direct change of value placed on one of the objects), *bolstering* (adding perceptions to one of the objects), *differentiation* (splitting one of the objects into two parts, each of which is perceived differently, and then achieving balance with one of the new notions), or *transcendence* (perceiving the two inconsistent objects as a whole, and relating them together to a third object in a balanced way) (Abelson, 1967). In the student-professor example, denial might occur by an internal attitude adjustment in one direction. Your position toward the professor might change (e.g., "Maybe she just fooled me and isn't as nice or as effective as I'd thought"). If you choose bolstering, you might attach additional perceptions to your original ones to achieve balance: "I never realized how much pressure professors must feel in doing their research, if even Dr. Samily feels like she has to stretch the rules." Using differentiation as your cognitive tactic, you would separate one side of the imbalanced system into two or more distinct parts and then define one subpart as relevant: "Actually, it's not the university that's accusing her but only that jealous colleague." Finally, if you opted for transcendence, you might make this rationalization: "I see both Dr. Samily's classroom success and her alleged plagiarism as two parts of what makes a university so complex. Besides, universities are still better places to be than corporations." Of course, our statements in this paragraph are only examples and cannot begin to indicate the full complexity of human attitudes.

Language In-Forms Personal Experience

Some communication-related theories focus on the role of language in inner experience. They ask important questions: Does the human capacity for language form the groundwork for effective thinking? Or is thinking itself linguistic, our only basic way to process information? Although theorists address these issues somewhat differently, they generally agree on the importance of language. Whether thinking *is* language itself or is simply assisted or enabled by language, we cannot conceive of human life apart from considering language.

After considering the theories, we'd like to suggest a middle position. That is, **language**—"a potentially self-reflexive structure system of symbols that catalogue the objects, events, and relations in the world" (DeVito, 1986, p. 176)—plays a formative role in consciousness. In discussing language, most theorists emphasize the elements of DeVito's definition: self-reflexiveness, interconnected structure, and symbolic meaning. Considering these factors one by one will clarify why language is at the core of human experience.

Self-reflexiveness, or what we discussed earlier as *reflexivity,* means that something is potentially capable of commenting on or referring to itself (Blum &

McHugh, 1984; Lawson, 1985). With language, we can speak about our speaking or reflect on our ability to reflect. Thus language allows us to move to another level of experience, one level removed from direct involvement with the outer world.

When we say that language has an interconnected structure, we mean that it has system properties. The organization of language (its grammar and syntax) cannot be separated from its collection of meanings and referents (its semantics). The French linguist Ferdinand de Saussure (1966), who established many of our modern ways of understanding language, viewed language not only as composed of the overall system of symbolic message structures, which he called **la langue**, but also as having a particular and unique property of spokenness, **la parole**. Language involves both the pattern of what can be said *(la langue)* and the immediate speech of communicators *(la parole)*. Saussure's distinction is similar to the differences between structure and process, in that language has both an overall form and a particular life as it is spoken. However, you may wonder, as some critics do, whether the concepts of language structure and speech can be separated this neatly.

Language by definition involves *symbolizing*. When humans speak, they enact a set of agreements that many of the sounds they utter and the marks they make on paper will be taken as substitutes for objects, relations, and experiences. Rarely is a language the product of individually negotiated agreement, however; a person is born into the stream of an already agreed-upon language. Therefore although we have many choices of speech within a language, the language itself more or less predetermines what those alternatives will be.

Communication theorists, in tune with philosophers and linguists, usually distinguish between signals and symbols (Langer, 1951). **Signals** stand in a one-to-one unambiguous relationship to what they represent. For example, the movement of branches in a tree is safely taken as a signal that the wind is blowing, because whenever one thing happens, the other happens.

Symbolic life is different. **Symbols** suggest, rather than verify, the relations between things. For example, the red-white-and-blue flag has become a visual symbol of the United States, but not all citizens think the same things when they see the flag, and they could salute other flags if they wanted to. A creative combination of shapes and colors *becomes* a flag, therefore, when people agree that it symbolizes some persistent meaning that they believe is important. In addition, we can say that the sequence of four marks *f-l-a-g* creates in English, along with the corresponding pronunciation of the letter sounds, a symbol of the red, white, and blue cloth we call the American flag. This arbitrariness is not decreed by any linguistic royalty; its symbolic origins are shrouded in living historical precedent. Although we create and change our language as we talk, it is important to remember that we are born into a society and a culture with an already existing set of linguistic rules.

The Centrality of the Symbol: The Language Bridge to Social Life

The preexisting rules of language also suggest that our lives are fundamentally social, and that language can never be wholly private, even if you're thinking to yourself about what you'll say to a friend this afternoon. If you are especially interested in the nature of language and its influence on social communication, eventually you'll probably want to look more deeply into three areas of contemporary theorizing—speech act theory, semiotics, and postmodern language theory.

Speech Act Theory. Have you ever been tempted to say, "You're a big talker, but you never do anything about it"? Have you ever heard someone say "Talk is cheap," or "That's just empty rhetoric," or "I hear you say it, but will you do it?" Some people assume that life can be lived in one or the other of two extremes—talking about things or doing them. Talking about things, we sometimes assume, is passive, while only physical accomplishments are active. Some communication theorists challenge this distinction. Searle (1969), for example, suggests that any assumed distinction between words and actions is illusory. Although many people assume that communicators can either speak or act, Searle argues that by speaking we engage in significant action, a **speech act**. That is, spoken words are literally actions because they require energy and affect others. Speaking is not merely preliminary to acting or a substitute for reality—speaking is itself an act performed by one person with another or others. Through speech we can assert a truth, direct or request a listener to act in a certain way, commit ourselves to future acts, indicate psychological dispositions, or perform a symbolic accomplishment, such as saying "I do" during a marriage ceremony.

Semiotics. Symbols and signals can be considered subcategories of a larger conceptual category of messages known as signs. **Signs** are those aspects of the human environment that take on the value and function of a message because they stand for or refer to something else. Semiotics is the study of such signs and their arrangement into codes by which people come to understand their daily lives. Any sign takes on a particular form that comes to be understood by people in certain ways that wouldn't be predicted by that form alone. Words, as symbols, obviously, are signs. The word *panic* is not inherently more stressful to read than the word *serenity,* but it has assumed such associations because of our mutual interpretations of what *panic* might refer to. Less obvious are how the nonverbal aspects of our lives also function as signs. How your friends or your parents set the table for dinner can indicate the kind of order that is expected in the communication episode we call a meal.

According to Saussure (1966), a sign exists as a relation between a **signifier** (something that calls attention to, or stands for, something else) and a **signified** (our sense of what it stands for or refers to). Although as a linguist he wasn't terribly interested in whether a sign closely resembled the reality that it presumably represented, other theorists have explored this relationship more fully (Eco, 1976; Peirce, 1931–1958). As Olson (1994) observes, "The basis of Eco's semiotics is a system for denoting the relationship that exists between the signifier and signified, their sign-function. Eco asserted that the content of a sign is not the signified itself, but a cultural conception of it" (p. 72). In this sense, then, the word *panic* has as its semiotic content not the actual somatic experience of distress but the sum of our cultural connotations for what it means to be panicked—including the associations we develop through watching movies, reading novels, and participating in other forms of popular culture—as they are interpreted by the human mind.

⬅LINK

Semiotics, which involves studying verbal and nonverbal signs, and often their interaction, has implications for how we understand communication contexts, discussed in Chapter 3, and cultural communication, discussed in Chapter 7. Wendy Leeds-Hurwitz (1993) claims: "Just as the proper context for understanding a single sign is a code (a set of signs and rules for their use), so the proper context for understanding a single code is a culture (a set of codes and rules for their use)" (p. 155). Although we have chosen to discuss semiotics in terms of personal experience, we could easily have included it in our discussions of context, culture, or media.

Postmodern Language Theory. In recent years, hundreds of authors have attempted to explain a shift from the assumptions of traditional modern thought to a newer set of social assumptions they call **postmodernism** (see Reviewing Key Ideas, p. 116). The topic is broad and difficult to summarize because scholars disagree on what postmodernism is and even whether it exists. Despite scholars' lack of agreement about definitions, the controversy is important for communication theorists and researchers to consider, especially in its implications for language study.

The term **modernism** refers to the post-Enlightenment view of rationality in Western culture, which has long been applied by science in its attempt to probe cause-effect relationships more predictably. Modernism assumes that those relationships are real and "out there" waiting to be discovered, and that they can be measured by precise research methods. Such methods lead us ever closer to the "truth," in this view, because science could be advanced by a single set of rational criteria, and society could be governed by compatible assumptions of order.

Postmodernism, in contrast, holds that, because rational order has begun to fall apart, a singular or universal understanding can no longer be applied. Lyotard (1984), a prominent postmodern theorist, contends that people no longer have faith in what he calls **metanarratives**, or **grand narratives**, the belief systems that once clearly defined—supposedly—how everyone was supposed to honor similar definitions of good and evil, right and wrong, and efficient and inefficient. In metanarratives, complex social structures were presumably explainable by a single story or a limited number of high-authority stories. In the postmodern world, though, people can't all subscribe to the same theories. The modernist grand narratives that once offered the promise of holding us together have splintered, we are told, into fragmented **language games** in which different groups develop different voices and rules for understanding. Obviously, such a philosophy resists clear definition, but a particularly helpful description of postmodernism stresses the same kind of fragmentation that Lyotard described: "Postmodernism . . . is committed to modes of thinking and representation which emphasize fragmentations, discontinuities and incommensurable aspects of a given object, from intellectual systems to architecture. . . . It prefers montage to perspective, intertextuality to referentiality, 'bits-as-bits' to unified totalities" (O'Sullivan et al., 1994, p. 234). A postmodern communication theorist would be unlikely to ask of a series of political campaign speeches, for example, "What's the basic theme here?" or "How does all this fit together?"

The postmodernist's assumptions about language are exceptionally interesting, if not persuasive to everyone. Many postmodernists assume that ours is a time in which signs no longer refer to things but only to other signs in infinite regression. A solid sense of connecting words to reality is no longer possible, if it ever was, because our world has become a "hyperreality" composed of words and claims. Language has become the new reality for the postmodern world. Therefore we should adapt ourselves to an existence in which meanings just can't be specified. Meanings are contingent upon other meanings, and concepts are never definable in a final sense. A form of postmodern criticism known as **deconstruction** (Derrida, 1982), for example, attempts to show that many messages can simultaneously mean what both they appear to mean and the opposite of what they appear to mean. Nor do words necessarily mean what their speakers or writers intend for them to mean. The postmodern theorist presumes that speaker, author, listener, reader, and critic are all equal judges of meaning. In postmodern criticism, the deconstruction of a message is a way of demonstrating its inherent ambiguity and self-contradiction. As Rosenau (1992) describes it, the analytical method of deconstruction aims to "undo all constructions. Deconstruction tears a text apart, reveals its contradictions and assumptions; its intent, however, is not to improve, revise, or offer a better version of the text" (p. xi). Thus Poster (1990) believes that to Derrida, "a reader of texts or an interpreter of culture who attempts to uncover stable, closed meanings cannot at the same time elucidate the 'textual' conditions under which alone it is possible to have meanings at all" (p. 102).

Lynn (1990) observes that deconstruction studies often appear to use a three-step process: "First, a deconstructive reading must note which member of an opposition in a text appears to be privileged or dominant (writers versus editors, error versus correctness, men versus women, etc.); second, the reading shows how this hierarchy can be reversed within the text, how the apparent hierarchy is arbitrary or illusory; finally, a deconstructive reading places both structures in question, making the text ultimately ambiguous" (p. 263). While some communication theories attempt to show how certain messages work, deconstruction, according to Lynn, "points out how they fail" (p. 263). To assume that language is "for" delimiting meanings, or "for" achieving complete clarity, is to miss much of the essential power of language, a power that can be traced more to its ambiguity than to its clarity. "Deconstruction," Lynn (1990) says, "typically leaves us in uncertainty, but with a richer understanding of the categories we have put in motion" (p. 264). Deconstruction is difficult to grasp because it counters many of our commonsense assumptions about meaning. ("Do you mean that someone who is asking me to go to lunch may also be asking me not to go to lunch?") However, in a sense, it is a good way to remind ourselves that communication is

---

REVIEWING KEY IDEAS

ASSUMPTIONS OF POSTMODERN LANGUAGE THEORY

- *Grand narratives* are no longer persuasive or essential.
- The voices of different groups have been fragmented into different *language games,* each with its own set of rules.
- No reliable connection exists between meaning and either authors' intentions or external reality.
- Postmodern reality is based on surfaces and differing layers of meaning.
- Messages are inherently unstable and unspecifiable; *deconstructing* them shows how they are ambiguous and capable of undermining or contradicting themselves.

more radically complex than it is sometimes assumed to be. Postmodern theory emphasizes the inherently unstable meanings of language and the complex social and personal practices through which we attempt to communicate.

Inner Speech Theory

Do you talk to yourself? Do you fear, as many people joke, that this is a sign of mental instability? Consider the possibility that self-talk is actually a hallmark of human intelligence. Feel better? It is easy to assume that the primary purpose of language is to talk with other people. That makes a kind of sense…even according to the cognitive evidence we've surveyed up to this point. But inner speech theory examines the talk we do with ourselves and how it helps us to think. The theoretical works of Dance (1982), Vygotsky (1962), and Bakhtin (1981) have been particularly important in developing theories of inner speech. Not only is human interaction not the sole function speech serves but it may not even be the primary one.

Mentation. After synthesizing research from a variety of disciplines (Dance & Larsen, 1976), Dance (1982) concludes that **mentation** is crucial:

> *The raison d'être of human communication, rather than being primarily transactional or interactional, is primarily mentation. In the earliest stages of human development, interaction may dominate mentation so that the behavioral ratio looks something like interaction/mentation. When human communication becomes fully constituted (at about the age of 7), mentation becomes and remains paramount as the primary raison d'être of human communication, and the usual behavioral ratio then looks more like mentation/interaction. This statement is not meant to slight the importance of interaction in human communication but to highlight that one of the unique aspects of human communication, as contrasted with the communication of other than human animals, is to take thought, to ratiocinate, to engage in higher mental processes. (p. 137)*

With fully formed speech, then, not only can human beings connect with each other more effectively (which Dance calls the **linking function**) but we develop and lead increasingly more complex inner lives (which Dance and others call **interiority**). Thinking involves conceptualization, or the ability to create concepts, and rational thought, the ability to manipulate those concepts creatively, reasonably, and thoroughly.

Speech isn't only a bridge between people; it is also a bridge, or a mediator, between a person's inner existence and outer impact. What good would thought and planning be without the ability to imagine through speech the likely consequences of that planning? Many communication theorists, like Dance, therefore, stress that inner speech allows us to **decenter**, or place ourselves imaginatively outside of our immediate existence. Decentering enables us to empathize or identify with others, to consider other times and places that we have not experienced directly, and to plan contingencies for an uncertain future. In a very real sense, we can be said to have developed the basis for a "world of experience" when we passed through the stage of simple vocalization in order to create spoken language.

Without speech, we would have no "world." For Dance, speech is the key to understanding human communication. Dance (1982) has created a systematic "speech theory of human communication," and an impressive amount of evidence supports his general premise. However, the perspectives of other inner speech theorists differ somewhat.

Inner Socialization. Much of the research on inner speech and its consequences was conducted by psychologists and language theorists from the former Soviet Union many years ago and has gained acceptance in the West only in recent decades (Johnson, 1984). Luria (1961) summarized his own research as well as the research programs of Vygotsky (1962) and Sokolov (1972) when he wrote that the process of "internal speech" has been shown to be "an invariable part of the thought-process" and "characteristic of the development of almost all the higher forms of mental activity" (pp. 34–35). Most of this early research, particularly that of Vygotsky, challenged the prevailing notion that children learn language by progressing through a series of structurally similar and relatively invariant stages of development that are closely keyed to age level. In contrast, Vygotsky (1962) argues that children learn language in ways that are better predicted by social facilitation (by parents, for example), which interacts with the creative aspects of the inner voice the child tries to apply to all situations of thinking. In this sense, speech and thought are not identical processes to Vygotsky, but they are so closely related that it is not useful to consider one without the other. Therefore, because inner speech releases creative problem solving, the child's development isn't locked into stages determined by age and physiology. More specifically, Vygotsky (1962, pp. 119–153) showed that in inner speech language is less sequential and linear than the language of interpersonal speech. He identifies four characteristics of inner speech:

1. **Abbreviation:** Inner speech presumes its "audience'" (yourself) and therefore has no need for elaboration. (An exception occurs during those self-conscious moments when we lecture ourselves as we would another person.)
2. **Sense orientation:** Inner speech is not oriented toward precise definitions or specifications of meaning; instead, it operates in terms of what Vygotsky (1962) calls the "sense" of words—a holistic sum of whatever the words have "aroused in our consciousness" in "dynamic, fluid, complex" ways (p. 146).
3. **Semantic merger:** Vygotsky used the terms *agglutination* and *influx of sense* to describe the process by which several ideas become interassociated within a single word, almost as if they were contained by it. This process is very similar to the workings of literary metaphor.
4. **Predication:** Inner speech is oriented toward change and action and therefore tends to deal with "predicates" more than with "subjects." In terms of Chapter 2, inner speech is more "processual" than interpersonal speech.

A number of applied communication theorists tie Vygotsky's notions to practical concerns of teaching and learning about communication. Inner speech concepts, they argue, may be adapted to interdisciplinary programs in education and therapy that are designed to facilitate interpersonal dialogue and personal growth. Streff (1984), for instance, discusses how Vygotsky's work might be applied to the structuring of learning programs in secondary schools, while Dance (1982) notes its implications for the development of self-concept. Anderson and McClearey (1984) use Vygotsky's research to support their claim that inner speech is inherently "poetic" (i.e., human consciousness and creativity both depend on speech forms that closely resemble poetry in the world's literature).

Dialogism. Another Russian theorist who is closely associated with Vygotsky's ideas about inner speech is Mikhail Bakhtin (1981, 1986). The two never met, and Vygotsky probably didn't know of Bakhtin, although Bakhtin knew about Vygotsky's research (Clark & Holquist, 1984, p. 382). Although Bakhtin's work was overlooked for many years in Western theory, few intellectuals of the twentieth century have become as rapidly accepted across so many disciplines as he has since the 1970s. Some of his work in the former Soviet Union may have been published under the names of colleagues for political reasons; indeed, the scholarly debate over which books and articles can be credited to Bakhtin continues today. Nonetheless, contemporary cognitive psychologists, literary critics, and communication theorists (Baxter & Montgomery, 1996; Shotter, 1993; Todorov, 1984) widely apply his work in their own fields of research.

Bakhtin (1981) extends the importance of inner speech even further than Vygotsky. Inner **dialogism**, as Bakhtin termed it, complements the American symbolic interactionism (which we'll introduce later in this chapter), a theory that was developed independently. Whereas Vygotsky conceptualized inner speech as language *usage,* Bakhtin believed that it was not simply self-to-self speech. Instead, Bakhtin's inner speech concept is an internalization of society's outer dialogue. Whenever a word is spoken (whether outer or inner), that word psychologically contains all the voices of society that have previously shaped its use. This is not a private and isolated act, however privately it might be done. *Saying* (his translators use "utterance" more often) a word, then, is social participation at its most basic level, because words are inherently dialogical.

Bakhtin's view of literature is similarly broad (see, e.g., Bakhtin, 1981; Holquist, 1990). He believed that all perception was analogous to authorship; that is, the perceiver creates a "text" in response to the world, and then proceeds to "read" and offer that text as an interpretation (to which the self or others respond). He claimed that writers of poetry, short stories, and novels are simply doing at a more overt level what all of us do daily at covert levels—attempting to express our ideas about the world without overcompromising it. We will fail at this attempt, he thought. But, ultimately, inner speech helps us balance the more ordered properties of the word with the chaotic properties of the world.

With the theorists from the former Soviet Union, we can see more clearly how language "in-forms" personal experience. It is the medium, in fact, through which we can even *have* personal experience. Does this conclusion mean that a culture's particular language predetermines the reality that can be perceived by native speakers of that culture? If so, are speakers of a given language destined to be trapped within the categories that language creates? These are the kinds of questions that linguistic relativity theorists address.

Linguistic Relativity Theory

Some people may hold the stereotype that all communication scholars are university professors whose research is underwritten by public and private grants. You might be interested to know that one of the most famous and influential language researcher/theorists of his time was an executive for an insurance company. Benjamin Whorf started studying linguistics out of personal curiosity, but he later supplemented his informal training by studying with the renowned Yale linguist Edward Sapir. Together, they are recognized for what has come to be called the **Sapir-Whorf hypothesis**, or, because Whorf became its chief spokesperson, the "Whorfian hypothesis" of **linguistic relativity theory**.

Whorf's research into different cultures, especially the Native American Hopi culture in the U.S. Southwest, led him to wonder if language is more than a vehicle for sending and receiving information (1956). Of course, anthropologists can easily show that the language of a culture reflects the beliefs, behaviors, habits, mores, values, and feelings of the groups they study. Cultural differences and language differences appear to correspond. Each culture's unique language is sufficiently complex to handle the contingencies that arise within that culture. However, Whorf went beyond the obvious observation that human languages are distinctive to suggest a more radical hypothesis: that such language differences can create distinctive realities in the perceptual and thought processes of native speakers. Because of the nature of language, reality is relative and in some ways provisional. Not only are thinking and perception psychological phenomena but they are fundamentally based on cultural factors. Not only is language capable of reacting to and describing what we see, Whorf decided, but because language places categories in our heads, it tends to determine what we're going to see.

The word *determine* became a sticky point as the theory of linguistic relativity developed. Those who were commenting on and writing about Whorf's hypothesis tended to overstate his ideas and turn them into a kind of linguistic determinism. Determinists tried to claim that because people spoke different languages, they could never experience a shared reality because they could never escape from the prison of their own separate language systems. This became known as the "strong version" of the Whorfian hypothesis (see Schultz, 1990, for an account of how this strong version developed). Some critics even argued that if Whorf studied the Hopi and wrote a book that he claims is accurate, then he contradicted his own thesis. If linguistic relativity is as correct as Whorf claims, they suggested, how can Whorf claim anything about his research with certainty? Therefore, because he wrote persuasively about other cultures, linguistic determinism must not be a conceptually solid theory. Critics reasoned: "If Whorf is right, how can Whorf be right? Therefore, Whorf is wrong."

Other theorists, however, have replied that Whorf never claimed the "strong version" of the theory—that language totally determines cultural reality. According to Schultz (1990), "In his clearest statements of the linguistic relativity principle, Whorf seems to be arguing that speakers of different languages do *not* all share identical forms and categories of thought simply by virtue of the fact that they are all human beings. At the same time, Whorf refrains from suggesting that all human beings possess, *within the boundaries of their native tongue,* vast resources for categorizing experience in a variety of ways" (p. 27). Whorf evidently wanted to show that each culture is linguistically rich, but in its own terms—and that other cultures with other languages will not automatically have access to the perceptual and personal experience of its people. This insight, he thought, would ultimately increase cross-cultural respect. However, from the standpoint of communication theory, his chief contribution is to spotlight language as a link: It is simultaneously the key concept of culture and the key concept of individual human thought. Thinking is not independent but has to be accomplished within—and by—language. That language's unique rules will somehow affect the forms of thought. The study of language, Whorf (1956) writes, "shows that the forms of a person's thoughts are controlled by inexorable laws of pattern of which he is unconscious. These patterns are the unperceived intricate systematizations of his own language" (p. 252).

Symbolic Interactionism

George Herbert Mead, a professor at the University of Chicago from 1893 to 1931, set in motion another main current of thought about the influence language has on personal experience. The term **symbolic interactionism** was later coined by Herbert Blumer (1969), but Mead's ideas originally defined this intellectual movement. Blumer's label stuck because it suggested the theory's double reliance on language ("symbolic") and social communication ("interaction").

Mead (1934) believed, with Whorf, that individuals and societies are all part of the same basic process. Both believed, too, with American pragmatists, that the key to unlocking this process is to study language and how we use it. To Mead, human experience was a knotted but unbroken thread extending from the largest group experiences to the most private and personal ones. Although our focus in this chapter is on personal experience, many prominent communication theorists in various fields have applied symbolic interactionist thought to the interpersonal (Goffman, 1959; McHugh, 1968) and mass-mediated (Duncan, 1962; Klapp, 1969, 1978) realms of communication.

Symbolic interactionists tend to believe that Mead's (1934) three-part distinction of *mind, self,* and *society* highlights the three levels of communicative force. None of the three can be defined apart from the definitions of the other two. Let's start by explaining society, because individuals are born into already existing social relations. Mead defines **society** as the web of social relationships that human beings create and in which they engage through what he calls **acts**, which are behaviors chosen voluntarily by individuals. Society thus becomes an interlocking set of cooperative behaviors by which individuals actively adjust themselves to one another.

Surely, you criticize and congratulate other people on many social occasions. But you also criticize and congratulate yourself. Suppose, for instance, you get a B on an exam. You may be satisfied with the B because it symbolizes a lot of hard work, but at the same time you may be dissatisfied with the grade because you know that you could have done better. In effect, you're communicating with yourself as if you were both the subject (evaluator) and the object (evaluated) in this judgment. Although it feels normal to you to act this way, Mead believes that this deceptively simple act is one of the premier achievements of the human race.

LINK

You'll read more on symbolic interactionist theories, especially Erving Goffman's approach to "the presentation of self in everyday life," in the section on dramaturgical approaches in Chapter 5.

Self becomes possible for a person as a result of noticing that, just as others can be treated as objects of action, so can he or she turn messages reflexively inward for personal notice. In addition, a person learns through social relations that others' acts are directed toward him or her. Thus a sense of unique placement in the world develops, a sense of identity, in which language is the medium of discovery. As Anselm Strauss (1956) explains, "Mead makes action toward the self an integral facet of the act. One takes himself into account while acting toward the non-self. This self-reflexivity is dependent upon language and arises during childhood as a result of participation in groups" (p. xi). One implication of this view is that a self is neither inwardly set nor socially given; rather, it is the result of complex and ongoing transactions among individuals, their actions, and the larger social structures made possible by those actions. It's only a small oversimplification to claim that you develop a self by listening to your talk with other people and inferring what kind of person would participate in such interaction.

Interaction, therefore, is inherent in your self-concept. Mead (1934) accounts for this by explaining the two types of responsiveness that make up the symbolic self: the "me" and the "I." The **me** component is that aspect of the self that is responsive to the outside social network, the aspect that is shaped, controlled, limited, or accounted for by external forces. The **I** component is that part of the self that asserts unique points of view, responds to impulses, and creates individualized positions that may or may not be similar to those of others. While the *me* is a force for predictability and conformity, the *I* is a source of surprise and novelty.

Mind is a different level for considering the same basic processes of interaction and differentiation. Because we develop what Mead calls *mind,* we are able to create an interior setting for the society we see operating outside of ourselves. We can re-create intrapersonally the interpersonal "conversation of gestures" in which we participate in society. Mind, then, is *society as we internalize it.* It is the inner conversation we are able to have with ourselves as a result of language, which enables both the outer conversation and the senses of self that flow from it. In one sense, Mead presents yet another theory of inner speech. But it would be a mistake to think of mind simply as depending on self and society. Mead's thought comes full circle to remind us that a society as we know it would be impossible without the symbolic contributions of mind. Society is just as attributable to mind as mind is to society. In our brief account, we have tried to suggest this circular interdependence by reversing scholars' normal sequence for explaining Mead's mind/self/society distinctions, but ultimately either sequence is somewhat misleading. Society and self do not emerge developmentally from mind; nor can we start with society and then build selves and minds. (How could any group exist without its members being able to plan, symbolize, perceive, or anticipate a social future—all aspects of mind?)

Mead's contributions to symbolic interactionism do not end with his mind/self/society distinctions. He introduced a number of concepts that have helped communication theorists to understand symbolic functions. Most prominent among them are:

- **Generalized other:** Over time, people develop a generalized sense of how other people react to them, and of the social expectations of these

---

REVIEWING KEY IDEAS

MEAD AND SYMBOLIC INTERACTION

- Mead's basic distinctions: *society, self* ("me"/"I"), *mind*
- Mead's conceptual contributions and basic terms: *generalized other, significant symbol, role-taking*

---

others. The individual, in developing a symbolic mind, begins to create an overall sense of how someone else thinks or feels relative to self. This creation, which is very influential in developing what some call a conscience, is Mead's generalized other.

- **Significant symbol:** Mead's understanding of *symbol* was very much like that which we outlined in an earlier section of this chapter—it is something that comes to stand for something else at a representational level because of human agreement. Yet in society all symbols are not equally shared or understood. Mead reserved the term *significant symbol* for those symbols that evoke basically similar meanings for communicators. A significant symbol serves as both stimulus and response for individuals within what he termed a universe of discourse (Mead, 1934, pp. 71, 89–90).

- **Role-taking:** Mead's systematic observation of human behavior suggested a number of implications of symbolic communication. One of the most crucial of these was his concept of role-taking, a concept similar to what we have previously discussed as *decentering*. Mead speculated that the extended dependency of human children on their parents and other caretakers, combined with a developing capacity for active participation in a community's symbols, allows children to play games in which they take on the roles of other people and things. That is, they symbolically remove themselves from self and re-place themselves in an imagined self of another person or object, thereby stimulating a recognition that reality can be seen from differing perspectives. Far from resulting in a confusion of selves, this symbolic act can be a powerful social clarification of self, resulting in an increased capacity for sympathy or empathy later in life (Mead, 1934, pp. 364, ff.) (See Reviewing Key Ideas, above).

According to the symbolic interactionists, without language there would be no distinctly human experience of community or society, no sense of "we're all in this together," no conscience or sympathy for others, no sense of who we are in the first place.

Whether you agree with Mead and others that all thinking literally is speech, or whether you believe that thinking merely depends on a capacity for spoken language, it is hard to deny that personal experience (even at the most basic sensory levels) is interwoven with language concerns. Our species truly is *Homo loquens,* the "talking animal" (Fry, 1977), even when the speaking is within the self. If language is so basic to consciousness, therefore, it stands to reason that how we talk about an issue or a topic will strongly influence what we can think about it. In other words, language creates the boundaries of what is possible in human life.

Cognitive Organization and Planning

Psychologists and communication theorists have become increasingly curious about how the human mind works. This was not always so. Twentieth-century researchers who identified themselves as **behaviorists** argued vigorously that knowledge about humans was developed most reliably by simply looking at people's specific actions. It was the behaviors themselves that interested such scholars, who reasoned that the human mind was like a **black box** (their metaphor), into which we would never be able to see clearly. Therefore, although behaviorists acknowledged that *something* was inside the black box, the simplest methodological approach was to define mental life out of the picture and attempt instead to compare systematically the inputs and outputs of the box. This philosophical position (for it was a specific philosophy of science that was being implemented) became for a time closely associated with social science itself. Once researchers recognized the primacy of studying behavior, they had moved toward a realm where it was considered most efficient to rely on quantitative research. The underlying philosophical assumption was that reality was both external and knowable—if we could just get our instruments and methodologies for defining it fine-tuned.

In the history of social science, debates about the merits of behaviorism have been common (e.g., Wann, 1964). However, most contemporary theorists believe we can and should know more about the cognitive processes that contribute to how we send, receive, interpret, and store messages. This acceptance carries with it a counterbalancing philosophical position: that human reality is not so much discovered as constructed or built by the unique perspectives of people as they communicate. Even if we can't discover precisely how mental variables influence external behaviors, the search is worth the effort.

Difference(s)

Every child learns at school that movement is relative, something that can be perceived only in relation to a point of reference. What is not realized by everyone is that this same principle holds for virtually every perception and, therefore, the human being's experience of reality. Sensory and brain research have proved conclusively that only relationships and patterns of relationships can be perceived, and these are the essence of experience (Watzlawick, Beavin, & Jackson, 1967, p. 27).

Such a statement is dense with implications. One especially practical implication is that no object of perception can be perceived clearly unless it is placed in relation to another object of perception. Look at any word on this page, and look in a sustained way at only that one word. Is that word all you see? Surely not; the relation of the word to other words, of the word to the page, of the page to the book, of the book to the rest of the objects in your environment—all these relationships allow you to focus on that one word. Without the presence of other relationships, any focus on the single word would be impossible. We see relationships between objects, not the objects themselves. We hear relationships between sounds, not literally the sounds themselves. In this sense, we can even "hear" silence.

Watzlawick et al. (1967) suggest some other examples of what happens when we attempt to eliminate relational factors: a tone that is held at a steady pitch tends to fade from conscious awareness; an unchanging gaze at any given point will yield blurrier, not clearer, vision; holding your finger motionless on a surface supplies almost no information about the surface compared with moving your finger around on the surface (pp. 27–28). In each of these examples, the object's relation to other objects has been limited. Common sense might tell you that in order to hear a word you should concentrate hard on it. But this is not the principle on which perception seems to work. Ironically, more useful perceptual information is obtained when we are aware of differences between things than when we concentrate on the things themselves. You can estimate how far the stop sign is from your speeding car only because you know from previous experience how large it is, and how it compares with other objects (also remembered as certain sizes) in the immediate environment. You know what to make of your friend's comment, "Nice job," only because you are able to hear it in relation to other actual and potential comments.

Communication theorist Gregory Bateson has helped us understand contrast and difference in conscious communication. Initial sensory input, Bateson argues, is always data about *first derivatives:* "statements about differences which exist among external objects or statements about changes which occur either in them or in our relationship to them" (Ruesch & Bateson, 1968, p. 173). The phrase "our relationship to them" suggests that a perceiver is a factor in whatever is perceived. Much of Bateson's later work (1980, 1991; M. C. Bateson, 1984) explores how people actually create a mental model of their relationship to the perceived, and subsequently experience that image of relation instead of experiencing the other person or object directly. Bateson reminds us that communicators cannot avoid taking a stance, which will inevitably influence both what is perceived and how it is perceived.

As an example, let's consider whether you can be said to be reading this book right now. We would suggest that you are definitely reading, but what you are really reading is *your relationship to the book.* If you enjoy school and believe books are informative, you will not be reading the "same" book as a classmate who finds education unstimulating and books worthless. Your relation to the book will be psychologically different. You'll imagine that you have a clear perception of the book's value—but remember that you are a part of the relationship of book-to-environment that makes the book meaningful.

Another theorist commonly cited across the intellectual map—and earlier in this book—also comments on the perception of differences and the perceiver's relationship to the perceived. Physicist Werner Heisenberg (1958) describes scientific "indeterminacy" in advancing his **uncertainty principle** (see also Bohm, 1980). In a study of very small particles, Heisenberg and his colleagues found that the technology needed to illuminate and magnify these particles set the particles in motion. This motion would not have occurred had there been no observation.

▣LINKS

❏ Review the respective advantages of both quantitative and qualitative research methods in Chapter 1. In your opinion, can a behaviorist also be a humanist, a qualitative scholar? Why, or why not?

❏ The modern/postmodern distinctions described earlier in this chapter are also relevant here. How might a behaviorist's philosophy of knowledge (the scholar's epistemology) clash with the postmodernist's diagnosis of the contemporary world? Further, how does our treatment of the importance of "difference(s)" echo a postmodern tone?

Thus the would-be observer has two options: Don't investigate (and remain uncertain about the phenomena under study) or investigate (and still be uncertain, because no one can be sure of the precise changes introduced by the observation itself). Naturally, scientists opt for the second alternative, since it provides at least some information for making educated guesses about how much change is introduced by the observation. But scientists should investigate with full recognition that the results will necessarily be indeterminate and imprecise. The uncertainty principle means that the relation of the perceiver to the perceived affects the perception. The looking becomes a part of the looked at.

Observers don't just relate to differences; they also create them. The uncertainty principle operates in the human sciences as well. Thus, for example, when someone says, "Go ahead and run your laps—I'll just sit here and watch" or "You know, a lot is riding on this speech because of who is in the audience," the presence of the observer changes the event in subtle and significant ways (see Reviewing Key Ideas, below, for a review of this section).

Constructivist Theory

Over the past several decades, many communication theorists have participated in developing a line of research called *constructivism* (Delia, O'Keefe, & O'Keefe, 1982). Although its basic premises are relatively straightforward, constructivist thought has influenced how many researchers perceive the relationships among self, mind, and behavior. And, as you will see, this branch of theorizing pays a great deal of attention to the importance of differences in human communication.

Basic Assumptions. Researchers applying a constructivist perspective make three basic assumptions about how humans communicate (see Reviewing Key Ideas, p. 128). First, constructivists assume that communication is an interpretive process. Therefore communication cannot be oversimplified as a stimulus-response, cause-effect, or transmission-reception phenomenon. Messages do not bring meanings to receivers from senders; instead, messages are occasions for people to create—or "construct"—realities through their interpretation of the messages.

Second, constructivists assume that human beings can be active agents in determining how their worlds are constituted. Therefore, constructivists argue,

---

REVIEWING KEY IDEAS

DIFFERENCE AND PERCEPTION

- We perceive and organize cognitions by noting differences.
- We primarily perceive relations between things, not the things themselves.
- Attempts to perceive can introduce effects of their own, thereby changing the conditions under which perception happens (the uncertainty principle suggests that observers may perceive a phenomenon that wouldn't happen in the same way if an observer wasn't present).

any conception of communication should reflect this idea of humans as choosers rather than as passive observers or victims of fate.

Third, constructivism assumes that individuals order individual choices and worldviews through complex patterns of cognitive organization. People do not collect or maintain communication data randomly, but instead use the information to create and maintain organized patterns of knowing. In this way, new situations and unique challenges can be understood in terms of the existing cognitive organization. To understand such patterns, therefore, is to understand a communication "world" as a person creates, experiences, and uses it. Understanding the patterns also provides effective clues to how a person perceives a unique self.

Constructing Shades of Gray. Constructivism employs a specific vocabulary for understanding communication. **Constructs**, a concept extrapolated from the work of Kelly (1963), are most simply described as "recognitions of difference." The mind, as we saw earlier in this chapter, tends to order information in terms of distinctive categories. Human consciousness is alert not only to similarity but primarily to difference as a key signal. Thus, for example, you know that you have a construct for *woman* if you can perceive the difference(s) between a woman and a man. Most people can readily identify a piece of music as classical, rock, country, or jazz. We have immediate constructs available for these distinctions. However, some people claim that "all rock music sounds alike" or "all classical music is boring" or "all country music just sounds twangy"; these are individuals for whom the constructs within that particular area of experience have not been differentiated. **Construct differentiation** occurs when increasingly specific distinctions are made and then organized hierarchically—as when a rock fan discusses an appreciation for "grunge" or "roots rock" but puts down "art rock." Other listeners who wouldn't be interested in or able to tell the differences among these categories would be said to be lower in **cognitive complexity**. The more constructs you have available to describe the world or a particular aspect of it, the more "cognitively complex" you may be said to be.

A "So what?" question of practicality arises here. Because we can assume that people can be more or less cognitively complex at both general and specific levels of experience, constructivism provides a concept that helps to explain why we occasionally have great trouble communicating even when we seem to be using the "same" definitions for the "same" words, and even if we grew up within the same culture. People who are more cognitively complex have more complicated category distinctions, "schemes," and "models" for the world; thus they will perceive more gradations of meaning and more possibilities for acting within a situation. The cognitively complex person sees shades of gray where another person may see only black-and-white options. Good and bad are not as quickly labeled and identified; people with more sophisticated construct and interpretive schemes can begin to see potential for good in the bad, and bad within good, as well as a range of other possibilities within that continuum. Cognitively complex individuals therefore tend to avoid the condition Rokeach (1960) researched as **dogmatism** and what language theorists called General Semanticists (Hayakawa, 1941) term the **two-valued orientation**: simple explanations of something as being either this or that. What constructivists call communication "strategies" will

⬅️🔗 L I N K

The concept of *adaequatio* (see Introduction) is relevant to constructivism. As people become more cognitively complex, developing more *construct differentiation* in an area of study, for example, they increase the extent to which they may be "adequate" to the demands of complex messages. Some students who may previously have read only romance novels or *Sports Illustrated* because they dismiss the classics as boring might need only a few new skills or appreciations in a literature course to "open up" the novels of Jane Austen or Charles Dickens. As they glimpse more of what Austen and Dickens are trying to do, their learning potential as readers begins to widen. Thinking back over the past two or three years, in which areas have you become more cognitively complex, more adequate to the demands of difficult or complex messages?

become more sophisticated and adaptable to specific problems that arise. As concept differentiation increases, cognitive complexity increases, which in turn leads to more communicative flexibility.

In a sense, constructivism is a developmental approach to human maturity. Researchers use its concepts to guide investigations of how people form impressions of others, how people engage in "perspective-taking" by assuming the roles of others, how conversations are managed, and how attitudes change.

Action Assembly Theory

Constructivists, among other communication theorists, are interested in modeling the complexity of human cognitive structures. To do so, they look at how people use those structures to accomplish their practical everyday tasks. Constructivism explains how someone processes and categorizes information in constructing a common reality with others, but how that processing actually produces behaviors is left relatively unexamined. The situation is analogous to an automobile assembly plant that's fully tooled up for production, with plenty of materials and all shifts of workers efficiently scheduled, but with no instructions from the production managers on what kinds of cars should be made. How are the instructions, the action plans, arrived at? Although this metaphor is misleading if it suggests only that communication is like manufacturing, it does point to the importance of system output. How can we develop a complete understanding of inner cognitive processes without taking into account how those inner processes become externalized? John O. Greene (1984, 1989) developed his **action assembly theory** to fill this need, and to answer such questions as "How do human plans become actions?" Greene (1989) suggests that there are "only two fundamental problems in understanding human communication":

> *The first of these essential problems is that of meaning: How do people assign meaning to stimulus inputs such as the utterances and gestural activity of others? The second problem is that of action; that is, explicating*

REVIEWING KEY IDEAS

CONSTRUCTIVIST THEORY: AN OVERVIEW

- *Constructivism* assumes that:
  - Communication is interpretive.
  - Humans are agents (active choosers).
  - Humans organize their choices and worldviews in complex patterns that reflect how they recognize differences.
- *Constructs* are recognitions of difference.
- *Construct differentiation* and *cognitive complexity* develop as people make subtle distinctions by organizing constructs in more complicated ways.

the process(es) by which people produce the behaviors that constitute the signs and symbols of communication. A moment's reflection reveals that any substantive issue concerning human communication involves input processing, the production of responses, or a combination of the two. Thus whether one studies mass media effects, interpersonal compliance gaining, or cross-cultural nonverbal communication, the essential processes are those of input and output, meaning and action. (pp. 117–118)

Therefore, while constructivism focuses on the problem of meaning, action assembly theory tries to explain the problem of action.

Greene is much more interested in how cognition produces alternatives for action (behavioral plans) than he is in describing either the structures of cognition or the behavior per se. Put another way, Greene seems to claim that part of the structure of cognitive life is a kind of awareness that he labels **procedural memory**—that is, our recollection of how to do things and our sense of which things typically "work" and why. Greene distinguishes this memory system from its twin system, **declarative memory**, which is our recollection of what we know. Procedural memory is of the process of producing actions ("knowledge how"), while declarative memory concerns the content of memory ("knowledge that"). Although communication obviously involves both types, Greene centers his theory on procedural memory.

Yet procedural memory itself has content, which is composed of a system of **procedural records**. Although Greene and his colleagues are conceptually quite precise in their research, for our purposes simply assume that procedural records are memories of previous communication outcomes, along with the details of actions and whatever situational factors were relevant to the outcomes. Recall the last three major purchases you made, including who was with you, what was said to you, and what you said. As you think, you are using procedural records.

But how do we know, in a given situation, how to use these procedural records or even which ones apply? Greene suggests that you use an **activation** process to select and abstract salient or relevant records. The mind monitors the current situation in terms of the storehouse of procedural records held in memory. When a record is "activated," in essence it has matched at some level (called a **threshold**) the demands of the current situation.

In this sense, then, you compare "what's been done" and "what can work" with "what needs to happen." And in doing so you produce, through an **assembly** process, what Greene calls **output representations**, or planned actions that are yet to be taken. In this way the mind makes ongoing sense of the world while maintaining behavioral contact with it. As Greene (1989) explains, his approach is not simply metaphorical. "Once activated, procedural records are assembled, or integrated, to form an output representation of action-to-be-taken. It is the lower levels of this output representation that actually generate and control muscle movements" (p. 121). More recently, Greene (1997) has published an extended version of action assembly theory that incorporates even more sophisticated accounts—for example, of how some pathways between procedural records and output representations are more symbolically based, while others are based more on associative or relatively unmindful patterns. The newer version also places

---

REVIEWING KEY IDEAS

ACTION ASSEMBLY THEORY:

- Focuses not just on cognition or action but on how inner plans become action.
- Applies these basic concepts:
  - *Procedural memory* (our "how to" memory)
  - *Procedural records* (content of procedural memory)
  - *Activation* (selecting and processing records)
  - *Assembly* (integrating records coherently to produce action possibilities)
  - *Output representations* (planned actions yet to be taken)

---

more emphasis on how individuals internally represent situations and goals while determining their options for acting. The terminology on which the theory was founded remains valid, however. One simple way to remember action assembly theory's basic idea is to take the label literally. Action assembly theory views the internal assembly of actions as an inherent part of human behavior (see Reviewing Key Ideas, above, for an overview).

REVIEWING KEY THEORIES

If communication is primarily a process that happens between people, why do some communication scholars want to focus on inner cognitive processes, too? The answer has to do with context again. Theorizing that accounts for what happens in our heads can be extremely important in helping us to understand the relationship between the self and others. It appears that we perceive actively and selectively; develop our selves through social uses of language; test or compare our different conceptions of self with other people, both directly and indirectly; and construct schemes by which we not only organize our past experiences but plan for future ones. In this chapter you read about two general strains of theorizing—*theories of language,* which account for personal experience and self, and *theories of cognitive organization and planning,* which account, at least in part, for how we act in response to the differences we perceive.

The linguistic theories concentrated on the nature of language itself: *speech act theory, semiotics,* and *postmodern language theory.* Then you read about theories that explain the processes of inner speech: Dance's *mentation* approach, Vygotsky's *internal socialization,* and Bakhtin's *dialogism.* Using those theories as a foundation, it becomes easier to see how cultural systems of expectation and language usage actually influence how we perceive—the province of Whorf's *linguistic relativity theory.* Finally, the especially influential *symbolic interactionist theory* of Mead and others begins to account for how mind, self, and society are all interrelated with language.

The cognitive organization and planning theories depend on a simple insight: We perceive (see, hear, touch, taste, and smell) relationships and differences between things more than we perceive the things themselves. Difference matters. In this section you read about how perception is at the base of the interpretive approaches of *constructivist theory,* and how people don't need to rely on simplistic "this or that" explanations. *Action assembly theory,* on the other hand, can help to explain how we turn perceptions into plans of action in our lives.

TESTING THE CONCEPTS

"If personal experience is really as complex as you say it is, how can I ever hope to know exactly who I am?"

Maybe none of us has enough reliable information to be able to know "exactly" who we are. We cannot use exactness as a criterion for judging our sense of identity. After all, perception is inherently inexact and filtered; conditions and relationships are subject to constant change; and inner speech is often the result of previous biases. And, if role theorists like Goffman (1959) are right, it may be more accurate to talk about our several "selves," which emerge differently as we perceive different situations, than a unitary "self." What we call a "self" in everyday talk is both the result of our past selective processes of perception and the regulator of how perception operates in the present. In this way, a healthy self-concept is like a homeostatic feedback mechanism, our psychological thermostat in a sense, that keeps our perceptual systems balanced.

"Can I ever perceive myself as others perceive me?"

No, not entirely. However, the ability to decenter yourself, disengaging somewhat from your own self-centered perspective, can be nurtured. With practice in communicating across differences between others and yourself, you will probably become more comfortable and even more accurate imagining how you appear and sound to others. However, as you might guess, you will create subtle and perhaps serious distortions as a result of perceiving their perceptions. This is analogous to what audiologists tell us about human hearing; aside from recordings, none of us is able to hear our own voice as others do because we hear our own voice partially through bone conduction, which no one else can.

(V.R.): Undoubtedly, however, who others perceive us to be is relevant to who we have become. We observe how others treat us and, at best, infer how they perceive us. I believe I am a funny person. When people laugh at my comments, they are reinforcing my belief. Therefore I make even more humorous remarks when I'm around them. This process becomes cyclical. With other people, however, I may not make silliness a part of my routine, so they react by treating me with more seriousness. I find myself acting more seriously around them. Their perception of me has affected who I think I am, but just as surely, my perception of myself has affected who they think I am.

"Do postmodern language theorists believe that science is worthless? That a full or true understanding of communication is ultimately impossible?"

It depends on the version of postmodern thought you're consulting. Although some postmodernists vigorously challenge the merit of conventional scientific methods, few if any would argue that we shouldn't try to learn more about the physical world. In other words, it's not whether but *how* we conceive of science that's at issue. What kind of theorizing could we do in a different kind of science? Norman Denzin (1992), merging symbolic interactionism and postmodern theory, suggests that the postmodernist's sense of science assumes "there can be no science of the real, no theory of the totality, no cumulation of verified knowledge. There is only situated, practical activity, organized and legitimated under the heading of one theory or another" (p. 159). Stated in this way, a key message of postmodern theory might be: Don't squeeze fundamentally different processes into an artificial box to make them conform to a single set of explanations and definitions. Pay more attention to contexts, situated knowledge, and the ways in which meaning can leak around the edges of our explanatory boxes. Maybe, of course, our best scientists have always done this.

"Can inner speech help me cope with the world by making me more rational?"

Think of inner speech less as a tool and more as a constant process of consciousness. It's unlikely that you could "turn off" inner speech even if you wanted to (although some Eastern meditation disciplines aim to "clear the mind" occasionally). Through inner speech you solve problems creatively, rehearse future actions, and imagine yourself in other people's positions in order to empathize. Therefore inner speech does help you to take the irrational in the world, process it, and thereby make better decisions.

"How do theories of cognitive organization, such as constructivism, really help my communication?"

Theories of cognitive organization can provide you with more sophisticated ways of understanding and defining your interpersonal problems. Consider a hypothetical example: As the chairperson of a student disciplinary action board, you have been asked to explain a controversial board decision to a reporter from the campus newspaper. Your understanding of cognitive complexity helps you adapt your message so that it can be understandable at the same time to both audience A (whose members' cognitive schemes seem limited to a few constructs, such as "truth" and "deception" or "right" and "wrong") and audience B (whose members, perhaps because there is less ego involvement, can process information on the basis of more constructs and "shades of gray"). Being able to map the cognitive sophistication of listeners and readers is crucial for effective communication planning (Windahl & Signitzer, with Olson, 1992).

YOU, THE RESEARCHER

1. Try a brief replication of Bruner and Goodman's 1947 study of children's perception of coin sizes. In social science research, *replication* refers to the process by which scholars attempt to "try a study again," typically by using different subjects or conditions while focusing on the same or similar variables. This strategy is important, because any number of uncontrolled factors could influence the results of a single study—yet ideally we'd like to be able to generalize findings beyond single studies. (Think of

this as a "So what if it's true in San Francisco? I live in Peoria" issue.) Although some scholars seem to shy away from studies that replicate earlier ones, perhaps believing them to be less creative and interesting, replication plays an important role in social investigation.

Begin by reviewing our discussion of Bruner and Goodman's study in this chapter (see p. 110). Then follow these steps to conduct your own research on the topic (or ask your teacher to help you adapt these instructions to a different setting):

- Arrange visits to three second-grade classes—one in a low-income area, one in a middle-income area, and one in a high-income area. You should call first, asking principals and teachers involved for their permission to visit on a certain day.

- With the teacher's permission, pass out blank sheets of 8½- by 11-inch paper, one per student, and tell the class you'd like them to draw the shape and size of a one-dollar bill from memory. (To make it more interesting for the students, ask them to use their creativity by coloring in the bill in any way they'd like, and by drawing a picture of anyone they choose in the middle.)

- Before leaving, measure the length and width of each picture of a bill in centimeters and determine the mean (average) area of the bill for each class. (Leave the artwork for the teacher to display, to use for teaching a lesson on money and its value, on how people's feelings get reflected in their art, or any other points the teacher might like to make.)

- Bruner and Goodman's results provide the basis of your research hypothesis: that the one-dollar bills depicted by students in a low-income area will tend to be larger than the bills depicted by students in middle- and high-income areas. Did this hold true in your small and admittedly simplistic replication?

2. African American writer and actor Ossie Davis (1969) asserts that "The English Language Is My Enemy." Davis noticed that English dictionaries are filled with negative connotations for "black" and "blackness" (e.g., "sullied," "foreboding," "wicked"), whereas "white" is almost always associated with more positive connotations ("purity," "innocence," "genuineness"). He claims that both black and white native speakers of the language cannot help but be affected by their immersion in the values environment of language.

- Form two small groups, one all women and the other all men. Each group should catalog as much evidence as it can for the thesis that for women the English language is an enemy.

- Compare the results of your discussion with the position taken in Lakoff's (1975) critique of language and power in society, *Language and Woman's Place,* or another extended statement of feminist linguistic theory.

3. Manford Kuhn (Kuhn & McPartland, 1954; Hickman & Kuhn, 1956) was a symbolic interactionist who was especially concerned with how a "self" is

subjectively experienced. He and his colleagues developed a method called the *Twenty Statements Test* (TST), which attempted to make the concept of self more tangible and research on the self more empirical.

- You can easily administer a rough form of the TST to a friend who isn't taking this course. Hand your friend a stack of twenty blank index cards. Then simply ask him or her to answer the question "Who am I?" twenty times, each on a different card and with whatever responses come to mind.

- Later, when you're alone, sort the cards into as many logical categories (piles of cards) as seem appropriate to you. (Examples: all of the three or four cards in one pile seem to refer to social roles the person enacts, such as "I'm a good critic of my husband's work" and "I'm an excellent student." Another pile may seem to relate to self-judgments, such as "I'm confused about where I'm going with my life" and "I'm intelligent.")

- Finally, see if you can create tentative labels that characterize what makes each category of statements "hang together." As above, one pile might be labeled "roles," but with another person there might be no cards at all that would justify this term. Still another subject's responses might justify two different piles of "role" cards, each with its own distinctive characteristics (like "family roles" and "career roles"). Two final research points are important here. First, by creating these labels you are doing a very rough and simplistic form of what empirical researchers call *factor analysis,* or the identification of a set of variables that seem to underlie or give a pattern to the data a researcher collects. Second, your research has produced a tentative operational model of your friend's self-concept. Remember that this will be a representation of something that is in constant flux, so you will not by any means have pinned down who your friend is. Instead, you will have sketched an incomplete picture of how your friend's self-concept is displayed momentarily and in an artificial context. Nonetheless, communication researchers build such models in order to draw tentative generalizations.

4. The *black box* behaviorist approach to the human mind was thoroughly debated by prominent psychologists B. F. Skinner (1953) and Carl R. Rogers (1959, 1961, 1980). Check your library for either the set of audiotapes of their 1962 debate or excerpts from the transcript that has been published in several print sources. (Although we could give specific reference citations here, regard this as a library scavenger hunt.)

   - Listen or read carefully to determine which set of arguments seems most persuasive to you, and why. Which, if any, of Rogers's or Skinner's disagreements seem to be rooted in how each theorist defines terms differently? If so, which ones?

   - Although some words will seem like jargon, much of the interchange is remarkably clear even for lay audiences. List terms that are new to you, and look up their meanings in a dictionary of psychology or social science in the reference section of your library.

5. *Consistency theories* have several distinct emphases. Compare and contrast the basic assumptions of Fritz Heider (1958), Leon Festinger (1957), and Charles Osgood (Osgood & Tannenbaum, 1955) by following these guidelines:

- Consult a survey of theories of social psychology for an overview.
- Research at least one important journal article by each scholar to discover how he characterizes the unique perspectives of his approach.

Jill Fineberg/Photo Researchers

CHAPTER 5

"How and Why Do We Create Relationships?"

Theorizing Interpersonal Communication

> Our uniqueness is not *in* us. It is something which comes to be as we respond to what
> is not ourselves. This sort of love, this sort of relationship takes place *between* persons
> and cannot be counted on as a social technique at our disposal.
>
> Maurice S. Friedman, *Touchstones of Reality* (1974, p. 262)

Not long ago, a student we'll call Mary enrolled in an interpersonal communication class. Her contributions to class discussions and her papers were excellent. She took readily to the concepts of communication and understood them well. She came to believe that the course material was intensely relevant to her daily life and began to apply the concepts to her most important relationships, those within her immediate family.

So far, so good. Every teacher probably hopes to encourage just this kind of practical spirit in students. For such students, a class is not just about memorizing distantly formed sets of facts; it's an opportunity to try things out, to experiment with what works in daily life.

But Mary had a few problems. Although she found that her own communication skills improved, her goal of taking these improvements home with her was more difficult to accomplish than she had thought it would be. She became discouraged with other family members. In fact, she found them more annoying as the course progressed. For example, she learned how to improve her listening but became more upset than ever when her husband and children listened poorly to her. She tried out some basic conflict-management techniques from the textbook, but the family just thought she was "talking weird" and accused her of playing games with them. She tried "assertiveness" and "self-disclosure," as the text suggested, but found that her husband longed for the predictability of their former roles and wished she weren't taking those stupid university classes after all.

What went wrong? Were the theories and skills emphasized in class wrong? Was her teacher wrong for encouraging real-life applications and for stressing practical implications of the theories? Was Mary's family wrong in impeding her personal growth and development? Was Mary wrong, or just ineffective in trying out these skills? Did she (or her teacher) misunderstand what the theories really say? All of these are relevant questions, and they strike at the very heart of justifying communication study in the first place.

As we've seen in earlier chapters, people often assume that communication is an activity that you can train yourself to accomplish: "I communicated that to him, but he evidently wasn't listening" or "She's an excellent communicator—I know she'll do well in her job interview." This assumption is also reflected in how communication programs are sometimes assessed: People's behaviors or attitudes are measured in order to determine how much they—as individuals—have improved their communication skills.

But was Mary necessarily a better communicator for having taken the class? Maybe not. Possibly, if the class encouraged her to think too individualistically, to search for increased autonomy and independence from others' messages and expectations, and perhaps even to hope for more self-actualization and self-respect (as if these qualities could be quantified), then Mary's communication with others could have deteriorated in quality, even while her self-confidence was strengthened in the short run. Maybe the class didn't encourage this outcome at all but simply gave Mary the tools with which to lead herself in this individualized direction. Teachers, researchers, and theorists alike have become increasingly suspicious of communication measures that presume participants to be autonomous bundles of behaviors and skills.

A person may develop better skills in speaking and listening, but these skills do not necessarily translate into what is known in the literature as "communication competence" (Spitzberg & Cupach, 1984). Wiemann, Takai, Ota, and Wiemann (1997) surveyed earlier models of competence in the communication discipline and found that many have focused unproductively on individuals' psychological or behavioral dispositions—on their individual knowledge or skill, in other words. But as you know, communication is far more than trading behaviors or messages. A better, more relational approach to understanding communication competence, they claim, is to assert that "judgments of competence should be made in terms of systemic effectiveness, appropriateness and satisfaction. Our position is that competence is something that is created within a relationship" (p. 33). In fact, a clear definition of **communication competence** must be fundamentally relational: "the ability of two or more persons to jointly create and maintain a mutually satisfying relationship by constructing appropriate and effective messages" (O'Hair, Friedrich, Wiemann, & Wiemann, 1994, p. 32). Obviously, then, someone who has never even thought about communication theory—indeed, someone who could have severe mental health problems or a total absence of formal education—can be communicatively competent. Conversely, someone who has built an impressive repertoire of interpersonal skills and concepts may be, *communicatively* speaking, quite incompetent if she or he has trouble diagnosing the appropriate situations or relationships in which to apply those skills. As Maurice Friedman (1974) reminds us in the chapter-opening quotation, competence in communication finds its wellsprings in interdependence, not in techniques.

"Ensnared" in Narcissism?

Despite Friedman's suspicion of technique, much of American popular culture encourages an individualistic self-orientation. One sociological survey points to several dominant social trends, including a concern for managing others competitively and a desire to seek personal fulfillment therapeutically (Bellah, Madsen, Sullivan, Swidler, & Tipton, 1986). Both trends emphasize an autonomous self as the perceived avenue to success and as the most valid style of communication. Lasch (1979), although he often seems to exaggerate for effect, captures much of this trend in American culture when he describes our "culture of narcissism." Communication researchers motivated by such concerns (Vangelisti, Knapp, & Daly, 1990) have investigated what is called **conversational narcissism**, a construct they trace in part to the work of sociologist Charles Derber (1979). A conversational narcissist works to shift attention to the self and away from others or a shared problem orientation.

Both individual and community perspectives are important standards for making ethical judgments. In Chapter 10, under the topic of *communitarian ethics* in communication ethics, we suggest some ethical implications of Derber's point about individualism precluding community. Other theorists, as you'll note, are more concerned with protecting individual rights and the freedom of individual choices.

In discussing how traditional societies can survive only through a tradition of interdependence, Derber (1979) critiques American cultural trends: "America is developing...not toward greater community or cooperation, but toward an intensification of the entrenched individualism. The continuing decline of the family, the neighborhood, and other 'community' institutions along with the strengthening of capitalist values and institutions suggests the yet further ensnarement of the individual" in individualistic conditions. Moreover, Derber fears that social relations will become even more dehumanized as people become "preoccupied with...personal growth" and "increasingly incapable of transcending a highly complex but intensified egocentricity" (pp. 93–94).

Derber wasn't trying to make a complex theoretical point, but he was suggesting something more complicated than just that Americans are selfish. He sketched the backdrop for the kind of theoretical discussions we need to have more often in the communication discipline. If communication is seen simply as what an individual can make happen by using personal skills, we reinforce our "ensnarement" (to use his term) within individualistic assumptions. Such assumptions are deeply embedded in the culture. But, despite them, communication is not something *I* do; communication is a *we* process. The result (and, therefore, the criterion) of communication competence is not autonomy but interdependence.

Mary wasn't being selfish by trying out her newly found communication skills in her family life. She had every right to believe that she was better equipped to help establish effective communication. Studying communication is highly practical. But it isn't ultimately dependent on building skills if the appreciation of interdependence doesn't accompany those skills.

If you agree that autonomy is overrated and overemphasized, you're probably curious about which theories of interpersonal life are most helpful in addressing this imbalance. These may turn out to be the most practical theories of all for you. In this chapter we ask some basic questions about communication interdependence. We begin by discussing what needs people attempt to satisfy through communication. Next, we survey several different approaches to the fundamentally mutual and social nature of interpersonal communication: the relational/interactional theory of the Palo Alto Group; the interpersonal perception theory of Laing; the dialectical theory of Baxter and others; the dialogic theories as developed and applied in various ways by Buber, Rogers, and Gadamer; and the dramaturgical theories of Burke, Goffman, and Bormann.

What Do People Need as Communicators?

To anthropologist Ashley Montagu (1962), "the individual is a myth. There are no individuals. There are many persons, however, who try to be individuals, who endeavor to live their lives separate and apart from their fellow human beings" (p. 61). Are they successful in this attempt? Or do they need more? One group of theorists suggests that communicators use relationships to obtain the individual rewards they think they need. However, other theorists reply that motives for communication are more complicated, and that people need social contact itself, for its own sake. The answers to these questions are especially revealing when we consider whether there is such a thing as a particularly human nature.

Social Exchange Theory: Rewards

You may have said, or heard someone say, something like this recently: "Why don't you drop him? What are you getting out of that relationship anyway? He's just exploiting you." Such statements are common enough to suggest that we typically reflect on the quality of our communication and try to evaluate the cost of our relationships relative to their rewards. "Is it worth it?" we ask.

One possible answer to the question "What do communicators need?" comes from **social exchange theory** (see Reviewing Key Ideas, p. 142). Researchers and commentators from this tradition (Blau, 1964; Homans, 1961; Thibaut & Kelley, 1959) tend to answer the question in a relatively individualistic way. Despite the fact that most exchange theorists have taken a sociological approach to studying communication, they conceptualize dyadic communication as the individual's primary means of attaining desired rewards and reinforcements. However, their individualistic tone is tempered by a relational requirement. The viability of social exchange rests on the assumption that human beings recognize each other's life situations, notice each other's needs, and in some ways are likely to engage in **reciprocity**—a condition in which a response is correlated to the worth of the original message (Gouldner, 1960). "You scratch my back, and I'll scratch yours" is a common saying that captures this sensibility. In other words, humans interact with others in full recognition that their acts will be noticed and in some way acknowledged (i.e., that they will receive a return on their communicative investment).

According to Peter Blau (1963), this economic analogy is at the core of social exchange theory: "The distinctive character of a social exchange is that one person furnishes a service to another and, while there is a general expectation of some future return, there is no advance stipulation of the precise nature of the return" (p. 139). Thus, Blau continues, "social exchanges...entail services that create unspecified obligations in the future and therefore exert a pervasive influence on social relations" (p. 140). **Rewards** (outcomes desired by communicators) are constantly being compared with **costs** (what communicators must forgo or give up in order to achieve goals). It's not just the individual motive to get rewarded that is important here, Blau explains, but beyond that, the establishment of an economic base for the relationship in which the partner feels a "requirement to reciprocate in order to receive further benefits" (p. 140). What an individual feels rewarded by, of course, will vary from one person to another. Accompanying a roommate to a play may function as a reward for some people and as a frustrating cost for others.

Relational partners who compare rewards with costs will try to achieve a form of communication **profit**, according to exchange theorists; the communication rewards outweigh the costs. Thibaut and Kelley (1959) conceptualize this phenomenon in terms of the **comparison level (CL)** phenomenon. A CL, simply stated, is an inner standard set by the individual that indicates an acceptable level of satisfaction in a relationship or a situation, on the basis of various forms of social judgment and past experience. In effect, this means that people symbolically model how their needs should be met and create expectations below which they will not feel satisfied. For example, a classmate whose company you enjoy but who consistently forgets about you when she's promised to come over and share chemistry notes probably wouldn't meet your CL for friendship. The enjoyable and rewarding conversation you share is more than counterbalanced by a cost—the annoying inconvenience of waiting around for her all the time. However, does not achieving this CL standard mean that you'll end your relationship with her? Not necessarily. To answer this question, Thibaut and Kelley would theorize that you also generate another standard—a **comparison level for alternatives** (written as CL_{alt}). This means that you compare the rewards and costs of your existing relationship with the anticipated rewards and costs that you would receive if you ended the relationship. If the CL_{alt} is low, you might be willing to put up with her annoying and unpredictable behavior (if, for example, as a new student on campus you hadn't made many friends yet, you might imagine that without this classmate you'd have no one to talk with at school). Your relationship with her is below your CL for such relations (i.e., it is far from ideal), but it is above your CL_{alt} (i.e., it is better than you currently expect to be able to establish with other classmates).

Social exchange theory encourages an image of human interaction as a calculation and, to some extent, of human beings as interpersonal accountants. In suggesting that we monitor ourselves and each other in this manner, theorists seem vulnerable to charges that they demean or dehumanize communication. They might even be seen as contributing to the conversational narcissism we discussed earlier. Although social exchange concepts are individualistic in some ways, you shouldn't forget that the basis for exchange in the first place is an expectation of reciprocity. Humans ultimately are not individualized and isolated schemers; rather, they cooperate with, rely on, and need each other in a variety of subtle ways. Before examining the nature of relationships more completely, let's look briefly at two other views on what communicators need, one derived from philosophy and the other from psychology.

American Pragmatism: Social Contact

Although the human mind is capable of considering itself as a separate and independent unit, studies of culture and socialization demonstrate just how dependent individuals are on interaction with others, even for their sense of self. As people become more and more individualized (increasingly unique in personality

---

REVIEWING KEY IDEAS

SOCIAL EXCHANGE THEORY:

- Presumes that people communicate by trying to achieve relational *profit* by producing more *rewards* than *costs*.
- Depends on an expectation of *reciprocity* in maintaining relationships.
- Assumes that people evaluate relationships for their exchange potential by employing *comparison levels* and *comparison levels for alternatives*.

and in the experiences that differentiate them from others), they become less and less individualistic and more and more socialized (Montagu, 1962). Their interwoven connections with others make this inevitable.

Whether you like it or not, then, you are never totally separate from the interests, attitudes, actions, and, most important, the influence of others. This doesn't mean that you can't make your own decisions or try to gain more control over your actions than you had, say, last month. Our point is not that you are buffeted around in a sea of social forces and pressures, where waves take you in completely unpredictable and uncontrollable directions. Language gives you the potential to establish a personal direction. But interpersonal contact is the foundation for the differentiation that's possible with language. Without interpersonal contact, you could not think of yourself as a separate being. Yet with that contact you realize that you can never be truly separable.

One of the most influential social philosophies in twentieth-century American thought has been **pragmatism** (Dewey, 1927, 1934). Scholars in this tradition tried to test the findings of the natural and social sciences against the experienced effects of ideas, and they taught that the essential meaning of any concept or idea can be seen in the effects it is observed to initiate. Philosopher Cornel West (1993) claims that the best characterization of pragmatism is that of C. I. Lewis: "Pragmatism could be characterized as the doctrine that all problems are at bottom problems of conduct, that all judgments are, implicitly, judgments of value, and that, as there can be ultimately no valid distinction of theoretical and practical, so there can be no final separation of questions of truth of any kind from questions of the justifiable ends of action" (quoted in West, 1993, p. 109).

Pragmatists, therefore, including philosopher John Dewey (1927), psychologist William James (1896), and language theorist C. S. Peirce (1931–1958), look at how social effects are integrated into individual experience. Dewey's work is associated with the symbolic interactionist ideas we surveyed in Chapter 4. Although much American philosophy has taken an individualistic turn, Dewey maintains a balanced view of the link between the individual and society. Consistent with the ideas of George Herbert Mead (1934), Dewey (1927) thought that selves and social forces define each other: "Any human being is in one respect an association, consisting of a multitude of cells each living its own life. And as the activity of each cell is conditioned and directed by those with which it interacts, so the human being whom we fasten upon as individual par excellence is moved and regulated by his associations with others; what he does and what the consequences of his behavior are, what his experience consists of, cannot be described, much less accounted for, in isolation" (p. 188).

FIRO Theory: Inclusion, Control, and Affection

Psychologist William Schutz (1966), researching his **fundamental interpersonal relations orientation (FIRO)** theory, identifies three basic interpersonal needs: *inclusion, control,* and *affection* (see Reviewing Key Ideas, p. 144). Although he believes that people seek ways to fulfill these three needs, his system does not presume that everyone is equally motivated by them or that the needs can predict human behavior precisely in any given circumstance.

In Chapter 8 you'll read about the questions raised by theorists of persuasion. What does Schutz's work suggest about why people might feel impelled to try to persuade others to change their beliefs, attitudes, or actions?

Inclusion, as Schutz (1966) uses the term, is similar to the idea of interpersonal contact. It refers to people's need to be recognized as participants in human interaction. People generally need to associate with others and to have their associations noted. Although people also value privacy and aloneness on many occasions, they seem at the same time to have lingering fears of being abandoned, ignored, or renounced by others. An absence of inclusion, suggests medical researcher James Lynch (1977), can be fatal, because the human body and mind are linked in this need for interpersonal connection.

If feeling included is a baseline condition for healthy human existence, then the need to make a difference—**control**—is the next logical level. Schutz is not referring to a desire to have one's own way all the time or to manipulate others in a bossy manner. These aggressive desires have been studied elsewhere in the communication literature; for example, **Machiavellianism** (named for the sixteenth-century Italian author of *The Prince*) is the interpersonal willingness to manipulate others for personal gain. Schutz's use of the term *control* is more neutral, referring to people's desire to make a difference in their social environments and to have some say over what happens. If there is no such sense of control, people feel they are at the mercy of others or vulnerable to the whims of fate. They are less likely to attempt significant projects or to initiate interaction with others. They become, in other words, spectators and not participants in living.

Finally, according to Schutz (1966), people need **affection;** that is, they seek a sense of interpersonal warmth or of being liked or loved. Friendship and other intimate relations often serve this function, of course, and the absence of such relationships is a source of much of the alienation we feel from time to time. Even though someone might be noticed consistently, and even have a measure of power over others, existence still might seem empty. In this dimension of interpersonal need, as with the other two, people's behaviors and desires vary widely. Obviously, people don't just have (or not have) affection (or inclusion or control)—they experience it to some degree in relation to its opposite or its absence.

Relational/Interactional Theory

A touchstone of modern communication theory is Watzlawick, Beavin (now Bavelas), and Jackson's *Pragmatics of Human Communication* (1967). Its authors, therapists and researchers at the Mental Research Institute in Palo Alto,

---

REVIEWING KEY IDEAS

FIRO THEORY: INTERPERSONAL NEEDS

- *Inclusion* (remaining connected with others)
- *Control* (ability to make a difference in social situations; not necessarily manipulative)
- *Affection* (interpersonal warmth and satisfying relations)

California, are collectively referred to, along with other colleagues, as the **Palo Alto Group**. They wanted to construct a unified theoretical synthesis to explain the everyday conflicts that frustrate people in their families and workplaces. Although the authors discovered part of that synthesis from their mentor, Gregory Bateson, they decided to explore an even wider landscape of contemporary thought in the social sciences, mathematics, literature, and philosophy. As they write early in the book, "...a phenomenon remains unexplainable as long as the range of observation is not wide enough to include the context in which the phenomenon occurs" (pp. 20–21). The relationship between what is studied (whether it is a person, a behavior, an object, or something else) and its environment is where scientists must concentrate their attention. Although this insight had already taken hold in the natural sciences by the mid-1960s, the social sciences, they thought, were still searching for the "properties," "characteristics," or "traits" that were assumed to make people more or less social, more or less communicative. This stress on relationship function as a representation of communication, in contrast to the message transmission and reception model, is the most significant contribution of the Palo Alto Group. As the researchers explain: "The observer of human behavior...turns from an inferential study of the mind to the study of the observable manifestations of relationship" and "the vehicle of these manifestations is communication" (Watzlawick et al., 1967, p. 21).

Pragmatics of Human Communication is not a work of pop psychology. The authors wrote for professionals and translated and applied many concepts from general systems theory, information theory, existential thought, the philosophy of paradox, and their own intellectual base camp of psychological and psychiatric research. Gradually, they drew from and inspired an even wider range of colleagues and research (Watzlawick & Weakland, 1977; Watzlawick, Weakland, & Fisch, 1974).

Despite the technical, occasionally dense prose of *Pragmatics,* the book is surprisingly readable. The authors provide generally clear definitions of terms and use examples from the daily dilemmas of real people and from popular literature. For example, an extended analysis of Edward Albee's famed play (and later film) *Who's Afraid of Virginia Woolf?* shows how *systems theory* can help explain interpersonal conflict. Although the authors were modest about the completeness of their book (p. 13), there can be no doubt about the extent of its ambition. In many ways, the book is a model of interdisciplinary synthesis in the social sciences, and much of the current debate over how to define communication can be traced to the 1967 Watzlawick, Beavin, and Jackson position.

Although the discussions of psychotherapeutic implications and applications to family therapy are fascinating in this and other works by the Palo Alto Group, we will focus here on their five influential "axioms" (see Reviewing Key Ideas, p. 150).

Axiom 1: "The Impossibility of Not Communicating"

As mental health professionals, these authors were just as curious about the sources of misunderstanding as they were about how to achieve understanding. Obviously, these aren't different concepts but the same issue approached from different perspectives. Yet the different perspectives can yield different questions as well as different answers. If behavioral researchers assume, as most did before the publication of *Pragmatics,* that communication is only the receiver's achievement of the sender's understanding, then they will tend to study those acts that attempt to produce congruent understanding in senders and receivers. Some of those behaviors will be found to be communicative (i.e., "successful"), while others will not.

Pragmatics turns this perspective on its head. Watzlawick, Beavin, and Jackson note that because "full" understanding is not achievable (that would be mind reading), it is practical to think of any behavior that leads to an understanding of the relations between people as having message value. "Behavior has no opposite," they claim. It's impossible for silence or absence, for example, not to be perceived as messages by others who notice them, whether or not they were specifically intended as messages by the actors. (Are you avoiding communication by skipping class or by not turning in a paper, or are you just substituting new messages that you and your teacher might interpret in the relationship?) In recent years, some communication scholars have questioned Axiom 1 by stressing intention in message formation. But the axiom reminds us that listeners and receivers may, as a part of *their* intention, attach communicative significance to any behavior.

Axiom 2: "The Content and Relationship Levels of Communication"

Whenever people speak, they perform dual functions. Each communicator provides information (or "content") for the other, and each suggests (directly or indirectly) the type of relationship they share. Bateson (see Ruesch & Bateson, 1951) calls these functions the *report dimension* (content) and the *command dimension* (relationship). These are simultaneously present in communication, according to the Palo Alto Group. For example, take the simple statement "Lend me your car this afternoon." On the surface, the statement refers to a car and when it's needed for transportation. This is its **content level** of communication. The message is about a car. But what else is it about? Is there another level of description that would help communicators understand more thoroughly what is going on here?

The Palo Alto theorists would say that in this example the content of the statement is basically equivalent to, say, "I'd like to borrow your car this afternoon." But the two statements are experientially quite different at the **relationship level** of communication. The first one ("Lend me your car…") implies that the speaker has developed within the relationship a right to demand a loan of the car and, therefore, is in some ways more powerful than the listener. This message level can hardly be more important, for it is the way people often signal put-downs and even compliments without coming right out and identifying such messages as negative or positive. The relationship level is experienced as important, but it can be denied overtly by communicators if challenged or if it's convenient to do so. ("You were offended by what I said? Aren't you being a bit insecure?")

While the content level contains the appropriate "data" of communication, the rules by which we guide our interactions are often found at the relationship level. As noted in Chapter 3, the mechanism by which this happens is termed *metacommunication*. In the metacommunicative functions of interaction, therefore, people clue each other in on "how to take" the more obvious content messages. For example, you've probably had the experience of a good friend kidding

LINK

Metacommunication is important in social talk partly because of how we use *constitutive rules*—well-understood social guidelines that tell us whether to interpret or "take" a comment as an insult or as a friendly joke, for example. Later in this chapter we'll examine rules theory in detail.

you incessantly about a personal problem or fault. Yet you realize that this kidding isn't meant to be insulting or degrading. Another person, maybe a rival of yours on the basketball court or in the office, would not be able to say the same things without your feeling insulted or degraded. But what's different? At the relational level, you and your friend have learned the metacommunication signals, many of them nonverbal, that allow you to distinguish between positive and negative tones. Watzlawick, Beavin, and Jackson, too, later point out that in pathological family patterns, people can even compliment loved ones with words and nonverbal cues that ultimately signal relational animosity. Then they can deny the hostile intention, pointing instead to the overt content of the talk.

Axiom 3: "The Punctuation of the Sequence of Events"

Just as punctuation marks in sentences indicate starts, stops, and pauses, similar clues regulate relationships. In the study of communication, *punctuation* is a process of perception through which people organize their ongoing interactions into recognizable openings, closings, causes, and effects. The events themselves, viewed externally, may appear to be seamless. It's often unclear what "caused" what, but it's usually very clear what happened and in what order. However, people who are confronted with such experiences want to understand some things as responses to others and to organize the whys and wherefores of communication. "You started it!" and "No, I didn't—you did!" exemplify different punctuations of an argument between two children (or adults). Sports coaches and managers sometimes discuss a "turning point" in a game after which the momentum changes significantly. Group leaders and consultants are similarly alert to "critical incidents" such as arguments or emotional breakthroughs that, according to their punctuation, change the tenor of subsequent talk in the group.

Axiom 4: "Digital and Analogic Communication"

Watzlawick, Beavin, and Jackson (1967) claim that human communication messages take one of two forms:

> They can either be represented by a likeness, such as a drawing, or they can be referred to by a name. Thus, in the written sentence "The cat has caught a mouse" the nouns could be replaced by pictures; if the sentence were spoken, the actual cat and the mouse could be pointed to. Needless to say, this would be an unusual way of communicating, and normally the written or spoken "name," that is, the word, is used. These two types of communication—the one by a self-explanatory likeness, the other by a word—are . . . equivalent to the concepts of the analogic and the digital respectively. Whenever a word is used to name something it is obvious that the relation between the name and the thing named is an arbitrarily established one. Words are arbitrary signs that are manipulated according to the logical matrix of language. . . . In analogic communication, on the other hand, there is something particularly "thing-like" in what is used to express the thing. (pp. 61–62)

Digital communication, then, depends on arbitrary agreements like the all-or-none unambiguous digit-based system of computers. A digit, such as the number 1,

⬅️ **LINKS**

❑ Recall our discussion of punctuation in Chapter 2, when we introduced the concept of process.

❑ Do you have any experiences of attempting to metacommunicate in an unfamiliar culture? Chapter 7 will explore this challenge in greater detail.

can stand for one person, one fork, one desk…or it can simply stand for an option other than zero. It is the agreement between people that makes a digital message stand for anything they want it to, even for objects that are fantasized or not physically present. Through digital messages we may free ourselves from a now world, a prison of the present, in order to talk about events long past or about people we are yet to meet. Because of digital message agreements, we can plan for the future. This kind of understanding is the basis of our entire system of language—it is like a code that we try not to keep secret. It is essential to human communication about complex events and ideas.

Analogic communication is also essential but in a different way. Analogic messages are connected more fundamentally to the actualities of communicating and, therefore, they are said to be more immediate than digital messages. If someone says "I'm shaking your hand" without actually shaking a hand, the statement is digital. Actually shaking the hand is analogic. Because analogic messages are clearly related to nonverbal communication, and are clearly immediate in character, it should come as no surprise that they are crucial in the development of metacommunicational meaning. Analogic messages, in fact, are indicators *of* relationship, the Palo Alto Group authors assert, and are not statements *about* relationships. This explains why people, when faced with **mixed messages** (contradictions between the verbal/digital and the nonverbal/analogic types of communication) almost invariably believe the latter.

Axiom 5: "Symmetrical and Complementary Interaction"

Theorists of the Palo Alto Group researched two basic patterns of interaction. Symmetry in art and architecture implies an obvious balance among elements. Similarly, in **symmetrical interaction** each of the two parties essentially seeks to match or mirror the behavior of the other. For example, one person's shyness will be met by shy reactions from the other, or an angry tirade triggers an angry response. Symmetrical interaction may not be orderly or harmonious. It may result in competition, in which each message contribution is met by the other side with a corresponding attempt to keep up the prevailing pattern. Thus an insult often begets an insult, sulking might create more sulking, and you're more likely to receive Christmas cards from those to whom you send cards. Like the exchange theorist's norm of *reciprocity,* symmetrical interaction behavior can often be observed to generate its own reflection.

Complementary interaction is the behavioral opposite of symmetrical interaction. It, too, characterizes many human relationships and also can be destructive. Suppose, for example, you have an argument with a friend. Your friend yells at you during the argument, but instead of yelling back in a mutually escalating way (that is, in a symmetrical pattern), you react by withdrawing. What you've done is adapt your reaction not by matching your friend's behavior but by fitting your response to that behavior. In effect, you've accepted your friend's behavior relationally and adapted to it by producing its logical opposite behavior. In a complementary pattern, yelling may be met with silence or whispering, passivity with aggression, attempts to persuade with willing receptivity, dominance with submission, giving with taking, and so forth. Although complementary relations do not usually develop a sense of competition (although there may be other conflicts within the pattern), the long-term consequences of this type of relationship are interesting to conflict researchers. Such a pattern of behavior could produce **schismogenesis**, a condition in which the two complementary positions become progressively farther apart, each as a result of the other (Watzlawick et al., 1967, p. 68). For example, a demanding husband who persistently criticizes an accepting, passive wife (or vice versa) may find that the more he criticizes, the more passive she becomes. This response is not satisfying to him, however, and he feels a desire to criticize more often and more sharply. Her submission then deepens. In effect, their behavioral patterns diverge.

Symmetrical patterns, therefore, are based on relatively equal status and relatively similar behaviors, whereas complementary patterns are based on status differences and divergent behaviors. In all likelihood, everyone's communication lives are composed of mixtures of each of these types of interaction, and they are not necessarily destructive. Problems arise when symmetrical relations escalate out of control or when complementary relations become more and more rigid.

In this discussion, we've assumed that each partner in the relationship is aware of the other. That is almost true by definition: How can there be a relationship between people without their mutual recognition? Still, relations can weaken to the extent that people reduce their awareness (or their willingness to show their awareness) of the partner's definition of self. Relational/interactional theorists accept Martin Buber's (1965a) view that **confirmation**, the capacity to be noticed and perceived in both actuality and potentiality, is a distinguishing feature of mature, healthy communication. Conflict can result when one person rejects the other's definition of self, but that rejection still indicates an awareness of who the other person is. However, what happens when one partner communicates as if the other didn't exist?

This condition, not surprisingly, is known as **disconfirmation**. It can be psychologically damaging, especially for people who are otherwise vulnerable due to their relative absence of power, their age, or their mental condition. Psychiatrist R. D. Laing (1969), whose early work in this area is often cited by the Palo Alto Group, quoted psychologist and philosopher William James: "No more fiendish punishment could be devised, even were such a thing physically possible, than that one should be turned loose in society and remain absolutely unnoticed by all the members thereof" (pp. 98–99). Laing treated families in which children were not "subject to outright neglect or even to obvious trauma" but, instead, received "subtle but persistent disconfirmation, usually unwittingly" (p. 100).

Overall, the Palo Alto Group's premise is simple: A communication relationship is crucial in determining message meanings. However, a relationship is not just two people directing messages at each other from their separate home bases. We'll understand communication only by studying relations between individuals, rather than by analyzing the individuals themselves. People's perceptions of relationship become their primary clues for developing relational strategies, as well as their primary evidence for drawing conclusions about others. As we will see in the next section, Laing has been an important contributor to our understanding of relational perception.

◁ L I N K

Consider the highly verbal digitized environment of e-mail, in which discerning mixed messages is clearly harder than in everyday face-to-face interaction. What significant problems could be created by this context? What are the implications for developing online communities and friendships? Will such future technologies as streaming video software restore more opportunities to perceive mixed messages as they offer new multisensory forms of telepresence? In considering these questions, you may want to review the discussion of online communication context in Chapter 3.

REVIEWING KEY IDEAS

RELATIONAL/INTERACTIONAL THEORY: THE AXIOMS PARAPHRASED

- It is impossible to avoid communicating if people are aware of their relationship.
- All communication interchanges have both content and relationship levels; our talk reveals not only what we think about our *topics* but our relation to *each other.*
- Our communication is filled with attempts to *punctuate* sequences of events—that is, to identify openings, closings, starts, stops, causes, and effects.
- Messages can take either *digital* form, based on arbitrary agreements about meanings such as are found in language, or *analogic* forms, based on more immediate nonverbal relationships.
- Interaction can be either *symmetrical,* in which one person tries to match the behavior of another, or *complementary,* in which each person adapts to another's behavior by adopting its logical opposite behavior (such as when someone tries to put you down and you concede meekly instead of arguing).

Interpersonal Perception Theory

R. D. Laing (1969) was curious about how relationships form, but he was also interested in how people accomplish the complex psychological process of perception. Only when people can match or coordinate their perceptions (of each other, of the relationship, of the other's view of the relationship, and so forth) can there be what Laing calls a "genuine relationship":

> *Interpersonal life is conducted in a nexus of persons, in which each person is guessing, assuming, inferring, believing, trusting, or suspecting, generally being happy or tormented by his phantasy of the others' experience, motives, and intentions. And one has phantasies, not only about what the other himself experiences and intends, but also about his phantasies about one's own experience and intentions, and about his phantasies about one's phantasies about his phantasies about one's experience, etc. There could be no greater mistake than to suppose that these issues are mere "theoretical" complexities, of little practical relevance.... Family interactions are often dominated by these issues. (p. 174)*

As an example of interpersonal perception analysis, let's consider a hypothetical relationship involving a father and a daughter. The father sees his fifteen-year-old daughter, Carla, as an intelligent and independent young woman. But he wonders if his persistent reminders about not drinking will boomerang: Will they be interpreted as nagging? As sincere expressions of concern? As an indication that

Carla is untrustworthy? In order to decide, the father will, without planning to do so, use what Laing, Phillipson, and Lee (1966) call **metaperspectives**, or perspectives about perspectives. He will consider how he sees himself (maybe as a diligent parent), how he sees Carla (maybe as not only intelligent and independent but also vulnerable to peer pressure), and how he thinks Carla sees Carla (maybe as bright and mature). In Laing's (1969) notation procedure, how a person sees self is noted as [p→p]; how that person sees another is [p→o]; and how the person sees someone else's view of the other's self is [p→(o→o)] (pp. 174 ff.).

Therefore Carla's dad, if he is normally perceptive about his relationship with his daughter, can generate even more relational data through metaperspectives. He develops a judgment about how Carla believes he sees their relationship: "I think Carla understands that I love her and want her to be independent, so my concern for her will more likely be seen as love than as meddling." This could be identified in a complex but reasonably clear notation: [p→(o→(p→o))].

Using the metaperspectival approach, and assuming that each person's experience is all he or she can access directly as evidence in making relational decisions, Laing, Phillipson, and Lee (1966) developed the *Interpersonal Perception Method* questionnaire to explore how people in *dyads* (two-person relationships) perceive and define their interactions differently. Each person is asked to respond (on a scale of "very true" to "very untrue") to a series of questions. Here are a few sample questions from the instrument given to one member of a relational dyad:

A. *How true do you think the following are?*
   1. *She takes me seriously.*
   2. *I take her seriously.*
   3. *She takes herself seriously.*
   4. *I take myself seriously.*
B. *How would she answer the following?*
   1. *"I take him seriously."*
   2. *"He takes me seriously."*
   3. *"I take myself seriously."*
   4. *"He takes himself seriously."*
C. *How would she think you have answered the following set?*
   1. *She takes me seriously.*
   2. *I take her seriously.*
   3. *She takes herself seriously.*
   4. *I take myself seriously. (Laing, Phillipson, & Lee, 1966)*

With both persons' responses, the researcher has a reasonably thorough map of the perspectives and metaperspectives with which they approach the relationship. Using these data, a counselor or a therapist can focus on the areas in which the partners' metaperspectives are most inconsistent or incongruent (i.e., in those areas where each partner inaccurately perceives the perspectives and metaperspectives of the other).

One outcome of interpersonal perception research is a clearer picture of the roles people begin to define in relationships. A **role** is the set of behaviors that is expected of a certain person ("John's role in the group is to keep things light," we might say) or a certain position ("It's part of the role of a leader to keep our

Remember that in Chapter 2 we contrasted *rules* with *covering law* approaches to explaining communication. Whereas covering law approaches try to find explanations that relate to human experience or human nature generally, across contexts, rules theorists focus on very specific situational interactions in order to determine which explanations best fit those particular contexts.

discussion on track"). Husbands and wives, job applicants and interviewers, young and old, and many other social groups may find themselves in predictably different roles if their ways of developing and using metaperspectives differ. In many roles, a person's social behavior might be analyzed almost as if it were a theatrical performance, with the criterion for effectiveness being dramatic impact. Later in this chapter we examine a set of theoretical perspectives that use the metaphors of drama to illuminate the communication process.

Rules Theory

The doors slide open and you enter an elevator that is already packed with about ten strangers. They make a place for you by adjusting their positions relative to each other...but they do this so skillfully that they don't need to speak, touch, or even look at one another directly. In a matter of seconds, people who have never interacted before have transformed an already crowded environment in order to admit you. At the next floor, you yourself participate in this intricate dance. Without being told, you seem to know how to act, which way to turn, when and how to look toward others, and whether to talk. How does all this coordination happen so effectively, so gracefully, and so often? To explain such things, some researchers have relied on the concept of communication rules.

Defining Rules

Rules allow us to organize and coordinate our lives. They create order out of chaos, uncertainty, and confusion. Football, flirting, solitaire, business meetings, and even friendships are guided by different sets of formal or informal rules. They are rarely codified or even openly discussed. Although society operates in a systematic and seemingly predictable way most of the time, other people seldom literally instruct you in how to act. Your parents may have told you a bit about how to be "polite" or how to conform to "etiquette," but did anyone ever teach you how to stand in line at a fast-food restaurant? (In each culture, most people have similar habits for lining up.) How and when to nod while another person is talking? These things happen so naturally that they seem effortless, even trivial, but the extent to which they are patterned and orchestrated with others' behavior suggests that an important communication process is occurring. Rules theory attempts to define the nature of rule patterns specifically and concretely.

Margaret McLaughlin (1984) defines **rules** as:

> *propositions, which may or may not be explicitly available to consciousness, which model our understandings of what behaviors are prescribed or prohibited in certain contexts. Rules may be stored and retrieved in a variety of linguistic forms, but the canonical rule-statement is of the form, "If situation X occurs, do (do not do) Y." Rules may be followed, or not, as the actor chooses; they are value-expressions whose truth cannot be determined. The behavior they prescribe is situation-bound. Rules are subject to alteration by consent of those whom they govern. (p. 21)*

Rules, then, can be either *implicit* (understood at subtle levels) or *explicit* (obviously and consciously referred to). Some implicit linguistic rules help us interpret messages that could mean different things at a literal level than they do at the connotative or implicit level. Therefore we're successful at carrying off or regulating interaction in ways that would be confusing to someone who is just learning the language, or just entering the culture. If, for example, a member of the family asks, "Can someone pass the salt?" the person closest to the salt shaker is likely to pick it up almost automatically and wordlessly pass it around the table— instead of responding to the question that was actually asked. Of course, the person *can* (is able to) pass the salt, but the question is not interpreted literally. The "question" functions not as a real question but as a request. In the same way, someone calls on the phone and asks the person who answers it, "Is Rob there?" Is a simple "yes" or "no" all that is expected? Of course not; the question is used, in U.S. culture at least, as a request to summon Rob to the phone if he is available.

Shimanoff's (1980) survey of definitions leads her to conclude that four criteria are generally recognized by rules theorists. Rules, she concluded, are followable, prescriptive, contextual, and behaviorally based. First, rules must be *followable* in the sense of being understandable and accessible enough to allow a person to adhere to them. Long ago, a high school gym teacher, who has faded into the dim memory of one of your authors, tried to establish a rule in his class that punishment for "screw-ups" (his term) would be shinnying up a rope to the ceiling of the gym. His scheme of explicit rules, however creative and fearful it was, didn't succeed. The punishment simply wasn't possible for many of us, who were yet to develop our upper-body strength. No matter how much we may be motivated psychologically to do something, if we are unable to accomplish it the rule cannot operate. "Communication scholars associate rules with actions rather than motions, and actions are behaviors that one may choose to perform; hence a rule must be capable of being followed" (Shimanoff, 1980, p. 39).

Second, rules are *prescriptive*. As such, they can be phrased as "if…, then…" statements that tell what should be done to comply with the rule, or, conversely, what will happen if the rule is broken (including how the rule breaker will be held accountable). We infer how to state a rule from what we see happening over time in certain contexts; for example, "*If* someone wearing a baseball cap enters a church, *then* the person should remove the cap immediately." Or: "If a student has a complicated question for the teacher and there are only two minutes of class time left, then that question should not be asked." Note that with most rules there's no one to enforce the prescription, and that at times there are those (like some teachers) who will overtly invite "violations" (like questions that can't be answered in the amount of class time that remains).

Third, rules are *contextual*. As we discussed in Chapter 3, the interpretation of communication rules usually depends on our surroundings. Raucous or raunchy joke-telling might be appropriate or even expected during some parties, but not at public lectures. It's not the joke that's inappropriate but the combination of message and context. Interruptions during someone's extended statement might be appropriate in a courtroom or even in a lunchroom, but not while listening to an after-dinner speech at a conference or while interviewing your college president about the institution's financial status.

Finally, rules are *behaviorally based*. Shimanoff (1980) distinguishes between cognition and behavior when she says that rules "may be utilized in making

LINK

How are examples of these kinds of linguistic rules related to *speech act theory*, which is discussed in Chapter 4?

mental evaluations, inferences, judgments, and interpretations of behavior, but rules themselves do not prescribe what one must (must not) or should (should not) think" (p. 50). Because we can't read others' minds, she reasons, it is "vacuous" to believe that a system of rules can prescribe cognitions or interpretations. Not everyone agrees with Shimanoff on this point. For example, the theorists associated with *coordinated management of meaning theory*—which you'll read about next—believe that some rules function to constitute our inner interpretations, not to direct our behaviors.

Coordinated Management of Meaning (CMM) Theory

Rules acclimate people to each other and enable us to coordinate our behaviors. The social order is so complex that, according to some research perspectives, it must be constantly negotiated and renegotiated. This notion that communication is a continuous process of spontaneous on-site adjustments and calibrations is a central tenet of **coordinated management of meaning theory (CMM).** (See Reviewing Key Ideas, p. 157.) It offers a special perspective on communication rules because it does not presume, as some earlier rules approaches did, that rules are handy sets of already-in-place dictates for how we should act. We don't knowingly "consult" rules to imagine possible actions; we negotiate them in response to particular contexts, and their meanings and shape are never static.

CMM theory was developed primarily by W. Barnett Pearce and Vernon Cronen (see 1980 for an early statement). It integrates systems theory, speech act theory, symbolic interactionism, and other theoretical viewpoints. As Cronen, Pearce, and Harris (1982) summarize, "CMM theory describes human actors as attempting to achieve coordination by managing the ways messages take on meaning" (p. 68). Further, the theory accounts for why **co-orientation**—the mutual recognition of an understanding—is not a necessary prerequisite for developing well-coordinated conversations, for example. That is, the other person doesn't need to know exactly what you mean or what you intend in order for a successful communication episode to develop.

We can illustrate CMM with an example expanded from some of its founders (Cronen et al., 1982, p. 68). Explicit rules—traffic codes—are supposed to govern how people drive on city streets, and certainly implicit rules (when to honk and when not to, etc.) are in play as well. Yet when two drivers approach an intersection (say, at a four-way stop), they bring with them different interpretations of reality. One driver may be a compulsive follower of traffic codes and know them well. The other may be more of an intuitive driver who tends to respond to others' actions. Despite the differences in their knowledge of traffic codes and in their ways of defining and utilizing rules, and despite their inability to read each other's mind, they still manage to avoid hitting each other. Their safe and successful accomplishment of their different driving tasks isn't due primarily to similar definitions of the situation or its rules. Instead, it's due to their mutual and spontaneous recognition of a common situation. That is accomplished as each driver monitors personal behavior along with the behavior of the other, developing new and unique rule adjustments *in process* for what behavior "means" in that context. Meaning is thus managed in a coordinated way—and from this insight comes the label for the theory itself. Seen in this light, communication rules don't spotlight or dictate what people should do as much as they spotlight how people decide what to do. This difference is significant in CMM theory.

CMM presumes that communication is the fundamental experience on which human nature is based. It rejects more psychologically oriented, individualistic approaches to rules in which the individual either understands or doesn't understand the rule structure of a relatively predictable and knowable social order. Most other rules-based theories assume that society exhibits a **homogenous social order**, or one that's similar across contexts and in which society has pretty much the same features everywhere. In this way of thinking about society, people generally share similar assumptions about what is right and wrong, appropriate and inappropriate, expected and prohibited in communication situations. In contrast, CMM theory holds that this assumption of homogeneity, or sameness, is suspect because it can't account for the many times when, for example, students from New York City must talk with professors from Wisconsin or when an Oklahoma patient is treated by a doctor who is new to the United States. Instead, we have a **heterogeneous social order**, which, despite some similarities, is composed of multiple tastes, styles, assumptions, language habits, and expectations. CMM theory takes into account both commonalities and differences. Therefore it becomes especially useful for understanding communication in conflicts (Pearce & Littlejohn, 1997), highly ambiguous cross-cultural contexts (Pearce, 1989), and ethical quandaries (Cronen, 1991).

Three questions are central to how CMM scholars study communication events: (1) What is the *coherence*? (2) What is the *control*? and (3) What is the *valence*? **Coherence** is the extent to which actors within the situations make sense of the communicative episode. It does not have to be the same for each party, and, in fact, is likely not to be the same. **Control** is the extent to which actors are able to influence what happens in the episode. **Valence** is the extent to which the actors like or dislike the episode that develops. Rules in such a view account for how individuals are integrated into larger social and cultural patterns; they are for sense-making (achieving coherence), for mutually-oriented control (the management dimension), and for organizing patterns of affect (the valence of perceived interaction). Indeed, in CMM "the constitution of individuals as ends is itself a process that must be understood in its particular cultural and historical context. Individuality must have a social basis because it takes culturally unique forms no matter how it is developed. Conversely, social structure must be created by entities at least individualized by the unique locations of their actions and embodiments in time and space" (Cronen, 1991, p. 36).

Two types of rules manage meanings in communication: *constitutive rules* and *regulative rules*. **Constitutive rules** "organize actors' hierarchies of meaning. They specify how meanings at one level of abstraction may count as meaningful at another level of abstraction. For example, 'You are beautiful' counts as compliment" (Cronen et al., 1982, pp. 73–74). These rules are called constitutive because they "constitute," or make up, people's inner sense of meaning. They also account for why the comment "You are beautiful" might "count as" an insult if it is voiced sarcastically in the middle of an argument. **Regulative rules** organize the constitutive rules into guidelines for behavior. A regulative rule might, for example, suggest that in some contexts (such as a cooperative team presentation with other students in your public relations class), even though you recognize that you've probably just been insulted, it would be most appropriate to ignore it, behaving as if it hadn't happened.

Have you recently been in a situation in which you understood the rules and were able to conform to them or follow the implicit guidelines but didn't feel very much in control of the situation? This common human experience is also addressed by the CMM theorists. For example, Pearce (1994) explores this problem by distinguishing between what he calls *game playing* and *game mastery*. Here, "game" is not a negative or trivializing term (such as "I hate it when my roommate plays his 'I'm too busy to clean' games"). Instead, Pearce and other CMM researchers are interested in how communicators use language in patterned ways, coordinated by rules, that seem to have structures similar to organized games. Using the ideas of Wittgenstein (1953) and others, they try to find the **language games** that structure—and often limit—our social interaction, making it more predictable. People who coordinate their behaviors readily, then, are probably playing similar language games. The concept of **game playing** involves following the rules, helping yourself adapt to what's going on. This is a kind of minimal communicative competence, such as recognizing that you "shouldn't" wear your swimsuit to church, although you literally could do so, or that you probably wouldn't take out a John Grisham novel and start reading it during a class discussion on, well, rules theory. But Pearce wants you to know that rules don't just hem us in as social limitations.

Knowing the rules can also involve more than following preexisting rules; it can involve a communicator's full participation in the open negotiations that always constitute our conversations. Meanings are never finalized, so there is always room for effective communicators to develop **game mastery**, which, according to Pearce, "refers to the ways of moving within or among games for purposes not comprehended by the games themselves" (p. 84). "In conversation," he writes, "one person may attempt to initiate a sequence of events that will culminate in the other's spending money for a product; the other person may deliberately choose not to play that game by selecting another—for example, by analyzing the strategy of the first" (p. 85). Pearce points out that game playing might be effective when situations are clear and stable, but in situations of conflict, ambiguity, or moral decision making, game mastery might mean we'd want to break rules creatively, transcending them, in order to reach a newer and perhaps more helpful stability. This is not a matter of technical skill or simple communication competence; it is a matter of interpersonal theorizing, and of testing one's developing theory result by result. For CMM theorists, theory and practice are intricately connected—a point very carefully made in a recent extension of their theory to practical theorizing, specifically the process of facilitating large-scale community dialogue (Pearce & Pearce, 2000). CMM theorists are willing to go beyond campus experiments or paper-and-pencil studies to try out their ideas in the crucible of public life, as they have as consultants in Cupertino, California. (A description of the work of the Public Dialogue Consortium group, based largely on CMM principles, can be found in Pearce, 1998; Pearce & Pearce, 2000; Pearce & Littlejohn, 1997.)

Years before CMM theory was developed, Ruesch and Bateson (1968) asserted that "a social situation is established when people have entered into

REVIEWING KEY IDEAS

The CMM Approach to Rules:

- Assumes that people don't need the same basic understanding about their situation in order to coordinate their behavior through rules.
- Assumes that the social order is *heterogeneous*.
- Analyzes communication episodes by looking for *coherence, control,* and *valence.*
- Recognizes two types of rules: *constitutive* and *regulative.*
- Distinguishes between *game playing* and *game mastery.*
- Identifies a hierarchy of contexts extending from intrapersonal *content,* through *speech acts, contracts,* and *episodes,* to *life scripts.*

communication; the state of communication is determined by the fact that a person perceives that his perception has been noted by others" (p. 28). Clearly, social situations are held together by the coordination of rules: "Any social situation is governed by explicit or implicit rules; these rules may be created on the spur of the moment for a particular situation, or they may be the result of centuries of tradition. In the context of communication, rules can be viewed as devices which either stabilize or disrupt a given communication system, and they provide directives for all eventualities" (pp. 27–28). CMM research focuses on the immediate episodes in which rules are created and employed to manage meanings. However, it does not deny the existence of more persistent socially based rules.

Remember that Ruesch and Bateson's model was organized by the criterion of how many communicators were involved at each level. The CMM hierarchy of contexts emphasizes different factors, those that relate more to interpersonal meanings than to the number of people involved. Philipsen (1995) notes that although CMM theorists adapt their hierarchy differently for different publications and audiences, the levels can be summarized as: Level 1 (the *content* level of personal experience, such as perceptions or cognitions); Level 2 (the *speech act* level, such as whether an utterance counts as a question, a threat, or as another functional category); Level 3 (the *contract* level, the system of mutual understandings that characterize any specific interpersonal relationship); Level 4 (the *episode* level, which involves a series of speech acts that seems to participants to have an identifiable beginning and end); and Level 5 (the *life script* level, which involves how a person uses many episodes to create an identifiable style of managing meanings with others). Obviously, the higher context levels are in many ways more powerful in influencing how communicators choose to coordinate their communicative acts.

But we do coordinate them methodically, even when it's not very clear how we accomplish this. Another tradition of inquiry is primarily concerned with bringing these methods to the surface. Although it wouldn't be thought of as a comprehensive theory of rules by communication scholars, *ethnomethodology* is clearly important for how it enriches theorizing.

LINK

See Chapter 3 for Ruesch and Bateson's influential model of social contexts in communication.

Ethnomethodology

Sociologist Harold Garfinkel (1967) pioneered his own creative way of investigating communication rules, and it is important for theorists to note his contributions. He took a microscopic look at the common and ordinary ways in which people put their concepts of the world into action. Based on an experiential approach to symbolic interaction (Rogers, 1983), Garfinkel thought a particularly interesting research task would be to learn how people in everyday life, without realizing they're doing anything remarkable, make practical sense of their complex social experiences and translate that "common sense" into behaviors. He wasn't trying to develop some grand or elaborate theory, but his methods enrich our understanding of the human experience. **Ethnomethodology**, his label, which literally means "the people's methods," tries to uncover "the formal properties of commonplace, practical commonsense actions 'from within' actual settings, as ongoing accomplishments of those settings" (1967, p. viii).

The "folk communication" approaches of Garfinkel are sociological and communication examples of **phenomenology**, a branch of philosophy that seems intimidating and distant for many beginning students. In Garfinkel's kind of research, phenomenologists are those who "study situations in the everyday world from the viewpoint of the experiencing person. This experiential view helps phenomenologists understand people and human life so that they can work effectively with them" (Becker, 1992, p. 7). This brief definition does not capture the richness of phenomenological research, but it does clarify why many rules theorists believe that understanding communication involves studying real people's attempts to make everyday experience meaningful.

Garfinkel and other ethnomethodologists and phenomenologists who followed him (e.g., Sudnow, 1978) try to show that the most ordinary aspects of our daily lives are amazing accomplishments of coordination. Instead of using the "taken-for-granted" assumptions (Schutz, 1967) that most of us use, Garfinkel seems to ask, "What if we regard these acts as 'problematic'; that is, as a series of coordinated solutions to quite complex problems?" In this way, ethnomethodology studies the most mundane and trivial events (such as expressing agreement with others or walking into a room) in order to find their fundamental significance. Because many of these actions are so habitual or mundane that social communicators forget about them, Garfinkel's methods are designed to get people to unearth their buried and invisible assumptions about the acts. In one exercise, for instance, he asked students to engage their friends in ordinary conversations outside class, but with one important difference: "without indicating that what the experimenter [in this case, the student] was asking was in any way unusual, to insist that the person clarify the sense of his commonplace remarks" (1967, p. 42). Here's an excerpt from one case:

> *The victim waved his hand cheerily.*
>   *(S) How are you?*
>   *(E) How am I in regard to what? My health, my finances, my school work, my peace of mind, my . . . ?*
>   *(S) (Red in the face and suddenly out of control.) Look! I was just trying to be polite. Frankly, I don't give a damn how you are. (Garfinkel, 1967, p. 44)*

LINKS

❏ Note that Garfinkel's explanation attributes "accomplishments" to *settings*, rather than to the individual communicators within those settings. Again, we see the influence and theoretical importance of context, which was introduced in Chapter 3.

❏ You might want to review Mead's symbolic interactionist theory to see the extent to which Garfinkel's approach is indebted to it.

Only by interfering with normal rules and assumptions, Garfinkel argues, do we expose those rules for study. Otherwise, they simply blend into our cultural context as if they were unimportant. Garfinkel's research revealed what CMM researchers also found, that implicit rules prohibit taking literally the questions in some greetings, because to do so is to complicate interaction unnecessarily. The meaning of the interchange could not be inferred from the words alone; knowledge of the rules that manage everyday talk is also required. Although this may sound trivial, it's actually an extremely practical reminder to travelers in different cultures, for example, who carry their handy little phrase books or handheld computer translators and expect these tools to be enough to get them by.

Mitchell (1978) suggests that Garfinkel's ethnomethodology "would maintain that since no situation is completely covered by rules for 'communicative interchanges'…all members in all situations employ documentary methods for practical theorizing to ferret out and to communicate the sense of what is going on" (p. 153). Ordinary people in everyday situations, in other words, behave very much like social scientists. When it comes to communication, all of us are theorists, practitioners, and researchers—*at the same time.*

Dialectical Theory

Relational/interactional theory, interpersonal perception theory, and rules theory all set the stage for a group of theorists associated with the more recently articulated **dialectical theory** of personal relationships (Baxter, 1988, 1990; Baxter & Montgomery, 1996; Cissna, Cox, & Bochner, 1990; Rawlins, 1992). To conceive of communication as *dialectical* means that relationships result from the interplay of perceived opposite forces or contradictions, and from how relational partners negotiate these ever-changing processes. Clearly, this perspective builds on the work of theorists like the Palo Alto Group and R. D. Laing, so we needn't reintroduce their ideas here. At the same time, dialectical theorists focus on dialogic communication situations, using the ideas of theorists we'll consider in the next major section. What, though, can we understand about dialectical theory that both grounds other theories previously discussed and introduces theories that are based overtly on human dialogue?

Dialectical theory explains communicative behavior by avoiding several simplistic assumptions that many people tend to make about relationships. For example, at times communicators want to think that they can have a relationship that is fully open and disclosive ("I wish I had the kind of friendship where I could tell my deepest secrets to him, any time I wanted"). Or they'd like one with complete freedom ("I want a relationship with no strings attached"), or one with automatic feelings of safety ("I know I can always count on her to be there for me; I never have to doubt that"). Interestingly, some communicators want the freedom of total openness only sometimes; at other times, they expect to have their privacy respected. Many of us want to avoid being dependent on other people—until we need their help, of course, at which time dependence doesn't seem so bad.

However, these situations suggest only a handful of the many tensions of interpersonal life that concern dialectical theorists. To understand the nuances of communication, they argue, we should realize that relationships often develop

◄● LINKS

❏ See Chapter 10 for our discussion of *Taoist* philosophy, which holds that life's essential processes must be defined by referring to their opposites. Thus strength can't be known in isolation, but only by understanding and acknowledging weakness. Strength and weakness, though evidently contradictory terms, are mutually dependent because each depends on the other for its very existence. Taoists suggest that although such "oppositions" appear to be separate, they are essentially parts of the same process.

❏ In two recent books, Baxter and Montgomery (1996; Montgomery & Baxter, 1998) stress the importance of dialogue in explaining interactional dialectics. In addition to the dialogue section in this chapter, you might want to revisit the explanation of Bakhtin's *dialogism* in Chapter 4.

from people's negotiation of contradictory states, values, and desires. Baxter and Montgomery (1996) assume

> *that relationships are organized around the dynamic interplay of opposing tendencies as they are enacted in interaction.... The ongoing interplay between oppositional features is what enables a relationship to exist as a dynamic social entity. A healthy relationship is not one in which the interplay of opposites has been extinguished or resolved, because these opposing features are inherent in the very fabric of relating. Instead, a healthy relationship is one in which the parties manage to satisfy both oppositional demands, that is, relational well-being is marked by the capacity to achieve "both/and" status. (p. 6)*

What are some dialectical contradictions that mature communicators must reconcile in healthy relationships? In her work, Baxter (1988, 1990) suggests several primary ones: autonomy/connection, openness/closedness, and predictability/novelty. She studies how such seemingly oppositional pairs must be defined in terms of each other, and the extent to which they rely on each other in communication. For example, you probably value autonomy in the sense of being thought of as "your own person." But if you always define desirable behavior as "being your own person no matter what," you undercut the very notion of a relationship with another person. Partners in long-term marriages know that this process is more subtle than what's normally considered as "compromise." It is a negotiation of a constantly shifting balance—unique for each couple—between autonomy (as self-regulation) and connection (as system adjustment). Not all scholars in this area claim theory status for their work. However, dialectical theory has carved its own distinct niche in the realm of interpersonal concepts and theories.

Dialogic Theory

So-called commonsense notions of communication tempt people to concentrate on the individual's psychological perspective, as we've noted earlier. But if relational and dialectical theorists are on the right track, and if symbolic interactionist concepts are accepted, a person does not and cannot develop an identity except through communication with other social beings. Now, consider another group of theorists who claim "the fundamental fact of human existence is neither the individual as such nor the aggregate as such" (Buber, 1965a, pp. 202–203). Fundamental human reality, to theorists of **dialogue**, can be observed only during those occasions when people meet each other (Anderson, Cissna, & Arnett, 1994). The work of theorists Martin Buber, Carl Rogers, and Hans-Georg Gadamer represents this line of research (see Reviewing Key Ideas, p. 165).

Dialogic Meeting and a Philosophical Anthropology

Identity, language, and communication reside in what famed philosopher and theologian Martin Buber (1965a) calls *the between*—the region of human existence that links self and others. It is not possessed by individuals, although we sometimes speak as if individuals "have" selves, as if an identity or a self-concept could be possessed in a psychological, inner sense. Selves and relationships emerge from "between" people, Buber thought, not from within them. To Buber (1957, 1958, 1965a, 1965b), life is not at all a matter of inner experience but, rather, can be lived authentically only through meeting others.

In a wide-ranging series of books on religion, philosophy, literature, theater, and culture (1957, 1958, 1965a, 1965b), Buber developed his **philosophical anthropology**. By this he meant that he wanted to uncover the potentialities of human existence by investigating culture and human nature as if he were encountering them fresh. Although we will meet Buber again in Chapter 10's discussion of ethical perspectives, we'll introduce the foundation of his philosophy here. Buber's ideas are increasingly practical, we believe, in a world of cultural conflict. To Buber, not only is dialogue attainable but it can become a concrete presence in daily life.

Buber's (1958) most famous insight is his distinction between the basic human attitudes of *I-Thou* and *I-It*. He describes the **I-Thou** attitude (or, as some scholars believe to be a more accurate translation, the "I-You" attitude) as one that invites and allows dialogue; in it, the person sees and responds to the other as the unique person that he or she is, not as a representative figure, a stereotype, or an extension of one's own personality. In contrast, the **I-It** attitude assumes others can be treated as objects, as things that can be concisely described, measured, manipulated, and accounted for. With the I-It frame of reference, a communicator might easily justify generalizing another person into a stereotypical category or assuming the other is a predictable representative of a category. Buber does not criticize the existence of I-It relations in human life, because so many daily relationships necessarily involve surface contact with others, and in fact, the object world is important to human existence. However, he does show that an I-It orientation can preclude "genuine dialogue" when it dominates a relationship, or a person's outlook on the world.

By **genuine dialogue**, Buber (1965a) means "spoken or silent" communication "where each of the participants really has in mind the other or others in their present and particular being and turns to them with the intention of establishing a living mutual relation between himself and them" (p. 19). This contrasts with two other conditions: **technical dialogue**, which appears to have a give-and-take quality but is actually designed only to achieve a specified end through objective communication, and **monologue**, which describes a dominant voice divorced from the expectation of response. Genuine dialogue provides the important human experience of confirmation, in which we perceive that we are really uniquely valuable in the eyes and experience of others. Persistent messages of *disconfirmation,* like being objectified or ignored, on the other hand, can disable people both socially and psychologically, making us wonder whether we make any difference at all.

Critics (e.g., see the discussion in Glatzer, 1966) sometimes portray Buber as a mystic whose philosophy is practical only for people who already agree with each other or already share the same humanistic principles of dialogue, respect, and authenticity—but that it is impractical for communicators who disagree vehemently. Yet Buber (1965a) meant his ideas to apply, if anything, *more* to what he called "the conversation with the opponent" in a concrete encounter; the basis of that conversation is not the "demand" but the persistent refusal to withhold one's self from the dialogue (pp. 34 ff.). Buber believed that our habit of with-holding ourselves from response precludes genuine communication in our time.

The Person-Centered Approach

One professional communicator who tried to make dialogue practical in a variety of contexts is psychotherapist Carl Rogers (1959, 1961, 1980). For students inter-ested in studying the professional implications of dialogic philosophy, Rogers's work is an interesting place to begin. Throughout the world, Rogers is regarded as one of the most influential psychologists of the twentieth century. Although his later writings are very much influenced by Buber's dialogic insights, Rogers's early works also illustrate many dialogic principles. In essence, Rogers suggests that individuals are not automatically "persons" but that, instead, they become persons through their contacts with others. Or, in other words, "persons" are fluid processes shaped through interaction with other persons.

Although some critics accuse Rogers of advocating individualistic selfishness (Geller, 1982; Schultz, 1977), he was a serious researcher who tried to theorize dialogic human interaction in face-to-face settings. He derived his theoretical principles primarily from his counseling practice and his practical experience in facilitating groups, often in settings of intercultural conflict.

Rogers hoped to build a formal theory (1959), but he also believed that while we are engaged in meeting others, we need to be *atheoretical*. By this he meant that we should build and use theories to help us understand our relationships, but that we should not conform slavishly to principles, skills, and concepts *while we're with other people*. Theory, ironically, can deflect us from the immediacy of face-to-face communication. To the extent that Rogers consciously tried to prac-tice so-called Rogerian principles in therapeutic talk, he found that communica-tion was doomed to be of low quality. Instead, his theory of effective therapy emerged from analyzing countless hours of recorded sessions of himself and other counselors and therapists interacting spontaneously with clients who had diverse problems. To Rogers, the conditions of effective communication in ther-apy are more broadly applicable to nontherapeutic interpersonal communication. Therefore he altered the designation for his overall perspective from *client-centered therapy* (a term still in wide use) to the more inclusive **person-centered approach** (Bozarth & Brodley, 1986; Levant & Shlien, 1984).

Beyond recognizing the need for social contact in the way we discussed ear-lier (1959, p. 207), Rogers's theory identifies three essential conditions that can "free" interaction to become effective dialogue: *congruence, positive regard,* and *empathy*.

Rogers (1959) found that communicators more easily facilitate understanding if they can achieve **congruence**—or a matching of their inner experience (to the extent that individuals are aware of it) with their outer behavior. That is, if a teacher is bored with a particular topic but attempts to hide that feeling (pro-ducing incongruence), the quality of classroom communication will probably suf-fer as the students notice the verbal and nonverbal dissonance experienced by the teacher. Although some humanistic psychologists are said to advocate an "expressivist" perspective by stressing the advantages of self-disclosure (Hart & Burks, 1972), a close reading of Rogers's work on congruence suggests that he favors disclosure that is relevant, is appropriately timed, and fits the roles and contexts in which communicators find themselves (Cissna & Anderson, 1990, pp. 134–135).

The condition of **positive regard** is variously called "acceptance," "regard," "respect," and, consistent with Buber's work, "confirmation." Rogers (1959) notes that when communicators do not attach conditions to their acceptance of others, their relationships produce more effective understanding. The positive regard in Rogers's system attaches to the person, not necessarily to the person's behavior. This is an important point to remember, because many reactions to Rogers's label have focused on such questions as "How can I have positive regard for a neighbor who has cheated me out of my property rights? Or for someone who beats people up?" You do not need to like the other person in order to regard his or her personhood and human potential positively. To disqualify someone automatically for something he or she has done (or someone he or she is assumed to be) is to create a gulf across which understanding is unlikely to develop. A research tradition within interpersonal communication, *confirmation theory,* probes such concepts as Rogers's *positive regard,* Buber's *confirmation,* and Laing's *metaperspectives* (Cissna & Sieburg, 1981).

Empathy has a long and varied history in the disciplines of communication, psychology, and philosophy (Katz, 1963). Some scholars identify it with a mode of knowledge in which a person mystically transports his or her perception into the mind of another in order to "know" the other's subjective feelings. But Rogers (1959) is not among them. From his theoretical stance, **empathy** means "to perceive the internal frame of reference of another with accuracy and with the emotional components and meanings which pertain thereto as if one were the person, but without ever losing the 'as if' condition. Thus it means to sense the hurt or the pleasure of another as he senses it and to perceive the causes thereof as he perceives them, but without ever losing the recognition that it is *as if* I were hurt or pleased and so forth" (pp. 210–211; emphasis added). The implications for practical interpersonal communication are inescapable. Can one person, then, ever truly say, "I know exactly what you're going through after your father's death. My father died last year, too"? Rogers's definition of empathy suggests that you can't know another's experience with certainty because the other person couldn't have had exactly the same relationship with a parent that you had with yours. Empathy, therefore, is basically a process of imagining tentative clues, not one of gaining precise knowledge. Further, attempts at empathy serve as positive relational messages, because they advertise our willingness to grant full credence to another's uniquely different experience. This advantage is lost, of course, if you consider empathy to be a full identification with the exact feelings and thoughts of the other person.

Rogers developed his theory of interpersonal dialogue from years of personal experience in his own therapeutic practice. He uses that practical data to refine the theory. His work demonstrates a merging of the concerns of theory and practice into what has been called a **praxis**—or the conception of theory as practical, and of practice as theoretically informed (Cissna & Anderson, 1990; Williams, 1976, p. 268). Theory and practice are not opposites in Rogers's system; the two converge in a praxis of communication.

How do you think *empathy* is similar to, different from, or dependent on the mental adjustment of *decentering,* as described in Chapter 4?

Hermeneutics and Productive Communication

Many interpersonal theories focus primarily on the relationship between communicators, and thus they tend to downplay the mechanics of the message-interchange process. However, some communication analysts, as we've seen, are more concerned with communication as a mechanistic process. They implicitly assume that a major function of communication is to convey information accurately from one person to another.

Good communication in this conduit-like view consists of a message that is "encoded" for an identifiable purpose by a speaker and then received (accurately, adequately, or appropriately) by a listener. In many instances, such a view adequately identifies problems in communication that might need repair or additional attention. However, scholars don't assume that this is the most reasonable way to conceptualize the process. Seeing communication as interdependence, in fact, suggests that the misunderstandings might be as important as accurate understanding in the long run.

Hermeneutics, a perspective borrowed from philosophy and, originally, from theology, studies how interpretations are developed out of people's encounters with written and oral "texts." It has produced an alternative communication theory of meaning, as Deetz (1982) describes:

> *Most researchers have assumed a* representational view *of understanding. The listener is assumed to have understood when s/he can recreate what the speaker meant. The desire to avoid misunderstanding is central in this view. Modern hermeneutics demonstrates the possibility of a more* productive *view. The interest here in interpersonal interaction is with the development and unfolding of meaning which is not yet available to either interactant, rather than in a comparison of the speaker's psychological intentions with those of the listener. The nature of dialogue is to open that which is out of reach and beyond comprehension. (p. 8; emphasis added)*

Deetz's last sentence is especially helpful. When dialogue develops, the consequences are essentially spontaneous and unanticipated. The interpretations emerge from the moment of interpretation itself, and not from prior intentions of the speakers or from any special capacity of language to carry meaning. Thus, for the hermeneutical theorist, the real value of communication lies in how it uses all the resources of human experience (including misunderstanding and prejudice) to produce meaning creatively, meaning that was not present before the communication occurred. This is why Deetz argues for a view that is not merely *reproductive* (reproducing another's meaning) but for one that emphasizes **productive meaning**—that is, he wants a perspective that assumes effective communication is "for" producing fresh and new meaning more than it is "for" transferring old meanings from person to person or place to place.

One of the most influential representatives of the hermeneutical approach to communication is contemporary German philosopher Hans-Georg Gadamer (1982; Warnke, 1987). "Reaching an understanding in conversation," Gadamer (1982) writes, "presupposes that both partners are ready for it and are trying to recognise the full value of what is alien and opposed to them. If this happens mutually, and each of the partners, while simultaneously holding on to his own arguments, weighs the counterarguments, it is finally possible to achieve an imperceptible but not arbitrary reciprocal translation of the other's position (we call this an exchange of views), a common language and a common statement" (p. 348). When Gadamer mentions "the full realization of conversation," he means that something has been expressed "that is not only mine or my author's, but common" (p. 350).

Although Gadamer's concern with dialogue and his respect for the other's position echo in some ways Buber's philosophy and Rogers's concern with empathy, it would be misleading to suggest that this is all he is saying. He stresses genuine questioning. Out of every dialogic encounter, Gadamer maintains, some new understanding develops, and *should* develop. The new understanding happens through the text (message), however fixed it might seem, "questioning" the interpreter while the interpreter questions the text. To Gadamer, questions are genuine and dialogue is possible *only when the answers are not already known* (such as when a young student asks about a teacher's feelings about the Vietnam War, or when a lost traveler asks directions of a native resident). The opposite of dialogue, which in this sense is similar to Buber's view, is an argument in which both parties become so entrenched in their positions that their only questions to the other are ones designed to disclose flaws in the opposing argument. We can see this anti-dialogue clearly at work in the American judicial system. Attorneys are taught in law school never to ask a question of a witness to which they do not already know the answer. The last thing a trial attorney wants in most cases is a surprise disclosure from a cross-examined witness.

Gadamer (1982) offers communication students some surprising challenges. Students learn from some textbooks that "meanings are in people, not in words," and that "language is a system of signs that are used arbitrarily to refer to things." But Gadamer asserts that people do not use language to accomplish their ends; it would make as much sense to think of language using people to achieve its ends. Language is a living historical presence from which human beings could not escape even if they wanted to. If language were only a set of tools, Gadamer claims, people could choose to use or not to use it. Instead, people have no such choice, having been born into a preexisting linguistic world. The meanings available to

---

REVIEWING KEY IDEAS

DIALOGIC THEORY

- Buber's *philosophical anthropology* emphasizes *the between* and *I-Thou* relations.
- Rogers's *person-centered approach* emphasizes *congruence, positive regard,* and *empathy*.
- Gadamer's *hermeneutics* emphasizes *productive meaning, genuine questioning,* and *linguisticality*.

⬅️ LINK

Note how Gadamer's *linguisticality* assumes that all language is an integral part of our cultural context. It's not just a way of "in-forming" personal cognitive experience, as discussed in Chapter 4, but more broadly forms the fundamentally human aspects of all experience. Far from being merely our "tool," language to Gadamer is in some sense the basic source of our humanness. Indeed, in some religious traditions "the Word" and "God" are inextricably linked.

language are the ways available to people to live in the world. According to Gadamer, then, people don't have experiences first, then decide how to express them. Instead, the experiences themselves are already influenced by the language into which we're born. He challenges students of language to assume that in a very real sense words do have meanings independent of any one person's use of them. Language has a historical quality of "ongoingness" and *human beings belong to language.* Gadamer calls this phenomenon **linguisticality**.

The concept of linguisticality suggests interesting implications when we consider communicative interdependence. Earlier in this chapter we stressed that communicators are not autonomous but are fundamentally interdependent with other communicators. Gadamer extends this concept significantly. Communicators, because of their necessary immersion in language and particular historical contexts, are also interdependent with language itself. In other words, we are shaped by language, just as we help to shape language for future generations.

Dramaturgical Theory

The Theatrical Metaphor

Think back to the last time you attended a play. Sitting in the theater, you probably understood that you were watching a performance of a written text that had been presented many times before by different actors, directors, and technicians. Intellectually, you understood that the actors' comments and conversations, however spontaneous they sounded, were in fact a kind of illusion of immediate reality. In one sense, the actors' lines were said in the immediate moment, but the words were not spontaneous, nor were the actors free to be "themselves." The analytical side of your mind led you to this conclusion. Yet when the theatrical experience works, the illusion becomes its own reality and the boundaries between what is scripted and what is immediate blur. You experience what is true, and that drama is immediate and, in its own way, real.

Communication scholars who like the theatrical metaphor don't suggest that society is a completely predetermined presentation in which people simply mouth someone else's scripts. Instead, **dramaturgical theory** explores how spontaneous social action relies on the same bases as theatrical performance. In interaction, social actors try to (1) coordinate their behaviors convincingly, in order to (2) give audiences the impression that reality is present within the boundaries of the interaction. In this regard, the concept of *role* is central. Our roles are composed of the behavioral expectations that people associate with who we are and what positions we enact.

Sociologist Elizabeth Burns (1972) concludes that the theatrical metaphor may be more practical than people assume, especially in diagnosing communication effects:

> *In ordinary life each person is engaged in a constant endeavour to mark out his own role, his setting, his course of action and to distinguish between those who are to be fellow actors and those who are to be spectators.... In their most highly valued relationships and preoccupations people like to think of themselves as free of all the attributes of an actor. It*

is, however, possible to preserve the necessary sense of authenticity if "the-atricality" is seen not as a mode of behaviour but as a mode of recogni-tion. It belongs to the critical, judging, assessing "I" that stands aside from the self— as conscience or "ego." But its function is enriched by theatrical awareness and theatrical insights that take into account the self as a social being. (p. 232)

Dramaturgical theory, therefore, is useful as a metaphor to help us understand how we coordinate our lives. Just as actors on a stage cannot create their lines and lives autonomously without creating problems for their fellow actors, so we in everyday life sacrifice personal control over our "lines" in order to produce a convincing ensemble performance. The roles must be meshed.

Following Shakespeare ("All the world's a stage"), some communication the-orists have extended the theatrical metaphor. In this section we consider the con-tributions of three scholars: Kenneth Burke, Erving Goffman, and Ernest Bormann (see Reviewing Key Ideas, p. 174).

The New Rhetoric of Identification

The twentieth century knew only a few Renaissance individuals whose knowl-edge and understanding cut across almost all traditional disciplinary boundaries in the human sciences. Kenneth Burke is one of them. Is he a literary critic or a sociologist? A psychologist or a communication theorist? A poet or a historian? He is all of these.

Several of Burke's many contributions have deeply influenced rhetorical and communication theorists. One is his distinction between what he calls the old way of studying rhetoric and an emerging new rhetoric. The **old rhetoric** was based on persuasion, the ability to affect others' attitudes and behaviors through "deliberate design" (Burke, 1967, p. 63). But with the advent of such disciplines as anthropology, psychology, and sociology, investigators came to realize, Burke claims, that a better way to approach rhetoric is through identification. **Identifi-cation** provided theorists with the basis for a **new rhetoric**. In it, the object of communication is not to change another's attitude but to set up the conditions under which individuals can find commonality with each other's experience. This too can be deliberately designed, yet it goes much further in accounting for people's unconscious and transcendent motives in their symbolic environments.

For example, controversial advertisements for Benetton, a worldwide corpo-ration that markets clothing, have at times shown no clothing products whatso-ever and have included no verbal inducements to buy clothing. Instead, several campaigns focused on a controversial and colorful series of visual images called "United Colors of Benetton." While a few ads include surprisingly direct sexual images (of multicolored condoms, of a nun and a priest kissing) that have shocked some people, or, most recently, an equally shocking collection of photos of death-row inmates, most of the ads simply feature people of different races and backgrounds juxtaposed graphically. Communication across differences is therefore foregrounded. The *old rhetoric,* a rhetoric of telling, would have given us reasons to buy the clothes. The *new rhetoric* provides no such reasons, and might even attempt the opposite by being unreasoning and arational. Instead of

LINK

Chapter 8, which describes other theories of rhetoric and attitude change, will define *persuasion* in greater detail.

telling us about the clothing that's for sale, the rhetoric aims to create, encourage, or show an identification with the company itself. In this way, the ad campaign functions more like a theatrical production. Arthur Miller's *Death of a Salesman,* for example, doesn't tell us what to believe and change about modern society. Instead, the play shows society's effects on a man and a family, and trusts our identification with the acts, agents, scenes, agencies, and purposes of the theater.

Burke (1969) developed these major notions of dramatic identification to explain essential elements in human communication outside of strictly theatrical events. He refers to them collectively as the **dramatistic pentad:**

> **Act**—the behaviors; what is accomplished. (What happened?)
>
> **Agent**—the person(s) performing dramatically. (Who initiated the action?)
>
> **Scene**—the situation in which the action occurs. (Where and when did it happen?)
>
> **Agency**—the means used by the agent(s) to accomplish communicative goals. (How did it happen?)
>
> **Purpose**—the motivating reason behind the rhetoric. (Why did it develop as it did?)

These five elements help to explain how we identify, or fail to identify, with each other in social situations.

The first and most crucial concept for Burke is the act. *To act* implies that we make a specific choice to behave in a certain way. An act is based on the symbolic capacity of human beings, which grants us this freedom to choose. **Action**, to Burke (1969), can be distinguished from **motion:** Action is behavior that flows from choices we make about how we want to act, but motion is behavior or changes caused by external forces. Guitarists act (or choose a direction for their communicative behavior), but the strings can't act; they must wait to be put into motion. This distinction seems obvious and even trivial until you consider the number of times you've heard someone claim, "She made me angry" or "His insult forced me to retaliate." These conclusions are not true in a literal sense, but they can objectify human experience unnecessarily and perhaps justify the manipulation of others.

The elements of Burke's pentad are interactive; they cannot be isolated conceptually from each other, as if they operated separately. Therefore Burke suggests that analysts of rhetoric look for consistencies and inconsistencies among the elements of the pentad. For example, are there times during which the behavior of a dramatic performance (act) is inconsistent with the setting (scene) in which it occurs? You might ironically call a close friend by the nickname "Killer" because you know that he has a gentle disposition, but an introduction of this same man in a professional setting would more appropriately include his real name and perhaps even a formal title. Nothing is inherently wrong with either the official or the informal name. It's the potential combination of a name and a situation that could seem "wrong." Burke calls this kind of analysis the consideration of **ratios**—analyzing how two of the elements of the pentad link up or interact. He suggests that we look to such interactions as an *act–scene ratio* (as in the example of when to use nicknames) or *agent–scene ratio* problems involving "who you are, where you are" (such as when you forget that you were supposed to represent the student-based radio station today to a potential client who might place advertising, and you show up in your jeans, ball cap, and T-shirt).

Impression Management

Beginning in the 1950s, Erving Goffman observed and analyzed how ordinary people use complex strategies to achieve their conversational goals. Through an impressive series of works (1959, 1974, 1981), he has charted how we accomplish interpersonal goal attainment through how we present ourselves dramatically to others, developing an overall approach he calls **impression management**. His most influential book was his first, *The Presentation of Self in Everyday Life* (1959), in which he develops elaborate metaphors from the theater and supports them with a multitude of examples from daily living.

Goffman believes that people engage in **role enactment**. Have you ever accused someone of being phony or of pretending to be someone he or she is not? Certainly that person may have been a deceiver. But Goffman uses a series of role-oriented questions about communication to show that we are all phony in some ways, that we all play inauthentic roles to some extent, and that we are by nature inclined to pretend at times in our communication with others. Sometimes what seems like pretending is simply a process of playing out our identities. Another communication theorist within sociology describes Goffman's views in this way: "People are not, originally and in some factlike way, 'mothers,' 'surgeons,' or 'crazy.' Instead, they are cast into these roles by themselves and by others. Moreover, the actor always retains the possibility of a certain distance from the role" (Brown, 1977, p. 199). There are different ways that mothers can raise children and different ways that surgeons can perform operations. But with too much divergence or distance from the role, people risk being socially redefined in ways they don't like: "My education professor isn't really a teacher—he's more of a baby-sitter in class."

In Goffman's world, human beings almost always behave strategically with each other, although much of this strategy results from role enactment at very subtle levels. For example, although you might believe you are simply asking a question of your department manager, to Goffman you are engaged in **face work**, or maintaining an appropriate image or impression. Although you believe you are simply stopping your commentary briefly in order to change the topic, Goffman would say that by sustaining that otherwise silent moment with an "Ummm…" you are actually maintaining the **floor**, or your socially sanctioned permission to speak to others. And though some critics suggest that Goffman believes human existence is little more than a con job we pull off on each other, his unique contribution is to spotlight the intricate importance of the mundane. Often the larger significance of human life is best seen in the seemingly trivial patterns of small talk.

Goffman's view of human nature is very direct and role-related: Our symbolic capacity blurs the line between "real" and "deceptive" behaviors. How can we tell who is genuine and who is phony in a world where people can behave in almost completely different ways at work and at home? As Cuzzort and King (1989) note,

"…Goffman probes deeply enough to make us see that what we consider a 'real' performance has elements identical to those involved in the phony performance. This requires us to think in new ways about the essential nature of humanity" (p. 284).

Although *role enactment* is a central concept to Goffman, several other concepts are also important aspects of his approach to impression management: *personal front; expressions "given" and "given off"; footing; regions; teamwork;* and *frame.*

- **Personal front:** Goffman observes that we attempt to foster particular impressions we want others to have of us. When we act in strategic ways to encourage these impressions, we are said to be maintaining a *personal front.* We do this through some relatively fixed biological factors, as well as through more immediate tactical expressions, including "insignia of office or rank; clothing; sex, age, and racial characteristics; size and looks; posture; speech patterns; facial expressions; bodily gestures; and the like" (Goffman, 1959, p. 34).

- **Expressions given** and **expressions given off:** We can distinguish between those impressions we intend (those *"given"*) and those over which we're not in control and which our audience builds as a result of its interpretations of unintended cues (those *"given off"*) (Goffman, 1959). Normally, the cues "given" (you wear a suit for a job interview) are considered to be part of your personal front, and those "given off" (your voice quavers in the interview) might be analyzed as unintended deviations or slips from your strategic front.

- **Footing:** When two communicators seem to interact on the basis of different statuses or different assumptions about who has power, they are said to have different *footing* (Goffman, 1981). It's an interesting metaphor, suggesting a more solid conversational ground for some interactants than for others. That is, some people's roles in a given situation (e.g., parent, teacher, or minister) grant them a freedom to speak and act that distinguishes them from others. Chances are, your doctor calls you by your first name, whatever your age or status. But do you say "Thanks, Melvin" or "See you next week, Marcella" when you leave the doctor's office? The difference is in the subtle operation of footing.

- **Regions:** Goffman notes in his studies that people behave differently not only in terms of who they are with but also as a result of where they are. Generally, these two factors are merged: When someone is "on" in a *front region,* the audience for a personal front sees a relatively official performance designed for it; in a *back region,* or backstage, the front is dropped in favor of less guarded behavior. The American fascination for understanding this distinction can be seen in the desire to know what Britney Spears, Michael Jackson, or Tom Waits is "really" like. (Some broadcast profiles of political candidates appear to take viewers behind the scenes on a campaign bus or in meetings with local workers, but Goffman might be suspicious of how "backstage" a performer's behavior really is when a camcorder is present.)

- **Teamwork:** Goffman (1959) finds that people often depend on team cooperation, on each other, to present a coherent social performance. But this dependence does not always result from friendships or open collusion. In a small-group discussion among the members of a committee, for example, Connie may notice that Marsha persistently wants every member's opinion before ending a discussion. Thus Connie remains silent until she is asked specifically about her opinion. She therefore gains the floor in an uninterrupted and special way—and with greater impact—than would have been possible had she volunteered her ideas earlier in the discussion. Connie and Marsha have cooperated in a teamlike way to define a situation.

- **Frame:** Goffman (1974), as well as other symbolic interactionists (McHugh, 1968) and linguists (Tannen, 1989, 1990), examines how communicators define their situation(s). A *frame* is a definition or an interpretation of what a situation means, and *framing,* therefore, is the act of asserting such a definition. For example, do you always know when you're having an argument? If we were to present a transcript of a husband and wife talking about their budget for the coming year and ask you for a description of what the two people were doing, you might respond that they are "arguing," while others might say that they are "planning," "analyzing," "discussing," or "criticizing each other's spending habits"—or they might offer a variety of other attributions. But, emotionally, there is a significant difference between planning and arguing. These two different definitions could have drastically different consequences for the couple conversing as well. If the husband (or wife) frames the conversation as a planning session, he (or she) will be ready primarily to discuss in analytical terms the overdrafts and spending habits of the family. If the wife (or husband), on the other hand, frames the discussion as an argument with a series of criticisms being traded, emotional defensiveness is more likely.

Goffman's work, as highly specific and idiosyncratic as it sometimes is, has influenced a wide variety of scholars in conversation and discourse analysis (Nofsinger, 1991; Stubbs, 1983), in symbolic public leadership (Klapp, 1969), and in media communication theory (Meyrowitz, 1985). When Goffman assumes that we play roles as if we were performing for others, he does not see this as negating our humanity. Instead, his brand of symbolic interactionism locates humanity precisely in our ability to be flexible in roles and to adjust our behaviors in order to take others into account.

Symbolic Convergence

Building on the foundation established by symbolic interactionists, Ernest Bormann's (1972, 1983, 1989) **symbolic convergence theory** is based on his earlier analysis of rhetorical "fantasies." Bormann (1989) suggests that the "central focus of the symbolic convergence perspective is upon the communicative processes by which human beings converge their individual fantasies, dreams, and meanings into shared symbol systems" (pp. 188–189). Bormann also assumes that communication can only be understood by transcending the individual as a unit of analysis. He is primarily interested in how people communicating together develop shared stories that give meaning to individual experiences so that those experiences "converge" into something larger and more coherent than isolated feelings, thoughts, or explanations. People dramatize their interpretations of individual meanings in terms of group symbols—thus he arrives at the term *symbolic convergence,* claiming his is "a general theory built from social scientific and rhetorical studies of communication," one that "places the audience in the center of its communication paradigm" (Bormann, Knutson, & Musolf, 1997, p. 255). Bormann uses a number of specialized concepts in developing his theory: *dramatizing message, fantasy theme, fantasy type, chaining, script,* and *rhetorical vision:*

- **Dramatizing message:** The "central focus" of the theory is on how drama is built, constructed, and shared among audiences after communicators initiate involving and persuasive messages. "In all communication contexts where the source produces dramatic messages," write three symbolic convergence theorists, "the audience members may, under certain conditions, become involved in the dramatic action" (Bormann, Knutson, & Musolf, 1997, pp. 254–255). The *dramatizing message* has certain rich linguistic characteristics, they say, and often relies on such elements as "puns, word play, double entendres, figures of speech, analogies, anecdotes, allegories, parables, fables, jokes, gags, jests, quips, stories, tales, yarns, legends, and narratives" (p. 255).
- **Fantasy theme:** *Fantasy themes* are those topics that groups and communities construct as shared explanations for their communication. The focus of a fantasy theme is not so much the here and now as the remembered (and concocted) past and an imagined future. As Bormann (1989) explains:

> *Fantasy theme analysis studies the way communicators discuss fictitious and nonfictitious events in the past or in the future or at some other place than the here-and-now of the immediate communication episode. The ongoing flow of experience may seem chaotic or confusing; immediate behavior may seem impulsive; occurrences may seem accidental. The speaker who recounts such experiences (after the fact) places the events into narrative form and provides an explanatory structure for them. The narrative form implies or attributes motivations to the personae and may provide an explanation based on lawfulness or the will of a supreme being rather than on chance or accident. The same is true of an account set in the future. The group may come to share a dream of what they want to achieve in the future by means of dramatic portrayals of characters in that future scene. Such dreams of the future are also structured interpretations of events. (p. 190)*

Therefore fantasy themes are the ways in which groups order their experience by talking about it. One year baseball's Pittsburgh Pirates adopted the slogan and song "We Are Family" to create a different rhetorical tone for the season. A basketball team that considers itself a "team of destiny" and another team that considers itself "snake-bit" are each in the process of developing a group fantasy. Bear in mind that, to Bormann, the term *fantasy* does not have a negative connotation. It simply refers to a consistent organizing explanation that arises from the group's own talk and in which the group believes.

- **Fantasy type:** People in a group with fantasy themes often interact with others to extract common substory meanings from those larger narratives. This phenomenon is the creation of *fantasy types*. Thus the Old West in the United States includes the fantasy types of "mountain man," "homesteader," "outlaw," and "noble savage," among others. Klapp's (1962) analysis of dramatic types in sociology—heroes, villains, and fools—draws from a similar source.

- **Chaining:** When a group forms a fantasy that guides it dramatically in its relation to other groups, that fantasy becomes a basis for the talk of the group. When symbolic convergence theorists discuss "chaining out" fantasies, or the process of fantasy "chains," they are referring to the actual conversational dynamics involved in extending the fantasies. One element of a group's collective dramatic narrative is built upon a previous contribution, then that one stimulates another, and so on. Enthusiasm (or discouragement) may build as different comments link together to shape the story. Fantasies do not emerge spontaneously; rather, their implications are constructed and construed through communication itself.

- **Script:** Bormann's theory is more content-oriented than other dramatistic accounts, such as Goffman's. In the symbolic convergence process, the content that comes to be accepted and not debated is referred to as *script*. Individual scripts may be acted out in role-like behaviors, or group scripts may illustrate the status of a developing collective consciousness.

- **Rhetorical vision:** "When sufficient fantasies have been shared," Bormann (1983) claims, "and the members develop enough fantasy types they may begin to shape them into a unified symbolic system which portrays a broad and consistent view of much or a portion of their social and material reality. The result is a rhetorical vision" (p. 75). Such a broad-based narrative is what guides the American Dream, the New World Order, and many other ideologies. Religious denominations also develop their own rhetorical visions. Other researchers have extended Bormann's central ideas to attempt to categorize different types of rhetorical visions. Cragan and Shields (1981), for example, discovered that three general categories of rhetorical vision predominated in Western culture, obviously with many exceptions, crossovers, and idiosyncrasies. The *pragmatic rhetorical vision* is developed out of the shared fantasies of people who emphasize, as you might guess, practical and efficient decision making in the pursuit of goals. These people tend to appreciate traditional scientific reasoning, and continue to seek clear distinctions and definitions. The *social rhetorical vision* emphasizes a more cooperative interpersonal worldview, one in which human cohesiveness plays a predominant role. According to this vision, people and groups are especially responsive to attempts to manage conflict in terms of ethics and social justice. Finally, groups that share a *righteous rhetorical vision* are those who make decisions with reference to a single issue or commitment that is particularly crucial, correct, or compelling (for them), such as the survivalist movements or Greenpeace.

However, it would be a mistake to assume that a rhetorical vision always regulates individual behavior. It doesn't—Catholics might still obtain abortions, and Zen Buddhists might succumb to materialistic longing. What a rhetorical vision accomplishes, however, is to give meaning to individual behavior and symbolically integrate individuals into a larger community consciousness. A valuable function is served even when a rhetorical vision does not drive all the actions of the group members. Bormann's explanation of a complex and often ephemeral process is a unique contribution to communication theory.

REVIEWING KEY THEORIES

Because interpersonal communication is often seen as a defining context for all communication, theorists have been especially active in establishing different theoretical approaches in this area, using both quantitative and qualitative research methods.

We surveyed three theories that try to account for what people need as communicators. *Social exchange theorists* stress an economic analogy to explain how people desire communication "profit." *American pragmatist philosophy* stresses the basic need for social contact, combined with the need to assess consequences in order to attribute basic meaning to our actions. *FIRO theory* elevates the three criteria of inclusion, control, and affection to describe how we judge our relationships.

A major project started in the 1960s, the Palo Alto Group's *relational/interactional theory,* remains influential in combining systems theory with research into toxic family communication patterns. This research produced five "axioms" of, and reminders about, communication that the authors claim will apply to any face-to-face situation. R. D. Laing's *interpersonal perception theory* was in many ways closely aligned to the Palo Alto project.

REVIEWING KEY IDEAS

DRAMATURGICAL THEORY

- Burke's *new rhetoric* emphasizes identification over persuasion, and relies on the explanatory device of the dramatistic pentad.
- Goffman's *impression management approach* emphasizes role enactment.
- Bormann's *symbolic convergence theory* emphasizes the analysis of how dramatizing messages can lead to fantasy themes, and how they form larger rhetorical visions.

Rules theory was a major advance for the discipline of communication in its attempt to make concepts context-specific as well as broadly applicable. In some ways it was a reaction to the emphasis of earlier theorists on identifying covering laws, but both rules and covering law explanations are valuable in helping us to understand how social life develops. We discussed one exemplary rules explanation in this section, the influential *coordinated management of meaning theory,* and an interesting research method with theoretical implications, *ethnomethodology.*

Dialectical theory, which describes how our relationships are negotiations of seemingly opposite tendencies, serves as a bridge linking relational/interactional and rules theories with dialogic theories. You then read about three distinctive types of interpersonal *dialogic theory:* Buber's *philosophical anthropology,* Rogers's *person-centered approach,* and Gadamer's *hermeneutics.* All stress how communicators need to remain open to surprise and must fully recognize the uniqueness of other communicators, among other dialogic characteristics.

The *dramaturgical* family of theories concludes the chapter. In this view, human communication is compared to theatrical and dramatic presentations, in that we naturally respond to the stories and roles of others' lives. Burke explains this concept by stressing the *new rhetoric of identification,* in which the goal of talk is not to persuade directly but to increase identification of audiences with speakers and writers. Goffman's sociological concern with roles and realistic power relations led to his *impression management theory.* Finally, Bormann's *symbolic convergence theory* attempts to analyze the narrative structures that groups create interpersonally in response to messages; interacting together, group members chain out fantasies to help them explain ambiguous events.

TESTING THE CONCEPTS

"How can I keep from becoming a Mary?"

(R.A.): Mary, who is actually a composite of quite a few students (both male and female) in my classes over the years, represents an excellent student, one who takes learning seriously. Maybe every teacher would like to have such "problems"—not only does Mary do all her assignments but she persistently applies course ideas to her daily life. She takes the course so seriously, in fact, that she becomes a "true believer." I think I recognize part of myself in her, too, and ache with her at the problems she encounters. True believers not only believe in something; they desperately want others to believe in it, too. They have trouble understanding why anyone else would make a different choice.

Students who intend to become specialists in communication will ultimately realize, we think, that the new information they're learning is not a cure-all for relational problems, and that it should never be forced on others in their lives. Husbands, wives, children, friends, and "significant others" have not been sitting in on the classes, and they already have their own ways of communicating that probably make sense to them. They will not always see better communication students as better family members, for example—although ideally this is what could happen. In addition, if communicators find themselves in unhealthy and dysfunctional family systems, even "good" methods will not produce good results. Be careful not to invest too much faith in methods, techniques, and information. Because all of us have the potential to act like Mary, we should know that our excitement at studying communication should be tempered by a recognition that effective communication in everyday life is not something we can impose on other people.

"Do different cultures inevitably have different rules?"

Not inevitably, but they're usually different enough that you're likely to be surprised continually. When traveling or communicating cross-culturally, you should expect that you'll behave in ways that are quite natural, normal, and reasonable to you but that an observer from the other culture might consider ridiculous, thoughtless, or even insulting. Communication thus depends to a large extent on the implicit expectations that each culture builds into its everyday interaction styles—enacting its rules. Because many of these rules regulate nonverbal interaction, they tend to be subtle, contextually diverse, and difficult to control. At the same time, they define relationships powerfully. Perhaps the best rules for cross-cultural communicators to follow are (1) expect to be surprised, and (2) become a good ethnomethodologist.

"You claim that as communicators we are all theorists, practitioners, and researchers. I understand that I have to theorize, but when am I necessarily researching communication in everyday life?"

Each day, in your own way, you theorize about better methods for doing things or for thinking about things. For example, you suspect that a different style of shooting a basketball will help you hit more free throws, or that studying with your friend will improve your grades in Molecular Biology. To develop the theories, however, you must first have a need to change particular behaviors (your free throw percentage is lousy, or you need an assistantship that your current 3.1 GPA in biology won't help you get). Maybe you'll solicit the advice of friends ("Do you study better alone or in a group?") or note how specialists solve problems similar to yours (by observing the free throw shooting styles of professional NBA players). When you do this, you're conducting research.

Think of research, then, as the active link that narrows the gap between what you are able to do now and what you would like to be able to do. Similarly, rules theorists attempt to illuminate how humans act together to get things done. If the rules are functional (if the methods "work"), then teachers, trainers, students, and others will be better able to adjust their own behaviors accordingly.

"How do I know if I'm genuine or if I'm behaving like a scripted 'actor' with the people in my life?"

(V.R.): For more than ten years I worked with the elder members of my church, affectionately known as the Keenagers. I drove the church van and took them to various meetings and special events. When I met them in the church hallway or on the street, they'd hug me, pinch my cheek, or give me a kiss. Some years ago (long before I started college and chose communication as my major), while shopping with my husband, several of the Keenagers crossed the street just to talk with me and give me a hug. After they left, my husband responded, "Boy, do you have them snowed! You're really quite an actor." I was astonished by his remark and a little hurt.

After studying communication theory, especially Goffman's work, I learned that possibly I *was* acting with people, in ways that they expected me to act when I was around them. My mother sees me differently than my children do. While I was a student (admittedly a "mature" one), my classmates often viewed me as funny, outgoing, and the comedian of the group; now, however, the same kind of students tell me I'm "much too serious." We are flexible human beings who adapt to specific situations. Possibly we should not regard acting as a negative concept but as a necessary series of adjustments we must make with people in order to be as "real" as we can be in each specific relationship at specific moments in time.

YOU, THE RESEARCHER

1. Assume that you are interested in discerning whether people in your hometown are "narcissistic" in the communication sense described at the start of this chapter. Further, assume that you have a million-dollar grant allocated for a thorough study of this phenomenon, and that you have unlimited time and a flexible schedule for conducting it.

   - Create an operational definition of *narcissism* that will guide your research. An *operational definition,* as we suggested in Chapter 4, seeks to define something by recognizing how it works in actual practice. For example, one operational definition of the concept "potential for success in graduate school" is the achievement of a certain score on the Graduate Record Examination, combined with a certain level of undergraduate success measured by grade point average. In other words, an operational definition answers the question "How will I know it when I see it?"

   - Describe in detail four different research approaches you could use to explore this issue. What distinct purposes will each approach serve? What are its unique advantages and limitations? Most important, perhaps, how will the four approaches you've chosen work together to provide a more coherent picture of conversational narcissism in your hometown and, more generally, in contemporary American culture?

2. Do you believe that feeling included and being recognized in social interactions are bases for our physiological health, and that the opposite communicative conditions can lead to disease? What is the evidence for your opinion? Interview an experienced health-care practitioner (doctor, nurse, psychiatrist, social worker) to get her or his assessment of this issue. What evidence does this professional cite to support opinions? Compare what you believe and what you learn from the interview with Dr. James Lynch's evidence in his books of medical research, *The Broken Heart: The Medical*

Consequences of Loneliness (1977) and *The Language of the Heart: The Human Body in Dialogue* (1985).

3. As you saw in this chapter, Watzlawick et al. (1967) analyzed Edward Albee's play *Who's Afraid of Virginia Woolf?* to show how systems principles and relational/interactional theory can have practical applications in relationships. For a similar analysis of your own, choose any short story, novel, or play you've read recently (perhaps for a literature class), and write a five-part essay illustrating your understanding of how the five axioms developed by the Palo Alto theorists can be observed within the work. (If you need help in choosing a literary work, you might seek out several contemporary authors who specialize in probing the mysteries of interpersonal relationships. Look for the short stories of Ursula LeGuin or Raymond Carver, or novels by Anne Tyler, Barbara Kingsolver, or David Carkeet. Your teacher and others in class may have additional suggestions.)

4. Obviously, as a philosopher Martin Buber (1958) can theorize about the effects of the *I-Thou* relationship. But how can I-Thou dialogue be researched if its meaning generally resides in "the between" of the relationship, as Buber says, rather than in the psychological experience of the individuals who are communicating? Examine current issues of the journals *Human Communication Research* and *Journal of Applied Communication Research;* which article—if any—comes closest to focusing on "the between" as Buber would recommend?

5. As a result of being an alert observer of your communication theory class, you can describe the regulative rules that seem to guide when students ask questions or make comments in class. How do such rules help to predict when students will engage in or avoid class participation? How are the rules governing content, context, timing, tone, turn-taking, and topic relevance displayed in the classroom? List as many regulative rules as you can think of, and describe each one as an "If . . . , then . . ." statement.

6. Ethnomethodologists study familiar communication encounters by interfering with participants' normal routines. They want to discover what happens when taken-for-granted expectations are violated. They learn interesting things about the familiar by making it "strange." Try conducting a low-level ethnomethodological study of your own:

    -   During the course of one or more days, make a point of asking family members and friends to clarify comments that they expect you to understand without clarification (e.g., "You know what I mean" or "I bombed out on that test"). Avoid indicating that what you're doing is unusual. Present your inquiries as neutral, sincere requests for more information (e.g., "What do you mean, you 'bombed out' on the test?" or "What do you mean by 'I'm having a good time tonight?' What makes the time you spend 'good' as opposed to 'fair' or 'poor'?"). You might even choose to question the most trivial assumptions. If someone asks, "How are you?," answer something like, "How am I? Compared to what?"

- Immediately after each conversation, take notes on the other person's verbal and nonverbal reactions to your questioning. Also note whether the person expressed frustration with the interference you caused in the flow of the conversation.
- Examine the data you've collected. What conclusions can you draw about people's expectations for the *ease* of conversation? For the *accuracy* of conversation? What conversational rules are at work here? Discuss your findings in class. Consult Garfinkel's *Studies in Ethnomethodology* (1967) for some entertaining examples of how people demonstrate their underlying expectations when those expectations are violated.

Dick Luria/Photo Researchers

CHAPTER 6

"How Do We Work Together toward Common Goals?"

Theorizing Organizational Communication

Management is not simply a skill or a technique or a profession. Management is not simply something you do as a part of your climb up the career ladder. Management, approached properly and with the attitude required for excellence, is a calling.

JAMES AUTRY, *Love and Profit: The Art of Caring Leadership* (1991, p. 18)

You wouldn't expect to read about bowling in a communication theory book. But let's start this chapter on organizational life by considering a problem of social participation that can be approached either through popular culture—bowling, for example—or through organizational interactions in workplaces and large groups. Although it has enjoyed increased popularity recently, many people don't care much about bowling, much less about who bowls with whom. But "bowling alone," believe it or not, has become one of the most talked-about catchphrases among social critics in recent years. It has caught the popular imagination, too, and is commonly discussed in major newspapers and newsmagazines.

Harvard professor Robert Putnam analyzed bowling's relationship to society in his recent article (1995) and book (2000) about the phenomenon he calls *bowling alone*. This image has come to symbolize what Putnam and many others think is a disturbing social trend. We want to ask why this could be significant for communication theorists. And—equally important for the purpose of this book—what does bowling have to do with studying organizational communication, the focus of this chapter?

Organized participation in bowling is a fading—or, at least, mutating—culture. Many people who grew up as baby boomers (including your authors) recall evenings watching parents and their friends participate enthusiastically in bowling leagues. One of us bowled for years, in three different leagues at different times in her life. In fact, years ago, teams representing workplace groups or even neighborhoods or families would typically meet in friendly competition, bringing family members along to cheer them on. They socialized and swapped gossip with a wide variety of other employees and friends. Imagine Thursday nights, for example, highlighted not by "must-see TV" but by a gathering of nonathletes, only faintly serious about winning or losing, sporting brightly colored shirts with names stitched in cursive on the front pockets, talking about the week's daily dramas.

But before you dismiss this as merely sappy sentimentality, return to Putnam's point about the decline of bowling as a group-coordinated activity. The important thing isn't that people are necessarily bowling less (actually, bowling alleys are doing very well) but that they are participating separately, or spontaneously in ad hoc groups. After analyzing organizational membership rolls over time and examining their patterns, not just in bowling leagues but in other civic and community activities or organizations as well, Putnam found that "bowling alone" was a fitting metaphor for a much wider and more significant range of contemporary trends. If he's right (and we should point out that some critics have disputed how far he stretches his argument), generally people are scheduling fewer and fewer organizational commitments for themselves; they may bowl, or volunteer at youth centers, or help renovate homes in the inner city, but they do not want to be members of organized groups that coordinate these activities.

Forgoing the camaraderie of these activities is evidently a small price for people to pay for the increased freedom of deciding what to do with their time. The ready availability of personalized entertainment options such as cable or satellite TV, music downloads, computer games, inexpensive videos, and Internet surfing has probably bolstered the trend. Voluntary associations linking people with others outside their families, such as civic and veterans' organizations and special-interest clubs, are shrinking. Not all organizations are affected, of course, but American society, at least, appears to be moving toward looser and looser organized ties. People protect their freedom by reducing organizational commitments.

Putnam says democratic decision making is threatened by this trend, and he may be onto something. But this fear, despite its importance, isn't our point here. Instead, think about this problem in terms of where our everyday organizational contact now tends to occur—at work. At least in the United States, Putnam argues, more people are limiting their organizational contact to their place of employment. We focus on work "at work," but *then* we play separately and minimize our ties with others. In doing so, some would theorize, we lose a particular quality of conversational involvement with our communities that came naturally with less stressful and more voluntary associations.

Workplaces, with all their stresses, then become our primary, if not our only, contact with structuring and coordinating group action, and therefore with formal organizations. The quality of life in such complex job- and career-based organizations as corporations, schools, hospitals, agencies, and government bureaucracies will be more important than ever before in influencing our emotions, our identities, and our lives. When we compare this trend with another, the thinness of people's ties with their employers, we begin to understand why organizational life feels increasingly volatile for people. Mergers and buyouts, downsizing or rightsizing, along with myriad other contemporary buzzwords and strategies, all suggest that the world of the complex organizations in which we work is becoming more unpredictable even while it becomes more central to our identities.

What is the nature of this world? What can communication theory and research tell us about its assumptions, its practices, and its potential?

Defining *Organization* Is Tougher Than You'd Think

One of the most obvious features of communication is that almost all of it is organized somehow. What's wrong with the following statement? "Yesterday afternoon, I was thirsty, so I asked my boss to get up and get me a glass of water." Although it literally could have happened that way, the sentence—and the sentiment—sounds wrong because its content contradicts how most people organize their thinking, their talk, and their relations. Rules theorists show that everyday talk, for example, is organized by a complex set of implicit understandings of what should or should not be said in particular contexts, or to particular people, or at particular times. Theorists of cognition say that we fill in our perceptual gaps in organized ways. Conversations, and even personal relationships, exhibit subtle but real organizational patterns that can be discovered through careful study. Your boss may not have been busy, and may in fact be a nice and cooperative person who is willing to help you. But you're unlikely to ask a supervisor to go out of her or his way to bring you a glass of water. Your talk naturally reflects not just the words you choose but the roles we create in public, often at low levels of awareness. That's just how social life is organized.

If all communication is basically organized, why do we say that some forms of it are "organizational," implying that some forms are not? And why do we devote a separate chapter—and most departments devote at least one entire course—to it? What is an organization, and what sets organizational communication apart from ordinary groups of people communicating? The answers are surprisingly complex.

A prominent organizational theorist of the mid-twentieth century, Chester Barnard (1938), believed that "an organization comes into being when (1) there are persons able to communicate with each other (2) who are willing to contribute action (3) to accomplish a common purpose" (p. 82). There is nothing wrong with his definition as long as you regard it as partial and are willing to use a little imagination. It makes sense to stress, as he does, that organizations depend on their members being available to each other through well-defined communication channels. When he stresses their "willingness to contribute action," he's really saying that organizational communication depends upon voluntary participation, not just on passive presence, hanging around, or just being there. Finally, any organization, in his view, has to have some sort of commonly recognized goal. Members need to know not only why they're there but how their behavior interlocks with that of other people in order to achieve something important. Barnard was convinced that a prime responsibility of organizational leaders was to stress the commonality of goals, so members could identify with each other in an atmosphere of shared purpose.

So far, so good. But although this definition certainly describes what happens at CNN or Ford (if at a very abstract level), doesn't it also describe most bank robberies, student government meetings, and family reunions? After all, each of these situations also involves close coordination of communicative action, directed toward a particular end. By this definition, isn't a volleyball team also an example of organizational communication? Or a group of workers who remodel your basement or transport your family's furniture from Chicago to Atlanta? Yet communication departments don't normally include the study of such small, limited-purpose groups under the designation of organizational communication. Usually they reserve the term for examples of what have been called "formal organizations," like those that employ a large number of people. **Formal organizations**, in addition to Barnard's three criteria of organization, but unlike most task-oriented small groups, tend to exhibit the following principles:

- They are embedded in a history, and presumably anticipate a future (*the continuity principle*).
- They depend upon certain task specializations (*the task specialization principle*).

- They create internal control systems in the form of bureaucracies (chains of command, hierarchies, leadership) and reward structures (*the control principle*).
- They address multiple audiences internally and externally (*the multiple audience principle*).

These principles, combined with Barnard's definition, form the basic definition of organizational communication that guides us in this chapter. It is summarized in Reviewing Key Ideas, below. The communication subspecialty that's come to be known as *organizational communication* usually involves studying companies, agencies, governments, administrations, or other similar ongoing institutions that consist of more than a few people. They usually represent workplace contexts for people. As you will see, they depend upon many of the same kinds of interpersonal relating that you studied in earlier chapters, and every large or formal organization depends on smaller task groups or teams for its survival. Indeed, much of the extensive research into small-group decision making is also directly relevant to organizational communication (see, for example, Allen, Gotcher, & Seibert, 1993; Putnam, 1989; Seibold, 1998).

In the rest of this chapter we develop three traditions of theorizing about organizational communication, although the labels are somewhat arbitrary and their contents overlap at times. The order of our description is roughly chronological, sketching first the early stages of management-motivated organizational theorizing in the twentieth century and carrying through to recent trends of studying organizations more through the lenses of how participants interpret and talk about them. For each tradition, we will suggest a central metaphor that its characteristics resemble—but the metaphors are for illustrative purposes only, and you shouldn't assume that all people who appreciate a given position would agree with one another across the board. And, as with other chapters, it would be best not to think of the different perspectives as competing with each other but as different, and often complementary, ways of understanding communication processes.

REVIEWING KEY IDEAS

ORGANIZATIONAL COMMUNICATION, ESPECIALLY IN FORMAL ORGANIZATIONS, PRESUMES:

1. Available communication channels.
2. Voluntary and active participation.
3. Common purpose or identity.
4. Continuity.
5. Task specialization.
6. Internal control systems.
7. Relations with multiple audiences.

Management-Based Theorizing: Organizations Manage Their Members' Communication

The earliest and most basic of the major traditions of organizational communication theory, not surprisingly, originated in management's desire to understand how organizations could produce better products and services by improving their internal communication practices. Theorists working in this tradition were driven by the dream of increased productivity linked to clearly defined worker responsibilities and more efficient practices in the workplace.

Metaphor: The Machine

A *metaphor,* as we've pointed out in an earlier chapter, is a vivid linguistic comparison designed to highlight some features or important attributes of a complex phenomenon. To say that your fraternity or sorority meeting was a "three-ring circus," for example, might imply to a listener that you thought it was trivial, scattered, not well organized. If, however, you said it ran like "clockwork," the comparison would probably be interpreted as positive, relating the meeting to a clock's efficient and precise functioning. Sometimes it's helpful to think about complicated events by imagining which metaphors might be applied appropriately to them.

Most theorizing in the "management-based tradition" has been generated, directly or indirectly, by the image of the machine. In other words, organizations, like machines, have been designed to accomplish specific ends, and to do so reliably, efficiently, and with a minimum of troubleshooting. The human element, while respected, is also seen as introducing unwanted unpredictability into the system. In order to maximize efficient production, the machine should be maintained, of course, but once it's successfully in place the prime task is to fit newcomers and new problems into its requirements. Success, in fact, is defined in terms of mechanical follow-through. One interesting result of the machine metaphor is the assumption that studying organizations is best done in a "top-down" mode; to understand organizations, the thinking goes, you have to understand the goals, if not the motives, of the people who design them—managers. This assumption has become so ingrained in some corners of the business world that to question it (as later theorists have done) is to stimulate a perplexed response: "How *else* could we define organizations and their effectiveness?"

Research Assumptions: Quantitative Social Science

In *management-based theorizing,* researchers historically have defined their tasks as careful observation and measurement of variables. They want to know, for example, whether a worker's routine wastes time, energy, or resources, and scientific methods can help them discover these things. Instead of relying on intuition or a generalized sense that management is an art, theorists in this tradition want more concrete evidence to build on. They seek to research human communication in a relatively detached, objective, and controlled way, in order to avoid tingeing their results with their own expectations or biases.

The desire to study organizations as problems of efficient production from a

LINK

Review the discussion of differences between quantitative and qualitative research from Chapter 1. While quantitative researchers by definition rely on counting and measuring things or processes, they also must be able to analyze and interpret their results creatively. Just because a method or a process is "scientific," we should not assume that it is bloodless or unimaginative.

managerial perspective has led to two general strains of theorizing: classical management theory and human relations/resources theory.

Organizations as Producers: Classical Management Theory

What has come to be known as *classical management theory* largely refers to the pioneering work done by two men working contemporaneously in different cultures, F. W. Taylor in the United States and Henri Fayol in France. Both believed that too many decisions were made by leaders who didn't have a clue about what their changes would produce. Resources were squandered by ill-advised "real world" moves that were nothing more than guesses, instead of applications of methods of the scientific revolution to factories. In effect, if the managers had enough detailed information about how workers accomplish their jobs—both in actual and potential production—they could better compare the likely results of proposed changes without having to expend actual resources on experimentation. This was elemental cause-effect thinking. And, as you can imagine, it represented an attractive advance for management.

Scientific Management Theory. F. W. Taylor knew his industry, the late-nineteenth-century steel mill, from the ground up. Starting as a basic laborer and gradually working his way through the levels of management to the job of chief engineer, he never lost his interest in how the lowest level jobs were connected to the highest level decisions in an organization. Taylor noted with alarm that the normal management tactic was to demand higher output or productivity of labor, and to back those demands with pressures or threats. His alternative, which he called **scientific management** (Taylor, 1913, 1947), relied on gathering as much information as possible about how every job in the factory was being done, and could be done. Only then, he reasoned, could any realistic expectations or demands be made.

Taylor, and the many subsequent theorists he inspired, in effect changed the ground rules for studying organizational life. His emphasis on evidence actually opened the door to true organizational theorizing, grounding theory in actual practices. According to Burrell and Morgan (1979), his writings "bristle with a meticulous concern for the detailed analysis of everyday work activities, such as the process of earth shovelling, pig-iron handling, etc. Taylor realised that by matching men, tools, and the tasks they were required to perform, it was possible to increase productivity without placing increased physical burdens upon the men. He sought to convert the process of management from an art form based upon experience and rule of thumb to 'a true science, resting upon clearly defined laws, rules, and principles, as a foundation'" (p. 127). If his notion to theorize with specific evidence gleaned from worker performance sounds intuitively obvious today, we have to note that it was hardly as obvious before he demonstrated its predictive power. However, at the same time, he clearly left out of his equation the rich uniqueness of the individual human person. Taylor's faith in the organization-as-machine metaphor was automatic and nearly total. Organizations or factories were big mechanisms that fitted together smaller and basically interchangeable mechanisms known as workers. We will see that other theorists later mounted a backlash counterargument to Taylorism, at both the human and the productivity levels.

Administrative Theory. Meanwhile, in France, Henri Fayol (1949) was developing similar ideas that emphasized scientific decision making, but he applied them somewhat differently to the coal mining industry in which he worked for decades. Although he understood the importance of analyzing workers' performance, his primary goal was to apply scientific thinking to the work done by those who administer managerial practices. The distinction between the two classical theorists was subtle but important: Whereas Taylor analyzed workers' acts as evidence that would lead to managerial improvement, Fayol scientifically analyzed the managers' acts themselves, correlating them with organizational policies. Both, of course, were motivated by a desire to improve organizational productivity.

Eric Eisenberg and H. L. Goodall, Jr. (1997) suggest that Fayol's most prominent contribution was his five-part analysis of **administrative science** principles (p. 66) (see Reviewing Key Ideas, below, for a summary list). Managers, working with other employees, must: *plan* (anticipate a probable future); *organize* (create clearly understood divisions of labor in hierarchical or, in his terms, "scalar" form); *command* (set goals realistically); *coordinate* (relate diverse employees to each other's interests, and to those of the organization); and *control* (by which he meant the evaluation of work styles and subsequent rewards). Think of these as functions that should be performed efficiently and directly by those who oversee organizational life. Although contemporary theorists would perhaps use different labels and emphasize more cooperative approaches to teamwork, it's hard to imagine that these factors, as Fayol understood them, would be much less important today than they were when he was working and writing.

Organizations as Collections of Individual Needs: Human Relations/Resources Theory

The widespread adoption of the ideas of scientific and administrative management stimulated both successes and disappointments. On the one hand, companies, for example, were capable of creating internal communication patterns that supported their business goals much more effectively. Organizations increased their rationality and self-awareness, which produced better quality information.

REVIEWING KEY IDEAS

FAYOL'S PRINCIPLES OF ADMINISTRATIVE SCIENCE

- *Planning:* Leading for an organization that is ongoing
- *Organizing:* Creating hierarchies and divisions of labor
- *Commanding:* Setting goals
- *Coordinating:* Relating interests and people
- *Controlling:* Creating fair and reasonable reward systems to accompany evaluation

On the other hand, management theorists began to ask such questions as: "Does the worker's own attitude about his or her work affect organizational effectiveness?" "What increases worker satisfaction, and how is this related to productivity?" "Do organizations unnecessarily limit workers' humanness?" "If personal and interpersonal needs were better met within organizations, would the organizations themselves profit?" Although some analysts and communication historians distinguish between a "human relations" approach and a "human resources" approach, we have chosen to use only a combined label here, because the questions the two approaches ask tend to be so similar, because the latter developed from the former, and because both signal an increased interest in interpersonal communication in organizational life, as the famous research done at the Hawthorne factory in Illinois suggests. (You should bear in mind that in some surveys a "human relations" approach is considered more naive and less theoretically sound than what is termed "human resources.")

The Hawthorne Studies. Late in the 1920s, researchers in the classical tradition began to wonder about a somewhat different set of questions in reference to organizational life. In planning the so-called **Hawthorne Studies**, they were curious about how such things as monotonous tasks and fatigue affected work performance in cause-effect ways. Consistent with the classical management research inclination, researchers Roethlisberger and Dickson (1939) wrote that "[i]t was anticipated that exact knowledge could be obtained about this relation by establishing an experimental situation in which the effect of variables like temperature, humidity, and hours of sleep could be measured separately from the effect of an experimentally imposed condition of work" (p. 3). Their work, together with the contributions of Elton Mayo, formed the basis of the Hawthorne Studies, named after the manufacturing plant in which they were conducted. The researchers were somewhat disappointed because they didn't obtain precise information about specific causes that produce effects, but they happened upon something that was even more important in the long run (as often occurs in research).

The famous **Hawthorne Effect (HE),** to oversimplify a bit, was what they discovered, and attempting to explain it helped scholars and practitioners understand organizations better. You see, one of the conditions studied was lighting. Would increased lighting help boost productivity for some groups as compared with a control group that experienced no change? One set of findings seemed promising: Better lighting appeared to boost productivity. Another finding seemed initially baffling: The productivity of the control group also went up! Stranger still, productivity continued to rise, in both groups, even though the experimenters adjusted the lighting conditions progressively downward to a near-ridiculous level of semidarkness. This was the basis of the HE: Workers were evidently responding to the experience of social attention. Because they were being studied—paid attention to—their work norms improved.

The theoretical contribution of the Hawthorne Studies, despite some methodological flaws and other problems, was to show that organizations cannot be conceived as containers of simple or unidirectional cause-effect relationships. Instead, they are complex systems of variables and conditions, both internal and external, in which social expectations and the human factor must be theorized. Theorists now needed to account for such factors as employee attitude, along with the perceived social environment in which employees made interdependent organizational decisions. As Roethlisberger and Dickson (1939) wrote, "It is apparent that this way of thinking substitutes for a simple cause and effect analysis of human situations the notion of an interrelation of factors in mutual dependence: that is, an equilibrium such that any major change in one of the factors (interference or constraint) brings about changes in the other factors, resulting in a temporary state of disequilibrium until either the former equilibrium is restored or a new equilibrium is established" (p. 326). This insight should sound familiar to communication students; it is a clear, brief statement of systems theorizing.

Obviously, the interest in interpersonal questions suggests that the machine metaphor was beginning to lose its hold. Although workers were still seen as components in a larger structure, the presumed passivity of employees was being questioned along with the rigidity of the cause-effect reasoning that propelled management thinking. Organizations were still being analyzed, in effect, from the top down, but human needs were becoming more prominent. Sometimes surprises were the result. For example, the optimistic but naive assumption of some researchers that happy and satisfied workers were more likely to be productive workers has, by and large, not been supported. More complex explanations of interaction resulted, however, and it can hardly be denied that organizational effectiveness is closely tied to interpersonal effectiveness in many important ways. In this section we will not have the space to survey all the relevant research programs, so we'll have to be selective in focusing on one representative theory to supplement the contributions of the Hawthorne researchers—McGregor's Theory Y approach.

Recall the discussion in Chapter 1 of the heuristic function of theorizing. Especially effective theories stimulate later scholars to conduct additional research and to branch off their interests in a variety of new directions. A theory can be heuristically successful even if it has been supplanted by later theories.

Theory Y. In 1957 a management theorist named Douglas McGregor spoke at a major convocation at MIT's Sloan School of Management, capturing in his presentation what many managers and researchers were thinking about organizational communication at that time but had been unable to articulate. The success of that speech and his subsequent book, *The Human Side of Enterprise* (1960/1985), brought McGregor's concepts and his concern for persons into the national conversation. The distinguished management theorist Warren Bennis wrote that "this book, more than any other book on management, changed an entire concept of organizational man and replaced it with a new paradigm that stressed human potentials, emphasized human growth, and elevated the human role in industrial society.... Much of the work that goes on now could not have happened if this book hadn't been written" (Bennis, 1985, p. iv). That's powerful praise, but notice that Bennis is not suggesting either that McGregor's work was universally accepted or that the theory is equally persuasive today; what he's saying is that McGregor enabled future organizational theorists to define their studies in more human terms, and to ask somewhat different questions about experiences within organizations. His theory, in other words, was an exceptionally *heuristic* one.

McGregor's **Theory Y** could be summarized through the following major points:

- *A description of management assumptions about our human relationship to work.* McGregor called the scientific management assumptions **Theory X** (see 1960/1985, pp. 33 – 35). Among them were: People tend to avoid work if they can, because it is inherently dissatisfying; people must be "coerced, controlled, directed, [and] threatened with punishment" in order to get them to work (p. 34); and people in fact prefer to be directed by others because this helps them avoid responsibility and feel more secure. It's important to point out that McGregor didn't attack these as completely empty myths (some research supports some of them in some contexts) but suggested that it is a poor organizing theory overall if we want to understand how to improve organizations.

- *A description of his alternative explanation for human nature at work.* McGregor's Theory Y was a more optimistic view of how we accomplish organizational tasks that was consistent with Abraham Maslow's (1965) emerging discussion of self-actualization and Chris Argyris's (1957) analysis of how large organizations can be reconciled with individual personalities. He relied on research on small-group communication and interpersonal relations in addition to traditional management research in order to generalize: People don't usually need coercion at work because they are already looking for ways to be active and self-directed; self-responsibility leads to internal rewards that also serve organizational goals; and most people seek ways to be creative, and this potential is lost if we assume that they only want to be secure and directed by others.

- *A critique of scientific management theory's narrow definitions of efficiency and control.* Decision making, said McGregor, did not have to be a top-down, management-directed process but could be spread throughout the organization with good results. The role of management, then, was the proper coordination of people, information, and decisions so that as many organizational members as possible could achieve their own goals within the context of organizational goals. In more contemporary terms, he attempted to replace an either-or situation (either management gets its way or employees get their way) with a both-and situation (both management goals and employee goals can be met at the same time).

Theory Y's distrust of what McGregor called the "tactics of control" (p. 132) created a cultural space within which later approaches in collaborative management, team-building, and participatory leadership could thrive. Still, it is not exactly a comprehensive theory of organizational communication but, instead, a theoretical reply to classical management theories. It supplies a useful corrective. But for more comprehensive theories we must turn elsewhere.

Systems-Based Theorizing: Organizations Contain Communication Subsystems

Metaphor: The Organism

Thinking about the organization as if it were a machine predisposes you to think about communication in a certain way. To communicate is to direct or control

LINK

In Chapter 2 we illustrated the generally misleading *conduit metaphor* in communication with W. Charles Redding's example of how managers in his workshops seemed to define *communication* as a simple "point and shoot" notion—it's merely a problem of transferring an idea from here to there, or from there to here. This limiting conception, though, does not help organizational members to understand the complexity of their interaction. Organizations are rarely as predictable as machines, which are simple systems designed for predictable outcomes. Organizations are more like complex open systems, also described in Chapter 1 in the discussion of *general systems theory.*

something in this line of thinking: to gather, direct, and point meanings; to direct people to agree with you; to have intentions that can be tied ideally in a direct line with the efficient achievement of goals.

Instead of considering organizations as machines, could we think of them as organisms, systems of biology and intellect, in roughly the same ways in which people are organisms? How would your concept of communication have to adjust to match this new metaphor? An organism metaphor might not be perfect (organizations don't act as if they were simply large[r] persons, for example; they don't speak in a single voice, or "think" in any direct sense). Yet it does capture something seemingly more sophisticated than the machine metaphor. Stated simply, organisms are systems in which outcomes are complexly dependent upon the interaction of many components and their attributes. Changes in one small part of a system affect the functioning of other components throughout the system. Further, organisms are *open* systems, by which we mean that they are constantly exchanging information with their environment. In the academic world, sociologists and social psychologists appeared to reach this conclusion before theorists in most other disciplines in their development of what became known as the **structural-functional tradition**. As Burrell and Morgan (1979) observe, "It is through the notion of structural functionalism that the use of the biological analogy…has had its major impact upon sociological thought. Based upon the concepts of holism, interrelationship between parts, structure, functions and needs, the biological analogy has been developed in diverse ways to produce a social science perspective firmly rooted in the sociology of regulation" (pp. 49–50). Theories developed within this tradition assume that communication doesn't move, like an object, from person to person or from source to receiver but is a function of complex changes in a web of relationships.

Research Assumptions: Quantitative or Qualitative Social Science

Researchers who study the functions of relations continue to see the need for the kinds of close analysis and measurement that are provided by controlled quantitative studies. Indeed, the structural-functional tradition applies this kind of empirical method. Instead of looking at a person, role, or practice and asking, "How good (or ethical, or true, or powerful, etc.) is this?," for example, a structural-functionalist would tend to ask, "How does this thing or action fit into the larger structure, and what functions does it serve there?" However, nothing inherent in systems thinking makes quantitative social science the only option for discovering organizational insights. Studies of organizational systems can also be conducted through first-person accounts, interviewing and ethnographic methods, textual analyses, and other qualitative methods. The important thing is not so much the method chosen as the attitude of the researcher in keeping the whole organization in mind when studying its parts.

Organizations as Sets of Roles: Structural-Functionalist Theory

Although we will not take the space to survey the full range of structural-functionalist theorizing, we can highlight two examples that will help you to explain some basic features of this sociologically inflected tradition: the bureaucratic theory of Weber and others, and the homeostatic open systems theory of Katz and Kahn.

Bureaucratic Theory. Today, we tend to react to the word *bureaucracy* as though it inevitably suggested something negative or unpleasant about organizing human action. After any confusion about how to lodge a complaint against a department store, a person might say something like "I hate bureaucracy." Rarely do we stop to think that bureaucracy, taken in a more literal sense, is the actual reason that we can potentially identify exactly who could best act on our complaint. The major figure in the history of the concept, Max Weber (1946), assumed **bureaucracy** to be the rational structuring of organizational roles for maximum efficiency. It was not for authoritarian reasons that formal organizations need bureaucracy, Weber believed, but for clarity of purpose and production, equitable relations, and effective communication. People simply need to know what others are doing, even if they do not have close interpersonal relations with them. While Weber was realistic about the limits of what bureaucracies could do, he nevertheless could not conceive of a modern organization that did not depend upon bureaucractic procedures. Weber and his followers typically thought that a bureaucratic ideal included several assumptions about how organizations should be structured (see the accounts in Baughman, 1989; Blau, 1956; Eisenberg & Goodall, 1997):

- *Division of labor* (different organizational members do different things; functional roles are created).
- Clear, explicit *definitions of job responsibilities* (members understand what's expected of them).
- *Standardized procedures,* well understood by all (members who do similar jobs are expected to do them similarly).
- *Hierarchical structures of authority* (members are responsible to higher authorities, and responsible for coordinating members lower in the hierarchy).
- *Technical competence* as a criterion for the selection of personnel (members are selected and rewarded for what they do, not for who they are).
- *Management and other roles presumed to be ongoing responsibilties,* creating careers, barring ineffectiveness (members should not be terminated capriciously).

The concepts of bureaucratic theory have generated relatively little research recently in the discipline of communication, and are important largely for their historical and contextual value. Still, some theorizing in the areas of superior-subordinate relations, organizational network analysis, and structural effects (for summaries, see Allen, Gotcher, & Siebert, 1993) are extensions of the spirit of bureaucratic theory.

Homeostatic Theory. An excellent representation of theorizing about organizational systems is found in a research program whose focus is organizational systems, an approach we're labeling **homeostatic theory** in order to avoid confusion with the more generalized general systems theory approach upon which it is based. The name seems appropriate because, as you'll recall from Chapter 1, one of the characteristics of a system is a tendency to maintain *homeostasis,* which means an internal balance within the system. Daniel Katz and Robert Kahn published their influential book *The Social Psychology of Organizing* in 1966, and solidified homeostatic theory as a way of defining organizations both as systems of structural roles (as did Weber) and as human systems with symbolic needs that must be fulfilled for members (as did human relations/resources theorists).

Although their analysis is complex, it is based on a few simple ideas:

- *Organizations are open systems* (they cannot be understood except by referring to their relations with their environments and the way in which they exchange information with other systems across system boundaries).
- *Organizations are purposive systems* (they are created and exist to serve particular purposes, and system functioning is constantly being compared with this central rational purpose in mind).
- *Organizations are systems composed of certain types of subsystems* (Katz and Kahn, 1966 identify the following types: *production subsystems,* which are concerned not with what the organization uses (*input*) and what it creates (*output*) but with how its inner processes fulfill the organizational mission (*throughput*); *supportive subsystems,* which secure the proper inputs; *maintenance subsystems,* which maintain the social processes of organizational roles; *adaptive subsystems,* which coordinate change; and *managerial subsystems,* which coordinate all the subsystems).
- *Organizations are ordered systems* (they are effective to the extent that a dynamic state of internal control and balance is maintained; "dynamic" in this sense means that the organization must constantly adjust its inner working to allow for new information, but how that adjustment "works" or "looks" will always be at least somewhat different).

Once you become familiar with some of the jargon of systems approaches, homeostatic theory appears to be straightforward enough. It doesn't explain much about communication other than how it tends to be structured in support of organizational goals, but the theory is evidently primarily meant to be descriptive. It's helpful as far as it goes, but does it go far enough?

Organizations as Both Causes and Effects: Structuration Theory

A more recent theoretical development was born, in a sense, in structural-functional thinking, but its theorists have extended it so far and so well that it can serve as a bridge between this tradition and the newer brands of theorizing that claim that participants create the essence of their organizations out of their talk. To put this in context, imagine joining a new team in your favorite high school sport—say, soccer. The first time you showed up for practice, you noticed that other players talked to the coach with fear and deference, that the coach asked only experienced players their opinions, that strong player cliques and alliances were already in place, and that there were some explicitly stated rules that everyone usually followed (although, you observed, some were able to break the rules more easily than others). Did you assume that it was your task to *fit in,* or merely to *join* the team? Were the features you noticed structures you must conform to, or did they merely describe how things happened before you arrived?

Sociologist Anthony Giddens (1993) thought that the central idea of *homeostasis*—the balance of parts and functions within a system—was accurate in one sense but misleading in another. It is accurate in that the parts of a system do operate interdependently, and do establish an equilibrium of sorts. But the more he studied functionalist theory and its supporting research, the more he became convinced that, all protestations to the contrary, most social scientists regarded this structural homeostasis as static rather than dynamic, passive rather than active, and as a kind of ideal structural state that systems establish apart from people's participation. This kind of organizational structure, he observed, was almost always thought by other theorists to function as "a constraint upon action, rather than also as enabling" (1993, p. 2). Theorizing organizations as structures of homeostasis therefore seemed misleading to Giddens because it assumed that organizations were collections of prior restraints on behavior. Operating from this assumption, joining the soccer team meant that you adapted your individual behavior to the already-in-place rules and structures you found there. But close observation of individuals in groups also leads to another interesting question: Although structures change people, don't people change and create structures as well? How can structures have a reality that is independent of the active agency of the people whose behaviors create them?

Giddens wanted a new concept, and his first step was to note that while some structural-functional approaches were "strong on structure," they were "weak on action," as we noted in the previous paragraph: "Agents [by which he meant people deciding on how to act] are treated as if they were inert and inept—the playthings of forces larger than themselves" (1993, p. 4). On the other hand, some interpretive approaches seemed to be conversely "strong on action, but weak on structure" in that they don't deal realistically with issues of "constraint, power, and large-scale organization" (p. 4). In order to reject the artificial dualism of the question "Is the organization dominant, or the individual?," Giddens says that the answer is "both."

His concept of the **duality of structure** explains this inventively. To Giddens (1993), "social structure is both constituted by human agency and yet is at the same time the very medium of this constitution" (pp. 128–129); structure is "both the medium and outcome of…practices" (1984, p. 25). You were shaped by the structures you found in the soccer team…*as* your interaction with others shaped and changed the structures. Put another way, the acts of communicators, and participants' memories of how those acts played out, make up the structures of the team's organization, which then influence those acts in certain ways. Giddens's **structuration** concept explains that structures are not static and definitive but constantly in motion and contingent. Structuration means, in practice, that structures define what actions are appropriate, but the acts themselves—as we perform them—constitute the structures. In our soccer example, if you begin to talk differently with the coach and not participate in the cliques, new structures will begin to evolve. "To enquire into the structuration of social practices," Giddens writes, "is to seek to explain how it comes about that structure is constituted through action, and reciprocally how action is constituted structurally" (1993, p. 169).

Discourse-Based Theorizing: Organizations Are Constituted by Communication

Anthony Giddens's notion of *structuration* puts communication at center stage in theorizing organizations. With his work in mind it is difficult to think of the organization as an impersonal or inhuman entity that exploits people for "its" own ends. The existence of organizational structure is inseparable from the lives of organizational actors. To assume otherwise is to engage in organizational **reification:** giving our *constructs* for organizational thinking a kind of animated life of their own, and treating them as if they were important apart from the actual human beings of which they are composed. Instead, according to a new generation of organizational theorists, we should listen more carefully to how people talk as they organize their work and social lives with others.

Metaphor: The Conversation

The common denominator of discourse-based theorizing is, as you might expect, talk—but not just any talk. Instead, to illuminate organizations these theorists tend to pay attention to talk that is mutualized, sustained, focused, self-animating, and tied to people's identities. Think of times in which you and a friend "lost yourselves" in a conversation without ever having a guarantee of how it would turn out. One of you glances at the clock and says, "How could it be 2 A.M. already? The 10 o'clock news was just on!" Neither of you decided on exactly how to "structure" the conversation, but a structure emerged nevertheless. It wasn't goal-less, but it wasn't saturated with goal-definition, either. You wanted to be understood, but you wanted to give your partner opportunities, too. Neither of you was consciously using strategies to manipulate the other, but each of you was influenced by what the other said. You weren't straining to clarify any particular idea, or trying to accomplish any particular task, but things were clarified nevertheless. Good conversations are, at the same time, intentional and spontaneous; they are complex weavings of preferences, needs, opinions, and social rules that are possible because partners focus more on the ideas being explored together than on themselves as individuals. They create miniature cultures of connection, and for a while the partners are native to those cultures.

But all of us know that conversations click with some friends but may not be satisfying or successful with others. We adapt; no technique can ensure good conversations, because while they are regulated they're not controlled by either, or any, side. Conversation analysts show how they are ensemble achievements. Organizational life, many theorists claim, has so much in common with conversation that we could say that the conversation is a basic metaphor for understanding organization. IBM, or Kellogg's, or General Motors, or a soccer team can be understood by looking for their conversational elements.

Research Assumptions: Interpretive/Qualitative Social Science

Communication studies, taken as a discipline, has had a long history of humanistic and interpretive studies in rhetoric, as you will see in Chapter 8. Rhetorical critics have typically analyzed texts, often as a result of closely following rhetorical campaigns. These qualitative studies have advanced our understanding of persuasion and other rhetorical functions but are not designed to create scientifically verifiable generalizations. Yet in the 1970s and 1980s a group of organizational communication researchers helped to create a new set of assumptions for qualitative researchers. Studies of texts didn't have to concentrate on speeches but could focus instead on practices as they are constructed by individuals and groups in organizational life. These practices, such as what constitutes a business lunch, could be analyzed textually—as if they were coauthored written texts, meaningful and rich. Careful, systematic close-in observation and interviewing can produce communication case studies of extraordinary power. As Karl Weick, who is himself a theorist of organizational sense-making (1995), has written (1983):

> *Many people see the current fascination with fieldwork, naturalistic observation, and qualitative research as a fad that will soon pass when people come to their positivistic senses. I read the omens differently. Both labs and surveys, when used alone, mislead us because they do not capture context effects. The presumption that distance from the object improves objectivity has not worked. All that distance seems to improve is ignorance. Those respondents from whom we detach ourselves are not doing what we say they are doing. We are too far removed for them to tell us that. I think methodologists now want to answer the question, "How can I control bias, yet still work in close?" (p. 21)*

Context, then, is a key. In order to understand conversational talk, we need to understand it "locally"; that is, in its immediate context, including both what is said and—just as important to researchers like Weick—what is not said or not done. And this, as he points out in this quotation, is what positivistic quantitative studies can miss. Discourse-based theorizing about organizations stipulates that contextual understanding is more realistic than linear cause-effect reasoning because contexts should be understood as holistically as possible. Weick's point should not be taken as an argument against conducting quantitative studies but as a reminder that distance in studying discourse does not necessarily equate with objective research and closeness with bias.

Organizations as Conversations: Conversational Autonomy Theory

James R. Taylor, a Canadian organizational theorist, has decided that the notion of conversation offers the key to understanding how we should conceptualize organizations. He argues against the classical management models of machine-like organizations, and also believes that the homeostatic systems and structurational views do not go far enough in taking into account the fundamentally communicational nature of organizations. He does not want to theorize organizations as if they were containers of communication, or prior producers of it—as is the customary approach—but as what he calls *self-organizing systems*. The "organizations produce communication" worldview, which seems outmoded to Taylor, is what he calls a **heteronomous model** of organizing; by this he means that the control of the organization is achieved by inputs from outside the organizational boundaries, with the goal of adapting outputs to the needs diagnosed as a result of the inputs. A company's tires malfunction badly, causing many accidents; consultants must intervene on the basis of this input-feedback to restructure the company's procedures in order to stop the malfunctions and improve public relations.

Taylor (1995; see also Taylor, Cooren, Giroux, & Robichaud, 1996) acknowledges that it's simple to see organizations as inputs and outputs, but unfortunately it also objectifies the processes by which real people work together. Instead, he describes an **autonomous model**, a "communication produces organizations"

◘**LINK**

To clarify Weick's point even further, recheck your understanding of Chapter 3, "How Do Contexts Affect Our Meaning," and consider how contextual understanding might be more readily achieved through qualitative research methods. What would a quantitative researcher reply in defense of how he or she could also take context into account?

approach, in which organizations are seen as self-shaping. This shaping-from-within has several essential features:

- Each organization is basically self-organizing, as opposed to being shaped from outside itself. Each creates its own internal coherence through *conversations*—complex negotiations of identity that not only lead to communication and organization but *are* communicative organization. Taylor (1995) writes that "[c]onversation is an interactive flow of discourse, involving multiple participants in quasi-synchronized alternation of verbal and nonverbal expressions" (p. 15). The network-like notion of "information flow" does not fit well with this view, as meaning is suffused throughout the organization's processes.

- Taylor employs the speech act theorists' distinction between *locution* (speech as verbal description of an outer reality, such as "That sunset is beautiful") and *illocution* (speech as performance in which another person's response is appropriate and necessary, such as "We'd be able to see the sunset better if you moved your car," which functions as a request, although it is literally a declarative statement). Conversation creates organization because it is fundamentally illocutionary in this way: It presumes an organized and cooperative interpretation. Conversation is something we can do only together, not singly. No one person can direct—or "manage"—a conversation. Organizations operate as a result of a pattern of these implicit understandings that cannot be seen or heard clearly in isolated statements: "Illocutionary force, it seems, is a property of the transaction and not of the statement" (Taylor, 1995, p. 18).

- Each organization, as a self-organizing cell, creates its own identity, and it also shapes and reshapes its own boundaries. Relevant features of the environment are not considered to be informational input to be "processed" or "used" by the organization but as opportunities for **coupling**, encountering disturbances at system boundaries. Such coupling is necessary to the ongoing existence of the organization. Conversational autonomy theory does not see disturbance as necessarily negative but as the way in which a system can shift potentially into a higher and more creative level of functioning. It focuses on how the organization maintains itself from within, not on what the environment "does to" the system from the outside. The role of leaders at these times is not to "use information" but to create, acknowledge, and, through organizational conversation, facilitate such opportunities. The tire company's crisis of quality control, however tragic for victims, might be a turning point in achieving a more solid identity for itself both internally and in the marketplace. Taylor's conversational autonomy approach allows us to see organizations not as objects but as processes of talk that are reproduced differently and uniquely in different times and places. All organizations are not fundamentally alike; each develops its own unique interpretive system that helps it to survive. Contemporary organizations may depend as much on appropriate ambiguity as on clarity in maintaining the relations among their members, and they may depend as much on conflict, disturbance, and discontinuity as they do on rational predictability in their relations with environmental forces. In considering the implications of his theory, in fact, Taylor (1995, p. 28) aptly discusses how it suggests the possibility of a new *postmodern* style of organizational communication.

Organizations as Cultures: Organizational Culture Theory

In the next chapter we will introduce a series of terms and concepts that clarify how important culture and intercultural communication can be in defining human affairs. In some ways, this has been a theme of the book from the start, as we have persistently stressed the contextual side of communication—and culture is the always-present context for all human action. We could easily have placed the culture chapter before this one, but organizational communication topics link somewhat more tightly with the interpersonal themes of the previous chapter. Here, we'll define what is *cultural* generally, in a way that will be appropriate for this chapter, and leave more specific conceptual discussion for the next chapter.

For now, think of **culture** as the cohesive patterns of making sense of the world that characterize a particular group of people in a particular time and place. (We'll both complicate and exemplify this definition in Chapter 7.) These patterns are cohesive because they are really subtle systems of perception, language, and action, and because through them people establish shared identities. Although some people mistakenly assume that *culture* applies only to ethnic or racial differences, it offers communication scholars much wider and richer opportunities. Ethnic heritage establishes cultural differences, but so does participation within a particular, well-defined activity over an extended period of time. So, although Hasidic Jews obviously can be considered a cultural group, think about how professional athletes, or dancers, or truck drivers might also have developed shared perceptions and practices that are fundamentally cultural even if their bonds seem thinner and more transitory than practices rooted in ethnic traditions. Theorists who specialize in **organizational culture** have observed that some companies, for example, have developed their own particular roles, norms, rituals, and storytelling practices that distinguish them from other organizations even in their own industry.

Cultures establish ways of doing and being that can be so thoroughly integrated into people's lives that they may be invisible or unacknowledged from the inside ("What? Doesn't everyone do it this way?"). On the other hand, these "ways," when observed from within another culture's mind-set, may risk wildly unexpected interpretations when they are taken out of context ("Those people are animals—why do they eat like that?").

Cultural anthropologists and others who seek to understand the uniqueness of cultural systems see the world in terms of contexts (Agar, 1994). Many have found it useful to use two terms, *emic* and *etic,* that distinguish between kinds of cultural context-knowledge. **Emic** knowing is the understanding, more or less from within the assumptions of a cultural group, that you would achieve by knowing how an insider perceives as a member. Research based on emic knowing is subjective but is also highly contextualized. Some researchers call it "in here" knowing. By contrast, **etic** knowing is based on an "out there" assumption. It trades an awareness of deep context for a desire to observe the cultural group

LINK

See our introductions to *postmodern* thinking in Chapters 3 and 4. Researchers may find that postmodern organizations are guided more by dialogic processes of discovery—even if they seem ambiguous and chaotic at times—than by rational processes that may artificially overstate the degrees of control managers are able to exert. Also, J. R. Taylor's work is an extension both of *speech act theory* (see Chapter 4) and of the social constructionist frame of mind, in which reality is in part created interpretively from the inside—of a system—out, rather than from the outside in.

as much as possible as a whole, in its environment—which, one could argue, is just a different and wider context. Sometimes, too, there is another distinction, and it is relevant to the study of organizational culture. Research and theorizing in the emic tradition sets up a goal of what could be called immersive clarification: Get inside the culture and, using ethnographic methods of observation and recording data, establish as clearly as possible what that world feels, looks, smells, and sounds like. **Ethnography**, the preferred methodology of cultural anthropologists, is the approach researchers use when they attempt to participate within the culture's assumptions in order to write forcefully about it later. Establish its uniqueness, and this is in itself a valid research goal. You don't need to know *why* things happen as they do, just understand *that* they happen that way. You don't need to try to change or predict anything in order to make a contribution. If you aim for etic knowledge, however, you may hope to use your findings to diagnose, predict, or prescribe different relations between the culture and its environment.

Organizational culture theorists within communication studies (for example, see Pacanowsky, 1989; Pacanowsky & O'Donnell-Trujillo, 1982, 1983) have tended to start with emic assumptions, hoping to sketch organizations as they are experienced by members and workers at the level of everyday communication. For too long, they believe, organizations have been identified with their leadership or ownership. This top-down presumption emphasizes, as we have seen in classical management theory, the materiality of organizational life: production, efficiency, documentary records, output. While they are undoubtedly important, these factors miss crucial elements of organization as well. As Pacanowsky and O'Donnell-Trujillo (1983) say in an important article, many kinds of cultural performances are enacted by people as they informally interact in the context of their work environments. **Performance** in this sense should not connote anything false or negative but is simply an attempt to manage identities in public, as we all must do to some extent.

Of course, we don't stand by the water cooler and think, "Complaining with you for five minutes about the parking garage is one of my cultural performances for the morning, Harriet." Culture is powerful precisely because we usually don't pay direct attention to how it plays out; we usually overlook or miss those moments as participants unless we're acting as communication researchers. But, in fact, what is happening is that we are talking about parking *and* enacting a cultural ritual—one that someone new to the organization might find interesting or even puzzling, at least at first. To be alert to **ritual** is a basic form of organizational culture awareness, because rituals are the familiar activities we engage in with others at regular intervals. They may be importantly symbolic of something like inclusion, such as birthday celebrations for all employees whatever their job status, but often the ritual is more informally social in nature ("I look forward to those late Friday afternoons when Jane and Jared don't seem to mind if we goof around").

Rituals are common in cultures, and to some extent the stability of people's experience depends upon the reassurances that rituals provide. Early organizational culture researchers, and others who followed their ideas, also identified other types of cultural performance that contributed to organizational culture (see

Pacanowsky & O'Donnell-Trujillo, 1983), which they labeled "passion," "sociality," "organizational politics," and "enculturation" (see Reviewing Key Ideas, p. 202, for a summary).

Passion-related performances are those whose primary function is to give workers' lives a dramatic interest that helps people adapt within the culture. The most common type of passion performance is the organizational narrative in which workers tell and hear stories that serve to make their roles more manageable. Rumors, for example, may circulate about the possibility of a company's merger; by talking about—and, in a sense, within—the story, employees participate in developing alternative theories and thus might develop stronger ties to a group. Some companies also nurture a version of a founder's myth in order to help employees believe that the president or CEO was once poor, too (a recent Hewlett-Packard television commercial made reference to the story of the company's being founded out of a residential garage). Some communication theorists make even more of the narrative dimension of organizations. As Barbara Czarniawska (1997) has suggested, "Narrative enters organizational studies in at least three forms: organizational research that is written in a storylike way…organizational research that collects organizational stories…, and organization research that conceptualizes organizational life as story making and organization theory as story reading (interpretive approaches)" (p. 26).

Sociality performances are those that maintain the social roles and relationships within the organization. Coworkers greet each other, or fail to, in certain ways that become patterned over time. They may seek to share the lunch hour with each other, or go their separate ways. Their e-mail messages might be personalized, or officious. Much of organizational behavior is thus rule-governed and highly contextual. One organization's culture might come close to mandating the social sharing of some facets of your private life, while in another culture this might seem unusual or even taboo.

Performances of **organizational politics** are those that enact or demonstrate power relations. Who in the organization can realistically hint that others should work overtime, without ordering them to do so? How do people within the culture know what kind of celebration to plan for a supervisor's promotion? At what point are you powerful enough to argue for a major policy change in a department meeting? Even providing examples of power dynamics suggests how intertwined this category is with the previous one; rules of sociality are often infused with power relations.

Enculturation, the final type of cultural performance in organizations, can be seen in how new members are integrated into an ongoing social structure. Over time, organizations develop ways of helping people adapt to the uniqueness of the culture they find there. While this can be a formal training process (new faculty on a campus, for example, are usually asked to attend a one- or two-day orientation to the institution's resources and expectations), it's usually experienced in an ad hoc way, through the spontaneous interactions of everyday talk. Some interesting recent work in this arena has focused on the observation that organizations, like larger societies, are composed of "co-cultures," although most studies have presumed a norm of European American behaviors. Different "outsider" experiences of individuals from marginalized co-cultural groups such as

◁ LINK

It's reasonable to think that some researchers would want to study organizations with a narrative approach, given what you learned about dramaturgical theory in Chapter 5. Later in the book (Chapter 10), we'll discuss the ethical implications of narrative.

REVIEWING KEY IDEAS

CULTURAL PERFORMANCES IN ORGANIZATIONS

- *Ritual* (performances, regularly enacted, establishing cultural stability and predictability)
- *Passion* (performances creating dramatic or narrative interest)
- *Sociality* (performances maintaining individual or group social ties)
- *Organizational politics* (performances indicating power relationships)
- *Enculturation* (performances integrating individuals into the organizational culture)

---

women, people of color, disabled workers, and those with alternative sexual preferences must therefore become important in organizational studies as well (Orbe, 1998).

One of the more interesting developments in organizational culture theory has been a tension between (1) theorists who use these concepts simply to describe organizations as complex cultural achievements on the one hand, and (2) theorists who want to use the concepts to diagnose organizations and intervene as managers and consultants to improve the organizations. While the former is basically *emic* in its approach, the latter is unabashedly *etic*. One surprising example of a prescriptively etic approach to organizational culture is provided by a consultant who gets a phone call from a CEO who wanted someone who could "install a new culture" in his company (Eisenberg & Goodall, 1997, p. 133), as if a completely different culture could be plugged in as a quick-fix technique. Theorists of the first sort would deny that this is how cultures work. But theorists of the second, more management-driven group hope to turn knowledge *about* organizations into applied knowledge *for* organizations, perhaps with techniques for improving culture. What Deal and Kennedy (1982) call a "strong culture" is clearly a management tool: "A strong culture is a powerful lever for guiding behavior; it helps employees do their jobs a little better, especially in two ways: *A strong culture is a system of informal rules that spells out how people are to behave most of the time.... *[and] *A strong culture enables people to feel better about what they do, so they are likely to work harder*" (pp. 15–16). It's not surprising, then, to discover that to some organizational culture theorists of the first type, this management-directed branch does not represent a discourse-based theory well at all because it objectifies culture as a manipulable variable, rather than conceptualizing it as a context (Sackmann, 1990).

Organizations as Sites of Power: Democratic Participation Theory

Some discourse-based theorists have begun to ask how participation in formal organizations affects our public identities—our sense of ourselves as persons, as citizens, as neighbors, and as members of communities of emotional support. Many of these perspectives mirror other topics that we have described in the book, but we shouldn't ignore their relevance to this chapter as well. We won't spend as much time on them, however, as their basic tenets have already appeared in earlier chapters. Two of the most important perspectives that establish the organization as a site of power relations are associated with organizational democracy and feminist analysis.

Workplace Democracy Theorizing. Some theorists (Cheney, et al., 1998; Deetz, 1992, 1995; Eisenberg, 1994; Harrison, 1994) are now theorizing with more precision about what makes a formal organization such as a company a place of fairness, mutual respect, full participation, and synergic cooperation. A critical concept in this attempt is **voice**, by which they mean the willingness or the ability of workers to state desires or criticisms publicly, and to participate fully in self-governing relations. This is, of course, by analogy to democratic citizenship in which citizens ideally develop not only the opportunity but the expectation of communicative participation. George Cheney (1995) reports research that suggests seven themes that must be addressed in planning for workplace democracy: *support systems* (what supports workers' social needs?), *growth* (what stresses come as organizations are transformed?), *identity* (negotiating the relation between worker-member identity and organizational identity), *revitalization* (being able to avoid static organizational patterns), *managing competitiveness* (striking a balance between the energies of cooperation and competition), *implementing participation* (coordinating self-direction with holistic goals), and *dynamic communication* (ensuring that diverse perspectives have access to each other). The MIT Dialogue Project (Isaacs, 2000; Senge, 1991) has generated additional support for ideas associated with workplace democracy, but it doesn't apply this term directly. A combination of applied communication consultation and theoretical conceptualization, this work uses a mixture of systems theory and dialogic thinking to describe what is termed "the learning organization." The theorists' concept of a **learning organization** is one of a consistently self-renewing unit in which all components have access to other components, so that change is not merely a troubleshooting device but a constant reality for the organization.

Feminist Organizational Theorizing. Although you might think that laws and social pressures supporting gender equality would have changed complex organizations profoundly by now, researchers have not found that women and men are acknowledged or heard on equal terms in organizations. Judi Marshall's (1993) approach, she found, had to be one of "'adding in' women's meanings to established theoretical frameworks.... Taking a feminist perspective [on organizations] highlights how theory making is essentially an ideological process, an exercise of power that can privilege certain social groups, certain points of view. In male-dominated cultures this exercise of power will inevitably be gendered. We need to be explicitly aware of this" (p. 139). Marshall's appeal that organizational theory should be gendered is not an expression of essentialism (as if membership in a category like female or male makes someone more dialogic *in her essence,* or less open *in his essence*). Feminist theorists ask that we pay close enough attention to organizations to discover the tendencies, not the essences, of what Mumby (1996) calls "gendered rationality." "Gender," according to Mumby, "must be understood not as a peripheral, only sometimes significant feature of organizational life, but rather as a defining, constitutive feature of the organizing process" (p. 259). Framed in the terms of this perspective, gender is better conceived as something we "do" with each other in organizations, not something we are influenced by. Our behavior together enacts our gendered realities. Feminist organizational theorists do not presume that women are necessarily better organizational communicators, nor do they assume that men are necessarily trying to keep women out of powerful roles. Instead, they want to examine the organizing process to see how power might be enacted in gendered ways that reduce the impact of women's voices.

REVIEWING KEY THEORIES

This chapter has summarized three broad classifications of theorizing in organizations: management-based, systems-based, and discourse-based.

Management-based theorizing focuses on the goal of making organizations work as if they were machine-like, and it started, at least, with an inclination toward quantitative social science methods. Under this label, you read about two kinds of classical management theory, *scientific management theory* and *administrative theory.* They stimulated a reaction, *human relations/resources theory,* which was represented in this chapter by a description of the famous *Hawthorne Studies* and McGregor's *Theory Y.*

Systems-based theorizing conceptualizes the organization differently. Here, the theorists do not imagine a mechanized presence for the organization but use systems theory to suggest that organizations are more like living organisms. Methodologies differ, too, and here we saw the rise of qualitative methods to complement quantitative social science. In this section you read about two types of *structural-functionalist theory, bureaucratic theory* and *homeostatic theory.* We then explored a key transitional idea, *structuration theory,* that was also helpful for theorists of more conversational and interpretive approaches to understanding organizational communication.

Discourse-based theorizing introduces the metaphor of the conversation for understanding the essence of organizing. Organizations are self-defining and self-organizing identities composed of many different forms of internal and external conversations. In conversational organizing, change is preferred over predictability, but this change is constantly monitored for its effects. Theorists in this tradition are especially attuned to analyzing the impact of power, culture, and oppression on work group relations. Thus qualitative and interpretive methods are especially appropriate. In this section, you learned to distinguish among *conversational autonomy theory, organizational culture theory,* and two more specific viewpoints that have energized the field, *workplace democracy* and *feminist theory.*

TESTING THE CONCEPTS

"How can McGregor's Theory Y be accurate when I see so many lazy people where I work?"

We all know people who are unmotivated and appear lazy. On the other hand, we know that many people desire to succeed and perform to their highest potential. McGregor's point is that we shouldn't take individual laziness or the fact that individuals shirk work as evidence of how people generally feel about organizations; his point is that the climate of organizational leadership influences whether people will work hard to meet this fuller potential. McGregor merely theorizes that workers tend to look, in a positive way, for opportunities to work—not to look for ways to avoid that work. They feel greater personal fulfillment by working productively. The implications for leadership and motivation are enormous, of course.

"In biology class, I learned that an organism is a living entity. How can my college, my sorority, or my hockey team be compared to an organism?"

When many people think of organizations, organizational charts or hierarchies come to mind, and it becomes too easy to think in mechanical abstractions. Yet organizations, according to this form of theorizing, are engaged in constant, living adaptation with other systems in an environment. They are not closed systems, with clear and predictable internal relations, but open systems in constant adaptation to and with a larger ecology of systems—just like biological organisms. This is consistent with the process view of communication held by most communication theorists. An organization lives in the same sense that a person lives by way of the interaction of living subsystems; placed together within the same context, the whole transcends the sum of the parts. One of the authors is the faculty adviser of a chapter of Lambda Pi Eta, the International Communication Honors Society. As each graduating class exits the organization and a new group of students are inducted as members, she witnesses this living, growing process. The organization outlives the contributions of individual members.

"*Homeostasis* is a term used several times within this chapter and elsewhere in the book. So, is balance important to an organization or not? How is exact balance possible?"

Internal balance is important in allowing members to understand their relationship to the organization itself, their place in the scheme of things. Order, structure, and belongingness are important ways in which individuals experience the balance, or homeostatic structure, of organizations. But it is not something that individuals must "try" to achieve. Rather, this is something that effective systems tend to exhibit.

"There is so much talk today about 'culture.' I've always believed that culture had to do with my ethnicity. Now I read that organizations like Taco Bell and General Motors have cultures, too. Have I been led astray in the definition of the term?"

No, you haven't been led astray, because the term does relate to our ethnic backgrounds. But the basic features of culture can be applied to organizations as well. In terms of culture, my (V.R.) Italian heritage and the organizations to which I belong both refer to groups of people who share certain ideas and patterns of behavior, a set of guiding rules and norms, and a contextual knowledge base. My Italian relatives and I have many language values, rituals, and behaviors in common, while maintaining our individual uniquenesses. Most important, perhaps, cultures are not experiences that we plan intricately, or usually attend to with great care. They just are. We tend to move about within the contexts of our cultures without analyzing them or attempting to determine why they are the way they are. That may be the reason you have not made the connection until now.

YOU, THE RESEARCHER

1. Conduct a journal search on the Internet or in your school library, concentrating on journals that publish organizational communication research. What are the titles of these journals, and, judging from the titles of articles published there, what kinds of research are published in each? Be sure to consider journals published in communication, management, sociology, and political science. Can you see any trends in managerial styles or issues in recent years?

2. Observe any workplace for a two-day period, taking notes about behavioral performances that you suspect might qualify as *rituals*. Use your notes to compare similarities among the rituals, and then create and label your own categories of the different *types* of rituals. This is a *typology*. Compare your typology with the one Pacanowsky and O'Donnell-Trujillo developed in 1983.

3. Organizational charts do not provide direct information about the communicative life of organizations, but they do indicate how organizations want to represent their own formal structures. Based on what you now know about your college or university, but without doing any actual research, draw up an organizational chart that represents your best estimate of what the organizational hierarchy looks like. (For example, who, or what office(s), would appear at the top? Who, or what offices, do you think report to those higher offices?, and so on down the levels of organizational structure.) Then you could:

   - Find the *actual* organizational chart for your institution and compare the two. (These are sometimes on Web sites or in catalogs but are also commonly available through the campus public-relations office.) Is your estimate more or less complex than the actual chart? Why? What kinds of cultures and cultural performances might characterize various levels or positions?
   - Compare the organizational structure of your campus with another type of organization that also publishes an organizational chart, such as a corporation. Look for similarities and differences in division of labor, authority, and management roles.
   - How do you think issues of workplace democracy can be addressed within the hierarchical authority structures of such complex organizations? At which levels, and with what issues, do you think workplace democracy theorists hope to make a difference?

4. Investigate popular culture portrayals of organizational communication by watching several influential films from recent years. For example, some films (e.g., *Broadcast News, The Paper, The Insider*) have portrayed media organizations, and not always generously. Other films have skewered organizational life more generally (e.g., *The Hudsucker Proxy, Office Space*). Can you infer the authors', directors', and producers' assumptions about organizations from the content of the films? Your instructor might choose to show one of these in class; if so, see if you can identify concepts from this chapter in the portrayals of characters, styles, and behaviors you find there.

Hazel Hankin/Stock, Boston

CHAPTER 7

"How Do We Develop Cultural Flexibility?"

Theorizing Cultural Communication

In a novel of Africa, Ajofia, a leader of Umuofia, speaks through an interpreter to the new missionary:

"Tell the white man that we will not do him any harm," he said to the interpreter. "Tell him to go back to his house and leave us alone. We liked his brother who was with us before. He was foolish, but we liked him, and for his sake we shall not harm his brother. But this shrine which he built must be destroyed. We shall no longer allow it in our midst. It has bred untold abominations and we have come to put an end to it." He turned to his comrades. "Fathers of Umuofia, I salute you"; and they replied with one guttural voice. He turned again to the missionary. "You can stay with us if you like our ways. You can worship your own god. It is good that a man should worship the gods and the spirits of his fathers. Go back to your house so that you may not be hurt. Our anger is great but we have held it down so that we can talk to you."

Mr. Smith said to his interpreter: "Tell them to go away from here. This is the house of God and I will not live to see it desecrated."

Okeke interpreted wisely to the spirits and leaders of Umuofia: "The white man says he is happy you have come to him with your grievances, like friends. He will be happy if you leave the matter in his hands."

"We cannot leave the matter in his hands because he does not understand our customs, just as we do not understand his. We say he is foolish because he does not know our ways, and perhaps he says we are foolish because we do not know his. Let him go away."

Chinua Achebe, *Things Fall Apart* (1959/1969, p. 175)

Most people have no difficulty with cultural differences in the abstract. Most of us, in fact, believe *we're* reasonably open-minded, sensitive, and accepting of others—when *they* act reasonably.

We begin to have trouble at those points of encounter—such as the one Achebe describes in his novel—when each side believes it is as open-minded as it can possibly be, given the perceived narrow-mindedness of the stranger. As you've learned in earlier chapters, much of your communication behavior is based on an undercurrent of expectations, values, and premises about which you're barely aware, if you even think about them at all. This often invisible layer of experience is what we'll consider in greater detail in this chapter.

Defining Culture

Understanding another culture is not the same thing as understanding someone else's subjective, emotional, or cognitive experience. People do "carry" fragments of culture in their heads, to use a loose metaphor, but they also enact culture through their behaviors, artifacts, governments, religions, media choices, and systems of economic exchange. Culture is not primarily what people think about or believe as much as it is what they assume they *don't have to think about* in order to accomplish their daily business. Therefore understanding culture involves both psychological (mental and cognitive) aspects and communicational (interactional, relational, and social) aspects. It is reflected in tangible objects as well as in the intangibles of expectations, values, and attitudes.

For example, it's significant that the missionary in Achebe's (1959/1969) book brought to Africa physical artifacts of his religion, and that even in an alien (to him) environment the church building and the land on which it stood possessed a sacredness that could be "desecrated" by people who had lived on that same land with their own culture all their lives. One culture looked at a building and saw merely an unfamiliar structure it might be able to tolerate, while the other culture saw a symbol of the basic goodness of heaven and earth. Thus the dynamic of the missionary's culture was not just in his mind but could also be observed in his relation to objects—that is, to objects he expected to possess power even for people who were unfamiliar with the objects' importance to him.

Our language contains so many different connotations and potential definitions of culture that critic Raymond Williams (1976) calls it "one of the two or three most complicated words in the English language" (p. 76). Some definitions stress shared sense-making and process; for example, Bradford J. Hall (1997) says that when he uses the concept, *culture* refers to "a community specific system of common sense which facilitates shared meanings and coordinated actions. It is a system which is interdependently related to human interaction and which includes standards for appropriate and effective human interactions" (p. 16). Harry Triandis (1994), a cross-cultural researcher born in Greece, attempts to synthesize divergent definitions into a single starting point: "Culture is a set of human-made objective and subjective elements that in the past have increased the probability of survival and resulted in satisfactions for the participants in an ecological niche, and thus become shared among those who could communicate with each other because they had a common language and they lived in the same time and place" (p. 22). For communication scholars, one of the most interesting implications of Triandis's definition is that it demonstrates why and how cultures perform valuable functions for their members' everyday theories. In fact, communication researcher William Gudykunst (1997) observes, "culture is our implicit theory of the 'game being played' in our society" (p. 328).

People in groups develop culture because it simplifies their communicative tasks in several ways. First, culture creates a better chance of survival; similar people banding together for physical or psychological protection is an age-old communication strategy. Second, people find interaction within their own culture satisfying because to some extent it helps them to avoid uncertainties and to experience fewer interpersonal surprises that may lead to problems. Third, because culture is ecological, its shared attitudes, values, and customs provide its participants with a sense of identity. Culture can be understood best, according to Triandis (1994), as a "superorganic" phenomenon—that is, one into which individuals are born, and one that will outlive those individuals. This isn't to say that people don't influence culture by their actions but that culture is not under the conscious control of individual leaders, no matter how powerful others may believe them to be.

As anthropologist Clifford Geertz (1983) reminds us, cultures are so superorganic that people forget that their definitions aren't really universal. For example, the notion of the individual *person* is itself a cultural construction that is common only in some cultures. "The Western conception of the person," Geertz (1983) writes, "as a bounded, unique, more or less integrated motivational and cognitive universe, a dynamic center of awareness, emotion, judgment, and action organized into a distinctive whole and set contrastively both against other such wholes and against its social and natural background, is, however incorrigible it may seem to us, a rather peculiar idea within the context of the world's cultures" (p. 59). Although American students typically assume that one of the highest values of humanity is for an individual to be a separate communicator responsible primarily to the self, this goal wouldn't even cross the minds of most people in some non-Western cultures. As you can imagine, communicating across such assumptions presents problems of a fundamentally different order than you would encounter waiting on customers at a fast-food eatery in Omaha.

It seems to us that serious students have three particular kinds of questions when they encounter cultural communication problems for the first time. We have therefore organized this chapter around these questions:

1. What kinds of terms and concepts help communicators understand the importance of studying this rapidly growing area of cultural research?
2. What kinds of cultural theories best explain the public tensions that can develop across gender, ethnic, race, and class lines?
3. How can cultural communication theories be applied practically to help clarify and perhaps resolve cross-cultural misunderstandings?

As with earlier chapters, however, you should remember that our brief survey cannot represent the whole range of scholarly research in cultural communication theory. For each theory or position we stress here, several others could have been chosen.

Culture: Basic Theoretical Concepts and Approaches

Cultural Syndromes

Triandis (1994) classifies cultures according to patterns that are observable in one form or another in all cultures. A **cultural syndrome**, he writes, is a "pattern of beliefs, attitudes, self-definitions, norms, and values that are organized around some theme that can be identified in a society" (p. 2). While the patterns themselves are useful (see A Theory Extension, p. 213, for descriptions), perhaps it's even more important to think of cultures literally as patterns, probabilities, or systems of human experience and action, rather than as a series of immutable laws or inevitable occurrences. A culture doesn't make people behave in certain ways, but it does embed behavioral patterns in its worldview so that it usually doesn't occur to people to act otherwise.

With these reservations in mind, Triandis (1994) summarizes research that shows how cultures can be categorized in four different ways. There are cultures that can be typified (1) as more or less complex in the social distinctions they invoke (the **complexity syndrome**), (2) as more or less individualistic in the ways they attach importance to a single human being (the **individualism syndrome**), (3) as more or less interested in conformity based on interdependence and tradition (the **collectivism syndrome**), and (4) as more or less reliant on strict norms and roles for regulating behavior (the **tightness syndrome**).

Borderlands and Border Crossings

Some of the research summarized in the preceding section might suggest that it is relatively simple to measure or categorize cultures. You might also be tempted to jump to the conclusion that because such measures have been developed, higher scores on certain criteria might indicate that some cultures are "better" or more admirable than others, or that cultural differences present insurmountable problems for communicators.

A THEORY EXTENSION

CULTURAL SYNDROMES

Think of cultural syndromes as the tendencies or patterns that cultures develop to organize communicators' behavior and meanings along certain dimensions. Although any single culture will inevitably be a mixture of patterns, each dimension may be considered a continuum.

- The *complexity syndrome:* Some cultures rely on a great number of distinctions and complex relationships among different individuals and groups (such as extended families and diverse occupations), whereas other cultures are comparatively simpler.
- The *individualism syndrome:* Cultures grant greater or lesser importance to the relatively independent rights and goals of individual actors.
- The *collectivism syndrome:* Cultures grant greater or lesser importance to conformity with larger social groups; this tendency can take either a *horizontal* form of high interdependence and cooperation with the group or a *vertical* form that emphasizes service or conformity on the basis of authority, structure, and tradition.
- The *tightness syndrome:* Cultures differ in the extent to which they implicitly regulate behaviors by norms and roles. Tighter cultures prescribe relatively narrow norms of behavior and strict sanctions for deviating from them, whereas looser cultures tolerate or accept a range of conflicting or pluralistic norms. According to research in this area, tightness appears to correlate with homogeneity—that is, the more similar a group's members are, the tighter the norms of behavior are likely to be.

Source: Triandis, 1994 (pp. 144–180)

 **LINK**

See Chapter 5 for more information about the communication rules that govern how these patterns develop distinctively in different cultures.

However, cultural differences may not be as isolating or as disabling as some people assume. In one sense, it's intuitively obvious that cultural comparisons, such as comparing people's expectations for appropriate behavior in Russia and Rio de Janeiro, will involve differences. But does this mean that everything is different? Clearly not. We live in an age of media involvement that cuts across historical, national, and cultural boundaries. Many, if not most, people live at the intersections of a variety of cultural traditions and become competent in a variety of cultural vocabularies. Albert Murray (1970) observes that blacks and whites in the United States have evolved traditions that differ from each other, but they have also co-created such traditions as jazz and forms of everyday talk that thoroughly interfuse blacks and whites with each other. Murray believes that African Americans and white European Americans, despite their many differences, are culturally more similar to each other than either is similar to any other cultural group in the world.

When cultural practices mix vigorously, we can expect extraordinary communication. Literary theorist Mikhail Bakhtin (1986) believes that cultural boundaries are especially important for understanding what motivates writers. He thinks that critics "have not taken into account that the most intense and productive life of culture takes place on the boundaries of its individual areas and not in places where these areas have become enclosed in their own specificity" (p. 2). The same reminder applies to communication theorists.

A similar idea advanced by other cultural theorists (Anzaldúa, 1987, 1988; Rosaldo, 1989), helps us to understand not only the important differences themselves but also the overlaps and profound interpersonal challenges of cross-cultural living. Gloria Anzaldúa (1987) suggests that to focus on "borders" is to "define the places that are safe and unsafe, to distinguish *us* from *them*. A border is a dividing line, a narrow strip along a steep edge" (p. 3). We won't get very far in understanding cultural identity if we think only in terms of divisive borders. The definitions and demarcations are just no longer this precise (if they ever were). Instead, Anzaldúa (1987) finds it useful to use the term **borderlands** to refer to those places where there are people living (physically, socially, psychologically) near borders, people who are affected by the different sides of presumably border-like differences. That is, such people don't find their identities defined exclusively from within cultural enclaves. Instead, identities are defined by contradictions and tensions in borderlands where cultures contact each other. The borderlands concept means that our future will not be in the hands of people whose identities are culturally insulated or purebred but will be defined increasingly by "a new space: a new field of identity" (Sanchez-Tranquilino & Tagg, 1992, p. 560). This new kind of vigorous if often tense cultural environment will place a premium on flexible communicators—those who are able to switch freely between cultural codes of language and behavior, and live with ambiguity and contradiction. The borderlands concept thus invites students of culture to imagine how people exist and live not just within but also across older definitions of cultural borders.

Renato Rosaldo (1989) reinforces Anzaldúa's insight:

In rejecting the classic "authenticity" of cultural purity, she seeks out the many-stranded possibilities of the borderlands. By sorting through and weaving together its overlapping strands, Anzaldúa's identity becomes ever stronger, not diffused. She argues that because Chicanos have so long practiced the art of cultural blending, "we" now stand in a position to become leaders in developing new forms of polyglot cultural creativity....

A renewed concept of culture thus refers less to a unified entity ("a culture") than to the mundane practices of everyday life.... Ethnographers look less for homogeneous communities than for the border zones within and between them. Such cultural border zones are always in motion, not frozen for inspection. (pp. 216–217)

In other words, you should temper your understanding of Triandis's (1994) cultural syndromes with an understanding of how difficult it is to assess cultural differences with precision. The borderlands idea allows us to transcend the assumptions of narrowly defined "identity politics" as well.

Of course, the concept of borderlands does not mean that there are no more dominant groups in society, nor that some groups aren't silenced by other more powerful groups. Working from some of the same premises as borderlands theorists, Mark Orbe (e.g., 1996) seeks to establish what he calls **co-cultural theory**. In one way, he reacts to former labels that at times suggested that minority or marginalized groups were inferior (they were called "subcultures," for example). Instead, not only are these multiple cultures diverse but they are also vigorous contributors to the overall cultural environment. He also notes how his analysis extends feminist *muted group theory* (to be described in more detail later in the chapter), and defines how group voices can be silenced—muted—by dominant social expectations. Co-cultures are groups whose members must develop specialized communication strategies to ensure survival in the larger society.

REVIEWING KEY IDEAS

THE BORDERLANDS CONCEPT

- Reminds theorists not to assume that cultural differences are pure or contained within borders, but that most people live in the vicinity of various borders and are inevitably affected by simultaneous cultural influences.
- Reminds theorists that cultural differences cannot be measured precisely, because social actors always absorb a variety of cultural influences within a pluralistic society.
- Reminds theorists that most people live in many different borderlands, and that they will be increasingly challenged to negotiate competing demands for their communicative energies.
- Reminds theorists to take a process perspective on communication, one that emphasizes change, adjustment, ambiguity, and flexibility over static definitions of what a culture "is."
- Reminds theorists that a new kind of cultural identity can emerge from the tensions caused by blending different codes and cultural patterns.

⬚LINK

Communication theorist Mary Strine (1997) is strongly attracted to the *borderlands* concept because it underscores an important concept of Chapter 5—*dialogue*. She writes: "Just as borderlands functions to decenter cultural differences and reorient thinking in the direction of dialogue and new integration, it opens new spaces of inquiry to dialogic interaction as well" (p. 183).

High- and Low-Context Cultures

Although the borderlands concept warns us not to overgeneralize the importance of a culture's borders, researchers remain interested in how patterns of verbal and nonverbal communication vary among cultural groups. Remember that verbal and nonverbal messages cannot be considered separately, because each message code operates as the context for the other code. Thus, for example, a comment expressing your confidence about an upcoming exam will always be interpreted in the context of some nonverbal message, such as a furrowed brow that suggests to the listener you're worried about the exam. Similarly, the nonverbal message of a handshake is usually embedded in a sequence of talk that lets an observer know how to "take" the handshake.

Edward T. Hall (1992), whose work has influenced generations of diplomats, travelers, and scholars, has devoted his professional life to a form of scholarly empathy. He attempts to place himself within the standpoints of non-Western cultures in order to make their everyday habits and interpretations seem less "strange" and more accessible to the European and North American mind. Among his other contributions, Hall (1977) has popularized the distinction between **high-context (HC) cultures** and **low-context (LC) cultures:**

> *A* high-context (HC) *communication or message is one in which most of the information is either in the physical context or internalized in the person, while very little is in the coded, explicit, transmitted part of the message. A* low-context (LC) *communication is just the opposite; i.e., the mass of the information is invested in the explicit code. Twins who have grown up together can and do communicate more economically (HC) than two lawyers in a courtroom during a trial (LC), a mathematician programming a computer, two politicians drafting legislation, two administrators writing a regulation, or a child trying to explain to his mother why he got into a fight. (p. 91; emphasis added)*

Hall's context distinction depends on understanding the relationship between verbal and nonverbal message systems. To a large extent, what a person says to a listener is based on what the speaker presumes the listener knows or is able to figure out from the context, and therefore what doesn't need to be specified overtly. Cultures differ in the extent to which their actors depend on nonverbal messages to clarify verbal messages. Some cultures (HC) rely heavily on such nonverbal messages as object language, tone of voice (a form of paralinguistics), and timing (chronemics) to alert listeners to what needn't be said in order to presume understanding. But other cultures (LC) socialize speakers to approach talk in a more explicit and elaborated way; low-context cultures expect listeners to supply fewer elements of context as essential message features (see A Theory Extension, p. 217).

Hall's distinction between HC and LC cultures extends the linguistic research (Bernstein, 1960) that distinguishes between *elaborated* and *restricted* codes (see Reviewing Key Ideas, p. 218). People speaking in an **elaborated code** supply a great deal of verbal explanation and information because they are expected to do so. Receivers in elaborated code situations cannot be expected to make connections easily or to have a storehouse of concepts with which to contextualize the new message. Let's consider an appropriate and very immediate example: In writing this textbook for students of communication, as authors we must use a relatively elaborated code. Even though some readers might be comfortable with less explanation, we would risk not reaching other readers who might have less background in the field if we used a less elaborated code. The classroom, therefore, is often an elaborated code situation, analogous to Hall's idea of a low-context culture. In other words, teachers can't assume too much about what students will understand through context without verbal elaboration, because they can't be sure of all the different experiential contexts of their listeners.

A **restricted code**, by contrast, probably characterizes the talk of sorority sisters if, for example, they have lived together for an extended period. Over time, individuals who frequently interact with each other develop special streamlined speech forms that rely heavily on context. In such relationships, less needs to be verbalized in order for others to understand and identify with a speaker. Twins, to

---

A THEORY EXTENSION

THE CULTURAL IMPACT OF CONTEXTING

Hall's theoretical distinctions suggest a highly practical interpersonal skill that he calls *contexting:*

> Japanese, Arab, and Mediterranean peoples who have extensive information networks among family, friends, colleagues, and clients, and who are involved in close personal relationships, are "high-context" (HC). As a result, for most normal transactions in daily life they do not require, nor do they expect, much in-depth background information. This is because it is their nature to keep themselves informed about everything having to do with the people who are important in their lives. Low-context people include the Americans and the Germans, Swiss, Scandinavians, and other northern Europeans. Within each culture, of course, there are specific individual differences in the need for contexting—that is, the process of filling in background data—but it is helpful to know whether or not the culture of a particular country falls on the high or low side of the scale. . . .
>
> HC people are apt to become impatient and irritated when LC people insist on giving them information they don't need. Conversely, low-context people are at a loss when high-context people do not provide enough information. One of the great communications challenges in life is to find the appropriate level of contexting which is customary both at home and abroad. Too much information frequently leads people to feel they are being talked down to; too little information can mystify them or make them feel left out.

Source: Hall and Hall, 1987 (pp. 8, 11).

use another fairly obvious example, may know each other well enough to be able to finish each other's sentences accurately; they share a restricted code.

Anthropologist Mary Douglas believes that all language depends to some extent on unspoken assumptions but that it takes a sophisticated understanding of communication to be able to study what's *not* said as well as what is said. This is why she titles one of her books *Implicit Meanings* (1975). Researchers such as Bernstein (1960) and herself, Douglas writes, are "interested in the dark side of the moon, in the meanings that are conveyed without being spoken" (1975, p. 173). Studying culture means explaining how people decide on mixing the spoken with the unspoken, which is another way of stating that "culture is communication" (Hall, 1959).

Theorizing about Cultural Dilemmas

Some people assume that the role of theories is to aid in the description of the world. Through theories, the assumption goes, we discover more and more about how complex processes work, which, in turn, better enables us to know what we want to do about them. This assumption certainly describes a major function of theorizing, and most social scientists are guided by it. Surely most of the theorists discussed in *Questions of Communication* have been motivated by this goal of discovery.

The Role of Theoretical Critique

Some theorists, however, also recognize that theories themselves are potent social forces. Sometimes, in fact, our theories are so interwoven into our lives that we lose sight of them as theories and act as if they were the realities they supposedly represent. Recall from Chapter 1 that a theory will never be completely value-free; instead, it always involves the value assumptions of the theorist at some level. Remember, too, that once a theory becomes widely discussed and acceptable (if not fully accepted), it can create blinders for some researchers and ana-

---

REVIEWING KEY IDEAS

HALL'S CONTEXT DISTINCTIONS FOR CULTURES

- *High-context cultures* rely more on context to help communicators understand the intended meanings of messages. These communication systems depend more on *restricted codes* of language.
- *Low-context cultures* rely more on verbal description to help communicators understand the intended meanings of messages. These communication systems depend more on *elaborated codes* of language.

Source: Hall, 1977.

lysts, who might find the theory so persuasive that they're unable to think outside of its suggested parameters.

Whether such blinders are big or small problems often depends on whom you ask. Some theorists, especially in the broad field of cultural communication and criticism, approach theory not as a method of empirical discovery but as an ideological playing field. To them, various practices become widespread not just because they illuminate some truth but also because they are politically comfortable or beneficial to groups in power. These theorists ask unsettling questions, such as: Who profits from the belief that large-scale studies of men's moral decision making can be generalized to explain women's ethical choices as well? Who profits from the belief that the essential standards for assessing world civilizations seem to have been developed in the European context of ancient Greek and Roman civilization? Thus, some very intriguing theorizing in communication and other social sciences focuses on where the interpersonal dimensions of culture meet the interpersonal implications of cultural politics.

Communication students who are curious about social practices will generally want to understand the basic vocabulary of the vigorous dialogue about multiculturalism that is now taking place in the intellectual world. A look through communication journals in recent years should convince you that our discipline is immersed in such a dialogue, yet the controversy rages widely across disciplinary boundaries. Some theorists seek to uncover hidden assumptions in so-called neutral or scientific or observational theorizing, and want to call attention to the far-from-neutral political consequences of communication theories. In other words, their theories critique the ideologies and hidden assumptions both of other theorists and of the social science disciplines.

We suggest that students learn about theories of cultural critique in order to become better informed participants in this important social conversation, and not because we want to push our own agenda. For example, we believe that you should learn how Molefi Kete Asante develops his theoretical perspective of Afrocentrism because his ideas are discussed by many other theorists and political figures, and not necessarily because we are convinced that you yourself should become an advocate of Asante's position. Be aware, too, that different theorists/critics may use the same terms differently. Asante's theory is a good example. The Afrocentrism label doesn't simply denote a communication theory; it is applied by some who make bolder claims about African history than Asante does, for example. Simply read with an open and critical mind, and you will be rewarded. We need informed participants in a cultural dialogue of theories, communicators who are knowledgeable enough to be fair to both positions that are personally near and positions that are, culturally speaking, more distant.

In this section you will learn about three theoretical positions that respond to somewhat different yet interconnected cultural dilemmas. Despite their differences, you will note similarities in how the theorists create their arguments and develop their conceptual systems. All of the authors, for example, agree that the issues of power and domination of certain groups over others should be central concerns in cultural theorizing. They also believe that cultural critique can be a valid part of theorizing, in that valid evidence can come from synthesizing historical and critical sources, as well as from the more traditional methods of social science research. We explore how articulation theory responds to dilemmas of class and social distinction, how feminist theorizing and muted group theory respond to certain dilemmas of contemporary gender relations, and how Afrocentric theory responds to the dilemma of race.

Articulation Theory: The Dilemma of Power

A new cross-disciplinary area called *cultural studies* has developed over the past several decades as a perspective on how communicative power becomes identified with broad social and cultural patterns of understanding (Carey, 1989; Grossberg, Nelson, & Treichler, 1992). McQuail (1997) believes it is "firmly established as an academic discipline and major publishing project" (p. 46), and that it is currently expanding its influence with students and within other disciplines. Sociologists, political scientists, psychologists, literary critics, philosophers, and communication scholars from a wide range of traditions have been attracted to cultural studies approaches, with most of their works characterized by an intense interest in media influence, popular culture, and interpersonal communication. Although Lawrence Grossberg (1993) is not anxious to lock down a formal definition, he nevertheless points out three features of cultural studies practice: (1) It recognizes the constant making and remaking of social practices, and therefore, the inevitability of "contestation" or continual arguments about them; (2) it focuses on popular forms of entertainment as a "terrain" for political power struggles where people actually live their lives; and (3) it is committed to a form of "radical contextualism" in which it's impossible to define culture's importance except locally and concretely, in immediate context.

For these reasons, cultural studies scholars tend not to be quantitatively oriented in their methods (many even see cultural studies as a countermovement to traditional social science, and thus ignore or renounce surveys and experimental designs for gathering communication data). Instead, they prefer qualitative methods of critical analysis and diagnosis. To them, "theorizing" suggests a somewhat different enterprise than it does to quantitative social scientists. As Slack (1996) explains:

> *"Theory" is a term that often connotes an objective, formal tool, or even a "value-free" heuristic device. Cultural studies resists thinking in terms of the "application" of theory in this sense.... In place of that conception of theory, cultural studies works with the notion of theory as a "detour" to help ground our engagement with what newly confronts us and to let that engagement provide the ground for retheorizing. Theory is thus a practice in a double sense: it is a formal conceptual tool as well as a practising or "trying out" of a way of theorizing.... Successful theorizing is not measured by exact theoretical fit but by the ability to work with our always inadequate theories to help us move understanding "a little further on down the road." (p. 113)*

The theorist Slack has in mind when discussing this approach is perhaps the most influential representative of contemporary cultural studies, the British intellectual Stuart Hall.

Among Stuart Hall's (1989, 1992, 1996) many enduring contributions to this area of research is his application of **articulation theory**. Cultural studies theorists use articulation theory to explain power relations as communication phenomena, not as mere exercises in overt manipulation or coercion. We discuss Hall's approach to articulation theory first because it provides a useful context for the other, more specific gender and racial approaches, as you will see later in this section.

By **articulation**, Hall (1996) means the process by which ideas and cultural concepts—that may or may not otherwise be closely related—are linked through public discussion into complex clusters that then appear to be unified and whole. His use of the word *articulation* implies two meanings: (1) The more obvious sense of something related to talk (e.g., people are said to "articulate" well if they talk plainly and to be "articulate" if they speak intelligently), and (2) the less common sense of how things can become connected, attached, or adjusted together (e.g., in a company, the research and development department has to be "articulated" with the marketing department in order for its products to be successful). Hall (1996, p. 141) points out that in Britain, an "articulated lorry" (a truck) is what people in the United States would call a trailer; the front cab of the truck is connectable to any number and kinds of trailer loads, depending on the choice of the company or client.

Articulation, then, is a rich metaphor for ideas. Political and advertising campaigns can be articulated—hooked, in a sense—to a wide range of discursive appeals based on different cultural values. In American presidential campaigns, for example, Republicans try to articulate, or link, their opponents in voters' minds with the slogan "tax-and-spend." "It's your money," they say, "not the government's money." In this way, they want to bolster the notion that Democrats uncritically and selfishly favor a wasteful big government at the expense of hardworking and successful individuals. On the other side, Democrats typically try to articulate Republican policies and candidates with only the wealthy and comfortable segments of society by using such terms as "special corporate interests" and the "wealthiest one percent." In this way, Democrats portray their own party as speaking for the common person and being sensitive to groups who have no other political voice.

Although articulation theory has not always been applied in precise ways in cultural studies (see Hall, 1996; Moffitt, 1993; O'Sullivan, Hartley, Saunders, Montgomery, & Fiske, 1994, pp. 17–18; Slack, 1989, 1996), it is especially useful in analyzing cultural problems in contexts where there are competing interests with different investments of power and domination. As Stuart Hall and other theorists apply the concept of articulation, it appears to have the following characteristics (see also Reviewing Key Ideas, p. 223).

1. ***Articulations are shifting, temporary phenomena, constantly in flux.*** An articulation that once served a cultural purpose may be rearticulated when power bases and group goals change. In the 1960s, for example, Jews were the non-black minority most closely aligned with the civil rights movement in the U.S. South; in the 1990s, many African Americans sought different cultural alliances.

⬡LINKS

○ Does Stuart Hall's articulation theory remind you in some ways of the *general systems theory* discussed in Chapter 1? Both discuss the relation of wholes to their parts. After reviewing systems assumptions in Chapter 1, and after reading this chapter's section on articulation theory, decide for yourself what their similarities and differences might be.

○ Does articulation theory also remind you of some of the problems associated with the social context of communication as discussed in Chapter 3? How might the articulated whole become the context through which its linked parts must be interpreted? Review Chapter 3 for clues to this interesting question.

2. ***Articulations are arbitrary features of discourse; they are not necessary or inherent in the phenomena being described.*** In other words, articulations are not the properties of unified wholes but are characteristics of how we talk about phenomena we consider to be whole. Consider, as an example, a train that travels between Philadelphia and New York. "It" has a number and a schedule, and regular travelers are used to saying that "it" is later or earlier today than "it" was yesterday. However, in terms of its actual components, today's train may be composed of a very different set of cars, coupled (articulated) in a very different way, than yesterday's train. But the travelers are convinced that, even though the physical identity of the train's components may be quite different, the essential identity of the train remains the same. Of course, the potential identities of a number of trains are highly variable, depending on the articulations decided on by those who have the power to determine the trains' couplings. The Republican Party identifies itself as the party of Abraham Lincoln, which appeals to minority voters, while the ACLU identifies itself as an organization that protects both conservative and liberal free speech. Both organizations want to be perceived as unified wholes, but articulation theory suggests that they—and all groups and ideologies—are formed by articulated links among shifting components. Such theorists and critics analyze the articulations through which today's train might be differently coupled than yesterday's train.

3. ***Articulations depend on hierarchical relationships.*** Articulation theorists note that although a truck's trailer may be larger and heavier than the truck's cab, its movement depends on decisions directed from the front. Therefore articulation theory asks such power-based questions as these: Who gets to define the relationship between two ideas? Who relies on whom for assent or acquiescence? How do groups come to understand that their voices have more or less impact than the voices of other groups? Who profits from seemingly innocuous or neutral policies? Not surprisingly, many articulation theorists are at least somewhat motivated by Marxist social analyses, in which *ideology* is an important concept. **Ideology** is a set of ideas that is so thoroughly accepted by its believers that they do not question its existence or importance. Some would argue that American individualism is an ideology within the social sphere, and that American capitalism is an ideology within the economic sphere. According to Slack (1989), ideology "is the mechanism that organizes the multiplicity of connections into a temporarily essentialized system of representation within which we live out those connections as real. Ideology is…of particular importance, for it is within ideology that relations of power are presented, represented, contested, and rearticulated" (p. 333).

4. ***Articulations potentially tie together both similarity and difference,*** allowing theorists to describe how cultural phenomena are often composed of both unity and distinctiveness, the harmony of sameness and the tension of difference. Hall (1996) cites singer Bruce Springsteen's appeal as one that "can be read, with equal conviction, in at least two diametri-

cally opposed ways. [Springsteen's] audiences seem to be made up of people from 5 to 50, busily reading him in different ways. The symbols are deeply American—populist in their ambiguity; he's both in the White House and On The Road. In the 1960s, you had to be one or the other. Springsteen is somehow both at the same time" (p. 138). The concept of articulation thus allows us to think of a complex cultural phenomenon both as a unified whole and as composed of different parts, perhaps even inconsistent or contradictory parts. Once you begin to sense how common articulations are, it is logical to ask who in society has the power to disseminate their articulations of events and how they put that power into play.

Articulation theory, then, gives students of communication a useful vocabulary for describing how communicative power is expressed and perceived—or, as Hall puts it, how that power is "read."

Feminist Theorizing and Muted Group Theory: The Dilemma of Gender

"The modern women's movement," wrote linguist Robin Lakoff in 1990, "now has behind it some twenty years of theoretical thinking about the many aspects of 'the woman question,' one of the most important and agonizingly insoluble issues among them being language. From early on, women have recognized the need to take back the language, reclaim it or parts of it, get a right to decide about how to speak and be spoken of and to" (p. 198). Talk about women and men leads us to distinguish sex from gender, a very important distinction to cultural communication theorists. They typically distinguish between sex and gender, although most people in everyday life do not. **Sex** is a biological and physiological condition into which a person is born, and **gender** is a cultural and social construction created by how people talk about different kinds of male and female behavior. As Wood (1996) observes, "Biological sex is transformed into culturally constructed gender as we interact with social structures and practices

---

REVIEWING KEY IDEAS

ARTICULATIONS:

- Are links or connections between phenomena or groups that structure our cultural understandings.
- Are shifting and temporary.
- Are arbitrary constructions that can be observed in the discourse about events, groups, and texts.
- Are dependent on social hierarchies and distributions of power.
- Are links forged between dissimilar, as well as between similar, elements.

that express, uphold, and encourage individuals to embody prevailing views of women and men" (p. 4).

One approach to understanding culture is to understand how it structures language and nonverbal practices between and among its various subgroups. A related issue of great cultural significance is how cultures make meaningful (or even validate) the differences between women's and men's communication habits. In some cultures, Lakoff (1990) reports, anthropologists have found that men and women claim to have developed separate languages that are unintelligible to each other. Lakoff, however, suggests that at most, such men and women have decided to pretend that they can't understand each other when in fact they actually can. In a predominantly Western model of gender, though, they often *don't* understand each other well, although they pretend they *do*. Lakoff (1990) notices that "there are deep and subtle differences that lead to more serious kinds of misunderstanding: both sexes use the same words in the same constructions, but understand them differently. This misunderstanding is serious: we think we understand and have been understood, when we really don't and haven't. The differences lie in areas that are not explicitly available for inspection, that require metacommunication to be fully examined. And…metacommunication is not something this culture (like most) values or is comfortable doing" (p. 201). Some researchers and theorists disagree with Lakoff. They argue that differences between male and female communication patterns in Western life have been exaggerated by a noncritical acceptance of some early research in the field.

Women and men who grow up speaking English are likely to believe that certain differences in female and male communication are natural. They may hear men and women speak somewhat differently, use what are perceived as different strategies in their speech styles, choose different adjectives in certain situations, have somewhat different communicative goals and motives, establish different nonverbal patterns, and, further, hear males and females talked about by others differently. Indeed, some research points in this direction (Frank & Anshen, 1983; Kramerae, 1981; Kramerae & Treichler, 1990; Wood, 1996). However, some celebrities in the popular culture have exaggerated the extent to which men and women therefore live in different kinds of communicative worlds. John Gray (1992), for example, has premised his career on talk shows and best-seller lists on the supposed metaphorical distinction that men are "from Mars" but women are "from Venus." Clearly, from his perspective, dealing with such huge disparities demands expert assistance, or ordinary people will make huge errors that will keep them from understanding, relating to, or resolving conflicts with, the "other" gender. Interestingly, careful academic theorizing leads us to a more hopeful sense of how important the differences may be. According to Canary, Emmers-Sommer, and Faulkner (1997), recent research casts a great deal of doubt on the assumptions that women are social, communal, and sensitive, and men are self-reliant, instrumental, and tough. Summarizing studies reported in their anthology, Kalbfleisch and Cody (1995) suggest that "men and women tend to use many of the same behaviors to express dominance, and…women can and do communicate dominance behaviors with some frequency. However, gender differences persist in that males and females differ in their ability to intensify or modify messages being sent. Males more effectively communicate dominance, whereas female behaviors reflect more solidarity and intimacy" (p. 7; see also Burgoon & Dillman, 1995). Similarly, in the matter of speech usage, an overview of recent research suggests that "some of the earlier research from the 1970s is too often accepted at face value or is rarely challenged, despite the fact that many of these early investigations were limited in a number of ways" (p. 7; see also Mulac & Bradac, 1995).

In fact, research in gender roles suggests that many male-female differences can be attributed to conditions of power and powerlessness. That is, while some women's speech has been found to include more hesitations, qualifiers, and tag questions than men's speech, Frank and Anshen (1983) summarize research that suggests these features are also characteristic of the speech of other power-diminished groups: "The use of the stereotypically women's language features is correlated more with social powerlessness than with sex" (p. 46). Mulac and Bradac (1995) found from their study of other published research that male and female power differences themselves tend to disappear over time as individuals communicate more with each other, suggesting that the beliefs and expectations we hold about what it is to talk "like a man" or "like a woman" may be overly simplistic.

It's interesting that some early research may inadvertently have caused us to overstereotype gender relations. But does this mean that for all practical purposes men and women are communicatively pretty much the same? No; important differences remain, as feminist theorists remind us. **Feminist theory** points to sexist distinctions inherent in the English language, a phenomenon that children growing up in families and schools cannot avoid. Remember that language structures personal experience, as we have stressed in this book. Language is our agency of socialization and the prime criterion by which progress in the school system is judged. As male and female children become proficient in language, they become attuned to the power differences that distinguish the sexes. Although we do not have the space in this book to summarize the full argument, feminists theorize that subtle and not-so-subtle linguistic features, such as the use of "he" and "mankind" to refer to women as well as men, and the tendency to call professional women by their first names while using titles for their male counterparts, all support the presumption of power inequality between the genders (see Pearson, Turner, & Todd-Mancillas, 1991, pp. 79–102).

While there may be no *essential* or inherent differences between the communication styles of particular men and particular women, there are certainly some power differences and powerful effects as men and women differently experience how they see themselves and each other, as genders are reflected in everyday talk. Pearson and Cooks (1995) claim that "traditional scientific research is a patriarchical enterprise, that information pertaining to women has been viewed through an 'ideological' lens, and that male experience has been the panorama from which others—both male and female—have been judged. Feminists discourage researchers from seeking additional answers to old questions, but encourage investigators to pursue new questions about women's experiences from their own positioning" (p. 334).

One particularly focused approach that attempts to account for some gender differences is **muted group theory**, originally developed in the writings of anthropologists (Ardener, 1978) and extended in the communication field by Cheris Kramerae (1981). Kramerae argues that women's language is often effectively silenced or redirected relative to the power of men's language. Muted group theorists assume that the differently socialized gender experiences of men and women create different perceptions of how the world works. Further, they assume, in Kramerae's account, that the "political dominance" of men's perceptions translates into the linguistic habits of individual speakers, "impeding the free expression of women's alternative models of the world," and that women are implicitly required to alter their models to reflect male communication patterns or to become "mute" or inarticulate (p. 3). Men then use women's muteness or inarticulateness in such situations to support the existing structure of interpersonal politics.

In a review of muted group theorizing and associated research on women's talk, Kramerae (1981) notes that the theory also suggests the following hypotheses:

- Females are more likely to have difficulty expressing themselves fluently within dominant (public) modes of expression.
- Males have more difficulty than females in understanding what members of the other gender mean.
- Females are likely to find ways to express themselves outside the dominant public modes of expression used by males.
- Females are more likely to state dissatisfaction with the dominant public modes of expression.
- Women refusing to live by the ideas of social organization held by the dominant group…will change dominant public modes of expression as they consciously and verbally reject those ideas.
- Females are not as likely to coin the words that become widely recognized and used by both men and women.
- Females' sense of humor—what relationships between persons, places, and things they consider incongruous—will differ from males' sense of humor. (p. 4)

In the Introduction to this book, we discussed Belenky and colleagues' *Women's Ways of Knowing* (1986) study. Although they do not test muted group theory directly, their extensive interviews reinforce Kramerae's point. Belenky et al. (1986) note that silence is a position that characterizes many women's reaction to public life, at least at the beginning of their involvement in it. The researchers also describe a "continued injunction against articulating needs, feelings, and experiences" among women, an expectation that women should "curtail their voice," and a "tendency to allocate speaking to men and listening to women" (p. 167). One interviewee, a successful professional woman, made these revealing comments: "You know, the older I get the more I realize that I'm willing to talk about things I care about only if I know the other person is really listening. If I don't feel that, I find myself falling into a silence, even when I'm at work or in the middle of a professional meeting" (p. 147).

Obviously, feminist theorists believe that reality looks different depending upon where you "stand," as cognitive and perception research would suggest. One other strain of feminism has been termed **feminist standpoint theory** for this very reason. Although a more general stance of standpoint theorizing can be applied to virtually any cultural issue, much of the impetus for this work comes from feminist theorizing, so let's look at its implications here. According to Julia Wood (1999), a prominent spokesperson for this position, it "traces the ways in which the locations of distinct social groups within a society shape members' experiences, knowledge, and ways of interacting" (p. 219). Specific work within feminist communication theory (e.g., Mathison, 1997) suggests that this perspective, which might seem unremarkable at first glance, actually undermines much of the scientific enterprise that presumes we can determine exact definitions of what objects and processes are, and determine them through neutral or disinterested inquiry. The knowledge claims that flow from this potential certainty, standpoint theorists argue, fundamentally present a masculine perspective or standpoint as the "correct" one, as Maureen Mathison (1997) suggests:

> Standpoint theorists...argue that this position of disinterestedness is untenable and contend that all knowledge derives from location. This is not to say that knowledge claims are arbitrary. There is a world in which observed phenomena may be agreed on.... What is at issue is who are permitted to identify, define, interpret, and act on such phenomena, and how they do so.
>
> According to standpoint theory, one of the primary problems with scientific inquiry is that it has been practiced by a limited group of privileged men who have narrowly construed and subsequently constricted what counts as knowledge....
>
> To amplify the manner in which things are named and imbued with meaning, many feminist scholars in communication have relocated their inquiry in women's lives. These scholars propose (explicitly or implicitly, consciously or unconsciously) that in establishing women's gendered experiences as the starting point for inquiry, accounts of knowledge can be more sensitive to and more inclined to include those who have been marginalized. (pp. 149–150)

Although Mathison is convinced that feminist standpoint theory makes an important contribution, she cautions that it should resist the impulse simply to "reinscribe" old categories of knowing with new, different ones. She wants to remind us that its purpose should not be to elevate women's perspectives as automatically better perspectives but to contribute to a scholarly dialogue in which a better and more balanced overall **epistemology**—or system of knowing—can be established. Knowing the differences between standpoints is not "an end in itself. It is a beginning" (p. 158).

Afrocentric Theory: The Dilemma of Race

Almost every day people in workplaces, classrooms, and families discuss *race* as though the term had a consistent and clear meaning for contemporary society. Most people seem to talk as though "race" were a biological or scientific label for a

⬅LINKS

○ Standpoint theorists base their thinking on the same reasoning we discussed in Chapter 4: that perception is not directly *of the characteristics of objects or events themselves* but a perception *of the relationship between perceiver and perceived.* If "I" look at "you," my perception is necessarily partial and dependent upon the aspect of you that I can see from my own perspective; there is much more to you that I can't see—and others looking from different perspectives will not be able to see exactly what I do.

○ Some feminists (Collins, 1991) have identified themselves specifically as black feminist theorists. One prominent feature of this approach is its consistent reliance on dialogic principles. See the related discussions of interdependence in Chapter 5 and of dialogic ethics in Chapter 10.

set of clearly defined characteristics that differentiate human groups. Even though people usually aren't sure of the science behind the label "race," we continue to use it as though we, and all our listeners, know exactly what we're talking about. However, as a number of commentators argue, race has largely lost its status as a precise biological concept and may instead have become one of our most prominent social myths. **Race**, in effect, has become a shorthand way of referring to differences in our cultural and social patterns of communication, as they are linked (rightly or wrongly) to visible physical features such as skin color (for further explanation and a supplemental definition, see A Theory Extension, below).

A THEORY EXTENSION

WHAT IS RACE? BACKGROUND FOR COMMUNICATION THEORISTS

- Race is "a social category of people who are supposedly distinguished by inherited and invariable characteristics. Whereas race can at first glance be viewed as an innocent description of what certain people look like, it carries a hidden agenda about their 'nature,' how they behave and are expected to behave." Further, "ultimately we have to identify an unofficial package of ideas and assumptions that go with race: that a racial group has historical legacies associated with a geographically defined area and culture of origin, and that usually such groups can be identified by skin colour. The stage is therefore set for xenophobia and bigotry" (O'Sullivan et al., 1994, pp. 255, 256).
- "'Race' as a meaningful criterion within the biological sciences has long been recognized to be a fiction. When we speak of the 'white race' or the 'black race,' the 'Jewish race' or the 'Aryan race,' we speak in misnomers, biologically, and in metaphors, more generally. Nevertheless, our conversations are replete with usages of race which have their sources in the dubious pseudo-science of the eighteenth and nineteenth centuries" (Gates, 1992, p. 48).
- "The term 'race' itself has become suspect in scientific circles" (Montagu & Matson, 1979, p. 175).
- "There is no doubt that all human beings descend from an original population (probably, as it happens, in Africa), and from there people radiated out to cover the habitable globe.... In a sense, trying to classify people into a few races is like trying to classify books in a library: you may use a single property—size, say—but you will get a useless classification, or you may use a more complex system of interconnected criteria, and then you will get a good deal of arbitrariness. No one—not even the most compulsive librarian!—thinks that book classifications reflect deep facts about books" (Appiah, 1992, pp. 37, 38).

We are not suggesting that people should stop using the word *race*. We only suggest that you remember how the term is used in contemporary theoretical and conceptual discussions; that is, it refers to very rough generalizations about the cultural patterns of communication used by different groups. If you're interested in a challenging summary of recent discoveries about what we term race, see Kwame Appiah's (1992, pp. 28–46) essay "Illusions of Race."

Clearly, different groups develop different cultures, and the rules and expectations of those cultures color their perceptions of the world. What is less clear is how communicators might try to avoid using their own culture's pattern as the standard for how all people should communicate. Molefi Kete Asante, writing as Arthur L. Smith, published one of the first books in the field of communication on interracial interaction, *Transracial Communication* (1973). In recent years, he has become a foremost critic of **Eurocentrism**, the tendency to explain and judge all cultural phenomena in terms of standards developed within traditional European art, science, literature, and philosophy.

For example, a public speech considered by most teachers in the United States to be organized, rational, well supported, and effective tends to conform to rhetorical standards developed in ancient Greece and Rome by Aristotle, Cicero, Quintilian, and other classical teachers. In addition, the European world tends to regard a speech as the speaker's uninterrupted possession, undertaken while a passive audience attends to the message. Asante does not argue that these standards are wrong; rather, he points out that they are not universal. Thus what he questions is not the application of European theories of communication and science to many people and situations but aggressive attempts to impose those standards on all people and all cultures. There is no single right way to give a speech, but many ways that will lead to different kinds of effectiveness depending on the cultural context. To extend the speech example, Eurocentric analysts have a difficult time understanding a shared-responsibility speech situation, where an audience actively cooperates verbally with the speaker (as in the African American *call-and-response* tradition; its enthusiastic audience responses often sound like interruptions to Europeans and others outside the tradition).

Similarly, Asante (1987) contends, European thinking should not be the presumed benchmark for all questions of science, politics, religion, and social policy. We stressed in Chapter 1 that theories involve the values and assumptions of the theorists and researchers who develop them. Thus, understanding Eurocentrism has implications not only for the theorizing done by scholars in the past but also for the theorizing that we are able to imagine doing in the future. For example, social psychology, which in many ways is related to the study of interpersonal communication, "is a product of Europe and North America. Almost all that we know systematically about social behavior was derived by studying individuals and groups from those regions of the world. However, 70 percent of the earth's population lives outside Europe and North America, in cultures that are quite different from those of the 'West'" (Triandis, 1994, p. xv).

Asante (1980, 1987) responds to Eurocentrism with the theoretical counterposition of **Afrocentricity**, which is based on the alignment of African Americans and others in the world with African cultural origins. (Following Asante's

⬅LINK

In Chapter 8, we will explain the European rhetorical tradition in more detail. Aristotle, an ancient Greek philosopher, defined *rhetoric* as the art of finding the available means of persuasion in a situation. European styles of theorizing and teaching rhetoric emphasize the ability to change someone else's mind. In contrast, Asante's (1987) *Afrocentric* definition of *rhetoric* is "the productive thrust of language into the unknown in an attempt to create harmony and balance in the midst of disharmony and indecision" (p. 35). Do the two positions on rhetoric indicate fundamentally different ways of defining what communication should accomplish in a society? Fundamentally different ethical positions?

reasoning, Asians [see Cheng, 1987; Kincaid, 1987b], Arabs [see Hasnain, 1988; Said, 1978, 1981, 1993; Tehranian, 1988], and others in the world may find themselves in unique rhetorical and cultural situations not easily couched in terms of European ideals.) Asante's theoretical position involves "placing African ideals at the center of any analysis that involves African culture and behavior" (1987, p. 6). Note that in response to what Asante perceives as the Eurocentric tendency to place European thinking at the center of all cultural understanding, he does not assume that we should substitute African thinking to bump Eurocentrism from that center. Asante's historical and critical synthesis of evidence suggests that people of African descent will never find an authentic cultural existence while denying the influence of African cultural experience. Empathy, not domination, appears to be Asante's (1987) essential motivation: "Ascertaining the view of the other is important in understanding human phenomena. African responses and actions, however, have too often been examined from Eurocentric perspectives. The misunderstandings between Europeans and others have provoked in me an interest in alternative perspectives" (p. 11). Although some theorists who label themselves Afrocentric are more politically oriented, and some Afrocentric historical summaries have been criticized (Coughlin, 1996), Asante tries not to substitute one form of overgeneralization for another. He simply wants to get beyond what he terms the intellectual colonialism of Europe.

Many concepts are important in Afrocentric theory, and each seems to be closely related to the others. In one of his touchstone works, *The Afrocentric Idea* (1987), Asante stresses these communication concepts:

1. ***Rhetorical condition.*** Asante suggests that we should pay less attention to what is said in various situations and more attention to the conditions in which talk (and the designation of who is able to talk) is governed by power and dominance relationships. A theorist understands communication and social rhetoric not just by listening to the content of words but also by focusing on the structural assumptions of power that govern any cultural situation.

2. ***Orature.*** This term refers to "the sum total of oral tradition [in African-based culture], which includes vocality, drumming, storytelling, praise singing, and naming" (Asante, 1987, p. 60). Even though there is an important historical legacy of literature in Africa, the Afrocentric perspective fundamentally values talk over writing. The spontaneity, immediacy, and narrative base of the spoken word reigns over the sequential, linear, writing-oriented rationality of European cultural standards. An oral tradition values a wider range of rhetorical effectiveness than the narrow persuasive ideals of traditional rationality; it also invests the audience with much of the rhetorical power that European systems attribute to the individual speaker. Further, Afrocentric theory tends to presume—contrary to the European perspective—that arguments themselves have no power apart from how they are said and by whom.

3. ***Nommo.*** A powerful aspect of Afrocentric orature is a kind of reverence for the spoken word as an instrument of *nommo,* which Asante (1987)

◁ LINK

Contrast the notion of *nommo* with the assumptions of the *conduit metaphor* discussed in Chapter 2. Recall that the conduit metaphor and its linear way of depicting communication is presumably built into the structure of the English language. It assumes, contrary to Asante's views and contrary to contemporary theories emphasizing *process*, that we act as if words were packages of meaning that can be delivered at will. Do you think Afrocentric theory is, in this way, similar to the process-centered view of communication described in Chapter 2? Do you believe Asante is suggesting that people who trace their roots to Africa don't just use language differently but think of language in different ways? Why, or why not?

describes as "the generative and productive power of the spoken word" (p. 17). When speakers are immersed in *nommo,* Asante says, they understand that "all magic is word magic" (p. 49). It involves not only what words mean but also how they are said through "intonation and tonal styling," which are "*substantive* parts of most African American oratory" (p. 48). We can hear *nommo* in action in rap music and in how African American disk jockeys present the music. McPhail (1994) believes that *nommo* is a form of rhetoric that "offers some important theoretical directions for a discussion of race based upon parallel conceptions of communicative action" (p. 106). The Afrocentric assumption is that the word is never conceptually static but is always changing, acting as a stimulus to further meaning. It is in no sense a package or object of meaning whose force can be predetermined.

Kinds of Cultural Communication Theories

Clearly, many cultural theorists are interested in clarifying basic communication concepts and in developing critiques of the power structures of class, gender, and race. Students should understand that communication theorists are active participants in the wider intellectual dialogue about culture—a dialogue that sometimes gets so heated that some have termed it the "culture wars." Nevertheless, communication theorists go beyond merely developing concepts or taking critical positions. They want to examine what culture is like from the inside, and they want to understand what culture is like from the outside. Social science traditions such as anthropology, sociology, and, of course, communication, typically distinguish between the *emic* approach of participation within a single system and the *etic* approach of studying cultures and cross-cultural problems from external perspectives, or from the perspective of attempting to compare cultures.

Emic Theorizing: Revisiting Organizational Culture

Emic theorizing depends on research that focuses on getting an "inside" look. What is the culture like from the experience of its members or participants? How does it feel to live within this set of behavioral patterns or assumptions? At a more basic level, how can an outsider ever determine the assumptions, mind-sets, or sense-making habits that are so crucial but often so unexamined by members? Other than the frivolous answer that an outsider can never determine such things for certain, emic theorizing demands that researchers participate as fully as possible within the culture, even to the point of immersing themselves in the everyday lives of cultural members. Much of our knowledge about the earth's cultures generated by anthropologists in the last century was obtained by direct participation in unfamiliar cultures over long periods of time. The term *ethnography* is an overall label for the direct and immediate "I lived there" experience of researchers. Before we can know how cultures vary, we need to discover what each one is uniquely like, from within.

LINK

We introduced the distinction between *emic* and *etic* in Chapter 6, in discussing organizational culture research.

In other words, effective emic theorizing depends on:

- A commitment to study from within a single culture
- A commitment to immerse oneself in the study not only as an analyst but as a participant
- An assumption that cultural patterns are not to be judged but understood; criteria for evaluation should be internal (i.e., what function does this behavior or interpretation serve for members?) rather than external (i.e., are these people smarter or more ethical than the people of a different culture?)
- An assumption that the patterns encountered by the ethnographer may or may not be analogous to the patterns of other cultures

Of course, it takes a special kind of alertness and self-awareness for a communication researcher to be able to contribute to emic theory in this way. It is not a matter of making sure you are neutral; it is a matter of making sure you are participating as fully as possible while maintaining the kind of "field notes" or other recording that will allow you to theorize later with sufficient evidence.

As we discussed in the previous chapter, organizational communication researchers note that people working on common tasks tend to develop cultures. Most theorists in this area suggest that the primary goal of cultural research in organizations is to probe how each organization uniquely addresses the dilemmas of its environment. It might be tempting to assume that research into organizations explains organizational communication generally, but organizational culture research warns against such an easy explanation. Instead, it portrays the organization not only as a site of many shared assumptions unique to that particular organization, but also as a site of conflicting messages, multiple interpretations, and contested meanings (similar to the borderlands concept discussed earlier in this chapter). Organizational researchers interested in culture (e.g., Goodall, 1991) therefore see organizations as places that both maintain cultural boundaries of their own and—because of workers' external relations—necessarily bring into contact many other kinds of overlapping boundaries.

We will not focus on or exemplify emic approaches in detail here, because a good example of one form of emic theory was examined in detail in Chapter 6.

Etic Theorizing: Cross-Cultural Contexts

Etic theorizing, as you might expect, depends upon different assumptions about studying culture. Specifically, effective etic theorizing depends on:

- A commitment to studying culture from standpoints outside the cultural system
- A commitment to maintaining a relatively objective overview of cultural characteristics
- A willingness to compare cultures and cultural patterns
- A sense that cultures may have analogous features and criteria that could apply cross-culturally

The etic researcher, then, tries not to operate within a culture or within cultural constraints but outside culture as much as that is possible. Etic research attempts to adopt an overview mentality, although its advocates will readily admit that on one level it is impossible to remove your own cultural patterns from your experience. One of the unique contributions of etic theorizing is the possibility of examining cross-cultural encounters more effectively by generalizing about them.

Both emic and etic theorizing are important. We get certain kinds of information about cultures only through the work of ethnographers, and it is important in its own right. But sometimes this kind of information can also be applied to help people adapt to new cultures. Historically, the study of intercultural communication has involved the highly pragmatic task of adapting communicators from one culture to the demands of others (see Leeds-Hurwitz, 1990; Moon, 1996). Whether theorists want their theories to change society or not, individuals still must develop skill in cross-cultural communication and understanding. We have chosen one major theory to represent how powerful this kind of question of communication can be: Young Yun Kim's (1988, 1991) *cross-cultural adaptation theory*. Many other theories could serve the same function, but we find Kim's wide-ranging and rich theory particularly useful in showing how many communication factors are involved in understanding culture. You'll also see again, in the context of this theory, how practical a solid theoretical perspective can be.

Imagine that a young Japanese woman named Yuko is about to come to the United States to study at a prominent Midwestern university. Although she has taken English throughout most of her schooling in Japan and has thoroughly investigated U.S. culture, she is quite nervous. She has heard stories of other Asian students who were equally talented but had bad experiences in America. They got homesick, felt awkward and disconnected, and found that they could barely concentrate on their schoolwork. Although Yuko is happy to have the opportunity to study overseas, she almost wishes she had never applied for the program that supports her studies. She knows she'll be challenged in ways she can't even begin to imagine (see A Theory Extension, p. 234).

Kim (1988, 1991; Gudykunst & Kim, 1984) has applied her interest in cultural issues to the specific practical question that worries Yuko: How can someone successfully adapt to a new cultural situation? Research in cultural communication, Kim believes, must examine more than the differences between cultures; it should also try to illuminate the practical human problems of what it takes to move from a set of comfortable cultural assumptions—an experience of feeling essentially "at home"—into new cultural assumptions that are experienced as alien and challenging. How does this shift happen for strangers, immigrants, refugees, sojourners, and travelers? In other words, not only is Kim fascinated by cultures but she wants to develop a **cross-cultural adaptation theory**—a systematic explanation of how individuals learn to reorient their communication assumptions in new cultural contexts.

In an increasingly interdependent world, networked with rapid transportation and communication systems, every person becomes a potential cross-cultural visitor, often unexpectedly. For example, one recent study (Ross, 1996) reports that an increasing number of global firms send executives to other countries to gain competence in cross-culturally ambiguous situations and add to their knowledge about other cultural systems. Many more firms now also bring foreign nationals to

---

A THEORY EXTENSION

DISORIENTATIONS FOR JAPANESE SOJOURNERS IN THE UNITED STATES

- "The Japanese are likely to be startled at the ease with which Americans approach and enter into intense conversations with people they scarcely know. Americans' lack of sensitivity to protocol and to status differences, or their deliberate efforts to undermine them, may appear naive or downright insulting. Their constant questions and revealing disclosure may seem intrusive and overbearing, forcing the Japanese to discuss matters they regard as private. The extent to which Americans recount their experiences, failures, and successes may sound self-centered and pompous. Their informality and impulsiveness may deprive social occasions of their congenial predictability. The pace at which Americans move and talk, their verbal and physical flamboyance, may be unnerving. Their eagerness to contradict, even to argue bluntly, disturbs the harmony that should prevail. Equally astonishing is their ability to engage in such conflicts without it impairing their feeling for each other. Their endless analyzing, insistence on verbal precision, and binding agreements reveal an incredible trust in words over people. They are prone to error because they are always in such a hurry" (Barnlund, 1989, pp. 190–191).

- "People often tell me that I am lucky to be bilingual, but I am not so sure. Language is like a radio. I have to choose a specific station, English or Japanese, and tune in. I can't listen to both at the same time. In between, there is nothing but static" (Mori, 1997, p. 17).

---

the home country to gain the same kind of experience. To understand the cultural disorientation that these managers will face, or that Yuko will face in her student experience, demands a multidisciplinary integration of research ranging from individualistic psychological constructs to large-scale anthropological research (see Reviewing Key Ideas, p. 236). Kim (1984, 1988, 1991) suggests that it is not enough simply to believe that the stranger learns culture in a linear way by adding information to previous information, or that adaptation primarily depends on people being tolerant of, or friendly toward, each other. Instead, Kim's theory is "integrative." Yuko's kind of question won't be answered by using the individual person as a unit of analysis. A broader theoretical base is needed—the "creative integration" of a systems approach (Kim, 1984).

Kim's theoretical base has several important features, which we have abstracted from a more complex description in her first book-length statement of the theory (1988).

Assumptions. Individuals within cultures are "open systems" who inherently seek an internal homeostasis, or balance, in order to avoid stress. As "open

Review the principles of *general systems theory* **in Chapter 1 to aid your understanding of Kim's** *cross-cultural adaptation theory.*

systems," people make decisions about how to act in terms of a continual inter-change of information with their environments. They develop cultural identities by developing competent communication and information interchanges with that environment. When the environment changes, however, people—as living systems—seek to grow and adapt to those changes. For example, if you have had the experience of studying in another country or culture, you know it was not easy to study while adapting to a new culture, but improvement in studying probably came along with an improvement in your cultural competence. Yet you weren't wholly in charge of your own level of cultural competence because you had to depend on others in the environment in order to know how to react. No one can bring into a new environment all the resources necessary for adaptation. Yuko is right to be worried.

Kim's meanings for the concepts "stranger," "host," and "ethnic" may seem unfamiliar at first. A **stranger** is her overall term for someone who comes into an immersive cultural situation without much background for understanding that culture; strangers can be immigrants, travelers, diplomats, or exchange students. **Host** generally refers to the new cultural experience for the stranger—its people, its practices, and its media—taken, for the most part, as a whole. Just as *stranger* doesn't have negative connotations for Kim (as it sometimes does in everyday English), the concept of host doesn't necessarily have positive connotations. **Ethnic** refers to the cultural origin of the stranger and, to the extent that there are traces of that origin in the host culture, to the intracultural support groups and neighborhoods that are part of the adaptation process for many people. For example, Yuko, our hypothetical Japanese student, flies into Chicago to begin her yearlong adventure as a Northwestern University student. Although she knows English well, she feels like a *stranger* at first, and is considered one in Kim's terms. Gradually, as Yuko encounters the *host* environment more and more deeply (campus, city, national television networks, and so on), she begins to notice more diversity in the host culture, whereas at first she saw primarily how different she was from a uniform culture in which everyone else seemed competent. She is aided in the transition by *ethnic* communities of Japanese students on campus in Evanston and by Japanese Americans she meets in the city.

Dimensions. Kim organizes her theory in six basic dimensions. Although they can be separated for purposes of analysis, remember that in a systems approach each dimension (and its subprocesses) will be related in a variety of ways to all other dimensions. Remember, in other words, that these dimensions are not separate categories or steps in a sequence (see Reviewing Key Ideas, p. 236, for an overview).

1. ***Personal communication.*** In this dimension Kim presents research describing the many factors that influence whether a stranger will be competent in knowing the basic communication expectations of the host system. This aspect of her theory draws on general communication competence literature in order to show the extent to which competence (knowing how to communicate effectively) depends on *cognitive* (mental), *affective* (emotional), and *behavioral* (action) factors. Updating Kim's concerns about

intercultural communication competence, Chen and Starosta (1996) have recently synthesized the cultural communication literature into three similar categories: *cognitive process, intercultural sensitivity,* and *behavioral process.*

Yuko, having talked with a variety of former international students from Japan, begins to believe that she is intellectually well prepared to come to the United States. She reads and writes English as fluently as any of her peers. She has studied with an English tutor who has helped her role-play different conversational situations, such as an advisement appointment in which she chooses classes. However, she is concerned about her emotional readiness and fears that she will feel off-balance at the boldness of American students. Although she knows she is linguistically competent, she feels awkward.

2. ***Host social communication.*** Much of the cross-cultural adaptation research Kim summarizes describes the extent to which successful adapters participate directly in the social communication processes of the host culture. This includes both interpersonal communication processes (often researched in terms of the number and strength of host relational ties, such as friendships and close working relationships) and mass communication processes (strangers who watch, listen to, and read a great deal of media content may find themselves better adapted to the host culture, thereby increasing their media involvement). The mass communication involvement seems to be especially important as a mediating factor of adaptation in the early stages of cultural transition, before the stranger has had a chance to establish interpersonal ties. Kim's (1988) metaphor helps us to

---

REVIEWING KEY IDEAS

BASIC DIMENSIONS OF CROSS-CULTURAL ADAPTATION

- *Personal communication:* how competent the stranger is in the expectations and behaviors of the host system
- *Host social communication:* how the stranger becomes tied to host-system relationships and mass communication content
- *Ethnic social communication:* how the stranger remains tied to representatives and messages of the stranger's own ethnic group
- *Host environment:* how receptive the host environment is to strangers, and how much pressure for conformity it exerts
- *Predisposition:* what the stranger brings as "baggage"—background, preparation for change, openness, and resilience
- *Adaptation outcomes:* how successful adapters achieve functional fitness, psychological health, and an *intercultural identity* that creates a *third-culture perspective*

understand the crucial importance of social communication: "The process of migration from society to society can be compared to the up-rooting and re-rooting of transplantation. All migrants are removed from most, if not all, of the long-standing friends, family, relatives and co-workers with whom they participated in interpersonal communication activities. In the new society, they are faced with the task of constructing a new set of relationships that is critical to meeting their personal and social needs: making a living, learning the new language, seeking companionship and emotional security, or finding a new social identity" (pp. 105–106). The transplanting metaphor suggests the importance of culture to defining the quality of our lives. Most strangers, immigrants, and other travelers adapting to new cultures have moved from a sense of comfort to one of disorientation, even trauma. They face challenges that they were unprepared to anticipate before entering the new culture. However, participation in host-based social communication can provide some of the information necessary to meet those challenges.

Yuko decides not to eat by herself in the dorm, even though she doesn't know anyone. Although it takes enormous courage for her, during the first few days she notices several women who appear ready to eat alone; Yuko asks if they'd like to eat with her. They are curious about her motivations for studying at Northwestern, and ready to introduce her to Chicago. Already familiar with some strains of American popular culture (rap music, jazz, Bruce Willis films), she sets out to explore other kinds of radio and television programs.

3. ***Ethnic social communication.*** Many strangers in a new host environment are helped by groups who have already experienced varying degrees of adaptation to the new culture. The stranger's interest in finding and joining such groups may be explained by a human tendency to reduce uncertainty in interaction. However, researchers are divided about whether this is a negative factor that inhibits cultural adaptation or a positive factor that helps to maintain ethnic identity for the stranger during the difficult transition period. (See Kim, 1988, pp. 118–119, for a summary.) Kim's (1988) systems theory, however, suggests that strangers' social communication within ethnic communities "can *both* promote *and* impede their adaptation process depending on the extent that it replaces their host communication activities over time" (p. 119). In the short term, ethnic communication appears to promote adaptation, but over longer periods of time it maintains previous cultural ties that, if they're with other inadequately adapted strangers, hurts the adaptive goals of the stranger.

Yuko is approached by representatives from the Asian Student Association, and she appreciates their invitation to join. Although she was warned before leaving Japan about relying too much on other Japanese students, she is grateful for conversations with people who have faced the same dilemmas she is facing. Their support becomes important to her, but she resolves not to narrow her own experiences too much. She accepts several invitations to dinner with friendly Japanese families in the community, but she makes sure that she attends soccer and volleyball matches with a circle of American friends as well.

4. ***Host environment.*** Adaptation is also influenced by many factors reflecting the kind of environment the stranger encounters. Kim's theory accounts for this with predictions based on two aspects of the host culture, receptivity and conformity pressure. *Receptivity* refers to the extent to which cultures welcome and communicate readily with the cultural "other." *Conformity pressures* within host communication patterns describe the expectations that strangers should rapidly adapt and understand the locally accepted ways of doing things. Kim (1988) notes that some societies value and readily accept cultural diversity, but others are more homogeneous and controlled (p. 130); this appears to be roughly the same phenomenon described by Triandis (1994) as the *tightness syndrome* (discussed earlier in this chapter). Kim's theory suggests that receptivity is often perceived in the social practices of a society, such as in the integration or segregation of its housing patterns, while conformity pressure is often reflected in language practices (1988, pp. 129–130).

At first Yuko senses that some of her instructors and classmates are not excited about having her in their classes. In her public speaking course, for example, the teacher has repeatedly asked her to look at others directly, eye to eye, when speaking, to increase the volume of her voice and use more vocal inflection, and to move around more when using visual aids. But these instructions don't seem to fit her personality. Still, Yuko gamely tries to comply. She also notices several students in the back row who, instead of listening closely to her speeches, read the student newspaper and whisper to each other as she speaks.

5. ***Predisposition.*** Not only do strangers encounter a new context in the host culture but they also carry along some "baggage" from their home culture. More specifically, strangers bring with them to the new culture several predispositions that can help or hinder their adaptation to the new cultural demands. Two are straightforward: *cultural/racial background* may be relatively similar (or dissimilar) to the requirements of the host culture, and what Kim calls *preparedness for change,* which formal or informal education may help foster.

The problem of the third predisposition, *personality attributes,* is more complex. The adapting individuals are successful to the extent that their personalities exhibit the qualities of openness and resilience. *Openness* means that strangers honestly and accurately assess the feedback they receive in response to their attempts to adapt. The successfully adaptive stranger avoids the extremes of closed defensiveness about the new challenges on the one hand, and an unreflective acceptance or acquiescence about the new culture on the other. *Resilience* refers to the inner strength that strangers need to accept cultural misunderstandings and defeats and still bounce back. Kim (1988) is quick to note that resilience should not be equated with "stubbornness and tenseness" but with a relaxed, persistent flexibility when encountering difficulty: "Without openness and resilience, [strangers] are less capable of absorbing culture shocks and withstanding

Kim's theory underscores the importance of understanding the physical and social contexts of communication, discussed in Chapter 3, in both the nonverbal and verbal realms. The theory also begins to account for how individuals internalize such features of context in their thought processes (see Chapter 4).

challenges of the adaptation process, just as a building without give in its structure will easily collapse in a storm" (p. 135).

Yuko is upset at the rudeness of some of the students in her public speaking class, and the unwillingness of the teacher to adapt the speaking assignments to the needs of her cultural group. However, after thinking long and hard about her problem, she tells herself that although this treatment seems unfair she does not have to be demoralized by it. She decides to experiment a bit with her speaking style in the ways recommended by the teacher, just to see what happens. During a long-distance phone conversation with her parents, Yuko reports that some of her classmates seem selfish but that they don't seem to be doing as well in the class as the ones who are more friendly toward her. She agrees with her parents that these rude students shouldn't be able to affect her negatively.

6. *Adaptation outcomes.* Kim (1988, pp. 139–146) identifies three primary outcomes of successful adaptation: increased *functional fitness, psychological health,* and *intercultural identity.* As strangers become more functionally fit, they may find that their inner resources become more congruent with the demands of outer reality in the host environment. However, the converse can also be true. An increasingly good fit between stranger and host system can help to change the system, too—the effects go in both directions. At the same time, adapters tend to experience more psychological balance and to avoid the high-stress experience of **culture shock**, in which individuals begin to isolate themselves out of feelings of despair.

Although not all strangers adapt this effectively, those who do adapt well will build a new intercultural identity, what Kim also calls a **third-culture perspective**: "an inclusive viewpoint that represents more than one cultural perspective—either the home culture or the host culture, but, at the same time, transcends both groups" (Kim, 1988, pp. 144–145). This does not mean that strangers give up their original ethnic identity but that they gain a wider perspective, or intercultural identity, that includes elements of the home and the host cultures' perspectives. This broader perspective is similar to the borderlands concept discussed earlier in the chapter. This third-culture position is neither a simple maintenance of the old ethnic perspective nor an assimilation into the new host perspective. Instead, third-culture communicators hold elements of both, and they do so by *articulating* (in Stuart Hall's terms) their perspectives in new ways.

Yuko becomes increasingly confident as the semester progresses, and she even decides to join several other organizations. She's still frustrated by how easily some students assume that she's unintelligent just because her competence in English doesn't match theirs. Occasionally, she suspects that some people avoid her because they've prejudged her culture. Although she still experiences conflicts, her initial feelings of queasiness and culture shock have diminished, and she believes she belongs at Northwestern now. She rarely feels lonely, even when she misses her family and friends back home. Although her grades could be improved, Yuko knows that she's gaining an even more valuable kind of education than most of her classmates. Now she has transcended a Japanese experience without giving it up, *and* achieved a midwestern U.S. cultural experience without being limited to it. Although most of her peers settle for a single cultural life, she has managed to build a multicultural life. Yuko doesn't have to choose between keeping her Asian identity and submerging herself to become completely "American." She is both Japanese and knowledgeable within a U.S. cultural setting—and more. Yuko has developed an intercultural identity, in Kim's terms a *third-culture perspective*. She has adapted cross-culturally.

REVIEWING KEY THEORIES

Studying cultural communication is a difficult challenge. In this task we encounter not only some of the most complex distinctions in the human sciences but passionate voices and social controversies as well. Many positions and concepts that were originally meant as descriptions, such as *race* and *multiculturalism,* have become politicized. Human identities, rightly or wrongly, have been invested in cultural differences, and it's no longer clear—as society used to think it was— that these differences are inherently problems or roadblocks for human understanding. Indeed, the differences appear to energize our interaction and enrich our experience as communicators, if we understand the conditions of "otherness" empathically enough.

This chapter divides the study of culture into three basic tasks. First, we consider the foundational concepts and theorizing that can guide the study of any cultural communication situation. Although they don't rise to the level of comprehensive theorizing by themselves, a number of concepts are especially important: *cultural syndromes, borderlands and co-cultures, high/low-context cultures,* and *elaborated/restricted codes.*

Second, we justify why theoretical critique, often known by such labels as *critical theory,* plays an important role in academic life; in this section we describe theories that address three especially important cultural dilemmas. *Articulation theory,* an outgrowth of the interdisciplinary area of *cultural studies,* addresses the dilemma of power. *Feminist theory,* along with its variants of standpoint theory and muted group theory, addresses the dilemma of gender. Finally, *Afrocentric theory* addresses the dilemma of race by offering a perspective that doesn't rely on Eurocentric assumptions.

Third, we re-establish the distinction between *emic* (from within the culture) and *etic* (from outside the culture) approaches and demonstrate the complexity of cross-cultural theorizing by taking you inside the logic of one particular theory, Young Yun Kim's *cross-cultural adaptation theory.* Kim attempts to account for how a cross-cultural traveler adjusts to the change from a relatively safe cultural experience to a new set of experiences in which everyday life is suddenly strange. What happens, her research shows, is that successful adapters create for themselves a *third-culture perspective,* a unique mix of behaviors and attitudes in which they depend neither on their home culture nor on their host culture exclusively for guidance in communicating.

TESTING THE CONCEPTS

"Is what we call 'American culture' a part of the 'borderland'?"

If you think of "America" as a country (some people do not, because there are many countries in the Americas), then there are many pockets of protected group identities that seem not to have much to do with different cultural groups—some rural areas, gated subdivisions, and segregated neighborhoods come to mind. To call American culture a "borderland" in the sense of this chapter's theorists might be a bit misleading.

On the other hand, American culture, when considered more broadly, seems to be in the forefront of an emerging borderlands mentality, both in the United States and across the world. Although Americans often segregate themselves into neighborhoods and locales that think and behave similarly, the lines are blurring and each unique cultural identity must now increasingly confront a broader context of integrated culture as well as other cultural groups. Further, in an era of international business, frequent and relatively inexpensive travel, and the availability of virtually instant global communication, the ambiguities and merged identities of the borderlands experience are expanding. So are the challenges. W. Barnett Pearce (1989) advocates what he calls *cosmopolitan communication,* which "enables coordination among groups with different, even incommensurate, social realities" (p. 169). He believes this approach allows us to respect differences while also finding ways to coordinate our communication practices across those differences.

"What is the difference between race and culture?"

The term *race* is currently being contested by a variety of theorists, almost as if it were the ground or terrain on which groups can fight their verbal battles. It's safe to say that today race is no longer the precise scientific concept it was thought to be in the early part of the twentieth century (see the definitions in this chapter). Then, it was assumed that races "had" certain biological characteristics and potentials that did not characterize other races. Now, when people refer to race, they are usually referring to a mix of ambiguously defined biological characteristics and a wide range of cultural cues and communication styles generally associated with certain groups. What we call race is a kind of verbal and conceptual shortcut to discussing culture. Still, as we stress in the text, race and racism are real because people talk about and experience their reality.

"Yuko chose to come to the United States and attend college. Why didn't she see what she was getting herself into?"

Yuko did all that she felt was necessary to prepare for the culture shock she would experience in the United States. Usually that is not enough to guarantee feeling comfortable, however, because discomfort naturally comes with any venture into new territory. The best and most thorough way to understand a different culture is to immerse yourself in that culture. It was impossible for Yuko to grasp the entire new experience ahead of time because any culture involves not only a recorded history; a language with grammar, syntax, and vocabulary; and a set of artifacts (all of which Yuko could study ahead of time) but also patterns of subtle and usually implicit interpersonal relations (which she couldn't anticipate precisely before she arrived). Kim's (1988) research demonstrates how disorienting a stranger's experience can be, as well as how successful adaptation to a new culture can occur.

YOU, THE RESEARCHER

1. On your own campus, interview three students or faculty members (not from your communication class) who represent three different cultural backgrounds. For example, you may know of a physics professor from Jamaica who has just been hired, or a student from Pakistan who has also studied in London. Ask the interviewees to describe how cultural assumptions did or did not help to prepare them to face power issues (concerning gender, race, class, and ethnicity) on campus. Here are some other suggestions for doing this research:

   - Approach this project as if you were a journalist preparing to write a human-interest story. Carefully prepare a set of four or five basic questions that will guide your interviews, but beware the tendency to channel the interview only along these lines. Your interviewees may want to take you in equally good, but different, directions. Take careful notes or, with the others' permission, tape the interviews.

   - Remember that your task is just to discover the persons' perspectives, not to persuade them that they're victims, members of dominant classes, or stereotypical representatives of cultural groups.

   - Look for similarities and differences in your interviewees' comments. Does your interview data reflect any of the concepts described in this chapter? Discuss your findings in class.

   - Consider the possibility that you could turn your research into a feature story for your campus or local newspaper, perhaps by collaborating with one or more of your classmates. If you do write such an article, you could use your three interviewees as focal points for the story, but you'll probably want to add extra information, too.

2. For one week, watch several television news programs carefully. Record in a notebook how the programs portray cultural differences in their coverage of the news. For example, apart from the weather report, how many stories make up a nightly local newscast? Of these, how many concern themselves with confrontations or collaborations between gays and straights, between blacks and whites, between representatives of ethnic neighborhoods and wealthy areas, or other cultural issues? Then, view five half-hour sitcoms to see how these programs portray cultural encounters and the identities of the people involved. Compare and contrast how the television news and situation comedies portray cultural differences. Discuss your findings in class.

3. Visit a local video store or library and select several movies produced in countries, and languages, other than your own. While viewing each one, look especially for portrayals of female/male role differences and their effects. You don't have to assume that the writers, directors, producers, and actors intended to present these differences in the way you interpret. Discuss with other students how much of what you see in the films represents the unspoken assumptions of the cultures in which they were filmed, and how much of each portrayal comes from the unique vision or agenda of the filmmakers. For example, a Japanese film from 1960 might cast women in roles that are subservient to men, but a contemporary Japanese filmmaker might consider the tension between women and men in the workplace to be dramatically interesting and might consciously try to advance a personal agenda that differs from that of the overall culture.

Bob Daemmrich/Stock, Boston

CHAPTER 8

"How Do We Allow Rhetoric to Change Our Minds?"

Theorizing Persuasive Communication

> Being the product of conditioning and being free to change do not war with each other. Both are true. They coexist, grow together in an upward spiral, and the growth of one furthers the growth of the other. The more cogently we prove ourselves to have been shaped by causes, the more opportunities we create for changing. The more we change, the more possible it becomes to see how determined we were in that which we have just ceased to be.
>
> ALLEN WHEELIS, *How People Change* (1976, pp. 87–88)

C. P. Ellis changed his mind. Ellis is one of many ordinary Americans profiled in Studs Terkel's book *American Dreams: Lost and Found* (1981, pp. 221–233). All of Terkel's subjects are noteworthy, but Ellis stands out because his story clearly demonstrates the power of public and interpersonal persuasion in a country that says it values free speech.

Born and raised in the textile culture of Durham, North Carolina, Ellis tried a variety of working-class jobs in search of the American dream but never found it. Instead, he found bitterness and disillusionment while working in the mills, on a bread route, at a gas station, and on the maintenance staff at Duke University. But he still didn't have enough money at one time even to fill the fuel-oil tank at his family's house. This wasn't the way America was supposed to be at mid-century if a person went to church, worked hard, and felt patriotic. Something was wrong; someone had to be blamed. Ellis's father, a member of the Ku Klux Klan, blamed blacks, Jews, and Catholics. The younger Ellis found his niche there, too, and with the habit of blaming others came an entire worldview. Klan members eventually respected him enough to select him as leader of the Durham chapter.

In a series of interracial civic meetings, Ellis was exceptionally open about his negative feelings toward blacks—so much so that he was admired by both sides for his honesty. He was asked to coordinate policies with a black activist woman he'd learned to hate. As co-chairs of a human-relations committee, each was criticized for being willing to work with the other. The Klan members couldn't believe their man was doing this: "C. P., what the hell is wrong with you? You're sellin' out the white race" (Terkel, 1981, p. 229). At the same time, "Ann was gettin' the same response from blacks: 'what are you doin' messin' with that Klansman?'" (p. 230). Eventually, each discovered that their children were being harassed by other children at school, and they began to notice each other's reaction to their parental agony. They had much in common after all.

Ellis still didn't favor integration, but he supported the resolutions that the integrated committee came up with. When the all-white school board refused to take the resolutions seriously, Ellis decided to run for the board himself. The Klan had turned against Ellis, as had many low-income whites. Blacks and liberals were suspicious, but Ellis shook a lot of hands and met a lot of everyday people. He lost the school board election, but not by much. In losing, however, he seemed to gain the enthusiasm he needed to return to high school through an alternative program and graduate. All the while, his attitudes toward social conditions and racism were slowly changing.

Ellis, now an ex-Klansman, also began to imagine more possibilities for structural change. At work he ran for president of the union, even though he thought he had no chance of winning the election. His opponent was black, as was 75 percent of the membership. Moreover, the company executives didn't like Ellis, and they advertised his racist past by posting signs and flyers. In response, Ellis called a mass meeting:

> *I invited some of my old black friends. I said: "Brother Joe, Brother Howard, be honest now and tell these people how you feel about me." They done it. (Laughs.) Howard Clements kidded me a little bit. He said: "I don't know what I'm doin' here, supportin' an ex-Klansman." (Laughs.) He said: "I know what C. P. Ellis come from. I knew him when he was. I knew him as he grew, and growed with him. I'm tellin' you now: follow, follow this Klansman." (He pauses, swallows hard.) "Any questions?" "No," the black ladies said. "Let's get on with the meeting, we need Ellis." (He laughs and weeps.) . . . It makes you feel good to go into a plant and butt heads with professional union busters. You see black people and white people join hands to defeat the racist issues they use against people. . . . Can you imagine a guy who's got an adult high school diploma runnin' into professional college graduates . . . ? I gotta compete with 'em. They say the older you get, the harder it is for you to change. That's not necessarily true. Since I changed, I've set down and listened to tapes of Martin Luther King. I listen to it and tears come to my eyes 'cause I know what he's sayin' now. I know what's happenin'. (Terkel, 1981, pp. 232–233)*

C. P. Ellis changed his mind. And his life. Not all of us make changes that are this dramatic, but the basic dynamics of attitude change are similar in most people's lives. What are those dynamics? How are people persuaded through others' rhetoric? These are the central questions we address in this chapter. As we progress, remember C. P. Ellis. We'll return to him occasionally to illustrate the practicality of rhetorical concepts.

In this chapter you won't receive a comprehensive catalog of contemporary research on attitude change. That has been done well elsewhere (see, e.g., O'Keefe, 1990). Our goal here is to pique your interest in theorizing about this important subfield of communication. You'll discover the role persuasion plays in the overall development of communication theory. As the chapter-opening quotation from psychotherapist Allen Wheelis suggests, human beings are simultaneously free and determined, and studying persuasive communication messages illustrates how this is true. We will develop this notion in three additional sections. First, we'll examine the relationship between mind and persuasion. Second, we'll begin our conceptual survey with the *rhetorical tradition* of persuasion, focusing on the contributions of such ancient theorists as Plato and Aristotle. In this survey you will see how classical rhetorical theory has influenced what we define as persuasion theory today. Then we'll show how interpersonal communication theorists understand persuasion through a *compliance-gaining tradition*. We'll consider examples from the field of medicine in which persuasion can best be understood as a "helping relationship."

◁ L I N K

In a sense, topics associated with persuasion and attitude change appear throughout this book because persuasion involves many other conceptual areas. In fact, some scholars argue that all intentional communication includes some sort of persuasive element.

○ Chapter 4 reviews cognitive and social psychological factors that influence persuasion.

○ Chapter 5 discusses such aspects of interpersonal persuasion as social exchange.

○ Chapter 9 evaluates the so-called media threat of powerful propaganda, which people once feared could sway the masses.

○ Chapter 10's treatment of ethics theories presents the ethical and moral dimensions of manipulation, power, control, choice, and self-determination.

Changing Minds and Minding Persuasion

Mind

The human mind is often discussed as if it were the cockpit, central processing unit, or control center of the body. When everything seems to be working predictably, we say people are "minding their manners." Mind is also invoked if things go badly. If we want others to stop doing something, we might say we "mind" their actions. Children who don't comply with family rules are described as "not minding their parents." When your friend won't accede in an argument, you might say he or she "has a mind-set." People who are excessively worried and express it in unconventional ways are said colloquially to have "lost their minds." Our society values people who can "make up their minds."

So, what's a *mind*? Is it a synonym for "brain," or is it something more? (See Reviewing Key Ideas, below.) Recall from Chapter 4 George Herbert Mead's (1934) claim that language allows us to imagine internally the shape and complexity of our external society—and this, to him, is the basic phenomenon of mind. In effect, mind allows us to plan and decide, even to try things out imaginatively, before we engage in overt behaviors. For summaries of current research in discursive, language-linked theories of mind, see recent books by Harré and Gillett (1994) and Wertsch (1991).

Biologist J. Z. Young takes a slightly different, but consistent, perspective in his influential book *Programs of the Brain* (1978). His central analogy—the idea of a **program**—is not derived primarily from computer programs but from the pre-Victorian sense of an organized plan for accomplishing a particular end. According to Young (1978), scientific researchers have found that "the brain operates in certain organized ways that may be described as programs, and the actions of these programs constitute the entity that we call the mind of a person" (p. 8). Some researchers in communication and psychology (see, e.g., Goss, 1989, pp. 133–137) use the term **schema** to refer to an organizing concept similar to Young's use of *program*. The concepts of mind, program, and schema, therefore, are teleologically important; they refer to the ability of the conscious organism to accomplish its objectives and goals. In fact, without this symbolic capacity, it's hard even to imagine having or setting objectives in anything other than a mechanical sense.

We could say that C. P. Ellis's mind changed when his program for deciding how to organize his actions changed. Or we could say that his program changed when his mind did. Mind and action are intimately connected; each helps to con-

---

REVIEWING KEY IDEAS

THE MIND:

- Uses language to help people re-create internally the complexity of society (Mead).
- Is the disciplined set of programs or schemata (plural of *schema*) by which people organize their plans for action (Young).

struct the other. This is why it's useless to try to explain a person's behavior by saying, for instance, "I know why he's not getting As in school anymore—he changed his mind about the importance of studying," as though the changed mind caused the changed behavior. In fact, from Young's (1978) program-oriented standpoint, the changed behavior and the changed mind are two facets of the same phenomenon. That phenomenon, consciousness, is language-based and communication-based: "Life is guided by programs and...programs are written in languages," Young writes; and "indeed our thesis is that the faculty of communication pervades all of living" (p. 9).

Persuasion

Herbert Simons (1976) long ago defined **persuasion** as "human communication designed to influence others by modifying their beliefs, values, or attitudes" (p. 21). Although this definition seems to refer more to messages than to communication as an overall process, it emphasizes that persuasion implies a kind of intentional behavior with reference to a plan or a goal, at least on the part of a speaker. However, Burgoon and Miller (1990), drawing on Langer's (1978) work on *mindfulness,* suggest that not all persuasive attempts are mindful, rational acts orchestrated by a knowing persuader. They admit that some level of intention is required in any definition of *persuasion,* but they find it fallacious to overemphasize highly rational elements in the definition. According to Burgoon and Miller (1990), scholars shouldn't assume "that persuaders are constantly in the highly mindful state of making rational choices, deliberating about alternatives, and rehearsing strategies." Instead, we should more often consider "the everyday world of persuasive discourse where many attempts at change, or reinforcement, consist of relatively mindless acts. Habituated behavior, whether successful or not, is the symbolic staple of would-be persuaders in many, if not most, daily persuasive encounters" (p. 157).

Every four years a national presidential election reminds us of the variety of possible avenues for gaining influence, or at least for securing our acquiescence (Edelman, 1964). Many of these avenues have not changed significantly over the past two thousand years. However, in the twentieth century, the means and media for conveying influential messages have changed radically. Political candidates, for example, no longer advertise themselves from a tree stump, the back of a wagon, or the bunting-laden caboose of a train on a whistle-stop campaign. Television and other electronic media supplement the print media in providing more news and more advertising than audiences can ever hope to assimilate. As technology advances, so, apparently, does the public's reliance on it. The modern audience seems to be an inviting and fertile ground in which persuasive messages can take root.

Political campaigns might also remind us of how much persuasion already exists in our everyday relationships. It's not just senators and governors who want to be "elected." All of us might be considered informal politicians as we go through each day trying to be tactful to some people, confrontive with others, and strategic toward still others. You may hope to persuade a job interviewer that you're the best potential employee among the applicants. Your teacher may hope to persuade you that the reading assignments are helpful and necessary. Parents may hope to convince teenagers that drugs and alcohol are dangerous. You may hope that your statistics on smoke alarms will be believed in your speech for public speaking class.

◄▢**LINK**

How might Greene's action assembly theory, discussed in Chapter 4, contribute to the study of mind? To our understanding of how people change their minds?

Concepts from the Rhetorical Tradition of Persuasion

Communication theories have focused on the problem of persuasion for centuries. Therefore the classical rhetorical tradition in Western civilization has had a long and influential history in the education of communicators (see Reviewing Key Ideas, p. 255). The advice and analyses of such early theorists as Aristotle, Plato, Isocrates, and others have been so persuasive that they are still studied intensively by scholars and students today. (Some excellent summary sources include Harper, 1978; Hauser, 1986; Kennedy, 1963; and Kinneavy, 1980.)

Classical Rhetorical Theory

Rhetoric, defined by Aristotle (384–322 B.C.) as the faculty or ability to find "the available means of persuasion" in a situation (1954, p. 24), was accorded a central role in ancient Greek civilization. Aristotle's work, which we will survey and extend in this section, became the basis of what we now term **classical rhetorical theory**, although many other Greek and Roman orators and philosophers contributed to it as well. Although some contemporary treatments of rhetoric emphasize its functions in constructing social reality, in helping people make sense of others' behaviors, and in coordinating social action, Aristotle's concern with the impulse for influence persists in rhetorical theory today. Because each male (yes, male!) citizen in Aristotle's Greece was expected to be able to argue his case in the public forum, rhetoric became an essential discipline in the education of that time. Rhetoric is still considered a specialized study of communication, one that emphasizes humanity's symbolic capacity to plan messages for practical ends.

By now you probably understand that our use of the term *rhetoric* does not include its modern pejorative connotations. If a contemporary politician says, "My opponent is engaging in mere rhetoric" or "Enough rhetoric! Let's talk real issues here!" the implication is that rhetoric is empty talk unsupported by solid reasoning or evidence. This negative or superficial usage is not what we mean by rhetoric. Like Aristotle, contemporary rhetorical theorists have the utmost respect for the study of intentional talk—talk that is expected to help people respond to ideas.

One ancient rhetorician, however, was more skeptical about the potential power of a skilled **rhetor** (one who uses rhetoric). Plato (c. 428–348 B.C.), a Greek philosopher and one of Aristotle's teachers, was suspicious of the **Sophists**, itinerant teachers who specialized in teaching people the practical everyday applications of rhetoric. To this day, Sophists have bad press; our politicians often accuse each other of "sophistry," which has come to imply the deceptive and biased use of rhetoric. In his dialogue *The Gorgias,* Plato pointedly criticized the frequent misuse of rhetoric. He said that it wasn't so much a genuine area of study as it was a simple knack for impressing or fooling other people. This knack for rhetoric, Plato argued, was not much more complicated than the knack for cooking. Although he later adjusted his philosophy to advocate a more comprehensive approach to human communication based on dialogue and the testing of ideas, his warning about an uncritical faith in rhetoric remains appropriate today.

A contemporary of Plato, the Athenian orator Isocrates (436–338 B.C.), took rhetoric more into the political realm in his teachings. Isocrates helped to educate the political decision makers of his day, stressing that only through rhetoric could

▣LINK

Consider this interesting connection between classical rhetorical theory and inner speech theory, surveyed in Chapter 4: To what extent do you think persuaders have a responsibility to be introspective about their interior dialogues? In other words, should rhetors become more *mindful*?

a society maintain social order or a group maintain cooperation among its members. In this sense, then, rhetoric is the glue that holds the political process together, not a threat to that process (as Plato asserted in *The Gorgias*). In the program for training rhetors described in his *Antidosis*, Isocrates claimed that rhetoric could be found in the thought processes, in the intrapersonal realm, of communicators. Therefore, in this view, we use language not just to influence others but also to conduct internal dialogues for the purpose of solving problems. Our thoughts and our rhetoric are interdependent.

Isocrates and Plato sketched the outline of a body of thought, and Aristotle filled in much of that outline. Many of our basic concepts of rhetoric thus emerged from the Greek and Roman classical rhetorical tradition.

Occasions for Rhetoric

Three basic types of occasions call for rhetoric, according to classic rhetorical theory. **Deliberative rhetoric** is seen in discussions of public policy in legislative groups; it basically concerns itself with such questions as "What do we do about...?" and similar inquiries. **Forensic rhetoric** occurs in courtrooms and other places where the facts and interpretations of individual cases are argued. This term persists today in the organized competitive speech activities known on many campuses as forensics programs. **Epideictic rhetoric** refers to the ceremonial speaking in public forums that praises or blames individuals for their virtues or vices. Epideictic speaking can be expected at funerals, weddings, and other special occasions where people gather to honor or celebrate a person, a group, or an event.

When we consider these occasions for rhetoric in the context of contemporary persuasion, they hardly seem stale. For example, although we like to think of political campaigns as opportunities for deliberative rhetoric, they often shift rapidly toward epideictic rhetoric when an opponent's character is being discussed as much as content. Similarly, when ex-Klansman C. P. Ellis called a meeting of his union during his campaign for union president, he himself brought up the charges the company had made against him and invited the members to consider and debate the truth or falsity of those charges. He also enlisted the aid of several black colleagues to testify to his open-mindedness and honesty. He invited debate at the meeting about what kind of leadership the members wanted. Ellis, in other words, constructed a situation that melded all three types of rhetorical occasion—people examined and evaluated his character, debated their different interpretations (forensic), and attempted to coordinate their views through rhetorical deliberation (deliberative).

Inartistic and Artistic Persuasive Appeals

Classical rhetorical theorists distinguish between inartistic and artistic persuasive appeals. They consider **inartistic means of persuasion** as the less interesting and effective of the two, because inartistic approaches emphasize the discovery of the facts of a given case that are largely external to the choices of the individuals concerned. Inartistic methods of proving a case are simply "found" in the situation or in the external inducements (Aristotle mentioned oaths and torture as examples); they are not the result of the creativity or imagination of the communicator. For example, has a professor "persuaded" students to study in a required class when everyone knows that grades will be recorded on student transcripts

Think back to what you learned about context in Chapter 3. How do you think the contexts known as "occasions for rhetoric" would necessarily influence the content of what is said within them, and even influence the goals of speakers and listeners?

and may be important in future job searches? A professor's reference to grades can be an inartistic means of persuasion, because grades are situational threats that aren't based primarily on the professor's own rhetorical skill. Of course, many professors do motivate students creatively to study, apart from the threat of grades. On what does their persuasiveness depend?

Artistic means of persuasion are characterized by creativity and genuine persuasion. Although the facts of a case are important, they don't (as we sometimes wish) "speak for themselves." Facts must be interpreted and presented creatively in order for them to have influence on an audience. The distinction can be seen in what is perhaps an apocryphal story told about the famous defense lawyer Clarence Darrow. Asked to describe how he chose the reasons for acquittal to include in his summation to a jury, Darrow replied that he didn't try to give a jury any reasons to free his client. Instead, he made the jury want to free his client, and trusted that the jury would find its own reasons. Darrow's approach, in other words, relied on the artistic rhetoric of interpretive appeal that he helped to construct with the jury, not on the naive assumption that the inartistic factual and rational proofs of the case could be persuasive in their own right. People who have followed recent murder cases closely, including the JonBenet Ramsey and O. J. Simpson cases, undoubtedly noticed a similar reliance on artistic means of persuasion by lawyers and spokespeople for those under suspicion. In discussing the cases, advocates vividly describe not only the facts and proofs of these situations but also the possibilities, thereby inviting the jurors or the wider public to form their own interpretations of "reasonable doubt."

For Aristotle, Darrow, and any advocates in controversies, persuasion develops from how listeners use artistic messages to change their minds and behaviors. Similarly, C. P. Ellis's persuasive power didn't come from coercing others to see things his way or from the obvious power of the facts he espoused. Instead, to put it in an unusual but appropriate way, he spoke his life in the public arena and relied on his knowledge of how the members of his audience made their decisions. In much the same way, no one made Ellis change his mind in a simple cause-effect manner. He persuaded himself, slowly building a new worldview from the messages that others (intentionally and unintentionally) provided.

Types of Artistic Proof

Aristotle described three general artistic proofs, which were for him the different choices rhetors make when they seek to persuade others. They can rely on *ethos, pathos,* or *logos.*

Ethos. As Aristotle observed, the force of a message's content is often not enough to sway an audience. The audience hears arguments and messages in the context of who is proposing them. A person of high prestige and reputation might be believed sooner and with deeper conviction than someone who is not seen as credible by an audience. **Ethos**, meaning "personal proof" or "ethical proof," is tied to the character of speakers, who simultaneously offer themselves to audiences alongside the words they speak. Indeed, a vital part of the Roman tradition of classical rhetoric was an extension of this notion. Quintilian and Cicero, among others, thought virtue should be assumed in the definition of a rhetor, that a skillful Roman rhetor was—we note, with apologies to skillful female rhetors—a "good man, speaking well." It was not enough merely to speak well.

The classical theorists thus created a foundation for what modern theorists describe as **credibility**. The speaker's reputation, experiences, and knowledge are taken into consideration by audiences, as is how much the rhetor can be trusted in a given situation. Although modern studies differ somewhat in how they define *credibility* (see Andersen & Clevenger, 1963; Delia, 1976; Infante, Parker, Clarke, Wilson, & Nathu, 1983), two issues usually emerge as most important: **expertise** and **trustworthiness**. Generally, these labels ask the implicit questions "Does the speaker know what he or she is talking about?" and "Can the speaker be trusted to be honest, accurate, and unbiased in the rhetoric?" A third factor often discovered in credibility studies, **dynamism**, suggests that many auditors admire rhetors who have enthusiastic and animated presentation styles.

Three reminders are important in considering the dynamics of personal proof. First, because audiences often don't make credibility assessments rationally, a speaker's physical appearance, clothing, ethnicity, group associations, and body type may affect his or her *ethos*. Second, remember that *ethos,* or credibility, is basically an audience-based phenomenon. We may often talk colloquially about a speaker's "possessing" a high degree of credibility or even charisma, but this kind of reference is conceptually misleading. It's actually the audience that develops and sustains a rhetor's *ethos*. High *ethos* remains as long as the audience sustains its belief in the rhetor's expertise, trustworthiness, and dynamism. Finally, remember that *ethos,* like all communication, is a situational issue. While C. P. Ellis attained a high degree of credibility with some (but not all) audiences when speaking about race relations in Durham in the 1960s and 1970s, this does not necessarily mean that he would maintain that credibility in other situations (e.g., at a KKK meeting, a National Organization of Women seminar, a convention of academic sociologists studying inner-city problems) or even with the same audience types in the 1990s. Credibility, therefore, depends much more on the audience and the situation than on the speaker's dynamic style or sincerity.

Pathos. Discussions of rhetoric prior to Aristotle probably emphasized emotionally based persuasion (Harper, 1978, p. 38). This explains, perhaps, why Aristotle wanted to create a more balanced view of this mode of proof. It is neither the type of appeal that necessarily should be a rhetor's first choice nor the type that necessarily will produce results with all audiences. *Pathos* refers to the rhetorical use of messages that appeal to an audience's emotions and passions. C. P. Ellis became a willing convert to the Klan because he felt bitter about what he perceived as the dismissal of white people's concerns. He wanted to blame someone in order to feel better, and the Klan's rhetoric gave him that outlet. Similarly, in changing his mind it was his sadness about the common economic plight of many blacks and whites that became the soil in which his new and more generous rhetorical assumptions were planted.

Advertisers use emotional appeals to promote their products, and political campaigners usually presume that the public's emotional involvement with a topic should be factored into the overall campaign strategy. As Democrats and Republicans argued in November of 2000 about crucial counts and recounts in determining the status of Florida's electoral votes, a national presidential election hung in the

◁▷ **LINK**

Chapter 5 examines concepts associated with communication rules. What rules, in your opinion, govern how speakers can talk about their own credibility in public, without seeming to brag or to be too arrogant? Consider public self-references to credibility in such situations as political campaigning, job interviews, and teaching Sunday school. Which rules seem to apply in each of these situations?

LINK

When you read Chapter 10, on communication ethics, consider which theories of ethics best help you sort out the issues of emotionality and negative advertising in political campaigns.

balance. Both sides argued the issues, and both sides made legal moves to establish their interpretations. However, both sides also appeared on thousands of interview shows urging that the "American public" must *feel good* about the election (taking into account public confidence in the system, public suspicions about whether one side or the other "stole the election" [to use their own heated rhetoric], etc.).

All significant issues, the argument goes, involve emotions. In Chapter 10 we'll discuss ethical criteria for communication. At this point, though, you might consider whether you find political campaign commercials that appeal to emotions ethical or unethical. Is it the emotional appeal itself that's ethical or unethical, or is it the situation or context in which the appeal is made? Many persuaders attempt to appeal to our needs to be first, best, part of a group, and so on. Muscular dystrophy telethons appeal to our emotions, too. Are they unethical? Television viewers are familiar with photographs and videos of starving children across the world, with their distended stomachs and emaciated faces, looking longingly toward the camera. Promoters of many causes—good and bad, necessary and trivial—have understood Aristotle's concern with appealing rhetorically to audience emotions.

Hauser (1986, pp. 110 ff.) points to two common misconceptions about the role of emotions in persuasive communication. First, emotions, he writes, are not "things" that can be stored up (like "pent-up" feelings or "repressed anger") or expended like commodities. They are better understood as judgments and interpretations, unique to each individual, that develop as a result of a complex interplay of psychological and physiological factors. This insight leads to the other misconception: that many people believe emotions come largely from outside the self. Hauser (1986) believes it is more productive to see emotions as specific and pointed toward referents: "We don't feel love in general. We love Dad, we love Kirsten, we love our dear friends who have shared so many rich experiences with us" (p. 111). Emotions are inner interpretations affectively tied to outer experiences. Just as some philosophers believe that there is no such thing as "consciousness" in general, but that consciousness must always be "consciousness-of-something" (they call this the concept of **intentionality**), Hauser is saying that emotions must be of and about referents.

Logos. Aristotle understood that, ideally, persuasion should be based on the logical arguments and reasons that a rhetor can present to an audience. Information that is presented in a precise order and accompanied by statistical support, examples, and relevant testimony encourages listeners to arrive at a specific conclusion recommended by the rhetor. This kind of "logical proof," called *logos,* makes sense and is rational. But is it always possible or practical?

In the Aristotelian theory of communication, human beings often use shortcut versions of rational processes. For example, a **syllogism** is a form of logical reasoning that moves from major premise through minor premise to conclusion. Regardless of the actual truth of the claims of the premises, therefore, one could at least trust the reasoning mechanism. A parent might reason with a child (validly): All cats are going to die (major premise); Rascal is a cat (minor premise); therefore (Rascal is going to die someday (conclusion). Or a parent might reason (with suspicious validity): All religious people are narrow-minded; Sister Margaret is a religious person; therefore Sister Margaret is narrow-minded (and presumably we shouldn't trust her). Maybe the world would be a better place if everyone reasoned with one another carefully and precisely; then again, maybe it wouldn't. Careful reasoning doesn't guarantee good results if rhetors aren't knowledgeable. As Aristotle noted, the world isn't a place where everyone reasons syllogistically with accurate information. Folks in everyday life tend to be persuaded more by their own reasoning than by logically "correct" reasoning imposed from outside their own experience. In this imperfect world, we often assume that there are some things in communication that we don't need to say or prove.

Realizing the alogical character of much human communication, Aristotle proposed that people typically engage others with examples and enthymemes. The rationale behind producing **rhetorical examples** is similar to the inductive assumptions of qualitative social scientists, who study human interaction using an accumulation of case studies or ethnographic methods of observation (see Chapter 1). With rhetorical examples, beliefs can be supported concretely and specifically. **Enthymemes** are similar to syllogisms, except that in an enthymeme one of the two premises is implicit. Because the rhetor will tend to assume that a listener can fill in some of the assumptions, all the dimensions of the appeal don't need to be made explicit. For example, in C. P. Ellis's case, the company executives decided that all they needed to do to block his election was to let the predominantly black union membership know of Ellis's past ties with the KKK. The rhetorical reasoning went something like this: "C. P. Ellis is a white man who once led an anti-black group; therefore you would not want him representing you." A premise, a step in the reasoning, has been omitted here. The company executives expected this message to be persuasive because it more or less created a psychological "space" into which audience members could insert their own assumptions, fears, suspicions, and, perhaps, hate. However, the company's message didn't mention fear or hate directly. Further, although this example might seem to imply that persuasion by enthymemes involves poor reasoning, this is not necessarily the case. In fact, this form of *logos* is most common in human affairs and is not necessarily negative. "We need to practice more so that we can win the big game Saturday night" is enthymemic reasoning, too.

Probably the most important contribution of Aristotle's theory in this regard is that it takes audiences very much into account. The validity of an enthymeme

---

REVIEWING KEY IDEAS

CLASSICAL RHETORICAL THEORY:

- Defines the study of *rhetoric* as finding "the available means of persuasion" (Aristotle).
- Analyzes *deliberative, forensic,* and *epideictic* contexts for rhetoric.
- Elevates *artistic* over *inartistic* means of persuasion.
- Distinguishes among different types of proof: *ethos, pathos,* and *logos.*

isn't in its logical form (as with a syllogism); rather, validity resides in the shared social meanings, interpretations, and assumptions by which people together make decisions. In this sense, persuasion is not primarily a psychological process but a process of social communication.

Concepts from the Interpersonal Tradition of Persuasion

Thoughtful students in any field of study should persistently ask themselves this question: How does what I've learned in class relate to real-life problems and situations? We firmly believe that the whole world is a classroom, and that you don't stop learning after you've earned your college degree. If learning is directed only toward achieving a grade or a degree, then that insight is likely to fade after the end of the semester or after graduation. How can communication theory or, more specifically, persuasion theory guide how you address the practical problems that complicate human life?

Persuasion as a Helping Relationship

Some years ago, one of the most famous and popular celebrities in the world, Earvin "Magic" Johnson of the National Basketball Association's Los Angeles Lakers, announced that he had tested positive for the HIV virus. One of the most feared and mysterious medical dilemmas of the modern era, AIDS remains a disease that researchers know too little about. Public education and public communication programs have in some cases been confused and contradictory. Although the disease had already created horrible suffering in the lives of millions of private and public individuals, Johnson's announcement that he was retiring from the NBA galvanized public opinion and sensitized many people to the immediate need for open communication about AIDS. Johnson decided to become an advocate for AIDS education and research in order to mobilize and humanize public concern. Since his announcement, he has done much (including coming out of retirement briefly to resume his career) to demystify the disease.

Johnson's experience spotlights the relationship between medical professionals and their public. To what extent should doctors and public-health officials also go beyond their traditional roles of treating and informing the public, given the constraints on their time, energy, and financial support? Should they become active persuaders? And if so, how should the public react? Should the public continue to be guided by the traditional medical model that implies that physicians are experts who consider the complaints brought to them by patients and then prescribe treatments with which patients should comply? This implies a linear, one-way model of communication that may be seriously outmoded. Maybe we can never go back to that way of thinking about medical problems. Maybe we're now too interconnected in our society.

The medical dilemmas of the late twentieth century illustrate the extent to which persuasion must be approached as a "helping relationship." Linear assumptions of persuasion no longer apply, if they ever did. Currently, as many articles in journals such as *Health Communication* and the *Journal of Applied Communication Research* demonstrate, we attempt to marshal public and private resources in order to communicate *with* people, interpersonally if possible, not *at* them, impersonally.

The most effective and lasting persuasive messages give people a voice in their own fates and encourage them to use that voice. Effective rhetoric thus encourages response and reality testing at interpersonal levels of communication, not unthinking acquiescence or mere compliance with a rhetor's suggestions or prescriptions.

Miller and Boster (1988) point out that most previous persuasion research was either done within the rhetorical tradition, based on the work of ancient Greek and Roman orators and philosophers, or in the mass media effects tradition that we'll summarize in the next chapter. One-to-many situations are important, but studying them exclusively overlooks the uniqueness of face-to-face interpersonal talk. To highlight this point, Miller and Boster discuss three uniquely important characteristics of personal occasions for persuasion:

- *The existence of a relational history* (we more readily take into account details from our past encounters with the other person)
- *The opportunities for interaction* (we can more easily adjust our approaches while we're applying them, because we're aware of the other's ongoing reactions)
- *The concern for relational outcomes* (rhetors in personal relationships attempt to influence the other while being fully aware of how much the attempt could change the relationship itself)

In other words, interpersonal persuaders communicate with somewhat different ground rules than those used by other persuaders in the wider, one-to-many public sphere.

Compliance-Gaining Theory

Social psychologist Herbert Kelman (1966) gives us a historical perspective on compliance as a form of social influence. He believes **compliance** occurs when one person does what another person wants done "to achieve a favorable reaction from the other. He may be interested in attaining certain specific rewards or in avoiding certain specific punishments that the influencing agent controls" (p. 152). Clearly, then, compliance is conceptually linked to the presence of the agent as well as to the agent's ability to provide rewards or punishments. The changed behavior is exhibited, Kelman believes, only under the public "surveillance" of the agent (p. 160), and it is unlikely to be integrated into the influenced person's attitude structure. In other words, compliance describes those situations that do not rise to the level of C. P. Ellis's change of mind. Kelman's perspective is that compliance is not a very deep or important facet of persuasion. He thought that deeper changes come from two other processes of influence: **identification** (in which people change behavior and attitudes to conform not only publicly but also privately in order to identify with the persuader in a certain way); and **internalization** (in which the person is influenced and conforms because he or she perceives a deeper congruence between personal values and the behavior suggested).

Other scholars, however, most notably Marwell and Schmitt (1967), have built **compliance-gaining theory** into a distinctive perspective on interpersonal persuasion. They believe it's important to discover the conditions under which people adapt behavior to others' suggestions and stipulations, even if deep attitude or value changes don't follow. Wilson (1998) observed that "compliance-gaining interactions unfold whenever a message source attempts to induce a target individual to perform some desired behavior that the target otherwise might not perform" (p. 273). The compliance-gaining approach has been so pervasive that without it we wouldn't have had much of an emphasis at all on interpersonal persuasion in the past forty years. We will briefly summarize its main themes, and then discuss it in terms of relational criteria.

Marwell and Schmitt's (1967) stimulus research synthesis identified 16 "strategies" of compliance-gaining after analyzing work in power and persuasion. As we paraphrase them here, these are the basic ways in which we try to persuade others interpersonally:

1. **Promise** (we promise to reward others if they comply)
2. **Threat** (we promise to punish others if they don't comply)
3. **Positive expertise** (we suggest that we know that good things will happen if they comply)
4. **Negative expertise** (we suggest that we know that bad things will happen if they don't comply)
5. **Liking** (we act so as to be pleasant, helping them to decide to comply with someone they like)
6. **Pre-giving** (we give a reward before suggesting that they comply)
7. **Aversive stimulation** (we continually punish them, so that only compliance will bring relief)
8. **Debt** (we suggest that they owe us compliance because of previous situations)
9. **Moral appeal** (we say they will be immoral if they don't comply, or more moral if they do)
10. **Positive self-feeling** (we show how they will feel better about themselves if they comply)
11. **Negative self-feeling** (we show how they will feel worse about themselves if they don't comply)
12. **Positive altercasting** (we suggest that "good" people would wish to comply)
13. **Negative altercasting** (we suggest that they would have to be "bad" people not to want to comply)
14. **Altruism** (we claim that we very much need the compliance)
15. **Positive esteem** (we show how others will think well of them after they comply)
16. **Negative esteem** (we show how others will think worse of them if they don't comply)

Our advice is not to try to memorize this list, because it is not important in itself. It simply catalogs the diverse ways in which we might frame persuasive messages for others.

If you think that some of the compliance-gaining strategies are similar or even overlapping, you're right. After analysis, Marwell and Schmitt broke the list down into five major factors: *rewarding activity, punishing activity, expertise, activation of impersonal commitments,* and *activation of personal commitments*; much of compliance-gaining research has attempted to compare the effectiveness of the different strategies in differing contexts. But although the list seems long and, at times, complicated, you should be able to translate it fairly directly into real-life situations such as your communication with teachers or family members, with religious leaders, or with health-care personnel. Which ones have you "used" recently? Which ones have been "used" on you? Do people in different organizational or interpersonal roles tend to rely on only some of the strategies? Or are there contexts of interpersonal persuasion in which compliance-gaining assumptions don't give us a full enough picture of how communication processes work effectively?

In this regard, it is useful to think about contexts in which well-meaning people in very different roles meet and work through how they imagine themselves as persuaders and persuadees. One good example is the health-care context. In one recent naturalistic study of doctors' compliance-gaining strategies in medical interviews with patients, for example, Schneider and Beaubien (1996) found that doctors didn't concentrate on the full range of compliance-gaining strategies but, instead, focused over 80 percent of the time on two that Marwell and Schmitt described—*positive expertise* and *liking*—as well as on *legitimacy,* one they did not address directly. Appeals to legitimate power are fundamentally techniques that affirm the patient's belief that it is consistent with the doctor's role, or "legitimate," for the doctor to support the opinion expressed. However, other researchers don't want to study compliance-gaining as a source- or speaker-based phenomenon, in which a doctor or a nurse treats patients as persuasive "targets." Instead of this narrow look at achieving changed behavior in others, these researchers (e.g., Vivian & Wilcox, 2000) are convinced that the relationship between the parties must be taken into account in a process of mutual and collaborative persuasion.

In fact, medical provider–patient interaction illustrates several dimensions of interpersonal persuasion very concretely and might expand how you conceive the dynamics of interpersonal persuasion.

Mutual Persuasion Theory

Michael Garko (1990) critiques how closely researchers have linked compliance-gaining to theories of exchange and power, and how reliant their theories have become on unidirectional influence. In the literature, the person who is asked to comply is typically termed a "target," suggesting a *conduit model* approach that cuts out many dialogic possibilities for communicators. Garko suggests that theories of interpersonal influence should become more transactional and mutualized. In an increasingly complex contemporary culture, where social problems, medical problems, political problems, scientific problems, and issues of personal morality cannot be separated realistically, only an interpersonally responsible mutual persuasion seems appropriate for energizing public policy. Society must have persuasion, but it must, in a sense, become mutualized.

Communication theorists David Smith and Loyd Pettegrew (1986), writing in the journal *Theoretical Medicine,* explore the differences between the traditional medical model of doctor–patient talk and a rhetorically based model they call mutual persuasion. They point out that although the doctor role tends to be quite caring, concerned, and well-meaning, a medical model of doctor–patient persuasion assumes the doctor will emphasize diagnosis, prognosis, and directives aimed at a relatively passive patient whose role, in turn, is to comply with the prescribed treatment. Compliance here, as in compliance-gaining theory, refers to the extent to which the patient does what the physician directs, regardless of his or her own attitudes, beliefs, or values. In fact, the medical field even publishes a journal, the *Journal of Compliance in Health,* which reports on research into how doctors, nurses, and other health professionals can attain higher degrees of compliance from their patients. However, as Smith and Pettegrew (1986) note, only about half the time do patients comply with "doctors' orders." They write, "From an ethical perspective this may be good news. We can applaud patients' resistance to the undermining of their own autonomy. From an efficiency perspective, the news is bad" (p. 130). Noncompliance could result in further illness.

If health-care professionals rely on the medical model's directives and prescriptions to enforce compliance, they do have some support that persuasion theory would predict: the patient's faith in the doctor's authority and the personal respect he or she tends to hold as a result of public admiration for the profession. In rhetorical terms, the physician brings to the relationship a degree of *ethos,* which causes some patients to accept the doctor's orders unquestioningly. After all, doctors often have something akin to an information monopoly concerning health care in general and the medical histories of their patients in particular. In the traditional medical model, the doctor controls the questions that elicit the patient's medical history and then controls the information that is to be applied toward a diagnosis. Finally, the information is presented to an acquiescent patient in a digestible form that is designed to justify the doctor's assigned treatment. Bear in mind that Smith and Pettegrew are not critical of physicians' motives or personalities here; they only mean to describe the accepted medical practice that has evolved over the years in most Western cultures.

The doctor serves as a benevolent but thoroughly rational persuader who objectively "knows the appropriate values and acts [in] patients' best interests" (Smith & Pettegrew, 1986, p. 131). In fact, much medical theory encourages this approach to avoid the possibility that doctors could lapse from rational decision making into subjective manipulation, thereby undermining a patient's "informed consent." According to law, patients must understand enough about their treatments and illnesses to agree in an informed way to what physicians might prescribe. Some authorities, including a presidential commission, have urged doctors to adopt a totally neutral, affectless style of presenting information to patients in order to avoid influencing their choices too much. Thus in this setting a generalized medical model of communication puts doctors in an untenable position: They must inform and direct patients, yet the patients must have a say in the treatment; doctors must be caring, yet they must be careful not to let their treatment preferences be communicated by subtle manipulation, such as through tone of voice or gestures (Smith & Pettegrew, 1986, p. 135).

Notice how the medical model described here resembles Aristotle's description of inartistic bases for communication. Either the older form of the medical model is used, in which physicians are granted the presumed power to manipulate, or the newer form of the model is advocated by some reformers, in which manipulation is supposedly avoided by physicians who simply present the alternative treatments and their probable outcomes for patients. The assumptions of the reformed medical model are (1) that the facts should speak for themselves and (2) that the inherent logic in certain treatments should be clear to patients as a result of doctors' dispassionate presentation of the information. If artistic persuasion is present, it is primarily in the forms of *ethos* and *logos.* According to

Smith and Pettegrew (1986), the guidelines of the President's Commission for the Study of Ethical Problems in Medicine and Biomedical and Behavioral Research suggest that "no tone of voice, word choice, or nuance which could influence the patient is to be used lest the communication fall short of rational persuasion and become manipulation" (p. 135). However, this stipulation is obviously futile, if not silly, given what you now know about the conditions of human interaction. As many concepts discussed in this book demonstrate, human beings cannot help influencing each other verbally and nonverbally during their communication. Even the absence of certain facial expressions will be interpreted in some way by the conversational partners.

Smith and Pettegrew (1986), therefore, build a case for **mutual persuasion** as an alternative model for doctor–patient communication. In this model, both parties are expected to make influence attempts, and both parties will recognize that influence is an inevitable result of interpersonal communication. The authors base their reasoning not on contemporary attitude-change research or compliance-gaining theory but on the oldest Western tradition of rhetoric, whose theorists "attempted to describe how the citizenry could arrive at decisions in the absence of certainty and where the assent of a number of individuals was required" (p. 138). The mutuality model must assume choice on the part of both parties. In fact, as we've seen in our account of classical rhetorical theory, the role of the audience is crucial even in the definition of *rhetoric*. If an audience doesn't hear and respond freely to a speaker, then what we're talking about is not rhetoric but coercion.

The mutuality model also assumes that people involved in genuine conversation are not able to make, nor are they interested in making, clear-cut distinctions between reason and emotion. Therefore doctors and patients alike are active symbol users, speakers, and listeners; neither is controlled by the other. It is only under these circumstances, Smith and Pettegrew argue, that the medical field can hope to gain a higher rate of patients who follow through in response to agreed-upon treatments. This isn't mere patient compliance but the coordinated actions of doctors and patients. In the mutual persuasion approach, the patient responds not just to a doctor's orders but also to an agreement in which both parties have a personal investment. In a sense, this is not compliance as Kelman (1966) defines it but behavior that is consistent with a personal decision. As C. P. Ellis discovered in a different setting, ultimately we all persuade ourselves or we're not persuaded at all.

REVIEWING KEY THEORIES

This chapter has emphasized how persuasion is necessarily interrelated with almost the full range of topics covered in communication theory. Within the discipline of communication studies, however, there are two general approaches to studying persuasion outside the context of mass media (a topic we've saved for Chapter 9): the *rhetorical tradition of persuasion* and the *interpersonal tradition of persuasion*.

In our discussion of the rhetorical tradition, we highlighted the work of Aristotle and others in establishing *classical rhetorical theory*. This theory illuminates such concepts as the *occasions* in which rhetoric develops in public forums, the difference between *inartistic* and *artistic appeals,* and the types of *artistic proofs* that speakers commonly use as evidence in persuasive situations.

LINKS

○ The mutual persuasion model appears to be closely related to the concept of dialogism in inner speech theory (Chapter 4), and the concepts of dialogue and dialectic (Chapter 5). As Geist and Dreyer (1993) write, "A dialogic view holds that the medical encounter is a co-constructed process between provider and patient that takes into account multiple socially constructed selves of the patient. The selves of the patient also include the social context of their relationships at work, in the family, and in the wider community.... Absent from the dialogic perspective is the naive view of the patient as an unbiased reporter of biological facts and the view of the provider as an unbiased listener objectively constructing scientific truth" (p. 235).

The interpersonal tradition, on the other hand, doesn't assume that persuasion takes place in a broad public forum. It helps us to understand how we persuade and are persuaded in such everyday face-to-face situations as families, classrooms, stores, and sports teams. Here we highlighted two areas of theorizing that are perhaps not fully compatible—the *compliance-gaining theory* of Marwell and Schmitt and others, and the *mutual persuasion theory* of Smith and Pettegrew.

Throughout, our own perspective has, we hope, been clear: that persuasive communication is most usefully seen as a helping relationship in which one person or group intentionally tries to affect the behavior and attitudes of others... with the participation of those other people.

TESTING THE CONCEPTS

"Why the emphasis on ancient rhetorical theory? Haven't we learned anything more about persuasion since ancient times?"

Obviously we have progressed very far in our ability to predict communication effects, and many modern theories are far more sophisticated than Aristotelian theories. Yet most students who read Aristotle are surprised at the quality of his insight into the human predicament. He wrote in a very different era and in a very different culture, with communication rules that undoubtedly contradict many that are prevalent in the contemporary United States (e.g., Aristotle did not question slavery or the second-class status of women in ancient Greece). At the same time, however, few communication theorists in the history of the world have been as persuasive as Aristotle.

"Is it good that *ethos*, or *credibility*, can be so persuasive? After all, don't we already put too much emphasis on image politics?"

This would be an especially good question for classroom discussion. Whether or not we like modern methods of media campaigning, the phenomenon of personal credibility will persist. It's not so much an issue of good or bad as it is a question of emphasis. If so-called ethical proofs (the appeal of who a speaker is) are effective, and even differently effective with various audiences and across various situations, communication theorists need to account for these variables.

"How can I get my friend to quit smoking (or overeating, or gambling)?"

You probably can't, although compliance-gaining research certainly suggests some strategic and potentially effective ways for you to structure your messages. But by claiming "*You* probably can't," we are saying that you (from the outside) probably can't create the perfect message that will change your friend's mind about smoking. Persuading someone isn't a matter of just flipping the right switch; it tends to be an emergent mutual process in which both parties are active participants. Rhetors can supply reasons, resources, and possibilities, and should do so if they feel strongly about a social issue (such as smoking), but they cannot cause others to change in a linear way.

YOU, THE RESEARCHER

1. We sometimes refer to a speaker's credibility, or *ethos,* as though it were a possession. However, most communication research focuses on credibility as an audience-based process. That is, no leader can be thought of as having uniformly high or low credibility across all situations; rather, she or he is more or less credible depending on the audience, the topic, and the context. Conduct a brief study of credibility on your own:

   - List three national figures or celebrities who are regarded by you and your friends (an implied audience for the celebrities) as highly credible in their respective fields.
   - For each high-credibility figure you selected, identify an audience, a topic, and a context where you would predict the person's credibility to be quite low. Explain why you chose the audience, topic, and context for each person.
   - Using basic methods of communication research, how could you determine if your reasoning is accurate in these instances? Discuss your proposed studies in class.

2. Interview three people in helping professions, such as counselors, doctors, nurses, and social workers.

   - Ask them to describe how often they think their clients and patients change attitudes and behaviors as a result of communication with the "helper."
   - Ask them to what extent such attitude change in others is specifically intended by the professional. In other words, are the effects of helping outcomes of the relationship or are they the result of a persuasive strategy consciously employed by the professional?
   - The medical profession studies the effectiveness of intentional persuasion, which it calls "patient compliance." Research is conducted on how health-care providers can more effectively persuade patients to follow through with treatment directives. How can the model of mutual persuasion be researched, given its different assumptions about causality?

3. Research the conditions of Greek culture in Aristotle's time. How did men and women regard each other? Were all people regarded as equal? Did some people not have the same rights as others? What power inequalities and elitist assumptions existed in Aristotle's time? Consider whether the culture in which Aristotle wrote affects your opinion of his theory of rhetoric. Why, or why not?

4. At your campus library, trace a public information campaign about the effects of smoking. Analyze advertisements, interviews, and news releases. Explain where you see the following phenomena at work:

   Ethos   Enthymemes
   Pathos   Rhetorical examples
   Logos   Mutual persuasion (or a lack of it)

Richard T. Nowitz/Photo Researchers

CHAPTER 9

"How Powerful Are Mass Media?"

Theorizing Media Systems

Super media are sounds we wake to from a clock radio. They ride with us in the car. In office and classroom, they are the sources of information. They occupy our home as an electronic window and printed page. Super media bring us the news, scare us, relax us, and at times inspire us. We cannot live without them, and we sometimes fear we cannot live with them.

MICHAEL R. REAL, *Super Media* (1989, p. 7)

Media are not fixed natural objects; they have no natural edges. They are constructed complexes of habits, beliefs, and procedures embedded in elaborate cultural codes of communication. The history of media is never more or less than the history of their uses, which always lead us away from them to the social practices and conflicts they illuminate. New media, broadly understood to include the use of new communications technology for old or new purposes, new ways of using old technologies, and, in principle, all other possibilities for the exchange of social meaning, are always introduced into a pattern of tension created by the coexistence of old and new, which is far richer than any single medium that becomes a focus of interest because it is novel. New media embody the possibility that accustomed orders are in jeopardy, since communication is a peculiar kind of interaction that actively seeks variety.

CAROLYN MARVIN, *When Old Technologies Were New* (1988, p. 8)

Media communication—for us, by us, and about us—seems to envelop contemporary culture. Theorists try to understand how the media might change the entire social fabric, and individuals in daily life often wonder how the media might affect them personally. Parents worry that violent television shows might affect their children in negative ways. Will children who watch such shows grow up to become violent adults? If a situation comedy portrays a racist (even a bumbling and foolish one) as a protagonist, will viewers understand the satire, or, instead, get the impression that racism isn't a terribly serious issue? Can modern advertising techniques manipulate people into buying products or candidates they wouldn't otherwise choose? What about the values and beliefs we bring to our media exposure? How successfully can we separate the effects of watching television, for instance, from the effects of talking about television with friends and neighbors? Have our own communication habits as media audiences helped to create the kind of media system we sometimes criticize? Could audiences have more power than we realize? Do we, in other words, sometimes get the media environment we deserve?

Such questions are difficult to answer because we don't have a clear lens with which to observe the mediated world. Because we exist only in that environment, we can't observe it in comparison with other environments. As communication theorists often say, you have to remove yourself from a given frame or system in order to perceive it more clearly. Yet the media seem to occupy a nearly all-encompassing frame.

Most of us find ourselves immersed in media messages every day. People wake up to alarm clocks that are tuned to their favorite radio stations; the night before, they fell asleep watching David Letterman. They read morning newspapers to scan more news than they can possibly assimilate. While traveling to work they strain to listen to radio traffic reports, more news, and entertainment programs. Over lunch, people talk about films, television series, and the insults of outrageous radio personalities. They also talk about distant world leaders, usually on the basis of forty-five-second "news bites" chosen by distant, anonymous network producers and directors. How would modern executives manage without telephones and fax machines? Computer access to information is now taken for granted, not just in businesses but also in many homes throughout society's strata.

Entertainment options continually expand through the media. Cable television and satellite dishes supplement local stations in most areas of the country. Global access is assured, even if global contact isn't. A media consciousness shapes the kinds of futures people can imagine and the kinds of planning they can attempt (Brand, 1988; Negroponte, 1995; Taylor and Saarinen, 1994). **Media events**, Dayan and Katz's (1992) term for the broadcast of special, one-of-a-kind occasions like a royal wedding or the funeral of a head of state, to a certain extent become highlights of our own everyday lives as we talk about them at work, on the street, and while grocery shopping. An anthropology of contemporary society, then, must include media. Without taking media influence into account, an analyst would miss the most pervasive aspects of everyday experience.

Yet within this media environment individuals often feel small and insignificant: "What can I do? I'm just one person." Some critics claim that the technology of the media depersonalizes people, making us less humane, less connected to one another, and more dependent on the decisions of powerful people we will never meet (Berger, Berger, & Kellner, 1974; Ellul, 1964, 1985; Ferrarotti, 1988). Some people believe they are at the mercy of a media-controlled coalition that conspires to shape how its audience thinks. Or, in an anthropomorphic way, people assume that the media have an independent and malevolent existence, that technology is somehow inherently evil, and that the most dangerous technologies are those that disseminate information.

Media theorists provide surprising insights for those in mass audiences who are willing to pay attention. The information media become more powerful in an age that treats information as a commodity. Audiences expect media to have that power, so it exists. To some extent, however, familiarity with the theories of mass communication and other mediated systems can allay some of the fears associated with the idea that the modern media engage in manipulation. To some extent, too, familiarity with media theories can provide a survival kit for dealing with **super media**, a term used by Michael Real (1989) to refer to media that pervade an entire culture.

Before continuing, we should define what we mean by "manipulation" and compare it to some other processes of social communication. Obviously communicators affect each other, often deeply so. You may have been profoundly influenced by a special teacher, by a member of the clergy, or by role models in public and private life. Such influences are natural and normal. While people should admit that they can be influenced, we should also admit the constant potential for influencing others. Even the tiniest conversational pebble we toss creates ripples. Thus influence can be unplanned or accidental. So we shouldn't be surprised that

◀▶**LINK**

Remember that the previous chapter analyzed persuasion as intentional communication in which attitudes and behaviors change. but not in a way that's directly "caused" by something outside the person.

people in families, organizations, and societies can make big differences in one another's lives; it is impossible to avoid having an effect. Human beings constantly adjust to the actions of others. Persuasion happens when people voluntarily change their ways of thinking and feeling (usually intentionally) as a result of the (usually intentional) messages of others. But what about the persistent fear of some people that they're being taken advantage of or manipulated by others' communication? What, if anything, do they fear beyond the suspicion that their attitudes, values, and beliefs are subject to change?

The word *manipulation* is derived from the Latin *manus,* "hand." In human affairs, it has come to refer to a process of taking control over someone's or something's fate—as in picking up an inert object and placing it elsewhere, at your will. Manipulation, then, describes a situation in which one person or group expects automatic reactions from another person or group. Realistic choice seems removed or reduced. No wonder people became frightened when they heard of the "mind control" and "brainwashing" techniques that were supposed to have been so effective in the mid-twentieth century (Brown, 1963). The public began to wonder if a powerful system of mass media (newspaper and magazine empires, then radio, then television) could systematically undermine its ability to make personal choices. Although modern societies wanted more sophisticated and direct means of communicating with diverse groups, they also feared that the systems they wanted could manipulate people directly through propaganda and thought-control methods. This concern with manipulation led, in the 1940s and 1950s, to what is retrospectively called the *magic bullet theory* of media effects, which we discuss in detail later in this chapter.

Although this simplistic "hit the target" analogy is no longer influential, the concern about media manipulation continues to fuel many media-reform efforts. How far should advertisers be allowed to go in promoting their products before they cross an ethical line into manipulation? Is it possible for subliminal communication messages to cause us to buy certain products? Are society's power relationships (haves/have nots, male/female, majority/minority, and so on) inherently reflected in the corporate nature of media conglomerates, reducing our choices and thereby manipulating our social and political preferences? Although this chapter can't answer these questions definitively, it will introduce you to many of the theorists who are grappling with them. Using their concepts and propositions, you will become a better decision maker about the effects of the media, and a media theorist yourself.

In this chapter we will look at three issues of media theory. First, we summarize how people make sense of media messages—that is, how they receive, process, and use such messages in their daily lives. Second, we examine some emerging theories of how media become cultural agencies. Because the media both shape and are shaped by the general culture in which they exist, understanding the media may provide the best clues to understanding contemporary life. People are socialized and acculturized in part by attending to the media. Third, we examine in greater detail those theories that help us relate interpersonal communication to mass communication problems. The connections among the different levels of communication study are important. Yet they are often neglected, because individual researchers might focus solely on either interpersonal or mass communication. This dichotomy, in fact, is often reflected in the splitting of academic communication departments on college and university campuses.

Have Media Changed How We Make Psychological Sense?

Edmund Carpenter, a media theorist who attempted to grapple with the differences between older and newer forms of mass media in the mid-twentieth century, claimed that the media we invent to help us communicate become similar to new "languages" that then structure our experience. The media, therefore, can't be understood as simple pipelines or channels carrying the same messages to different people. He wrote:

> *Each medium, if its bias is properly exploited, reveals and communicates a unique aspect of reality, of truth. Each offers a different perspective, a way of seeing an otherwise hidden dimension of reality. It's not a question of one reality being true, the others distortions. One allows us to see from here, another from there, a third from still another perspective; taken together they give us a more complete whole, a greater truth. New essentials are brought to the fore, including those made invisible by the "blinders" of old languages. (Carpenter, 1960, pp. 173–174)*

A number of theories, then, go beyond the claim that the public's attitudes and beliefs are changed by media messages. These theories suggest instead that something more fundamental occurs, that how people perceive and make sense of the world is affected by the introduction of different media into human experience (see Reviewing Key Ideas, p. 275). Stated somewhat differently, it's not just the power of the messages to change *what we think* (a content issue) that must be analyzed, but we should also recognize the power of the media themselves to change *how we perceive* (a process issue). Joshua Meyrowitz (1994) recently used the term **medium theory** to describe the efforts of a number of scholars to solidify this point, most notably Marshall McLuhan and Fr. Walter Ong.

Medium Theory: Media Extend and Change Our Senses

An intriguing and controversial landmark of twentieth-century communication theory is Marshall McLuhan's *Understanding Media* (1964). His basic idea, developed in earlier work as well (1962), is that media restructure the human consciousness in surprising ways. If European and American cultures revere linear and sequential analysis, we can trace this, according to McLuhan, to the invention of movable type and the institutionalization of writing. *Media,* says McLuhan, are nothing more than extensions of human senses. For example, clothing is a medium extending the skin, and radio and television extend the reach of hearing and vision (simultaneously, in the latter case). Drawing in part on the earlier work of his Canadian countryman Harold Innis (1951; Carey, 1989, pp. 142–172), McLuhan (1962) asserts that "…if a new technology extends one or more of our senses outside us into the social world, then new ratios among all of our senses will occur in that particular culture. It is comparable to what happens when a new note is added to a melody. And when the sense ratios alter in any culture then what had appeared lucid before may suddenly be opaque, and what had been vague or opaque will become translucent" (p. 41). DeFleur and Ball-Rokeach (1982), in their summary of Innis's notions (as elaborated by McLuhan), call this an issue of "technological determinism." The "nature of the media technology prevailing in a society at a given point in time greatly influences how the members of that society think and behave" (p. 184). Perhaps the word *determinism* is an overstatement, just as most commentators on communication have recently claimed that McLuhan's thesis—"the medium is the message"—exaggerates the importance of the media and underplays the importance of media messages.

But McLuhan was onto something important, even if he exaggerated at times; in fact, he thought that his large theoretical guesses and overstatements, even if seemingly outrageous, functioned as valuable "probes" to open up calcified thinking among other scholars. Indeed, it worked. Without the insights of McLuhan and Innis, theorists might not have paid as much attention to the message value of the different media themselves. For example, television *shows* can be "about" crime, or cartoons, or news. But, McLuhan asks, What is *television itself* "about"? Does the existence of television encourage us to think about and evaluate our world more in some ways than in others? McLuhan (1964) reminds us that literal content isn't as important as most people assume: "the 'content' of a medium is like the juicy piece of meat carried by the burglar to distract the watchdog of the mind" (p. 32). To think of content as the most important meaning of media is to mislead yourself, in McLuhan's theory.

His *Understanding Media* (1964) builds on this basic idea that the media themselves *are* messages. It also integrates tremendously diverse sources from history, literature, and social criticism to demonstrate how the electronic media affect modern sensibilities. Although some of McLuhan's distinctions no longer motivate researchers and creative theorists, they remain historically interesting, and in their time they were exciting and heuristic ideas. Contemporary theorists are finding new relevance in many of his ideas, as the Internet further changes how we think about connectivity and interaction. In a recent book, one analyst (Gordon, 1997, pp. 341–349) has written an entire chapter in Q&A form, articulating the kinds of issues—e-mail, *Wired* magazine, interactive CD-ROMs, graphic morphing, spell-checkers, computer commuting, and tattoos—McLuhan would be interested in if he were alive today. In his own era, McLuhan became a pop culture hero, as his ideas were debated on talk shows and in the popular press; he even appeared in a cameo role—as himself—in a Woody Allen movie. In addition to his central thesis, McLuhan's ideas about *hot and cool media* and the *global village* have been highly influential.

Hot media, to McLuhan, are those that demand relatively little of audiences; they supply or attempt to supply a great deal of information while leaving little for the listener, viewer, or reader to "fill in." Hot media are highly definitional and intense. In a sense, they tell listeners much of what they need to know in a situation and leave little to their imagination or participation. Compared with the English language, Asian alphabets that are pictographic define meanings less precisely for readers, "spelling fewer things out," and thus are, in McLuhan's sense, not so "hot." (Books tend to be "hotter" media than radio or television, since print seeks to "tell" readers more definitive detail than they literally need for purposes of interpretation. And textbooks tend to be hotter than novels.) Those media that require (or invite) more audience participation in creating meaning are said to be **cool media**.

Compare McLuhan's hot media and cool media distinctions with the discussion of elaborated and restricted codes in Chapter 7. Are the concepts similar? Analogous? What are the important differences?

How can McLuhan's concepts of hot and cool media help people understand today's culture? Most of the modern electronic media seem to be moving in "cooler" directions, with interesting implications. The cooler media climate invites an ambiguity of style that we can see at work in the political arena. A politician who defines issues too precisely may be seen as logical, but not in tune with the thought patterns that the electorate has come to expect. People feel more included by the cool media, more likely to want to feel a part of what's going on. Their expectations change, sometimes subtly, for what defines public discourse. Other implications McLuhan attributes to the emerging cool media are the modern concerns with total effects rather than isolated meanings, and the concern with processes rather than products.

According to McLuhan (1964), an outgrowth of this emerging "coolness" in the media is the interwebbing of the entire world into a **global village**. Making strong and individualized statements is appropriate to a "hot" medium, but a different rhetoric better fits a world increasingly linked by computers ("extensions of our central nervous systems") and other electronic mass media (McLuhan & Fiore, 1968). Whereas in the first oral cultures villages were places of immediacy and interdependence, the innovation of the printing press and other industrial sophistication made it possible for people in faraway places to trade messages with one another. McLuhan (1964) believes that the new electronic media have returned the communication environment to a state of immediacy:

> *The immediate prospect for literate, fragmented Western man encountering the electric implosion within his own culture is his steady and rapid transformation into a complex and depth-structured person emotionally aware of his total interdependence with the rest of human society. Representatives of the older Western individualism are even now assuming the appearance, for good or ill, of Al Capp's General Bull Moose or of the John Birchers, tribally dedicated to opposing the tribal. Fragmented, literate, and visual individualism is not possible in an electrically patterned and imploded society. So what is to be done? Do we dare to confront such facts at the conscious level, or is it best to becloud and repress such matters until some violence releases us from the entire burden? For the fate of implosion and interdependence is more terrible for Western man than the fate of explosion and independence for tribal man. (p. 59)*

Obviously McLuhan comes down on the side of confronting the implications of our interdependence, since it was our own invention of certain types of media that led us to our retribalized "village"-like state of consciousness, changing us forever. McLuhan, in effect, argues that we cannot return to a primarily linear, sequential, "literate" consciousness because we've become "holized." Instead of scholars analyzing parts more efficiently, McLuhan wants theorists to understand wholes more effectively.

←LINKS

○ Review the discussion of *immediacy* in Chapter 3. How might Mehrabian, for example, predict the differences between the immediacy of face-to-face interaction and the immediacy of electronically linked communication in e-mail or online chat rooms? Many theorists are now struggling to describe the differences between face-to-face and digital forms of presence (Anderson, 1994; Gozzi, 1999; Gozzi & Haynes, 1992; Jones, 1994; Strate, 1999; Strate, Jacobson, & Gibson, 1996; Turkle, 1995; Walther, 1993, 1996).

○ Should McLuhan be considered one of the first *postmodern* communication theorists? Reread his claims in the context of Chapter 4's treatment of the postmodern challenges for theorizing.

Medium Theory and the Human Sensorium

McLuhan's early interests made him a scholarly role model for one of his students, Fr. Walter J. Ong, who has assumed significant intellectual stature in his own right. In a manner somewhat similar to McLuhan's, Ong attempts to synthesize literature, history, the arts, and the social sciences to discover larger patterns. Some of his work on print culture in Western thought was published early enough to influence McLuhan's *The Gutenberg Galaxy* (1962). In two of his most admired books, *The Presence of the Word* (1967) and *Orality and Literacy* (1982), Ong effectively uses McLuhan's themes as foils or touchstones for his own creative thought.

Ong (1967) describes what he calls the human **sensorium**: "the entire sensory apparatus as an operational complex" (p. 6), or the network of habits by which people employ their senses of sound, sight, touch, smell, and taste. The relationships of the senses to one another (whether a given group, for example, emphasizes sound over touch in its way of prioritizing experience) to a large extent define human cultures. Ong (1967) believed humankind has experienced three stages of language transformation: (1) the *oral* (or *oral/aural*) stage; (2) the *script* stage, including the inventions of the alphabet and typography; and (3) the *electronic* stage (pp. 17–110).

The **oral stage** consisted of using language not as records or packages of meaning but as immediate experience. Language was not used to "keep" knowledge, exactly, because even the storytellers and singers of earlier cultures—who were responsible for maintaining the group's culture—typically "retold" stories inexactly. Instead, the word was experienced as a celebration of life, not as a tool for its manipulation. The **script stage** changed that somewhat. With the alphabet came a switchover in human consciousness. Human beings gained more control over sound by representing it visually, as well as by achieving more control over time. The order in human affairs that resulted changed consciousness because it changed the sensorium. "It appears no accident that formal logic was invented in an alphabetic culture," writes Ong (1967, p. 45). Typography increased people's reliance on visualization in the sensorium, but it did not create this reliance, because earlier peoples also had to be keen observers. Instead, typography married visualization with the word. Statements and representations could be repeated exactly. This made the word more believable, increasing people's trust in "the isolated thinker, the man with the book, and downgraded the network of personal loyalties which oral cultures favor as matrices of communication and as principles of social unity" (Ong, 1967, p. 54).

Ong questions McLuhan's belief that media in the **electronic stage** have created the equivalent of a retribalized and orally centered global village. The current electronic involvement with the word has features similar to the oral stage, of course; it makes communication less reliant on formal literacy. But contemporary people cannot, will not, and should not forget literacy. The new electronic culture extends people's sense of being "present" for one another by merging print and orality into human consciousness. Whereas humanity started in a period of **primary orality** associated with the oral stage of language transformation, we progressed to the grasp of **literacy** associated with the script stage, an ability that profoundly changed how we perceived. Now we are in an age of **secondary orality**, Ong believes, which differs considerably from our earlier dependence on orality. It is a new consciousness with a different set of ground rules. Here's why:

> ... *before writing, oral folk were group-minded because no feasible alternative had presented itself. In our age of secondary orality, we are group-minded self-consciously and programmatically. The individual feels that he or she, as an individual, must be socially sensitive. Unlike members of a primary oral culture, who are turned outward because they have had little occasion to turn inward, we are turned outward because we have turned inward. In a like vein, where primary orality promotes spontaneity because the analytic reflectiveness implemented by writing is unavailable, secondary orality promotes spontaneity because through analytic reflection we have decided that spontaneity is a good thing. We plan our happenings carefully to be sure that they are thoroughly spontaneous.* (Ong, 1982, pp. 136–137)

Ong illustrates both his similarity to and his disagreement with McLuhan. At the same time, his last several sentences eloquently suggest the paradoxes of modern living. As Ong's foremost commentator, Thomas J. Farrell (2000), observes, "If Ong's analysis of the human sensorium...is correct, then for centuries most people in Western culture have not experienced the ineffable depths of the human psyche because of their cultural conditioning accentuating visualism and visualist modes of thinking" (p. 194).

Ong has been increasingly influential in the current intellectual community (Dance, 1989; Farrell, 2000; Gronbeck, Farrell, & Soukup, 1991; Havelock, 1986). He undoubtedly influenced the prominent contemporary media theorist Neil Postman, whose recent work explores television's new emphasis on visual presence to the exclusion of analytic thinking. Postman (1985) does not attempt to show, as do Ong, McLuhan, and others, that perception and modes of consciousness themselves are changed by technology; instead, he claims that each new technology changes the "structure of discourse" that people believe to be appropriate. Yet he also believes that there is a relationship between technological advances in the media and human consciousness (p. 27).

Postman (1985) provides an interesting example that is relevant to students and teachers. If you agree with his reasoning, the example demonstrates a shift in the modern consciousness—from print-oriented to television-oriented thinking. In print-oriented thinking, according to Postman, a reader or other message recipient usually assumes that the message should be internally consistent and without contradiction, because the context of the communication is assumed to be singular. In other words, "where the author is coming from" is assumed by the typographic mind to be one place. Postman (1985) often points out to his younger students that what they write in one part of an essay is inconsistent with other parts: "'I know,' they will say, 'but that is there and this is here'" (p. 110). The teacher assumes that students should be writing from one coherent and cohesive

⬅ **LINK**

The new tolerance for inconsistency and contradiction that Postman (1985) describes may help to explain the theoretical appeal of contemporary postmodern thought. In Chapter 4, we discuss the scholarly debate over postmodern theoretical assumptions about language. You may find it interesting to reconsider postmodern theory in the light of media theorizing. Kellner's *Media Culture* (1995), Poster's *The Mode of Information* (1990) and *The Second Media Age* (1995), and Taylor and Saarinen's *Imagologies* (1994) all examine media contributions to a changing postmodern world. McLuhan, Ong, and Postman all range widely over the terrain in drawing connections between mediated communication and the basic ways in which we construct perceptual worlds. Do you believe the electronic media and the new online culture will continue to erode the older, linear rationality of modernism? Why, or why not?

point of view, connected by threads of meaning, which is a very print-oriented way of thinking.

However, Postman points out that television has changed the styles of modern discourse, so that the contexts for any opinion now seem "discontinuous" and constantly shifting. Yesterday cannot be compared with today because a person's stance or opinion could shift at any minute. Postman's students, raised in the age of television more than he was, have incorporated an expectation for discontinuous thought. Television moves abruptly from violent tragedy to giggly comedy with almost no transition, and nothing is perceived as being wrong or amiss; after all, the network is not assumed to be advancing a singular position. As Postman (1985) notes, "...in a world of discontinuities, contradiction is useless as a test of truth or merit, because contradiction does not exist" (p. 110). Perhaps, he speculates, this is why the American public seemed relatively unconcerned when President Reagan repeatedly made public statements that were seemingly mutually exclusive or inconsistent.

Have Media Controlled Our Social and Cultural Behaviors?

Up to this point in the chapter we've discussed theories of how the media alter how we think and, therefore, how we talk. Media do not function as neutral conductors of messages from sources to receivers, in other words. They are, instead, an inescapable part of our social environment. Beyond that, the medium with which we choose to communicate a message inevitably becomes a part of the message itself. In systems theory terms, the medium is a component of the whole communication system, one that bears a relationship to all other components.

If we hope to answer, even tentatively, the question that heads this chapter— "How powerful are mass media?"—we need first to acknowledge that the media are perceptually influential, and then to consider the consequences of that influence on human affairs. Since it's impossible in a brief book to survey all the theories that attempt to account for media impact, in this chapter we'll summarize representative theories that indicate the range of historical, conceptual, and political concerns in this growing area of communication research.

Shot with a "Magic Bullet"?

As the twentieth century became more technologically sophisticated, observers of the mass media began to worry. They feared that individual citizens would be highly vulnerable to persuasive messages from powerful media sources. In the introduction to this chapter we referred to this as the **magic bullet theory** of mass-mediated communication, although it has also been called the **hypodermic needle approach**. By analogy, listeners, viewers, and readers were seen as targets of the media "bullets" (messages), which, if accurately sent, could produce certain desired results. Or, in the second analogy, the audience is conceptualized as a patient who receives an inoculation of persuasion from the media, which, in turn, hold the audience's fate in their hands.

The magic bullet approach is based on a number of assumptions. Although the theory may at first seem simplistic, it was highly believable in the post–World War I age of unsettled international and interpersonal relations:

1. People in major industrialized societies (in which the mass media were developing) experienced feelings of disconnection and **anomie** (a sociological term that describes the breakup and confusion of values within a society) (Theodorson & Theodorson, 1969, p. 12). Traditional societies, with their strong bonds based on families and community affiliation, were changing rapidly after the First World War, and members of newly mass-mediated societies were in many ways presumed to be disoriented and psychologically isolated from each other.

2. Although people in different groups of a society varied widely in their beliefs, attitudes, and values, they were thought by communication researchers to respond to significant messages in largely similar and predictable ways.

3. People were considered very persuasible, and their attitudes easily changed to quite different positions. This assumption, as well as the previous one, was thought to have been established by the success of international propaganda campaigns during World War I.

4. Cause-effect thinking—and its manifestation in the social sciences of the day, the stimulus-response assumption—tended to assign each effect to a specific and identifiable cause. In the case of media effects, the cause, or stimulus, was media content, and the effect, or response, was attitude (and often behavioral) change.

The presumption that audiences were fundamentally vulnerable to media power motivated many communication researchers for years, although, interestingly, many sociologists and other social scientists evidently understood that the mass media did not have the kind of direct and immediate influence that was sometimes attributed to them (Delia, 1987). Gradually, communication researchers in the areas of voting and marketing behavior began to notice effects that were not attributable to the impact of campaign messages on isolated voters.

Two-Step and Multi-Step Flow of Influence Theorizing

Using voting and marketing data, some theorists began to speculate that the media audience was not as atomized—that is, not as spread out and isolated—as

LINK

More attention to rhetorical theories, discussed in Chapter 8, might have helped early theorists predict that audience effects of media messages were less automatic, and audiences were more active and "obstinate," than critics initially presumed. Rhetorical and social science theories clearly can complement each other.

REVIEWING KEY IDEAS

MEDIA CHANGE OUR WAYS OF PERCEIVING

- Innis and McLuhan: Media radically extend our senses, with the media themselves becoming messages that transcend the importance of the content they are presumed to carry; the electronic media help to create a new *global village.*

- Ong: Media adjust the human *sensorium,* changing the relationship of the senses to one another; this is seen in stages of orality (a "primary orality"), script ("literacy"), and electronic ("secondary orality") experience.

they had previously thought. Nor were they as malleable. Theorists began to talk of *"the obstinate audience"* (Bauer, 1964), how audiences were capable of standing firm in the face of persuasive attempts, and of how interpersonal variables intervened between sources and receivers of media messages. It became clear that everyday face-to-face talk about mass communication sources was a vital part of the communication system.

Opinion Leaders in Personal Relations. The most influential scholarly attempt to revise the magic bullet theory was the book *Personal Influence,* by Katz and Lazarsfeld (1955), although an earlier book laid its conceptual groundwork (Lazarsfeld, Berelson, & Gaudet, 1948). Basically, these authors argue that we cannot understand the media system either by looking to media content for its inherent effects or by looking to media audiences for their vulnerability. Instead, a third major variable, interpersonal relations, must be factored into this seemingly simple equation. Their research suggested that the most significant media effects are not directly caused but, instead, come from relationships with influential people in an audience member's own everyday experience.

Katz and Lazarsfeld (1955) call these persuasive agents **influentials**, or **opinion leaders**. Most audience members are not directly addressed or changed by media messages, but their discussions of the media with others subsequently form or change their opinions. Moreover, certain people in this interpersonal system become influential because their opinions are listened to and heeded carefully by others. Opinion leaders also tend to be more exposed to the mass media than other people, and they specialize in specific areas of media coverage to which they have paid particularly close attention (e.g., someone might be an opinion leader in politics but not in fashion). Only rarely is an opinion leader found to be influential across the board.

The **two-step flow theory** thus takes mass communication beyond a simple stimulus-response model, in which the process was seen as a simple one-step or linear injection of attitude. Instead, it looks at mass communication from the point of view of a single audience member, and media messages are seen as filtered through an intermediate step, in which influential others monitor and interpret media content and then disseminate that content interpersonally.

Ironically, the researchers of personal influence in media systems were really demonstrating that many of the most important effects of the mass media are not mass effects at all but a complex and subtle web of interpersonal effects. They showed that part of our understanding of any level of communication must be based on understanding the other levels. But what does this mean in practical everyday terms? It means, for example, that your reaction to *Will & Grace, ER,* or *Good Morning America* is not attributable solely to the show, or to you, or to a straightforward interaction of the show and your attitudes. Instead, your reaction to a television show or other type of media content has to be considered in terms of your interpersonal relationships; your friends and acquaintances, whether they know it or not, are probably exerting some type of opinion leadership.

Subsequent theorists, considering the two-step flow model of mass communication too simple, developed **multi-step flow theories.** Although the basic philosophy is similar, interpersonal influences are seen as being more intricate and multilayered than in the two-step flow theory. In addition, mass communication content depends on many other factors of interpersonal influence for its effects. This can be seen in practical terms by a simple hypothetical example: Think about your experience with an innovative or controversial television show, such as *Buffy the Vampire Slayer, South Park,* or *The Sopranos*. Did you happen to discover the show by chance and watch it before any of your acquaintances did? Or did you hear about the show from one of them? "Hey, did you see that strange new show on Fox network last night?" or "I know you're interested in medical shows; you ought to watch the new one on Monday nights," or "Can you believe something that obnoxious got on the air?" For whatever reason, you decide to tune in. Aside from the personal preferences and values that you brought to the occasion, and aside from the actual content of the show and the intentions of its producers, directors, actors, and network executives, several other facts are already relevant for any theory of the media system:

1. Interpersonal factors probably influenced your decision to watch the show (e.g., "I like Tamara, and I'd like to have more to talk with her about. I think I'll watch *The Sopranos,* too").
2. While watching the show, your friend's recommendation, warning, or enticement about it probably affected your reactions. To the extent that your friend had high or low credibility for you, your judgment was influenced in a positive or negative direction by associating the (impersonal) television program with that (personal) direct experience (e.g., "I don't get it. This seems so offensive. But Tamara thought it was sophisticated and deep. She's probably seeing all the ironic twists more clearly than I do. Come to think of it, I guess I like this show more than I thought I would").
3. While watching the show, you will be formulating and perhaps rehearsing the reactions you'll share with the person who suggested your viewing choice, and you might be anticipating further communication with others about the show as well. This doesn't need to be a conscious process. Overtly or covertly, all healthy individuals process personal experience within the context of anticipated future social interaction (e.g., "I think I'll tell Tamara how fascinating the show was, and how I'm planning to watch it next week, too. I'm really looking forward to it. Maybe Jim would like to know about it, too; I'll call him").
4. After watching the show, your talk about it with others becomes a part of the mass communication system. Advertisers, celebrities, and public relations specialists are well aware of the value of "word-of-mouth" information, and the multi-step flow model is more or less a theoretical form of this process (e.g., "Simone, have you seen *The Sopranos* on HBO? It's weird but really involving, getting to know a mob guy like this. I think you'd like it."..."Thanks. I've already heard about it from people at the office").

Therefore what may seem to be a simple process of receiving messages directly from media sources is clarified to be what it actually is—a complex web of interpersonal processes operating within the context of media topics and choices. Causes and effects are difficult to pinpoint in this multi-step web of influences.

One model of communication that attempts to take interim influences into account is based on the gatekeeping role of the media.

A prominent and currently influential extension of multi-step flow theorizing is Everett Rogers's **diffusion of innovations theory**. Rogers (1995) is interested in discovering how social and cultural *innovations*—new ideas, technologies, and practices—become disseminated to, understood by, and adopted within new audiences. For example, how did the patches designed to help people stop smoking become so rapidly adopted? What did car manufacturers try to do to facilitate buyer acceptance of the airbag innovation? How do multinational companies like Monsanto encourage markets to accept new forms of genetically altered foods? To research such processes, Rogers and other diffusion researchers attempt to learn more about why some innovations are perceived by audiences viewing media messages as more advantageous or more compatible with their values, why some seem relatively simple to try out and adopt, and why some have more immediately observable effects than others. All these aspects of the innovations themselves will influence rapid diffusion.

But these aren't the only factors that influence successful diffusion, of course. Rogers discusses the crucial role of **change agents** (a professional persuader who consciously attempts to coordinate *influentials,* or *opinion leaders*). Rogers believes that persuasion is influenced by both *homophily* and *heterophily*—imposing-sounding terms for a fairly simple distinction. **Homophily** refers to how similar the persuader and persuadee (or any people) are on such basic dimensions as attitudes, values, or socioeconomic status. We often change our attitudes or practices on the basis of the advice or testimony of people who are like us; homophily is an important aspect of trust, according to diffusion research. Thus change agents face a particular problem because they are often perceived as being quite different from the ultimate adopter audiences. **Heterophily** is the concept that describes such differences. For example, the executives, scientists, and marketing professionals who encourage the adoption of genetically engineered seed corn are perceived as having values and life-styles that are quite different from those of the farmers who must choose to plant the new strains of corn. Thus, Rogers found, the successful change agents were those who supplemented their expertise with locally credible influentials as well.

It is not necessary here to discuss all the distinctions Rogers makes, but the range of his research and theorizing is impressive. He created a useful typology of the different types of adopters based on their willingness to adopt new ideas: *innovators* were more cosmopolitan and willing to experiment; *early adopters* tended to be local influentials, or opinion leaders; *early majority adopters* were not necessarily leaders but were active in their social systems; *late majority adopters* were fairly skeptical, often adopting only when they felt forced to change their previous practices; and *laggards,* those whose primary point of reference was a traditional past, and who tended to be system isolates. It's obvious that diffusion-of-innovations research attempts to take into account elements of media content, the credibility of persuaders, and forms of social interaction among audiences. A useful concept in explaining how such content reaches its audience is the notion of *gatekeeping*.

Gatekeepers in the Media System. Westley and MacLean's (1957) model of *gatekeeping* helps to clarify the concept of interim decision makers, or gatekeepers, in combined mass communication and interpersonal communication systems. **Gatekeepers** are those individuals, groups, or roles that control the kind and amount of information receivers can receive, supplementing an audience's direct knowledge of its communication environment. Whether they do so officially or unofficially, gatekeepers monitor the range of messages that might be relevant to a given audience, select and abstract the portion of that range they believe will fit the audience's needs, and relay only those messages to the audience. Gatekeeping is relevant to what media researchers call the **agenda-setting theory** of the media (McCombs & Shaw, 1972). In brief, this approach suggests that media sources don't force us to believe certain things but, instead, by the nature of the profession they must give us a selective, limited set of options to think about. No news medium, for example, can report all that happens in a given day. Certain stories make the newscast or the paper, and others don't. Media gatekeepers therefore set the agenda for social and political life without necessarily being manipulative in doing so. Gatekeepers, whether we like it or not, are an inevitable influence on what we know, or what we think we know.

Informal opinion leaders who communicate interpersonally at the office, in the factory, or at school can also be gatekeepers, as Katz and Lazarsfeld (1955) suggest. Or gatekeepers can have more official roles within the mass media: The producer of *NBC Nightly News,* the managing editor of the *New York Times,* and the manager of your campus radio station can all decide what information gets reported and what information doesn't get reported, based on their interpretations of the relative importance of that information.

Westley and MacLean's (1957) model of gatekeeping is illustrated in Figure 9.1. Although the diagram may look confusing at first, it illustrates a basic process: the intentional attempt of person A to create with person B a certain communication relationship with a certain symbolic content. This is not the kind of transactional model we discussed in earlier chapters, but it does indicate some of the directional factors that people have in mind when they try to create a certain effect with their messages (as shown by the arrows in the figure). Further, the Xs at the left of the figure designate what the authors call *objects of orientation,* or the infinite range of available objects and events capable of being transformed into symbolic messages and stimuli. Both person A and person B, of course, can select from this experiential environment of Xs those objects of orientation they want to attend to; but no two people will select the same Xs, nor will they make their selections for the same reasons. Person A's selection of certain objects of orientation forms the basis for his or her message to person B.

So far, the model is very straightforward. But Westley and MacLean point out that there is often another communication role fulfilled by a person or a group whose purpose is to expand the message environment of the audience (B). Bs can't successfully monitor the incredible diversity of the media world, and thus won't be able to process successfully much of what A is creating. Enter the gatekeeper role, C, which operates much like B's (unappointed) agent in selecting information about objects and relationships. Much of the world's information

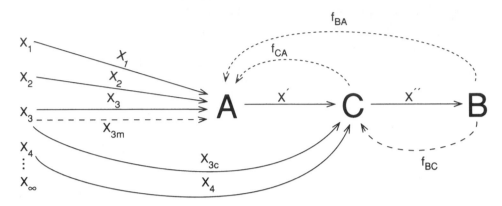

FIGURE 9.1 Westley and MacLean's Model of Gatekeeping

SOURCE: "A Conceptual Model for Mass Communication Research," by B. H. Westley and M. S. MacLean, Jr. In *Journalism Quarterly*, vol. 34 (pp. 31–38). Copyright © 1957. Reproduced with permission of the Association for Education in Journalism and Mass Communication.

potential (Xs) and influence potential (As and the AX relations) are thus filtered through this gatekeeper (C) to an audience.

A few examples will illustrate the importance of the gatekeeper's role in a society dominated by the mass media:

1. Your friend living in Milwaukee is keeping you abreast of neighborhood gossip that it would be very hard for you, living in Chicago, say, or Walla Walla, to collect. But your friend, as your gatekeeper, is inevitably leaving out some things and probably overemphasizing others.

2. This textbook is a message that operates within a mass medium—the publishing industry. If you can imagine that Westley and MacLean occupy the A role and you as a reader occupy the B role (in that they have a particular point of view they'd like you to understand), then we, as this text's authors, occupy the C role. Whether an audience's interest is communication or internal medicine, most audiences can't check independently on everything they read or hear, so they end up trusting strangers who claim to abstract and present this other message faithfully and helpfully. Therefore as a reader you are our audience, and even though we think we are well informed, we will undoubtedly select different features of the model to explain than other authors would choose. We will also emphasize certain issues more than others would. Remember, then, when analyzing mass communication systems, that gatekeepers are everywhere, and no one can avoid them.

3. During the Persian Gulf War, newspapers served as gatekeepers for the public, military briefers served as gatekeepers for the press, generals and the commander in chief served as gatekeepers for the briefers, and the intelligence-gathering community served as gatekeepers for the generals and the president.

4. TV personalities, such as Oprah Winfrey, Larry King, and Geraldo Rivera, also mind the public's gate, promoting some informational and entertainment trends in American culture while blocking others.

As people who attend to the mass media, therefore, we should strive for a realistic understanding of who our opinion leaders and gatekeepers in the media are and of how gatekeepers influence the persuasive impact of media messages. It's not enough for us, as informed citizens, to know what we believe; we should be more attuned to how we come to believe what we do, and to how our beliefs are constantly shifting in response to mediated communication messages.

You've probably noticed that the media theories discussed so far tend to look at effects from the standpoint of the media, which initiate messages for and have effects on audiences. This tendency is perhaps natural. But now let's reposition our theoretical stance to consider the media system more from the vantage point of its audiences.

Uses and Gratifications Theorizing

Probably the most prominent of the recent advances in media theory has come from research in the **uses and gratifications** approach, which examines what audiences have in mind when they expose themselves to the media (Blumler & Katz, 1974; Palmgreen, 1984). In other words, to what uses do audience members put media messages as they see, hear, or read them? And what personalized or social gratifications do audience members attempt to gain from their use of media messages?

The emphasis of uses and gratifications research is on what audiences attempt to do with media messages, not on the effects the media have on audiences. This distinction is important. Unlike some other media theories, uses and gratifications theory does not assume that media audiences are basically passive. Media audiences are conceived as active agents in control of their own destinies. Let's consider a simple example: Imagine that a younger brother, who seems generally healthy and happy, has a habit of attending films that you believe are too violent and gory. Naturally, you're worried about the outcome of his interest in such movies. Will he be psychologically affected by them? Is he in danger of becoming more violent himself, or of condoning casual violence in society? Some media-centered theorists would examine such questions by looking for the effects these movies have on people like your brother. They might perform short-range studies, administering attitude test instruments before and after people's exposure to violent films. Or they might seek to discover longer-range effects through **longitudinal studies**, which follow a group of subjects over a specified period of time and chart (through focused interviews, journals, and similar methods) their media choices and changed attitudes, beliefs, values, and behaviors.

A uses and gratifications theorist, however, would take a very different approach to examining the same issue. Although these theorists have diverse ideas, they tend to assume that it's more important, conceptually and analytically, to start any analysis with the audience. Before we can know whether media messages

⏴**LINK**

Recall the discussion of Schutz's *FIRO theory* of interpersonal needs in Chapter 5. Do *inclusion, control,* and *affection* also apply in mediated situations? Why, or why not? Uses and gratifications theorists try to understand human motivation at basic levels. How might this important point represent a connection between psychological and media studies?

are harmful, they claim, it's necessary to know what the audience members are "doing with" the messages. Is your brother watching the films as indications of the way society should solve problems, essentially using the story line on screen or video as a training film? Are his gratifications those of personal esteem, which he gets by identifying with killers and asocial law-and-order types? Or is your brother using the films as mechanisms for escapism and fantasy, understanding full well that they bear no necessary resemblance to a healthy social existence? Are his gratifications basically social ones, in that he simply wants to be able to talk about the films knowledgeably with friends at school? In that case, he wouldn't be identifying with the film's characters; he'd be using the film's characters to identify, perhaps in healthy ways, with people in his immediate interpersonal environment. He might even watch violent heroes in order to make fun of them, and therefore fit in with a clique of friends.

Among the most important assumptions of uses and gratifications research are the following (adapted from Palmgreen et al., 1985):

- Audiences are active and goal-directed.
- Audiences want personal needs satisfied, and they approach media with that goal in mind.
- Media compete with other sources for people's need satisfaction.
- Media content and structure can't by themselves predict how audiences will develop patterns of gratification.
- Gratifications "can have their origins in media content, exposure in and of itself, and/or the social situation in which exposure takes place" (p. 14).

These assumptions remind us of several important aspects of uses and gratifications theory. For one thing, even though theorists emphasize different areas of the theory, they generally do not claim that psychological factors almost solely influence media impact or that the media are themselves powerless (Blumler, 1985). Instead, media content (i.e., what the media "say") has to be considered along with media characteristics and structures (i.e., how each medium "packages" and presents its messages) and in the context of audience activity.

Palmgreen et al.'s (1985) general media gratifications model, illustrated in Figure 9.2, shows the various factors that the gratifications theorist must consider, as well as the relationships among them. The single-direction arrows, of course, indicate effects and influences; double-direction arrows indicate mutual effects. Although a full description of this model is beyond our purpose here, you should consider three important ideas that are illustrated in Figure 9.2: (1) "Society" and "Individuals" (shown in boxes 1 and 11) are far from separate concepts; (2) "Effects" (in box 10) are not directly influenced by "Media Content" (box 3), nor do effects directly influence media content; and (3) "Gratifications Sought" (box 8) can be affected not only by individuals and their attitudes but also by "Beliefs and Expectations about Media and Alternatives" (box 5).

Thus one question we might ask in media analysis is "To what extent does the mediated environment change an audience's notions and evaluations of what to expect in daily life?" This is the central question addressed by cultivation theory.

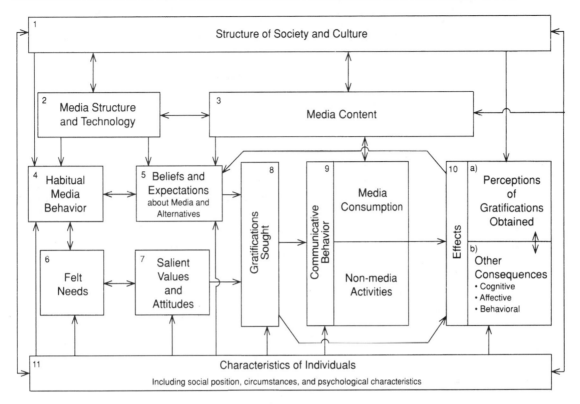

FIGURE 9.2 A General Media Gratifications Model

SOURCE: "Uses and Gratifications Research: The Past Ten Years," by P. Palmgreen, L. A. Wenner, and K. E. Rosengren. In K E. Rosengren, L. A. Wenner, and P. Palmgreen (Eds.), *Media Gratifications Research: Current Perspectives* (p. 17). Beverly Hills, CA: Sage Publications. Copyright © 1985. Used with permission.

Cultivation Theorizing

Cultivation analysis, largely identified with the work of George Gerbner (1970) and his "cultural indicators" research into television's role in society, recognizes that media do not necessarily have a direct "magic bullet" effect on audiences; even so, the media can still be powerful agencies of modern life. Cultivation analysis rests on the basic notion that the media don't change people as much as they change the ground rules by which people define reality. That is, the media change our social expectations. The metaphor implies that media content, like a farmer in the field, cultivates, readies, and assists some developments while discouraging others. The farmer doesn't literally make seed crops grow, or even literally keep individual weeds, should they pop up, from draining nutrients away from crops he or she wants to grow. The farmer simply creates the conditions in which one set of outcomes is much more likely to occur than others. In much the same way, media structure and content "cultivate" modern audiences with particular expectations and definitions of reality.

The questions of cultivation theorizing maintain a dual focus on media and the people who utilize them. According to Signorielli and Morgan (1990), cultivation researchers ask:

1. *What are the processes, pressures, and constraints that influence and underlie the production of mass media content?*
2. *What are the dominant aggregate patterns of images, messages, facts, values, and lessons expressed in media messages?*
3. *What is the independent contribution of these messages to audiences' conceptions of social reality? (p. 9)*

A researcher engaged in a cultivation analysis of television might compare media content with the viewing habits of heavy viewers and light viewers to see if heavy viewers are more likely to reflect, in their own views of "real life," the patterns of reality presumed and presented on television. For instance, does the fact that televised entertainment programs disproportionately feature violence encourage violent behaviors among viewers? Cultivation research (Gerbner, Gross, Morgan, & Signorielli, 1980) tends to show that instead of this kind of overt effect, the media "cultivate" and viewers develop a view that the world is "mean," "dangerous," and difficult to understand. The prime outcome of this **mean world thesis**, then, is that people who are heavy viewers tend to feel defensive, mistrustful, alienated, frustrated, and often uncooperative. Does the television medium cause this? Not exactly, but it is an accomplice.

Gerbner (1990, p. 257) refers to two types of cultivation. **First-order cultivation** refers to the literal beliefs people hold about the world. Some people, for example, may think that because they see more Hyundai ads this year, this suggests that Hyundai must be establishing a foothold in the American automobile market. **Second-order cultivation** has a symbolic dimension, and more far-reaching implications. Gerbner's (1990) explanation of a specific example is extremely relevant for modern society. Second-order cultivation involves:

> *the symbolic transformations . . . that exhibit the special power of symbolic life over and above verisimilitude. That is the special characteristic of terms of discourse to shift from specific cases to general classes and to be understood symbolically rather than literally. For example, in the television world, men outnumber women at least three to one. Taken literally, this would suggest that heavy viewers would underestimate the number or proportion of women in the world, which is not the case. Relative under-representation in the fairly rigidly structured symbolic world, however, is not only a question of numbers. It translates into differential "quotas" of life chances, ranges of activity, stereotyped portrayals, and levels of occupations. Questions dealing with these symbolic transformations of numerical deviations from statistical norms tap dimensions most relevant to cultivation. (p. 257)*

Therefore, the fact that a child viewing television regularly would see fewer women on television would easily be counterbalanced in the first-order realm by his or her direct experience with approximately equal numbers of men and women in everyday life. At the symbolic (second-order) level, however, the media cultivate a set of cultural expectations about the diminished importance, prominence, and centrality of women's contributions. This is disturbing because the symbolic level, almost by definition, is harder to recognize, analyze, and change. The child may internalize these shadow distinctions that have been cultivated and build behavioral patterns that reflect them into his or her life.

Some theorists and philosophers of communication focus on the power relations that have become institutionalized by such distinctions among social groups. They suggest that their mission is primarily a "critical" one: to critique the power relationships within the media system.

Cultural Studies, Critical Theory, and Critical Theorizing

A currently influential strain of work in media theory can be traced to the Centre for Contempory Cultural Studies, located at the University of Birmingham in England (Ferguson & Golding, 1997; Grossberg, 1984; S. Hall, 1989; Hoggart, 1972; Kellner, 1995; Williams, 1981). Although it is generally known as the *cultural studies* approach, this theory is less a unified method for analyzing social processes than it is a broadly defined interdisciplinary stance adopted by some theorists commenting on the modern media.

Cultural studies approaches to media theorizing are usually characterized by the following:

1. They tend to deny that "communication" or "mass communication" should be considered as discrete fields or disciplines of study that can be analyzed apart from other aspects of culture. These scholars study culture as a total life system. Cultural studies proponents therefore tend to believe that too much of twentieth-century communication theorizing and research uses a somewhat restrictive "transmissional" definition of communication (Carey, 1989).

2. Despite a broad cultural conception of communication that could potentially analyze nonverbal messages and artifacts, cultural studies theorists stress the historical role of language in forming both culture and its human institutions (Williams, 1981).

3. Cultural studies approaches tend to take value positions into account in theoretical explanations of social power. This is another way of saying that they often take the form of *critical theory,* a term that we introduced in Chapter 7. This doesn't mean that they are negative (a connotation some people have for "critical"), though critical theorists do often take oppositional stances and may take certain positions to point out or counter established institutional meanings and methods.

4. Many cultural studies theorists, especially the critical theorists, tend to be Marxist in political orientation and therefore focus on power, class, and economic distinctions in social life. These theorists describe society with such terms as **ideology** (a set of widely held beliefs whose validity is not questioned) and **hegemony** (the usually institutionalized and in-place distribution of power that makes one social group dominant over another or others, often with the implied acquiescence of the dominated). For example, if it's impossible almost by definition for poor or middle-class people

**LINK**

Cultivation analysis and *cultural studies* are relevant to multicultural and intercultural communication, discussed in Chapter 7. For example, cultivation research might provide evidence that feminist theorists can apply within their framework. Critical theorists often focus on the social centrality of media in critiquing culture.

⊟ LINKS

○ Cultural studies scholars blend theorizing with social criticism in order to reveal the often hidden distinctions in our power relations. Theorists who specialize in probing race, class, and gender distinctions thus often build on the contributions of critical theorists operating within the cultural studies tradition. See Chapter 7 for a discussion of how theory can function as cultural critique.

○ The cultural studies tradition in media studies has also been linked to postmodernism; review Chapter 4 for some relevant details.

to own newspapers and television stations, then doesn't this fact influence the rhetoric—news, advertising, programming—that characterizes those institutions? Doesn't the extent to which the language and the concerns of the "community" are represented, then, become more a matter of guesswork or condescension than of anyone's direct responsibility, duty, or influence?

5. Cultural studies theorists tend to focus on creative explanation in social science, rather than on precise prediction. Cultural studies thus seems quite different from many other theoretical perspectives when it is first encountered. These works read more like communication commentary or social criticism than like what some people would identify as "theorizing." As Carey (1989) writes, "[C]ultural studies does not attempt to predict human behavior; rather, it attempts to diagnose human meanings. It is, more positively, an attempt to bypass the rather abstracted empiricism of behavioral studies and the ethereal apparatus of formal theories and to descend deeper into the empirical world" (p. 56).

One exemplary and provocative excursion into media-based cultural studies is Douglas Kellner's (1995) *Media Culture*. Starting from the premise that the best way to learn about our own culture is by studying its popular media images and texts, he analyzes prominent features of '80s and '90s popular culture: films such as *Rambo, Top Gun,* and *Do the Right Thing;* celebrities such as Madonna; cyberpunk novels like *Neuromancer;* subtle methods of recasting Gulf War journalism as patriotic entertainment; rap music as "contested terrain" on which the struggles of different groups might be observed; and the role of iconic visual images in cigarette advertising. Kellner assumes that these phenomena are not merely meaningless or trivial "innocent entertainment" but "thoroughly ideological artifacts bound up with political rhetoric, struggles, agendas, and policies" (p. 93). For example, using cultural evidence, he claims he can show "how certain Hollywood films produced images that could be mobilized to produce consent to the U.S. war against Iraq in the early 1990s" (p. 6). He doesn't "read" these texts (analyze them) for the immediate authors' intentions but for how the texts take on meanings for audiences, almost without anyone's intending them to do so. It doesn't matter to him what a screenwriter intended to do, for example; he or she may have produced a text that has been intimately shaped by a variety of potent cultural factors far beyond the writer's knowledge or control. For example, Kellner finds that such texts often "advance specific ideological positions which can be ascertained by relating the texts to the political discourses and debates of their era, to other artifacts concerned with similar themes, and to ideological motifs in the culture that are active in a given text" (p. 93). How does he do this? His theoretical approach, though admittedly subjective, is also powerful because it is

- *Contextual* (He examines the **social horizon**—what else is happening in the culture?—and the **discursive field**—how do people talk or behave within the texts with reference to their situations?)
- *Political* (Whose power is advanced by popular acceptance of the texts? He examines the **resonant images** of texts in order to discover evidence

for *ideologies,* idea systems about power that are so pervasive that they're rarely questioned. *Resonant images* are those that stick in your mind, playing and replaying, whether you want to remember them or not. A contemporary example would be David Letterman's "Top Ten" list, a television show feature that has now made its way into a wide range of books, editorials, sitcom jokes, and political conversations; it is, at the same time, a visual image, a concept, and a form/structure for content of all kinds.)

- *Multicultural and multiperspectival* (Can we look at the so-called same text from a variety of different vantage points, showing how it operates differently in engaging different meanings for different audiences?)

Kellner and many other cultural studies theorists believe that media don't need to be directly or intentionally manipulative in order to have deep and lasting effects on the behaviors of audiences. Rather, they want to unearth the nearly invisible and often politicized assumptions that operate through media culture to structure our lives. As such, this is a far different version of media power than the one the magic bullet theorists envisioned; see Reviewing Key Ideas, below, for an overview of approaches to media power.

Are Mass Communication and Interpersonal Communication Different Processes?

Remember that the two-step flow and the multi-step flow of information concepts are based on systems of interpersonal influence. When describing them, we

---

REVIEWING KEY IDEAS

AN OVERVIEW OF TWENTIETH-CENTURY VIEWS OF MEDIA POWER

- *Magic bullet theory* focuses on the power of sources or messages to influence individuals directly.
- *Two-step* and *multi-step flow theories* focus on the influence of everyday opinion leaders in creating media effects within audiences. Examples include *diffusion of innovations theory* and *agenda-setting theory.*
- *Overtly audience-based* and *culture-based theories* focus on how audience needs and cultural values contribute to the nature of media effects. Examples include *uses and gratifications theory, cultivation analysis,* and *cultural studies.*
- *Reintegration of the interpersonal dimension in audience theories* focuses on how media audiences make mass media content and interpersonal communication interdependent. Examples include *parasocial interaction, play theory, spiral of silence theory, public journalism theory,* and the *theory of mediated place.*

contended that it is impossible to understand media effects without taking personal relationships into account. Indeed, *Personal Influence* is the title of Katz and Lazarsfeld's (1955) groundbreaking book in media theory. But what other theories and concepts can bring this interpersonal dimension into sharper focus? Although many could be discussed, we'll highlight para-social interaction, play theory, spiral of silence theory, public journalism theory, and the theory of mediated place. These contributions help us to understand the so-called new media of electronic technology—including interactive video systems, computer-mediated communication, teleconferencing, and others (see Brand, 1988; Chesebro & Bonsall, 1989; Hawkins, Wiemann, & Pingree, 1988; Kaplan, 1990; Rice & Williams, 1984; Walther, 1996).

We've already introduced Real's (1989) concept of *super media*. By using this term, Real doesn't intend to evoke trivial comic book images but to suggest the root sense of "super," the sense of something covering or including other things. The electronic media in modern society have become an encompassing and overriding environment for all communication, interpersonal and mass. McLuhan (1964) and Ong (1982), of course, would not argue with Real's conclusion.

Para-Social Interaction

Television executives understand that dropping a major character from a popular television series is a risky decision, one that could spark a firestorm of viewer protest. Viewers might react with anguish, as though they had lost a relative or a friend. Indeed, they have.

Horton and Wohl (1956) describe how media audiences project feelings of friendship and affiliation onto media personalities. In effect, audiences listening to radio or watching television form psychic relationships, engaging in **para-social interaction**, with soap opera actors or news anchors. These relations are strikingly similar in emotional tone and psychological consequences to face-to-face relationships with "real" people. Of course, the media figures, even if they are fictitious, become real to audiences as soon as they are considered to be real. As sociologists have long suggested, in some situations it doesn't matter if what someone believes to be real actually matches an objective reality; if it's acted on as if it were real, it becomes real in its consequences. It isn't pathological and rare but normal and common to form such para-social relations, even if it's a one-way process.

Of course, it's not normal or healthy to become obsessed with media figures, losing track of one's own life. The entertainment press is routinely filled with stories of "stalkers." While many of them are motivated by a love of or reverence for the celebrities they follow, most public figures justifiably feel threatened by audience members who have lost their sense of balance. An extreme case of para-social interaction occurred in the 1980s, when a young man became obsessed with actress Jody Foster and sought to gain her attention by attempting a presidential assassination.

Play Theory

William Stephenson (1967) developed his **play theory** of mass communication to explain how people react to the media subjectively. Even in reading the news in a newspaper or magazine, Stephenson contends, a citizen is largely motivated by a desire to engage in what he calls subjective play, fantasy, and personal myth-making (p. 3). Later in his book, Stephenson contrasts subjective play that leads to **communication-pleasure** with the **communication-work** assumptions of those who advocate persuasion and social control theories of media. Although his concepts are not referenced often in recent mass communication theory—despite the fact that his method of researching play theory, *Q-methodology*, remains popular—play theory is a helpful way to understand what we do, as audiences, with media content. As such, it is a useful complement to uses and gratifications research. Dayan and Katz (1992), in their influential research on unique media events, pay a tribute to Stephenson: "Stephenson's...'play theory of mass communication' anticipates our discussion. Almost alone among students of opinion and communication, Stephenson's theory views the media as agents of play, and play as an agent of socialization" (p. 29).

"Play," Stephenson (1967) writes, is what people do when they feel "self-sufficient" and relatively free. "Work is not disinterested, is not an interlude in the day for most people. It produces goods, services, or ideas...by application of effort for a purpose" (p. 193). Stephenson considers it obvious that few people in a mass audience use media for "communication-work." Instead, they try to use mass media messages (as Horton & Wohl, 1956, coming from a psychiatric per-spective, would agree) for "sociability and self-existence" purposes (Stephenson, 1967, p. 194). Although some communication trends in the 1990s have made the home more of a viable workplace with the introduction of such "new media" options as e-mail, Internet research, voice mail, and fax capabilities, Stephenson's supposition probably still holds true today.

The most basic media effects come from media structures and messages that encourage what Stephenson calls **convergent selectivity**. *Selectivity* implies that, psychologically speaking, individuals can roam freely and select, frame, and toy with messages, and *convergent* implies that such choices will converge around their distinct or idiosyncratic emotional needs. According to Stephenson (1967), people don't play to attain conscious rewards but to entertain themselves, enhance their self-concept, and exercise their freedom of inner choice. Thus, what can sometimes seem to be the most superficial aspects of mass communica-tion are potentially the most important:

> *Reaching the truth is a matter for science, technology, reason, and work. Charisma, imagery, and fiction are characteristic of convergencies.*
>
> *But this is not to be despised. On the contrary, reality is so complex that its symbolical representation is essential to give it meanings that ordi-nary people can appreciate. Politics is conversation about freedom, liberty, fundamental rights, and the like— issues which need bear little relation to ongoing real conditions or legislative actions. But all these can be good fun, that is, good communication-pleasure. (Stephenson, 1967, p. 195)*

Small wonder, then, that normal viewers might identify psychologically through para-social interaction with media figures and feel a real sense of personal loss, perhaps, when a favorite news anchor gets fired or a favorite sitcom is cancelled.

Spiral of Silence Theory

German researcher Elisabeth Noelle-Neumann (1984) explored what happens when people are asked to give their opinions on public issues. Not surprisingly, she discovered that people do not express their opinions as if they issued directly from some inner true self. Instead, as we've seen, people psychologically evaluate and identify with others' positions, and then consider the social and interpersonal consequences of voicing their own opinions publicly. People who believe they belong to a majority are more likely to feel bolstered by numbers, more likely both to speak up in the first place and to speak assertively about the beliefs and values behind their opinions.

Noelle-Neumann's work asks us to consider what happens when the media polls and news accounts publicize public opinion so effectively that they make it clear (perhaps clearer than it "really" is) which side of a controversial issue is in the majority and which is in the minority. Her **spiral of silence theory** describes the phenomenon that develops: People who perceive themselves to be in a minority inhibit their communication, and those who perceive themselves to be in the majority are more motivated to speak. Thus those in the minority, who speak less, will be relatively underrepresented in the media and audiences will tend to underestimate their impact or influence—leading to a downward spiral of less and less assertiveness from such groups. Conversely, once a group believes its side is ascending, it becomes bolder, more likely both to communicate openly and to overestimate its own influence.

An interpersonal tendency to save face in effect interacts with a media tendency to stifle dialogue. The gap between the haves and the have-nots potentially widens as the latter group wonders, "What's the use of speaking out? We've already lost." The implications of Noelle-Neumann's theory are obvious for presidential election polling and large-scale social issues such as public sentiment for or against a war. Less obviously, the theory also applies to a group in a small town that might wish to take a stand on library censorship but believes it is in a tiny minority. The local paper and radio station may have editorialized emphatically for the banning of Mark Twain. But if the group speaks out in spite of its estimation of failure, breaking the spiral of silence, the members might discover that they have more allies than they thought, allies who also had been silenced. Noelle-Neumann justifiably questions the compatibility of mass communication systems with some aspects of democratic theory.

Some recent commentators, while acknowledging the impact of her work, have questioned why Noelle-Neumann, a journalist during the Nazi regime in Germany, largely neglects what is perhaps the most obvious example of the spiral of silence—the silence found in German mass assent to Hitler's policies (see, e.g., Simpson, 1996).

Public Journalism Theory

Noelle-Neumann attempted to explain some persistent problems in our understanding of how the institutionalized press (including both print and broadcast journalism outlets) is related to public concerns and public opinion. Whether we agree with her conclusions or not, a wide range of theorists agree that the public must be understood within the context of media decision making. A theoretical and pragmatic movement of the 1990s has worked explicitly from this premise. Known also by several other labels (among them *civic journalism, communitarian journalism,* and *conversational journalism*), advocates of *public journalism* attempted to redefine the potential relationships between journalists and their readers and listeners (for accessible review articles from a communication theory perspective, see Anderson, 2000; Gunaratne, 1998; Hardt, 1997; Pauly, 2000; Schroll, 1999). What, specifically, is the definition and theory of communication that supports this new movement?

So-called traditional journalism itself is hard enough to define. For example, is *Entertainment Tonight* a journalistic venture? Is Geraldo Rivera a journalist in the same sense that Cokie Roberts is? What distinctions make George Stephanopoulos a presidential adviser one month and an ABC correspondent/reporter the next? Nevertheless, even given normal difficulties of definition, it's possible to observe some differences between traditional journalism tasks and public journalism tasks. If *traditional journalism* defines its goal as presenting accurate and balanced factual reports of what happened in the world, without intruding on those happenings, **public journalism** attempts to go beyond those facts to seek ways to help the public talk about them. In public journalism theory, the newspaper or other journalistic institution continues to report on newsworthy events but defines a wider role for itself than that of a simple news conduit to the public. Public journalists suggest that journalism should define itself as a site or a forum in which citizens can express their own voices in participating in civic life. Therefore public journalism papers, for example, sponsor public dialogues on controversial issues, integrate citizen columnists into the newsroom, conduct focus groups to determine which issues the public is most interested in learning about within political campaigns, and widen their frames for what counts as news. Opponents of public journalism contend that such moves threaten to compromise the objectivity with which journalists have defined their mission in the past.

The movement has been energized not only by newspaper professionals like Davis "Buzz" Merritt (1995; see also Charity, 1995) but especially by media intellectuals like Jay Rosen (1994, 1999), working from a historical base articulated by James Carey. Carey (1989; Munson & Warren, 1997) has often analyzed the famous early-twentieth-century debate between journalist Walter Lippmann and philosopher John Dewey. While Lippmann (1922) argued that the modern world was so complicated that people needed to have it interpreted for them by a cadre of experts who were specially trained to understand it, Dewey (1927) replied that the basic problem of democracy was not simply deciding how to relay accurate information and interpretation; instead, it was how to get ordinary everyday citizens to engage in civic conversations in helping to determine their own fates. Whereas Lippmann argued for a journalism of expertise and objectivity, Dewey implicitly mistrusted that model because he thought it short-circuited public dialogue. As the Dewey model has been implemented in public journalism, it seeks to do the following things, according to Edmund Lambeth (1998):

⟨◌⟩ LINKS

○ Review Chapter 2 for a definition of *communica-tion* as a mutual-ized process. To what extent do you think public journalism can succeed in applying this approach to the everyday jobs of professional newsworkers?

○ The next chapter will discuss the *discourse ethics* of Jurgen Haber-mas. Some theo-rists believe his theory supports the notion of public journal-ism. After you read Chapter 10, you may want to review the goals of public journalism.

1) *listen systematically to the stories and ideas of citizens even while pro-tecting its freedom to choose what to cover;*

2) *examine alternative ways to frame stories on important community issues;*

3) *choose frames that stand the best chance to stimulate citizen delibera-tion and build public understanding of issues;*

4) *take the initiative to report on major public problems in a way that advances public knowledge of possible solutions and the values served by alternative courses of action;*

5) *pay continuing and systematic attention to how well and how credi-bly it is communicating with the public. (p. 17)*

Thus public journalism also seeks to bring the profession more in tune with two-way models of communication rather than linear or conduit models, to help the profession integrate its audience more actively with its process. This is not the only trend in which this emphasis on process and activity is becoming more prominent. In a way that is similar to public journalism's sense of journalism as a space or a place for dialogue, Joshua Meyrowitz establishes the importance of broadcast media as a place, rather than just a channel, for communication.

The Theory of Mediated Place

The research on television has been severely limited to the extent that it views electronic media merely as new links among pre-existing environ-ments. That is, such research ignores the possibility that, once widely used, electronic media may create new social environments that reshape behavior in ways that go beyond the specific products delivered. (Mey-rowitz, 1985, p. 15)

In what we might call a **theory of mediated place**, communication scholar Joshua Meyrowitz (1985) blends and extends the work of McLuhan (1964) and Goffman (1959) to show how a new **media matrix** (the whole system of individ-ual media acting interdependently) has changed our expectations of what consti-tutes a "place" or a "social situation."

People used to define places in physical terms. You and I were in the same "place" if we could talk with each other directly and with maximum sensory involvement. We weren't in the same "place" if one or both of us moved our loca-tion in physical space. But what of media that create new extended informational settings that are also extended "places"? To use Meyrowitz's analogy, it is as if modern technology had torn down some walls that we once used as demarca-tions of separate places—this is "family life," that is "work life," there is "politics," here is "personal decision making," and so forth. In other instances, the media have erected new walls. Since the media matrix extends access to information and extends it simultaneously, the lines between the public and private spheres of life are now blurred.

Consider, for example, the recent social preoccupations with the private lives of politicians, the undermining of authority, the blurring of distinctions between parental and children's roles in families, openness in discussing sex and personal problems publicly, and people's increased willingness to discuss empowerment in gender, social class, and ethnicity issues. All such changes have become possible, at least in part, because media, according to Meyrowitz (1985), have "combined previously distinct social settings, moving the dividing line between private and public behavior toward the private, and weakened the relationship between social situations and physical places. The logic underlying situational patterns of behavior in a print-oriented society, therefore, has been radically subverted. Many Americans may no longer seem to 'know their place' because the traditionally interlocking components of 'place' have been split apart by electronic media. Wherever one is now—at home, at work, or in a car—one may be in touch and tuned in" (p. 308). Television makes it harder for an aristocracy or a repressive regime to maintain power. When people no longer "know their place" in physical terms, they also no longer "know their place" in terms of social position. The electronic media matrix makes information about each social reward and each social danger much more equally available across the spectrum of social differences. The matrix also makes it possible for the public to worry in new ways about whether to elect a president who has cheated on his or her spouse or to approve a judge who has smoked marijuana. Who would have known enough to care before the new technology? Their place, "over there," has become our place, "over here."

Meyrowitz's theory is a good place to wrap up our discussion of mass communication theorizing. He draws on almost all the themes we've surveyed. He assumes that the media become messages in their own right, and that these messages affect human perception. He believes that social class and power relations in society are traceable to a mediated environment, as well as to the individual actions of political and social figures. He understands why interpersonal behaviors and mass media phenomena must be studied as different aspects of the same process. Most important, perhaps, he shows the extent to which the whole fabric of a society is influenced by communication. Communication is not just one component of a society but the basis for constituting a society in the first place.

> ⬅️**LINK**
>
> How does Meyrowitz's view of non-physical place change your understanding of communication context and ecology as discussed in Chapter 3? For example, in terms of his *media matrix*, what would constitute "crowding"?

REVIEWING KEY THEORIES

In this chapter you read about three basic questions of media theorizing: How have the media themselves changed how we make sense of the media's messages? Do the media control us, and, if so, why? And, finally, what connections can link mass media to interpersonal communication, two processes that are sometimes thought to be separable?

In response to the first question, we surveyed *medium theory,* including two major approaches that are conceptually related to each other. Both McLuhan's notion that the "medium is the message" and Ong's idea of the human sensorium show how our senses and sense-making are changed by the very media we participate in and through.

In response to the question about media controlling audiences, we started by surveying unsophisticated early *magic bullet* theories of direct influence. These gave way to *two-step* and *multi-step flow theories,* notably Everett Rogers's *diffusion of innovations theory,* that showed how media influence is not direct but is effected through interim interpersonal communicators. *Gatekeeping* and *agenda-setting theories* show how certain roles in the media are more important than others in determining how the public is influenced. *Uses and gratifications theory* suggests that the audience may be more "in charge" than previous researchers believed; it's not a question of what the media content does to us but of what we do with the media content. In a different way, *cultivation theory* further suggests how the effects can be extremely potent but still indirect. Finally, *cultural studies theory* takes us into the realm of popular culture, demonstrating that what we buy, watch, and enjoy can tell us much about the power relations and even politicized domination that are usually invisible in everyday life.

In response to the third question about the mass communication/interpersonal communication link, we looked at the concept of *para-social interaction,* through which individual media watchers identify with celebrities almost as if they were immediately present—as friends, for instance—in the individuals' lives. Stephenson's *play theory* suggests that we try to achieve communication-pleasure through our relations with media content, similar to the way we assess interpersonal relationships. Noelle-Neumann's *spiral of silence theory* provides a mediated "public opinion" explanation for why people may be silent even though they may feel passionately about social and political issues. *Public journalism theory* seeks to reinvigorate the public dialogue so that public voices are more likely to be heard, heeding a democratic philosophy based in Dewey's work. Finally, Meyrowitz's *theory of mediated place* reminds us of all the ways that media cannot simply be channels but must be thought of as places for our existence.

TESTING THE CONCEPTS

"I still don't know if the media primarily influence me and the rest of their mass audience, or if I primarily influence the media. Which is it?"

This doesn't seem to be an either-or issue. The answers, we're finding, are more complicated. You can assume, with some assurance, that the media do not have the power to manipulate people directly, as was feared in the early decades of the twentieth century. Because people both select and subsequently talk about media content in their own ways (in order to achieve their own "gratifications"), audiences exert a powerful influence on the media. Perhaps the most powerful influence the media have on your life is in the subtle adjustments they make in your perceptual process. But if you accept the hypotheses of Ong, McLuhan, and Meyrowitz, for example, it's not only what you perceive that should be considered but also the bases on which you claim to perceive at all.

"Isn't McLuhan's theory just a cultural fad from the '60s?"

Contemporary communication theorists are in something of a dilemma when considering McLuhan's work. On the one hand, some of it seems dispensable as an artifact of an earlier time. Although McLuhan was no flower child, his kind of intellectual adventure seems more congenial to that era, and his kind of hyperbole seemed more acceptable in the late '60s. McLuhan's wilder claims were not always taken seriously, and "McLuhanisms" were controversial even then. But, on the other hand, he replied that his mission was as an "opener," or intellectual prod, whose mission was to liberate other people's thought. He wasn't so much concerned with being right as he was with being stimulating. We usually get our most creative innovations not from people who are concerned with being pristinely correct or playing it safe but from people like McLuhan, who are willing, if necessary, to be wrong in creative and expansive ways. McLuhan's probes led us to new and important territories of understanding. This is a crucial role of any theory, a heuristic one that jostles other researchers' interest in previously unexplored ideas. Interestingly, current theorists of digital culture have rediscovered the relevance of McLuhan's work: "...in recent years, the explosion of new media—particularly the Web—has caused new anxieties. Or to put a more McLuhanesque spin on it, the advent of new digital media has brought the conditions of the old technologies into sharper relief, and made us suddenly conscious of our media environment. In the confusion of the digital revolution, McLuhan is relevant again" (Wolf, 1996, p. 124; see also Press, 1995.)

"Even if the media don't exactly control us, is it fair to say that violent content in media can cause violence in everyday life?"

One of the most distinguished researchers in this area, Ellen Wartella, takes a strong position about media violence, but one that recognizes a wide variety of contextual factors. While specific programs do not cause specific individuals to behave in particular violent ways, there can be little doubt, she concludes, that it has contributed to our culture of violence. Wartella (1997) succinctly describes a "wide consensus among the experts that, of all the factors contributing to violence in our society, violence on television may be the easiest to control, the most tractable" (p. 4). She writes that the literature shows three major effects of televised violence: the *learning effect,* in which viewers see the possibilities of violent aggression; the *desensitization effect,* in which "prolonged viewing" leads viewers to become emotionally detached from the real and painful consequences of violence; and the *fear effect,* in which seeing televised violence increases our distrust of others, predisposing us to "self-protective" behaviors that, ironically, may increase violence in the long run (p. 6).

YOU, THE RESEARCHER

1. Chart your media usage for a week. Every four or five hours, update an informal log to show the minutes you spend:
   - Reading: books _____   newspapers and magazines _____
   - Watching: films _____   rented videos _____   TV networks and cable stations _____   video games _____
   - Listening: to radio _____   to audio systems _____
   - Talking interpersonally about: media programs, films, and characters _____   media accounts of political and social issues _____
   - Communicating with others, using: telephone _____   fax _____   mail service _____

- Working individually with computers: on individual creative tasks _____ on bulletin board systems, chat rooms, or e-mail _____ using online databases or searching the Internet _____

Compare the media distribution and investment of your time with that of other students. Are some of your different habits rooted in family traditions? In job responsibilities? In personal preferences? What do the class logs suggest about the pervasiveness of media influences in modern society?

2. Media theorist Arthur Asa Berger (1982) warns that "the danger for the Marxist media analysts is that they know the answers before they ask the questions" (p. 64). This is another way of suggesting that at least some critical theory research has an ideological agenda of its own, and a point of view that it is ready to protect and defend. In your college library, locate the spring 1993 issue of the *Western Journal of Communication*, which examines this issue of ideology from a variety of angles. Read the articles by Condit (1993), Wood and Cox (1993), and several other contributors. Then, based on your reading, consider whether you think Berger's criticism is fair or unfair. How might the researcher in this tradition best maintain both an open mind and an ideological commitment simultaneously? Or, conversely, why might this task be impossible, unrealistic, or unnecessary? Explain your reasoning.

3. Confront the para-social interaction phenomenon by introspection. Among television personalities, such as interview journalists like Charlie Rose, sitcom characters like Dharma or Greg, and hosts like Oprah Winfrey or Judge Judy, which ones seem to be your friends? Your enemies? Confidants or allies? A secondary question: What personal needs do you fulfill through such psychological identification with these people whom you don't know and probably will never meet? What do your answers tell you about the relationship between para-social interaction and uses and gratifications theories of the media? Would a large-scale research study of such personal introspections be helpful in deepening our theoretical understanding of everyday media use? Why, or why not?

4. Use Westley and MacLean's model of gatekeeping, shown in Figure 9.1, to illustrate the process of an evening newscast. For each component of the model, identify the corresponding person(s), group(s), or message(s) in the newscast.

5. Explore how advertisers promote products in the new medium of cyberspace. On the Internet, find five advertisements that appear on a search engine or on nationally based home pages. (What, for you, counts as an advertisement, and why?) Look at how the products are advertised—their association with their sites, their graphic design, and the different types of appeal they seem to make. Also consider these questions: To whom do the advertisers appeal? Why are the ads placed in certain locations? How might this new advertising on the Internet affect our perception of the media in general? McLuhan (1964) argues that certain types of advertising

are best suited to the print and electronic media: "The continuous pressure is to create ads more and more in the image of audience motives and desires," "the need is to make the ad include the audience experience," and "the steady trend in advertising is to manifest the product as an integral part of large social purposes and processes" (p. 201). Do you think his conclusions hold true for online advertising? Explain your reasoning.

Frank Fournier/Contact Press Images

CHAPTER 10

"When Is the Effective Choice the Ethical Choice?"

Theorizing Communication Ethics

> Entire new professions are now being trained to use . . . methods for probing or concealing secrets. Government surveillance and information-gathering ha[ve] reached unprecedented dimensions throughout the world; so have infiltration by social scientists for scholarly or commercial purposes, undercover journalism in search of exposés, investigation by private agents and underworld sources, and industrial surveillance and espionage. These practices invite imitation and retaliation, and thus in turn generate a need for still more effective and more secret prying.
>
> The new techniques and the changes they make possible join with the long-standing personal and professional conflicts over secrecy to raise practical moral problems for us all. Yet these problems are often postponed or explained away or dismissed altogether.
>
> SISSELA BOK, *Secrets* (1983, p. xvii)

If the discipline of communication can be said to have a personality, it is definitely a complex one. At times, the reputation of a communication department is that its faculty is primarily interested in the applied aspects of human behavior—teaching and learning about how people can put into practice "better" or "more competent" or "more effective" communication strategies. This takes many forms: Classes in public speaking, reporting, interviewing, listening, small group communication, broadcast management, public relations, and other areas all display this ongoing interest in "what works" in human communication behavior. The pragmatic personality of the communication discipline has been one of our strongest and most needed contributions to academic life, because it counterbalances the "ivory tower" or "egghead" image with which some social critics dismiss professors and their classes.

The "Whether" Question

At other times, however, the discipline is challenged to show another side of its personality. Scholars recognize that any discipline of study must be based on more than an understanding of everyday practical effectiveness. People who are genuinely interested in learning about communication, then, are not just interested in implementing strategies to accomplish goals in particular instances. They are also concerned with why those strategies work. As we discussed in Chapter 1, a body of knowledge about any area of study has to be buttressed by a body of theory that can explain why and how specific learnings can be generalized and transferred to new situations. This foundation for practical application goes beyond that "What works?" question to another issue: "Why does it work?" We've written *Questions of Communication* for students who have, or are on the road to having, this type of deep curiosity about communication. An education without either practical application or theory would be fragmented at best.

However, yet another facet of the discipline's personality remains to be considered. In some ways it is simply an additional area for theorizing. But in another sense it is a separate question, substantially different from the "What works?" and

"Why does it work?" questions. A comprehensive communicator should also be able to ask what we call the *"whether" question*. When we know something about what works and why it works, we still need to ask whether to act in the indicated ways: Is it right? Is it fair? Is it restrictive or deceptive to others? As Bok points out in the chapter-opening quotation, such questions, especially when they are considered in the context of new techniques for invading privacy and violating freedoms, define the domain of ethics. In their examination of ethical problems in the mass media, Christians, Rotzoll, and Fackler (1991) define *ethics* as "the liberal arts discipline that appraises voluntary human conduct insofar as it can be judged right or wrong in reference to determinative principles" (p. xvii). Their emphasis on "voluntary human conduct" is pivotal. Ronald C. Arnett (1991), in reviewing communication scholarship in ethics, points out that the concepts of *choice* and *choice making* seem to be the distinguishing features of a communicational approach to ethics.

This chapter begins with a survey of the general theoretical and philosophical foundations on which ethical communication decisions may be built. It then discusses in more detail some specific ethical systems that are especially relevant to communication in our increasingly complex society, one in which we are simultaneously expected to be able to affect others' behavior and maintain our own psychological health.

In a massive study of American character directed by Bellah, Madsen, Sullivan, Swidler, and Tipton (1986), researchers found that many U.S. citizens tend to discuss communication only in terms of its "managerial" dimension (how can someone use communication techniques to gain the cooperation or compliance of others?) or its "therapeutic" dimension (how can someone enhance her or his "self"?). Both dimensions could potentially ignore the ethical dilemmas of what to do as a communicator when self-interests and community interests are to be—or ought to be—balanced. Kenneth E. Andersen (1991), working from an ethical perspective, has surveyed the literature of communication theorists and found that "individual theorists...rarely address ethical issues directly in terms of the role and function of communication in a society and for individuals" (p. 6). Even for a clearly ethics-related concept such as a speaker's *credibility,* he notes that "the emphasis is more typically on the impact of the credibility of the source in terms of outcomes, rather than the impact on ethical quality of a particular choice or practice," and that "pragmatic questions of effect, rather than ethical quality, are the usual concern" (p. 6).

Researching the practical matter of communication effects does not necessarily lead to an awareness of ethical implications. Though it would be encouraging to think that behavior and ethics go hand in hand, what happens on the one hand and whether it should happen on the other are usually divorced issues in communication studies. A number of ethicists, however, have attempted to develop coherent theories for analyzing ethical concerns in tandem with pragmatic effects.

As teachers and authors, we do not believe the study of communication is an amoral or ethically neutral activity. But neither are we ready to assume only one moral and ethical stance and teach it as the necessarily correct one. Instead, what we intend to do in this chapter is set the table for you, introducing some of the enduring traditions of ethical decision making that have engaged communication scholars. We describe their similarities and differences, and will confront you with some difficult personal choices. If you feel uncomfortable or even squirm a bit while reading this chapter, then we've done our job as authors. You may be forced to rethink some of your beliefs and choices. As ethicist Michael Josephson once said in an interview, "I want to make you uncomfortable, because growth will only come out of a little level of discomfort" (quoted in Moyers, 1989, p. 17). Does it make you uncomfortable, for example, to learn that a recent study found that 61 percent of high school students and 32 percent of college students admitted cheating on an exam within the past year, that more than 33 percent of students said they would lie, if they had to, to get a job, and that 21 percent of college students reported they would falsify an organizational report in order to keep a job ("Ethics of Young," 1992)? At times, ethical discussion is difficult because we are uncertain about what to do. Ironically, discussion is sometimes also difficult because we feel certain that our own positions are justified, correct, or necessary under the circumstances, and that no alternatives are reasonable.

Few thoughtful people who have read widely in ethics give themselves the luxury of certainty, as though they could be absolutely convinced that one system is invariably correct while all others are misguided. An argument can be made for each system. In any case, ethical theory is fascinating because it is the area of communication studies that helps us to integrate the "what works," the "why does it work," and the "should it happen" questions.

Theoretical and Philosophical Foundations for Ethical Communication Decisions

In the film *Do the Right Thing,* writer, director, and actor Spike Lee explores the inner turmoil of an urban neighborhood and the people who live there. Against the backdrop of community and racial violence, Lee projects a story of simmering tensions—tensions that eventually boil over. Whites and blacks, angry for different reasons, are both confronted with the question implied by the film's title: What is "the right thing" to do? How should we talk to each other? How tolerant and accepting should we be in the face of oppression? Although sensitivity, acceptance, and openness are nice, when might intransigence, standing one's ground, or even attack also be justifiable as communication behaviors? Lee is smart enough not to deliver final answers to us. He is content to frame the questions eloquently.

In fact, the ambiguity of Lee's title in some ways mirrors our lives. We often talk about the "right" (or "wrong") things to do as though we were able to match our decisions to an absolute standard or to have our choices judged by an impartial moral tribunal. Although religious and spiritual dogma might serve this function for some people, the supposedly clear-cut lines of right and wrong that are proclaimed by adherents often blur. Increasingly, even intradenominational church conventions are places of questioning, argument, and contention.

Are there foundations or guidelines for coming closer to the "right thing" in human communication? While a number of guidelines have been offered, they are not literally theories of communication ethics. However, they do apply equally well to interpersonal communication, social policy, politics, and other realms of human interaction.

Deontological Approaches

Imagine this situation: You are enrolled in a course taught by a professor whom you admire and like personally. The professor has advised, encouraged, and guided you through the course as well as through the maze of university requirements. But you've just accidentally discovered that a classmate has purchased an already prepared term paper from a "research company" near the university, which the student intends to turn in as the final assignment for the course. You know that other students also engage in this sort of activity. You also know that your classmate's grade is unlikely to influence your own grade. What should you do?

Deontological ethics, also called *deontology,* is that branch of ethical study that asserts that ethical choices arise from personal allegiance to principles that are relatively unchanging and ongoing. In the preceding scenario, then, to the extent that you're guided by an appropriate principle, your decision will be ethically based, whatever you ultimately decide. A deontological approach to your dilemma might mean that you would rely, for example, on a principle of truth-telling. Further, you would probably assume (as an informal deontologist) that all students should be subject to the same rules and should have equal chances to obtain high grades based on their intelligence and effort, not on their checking accounts or their willingness to cheat. Your allegiance to this principle might lead you to make the ethical decision to report the student's intentions to the professor. (Of course, your allegiance might be to an entirely different principle, like "Never turn in your peers," and you'd still be reasoning deontologically.)

Many social groups organize themselves around the deontological concept that right and wrong are based on a recognized moral authority such as church dogma. Right and wrong, when determined prior to behavioral dilemmas, can be used as moral benchmarks for personal decision making. Society itself, deontologists believe, is founded on the rational assumption that humans will recognize the need to submit to principle. Only then will social communication be both fair and reasonably coherent. This is the basis, for example, of the service academies' reliance on an "honor code" in which a cadet violator must be reported by innocent observers or else the witnesses have also violated the code.

Probably the most famous of the deontological theorists is the eighteenth-century German philosopher Immanuel Kant, whose principle of the **categorical imperative** has guided countless decision makers. Kantian theory suggests that a fundamental decision made about one member of a group ought to be "universalizable"—that is, to be applied equally to all members. Any deviations from this application of principle would need to be established as exceptions. Further, he extended his imperative to claim that people should not be treated merely as means to an end, nor should people decide moral questions on the bases of convenience or self-interest. Instead, Kantians hold that moral laws are often internalized in the human conscience, providing access to ethical principles.

Teleological Approaches

Teleological ethics, or *teleology,* is the philosophical study of how goals and outcomes can shape human behavior. According to Flew (1984), "...characteristically, certain phenomena seem to be best explained not by means of prior causes, but by *ends* or aims, intentions or purposes. Teleological explanation seems typical of living or organic things—plants, animals, people. Thus an animal's behaviour is sometimes best described in terms of its goal (food seeking, for example); a chess player's activity can be understood in terms of his purpose—to win" (p. 350). An analyst taking a teleological position believes that people are proactive, not just reactive, in accomplishing their goals. That is, people are aware not only of what influences them at any given point in time but also of wanting their acts to influence a changeable future.

Obviously, teleology provides future-oriented explanations, and therefore it is often known as a **consequentialist ethic**. Consequences, rather than motivations, principles, or causes, are paramount. How might teleological ethics help you make the decision about whether to report the student in our earlier example? In a consequentialist approach, you would probably assess what is likely to happen as a result of your action (reporting the student, staying silent, or finding another option). Then you would compare that consequence with its alternatives to determine what good would come from each. No principle can tell you this reliably; you must become immersed in the dynamics of each social situation.

The most notable teleological position, **utilitarianism**, is associated with the work of nineteenth-century British philosopher John Stuart Mill. In this view, the most ethical human actions are those that produce "good" consequences for the greatest number of people. You can see how Mill's approach and Kant's approach—both reasonable in their own ways—might easily produce contradictory advice about how to address your term paper predicament, however. As a duty-directed deontologist, you could suggest that the principle of truth should be maintained as a first ethical criterion, and you would probably tell the truth about the other student's cheating. However, as a utilitarian, you wouldn't necessarily be convinced that telling the truth is the most ethical action. Who would ultimately be helped by the informing? Who would be hurt? It's possible for you to reason teleologically that it is ethical to report the cheater so that everyone else's grade in the class would remain relatively higher (a fair or good consequence for a greater number of people). Or you might reason that reporting the cheater would result in a severe penalty for that student, but no one else would really gain much from it. In this last interpretation, failing to report the student's cheating would be seen either as ethically sound behavior or, at worst, as not unethical.

Presumably, *Washington Post* reporters Bob Woodward and Carl Bernstein acted from a teleological ethic when they used deceptive interviewing practices to break the Watergate story about political espionage in the early 1970s. Some informants were told that their statements were not the primary investigative breakthroughs but, instead, were secondary corroborations of accounts the reporters had already received. Under this false understanding, the sources talked more freely. In fact, however, their stories formed the informational structure of the entire narrative—the basic argument that persuaded later interviewees to talk. The magnitude of the Watergate story and the degree to which the facts were submerged, combined with the assumption that "the greatest good for the greatest number of people" would be served by publicizing the wrongdoing, led Woodward and Bernstein to a consequentialist criterion of ethical communication.

Egalitarian Approaches

Combining some aspects of both duty-based ethics and utilitarian ethics, **egalitarian ethics,** or *egalitarianism,* attempts to evaluate communication by the criterion of equality. The central question usually becomes: Have the conditions produced by the communication enhanced or hindered equal treatment for the individuals who are affected by it?

Egalitarian ethicists sometimes discuss their position in contrast to a kind of ethics that is occasionally treated as a separate category—**egoistic ethics**. An egoistic ethic basically asks if the outcome is good (or positive, or helpful, or gratifying) for the person doing the evaluating, quite apart from human issues of altruism (Singer, 1986). To return to our example, if you ponder whether to report your classmate's cheating on the basis of egoistic ethics, you would primarily wonder if doing so would improve your own status in the class; if so, then the message will be treated as a reasonable and ethical thing to do. Ironically, the cheating student evidently reasoned egoistically also.

Since human beings don't live or even think in isolation, however, egalitarians wonder if it is ethical to encourage people to act as if they were isolated from society or from the social consequences of their actions. Each of us is constantly affected by those whom we constantly affect, even if that connection is only dimly seen in a given context. Instead of the unquestioning acceptance of external duty advocated by deontologists, or the social calculation urged by the consequentialist ethic, or the selfishness of the egoistic ethic, egalitarians theorize that human affairs are better served by an ethic that prevents the weaker or less protected members of society from being taken advantage of by the stronger members. Only in this way, egalitarian theorists argue, can all of us have equal access to the communication information, channels, and interpretations that keep a society viable.

The most famous proponent of this position is contemporary philosopher John Rawls. In *A Theory of Justice* (1971), Rawls develops what he refers to metaphorically as the **veil of ignorance** criterion, which communicators can use to evaluate their social acts. When considering how to act or speak toward others, Rawls's theory of justice requires individuals who are self-interested in a particular social outcome to place their acts on one side of a metaphorical curtain and everyone else who could possibly be affected on the other side (including themselves), regardless of race, class, gender, power, or other distinctions. Rawls suggests that ethical communicators who are about to make a decision should remove themselves mentally from their actual circumstances in order to enter a hypothetical reality (behind the "veil") from which they are as likely to emerge weak and dependent as powerful and independent. Decisions made on one side of the "veil of ignorance," therefore, could not take such distinctions or the biases arising from them into account. Subsequent communication decisions would potentially influence all parties equally and fairly, and justice would be the theoretical result.

What could be the consequences of applying Rawls's veil of ignorance criterion to your decisions about communicating ethically across cultural boundaries? Given what we know about how cultures shape people's values of right and wrong, can we agree on a cross-cultural ethic? See Chapter 7 for clues for addressing these difficult questions. We'll return to them in our discussion of Taoist thought later in this chapter.

For example, in our student cheating incident, would it be any more or less ethical to report the matter to the professor if the student was your personal friend? As a Rawlsian egalitarian, you'd have to place that friendship on the other side of the "veil" and make the ethical decision on how to communicate without recourse to either the fact of the friendship or your egoistic desire to maintain it. The social fact of friendship would have no fundamental relevance to the ethical decision. Rawls's metaphor of the veil of ignorance would remind you of this by stipulating that the cheater would be as likely to emerge from behind the veil as a stranger as to emerge as the friend he or she "really" is. The "right thing" has more to do with maintaining a just or fair social community than it does with maintaining special privileges or special information such as who are friends and who aren't. Such distinctions should not be critical in ethical decision making in this view. Through such egalitarian reasoning, democratic governments justify legal systems protecting the rights of the accused, even if the accused in a particular case represents a social or economic group that is often unfairly associated with crime. Opponents of capital punishment also appear to use a "veil of ignorance" ethic in their reasoning: "That person in prison could be you or me. Wrongful accusations can victimize *anyone*. What policy best guarantees a process of justice, regardless of our knowledge about someone's past criminal record, socioeconomic class, ethnicity, or other factors that may not be relevant to this case?"

Although the deontological, teleological, and egalitarian theories of ethics are only generalizations that summarize complex systems of philosophical thought in ethics, they provide a background for our survey of ethical systems with more specific application to communication theory.

Beyond "What Works": Specific Theories of Communication Ethics

Students of philosophy and students of communication theory have much in common, probably more than they (or some of their professors) realize. After all, what is philosophy but an attempt to systematize our overall but tentative wisdom concerning how people communicate their ideas and feelings in various

---

REVIEWING KEY IDEAS

PHILOSOPHICAL QUESTIONS FOR ETHICAL COMMUNICATORS

- To what extent should ethics be *deontological,* or based on following relatively unchanging principles?
- To what extent should ethics be *teleological,* or based on analyzing the consequences of messages?
- To what extent should ethics be *egalitarian,* or based on maintaining justice and equality among communicators?

contexts? Philosopher Abraham Kaplan (1961) described the connection between philosophy and everyday communication (although he did so in an era when the importance of gender-neutral language was not yet recognized):

> *A philosophy which speaks, even indirectly, only to philosophers is no phi-losophy at all; and I think the same is true if it speaks only to scientists, or only to jurists, or priests, or any other special class. For the business of phi-losophy, as I see it, always was— and remains— to articulate the princi-ples by which a man can live: not just as a scientist, citizen, religionist, or whatever, but as the whole man that he is. To describe a man's philosophy is to say how he orients himself to the world of his experience, what mean-ings he finds in events, what values he aspires to, what standards guide his choices in all he does. (p. 4)*

Communication studies and philosophy are thus cohorts in the human "orienta-tion to the world of…experience" and in the discovery of "meanings" in the everyday world of communication events and choices.

We do not mean to suggest that philosophers and theorists of communication ethics are unconcerned with "what works," but that they tend to go beyond that level of analysis or questioning to ask the "whether" questions we discussed ear-lier. They want to go further in order to unearth other dimensions in the commu-nicative realm, such as whether some possible actions might accomplish one's ends, yet at the same time be undesirable or harmful within the communicative matrix of society. Such an overview of communication effects is barely different from the transactional perspective we discussed in Chapter 2. An analyst may dis-cover quite a bit about *behavior* by researching individual people, but he or she might miss the importance of *communication* by doing so. Communication focuses on relationships (and vice versa). As such, it has multiple dimensions, only one of which is pragmatic in the technical sense. The other major dimension is, and must continue to be, ethical. Even if we know how to act in order to achieve a desired objective, we're still left with choices about whether it's right or appropriate to act in that manner. In other words, then, learning about communi-cation is simultaneously a study of actions and reasons. It is important not to lose sight of this distinction. As you will see, one important classical treatment of rhetoric emphasizes the unity of acts and reasons (Aristotle, 1954). Others we'll summarize will stress a dynamic ecology of values (Taoist ethics), the importance of avoiding manipulation and objectification (dialogic ethics), the openness to ideas (marketplace of ideas ethics), and the place of stories in informing our ethi-cal decisions (communitarian ethics).

Virtue Ethics

Aristotle's famous definition of the scope of rhetoric—"the faculty of observing in any given case the available means of persuasion"—shows his intense interest in "what works" in communication (1954). Indeed, in some ways his *Rhetoric* served as a manual of persuasion for communicators in ancient Greek civilization. As Solmsen (1954) writes in the introduction to a translation of *Rhetoric and Poetics,* "Aristotle certainly visualizes a speech not as composed for the admiration of literary connoisseurs through all time but as designed for a specific, practical end, as delivered before an audience, as calculated to prove and to convince" (p. xii).

Yet Aristotle also generally recommends that communicators relate to each other in nonmanipulative ways. In a discussion of **virtue ethics**, he defines his central term, *virtue,* as the way people create and preserve "good things; or a faculty of conferring many great benefits…" (Aristotle, 1954, p. 57). Common virtues are justice, courage, temperance, magnificence, magnanimity, liberality, gentleness, prudence, and wisdom. But Aristotle goes on to show that "virtue"—which sounds so much like a trait or a series of principles—is in some ways a relational term: "If virtue is a faculty of beneficence, the highest kinds of it must be those which are most useful to others" (p. 57). Further, *justice* can be defined only through the development of an interpersonal ethic: "Justice is the virtue through which everybody enjoys his own possessions in accordance with the law; its opposite is injustice, through which men enjoy the possessions of others in defiance of the law" (p. 57).

Aristotle's position on moral virtue in situations involving ethical choices falls somewhere between the extremes of action. Referred to by contemporary scholars as the **principle of the golden mean**, it suggests that when people are faced with ethical choices in a situation, the most ethical action is often the one at a midpoint between two extremes; for example, between being foolhardy and rash on the one hand, and totally passive on the other. According to Aristotle in *Nichomachean Ethics* (1947), "virtue…is a state of character concerned with choice, lying in a mean, i.e. the mean relative to us, this being determined by a rational principle, and by that principle by which the man of practical wisdom would determine it. Now it is a mean between two vices, that which depends on excess and that which depends on defect; and again it is a mean because the vices respectively fall short of or exceed what is right in both passions and actions, while virtue both finds and chooses that which is intermediate" (p. 340). Under the principle of the golden mean, then, total commitment to extremes of one side or another in a controversy indicates an ethically suspect lack of discernment. Aristotle discusses extremes in terms of excess and deficiency. Communicators concerned with ethics might reassess their positions to see if a middle ground might be more appropriate. Although meeting in the middle may not result in total agreement, it is a hallmark of the rational society and a sign of ethical communication.

Taoist Ethics

Chinese Taoism (pronounced as if it started with a *D*) is a much older system than Aristotle's ethical guidelines, though it obviously is far less influential in Western civilization. This ancient philosophy is largely based on two works: Lao Tzu's *Tao Te Ching,* which is more than two thousand years old, and the *Chuang Tzu,* a book that has come to be known by the name of its author. The **Tao** ("Tao" is often translated by Western scholars as "The Way," despite Taoism's mistrust of the ability of language to capture reality) is thoroughly culture-specific in its Eastern origin. However, its applications to Western thought have been noted consistently (Bynner, 1962; Cooper, 1972; Kohn & LaFargue, 1998; Zhang, 1988).

In addition, references to Taoist concepts have been increasingly prominent in contemporary Western communication and rhetorical theories (Cheng, 1987; Crawford, 1996; Jensen, 1987; Kincaid, 1987a; Oliver, 1962).

Taoist philosophy is suspicious not only of language as a mirror of reality but also of any system of "shoulds" that purports to tell people how to behave. Although this may seem to make Taoism an unlikely source of an ethic for communication, its rich thought is actually quite similar in many ways to some of the basic insights of contemporary communication theory. As such, Taoism offers the student of communication an array of fresh insights that also seem somehow familiar.

The basic assumption of **Taoist ethics** is that life is an organic whole with its own dynamic ecology. Within this holistic system, no individual person or thing exists except in relation to others; thus, no action can be taken egoistically. In contrast to a deontologically defined principle or duty that guides an individual's decision making, harmony with the whole is the criterion by which a Taoist begins to generate communicative decisions. This does not mean, in the words of the "me generation," that one must always "go with the flow" or never confront another, but that a person must always take into account the ways in which individual action may be counterproductive when considered holistically. Thus **yin** (the passive and receptive elements of living) and **yang** (the active and forceful elements) exist interdependently and dialectically.

In other words, *yin* and *yang* each come into being along with and because of the other. Neither is definable without reference to the other, and this seems to be the basis of Taoist skepticism about language. Logically, if no thing can be truly specified without references to the "not-things," then how can language capture reality? How can words ever encompass enough? Obviously, the ancient Taoist *yin* and *yang* philosophy of interdefinition predates Dewey and Bentley's (1949) twentieth-century transactional view of human experience. Alan Watts translates this transactional dynamic as "mutual arising" (1975, pp. 43, 53). The *Chuang Tzu* takes an interpersonal perspective on this concept: "If there were not [the views of] another, I should not have mine; if there were not I [with my views], his would be uncalled for —this is nearly a true statement of the case, but we do not know what it is that makes it be so" (Legge, 1962, p. 179). Thus, in dialogue, it is the sheer differentness of the other person's view that teaches me what I believe; my individual views arise not from within but from the connections between me and others. This linkage means that harmony is best established when it is accepted and allowed. Leaders don't need to rule or to force the action. Instead, they lead by noninterference and by not thrusting themselves unnecessarily into an artificial center stage.

Two basic features characterize the implicit Taoist ethic in a conflict situation. First, because the sides are mutually dependent, to the extent that different positions are clearly seen as isolated sides, the underlying unity is not experienced. Instead, the self is de-emphasized and transcended, although its uniqueness is constantly affirmed. Paradoxically, within such uniqueness is multiplicity; Lao Tzu said that "one who recognizes all men as members of his own body / Is a sound man to guard them," and that individuals are "members of one another"

LINKS

○ Taoist philosophy is fundamentally dialectical, depending on the same assumptions as *dialectical theory*, discussed in Chapter 5.

○ Review the section in Chapter 2 on *transactional*—as opposed to self-actional or inter-actional— relations. A Taoist ethic emerges from a transactional perception of reality.

(Bynner, 1962, pp. 8, 32). Taoism even suggests that a form of empathy can come from such experience: The Sage "does not view things as apprehended by himself, subjectively, but transfers himself into the position of the thing viewed. This is called using the Light" (Cooper, 1972, pp. 65–66).

Second, the attempt to force the other side into a predetermined position, capitulation, or solution is certain to fail. The more appropriate approach is **wu-wei**, an "effortless effort," or, more simply, effort that flows naturally from the demands of a situation. *Wu-wei* has occasionally been misunderstood by Western thinkers as mere passivity or nonaction—but it involves more context sensitivity than that. The ethical message of Taoism, often subtle and implicit, is to find the movement of the Tao and merge with it. Thus, the effective person is much like flowing water, the central symbol of Taoism; that person adapts action to already existing channels, and finds that, like flowing water, he or she can shape the environment in turn. Water, the weakest, softest, and most pliant substance known to the ancient Chinese, therefore, was also the strongest. The hardest substance they knew, stone, was weak by comparison.

Interestingly, then, Taoism seems to blend pragmatics with ethics, the "what works?" question with the "whether what works is right" question. In emphasizing the interconnectedness of living systems, and insisting that all facets of the world are always in a process of mutual definition, Taoism is similar to a modern-day Western philosophy of dialogue.

Dialogic Ethics

In 1922, a small and intriguing book by Martin Buber (1958) called *I and Thou* appeared in German and began to break its own ground for ethical discussion. Although Buber's writing style resembles mystical poetry at times, his views are rooted not in mysticism but in the concrete realities of everyday existence. The questions Buber asks about humanity are very practical ones.

Stated simply (perhaps too simply) in his **dialogic ethic**, Buber (1958) saw what is uniquely human as the relations between persons, not the individual persons themselves. As Chapter 5 noted, each of us, through concern for what Buber calls *the between,* or the relationship itself, can become a unique "you" for others (or, as it is usually translated, a unique "thou"), capable of being seen and respected in all our differences. Buber contrasts this uniquely person-with-person relationship, the **I-Thou relationship**, with the **I-It relationship**. I-It relations are those in which we regard the other side of the relation as an object or thing to be used, but we do not expect to communicate with it in meaningful ways. I-It relations may be normal and natural for certain portions of our lives; a craftsperson, for example, "uses" tools to make furniture. But when the assumptions of I-It unduly invade our consciousness while communicating, we renounce our human character and our potential to create a sense of community is diminished. As Buber (1958) explains:

> If I *face a human being as my* Thou, *and say the primary word* I-Thou *to him, he is not a thing among things, and does not consist of things.*
>
> *Thus a human being is not* He *or* She, *bounded from every other* He *and* She, *a specific point in space and time within the net of the world;*

nor is he a nature able to be experienced and described, a loose bundle of named qualities. (p. 8)

Clearly, the ethical implication of Buber's position is that we diminish others when we objectify or "use" them as we do objects. This implication also applies to the assumption that we can measure objectively the "qualities" or "nature" of human beings and the human spirit. Buber mistrusts **psychologism**, or the idea that all authentic human experience occurs in the inner self and can be measured or described by the concepts of psychology. Thus, from Buber's perspective it may be unethical to reduce our concept of human existence to a series of individuals who can be measured and known objectively.

Our identity is not housed within our minds but in *the between;* it is from human relations that identity develops. In effect, then, we owe ourselves to the grace of each other's speech, in Buber's (1958) view:

Through the Thou *a man becomes* I. *That which confronts him comes and disappears, relational events condense, then are scattered, and in the change consciousness of the unchanging partner, of the* I, *grows clear, and each time stronger. To be sure, it is still seen caught in the web of the relation with the* Thou, *as the increasingly distinguishable feature of that which reaches out to and yet is not the* Thou. *But it continually breaks through with more power, till a time comes when it bursts its bonds, and the* I *confronts itself for a moment, separated as though it were a* Thou; *as quickly to take possession of itself and from then on to enter into relations in consciousness of itself. (pp. 28–29)*

In essence, we become human through our communication with others, and we are responsible for maintaining our humanity through communication.

In his distinguished career as a theologian, an intellectual, a political figure, an educator, and an author, Buber (1965b) developed the implications of his dialogic approach. Two distinctions he drew are particularly important. In one of them, he described the difference between the conditions of "being" and "seeming" (1965b). The condition of **being**, he thought, was when persons respond to each other in terms of the demands of the immediate situation. It is basically an unstrategic condition or style of living and meeting others. In a condition of being, we do not decide beforehand how to behave or what to think or feel. These are simply outcomes of concrete situations, not objectified plans to be made and packaged. Interestingly, Buber's conception of authentic being includes the possibility that we may be called to oppose another; he was no hopeless romantic. In order to confirm our partners in communication, we must sometimes tell them directly that we believe they are wrong or misguided. Only in this way can we be real partners, real Thous, for others. **Seeming**, in contrast, was a human choice that grew out of the assumptions of I-It. In seeming, false impressions and guile are common and unquestioned strategies. When we are engaged in seeming, we give up the spontaneous authenticity of a meeting for the planned objectification of impressions. We try to manage and manipulate each other and each other's reactions.

Another particularly important ethical distinction for Buber is the problem of "imposing" ideas or actions on others compared with "unfolding" ideas for them

⏴LINK

Compare Buber's dialogic ethic with Goffman's theoretical concepts of *impression management,* discussed in Chapter 5. If these two scholars were to talk in dialogue, they might disagree about the fundamental nature of human existence. For example, Goffman might argue that an inherent part of human society is a kind of *seeming,* because we constantly dramatize ourselves for others and want to be seen in a positive light. Yet Buber appears to position his theory against seeming. In your comparison, try to decide if this disagreement is based on genuine conceptual disagreement or just different terminology. Given your understanding of Buber's approach to *I-It* relations, would he ever see a valid role for seeming in social life?

◀ L I N K

Seeming sometimes appears to be the preferred choice for media communicators, such as entertainers and broadcast journalists (see Chapter 9 for more on media communication). For example, you'll rarely, if ever, hear about Peter Jennings's or Oprah Winfrey's headaches; although they may be sick or in pain, they've trained themselves to speak on-camera or on-stage in much the same way they do when they feel healthy. Many widely admired broadcast interviewers also act as though they were friends with each interviewee, although you may later discover that the two had been feuding. Because many communication majors want to enter such fields, you might like to speculate about why audiences apparently don't believe that such *impression management*, to use Goffman's concept, in professional roles involves ethical dilemmas.

(1965b). The person concerned with **imposing** a point of view is basically acting as a propagandist. It is the acceptance of the idea rather than the value of the idea itself or the relations of the individuals involved that is foremost in the mind of the propagandist. Such a person is ends-oriented, and in many cases the means may be sacrificed for the desired ends. In contrast, someone interested in **unfolding** is primarily motivated by the relation itself. The unfolder stands on a personal ground of commitment but makes no attempt to change, add to, or impose on the other as if the other were a thing to be shaped. Instead, one's perspective is offered (unfolded) as a relational invitation for the other's full consideration. This in no way contradicts the potential for opposition discussed in the previous paragraph. Two people may engage in heated exchange from entirely different vantage points, each unfolding ideas while still respecting and addressing the experienced ground on which the other stands.

This brings us to what is in some ways the most important of Buber's (1965b) ethical concepts—**inclusion**, or, as he sometimes called it, "imagining the real." Persons engaged in inclusion maintain their own perspective while simultaneously imagining the experienced reality of the other communicators from their perspectives. The dialogic communicator thus knows firsthand that reality is differently experienced depending on who, and where, we are. Perception is both here and there. Discussions and decisions are potentially more thorough and informed, as well as more emotionally sound, when we engage in inclusion. Of course, inclusion is not mind reading; rather, it is a tentative but educated guess at an alternate possibility of "rightness" that is not the same as our own. It thus verifies and confirms humanness, not just a single human being.

Inclusion, as Buber uses the term, appears to be essentially similar to what some social scientists and psychologists call *empathy* (Anderson, 1982; Ayres, 1984; Cissna & Anderson, 1990; Johannesen, 1990). However, some other authorities disagree, reserving the term *empathy* for an identification in which one person attempts to gain knowledge about another by projecting into the other's experience (Arnett & Nakagawa, 1983; Stewart, 1983). The essential question for dialogue seems to be this: Does the dialogue partner try to meet the other person on his or her terms without pretense, without abandoning his or her existential ground, and without judging the other by the perceiver's own external standards? *Inclusion,* according to Buber, is essential to maintaining an ethical relationship. Ethical communicators understand the world as much as possible both from their own side and, imaginatively, from the other side.

Richard Johannesen (1990, pp. 62–63) has distilled the thought of Buber and other theorists into six characteristics of dialogue, which can also be considered ethical guidelines for communication:

1. ***Authenticity.*** Maurice Friedman (1960), a noted philosopher and Buber scholar, summarizes this feature: "Whatever the word 'truth' may mean in other spheres," he writes, "in the realm between man and man it means that one imparts oneself to the other as what one is. This is not a question of saying to the other everything that occurs to one, but of allowing the person with whom one communicates to partake of one's being" (p. 86).

2. *Inclusion.* A dialogue partner's life is included as a viable perspective from which someone can understand the world. Perception, therefore, can and should be more than a psychological phenomenon. Ethical communicators do not act as though they are isolated individuals.

3. *Confirmation.* In dialogue we verify each other's existence. Through speech and other forms of communication we demonstrate that we notice others and take them into account, even if we might not agree with them. The very human need to be confirmed, unfortunately, may lead some communicators to adopt behaviors of seeming to be what they're not, and they try to fake sincerity, interest, or competence in order to make the right impressions. Confirmation, you may recall, was discussed in Laing's interpersonal perception theory in Chapter 5.

4. *Presentness.* Johannesen (1990) explains that dialogue partners "demonstrate willingness to become fully involved with each other by taking time, avoiding distraction, being communicatively accessible, and risking attachment. One avoids being an onlooker who simply takes in what is presented or an observer who analyzes" (p. 63).

5. *Spirit of mutual equality.* Dialogic communicators avoid imposing their will on others; instead, they seek ways to allow and encourage others to express themselves more fully. The connection of dialogue to listening is affirmed by this spirit of mutuality. In fact, Buber and others have noted that the spirit most opposite to dialogue is that of *monologue,* in which a single voice dominates a situation. More important, perhaps, that voice—if spoken in the absence of mutuality—will discourage or preclude thorough listening. Some rhetorical and argumentation theorists have described this condition as *bilaterality,* or the mutual access of communicators to all the resources of talk; in a dialogue both sides are heard.

6. *Supportive climate.* Judgment of the other person is not a central characteristic of dialogue. Rather, the ethic of I-Thou recognizes the essential connection of individuals (symbolized by the hyphen in I-Thou) that makes dialogue more of a team effort than a transfer of psychologized meanings from one individual to another.

Many writers have applied dialogic theory to analyses of ethical dilemmas—in society, in political arguments, in cross-cultural encounters, and in ordinary conversations. Recently, the attempts of critical theorist Jurgen Habermas (1979, 1990), educator and philosopher Nel Noddings (1984), and communication scholars Charles Brown and Paul Keller (1979; Keller & Brown, 1968) have been notable.

Brown and Keller (1979) describe their **interpersonal ethic** in terms of the choices communicators have, and are able to develop, as a result of their dialogue. This **choice criterion**, as they describe it, has much more to do with the attitudes people demonstrate toward one another than with specific behaviors that might be prescribed or precluded. They agree with Buber that human interaction is not a matter of "do's and don't's." It involves genuineness and concern as imperfect persons do their best with imperfect means to give themselves and others a chance to make a difference in life. Thus Brown and Keller (1979) show that a dialogic ethic ultimately comes down to the choice criterion: "The ethic we are proposing is imbedded in the assumption that *whatever enhances that which is uniquely human in participants is ethical; whatever dehumanizes is unethical.* This assumption finds expression in one of the values held most dear in a democratic society, namely, that conditions of free choice be created and maintained in which it becomes *possible for the individual to realize his or her potential.* This is achieved to the extent to which others…*do not* try to control, coerce, manipulate, maneuver, or exploit him or her" (p. 277). Further, Brown and Keller point out, such behavior is unethical not only because it harms the other but also because it subverts the growth of the manipulator.

Nel Noddings built on Buber's notion of dialogue for the **feminine ethic of care** she developed for everyday relationships (Johannesen, 2000). Her book *Caring: A Feminine Approach to Ethics and Moral Education* (1984) has had a powerful effect on contemporary ethics as well as on the ongoing social conversation about gender relations. Noddings starts from a somewhat different premise than some other ethicists. She argues that caring is not just the outcome of an ethical relationship but also the genesis of ethics at its most elemental and crucial level. Further, she believes this insight is unusual within ethics because most ethical theory has been developed by men. Thus many ethical systems are dominated by the enunciation of relatively detached principles and "can/can't" or "should/shouldn't" guidelines (a typically male perspective, Noddings suggests), rather than by a more "feminine" assumption of the primacy of relational caring within social situations. From our earlier discussion, you should recognize Noddings's characterization of the male-dominated approach as primarily deontological. However, instead of arguing for a teleological criterion of judging the possible consequences of actions, she goes more or less outside the boundaries of the basic assumption. Noddings believes that women tend to approach moral problems from neither principles nor (necessarily) consequences but from emphasizing the crucial reality of the relationship itself. This is how she describes the problems of *caring* and being *cared-for.*

Bear in mind that Noddings does not mean to suggest that women are incapable of acting on principle or that men are incapable of being relationally sensitive. Rather, she merely asserts that ethical decisions are not made hypothetically but are embedded in real situations. Studies of gender differences in real-life contexts have shown that men and women tend to solve problems differently. Men generally apply previously developed principles, whereas women generally inspect the situation and the relationships for more information about "feelings, needs, impressions, and a sense of personal ideal" (Noddings, 1984, p. 3). Men answer hypothetical or imaginary questions more readily because the principles from which they tend to operate are thought to be invariable (i.e., they try to describe the situation and apply the rule to get the right answer). Women tend to balk more at hypothetical descriptions of behavioral problems because they want more information about the relationships involved. Therefore it makes a difference at the level of caring, for example, whether the people involved have been together for two months or two years, and it matters whether they feel strongly about each other or are only mildly attracted. It is from the immediacy of the more "feminine" condition that ethical caring develops, according to Noddings. In fact, she argues that an ethic of caring exists as a "natural inclination" once a person (female or male) is immersed in the immediacy of a given relation.

Like many other dialogic theorists, Noddings is suspicious of developing an action-based or a behavioral criterion for ethical living. What is right in one situation may be wrong or even destructive in another. The relation is primary, so the attitudes supporting relatedness are primary in moral dilemmas. As Noddings (1984) writes: "What we do depends not upon rules, or at least not wholly on rules—not upon a prior determination of what is fair or equitable—but upon a constellation of conditions that is viewed through both the eyes of the one-caring and the eyes of the cared-for. By and large, we do not say with any conviction that a person cares if that person acts routinely according to some fixed rule" (p. 13). An ethic of human communication instead requires **engrossment**, Noddings's term for becoming involved with the other's existence, a concept that suggests the dialogic ideas of *inclusion, imagining the real,* and *empathy.* When we experience engrossment in another person, we also notice **motivational displacement** (pp. 17, 25). That is, motivation no longer seems to come from within ourselves but seems to have been displaced to the "cared-for" person. Motivation is simultaneously within and outside the individual person; it is relational.

Noddings's ethic of care is primarily applicable to situations of interpersonal communication. But her emphases on real-life situations, relational motivation, and suspicion of invariant principles also apply to other approaches to communication ethics in the mass media and across cultures.

Although Jurgen Habermas's (1990) **discourse ethics** also recommends dialogue, it differs in interesting ways from other dialogic theories of ethics. Habermas, for example, stresses what he calls **communicative rationality** as a backdrop to social order. That is, he is especially interested in how problems are argued within the public sphere when communicators experience social and political conflict. As Habermas (1979) explains: "I...proceed on the assumption that 'moral consciousness' signifies the ability to make use of interactive competence for *consciously* processing morally relevant conflicts of action" (p. 88). For Habermas, then, unlike most other dialogic theorists, consensus is a desirable social goal that can best be achieved by communicators who choose clear rules for guiding the fairness of deliberations. Thus Habermas's discourse ethics has been characterized as primarily a procedural system for establishing rational access to dialogue for a wide variety of communicators.

Within the communication discipline, the most influential of Habermas's concepts has been the **ideal speech situation**. It describes what he considers to be the best dialogue conditions for argumentative deliberation. According to Habermas (1990), an encounter of "ideal speech" has four characteristics: (1) The "cooperative search for truth" results in a consensus, or a mutually agreed-upon interpretation, about that truth; (2) the "force of the better argument" transcends any kind of external or internal coercion; (3) all communicators have equal access to the discourse; and (4) all communicators have equal opportunities to question assertions, introduce their own assertions, and express personal attitudes and wants (p. 89). Over time, Habermas (1992) has clarified that he saw the ideal speech situation not so much as a set of concrete procedural rules but as an attitude of inquiry

⊙ **LINKS**

○ Habermas's *discourse ethics*, with its obvious attempt to extend dialogue into a reinvigorated public sphere, has also been a philosophical foundation for some *public journalism* theory (see Chapter 9).

○ Although Habermas, to his credit, advocates that all speakers should arrive at a dialogic forum that is equally able to listen, to speak, and to articulate the common concerns of a public, some cultural critics argue that such openness rarely reflects the real-world conditions of intergroup relations. Do you think there are times when dialogue may not be a reasonable ethical criterion? In light of the cultural theories of power and dominance you learned about in Chapter 7, do you think dialogic ethics can help guide communication forcefully in a pluralistic society? Why, or why not?

through which rational people attempt to structure how they should address their problems: "'Ideal speech situation' is somewhat too concrete a term for the set of general and unavoidable communicative presuppositions which a subject capable of speech and action must make every time he or she wishes to participate seriously in argumentation" (pp. 160–161). Further, it is "a description of the conditions under which claims to truth and rightness can be discursively redeemed" (p. 171). In conceptualizing an ideal speech situation, Habermas demonstrates his faith in procedures of dialogue for the purpose of attaining public justice. Discourse ethics seems to trust the creation of public argumentative norms over the clash of private values that may never contribute to a total consensus.

However, some scholars believe that this procedural faith, combined with Habermas's assumption about the desirability of consensus, may not always serve a pluralistic society well (see, e.g., Benhabib, 1990, 1992; Young, 1990; among others). Those arguers who are best able to articulate generalizable or universal interests in public can be expected to do better in Habermas's ideal speech situation than those who are uniquely and radically oppressed. In other words, although such critics may appreciate Habermas's dialogic tendencies, they fear that discourse ethics, almost paradoxically, is overly concerned with maintaining a public procedural image of consensus at the expense of the diversity of multicultural voices. To Iris Marion Young (1990), "such a desire for political unity will suppress difference, and tend to exclude some voices and perspectives from the public, because their greater privilege and dominant position allows some groups to articulate the 'common good' in terms influenced by their particular perspective and interests" (p. 118).

In many situations, articulations of "common" concerns will be more favorable to particular groups in power, which could help keep dominated groups at the rhetorical margins of society. In South Africa, for example, for years whites were able to argue that because of their European culture and education system, white perspectives were better suited than black perspectives to represent the political common good. Blacks were often invited to participate and negotiate, but they were not taken seriously. In many parts of the United States, too, the procedures for participation are in place, but dialogue by itself may not guarantee that marginalized groups will be heard adequately. Do the processes of consensus, compromise, and official dialogue themselves inherently favor some groups over others? Companies faced with strikes by workers often have public relations departments that tell the public (1) it is in the common good for workers to keep their jobs (working for less money) rather than push for more money that could force the organization to its demise, and (2) while the company is open to listening to both sides and considering the "common good," workers are not dialogic in that they make "demands."

Other interpreters defend Habermas's sensitivity to less powerful groups, suggesting that decentering and empathy are important to his discourse ethics: "Habermas's discourse model, by requiring that perspective-taking be general and reciprocal, builds the moment of empathy into the procedure of coming to a reasoned agreement: each must put himself or herself into the place of everyone else in discussing whether a proposed norm is fair to all. And this must be done publicly; arguments played out in the individual consciousness or in the theoretician's mind are no substitute for real discourse" (McCarthy, 1990, pp. viii–ix).

REVIEWING KEY IDEAS

FOUR APPROACHES TO DIALOGIC ETHICS

- Buber's *I-Thou* concept stresses the uniquely human relation as the basis for ethics (not *psychologism* or individualism) and distinguishes between *being* and *seeming,* and *unfolding* and *imposing.*
- Brown and Keller's *choice criterion* suggests that ethical communicating increases people's range of free choice.
- Noddings's *feminine ethic of care* emphasizes that caring communicators reduce their reliance on deontological principles of ethical choice making; it also focuses on how the caring person experiences *engrossment* in particular relationships.
- Habermas's *discourse ethics* elevates procedural standards for rational deliberation and advocates an *ideal speech situation* in which participants are equally able to contribute and to influence others.

Genuine empathy would seem to create a more open ethical climate in which diverse voices are not only heard but also invited.

Obviously many of the ethical systems we have surveyed thus far are not mutually exclusive. In many cases they overlap enough that their authors and other experts from "within" one system can find much to agree with in other perspectives. For example, although Martin Buber agreed with many of the philosophical aspects of Taoism, what he saw as its essential mysticism sent him to look for ethical insights in a somewhat different direction. This different direction is not an entirely contradictory one, however. As we will see, several of our remaining ethical theories also show a consistency of purpose even when theorists choose different terminology.

Marketplace of Ideas Ethics

In a widely read journal article published about four decades ago, Karl Wallace (1963) suggested that the essence of human communication understanding ought to be ideas—the *good reasons* that people give in support of actions. All discourse can be called into question, at least potentially. When this happens, its "substance"—its conceptual content and essential subject matter—has to be justified as leading to acceptable human behavior. The ideational substance of discourse is basic to Wallace, much more basic than the style, ornamentation, organization, or form in which messages are presented. Some of us might argue about how important it is to create clear-cut distinctions between content and style because they are often interdependent in communication, but Wallace in his time responded to studies that took a narrowly pedagogical approach to rhetoric by emphasizing *how* things are said rather than *what* is said.

People constantly make requests of each other as they try to convince, appeal to, be accepted by, or gain compliance from their listeners. Richard Weaver (1971) captures this in a striking metaphor: Language is "sermonic." It cannot be neutral. Each of us preaches. Human speech, even at its most objective, persistently asks to be believed. We normally think of religious rhetoric in this way, but Weaver expands the notion. Language is immersed in value orientations, and creates in both speakers and listeners a complex set of choices, values, and positions. Speech is inherently position-taking, and listening inherently involves developing positions as well.

But what kind of position-taking is Wallace advocating? If all rhetoric takes a position or expresses a value judgment, then society needs a way of evaluating such judgments. *Good reasons,* to Wallace, are those freely expressed, rationally based, and consistent supporting materials for the positions people assert. They mix traditional rational argument with the recognition that human beings are emotional creatures. "Good reasons" are what we use to support our "ought" statements. As critic Wayne Booth (1974) points out, "...the philosophy of good reasons leads us to a reaffirmation of those central human values that other philosophies and religions have reached by other routes: of tolerance, of justice or fairness, of 'democratic' equality of vote in all matters that concern all men equally" (p. 149).

In an earlier article, Wallace (1955) had already laid the groundwork for his ethical approach. Drawing on Aristotle and classical rhetoric, Wallace asked if modern society has become too preoccupied with its ability to persuade and too often ignores questions of "ought" and "what would be better?" in favor of "what works?" His concerns, among others, stimulated the questions with which we began this chapter. Communication theory and research should not settle for a body of "findings" that are not connected to a moral context of "good reasons." This doesn't mean that the same researchers have to conduct these kinds of ethical studies; rather, it means that communication scholars should not privilege one kind of study over the other, nor should they divorce the study of communication science from the study of value judgments.

Wallace (1955) suggests four practical principles for ethical rhetoric in a democratic society. Each of them, paraphrased here, has implications for communicators in all fields:

1. Communicators in a democratic society should uphold a *standard of knowledge.* Because audiences depend upon the information speakers present in public, ethical speech should demonstrate a thorough familiarity with the topic and its relevant implications. Communicators in public life must, in other words, have a knowledge base that supports their good reasons. We must know what we're talking about if we ask others to listen.

2. Communicators in a democratic society should exhibit a *habit of justice.* That is, they should be fair in their selection and presentation of facts. If public communicators are ethical in this way, their audiences will have a fair and reasonable opportunity to make up their own minds about the subject at hand. This idea is in many ways similar to a dialogic ethic. The habit of justice encourages the unfolding of ideas for others, rather than the imposing of ideas on them; it also preserves the choice-making criterion and reflects the concern for equal access in discourse ethics. If communication is ethical, it does not diminish the freedom of, or the equal treatment available to, its participants.

3. Communicators in a democratic society should enact a *habit of preferring public to private motivations*. An ethical speaker should be willing to discuss openly the sources for the positions offered by his or her rhetoric. This type of communicator does not merely speak but in addition speaks about the very origins of his or her speaking. An audience has a right to ask something beyond "What do you know?" The listeners in a democratic ethic need to hear answers to "How did you come to believe this?" and "Why are you telling us this?" A willingness to disclose such matters speaks directly to the issue of communicator credibility

4. Communicators in a democratic society should demonstrate a *habit of respect for dissent*. Following this ethical guideline, a communicator will not try to avoid or hide information that might counter his or her opinions. Rather, the communicator respects opposing positions, in the same way that beginning tennis players appreciate playing with more advanced players. It is the strength of the *other* position that ultimately can strengthen the communicator's position; after all, an untested belief has no strength or validity. This respect for dissent is not a passive tolerance but an active choice of communicators that supports dialogic principles and communicative rationality.

> ◁ L I N K
>
> See the discussion of *ethos* and credibility in Chapter 8. In what ways would more attention to *ethos* improve political campaigning? How might it improve the communication of teachers and students?

Wallace's four ethical principles for democratic rhetoric seem to elevate the needs of a communication system beyond the needs of the individual within that system.

Wallace's suggestions for rhetoric in a free society presume that ideas must be freely developed, freely shared, and freely confronted. Recently, rhetoricians and other scholars drawing on legal opinions and interpretations have extended similar ethical perspectives in philosophical and pragmatic studies of free speech, creating what has become known as **marketplace of ideas ethics** (Haiman, 1981, 1991; Schauer, 1982). The metaphor implies that ideas, like commodities, are differently attractive and influential to various publics. Further, like a market economy, a marketplace of ideas gains strength or influence by encouraging maximum access to the market and by maintaining an adversarial or competitive system for testing ideas against each other. The censoring of ideas is viewed as an impediment to the marketplace in its quest for truth.

Franklyn Haiman has clarified and applied the marketplace of ideas notion within the communication discipline. His book *Speech and Law in a Free Society* (1981) created one of the best extended justifications for the marketplace approach to free speech and ethical communication. In it, Haiman argues that a society is both energized and educated by the open interplay of ideas. While intervening to conceal or restrict discourse may occasionally be justified by a government in an emergency, in everyday affairs a relative openness is required for an informed citizenry to maximize its opportunities for making choices.

Ethicist Sissela Bok's highly regarded study *Secrets* (1983) does not presume that all concealment is necessarily unethical, but it does suggest that secrecy should be carefully balanced against its consequences. Bok offers two "presumptions," or ethical guidelines, for deciding whether secrecy or revelation is most appropriate: *equality* and *"partial individual control* over the degree of secrecy or openness about personal matters" (1983, p. 27; emphasis added). The equality guideline suggests that controls over whether information is open or secret should be relatively equally distributed among members of a group or a society, even though the kinds of information available to them may differ at times. Although some social roles grant high information access and, therefore, high control, Bok claims that such "special considerations" must be justified as valid exceptions to the presumption of equality. Her other presumption, partial individual control, articulates the relationship between information openness and personal choice. As a general rule, a just and free society grants individuals a large degree of control over information about private matters or personal experience. It sounds simple: People should, for the most part, be in charge of information that pertains to them personally. It is interesting to note one implication of this presumption: If in the interpersonal realm individual rights to privacy should be considered ethically primary, then the marketplace of ideas metaphor may be an inadequate rationale for requesting (or expecting or requiring) self-disclosure. However, as in Bok's earlier work (1979), public discussion and discussibility become the key criteria for ethical questions in communication. Extending Rawls's (1971) analysis, Bok argues that publicity and our willing submission to it are the best safeguards and checkpoints of ethical responsibility. "A moral principle must be capable of public statement and defense," Bok believes (1979, p. 97).

Four principles consistent with "public statement and defense" emerge from Haiman's (1981) study of cases and trends in American freedom of expression. Taken together, they can stand as propositions of a marketplace theory of ethical communication:

1. *Unless the harm done by an act of communication is direct, immediate, irreparable, and of a serious material nature, the remedy in a free society should be more speech. The law is an inappropriate tool for dealing with expression which produces mental distress or whose targets are the beliefs and values of an audience.*

2. *Unless deprived of free choice by deception, physical coercion, or an impairment of normal capacities, individuals in a free society are responsible for their own behavior. They are not objects which can be*

REVIEWING KEY IDEAS

FIVE THEORIES OF ETHICAL COMMUNICATION

- The *virtue ethic* of the golden mean
- The *Taoist ethic* of non-interference
- The *dialogic ethic* of mutuality
- The *marketplace of ideas ethic* of individual freedom and justice
- The *communitatian ethic* of community coherence and narrative rationality

triggered into action by symbolic stimuli but human beings who decide how they will respond to the communication they see and hear.

3. *So long as there is a free marketplace of ideas, where the widest possible range of information and alternatives is available, individuals will be the best judges of their own interests. The law is properly used to enrich and expand that communications marketplace and to insure that it remains an open system.*

4. *Government in a free society is the servant of the people, and its powers should not be used to inhibit, distort, or dominate public discourse. There must be compelling justification whenever the government requires unwilling communication of its people or withholds information in its possession from them (Haiman, 1981, pp. 425–426).*

Haiman's four principles represent a synthesis of both sensitive political theory and sophisticated communication theory. Notice how his second principle, for example, depends on a symbolic interactionist approach to communication, yet Haiman attributes a unique and subtle responsibility to government for determining exceptions. He concludes that people are actors, capable of determining their own symbolic realities. They are not, by and large, manipulable robots whose lives are determined and shaped by outside forces (as some propaganda theorists and strict psychological behaviorists might claim).

Communitarian Ethics

In recent years, theorists have rejuvenated an academic interest in stories and storytelling. Although some of them believe a full-blown explanation of human communication experience can come from narrative (Fisher, 1987), others seem to understand it primarily as a helpful organizing principle or metaphor (M. C. Bateson, 1984; Coles, 1989; Keen, 1970). **Narration**, or *narrative,* the human tendency to organize experience into stories with plot, characterization, chronology, conflict, and resolution, becomes the basis for an intriguing approach to ethics (Hauerwas, 1981; MacIntyre, 1984).

A **narrative ethics**, then, as Arnett (1991) points out in his synthesis of the work of Fisher, MacIntyre, and others, is important because it removes ethical discourse from the sphere of expert judges and from distant rules and principles and places it squarely in the experience of particular communities (pp. 65–68). A story does not and cannot develop merely as a product of one "teller," in other words; instead, a story can be considered a cooperative venture, in which individuals participate and to which they contribute. But the story is in many ways larger than what any single speaker or writer can tell, because what is heard, interpreted, and even imagined all contribute to the narrative as well. Because a story is more than its text and more than its telling, evaluating its power is not the province of experts but a collaborative community function. Stories invite evaluation through conversation. At its most basic level, then, narrative theory necessarily emphasizes conversational elements and (in the ways discussed in Chapters 2 and 5) transactional elements. It also portrays reality as constructed through talk and its consequences, through people seeking shared meaning.

⬛**LINKS**

○ To what extent does *multiculturalism*, discussed in Chapter 7, make up the narrative of America's history? In what sense might multiculturalism be an ethical perspective, in addition to a political controversy, a slogan, or an agenda?

○ Is a sense of self or a personal identity prior to social communication, or vice versa? Or is it a dialectical tension (see Chapter 5) in which both sides are true at the same time? Communitarians argue that if social life and its communities are thought to be "ontologically prior" (i.e., more fundamental for defining a uniquely *human* existence), then the major ethical responsibility is to the community and not necessarily or automatically to protecting individual self-expression. What do you think?

We explore ethics, our sometimes painful decisions about right and wrong, by paying careful attention to the stories that characterize a given culture. Analysts of popular culture chart deep currents of thought from seemingly trivial and superficial sources like soap operas, sitcoms, comic books, and music videos. One psychologist demonstrates this through an interesting methodology. Bruner (1986) tries to understand cultural values by having subjects hear or read a single story, and by then asking them to "retell" the story. The same "actual text" (literal words of an "author") turns into quite different "virtual texts" (the interpretive experiences of the retellers). A researcher won't discover an infinite variety of interpretations; the stories will be different, but they will still reflect a limited number of social and cultural community visions. A story, despite an identifiable individual authorship, transcends individuals to implicate them within a community ethic.

One implicit narrative ethical principle, therefore, seems to be a tolerance for diversity, or even an invitation to diversity. Precise formulas for social responsibility, in contrast, are not expected outcomes of narrative ethics. As Bruner (1986) explains, "…the function of literature as art is to open us to dilemmas, to the hypothetical, to the range of possible worlds that a text can refer to. I have used the term 'to subjunctivize' to render the world less fixed, less banal, more susceptible to recreation. Literature subjunctivizes, makes strange, renders the obvious less so, the unknowable less so as well, matters of value more open to reason and intuition" (p. 159). Narrative theorists might well ask: What will keep diverse people talking in spite of their differences? Making an "ethical" decision in some contexts might be nothing more than taking action to move the story along with the cooperative contributions of a given community.

Narrative principles are central to the recent development of a **communitarian ethic**. Communitarian ethicists downplay or reject the traditional liberal emphasis on individual **rights**, conceived as what people should be able to do as individual moral agents. Communitarians shift the emphasis to different ethical ground on which questions of community coherence can be considered (Christians, Ferré, & Fackler, 1993; Etzioni, 1993; Glendon, 1991). Discussing Stanley Hauerwas's (1981) analysis of character and community, media scholars Christians, Ferré, and Fackler (1993) write that appropriate forms of community are "grounded in stories of substantive morality and not merely in formal rules of proper procedure…. Moral power is inseparably connected to a body of language given us as a legacy; the legacy moves us toward a moral horizon, and thereby holds the whims of autonomous individualism at bay. Communities are woven together by narratives that mediate their common understanding of good and evil" (p. 115).

A communitarian ethic reminds us to elevate the values we have developed and hold in common to a more prominent decision-making position than the logical rationality we sometimes seek to protect. This is not an irrational approach but a holistic view of rationality. W. R. Fisher (1987) uses the term **narrative rationality** and describes it as intimately value-tied: "The concept of narrative rationality asserts that it is not the individual form of argument that is ultimately persuasive in discourse. That is important, but values are more persuasive, and they may be expressed in a variety of modes, of which argument is only one.

Hence narrative rationality focuses on 'good reasons'—*elements that provide warrants for accepting or adhering to the advice fostered by any form of communication that can be considered rhetorical"* (p. 48; note that this use of "good reason" is slightly different from Wallace's, as summarized earlier in this chapter).

Clearly, a narrative approach does not help you decide with precision whether a specific act you're contemplating will be "right" or "wrong" taken in isolation. In this sense, it has rather severe limitations as an ethical system (Rybacki & Rybacki, 1991, pp. 124–125). Instead of offering precision, the narrative paradigm contests the assumption that right or wrong can be isolated from the cultural context of stories in which decisions are embedded. Although this paradigm obviously denies a deontological (ethics-as-duty) assumption, it does not necessarily argue in favor of open relativism, in which all behaviors have the potential to be equally valid. Instead, ethical discourse is like a game played within the confines of ground rules—and the ground rules are constructed in the form of what Fisher calls "narrative rationality": stories that make sense, make a coherent community, and provide "good reasons" to support behaviors that are consistent with those stories.

REVIEWING KEY THEORIES

Interestingly, this chapter on ethics brings us back to several themes that were discussed in the Introduction. For example, while the learning styles of men and women appear to be somewhat different, they also share several similarities: They both move in the direction of an increasing acceptance of diversity and divergent points of view, as well as an increasing recognition that the individual is inherently important in the choices he or she makes. The direction most college students take in structuring their own learning also seems to reinforce the importance of searching for good reasons, expanded choices within community, and a tolerance of different perspectives. Although some reports on our ethical climate are discouraging, colleges and universities provide an encouragingly active arena for ethical discourse in society.

College courses in communication generally, and communication theory in particular, offer excellent opportunities for us to question our ethical commitments to other people, and to fair and just communicative choices. In this chapter we've tried to supply an accurate overview of the information you need to develop your own ideas on this crucial matter of interpreting right and wrong, appropriate or inappropriate, moral or immoral behavior. We started with three general alternative philosophical positions ethicists tend to take. *Deontologists* place their faith in prior principles that can be applied to new situations. *Teleologists* tend to suggest, however, that we can communicate with more moral justification if we take into account the consequences or outcomes of our proposed actions. Finally, *egalitarians* take equality, fairness, and justice to be the hallmarks of ethical behavior; the most ethical decisions tend to be those that treat people equally.

Beyond the general ethical philosophies, you read about five more focused theories of communication ethics. The *virtue ethic* depends on the golden mean of Aristotle and cautions against extremist positions. The *Taoist ethic* refrains from specific injunctions or ethical criteria by which to judge individual behaviors but suggests that *wu-wei,* or noninterference, be a guiding principle of our relations with each other. The *dialogic ethic* renounces manipulative attempts and elevates human confirmation, inclusion, openness and listening to others' positions as central ethical guidelines. The *marketplace of ideas ethic* sets standards for how we deal with ideas fairly and justly in the public arena; it assumes that freedom of speech is a primary good in our society. Finally, the *communitarian ethic* suggests that the coherence of the community—rather than individual rights—should be the prime standard with which ethical decision making should proceed; this ethical theory is supported by reasoning developed by theorists and ethicists of human narration.

TESTING THE CONCEPTS

"Early in the chapter you imply that ethics is a 'gray area' for discussion. But if I choose the 'deontological' position, for example, doesn't that eliminate the ambiguity? Won't the principles I believe in determine my choices?"

Not necessarily. Some choices may be simplified, but you still need to decide when a principle should be invoked. All principles are subject to interpretation as well, and even deontologists would find it hard to argue that all circumstances must be governed by rigidly defined duties. Christians are told, "Thou shalt not kill," yet most Christians interpret this as referring to human life exclusively (relatively few are vegetarians), and others may exclude supposedly "just" wars. Still others who believe in the same principle—pacifists, for example—draw their lines of interpretation differently.

"Doesn't the teleological position invite rationalization or self-delusion? Couldn't such communicators always fool themselves into thinking that some 'greater good' will be served by whatever decisions are made?"

Yes, but any other ethical paradigm may be rationalized in a similar way. The domain of ethics is intensely rhetorical, in other words; people constantly justify, confront, and rejustify their decisions. What may be a choice to one person could be seen as an inevitability by another. What matters, we would argue, is not that rationalization *could* happen (after all, self-delusion is a persistent human frailty) but that communicators should refer to ethical criteria to evaluate their choices and to minimize merely self-serving or convenient decisions.

"Does Aristotle's principle of the golden mean suggest that I always need to compromise a strongly held position?"

You may be strongly committed to positions without necessarily being unethical, according to Aristotle. He only reminds you to consider whether the stand you've taken is, in context, not close to the "vices" of *deficiency* or *excess.* Further, he does not suggest that as a communicator you should "always" compromise; rather, you should recognize the middle ground as a fertile territory for discussion. This, of course, is to some extent a judgment call. But what isn't?

"It sounds as if *wu-wei* might mean I should go along with unfair conditions even when I don't want to do so. How can this sort of non-interference be right or ethical? Didn't Nazi collaborators in France during World War II, for example, engage in *wu-wei*?"

Taoist philosophers urge that people can act in an organic way without interfering with the natural flow of their own experience, or interfering with or manipulating the behavior of others. Therefore, a primary Taoist response to your example would be to turn toward analyzing the Nazi invasion itself. From the individual's perspective, maybe the most ethical communication would be the one that is in accord with one's own inner experience. That is, if you indeed feel that the conditions are unfair, then the natural flow of your action within this holistic context might be to resist those conditions.

"Are communitarian ethicists opposed to preserving individual rights in society?"

Not according to sociologist Amitai Etzioni (1993), perhaps the most prominent spokesperson for communitarianism in the social sciences, who states that "our call for increased social responsibilities...is not a call for curbing rights. On the contrary, strong rights presume strong responsibilities" (p. 1). Communitarian ethicists do fear, however, that "people treat rights-based arguments, unlike many others, as 'trump cards' that neutralize all other positions" (Etzioni, 1993, p. 7). In other words, they argue, by paying too much attention to the rights someone supposedly "has," we may obscure a kind of communicative (and other) violence that's done to a community. For example, if we affirm an individual right to privacy, does that mean that a community cannot require that neighborhoods be informed when a convicted (and later released) child molester moves in? Communitarians argue that the community is "ontologically prior" to individual rights, and that we achieve such rights within the context of the community in which we communicate.

YOU, THE RESEARCHER

1. Public relations (PR) is an increasingly valuable organizational function in an information society. Organizations employ professional PR communicators to explain their internal policies, decisions, and dilemmas to external publics, and to decide on behind-the-scenes persuasive strategies for doing so. Occasionally these professionals may find that their responsibility to the organizations they represent (e.g., corporations, government agencies, and school districts) conflicts with their responsibility to relay accurate information to the public. For this reason, the Public Relations Society of America (PRSA) has long emphasized the ethical dimensions of public communication.

   - Get a copy of the PRSA's Code of Professional Standards for the Practice of Public Relations from your college library, your instructor, or the PRSA Web site.
   - Evaluate the document to see which theories of ethics are most consistently reflected in its recommendations.

- Analyze the code. Would following the advice in some sections mean rejecting or ignoring the stipulations in some other sections? If so, in which contexts are such double binds most likely to occur?
- Interview a PR professional. Ask what was the most vivid ethical dilemma he or she has ever faced, but do not press to find out what action was ultimately taken. Take careful notes.
- In class, discuss the incident with your instructor and your classmates in terms of the dictates of the code. Take a personal position: What would you have done? (Later, you may want to follow up with the professional to discover how the situation was resolved.)

2. Videotape the television commercials shown during a local station's children's programming on any Saturday morning from 8 A.M. until 12 noon. How do the persuasive appeals of these ads differ from prime-time ads designed for adults? Prepare a brief multimedia presentation for your class using the most illustrative commercials.
- What are the ethical implications of ads for toys, electronic gadgets, shoes, and clothes that target children rather than parents?
- Is this basically a bottom-line financial issue, one you might accede to if you were a network executive? Or is it a moral issue of right and wrong, one you would attempt to change if you were a media decision maker? Or is this dichotomy too simplistic? Explain your reasoning in your class presentation.

3. Communication researchers often face their own kind of ethical decisions. Twentieth-century social science research, in fact, often depended on the use of research confederates (e.g., "plants" in a group), invasions of privacy, misleading instructions, hidden cameras and microphones, dishonest role-playing, and other deceptive methods.
- Find a journal article in communication, psychology, or sociology that reports on a study in which you believe the deception of subjects was employed unethically or without justification. Which theory or approach to communication ethics best describes the criteria you use in making your judgment?
- Find another article on a similar research topic, but in this case you should agree with the researchers' use of deception as ethically justified. What, specifically, makes the deception of subjects seem ethical? Have you applied the same criteria that you used with the other article?

4. Sociologist Irwin Deutscher (1973) warns that the outcome of much of our theory and research in human studies is a "fiddling with people's lives" (p. 358), no matter how innocent or inoffensive individual research studies may be. Western culture does not lack manipulators who are willing to fiddle with the lives of others. Therefore theories in such areas as compliance-gaining, behavior modification, and public-opinion polling, for example, may be misused by powerful groups seeking to intervene in social situations or to manipulate individuals and the public in order to satisfy their

own goals. What, if any, are the ethical responsibilities of the communication researcher seeking to identify interaction outcomes precisely and, perhaps, even predictably? Should such researchers be concerned with the potential misuse of their findings and the consequences for society in general? Or should we allow science to progress, "letting the chips fall where they may"?

Courtesy of the University of South Florida

CHAPTER 11

"Why Does Communication Matter?"

The Status of the Discipline

> Were you to trace any life, and study even the minute consequences, the effect, for instance, of a three-minute walk over a patch of grass, of words said casually to a stranger who happens to sit nearby in a public place, the range of that life would extend way beyond the territory we imagine it to inhabit.
>
> SUSAN GRIFFIN, *A Chorus of Stones* (1992, p. 151)

> The aspects of communication to which scholars attend...have blossomed into a rich assortment of intriguing questions for which we continue to seek answers. Answers lead to other questions, pose new problems for future inquiry, and attract the attention of new generations of scholars. The evidence of activity indicates a field of study that is very much alive, maturing, open to different styles and methods of inquiry, and accommodating to a mixture of philosophical perspectives and world views.
>
> DENNIS S. GOURAN, "Speech Communication after Seventy-five Years" (1990, p. 27)

We started this book with a concern for questions, and that's how we'll end it. Where will the study of communication take us? How can we describe to others the depth of our interest in learning more about communicating? How can we, as teachers and students, structure this learning in a way that makes sense to our many audiences? Can we readily explain our departments and courses to employers, parents, and people from other college and university departments? You see, on almost all campuses and for almost all students, it matters what you choose as a major. Not only is communication study a preparation for a career but it is inevitably a topic for everyday conversation. Communication majors want to find good ways to explain their choices. You could spend your time explaining theories, but theories are only some of the building blocks of a major subject.

Those theories exist within a context of academic structure and a system of academic expectations, which we'll introduce in this final chapter. As you read, you should know that some of the topics here stimulate many different opinions; your teacher, along with others, may disagree with some of our conclusions. We doubt that most scholars would argue much about the historical facts and trends we summarize, but interpretations of disciplinary status and evaluations of potential for the future are fair game for vigorous debate. Find out where your teacher, or your department, stands on these issues. This chapter will serve its purpose if it helps to create a dialogue in which readers seriously explore and debate fresh positions. We don't need agreement as much as we need disciplined questioning.

Studying Communication in a Disciplined Way

You are studying a subject that is too complex by far to be contained within the boundaries of a limited list of classes. Ranging widely across the sciences, arts, and humanities, it challenges you to learn a variety of concepts, theories, and methods. Communication study is so broad, in fact, that some observers wonder whether it has any content that it can rightly call its own—whether communication should even be considered its own "discipline" of study. From this perspective, communication becomes a function of all disciplines and needn't be the special focus of any of them. Communication, these observers say, isn't really a discipline but a broad field of interest. Although some observers don't distinguish closely between a *field* and a *discipline,* others stress the distinctive qualities of academic disciplines. A **discipline** in the latter sense is a branch of learning that possesses its own content and relatively distinct curriculum, and prepares people for well-defined career responsibilities (e.g., engineering, physics, or accounting). A field, in contrast, may be defined as a loosely associated group of scholars working on similar problems, but not unified by consistently defined concepts and not necessarily tied to particular career responsibilities. For example, many campuses have cross-disciplinary programs in such fields as International Studies, Women's Studies, and African American Studies.

In some ways communication—the process of developing shared meaning through messages—should be a part of all other disciplines. Accountants calculate figures, but they also have to communicate about them in order for their work to be meaningful. Astronomers look for and study distant solar systems, but they also have to coordinate their work daily with colleagues. Literature professors read novels in private, but their analyses of the novelists' skills in sketching characters and creating dialogue must be based on real-life insight into everyday human communication. But if communication is part of everyone else's disciplines, why not let them teach it? Why do we need a separate communication department? Indeed, if one premise of *Questions of Communication* is correct— that communication theory is a broadly based liberal arts endeavor that can't be limited to research from one discipline—why should communication departments need to develop their own identities? Why not let the other disciplines study communication?

Give these questions some careful thought. Although the distinction between a discipline and a field appears tidy at first, that may be due primarily to the examples we've chosen. Consider the many other college departments we regard as disciplines whose content and concerns cut across the broad intellectual landscape. For example, is psychology not a discipline because researchers in all areas of study have (presumably) developed a capacity for thinking? Does sociology not have a content of its own because humans in all disciplines work in groups? Is management not a discipline because all people manage their decision making? Does biology fail to qualify as a discipline because all human life is made up of living systems? One prominent critique of the communication discipline created controversy a number of years ago because it was published in the *Chronicle of Higher Education,* a periodical read by many faculty and almost all college administrators across the country. In A Theory Extension, p. 332, Alan Fischler (1989) asserts that communication isn't a discipline because its title names an "act" rather than a subject matter. Yet more than a few respected academic units that are typically considered disciplines are similarly labeled; management, nursing, and engineering come to mind. Interestingly, Fischler's own department, English, taken literally, is inherently neither a subject matter nor an act but a language.

Some disciplines appear to be characterized by a particular focus on *processes,* not only by a particular body of *content* (at least as *content* is usually

A THEORY EXTENSION

COMMUNICATION AS A DISCIPLINE: VIEWING REALITY THROUGH DIFFERENT LENSES

- **A Criticism from Outside:** "The pre-professional gains nothing… from a series of courses in Communication theory, each of which is a replica of the others; one learns only how to become a replica of the teacher…. But that's the problem inherent in taking a verb, transforming it into a noun, and calling it an academic discipline. 'Education' is a similar case. The words 'education' and 'communication' define acts, not bodies of knowledge…. Communication professors who claim that theory and technique by themselves form a subject matter and constitute a legitimate discipline are reduced not only to studying themselves, but also to testing students on proper pinky placement in their handshakes and awarding college credit to those who have mastered the inflection of 'Uh huh'" (Fischler, 1989, p. A28).

- **A Description from Within:** "Communication, as an academic discipline, bridges the gap between the humanities and the social sciences. It focuses on the study of relationships among open systems, especially the relationships among persons, groups, and cultures, and the factors which influence the forming, changing, maintaining, and terminating of those relationships. Some of these factors are the nature of persons, the nature of groups and of cultures, symbolic discourse in various forms, communication media, and a variety of contexts or environments in which communication occurs…. In spite of the fact that communication has been the object of formal study for over two thousand years, there is still much to be learned. Communication in a changing environment with changing participants is not a fixed body of content that one can master, nor a closed system of laws or rules that one can acquire once and for all. Furthermore, advancing technology, cultural changes, increasing human mobility, and the mingling of persons from different socio-cultural backgrounds are placing ever-increasing stresses and strains on human relationships. It is, therefore, imperative that we continue to devote significant attention to this complex process in order to improve the effectiveness of communication, to enhance the quality of life for individuals, and to ensure the survival of the species" (Darnell, 1984, p. 11).

defined). Many disciplines deal with the content of people talking with other people. While studying the content of political campaigns, for example, economists follow the arguments closely for fiscal policy implications; doctors listen to the same political rhetoric to gain clues about what will happen in the health-care sphere; generals and admirals want to infer what a new president might do to military expenditure. Many thoughtful people attend to the content of politics, but they may focus on it differently, depending on their perspective. That's what we mean by process: A process focus emphasizes the *how* of our looking and the *how* of the relationships we study, in addition to the content.

A discipline may be characterized by its unique focus, even if it overlaps other studies. In fact, a discipline might be seen as especially crucial if it has both (1) a well-defined unique focus on process and (2) obvious threads of relevance stretching out to many other research and career traditions. To us, not only does communication qualify on the basis of these criteria but it also has the potential to become an even stronger contributor to campus life in the future. Perhaps because of the various threads of relevance connecting them to many other studies and professions, such disciplines as communication, English, sociology, and management might better be termed **interdisciplines**.

No single area of study can capture or package the knowledge that links the diverse applications to which we must put our knowledge. For example, economists must know about history, the psychology of consumerism, and the cultural habits of large social groups if they hope to understand the dynamics of a fiscal system. The categories of knowledge have thus begun to overlap as our world becomes more complex. Since all human activities in some ways converge in human interactions, communication might be the most fundamental of the interdisciplines that can respond effectively to an era of dissolving boundaries. In the rest of this chapter, we'll call communication a discipline (a familiar term on campuses), although we believe it best represents an interdiscipline—that special form of discipline that focuses on processes and linkages with other areas of study.

We'd like to help you theorize informally about your connection to communication studies. We suggest that you begin to ask questions about the uniqueness of communication studies based on the two factors mentioned previously— focus and relevance. We've divided this final chapter into two main parts. The first part describes the growth and status of communication studies in higher education, and the second discusses several components of what we call "healthy" disciplines. Your class may want to compare perceptions of your communication department's role on campus and in the professional community.

Communication Departments in Higher Education

The communication department is a relative newcomer to colleges and universities in the United States. Its history can be traced by two trends—one emerging from humanistic concerns and the other born in social science. Much of the discipline was solidly influenced by the first trend, which included an emphasis on speech by a few English teachers, who in 1914 created an offshoot organization that later became for many years the Speech Communication Association (and in 1997 became the National Communication Association). These teachers thought that the education of public speakers demanded approaches, techniques, and content that were different from the ones students learned in literature, rhetoric, and composition courses (see Reid, 1990). These scholars, many of whom traced their roots to Aristotle, established speech as a study of historical and critical methods for understanding persuasion in one-to-many public contexts. Later,

LINKS

○ You read about background for the humanistic history of communication studies in Chapter 8, on the rhetorical tradition of persuasion.

○ You read about background for some social science projects in media effects in Chapter 9.

speech scholars, influenced in part by the work of social psychologists, became interested in less formal, face-to-face speaking and listening. Interpersonal communication thus blended the humanistic concerns of psychologists, the group dynamics interests of sociologists and organizational consultants, and the behavioral and quantitative methods of social science.

The discipline was further influenced at mid-century by another group of social researchers who would foresee a wider role for communication emerging from the powerful new electronic media. Their methods were not primarily those of historical or rhetorical criticism but were developed from the powerful belief that society could be understood in scientific ways. As Cuzzort and King (1989) observed, from about the turn of the last century people expressed the optimistic view that "the entire range of human communal activities could be examined scientifically and that such scientific understanding would enable people to achieve better and more ideal social structures. The new society would be as radically rational and as well designed as a modern jetliner" (p. 7).

Scientific communication researchers borrowed concepts and quantitative methods from sociologists (also largely a twentieth-century discipline), from psychologists, from economists, and from other disciplines. (Of course, other disciplines also got their start by borrowing concepts and methods; scientific sociologists borrowed from economists and the natural sciences, psychologists borrowed concepts from philosophers, and political scientists borrowed insights from historians, for example.) Contemporary communication departments stress not only the humanistic principles that characterize English and other performance disciplines but also the systematic and often quantitative methods imported from the social sciences (see Powers, 1995). Later, many communication scholars interested in interpersonal communication primarily borrowed neither rhetorical methods nor methods for studying media effects; they focused instead on how social psychologists, psycholinguists, anthropologists, and other scientists did their work. As communication historian Hanno Hardt (1992) observed, "[M]ost recently, the boundaries of communication research began to shift when academic interests that were traditionally identified with speech or interpersonal communication moved on to the terrain of social communication and were joined by others whose intellectual curiosity about culture seemed to be met by the potential of communication research as a source of analysis. The result was encouraging in that the dominant perspective of communication research had to rethink its theoretical foundations" (pp. 21–22).

All disciplines borrow from other disciplines, or they ought to do so. Ideally, information is shared freely across disciplinary boundaries, without some groups either isolating themselves or marginalizing others. The research enterprise, in other words, is an *open system* (in terms of general systems theory). Yet, serious students wonder, if this is true, who decides how to categorize learning into coursework and students and faculty into departments on campuses?

Carving Knowledge into Slices: Who Decides?

Coursework at universities everywhere has probably been influenced—historically and at least indirectly—by a system of dividing knowledge into neat and teachable content categories originally inspired by French Renaissance philosopher Peter Ramus. Ramus (see Ong, 1983) believed that all subjects could be categorized so that the content of one would not overlap the content of others; what teachers need to do is decide where the boundaries are and then teach the boundaries. You can imagine what this kind of logic, known as *Ramism,* would have to say about the study of what we call interdisciplines.

Traditionally, the faculty of a college or a university is given the responsibility of structuring the curriculum, which is the range of courses the institution offers. In department meetings, faculty councils, and senates across the country, teachers typically torture one another in lengthy disputes about which programs should be added, trimmed, expanded, or even eliminated in any given year. Faculty members monitor their programs through internal and external reviews that are correlated with student needs, "market" patterns, and, perhaps most important, the traditional mission and structure of the academic institution. The twentieth century has seen, by and large, an increasing faculty acceptance of interdisciplinary ventures and an increasing suspicion of older, locked-in categories of learning.

Recently, however, many campuses have adopted a corporate administrative model in which faculty decision making about departments, majors, core curricula, general education, and similar matters has become less central. The trend in the past decade was to define campus decisions, even those involving coursework and majors, as administrative or consumer-based functions. Although this book is not the place to debate whether this trend is good or bad, students should understand that the shape of their department's offerings does not always reflect the preferences of all the faculty in that department. Occasionally college and university administrations will combine or merge areas of study based on financial reasons or reasons of efficiency.

Therefore, for a variety of reasons, communication departments are labeled differently. A few reflect a long-standing reliance on concepts and labels of Rhetoric. Others call themselves Speech Communication, reflecting a merged identity with a continued reliance on spoken symbolic interaction. Still others are known as Media Studies, Mass Communication, or Journalism departments. Recently, we've seen more departments (and even "schools" and "colleges") designated simply with the label Communication. Such blended-identity units, whether they're a result of a genuine appreciation of the overall interdiscipline or are simply enforced by administrators, emphasize what communicators have in common, whether the relationships they study are interpersonal, rhetorical, or mass mediated.

Communication Studies Departments and Majors

Certainly not all departments of communication are equally popular, effective, or useful. Yet in many ways they are all part of one of the great U.S. academic success stories of the century. Craig and Carlone (1998) recently studied the "increasing centrality in academe and in society" that characterizes the communication discipline (p. 67). They analyzed two trends: the growth in degrees granted over the years (which indicates its attractiveness to students and its relevance to both academe and the private sector), and the growth of published books and periodicals devoted to communication studies (which indicates its emergence as a "central category of cultural knowledge") (p. 75). Growth in each trend was quantitatively and qualitatively significant. Further, consider the dramatic growth of student majors. Drawing from different tables of statistics, which was necessary because of the differing labels for communication departments, the authors noted, "Rapid growth across the communication disciplines as a whole is apparent. Total communication degrees increased 534% in this 25 year period [between 1967–68 and 1992–93], which exceeds the growth of all bachelor [sic] degrees (84%) by a factor of more than six. Communication degrees grew from 1.85% to 6.37% of all bachelor degrees in this period" (p. 69). Undergraduate degrees in communication rose from 11,692 in 1967–1968 to 74,184 in 1992–1993. If you'd like to compare this growth with a somewhat similar academic discipline, consider that sociology granted about 36,000 bachelor's degrees in 1970 but only about 14,000 in 1993 (Rogers & Chaffee, 1993, p. 124).

Communication departments are now well established in most of the country's major universities and in the full range of public and private institutions at all levels. Communication students in these departments successfully prepare themselves for careers in advertising, education, the electronic media, journalism, public relations, the performing arts, and a wide range of private and government organizations.

A Healthy Discipline

It's hard to know how to gauge the health of a system—such as a discipline or an interdiscipline—that is so much larger than yourself, since your own perspective is, by definition, limited. Maybe the best you can hope for is to sample a wide variety of experiences within a system. As authors, we represent at least some of that variety. One of us started college right out of high school, whereas the other began college as a "mature student" after a series of successful job experiences. One of us attended a massive university, whereas the other started at a community college. We have taught at mid-size state universities, large public research universities, a private research-based university, and a small Christian liberal arts college. Both of us define ourselves first as teachers and learners, then as writers and researchers. But we've also participated at many levels of university governance—directing programs, chairing departments and committees, and managing a radio station, among other duties. In addition, we've received a vivid education by talking with a wide range of students and colleagues about their experiences at different schools.

What follows, then, is an idiosyncratic but—we hope—realistic and accurate explanation of why we are optimistic about the discipline of communication. We basically respond to these kinds of questions: Where did we come from? Who are our intellectual neighbors? What do we study? What is our future? (See Reviewing Key Ideas, p. 337).

Knowing Your Past: A Discipline That Charts Its History

Now that you have a sketchy impression of how communication departments got started, perhaps you're curious about more of the historical context for your learning.

A twenty-one-year-old Mark Twain supposedly observed that at eighteen he was sure his father was really ignorant, but that he was amazed at how much his

---

REVIEWING KEY IDEAS

A HEALTHY DISCIPLINE:

- Knows its *past* (it is aware of its own history)
- Knows its *neighbors* (it understands its pathways to related disciplines and how it is interdependent with them)
- Knows its *content* (it understands its distinctive core concepts)
- Knows its *potential* (it anticipates a productive future for itself)

◁ L I N K

Chapter 5 describes the dialectical questions in interpersonal communication. Does the process of disciplinary maturation which involves both *differentiation* (establishing a unique identity) and *interdependence* (relying on others to help shape identity and expecting that reliance in return) seem to reflect a dialectical way of thinking? Why, or why not?

father had learned in just three years. One mark of maturity in adolescence is the ability to compare realistically your own knowledge with the wisdom of those who came before you. Maybe, just maybe, Twain himself changed more than his father did during those three years. Interestingly, young teenagers typically are not interested in genealogy or even in an informal family history, but beginning in the college years adults express far more curiosity about their roots, asking, "Where do I come from?"

A similar process occurs in institutions and academic disciplines. As they mature, they find themselves becoming more curious about where they came from and to what extent they must rely on the support of others. In individuals or institutions, **differentiation** is the process of developing uniqueness in the context of recognizing one's dependence on larger patterns (Lewin, 1951). Academic disciplines experience differentiation; they also grow to recognize their reliance on their own history and their interdependence with other influential groups. In this and the following section, we chart some of these influences and give you other sources so that you can explore your own curiosities.

The communication discipline is now actively charting its own history, as we noted earlier (see also Chafee & Rogers, 1997; Friedrich & Boileau, 1999). Generally, that history reflects humanistic and social scientific concerns that were originally separated but are now increasingly merged. This doesn't mean, of course, that each researcher or each department emphasizes qualitative, critical, and traditional social science research equally, as you will discover later in this chapter and later in your coursework.

We don't have the space in this book to summarize all of the projects that attempt to trace the history of communication departments and research traditions. We can, however, recommend several sources to you. Most of them bemoan the fact that we've so far been largely unreflective about our history; however, the fact that so many questions are being asked now is surely a good sign. For an overall comparison of the different strains of communication studies, see Delia's (1987) extensive and detailed summary or Pearce and Foss's (1990) more succinct account. If you're more curious about the rhetorical and humanistic origins of the side of communication studies usually associated with speech, you may want to start with Herman Cohen's *The History of Speech Communication: The Emergence of a Discipline, 1914–1945* (1994), Work and Jeffrey's (1989) brief anthology published at the seventy-fifth anniversary of the Speech Communication Association, and Loren Reid's (1990) informal account of his own contributions to, and perceptions of, how a discipline interested in elocution and speech performance has matured into a discipline of teachers and researchers of communication. Communication scholars have long staked their territorial claims to include both the practical and the theoretical; more recently, they have also examined how the distinction between practice and theory may be somewhat artificial. Some scholars believe the discipline of communication gathered crucial prestige in the academic and political worlds when media systems began to be researched scientifically at mid-century. The foremost account of this social science strain of communication studies is Everett Rogers's *A History of Communication Study: A Biographical Approach* (1994). Interestingly, as Craig (1995) points out, Rogers's book only slightly overlaps Cohen's history—even though they were published in the same year and the departments in which they'll be read are finding that their concerns overlap more and more. Finally, for a history of communication studies that recognizes each of the other strains but gives more weight to the cultural impact of American pragmatism, symbolic interaction, contemporary cultural studies, and critical theories, see Hanno Hardt's *Critical Communication Studies: Communication, History, and Theory in America* (1992).

Knowing Your Neighbors: A Discipline of Connections, Not Boundaries

Although communication plays a role in all disciplines, not all other disciplines are equally relevant for communication researchers and teachers. This can be illustrated by our own personal experience. Your authors have given presentations on communication on various campuses for students in management, psychology, physics, theology, education, sociology, and accounting departments, among others. We have enjoyed these talks and workshops immensely, and built a wide variety of satisfying friendships and professional relationships through them. Everyone, whatever their disciplinary affiliation, profits from improved communication. Some of the students and faculty members we've met correctly assumed that communication scholars would be unlikely to borrow basic concepts from them (e.g., accounting techniques are unlikely to be a source of conceptual insight for communication scholars, even though the accounting profession would be a good site for applied communication studies). However, others assumed incorrectly that we wouldn't be interested in their research and theories. Perhaps they thought we were interested only in the performance aspects of speaking or in the "hardware" of media technology. Or, in other words, perhaps they thought we weren't theorizing about what we study.

However, as you've seen throughout this book, communication scholars have always been interested in applying ideas from other specialists. Some critics call this "borrowing," perhaps suggesting a derivative status. But academic borrowing is not unique to communication, nor is it a shortcoming. Rather, it's a necessary academic habit in the contemporary world. In fact, communication, because it's a discipline with permeable conceptual territories, is a good example of the contemporary social condition that anthropologist Clifford Geertz (1983) calls **blurred genres**. Geertz believes that it's getting harder to separate fields of knowledge because, for example, philosophy increasingly resembles literary criticism, science writing resembles personalized essays, history resembles fiction (and vice versa), "parables pos[e] as ethnographies," "ideological arguments [are] cast as historiographical inquiries," and so on (p. 20). Moreover, working with ideas in interdisciplinary ways creates fresh forms of knowledge. As Geertz (1983) writes:

> *What Clyde Kluckhohn once said about anthropology— that it's an intellectual poaching license— not only seems more true now than when he said it, but true of a lot more than anthropology. Born omniform, the social sciences prosper as the condition I have been describing becomes general. It has thus dawned on social scientists that they did not need to mimic physicists or closet humanists or to invent some new realm of being to serve as the object of their investigations. Instead they could proceed with their vocation, trying to discover order in collective life. (p. 21)*

When Geertz says that the social sciences were "born omniform," he means that versatility and flexibility in moving among many disciplinary forms is part of the identity of such disciplines. They thrive on pluralistic views.

Thus, as communication theorists, we try to know our closest scholarly neighbors and to monitor what they consider to be important, even as we proceed with our own work. Probably the neighbors closest to our current work are the social sciences of anthropology, sociology, political science, and psychology; the humanities of philosophy, history, and literary criticism and composition studies in English; and the professional applied disciplines that acknowledge communication research, such as education, management, social work, nursing, and law.

While scholars naturally borrow concepts, they simultaneously adjust those ideas to fit the unique demands of a particular focus on the communicative relationship. Rarely is a theory or a research tool simply imported by itself; instead, it is utilized in a new way, tinged with new meaning, applied to fresh problems.

The borrowing goes both ways. Increasingly, scholars who teach in communication departments are cited in the wider academic and popular discussion of politics and social policy. Rhetorical concepts have a widening influence in such fields as the philosophy of science, economics, and international diplomacy. Communication scholars and their research are becoming widely quoted in other disciplines and in popular media treatments of public problems: Kathleen Jamieson and Roderick Hart on political campaigning and media advertising, Molefi Asante on Afrocentric theory, Cheris Kramerae on gender-based power relations, George Gerbner on violence in the media, Lawrence Grossberg and Michael Eric Dyson on cultural theory and criticism, and James Carey and Jay Rosen on the public responsibilities of journalism.

Knowing Your Content: A Discipline with Core Concepts

Any attempt to isolate basic ideas in a discipline as diverse as communication seems a bit presumptuous at best and perhaps misleading at worst. Surely, important aspects of communication will be left out. However, some scholars have been bold enough to attempt such a difficult task. In a recent essay, Stamp, Vangelisti, and Knapp (1994) explain why four concepts are especially "foundational" for communication theorists in distinguishing a communication-based approach from the approaches of other disciplines. Although they intend for their discussion to apply especially to interpersonal communication research, we see their concepts of *meaning, relationship, process,* and *context* as also characterizing the discipline as a whole. In many ways, these have been recurrent themes in *Questions of Communication* as well. Summarizing them here may help you put the entire study of communication theory into a distinctive perspective.

Meaning. Communication theorists are especially interested in the question of where meaning is generated in human experience and where it can be found. Communication theorists, teachers, and researchers tend to assume that meanings are not the possession of a single person but are "negotiated phenomena" that "do not belong to [persons]," and are "pluralistic endeavors negotiated by participants within their relationship" (Stamp, Vangelisti, & Knapp, 1994, p. 170). This is not to say that individuals don't have unique experiences, but that meaning (as communication scholars tend to use the term) is not simply a psychological or cognitive phenomenon. Further, most communication theorists do not imagine messages as containing meanings but as evoking meanings when understood in relationships. Therefore relation makes meaning possible.

Relationship. The unit of analysis for a communication theorist is not generally the individual person, even though the behavior of individuals is certainly important. Instead, the acts of individuals are consistently thought to be characteristics of the relationships in which they are involved, rather than mere expressions of innate tendencies or self-contained personalities. To communication theorists, it isn't very interesting or conceptually helpful to ask. "What kind of person is she?" or "How does he act?" Rather, communication perspectives would reflect a curiosity about how he acts when he finds himself within a support group, or how she processes media messages on the evening news or in clothing ads, or how her presence affects others' talk. Relationships are hard to study, however, because they won't stand still for you to analyze them; they're always shifting in some way.

Process. Therefore communication theorists are as interested in social structures and enduring institutions and organizations as other social scientists might be. They are as interested in rhetorical texts, such as speeches and documents, as literary critics might be. One aspect of the culture of communication inquiry over the past 40 years, however, has been the emerging recognition that such phenomena cannot be viewed as static or immune to the influences of time. The process concept reminds scholars to look for evidence of change and changingness in whatever studies they conduct. We understand that today's IBM might resemble the "same" company we studied last year, but that subtle changes have affected its internal communication. When people talk—or read or write or listen—their communication changes them. In other words, the existing communication forms the basis for interpreting new communication messages.

Context. Therefore no message can be understood apart from the context in which it is interpreted. Contexts could include the physical surroundings within which we communicate, the temporal aspect of interaction, the relational expectations within which we interpret each other's behavior, the influence of background messages (often nonverbal) in any relationship, and the number of people present, among many other factors. The tradition of communication scholarship stresses context so much that it is often frustrating to our students, our trainees, or our clients in consulting relationships. We are asked questions like these: "What do I do when I lose my place in presenting my speech?" and "How do I talk to my father?" There are no good answers to such questions without asking other questions. You've lost your place in the speech, but who is your audience? Is your previous relationship with your audience informal or formal? What time of day is it? What is the seriousness of your task? Why are people listening to you? People who don't understand the impact of context often assume that communication teachers are indecisive or nit-picking when they're unwilling to give a quick answer to subtle problems. They don't understand that for many communication experts context is a core concept of the discipline, one that can't be ignored.

Knowing Your Potential: A Discipline That Anticipates a Future

The future seems secure for a theoretically sophisticated discipline or interdiscipline of communication. If communication departments continue to explore and integrate (1) theories emerging from empirical data-based social science research, (2) theories of meaning and ethical judgment from the humanities, and (3) theories of cultural critique—blending them with respect for both qualitative and quantitative studies—the academic and professional worlds will listen to us carefully. Communication scholars and departments make solid cases for their contributions. But this doesn't mean that the future of communication studies will automatically look like the past.

For example, the discipline's future has been questioned by a few administrators who assume that effective communicators in any given field can teach and research communication well enough, making departments of communication dispensable. Although this is hardly a nationwide trend, a few instances of departments being threatened by their administrators have left some students, faculty, and alumni agitated.

A second—and healthier—form of questioning the future can be seen in the journals and books of the field. There we find many clashing opinions about the shape of the future. We regard this as healthy because out of this dialogue and its different visions will come a future that is tested and usefully challenged as it develops. We find regular examples of this dialogue in the vigorous discussions of the nature of the discipline in its journals (for example, see the two-issue *Journal of Communication* investigation entitled "The Future of the Field—Between Fragmentation and Cohesion" [1993]). Because scholars disagree strongly, it's impossible to predict precise outcomes. For example, some might deny the premise of this chapter—that communication should claim a disciplinary status, although Powers (1995) cites a study that concludes "the preponderance of communication professionals...believe we are already a discipline, and even more believe that we should be considered one" (p. 213). Some faculty want a blended approach to departments, while others want to retain the special character of a speech/rhetorical or a journalism emphasis. All we can feel safe in predicting is that the study of communication will be stronger for having had these kinds of discussions.

In our senior-level capstone classes, we remind students that the image they currently hold about who and where they'll be five or ten years into their careers will shape in subtle ways the careers they actually create during that time. If a female public relations student, for example, believes that the field is too low-paying, or too limiting in its opportunities for women, then that perception will affect the kinds of jobs she'll apply for, and thus will change her actual future. Quite apart from the realities of her perceptions (pay can be low at times, and there is a residual sexism in many organizations), she will enfold her expectations into the realities of her jobs. Perhaps she'll limit herself too much. If a classmate has a different perception, her experience will probably be different, and perhaps more successful. So it is with academic life. If communication teachers and students sit around wringing their hands, wondering about how respected they are by others, this itself affects how we're seen. It affects how we're treated, too. How we talk about ourselves influences what we'll become. We talk ourselves into the future. The discipline of communication is alive and well, and certainly healthy enough to create a robust rhetorical future.

We hope you'll use what you've learned in this book to enter the conversation of a vital, vigorous, and important discipline of study. We also hope that you're beginning to build the personal discipline to study it well, in whatever direction it takes you.

Our final question for you: Which questions do you want to ask next?

TESTING THE CONCEPTS

"Even though I may know more about theories, and even more about the history of the communication discipline, how will this help me get a job?"

So many variables factor into job searches that it's impossible to cite only one as the crucial factor. Knowing the shape and the theoretical status of your own discipline is one issue, among many others, that will impress potential employers. Your writing and speaking skills are also important, but employers usually don't make their decisions on those bases alone, either, because so many applicants are good writers and speakers. Employers want to know if you're a curious and persistent learner who will continue to make contributions to the organization. Some of our former students have returned to tell us that employment interviewers often ask questions like "Why did you choose to major in communication?" If your answer to this question is a thin "I don't know; it just seemed interesting" or "I'm a people person," you'll undercut your chances.

If you want to know more about career possibilities in communication, we recommend that you read the latest edition of *Pathways to Careers in Communication*, a booklet published by the National Communication Association. Single copies of the booklet are available from the National Communication Association, 1765 N St., N.W., Washington, D.C. 20036; multiple copies are discounted.

YOU, THE RESEARCHER

1. Locate four articles that define the discipline of communication in past issues of *Communication Education, Journal of Communication,* or *Communication Theory.* In what ways do the authors advance similar positions? In what ways do they argue for different positions? How do you think disciplinary disputes could affect you as a student, directly or indirectly? Your teacher may want you to discuss these questions in class.

2. Brainstorm with a group of other students to identify three questions you still have about the discipline or about national organizations within the communication professions. Access the National Communication Association's home page on the World Wide Web: <http://www.natcom.org>. Try to find the answers to your questions either on the NCA's page or by tracking its links to other Web sites.

3. Interview three professors outside of the communication department. Ask them to define the discipline of communication or to describe what the communication department on your campus focuses on in its teaching. How are these professors' definitions similar or different? How do their descriptions compare with your definition of the discipline? With the views expressed in this book? With the attitudes of your communication professors, as you understand them?

4. Go online to find the Web site for one or two examples of each of the following types of institutions:

   - A community college (e.g., St. Louis Community College at Florissant Valley, Arapahoe Community College)
   - A small or mid-size liberal arts college or university (e.g., University of St. Thomas, DePauw University)
   - A mid-size state university (e.g., University of Northern Iowa, Central Connecticut State University)
   - A large research-oriented private university (e.g., Stanford University, Columbia University)
   - A large research-oriented public university (e.g., University of Arizona, University of Minnesota)

   Compare the Web pages for the communication departments at these schools or others you may want to explore. Note: (a) how the department names differ, (b) how the departments describe the rationale for their programs, and (c) the kinds of required and elective coursework they offer. How do you explain the diversity of courses you find? What courses or areas of study seem to be especially common in your limited study?

Glossary

An Access Vocabulary in Communication Theory

Answering several basic questions helped us decide what should be included in this glossary: Which terms are especially important for beginning students as they prepare to enter the conversation in communication theory? When professionals and academics in communication talk about theory and research, which terms do they tend to use again and again? Which general concepts used in this book might be unnecessarily intimidating or mysterious to undergraduate students and therefore need further clarification? In some cases we've essentially reproduced, for easy reference, the existing definition already given in the text, but in others we've added examples to make the definition more helpful.

We realize that many faculty members who teach communication theory would create somewhat different lists, and our brief definitions will almost certainly leave out important facets of some concepts. Some terms, too, seem to resist a definition that would be both reasonably accurate and accessible enough for new readers in communication. We decided that we should not attempt to present concepts in as much detail and as specifically as subject-matter specialists would but that we should try to give each term a conceptual handle that, if grasped, would give students preliminary access to the research interests suggested by the label—hence the term "access vocabulary." Neither do we attempt to include definitions for all of the terms italicized in the text, many of which are specialized concepts of particular theories and, we hope, sufficiently clarified in the context of those descriptions.

In addition to basic concepts in communication theory that might be found in any text, we've included a number of terms that are used somewhat uniquely in *Questions of Communication,* and that are unlikely to be found in most other treatments of communication theory. Many of these terms come from associated disciplines, and through them we hope to encourage a broadly based liberal arts attitude for studying theory. Taking a communication theory course gives you an especially inviting opportunity to notice how interconnected your studies can be.

abbreviation the phenomenon of inner speech in which language structure is shortened ("abbreviated") because the audience—the self—has no need of elaborated discussion. Representative theorist: Vygotsky.

access theory suggests that online communication habits subtly move us further away from "directedness," transfer, or conduit assumptions about mediated communication. An access approach foregrounds the availability of many kinds of computer-mediated messages that aren't literally "sent to us" and emphasizes the active/interactive choices of communicators who were often previously conceived of as "receivers."

act behavior chosen voluntarily by an individual.

action assembly theory explains the cognitive process by which people transform inner plans into communication behaviors. Representative theorist: Greene.

actional view of behavior (action) assumes that behavior is attributable to people's active choices, as opposed to being caused by outside forces that act on individuals. See also *motional view of behavior.*

activation in action assembly theory, the process of monitoring current situations in order to select and abstract relevant records.

adaequatio a classical concept that describes how a perceiver or learner must be adequate to the demands of a situation or message, or else it will seem relatively meaningless. Representative contemporary theorist: Schumacher.

administrative theory/administrative science an early application of classical scientific theorizing to understanding managers' decision making. It emphasized such leadership principles as planning, organizing, commanding, coordinating, and controlling. Representative theorist: H. Fayol.

affection in FIRO theory, the desire of people to be liked in social situations.

Afrocentricity places "African ideals at the center of any analysis that involves African culture and behaviors" (Asante, 1987, p. 6). Afrocentric theorists often contrast their concepts with Eurocentric tendencies to explain cultural phenomena only in terms of standards developed within traditional European art, science, literature, and philosophy. Representative theorist: Asante.

agency in dramaturgical theory (pentad), and other human sciences, the means used by an agent or agents to accomplish communication goals. See *agent*.

agenda-setting theory examines how mass media outlets' choice of stories and content "sets the table" for public talk, creating the prime information for public policy and entertainment. Media producers, therefore, are communication "gatekeepers," and the issues and stories they present (only a small fraction of those that are available) automatically provide a social and cultural agenda to which the public must respond. Representative theorists: McCombs and Shaw.

agent in dramaturgical theory (pentad), and other human sciences, a person or a group performing or initiating performance, creating messages, and setting a drama in motion.

analogic communication in relational/interactional theory, communication (generally nonverbally based) that is connected more immediately to the actuality of the interchange than to prior agreements about symbols or meanings. Analogic communication, such as shaking someone's hand in a "harder" or "softer" way, is more a *part of* a relationship than a *statement about* a relationship. See *digital communication*.

anomie sociological term indicating a general confusion of values within a society.

articulation see *articulation theory*.

articulation theory studies how ideas and cultural concepts are linked together through public discussion into complex clusters of meaning, which then appear to be unified and whole. *Articulation* in this approach suggests connectedness, in addition to its more common contemporary meaning of the ability to verbalize. Representative theorist: S. Hall.

artifact in the study of nonverbal communication, a displayed object that functions as a communication cue.

artistic means of persuasion in classical rhetorical theory, persuasion characterized by creative work from a communicator to interpret facts and present proofs relevant to the case at hand. See *inartistic means of persuasion*.

assembly in action assembly theory, the process of integrating records coherently to produce action-possibilities.

attitude human predispositions to act, choose, or evaluate in certain ways over time.

attribute a property that a theorist claims is present whenever a particular concept is discussed.

autonomous model in organizational communication, a model that describes how organizational units create their own identities through coherent conversations that cannot be "managed" by individual supervisors, and that ultimately constitute the organization itself. In this model communication produces organizations rather than the other way around. See *conversational autonomy theory*.

availability a person or group's flexibility or openness to being changed by new messages.

axiom a firmly established claim that, for the purposes of a given argument, needs no further support.

behaviorism/behaviorist a philosophical and theoretical position in psychology and other social sciences that regards actual human behavior—not inner feelings, goals, or values—as the most important data to gather. Behaviorism has been identified primarily with quantitative and empirical social science, and not with qualitative humanistic studies.

being a concept of ethics in dialogic theory that describes how people respond to each other in terms of the demands of the immediate situation.

believing game the choice of approaching new information by assuming that it has value and is sensible in the context of its authors or other communicators. Representative theorist: Elbow. See also *doubting game*.

between, the a term used by theorists of dialogue to describe the site or place of genuine meaning in a mutualistic orientation to communication. Human and dialogic meaning is not a psychologistic object to be possessed inside the mind but a relational process. Representative theorist: Buber.

bit in information theory, the amount of information necessary to reduce uncertainty by about half.

black box a behaviorist metaphor that suggests that the human mind's inner processes are not as important to know or study as the inputs and outputs (stimuli and responses). The mind was treated methodologically as if it were an unopenable "box."

blurred genres Geertz's concept that describes how fields of knowledge increasingly seem to blend together and overlap, depending upon each other's insights.

borderlands describes physical and social regions where people's identities are affected by a blend of communication expectations that originate on both sides of a given cultural border. Representative theorists: Anzaldúa; Rosaldo.

bureaucratic theory/bureaucracy the study of the rational structuring of organizational roles for maximum efficiency. A bureaucratic ideal includes effective division of labor, clear job descriptions, standardized procedures, hierarchical authority, criteria for technical competence, and ongoing organizational responsibilities. Representative theorist: Weber.

calling a situation to which someone feels he or she should or must respond with commitment. Usually used to describe longer-term commitments like vocations or social responsibilities, the term also suggests a combination of external invitation and developing personal response. Representative theorist: Polanyi.

categorical imperative in deontological ethics, the principle that an ethical decision applied to one person ought to be universalizable, or be able to be applied equally to everyone with few, if any, exceptions. In addition, people should not be treated as means to an end. Representative theorist: Kant.

causation assumed connection between two events, in which the first appears to make the second happen.

chaining in symbolic convergence theory, the process of forming a fantasy (and its details) through a progressive conversation-like elaboration of the theme. People "chain out" their dramatic interpretations of how the world works through social means, not individual psychological ones.

change agent in diffusion of innovations theory, a professional persuader who consciously attempts to coordinate influentials or opinion leaders.

channel a medium or route through which a message is sent for purposes of communication.

choice criterion see *interpersonal ethic*.

chronemics the study of how people develop meaning through the use of time variables.

classical rhetorical theory a traditional approach to rhetoric, based largely on the work of Aristotle and other ancient Greek and Roman rhetoricians.

CMM theory see *coordinated management of meaning theory*.

co-cultural theory examines those groups whose members must develop specialized communication strategies in order to establish themselves in the larger society. These groups, which were sometimes treated as marginal or inferior by earlier social scientific thinking, are considered "co-cultures" because they make positive contributions to the larger culture without being inferior in any way. Representative theorist: Orbe.

cognition the overall process of mind, including thinking, perceiving, judging, and consciousness.

cognitive complexity in constructivism, the presence of a wide variety of usable constructs that a communicator could use to understand and interpret messages and meanings. If you are more cognitively complex, you have more distinctions available with which to understand the world. Fewer available constructs might lead to dogmatism, thinking that a situation or a person is either good *or* bad, for example, instead of more nuanced or subtle explanations. See *construct, dogmatism*.

cognitive consistency theory explains the means by which people maintain inner balance, congruence, or consistency among attitudes, opinions, and beliefs. Representative theorists: Heider; Festinger; Osgood.

coherence in coordinated management of meaning theory, the extent to which actors within situations make sense of communicative episodes.

collectivism syndrome categorization of cultures by their greater or lesser commitment to group conformity, tradition, and the interdependence of members.

commitment in Perry's study of learning positions, the highest level; in this position students develop personal commitments to ideas, but are open to constant change and to being persuaded to adopt other positions.

commitment foreseen in Perry's study of learning positions, a higher-level position marked by students' ability to commit themselves tentatively to ideas with a stronger sense of personal identity than they started out with.

communibiology a theoretical position within communication studies that asserts that genetically determined individual traits or temperaments are more powerful in determining communication outcomes than environmental contexts. Representative theorists: McCroskey and Beatty.

communication the mutual process through which people interpret messages in order to coordinate individual and social meanings, and to develop shared meaning.

communication competence is "the ability of two or more persons to jointly create and maintain a mutually satisfying relationship by constructing appropriate and effective messages" (O'Hair et al., 1994, p. 32).

communication cue message or act to which observers can attribute meaning or significance; examples might include oral or written statements, as well as gestures, pictures, smells, tactile contact, and other sensory data.

communication-pleasure in play theory, a kind of subjective play people seek by attending to media messages. Audiences seek ways to enjoy their interactions with media.

communication-work in play theory, what people supposedly avoid by attending to media messages. People do not use media primarily to control things or to become more efficient, these theorists say, but to meet personal needs of entertainment and subjective involvement.

communicative rationality Habermas's concept of how rational dialogue can support social order by helping people to achieve a consensus.

communitarian ethics emphasizes an ethical standard that elevates community good and community coherence above individual rights. Representative theorists: Christians, Ferré, and Fackler; Etzioni; Glendon. See also *narrative ethics*.

comparison level in social exchange theory, a cognitive standard that indicates an acceptable level of satisfaction in a relationship or a situation.

comparison level for alternatives in social exchange theory, a cognitive standard for comparing the rewards and costs of an existing relationship with the anticipated rewards and costs of alternative relationships; the comparison level for alternatives provides a basis for maintaining or ending the relationship.

complementary interaction in relational/interactional theory, the situation in which one person's response is a logically opposite fit to the other person's behavior. For example, if your roommate is domineering, you may withdraw and not assert your rights. If someone yells at you, you may become even more silent. See *symmetrical interaction*.

complexity syndrome categorization of cultures by the greater or lesser complication of their social distinctions among members.

compliance-gaining theory/compliance explanation of the process of achieving—through various interpersonal strategies—the assent, agreement, or cooperation of others when the others might not necessarily want to cooperate on the basis of their own inclinations. Representative theorists: Marwell and Schmitt.

concept a process that is labeled and categorized by scholars in order that it can be studied more effectively; a concept (e.g., attitude) may have no tangible existence of its own, but it is useful as an explanatory tool if theorists remain aware of the nature of the abstraction.

conduit metaphor the persistent bias within the English language toward assuming communication is a transmission of meanings "contained" in words sent from "senders" to "receivers." Representative theorists: Reddy; Lakoff and Johnson.

confirmation/disconfirmation the process of being noticed and perceived in both actuality and potentiality. Disconfirmation, of course, is the absence of confirmation, but it has also been analyzed as an intentional communication strategy in its own right, as in put downs or "freezing out" others in groups.

congruence in the person-centered approach, the matching of one's inner experience, to the extent that a person can be aware of it, with outer behavior. For example, in ongoing healthy relationships we assume that people's behaviors accurately reflect their inner attitudes and values; we do not say we're happy when we're consistently sad.

consequentialist ethic see *teleological ethics*.

consistency theory see *cognitive consistency theory*.

constitutive rule organizes meanings by specifying "how meanings at one level of abstraction may count as meaningful at another level of abstraction. For example, 'You are beautiful' counts as a compliment" (Cronen et al., 1982, pp. 73–74). See *regulative rule, coordinated management of meaning theory*.

construct in constructivism, the mind's recognitions of difference in what is perceived. For example, if you can identify the difference between a car and a truck, that means you have developed a construct for each.

construct differentiation in constructivism, the ability to develop increasingly specific distinctions in constructs and to organize those distinctions hierarchically. See *construct*.

constructed knowledge in Belenky et al.'s study of women's learning perspectives, a perspective that involves integrating the voices of self and other in flexible and personalized learning. Learning is understood as constructed in the sense of being the result of personal decisions and commitments.

constructivism/constructivist theory a theoretical perspective in which communication is explained as a fundamentally interpretive process through which people organize and create personal reality. It examines the complexity with which people develop and organize different categories of perception called "constructs." Representative theorists: Kelly; Delia.

content level of communication in relational/ interactional theory, an emphasis on what's being discussed overtly, the "content." See *relationship level of communication*.

context in the study of communication situations, all features that frame or surround an analyzed object or event in time or space.

control in FIRO theory, the ability to make a difference in a social environment; *control* in this sense does not connote manipulation or authoritarianism. Coordinated management of meaning theory, similarly, regards control as the extent to which actors are able to influence what happens in a communication episode.

convergent selectivity in play theory, audience members' tendency to choose ("converge on") media messages that meet their own emotional needs and support their own enjoyment.

conversational autonomy theory suggests that organizations are self-organizing and self-shaping, and that organizations emerge through creative and coherent human conversations. Representative theorist: J. R. Taylor. See *heteronomous model, autonomous model*.

conversational narcissism the tendency of some communicators to monopolize conversations in order to prove that they are effective communicators. Representative theorist: Derber.

cool media in medium theory, media that require or invite high degrees of audience participation and interpretation in creating meaning. See *hot media*.

coordinated management of meaning (CMM) theory describes communication as people's mutual attempts to blend or negotiate individualized rules and meanings in order to achieve coordination in their relationships. Representative theorists: Pearce and Cronen.

co-orientation the mutual recognition of an understanding.

cost in social exchange theory, what a communicator must forgo, or give up, in order to achieve goals.

coupling in conversational autonomy theory, the process of encountering disturbances at the boundaries where systems come into contact. These disturbances can shift a system to a higher level of functioning.

covering laws See *laws (covering laws) approach*.

credibility a communicator's expertise, trustworthiness and, to a lesser extent, dynamism, as perceived by an audience. See *ethos*.

critical theory explains and critiques social communication by examining the implications of power relationships; Marxist and feminist scholars usually approach theorizing with these assumptions. Often identified with cultural studies approaches. Representative theorists: Kellner; Kramerae; Williams. See also *cultural studies*.

cross-cultural adaptation theory studies how individuals learn to reorient their communication assumptions when they become strangers in unfamiliar cultural systems. Representative theorist: Kim.

cultivation theory/cultivation analysis explains media, especially television, not in cause-effect terms but by describing the longer-term tendencies of audiences to adjust their expectations about reality in the direction of prevalent media content. Representative theorist: Gerbner.

cultural studies a broadly based approach to studying communication through its cultural implications; often studies in this tradition adopt the tone of social commentary or criticism; closely identified with critical theory. Representative theorists: Carey; Grossberg; S. Hall; Kellner. See also *critical theory*.

cultural syndromes the tendencies or patterns developed within cultures to organize communicators' behaviors. Examples include complexity syndrome (complication of relational patterns), individualism syndrome (extent of reliance on individual rights), collectivism syndrome (extent of conformity to larger social groups), tightness syndrome (extent of behavior regulation through norms and roles). Representative theorist: Triandis.

culture a "set of human-made objective and subjective elements" shared by a group and developed so that these individuals might communicate more effectively and efficiently with one another (based on a definition by Triandis, 1994).

culture shock cultural strangers' feelings of stress or despair at the challenges of adapting to a new culture, perhaps leading to self-imposed isolation.

decentering placing ourselves imaginatively outside our immediate existence; for example, imagining what life would be like for others in other situations.

declarative memory in action assembly theory, our recollection of what we know; this is memory's content, sometimes described as "knowledge that" memory.

deconstruction a form of postmodern criticism that attempts to undermine or "undo" supposedly obvious or overt meanings of texts in order to show that texts do not inherently contain meaning. Instead, to deconstructionists, texts may evoke meanings differently—and often evoke opposite ones—for different readers. Representative theorist: Derrida.

deliberative rhetoric in classical rhetorical theory, rhetoric typically exhibited in public policy and legislative situations.

deontological ethics/deontology a philosophy that relies on duties and principles as bases for making ethical decisions. Representative theorist: Kant.

descriptive research helps to build theory by gathering information. Descriptive research attempts to explain *what* is there but not necessarily *why* it's there.

developmental theories explanations that account for changes in communication or communication effects over time.

dialectical theory examines how relationships develop from the interplay of perceived opposite forces or contradictions (e.g., autonomy/connection, openness/closedness, predictability/novelty), and how communicators negotiate these ever-changing processes. Representative theorists: Baxter; Rawlins.

dialogic ethics advocates such conditions as open consideration of ideas, authenticity, and a caring respect for otherness as criteria for ethical communication. Representative theorists: Buber; Habermas; Noddings.

dialogism a concept of inner experience in which inner speech is presumed to be dialogic because it imports the society's larger dialogue. Language, whenever it's used to think with or describe reality, is thought to contain an inherently dialogic mix of social voices. This concept is similar to claims of symbolic interactionism but goes further in describing inner speech as dialogue. Representative theorist: Bakhtin.

dialogue a condition of quality communication in which each partner respects the uniqueness of the other and does not seek to predetermine outcomes of the interchange; the basic reality of human existence is assumed to be in "the between" of the relationship rather than in psychological variables. Representative theorists: Buber; Gadamer; Rogers.

differentiation the process of recognizing uniqueness in the context of larger patterns.

diffusion of innovations theory an extension of two-step and multi-step flow theories of mass communication in which researchers attempt to account for how new ideas, technologies, and practices are disseminated to a variety of audiences within a society. Representative theorist: E. Rogers. See *two-step flow theory, multi-step flow theory*.

digital communication in relational/interactional theory, communication that depends on arbitrary agreements like the all-or-none digit-based system of computers, or the agreements in languages that certain words will stand for certain things. See *analogic communication*.

discipline (academic) a group of teachers and learners sharing a common focus on the human condition. For example, the discipline of communication may be said to focus on the relationships and relational messages through which people share meanings. Psychology, although its concerns overlap those of communication, tends to focus on mind and mental or emotional processes and their effects on human behavior. Clearly, both deal with communication and both deal with psychological processes, but their interests often tend to be different. See also *field*.

disconfirmation see *confirmation/disconfirmation*.

discourse ethics attempts to ground dialogue in a form of rational communication by which a consensus about public problems can be reached. This involves trying to structure an ideal speech situation in which communicators have equal access to the sphere of public discourse and procedurally equal opportunities to test arguments within the dialogue. Representative theorist: Habermas.

discursive field Kellner's cultural studies concept, which refers to how people talk or behave within texts with reference to their situations.

dogmatism the belief that one is certain in making a strong distinction. See *two-valued orientation*.

doubting game approaching new information by noting and analyzing its flaws, deficiencies, and inadequacies. Representative theorist: Elbow. See *believing game*.

dramatistic pentad see *pentad*.

dramatizing message in symbolic convergence theory, a message with especially rich language that helps to increase audience interest in a drama: word play, metaphors, anecdotes, jokes, and so on.

dramaturgical theory explains how human interaction can resemble theatrical and dramatic conventions in its reliance on impressions, roles, and performances. Representative theorists: Burke; Goffman.

duality in Perry's study of learning positions, the initial position. In duality, students are certain about what they know and believe that certainty about knowledge is possible.

duality of structure the basic concept of structuration theory; duality of structure means that not only is social organization structured by agency (intentional actions), but it also shapes such actions.

dynamic objectivity a concept that considers traditional notions of objectivity to be incomplete without recognizing, at the same time, how personal subjectivity, and perceivers' relationships with the perceived, can affect external reality. Representative theorist: Keller.

dynamism a factor of credibility based on a communicator's perceived enthusiasm and animation.

ecology a natural system that emphasizes the interdependence of living things and processes.

egalitarian ethics relies on the criterion of human equality as a basis for making ethical decisions. Representative theorist: Rawls.

egoistic ethics ethical system that advances the criterion of which outcome is good for the person doing the evaluating.

elaborated code communicators using elaborated codes supply a great deal of information, assuming message receivers do not necessarily have sufficient context or background for understanding. See *restricted code*.

electronic stage/secondary orality Ong's third stage of human communication development, in which new electronic media reintroduced the spontaneity of oral communication but liberated human beings from the need for face-to-face contact, thus changing our perceptual abilities in new ways.

emic knowing/emic theorizing cultural understanding achieved by participating within the cultural group's own assumptions and practices; perceiving, inasmuch as possible, as an "insider" would perceive.

empathy in the person-centered approach and other social science traditions, "to perceive the internal frame of reference of another with accuracy and with the emotional components and meanings which pertain thereto as if one were the person, but without ever losing the 'as if' condition" (Rogers, 1959, pp. 210–211).

enculturation in organizational culture, a type of performance that integrates new members into an ongoing social structure.

engrossment in the feminine ethic of care, becoming involved in the other's existence and caring for and with her or him in a dialogic way.

enthymeme a form of logical proof, similar to a syllogism, in which a key element is omitted on the expectation that audience members will supply it from their own experiences.

entropy the tendency of a closed system to become increasingly disorganized and unpredictable.

epideictic rhetoric in classical rhetorical theory, rhetoric typically exhibited in ceremonial public forums; such talk usually focuses on praising or blaming individuals for their virtues or vices.

epistemology the branch of philosophy that examines how we gain knowledge about the world. In some contexts, the term is used to refer to a particular system of knowing as "an epistemology."

equifinality in general systems theory, a characteristic of open systems that suggests that any given state of the system can be obtained by various system interactions.

ethics the value-based consideration of right and wrong in deciding how to frame communication messages.

ethnic in cross-cultural adaptation theory, the term for the cultural origin of the stranger or traveler to a new culture—and, to the extent that there are traces of that origin in the host (new) culture, to the intracultural support groups and neighborhoods that are part of the adaptation process.

ethnography a method practiced by researchers who participate directly and intensively within a culture in order to write about its uniqueness.

ethnomethodology investigates the everyday sense-making rules of individuals by violating their expectations of normality. Representative theorist: Garfinkel.

ethos in classical rhetorical theory, a form of artistic proof that depends on the speaker's character and credibility.

etic knowing/etic theorizing cultural understanding achieved from outside the culture, perceiving the culture as a whole, perhaps in its relation to other cultures.

Eurocentrism the tendency to explain and judge cultural phenomena in terms of standards developed within traditional European art, science, literature, and philosophy.

expectancy-violations theory predicts that when nonverbal expectations are violated, the violator's credibility will be especially important. High-credibility violators may tend to be perceived as more effective, and to elicit more cooperation. Low-credibility violators tend to be more effective when they abide by expected social norms. Representative theorist: J. Burgoon.

expertise a factor of credibility that depends on a communicator's relevant knowledge in a certain area.

expressions given/given off in impression management, this distinction refers to the fact that some cues others could interpret are intentional ("given" in Goffman's terms), while some are unintentional ("given off"). In a public speech, your *expressions given* would include the posture and gestures you practiced, while *expressions given off* would include your shaking hands and sweaty armpits.

face work in impression management, the attempt to manage one's appearance and style in face-to-face encounters.

fantasy in symbolic convergence theory, a consistent organized explanation that arises from a group's own talk, and in which the group believes. Symbolic convergence theorists like Bormann do *not* use "fantasy" in one of its everyday meanings to refer to something that couldn't possibly come true.

fantasy theme in symbolic convergence theory, a topic that a group or community constructs as a shared explanation for their communication.

fantasy type in symbolic convergence theory, a recurring representation of certain forms of behavior or personality that enrich the group's story about itself. For example, with the U.S. vision of the Old West came fantasy types of mountain men, Native Americans as noble savages, mining towns as rowdy places, and so on.

feedback any message that aids a communicator in evaluating the success of previous messages. See *positive feedback, negative feedback.*

felt difficulty the realization that something is wrong or troubling about a situation. Representative theorist: Dewey.

feminine ethic of care grounds ethical decision making in the particulars of caring relationships rather than in the principles and duties of deontological ethics. Although exceptions are common, relational engrossment is identified by Noddings with feminine styles, while attention to ethical duty and obligation tends to represent masculine styles. Representative theorist: Noddings.

feminist organizational theorizing an attempt to define the ideological implications of gendered behavior in organizations, including how men's and women's power are framed differently. Rather than being considered simply as what we *are* in organizations (women or men), gender is conceived as something we *do*. Behavior enacts gendered realities.

feminist standpoint theory see *standpoint theory, feminist.*

feminist theory explains communication variables (e.g., language, nonverbal immediacy, media effects, and ethics) from the perspective of gender relationships; it often focuses on the overt and covert power implications of cultural patterns. Representative theorists: Belenky et al.; Gilligan; Kramerae; Lakoff; Wood.

field (academic) a loose affiliation of scholars broadly interested in studying similar phenomena; a field is often contrasted with a discipline, which presumes a well-defined focus on specific content or processes. See also *discipline.*

figure/ground relationship psychological concept describing how things on which you want to focus (*figures*) are always perceived against the backdrop of other things that are not focused on (*ground*). Changing your focus of attention will move a perceptual object from ground to figure, or vice versa.

FIRO theory see *fundamental interpersonal relations orientation theory.*

first-order cultivation in cultivation theory, how media influence the literal beliefs people hold about the world. See *second-order cultivation.*

floor in impression management, the socially sanctioned permission to speak to and with others.

footing in impression management, the assumptions that determine who has more social power in a given situation.

forensic rhetoric in classical rhetorical theory, rhetoric exhibited in courtrooms and other places where the facts and interpretations of individual cases are argued.

formal organization a social group that brings people together to accomplish a common purpose and exhibits these additional characteristics: embedded in a history and anticipating a future, task specialization, internal control systems and reward structures, and multiple external and internal audiences.

formal theory a set of tentative answers built in response to focused questions, often phrased as propositions and described systematically.

frame/framing a *frame* is a definition or interpretation of what a situation means, and the process of *framing* is the act of asserting such a definition.

fundamental interpersonal relations orientation (FIRO) theory explains the role of the human needs of inclusion, control, and affection in interpersonal communication. Representative theorist: Schutz.

game mastery in CMM theory, the creative response to rules that may take social situations in new directions—perhaps even by transcending or breaking existing rule structures.

game playing in CMM theory, following the rules of a social situation and adapting to what is happening.

gatekeeper a person, group, or role that controls the kind and amount of information audiences can receive.

gender a cultural and social concept based on how people talk about different kinds of male and female behavior; often, but not necessarily, related to the biological condition of sex. See *sex*.

general systems theory (GST) describes living systems by referring to the interdependence of their components and the relationships among components. Representative theorists: Bertalanffy; Fisher.

generalized other in symbolic interactionism, an overall sense of how someone else reacts to you, or thinks and feels relative to you.

genuine dialogue develops when "each participant really has in mind the other or others in their present and particular being and turns to them with the intention of establishing a living mutual relation" (Buber, 1965a, p. 19).

genuine questioning in Gadamer's philosophical hermeneutics, inquiries to which the answer is not already known.

global village McLuhan's concept that new electronic media have interconnected the world in ways that bring strangers and different cultures into essential interdependence, similar to the social contacts established in tribal villages.

golden mean, principle of suggests the avoidance of extreme positions ("vices") of deficiency and excess in the consideration of ethical decision making. Representative theorist: Aristotle.

grand narrative See *metanarrative*.

haptics the study of how people develop meanings for touch behaviors.

hard architecture refers to human-designed environments that make human contact more difficult by, for example, emphasizing uniformity, ease of maintenance, and clearly marked status levels over interpersonal contact. Representative theorist: Sommer.

Hawthorne studies/Hawthorne effect research studies that found workplace productivity improved when changes were made, in many cases regardless of what kinds of changes were introduced (both improving lighting *and* decreasing lighting, for example, improved productivity). Evidently workers experienced the social attention of being studied as an important and positive factor. The Hawthorne studies led to more sophisticated analyses of cause-effect in organizations. Representative theorists: Roethlisberger and Dickson.

hegemony in critical theory, the usually institutionalized and in-place distribution of power that makes one social group dominant over another or others, often with the implied acquiesence of the dominated.

helical spiral a model of communication that attempts to account for communication as a circular process that constantly changes over time. Representative theorist: Dance.

hermeneutics investigates the interpretation of texts; in one form popularized by Gadamer, hermeneutics emphasizes the historical and inherently linguistic nature of experience in denying a transmissional model of communication.

heterogeneous social order in CMM theory, the assumption that society is composed of multiple tastes, styles, assumptions, language habits, and expectations; we must assume that many distinctions and differences are at play in society.

heteronomous model in organizational communication, the belief that organizational control can be achieved by inputs from outside system boundaries. This model is critiqued by conversational autonomy theorists. See *autonomous model, conversational autonomy theory*.

heterophily dissimilarity between people on such basic dimensions as attitudes, values, or socioeconomic status.

heurism the ability to stimulate further research and speculation.

high-context (HC) culture emphasizes message processing in which relatively little meaning is obvious in explicit content and communicators are expected to rely heavily on context to interpret possible meanings. See *low-context (LC) culture.*

holism/nonsummativity in general systems theory, the reminder that systems must be understood as wholes ("holism") rather than as mere accumulations of added-together ("summed") parts.

holon in general systems theory, any system being studied within the context of associated larger and smaller systems; the theorist knows that any holon is a subsystem of larger systems, and that the holon comprises smaller subsystems.

homeostasis a balance of relations within a system.

homeostatic theory an approach to organizational theorizing that stresses the importance of dynamic states of balance in organizational systems. Balance to homeostatic theorists is not a simple state, to be achieved and then left alone, but a constantly shifting characteristic of open systems. Representative theorists: Katz and Kahn.

homogeneous social order the assumption that a society is composed of basically similar contexts, with similar assumptions about right and wrong, and appropriate and inappropriate behaviors. CMM theorists argue that this assumption overstates social similarities. See *heterogeneous social order.*

homophily similarity between people on such basic dimensions as attitudes, values, and socioeconomic status.

host in cross-cultural adaptation theory, the general term for the unfamiliar culture encountered by travelers and sojourners, including the new culture's people, practices, and media.

hot media in medium theory, those media that demand relatively little interpretation from audiences, because they supply a high degree of definitive information. See *cool media.*

human sensorium See *sensorium, human.*

hypertext a computer-based structure of information pathways in which different texts and ideas are linked electronically to offer a variety of nonlinear means of accessing information.

hypodermic needle approach See *magic bullet theory.*

hypothesis a tentative statement of expectation or truth.

"I" in symbolic interactionism, the component of the self that asserts unique points of view, responds to impulses, and creates individualized positions. Representative theorist: Mead. See *"me," self.*

ideal speech situation Habermas's concept in discourse ethics, emphasizing that public speech is ideally characterized by: a cooperative search for truth that leads to a consensus, the assumption that the better argument will prevail, and that there will be equal access to public forums and equal opportunities for people to speak and question others.

identification in interpersonal persuasion, changing one's mind in order to align oneself positively with the persuader. For another usage, see *new rhetoric/old rhetoric.*

ideology a system of ideas so thoroughly accepted that communicators don't question its existence, validity, or importance.

I-It/I-It relationship in dialogic theory, the treatment of others as if they were objects or things that can be described, predicted, or measured precisely. An I-It attitude is not necessarily an undesirable occurrence in itself, and can be necessary in some relationships; however, if the I-It attitude dominates personal relations, genuine dialogue cannot develop. Representative theorist: Buber. See *I-Thou.*

illocution in speech act theory, speech used to perform an act in which another's response is presumed to be appropriate and necessary. For example, while sitting with you in a movie, a friend says, "I'm tired and have a really bad headache"; this statement may be an illocution, suggesting that you should offer to leave with him or her. See *locution.*

immediacy theory demonstrates how people signal the emotional responses of attraction, dominance, and arousal through nonverbal and verbal messages related to physical closeness; for example, eye contact and movement toward another, indicators of immediacy, are correlated with desires for increased involvement. Representative theorist: Mehrabian.

imposing an attitude criticized by dialogic ethical theory, in which one person acts as a propagandist in trying to shape another's mind. In imposing, it is the acceptance of the idea that is foremost in the mind of the persuader, rather than a concern for the other as a person, or even a concern for the value of the idea.

impression management how people accomplish interpersonal goals by making strategic choices about presenting themselves, dramatizing themselves, in social situations. We try to control others' impressions of us. Representative theorist: Goffman.

inartistic means of persuasion in classical rhetorical theory, this is rhetoric based on methods of proving a case that are, for example, based on such external inducements as force, torture, bribes, or prior promises. Inartistic means, in general, are those that do not depend on the creativity or imagination of the rhetor, or communicator. See *artistic means of persuasion.*

inclusion in FIRO theory, the need to be recognized as a full participant in human interaction. In dialogic theory, similarly, *inclusion* refers to the ability to respect and understand others without necessarily agreeing with them or abandoning one's own position; Buber calls this "imagining the real."

individualism syndrome categorization of cultures based on the greater or lesser commitment to the importance of a single human being.

individualistic orientation defines communication itself primarily in terms of what one person does to others; it often reduces communication problems to aiming proper or effective messages at target receivers. Although this is a limiting and inadequate perspective for studying communication as an overall process, it is not an indictment of studying individual or personal decision making, for example. Many studies of individuals or individual behaviors still make valid contributions to the communication discipline. See *mutualistic orientation.*

influentials/opinion leaders in two-step or multi-step flow theories of mass communication, these are people who attend closely to media messages and then influence others through interpersonal communication.

information message that reduces receiver uncertainty.

information theory analyzes the sequences of message sending and receiving in terms of efficiency. Representative theorists: Shannon and Weaver.

inner speech theory a generalized perspective that emphasizes the importance of language in cognitive information processing, the development of self, the anticipation of dialogue, and the like. Representative theorists: Bakhtin; Dance; Vygotsky.

intentionality a philosophical concept that suggests that some processes must have an object in order for us to understand or talk about them. For example, it is said to be impossible to have "consciousness" without specifying its object: we must have "consciousness-of-*something.*"

interdiscipline (academic) a group of teachers and learners who share a common focus on the human condition but simultaneously emphasize its reliance on, and relevance to, a wide variety of other scholarly groups and disciplines. Compare with *discipline,* which is a more common designation. This book presumes that communication is both a discipline and an interdiscipline (see Chapter 11).

interiority the human ability, based on inner speech, to create a complex and rich inner life. Representative theorist: Dance.

internal socialization refers to how children learn language through a combination of social facilitation and creative linguistic play. Representative theorist: Vygotsky.

internalization in interpersonal persuasion, influence gained because an auditor perceives a relatively deep congruence between personal values and the suggested behavior.

interpersonal ethic the position that effective ethical decisions expand people's range of choices, while unethical decisions reduce choices (the *choice criterion*). In addition, theorists of interpersonal ethics generalize that "whatever enhances that which is uniquely human in participants is ethical; whatever dehumanizes is unethical" (Brown

& Keller, 1979, p. 277). Representative theorists: Brown and Keller.

intimate distance in the study of proxemic cues, the distance from touching to eighteen inches. See *proxemics*. Representative theorist: E. Hall.

intrapersonal refers to processes that occur within the person.

I-Thou/I-Thou relationship in dialogic theory, the attitude in which one person responds to another as a uniquely valuable individual, not as a representative figure, a stereotype, or an extension of one's own personality. Representative theorist: Buber. See *I-It*.

kinesics the study of the meaning of body movements.

la langue refers to the overall system of symbolic message structures; language as an abstract system. Representative theorist: Saussure. See *la parole*.

la parole refers to the particular and unique speech of individual communicators; how people actually use language in everyday life. Representative theorist: Saussure. See *la langue*.

language a socially agreed-upon code by which objects and relationships in the world are symbolized.

language game how language is organized and used to make social action in a given situation more predictable through rules. Representative theorists: Wittgenstein; Pearce.

law of the instrument the tendency of a theorist/researcher to view potential problems in light of only one technique, methodology, or perspective. This tendency is not generally advisable, because ideally researchers would start with questions about the problem they want to study rather than with a certainty about how they want to study a problem. Contemporary theorist: Kaplan.

laws (covering laws) approach searches for macroscopic, highly generalizable, and relatively invariant principles that apply across many different types of communicators and situations. See also *rules, general systems theory*.

learning organization a dialogic approach to organizational communication, treating an organization as a consistently self-renewing unit in which all components have access to other components. In learning organizations, change is expected because it is the basis for effective dialogue. Representative theorists: Isaacs; Senge.

linguistic relativity theory explains how the language of a culture affects (or, in the strong version of the theory, determines) the way a culture defines reality. Also known as the Sapir-Whorf hypothesis. Representative theorist: Whorf.

linguisticality in hermeneutics, the notion that language is an ongoing entity, and that in some sense humans "belong to language" because we are as much expressions of language as it is an expression of us.

linking function the ability to bring people together. See *inner speech theory,* which assumes that linking is not the only function, and may not even be the primary function, of human communication.

literacy See *script stage*.

literature, the body of existing research in a subject matter area, field, or discipline of study.

locution in speech act theory, speech used as a verbal description of reality. See *illocution*.

logos in classical rhetorical theory, a form of artistic proof that relies on logical argumentation and reasoning.

longitudinal studies research designs that follow a group of people over a specified period of time and note changes in their choices or behaviors.

low-context (LC) culture relies less on context for understanding than on explicitly stated messages. See *high-context (HC) culture*.

lurking describes the process of a person observing/reading/listening to an online "chat" without contributing directly to the conversation, or even necessarily informing others of his or her presence.

Machiavellianism the willingness to manipulate others for personal gain.

magic bullet theory early perspective on media effects; held that media caused direct and measurable effects in individuals in the mass audience. Also known as the hypodermic needle approach.

marketplace of ideas ethics advocates the open exchange of, and access to, divergent ideas in order to compare "good reasons" within a democratic climate. Representative theorists: Haiman; Wallace.

"me" in symbolic interactionism, the component of the self that responds to the outside social network; it is shaped, controlled, limited, or accounted for by external forces. Representative theorist: Mead. See *"I," self*.

mean world thesis in cultivation theory, the finding that heavy viewers of television tend to believe the world is more violent than it is when measured objectively.

meaning the patterns human beings create out of their interpretation of experience.

media events broadcasts of especially important, one-of-a-kind occasions. Representative theorists: Dayan and Katz.

media matrix the system of different media acting interdependently.

mediated place, theory of explains how electronic media alter the human experience of "place" by blurring traditional distinctions between public and private spheres. Representative theorist: Meyrowitz.

mediation/media the imposition of a new entity or process between communicators that may reduce the directness of their contact. For example, media technologies like television and the telephone mediate, but so does a third party who attempts to help arguing neighbors settle a property dispute.

medium theory suggests that media, far from being mere channels for conveying information, actually restructure how humans perceive. Representative theorists: McLuhan; Ong.

mentation the complex human thought process; in one form of inner speech theory, mentation is the basic reason for, and foundation of, human communication. Representative theorist: Dance.

message a stimulus to which meanings are attributed in communication.

metacommunication the process of communicating about communication.

metanarrative an influential belief system or social "story" that clearly dictates how people should define important issues in their lives, such as good/evil or right/wrong. Modernism relies on metanarratives supplied by institutions such as the church and the scientific establishment, while postmodernism holds that such metanarratives have largely lost their power and authority to guide our lives. Also referred to as grand narratives. Representative theorist: Lyotard.

metaperspective in interpersonal perception theory, a perspective about a perspective; for example, Jane's view of how John sees Jane.

metaphor a figure of speech that asserts a sameness about different things.

mind in symbolic interactionism, the way we recreate social communication patterns intrapersonally; it is society as we internalize it, allowing us to have inner conversations, to plan or rehearse social action, or to consider ourselves as others see us. Representative theorist: Mead. In the study of persuasion, *mind* also refers to the disciplined set of programs or schemata by which people organize their plans for action.

model a verbal or pictorial description or representation of a process designed to offer a simplified and more accessible explanation.

modernism a perspective that celebrates rationality and scientific method in the Englightenment tradition.

monologue in dialogic theory, a communication situation in which one voice or perspective dominates without any expectation of a response.

motional view of behavior (motion) assumes that behavior is caused, or set "in motion," by outside forces—as opposed to being actively chosen from within people. See *actional view of behavior*.

motivational displacement in the feminine ethic of care, the ability to experience motivation unselfishly; that is, motivation is displaced to the "cared-for" person and becomes a relational experience.

multiplicity in Perry's study of learning positions, a second-level position in which students believe all reality is fundamentally negotiable.

multi-step flow theory an extension of two-step flow theorizing; this approach suggests that many layers of interpersonal influence are necessary to an understanding of how media influence is disseminated. See *two-step flow theory*.

muted group theory studies how women's voices can be "silenced" by the political dominance of men's interpersonal perceptions and behaviors. Representative theorists: S. Ardener; Kramerae.

mutual control, principle of the idea that a field of study does not need to be unified or explained by only one theory. Instead, multiple and overlapping theories are capable of covering a field in a coordinated way. Multiple theories do not necessarily mean theorists are undecided, but that different theories may be accounting for somewhat different phenomena.

mutual persuasion theory/mutual persuasion in interpersonal persuasion, an approach that suggests the traditional roles of persuader-initiator and persuadee ("target") inaccurately describe the dynamics of communication. In mutual persuasion, both parties or sides influence the other. Representative theorists: Smith and Pettegrew.

mutualistic orientation defines communication primarily as a process of relationship awareness and relationship building. In this view, communicators are not autonomous individuals, but they are necessarily enmeshed in relationships where co-participants inevitably affect each other's identities, actions, interpretations, and potentials. See *transaction, individualistic orientation*.

narration the human tendency to organize experience into stories with plot, characterization, chronology, conflict, and resolution. Sometimes called "narrative."

narrative ethics locates ethical decision making in the context of group and community experience of common "stories," rather than within the traditional dictates of experts or logical rationality; narrative ethics elevates the consideration of values in the development of a "narrative rationality." Representative theorist: Fisher. See also *communitarian ethics*.

narrative rationality a concept from communitarian ethics suggesting that individual forms of reasoning and proving arguments are less persuasive for audiences than values embedded in stories. The ethical stance of narrative rationality "focuses on 'good reasons'—elements that provide warrants for accepting or adhering to the advice fostered by any form of communication that can be considered rhetorical" (Fisher, 1987, p. 48).

negative feedback inhibits or regulates a tendency within a system.

new rhetoric/old rhetoric in Burke's approach to dramaturgical theory, "new rhetoric" is more often associated with *identification* (people recognizing themselves within the experiences of others, establishing commonality) than with the "old rhetoric" preoccupation with overt *persuasion* (people attempting to change others' minds by convincing them of alternative views).

noise in information theory, internal or external interference with the sending and receiving of messages.

nommo in Afrocentric theorizing, a reverence for the generative and spiritual power of the spoken word.

null hypothesis an overt statement that reminds researchers *not* to expect significant differences in a given direction. Overtly stating null hypotheses reminds researchers of the need for fairness and objectivity, and of the need to check their own natural biases and expectations.

old rhetoric See *new rhetoric/old rhetoric*.

opinion leaders See *influentials/opinion leaders*.

oral stage/primary orality Ong's concept describing earlier stages of human communication in which we depended upon direct, face-to-face speech.

orature in Afrocentric theory, the fundamentally oral tradition, and its implicit criteria for communication, developed within African-based cultures; this assumption of the primacy of oral communication affects literature, persuasive public contexts, and forms of interpersonal communication.

organizational culture the communication habits, norms, and values within an organization that give it a distinct identity; this process is analogous to how larger cultures are distinguished by their unique patterns of social communication.

organizational politics in organizational culture, a type of performance that enacts or demonstrates power relations.

output representation in action assembly theory, planned actions yet to be taken.

overlap a conversational moment in which people find themselves talking simultaneously.

Palo Alto Group researchers responsible for the development of relational/interactional theory, most notably Paul Watzlawick, Janet Beavin (now Bavelas), and Don D. Jackson. The Palo Alto Group advanced the theoretical work of Gregory Bateson.

para-social interaction the tendency of some audience members to identify with media figures (celebrities, fictional characters) as though an interpersonal relationship had been established. Representative theorists: Horton and Wohl.

parsimony the condition in which an explanation is sufficiently complex to explain the processes it claims to explain but is not more complicated than it needs to be.

passion in organizational culture, a type of performance whose primary function is to give workers' lives a dramatic interest that helps people to adapt within the culture.

pathos in classical rhetorical theory, a form of artistic proof that relies on appeals to an audience's emotions and passions.

pentad, dramatistic a means of analyzing rhetoric in context by looking at five factors (pentad): act (what was done), scene (where it was done), agent (by whom it was done), agency (with what means it was done), and purpose (the goal that guided the action). Representative theorist: Burke.

perception the process by which an organism assimilates, interprets, and uses sensory data.

perceptual salience refers to the perceived importance to the self of a given object or event.

performance an attempt to manage identity in public.

personal distance in the study of proxemic cues, the distance from eighteen inches to four feet. Representative theorist: E. Hall. See *proxemics*.

personal front in impression management, the personal image people strategically attempt to create.

person-centered approach a dialogically based approach to interpersonal communication that emphasizes genuine concern for the messages and self-concept of the other person; it involves empathy, congruent behavior, and acceptance of the other's experience. Representative theorist: C. Rogers.

persuasion the communication process in which people influence the opinions, attitudes, beliefs, and actions of others. Communication scholars often, but not inevitably, study persuasion as an intentional process of affecting target audiences.

phenomenal field the array of cues available for individuals' perceptions and interpretations.

phenomenology the "study of phenomena, of things or events, in the everyday world… from the viewpoint of the experiencing person" (Becker, 1992, p. 7).

philosophical anthropology a perspective that seeks to examine human existence by investigating culture and human nature as though they were being encountered fresh. Representative theorist: Buber.

play theory explains how audiences use media messages to reinforce a tendency toward free choice and "subjective play." Representative theorist: Stephenson.

polysemy a characteristic of language through which multiple alternative meanings may be available at any one time for a message or a set of messages.

positive feedback enhances or reinforces a tendency within a system.

positive regard in the person-centered approach, the belief that effective communicators value other people, as individuals, even when they disapprove of their behaviors. Also known as acceptance, unconditional positive regard, respect, and a similar concept from another dialogic theory, confirmation.

postmodernism/postmodern theory/postmodern language theory a general theoretical perspective that contests the modernist view that reality is measurable and verifiable, that causes and effects can be specified, that meanings are stable and capable of being transmitted, and that science or other institutions can clarify the human condition rationally. Various versions of postmodern theory assume instead that linguistic meanings are contingent, transitory, and often contradictory, and that no grand narrative or story—including science—is capable of unifying the human experience. Representative theorists: Derrida; Lyotard.

pragmatism a philosophical and theoretical position asserting that the essential meaning of any concept or idea can be seen in the effects it is observed to initiate. Also known as American pragmatism. Representative theorists: Dewey; James; Peirce; West.

praxis the interdependent unity of theory and practice. Theory that is practical becomes practice that is theoretically sound.

predication in inner speech, the predominance of active language, which makes it somewhat more process-centered than face-to-face speech in everyday life. Representative theorist: Vygotsky.

primary orality See *oral stage.*

principle of mutual control See *mutual control, principle of.*

principle of the golden mean See *golden mean, principle of.*

procedural knowledge in the Belenky et al. study of women's learning perspectives, a perspective in which some women place faith in the "how to" procedures that have helped others become competent.

procedural memory in action assembly theory, our recollection of how to do things and our sense of which things typically work, and why. Procedural memory is remembering how to produce actions, sometimes referred to as "knowledge how," as opposed to the more content-oriented "knowledge that" memory.

procedural records in action assembly theory, memories of previous communication outcomes, along with the details of actions and whatever situational factors were relevant to the outcomes.

process the condition of constant, dynamic change.

productive meaning in hermeneutics, the communicative goal of communicators achieving a new meaning through dialogue, not just attempting to relay a previous one.

profit in social exchange theory, what is achieved when communication rewards outweigh the costs.

program in the study of mind, an organized cognitive plan for accomplishing a particular end.

proposition a formal claim asserted as true within the context of a theory.

proxemics the study of how people use distance as a communication cue.

psychological reactance a theory predicting that people tend to react to situations in ways that protect their range of options. Representative theorist: Brehm.

psychologism the belief, criticized by dialogic theorists, that reality is found and defined inside people's psyches and that personal experience is not fundamentally dependent on social interaction.

public distance in the study of proxemic cues, distances of more than twelve feet. Representative theorist: E. Hall. See *proxemics.*

public journalism theory/public journalism a theoretical movement that expands the role of news organizations to encourage a wider public responsibility. Public journalists generally go beyond traditional definitions of news reportage in order to establish newspapers, for example, as sites or forums in which citizens can express their own voices in civic life. Representative theorists: Rosen; Merritt; Carey.

punctuation how people structure experience in terms of their perceptions of starts, stops, and changes in processes. Even though reality does not inherently contain such markers, communicators structure their experiences by supplying them. For example, there is no objectively verifiable answer to the question "When did our argument start?," because different communicators will trace its beginnings ("punctuate it") differently. Representative theorists: Palo Alto Group.

purpose in dramaturgical theory (pentad), the motivating reason behind rhetoric.

qualitative research methodologies investigation by which the qualities of phenomena are discovered, observed, described, and analyzed; some forms may be referred to as "naturalistic" or "interpretive" methods. See *quantitative research methodologies.*

quantitative research methodologies investigation by which units of phenomena are isolated, measured, counted, and analyzed. See *qualitative research methodologies.*

race a set of social distinctions based on how people link, rightly or wrongly, cultural patterns of human communication to visible physical features such as skin color. Race, once thought to be a biologically inherited characteristic, has become increasingly suspect in recent years as a valid scientific concept.

rapport constellation a pattern of postures and nonverbal bodily cues that is associated with immediacy. Representative theorist: Scheflen. See *immediacy theory.*

ratio in dramaturgical theory, Burke's notion that communicators recognize the combinations of the elements of the pentad (act, agent, scene, agency, purpose), not just the elements individually. He called each combination a "ratio." For example, it's not morally wrong to wear a backward ball cap to a wedding, but don't expect to impress people—or even to be treated neutrally—if you do so. Both the act and the scene are appropriate; they're not appropriate *together,* in what Burke called an "act-scene ratio."

received knowledge in the Belenky et al. study of women's learning perspectives, the perspective in which some women believe they can receive knowledge from others but they themselves cannot develop knowledge on their own.

reciprocity a condition in which a response is correlated with the worth of the original message. For example, if you compliment someone, he or she is likely to reply with a compliment or another positive message.

reflection-in-action the constant adjustment of a communicator's theories while he or she is involved in practical interaction. It is based on a willingness to engage in an ongoing process of practical "research" from moment to moment, rather than relying on techniques. Representative theorist: Schön.

reflexivity the situation in which we attempt to use a skill or a capacity to explain itself. For example, *studying language* by *talking about it* is said to be a reflexive problem. Sometimes referred to as "self-reflexiveness."

refutability the criterion by which a theory can be judged by its ability to be disproved (sometimes termed *falsifiability*). In other words, if a theory is so broadly or vaguely stated that almost *any* result can be said to be accounted for by it, then ultimately it will not be a useful theory. Theorizing must, in other words, be specific enough to be open to contradictory evidence.

regions in impression management, this refers to the relatively public or private contexts in which strategic interaction occurs. *Front regions* encourage official performances; *back regions* encourage less guarded behavior.

regulative rule how constitutive rules are organized into guidelines for behavior. See *constitutive rule, coordinated management of meaning (CMM) theory.*

reification treating concepts and theoretical constructions as if they had an inherent life or importance of their own, apart from the meanings we attribute to them.

relational culture the phenomenon by which each interpersonal relationship develops many of the same kinds of patterns and features as do larger cultures. Representative theorist: Wood.

relationship level of communication in relational/interactional theory, emphasis on how messages affect or comment upon the relation between the communicators. See *content level of communication.*

relativism in Perry's study of learning positions, the third level of student learning, in which truth is thought to be necessarily relative to context and circumstance. Relativism has also been used by some philosophers to refer to the claim that moral truths are not absolute but conditional.

research question asks about what relationships between behaviors or processes could be found by doing a focused investigation.

resonant image Kellner's cultural studies concept: an especially striking textual image or example that sticks in people's minds and can support ideologies.

restricted code speakers and listeners using restricted codes tend to believe they already have specialized verbal assumptions in common (e.g., workplace jargon) and therefore don't need to verbalize as much information in order to achieve understanding. See *elaborated code.*

reward in social exchange theory, an outcome desired by a communicator.

rhetor one who uses rhetoric.

rhetoric the study of communication messages designed to affect specific listeners or readers in particular ways.

rhetorical condition in Afrocentric theory, the emphasis on the power-based conditions in which people talk.

rhetorical example in classical rhetorical theory, an inductive form of logical proof in which a communicator introduces illustrative instances that support the argument.

rhetorical vision in symbolic convergence theory, "a broad and consistent view of [a group's] social and material reality" (Bormann, 1983, p. 75).

rights what people should be able to do as individual moral agents. Some approaches to moral theory presume rights to be inherent in human experience and treat them almost as if they were individual possessions; this idea is critiqued by communitarian ethicists.

ritual in organizational culture, a type of performance that maintains familiar activities that the group enacts at regular intervals. Rituals may be symbolic at many levels, but an especially important function of ritual performance is to provide stability and reassurance within a complex organization.

role a set of behaviors expected of a certain person or a certain position.

role enactment in impression management, the strategic use of consistent social role behavior to encourage certain impressions in others. For example, parents (whether loving and attentive or uncaring and insensitive) may be aware of how others define "a good parent," and in public may attempt to act as they believe good parents do.

role-taking in symbolic interactionism, an inner symbolic decision by which people remove themselves from their own perspectives and re-place themselves in the imagined self of another person or group, in effect taking on an alternative role and thereby recognizing that reality can seem different from differing perspectives. Similar to decentering in inner speech theory. See *role*.

rule See *rules theory*.

rules theory explains the usually implicit understandings people develop for how to act and speak in social situations. Representative theorists: Ganz; Garfinkel; Shimanoff.

Sapir-Whorf hypothesis See *linguistic relativity theory*.

scene in dramaturgical theory, the situation in which action occurs.

schema See *program*.

schismogenesis in relational/interactional theory, a condition in which two complementary positions grow progressively farther apart, each as a result of the other. For example, I criticize you, and you withdraw. Then I criticize you for withdrawing, leading to further withdrawal on your part.

science methodical and systematic investigation of a topic.

scientific management theory an early approach to management that emphasized comprehensive information-gathering and close analysis of workers' actual job performance. Representative theorist: F. W. Taylor.

script in symbolic convergence theory, fantasy content of public dramas that comes to be accepted and is not open to debate.

script stage/literacy Ong's concept of the stage of human communication in which the technology of writing was invented and subsequently changed human consciousness.

secondary orality See *electronic stage/secondary orality*.

second-order cultivation in cultivation theory, how media influence the symbolic interpretations and expectations of media audiences rather than their literal beliefs.

seeming an attitude criticized by dialogic ethical theory, in which people create false impressions for each other; an expression of a fundamentally I-It attitude.

self in symbolic interactionism, a sense of identity or unique personal placement in a social world, discovered primarily through language-based interaction. It is through linguistic social participation that we discover who we are, developing selves. Representative theorist: Mead.

self-fulfilling prophecy when we seem to see, hear, or experience what we have already preordained for ourselves, perhaps through our expectations. Representative theorist: Rosenthal.

semantic merger in inner speech, the phenomenon by which meanings for several ideas and concepts become blended ("merged") within a single word; similar to how a metaphor works. Representative theorist: Vygotsky.

semantics the study of the patterns of meaning within a language.

semiotics the study of how signs (an overall term for both symbolic and nonsymbolic signal messages) in human environments form patterns or codes within which people come to understand their daily lives. Representative theorists: Barthes; Eco; Leeds-Hurwitz; Peirce.

sense orientation the phenomenon of inner speech that depends not on precise definition but on the more emotive or holistic senses of words. Representative theorist: Vygotsky.

sensorium, human Ong's description of how human senses and sensory capacities have been changed by the domination of different media in different eras.

sex biological designations of male and female. See *gender*.

sign aspects of human environment that take on the value or function of a message because they stand for or refer to something else. The word is often used as an overall term that is larger than both signals and symbols. See *semiotics*.

signal in information theory, an encoded message sent through a channel to a receiver. In theories of language, signals are those messages that stand in a one-to-one, unambiguous relationship to what they represent. See *symbol*.

significant symbol in symbolic interactionism, a symbol that evokes basically similar meanings for communicators in social situations. See *symbol*.

signified that which a signifier refers to or stands for. See *signifier, semiotics*.

signifier something that calls attention to, or stands for, something else. See *signified, semiotics*.

silence in the Belenky et al. study of women's learning perspectives, a perspective in which some women feel as if they cannot contribute meaningfully to intellectual or social conversation. Silence implies that one could choose to talk but does not do so perhaps because of a sense that others will not listen.

social distance in the study of proxemic cues, the distance of four feet to twelve feet. Representative theorist: E. Hall. See *proxemics*.

social exchange theory investigates how interaction is guided by the desire to maximize communication profits and rewards while minimizing communication losses and costs. Representative theorists: Blau; Roloff; Thibaut and Kelley.

social horizon Kellner's concept referring to the cultural context for actions.

sociality in organizational culture, a type of performance that maintains social roles and relations within the organization.

society in symbolic interactionism, the web of social relationships that human beings create symbolically through their use of language. Representative theorist: Mead.

Sophists itinerant teachers in ancient Greece who taught people the practical everyday applications and skills of rhetoric.

space-binding messages bring people in different places communicatively "together."

spatialization dividing reality artificially into static categories that ignore the process assumptions of communication and change.

speech act See *speech act theory*.

speech act theory studies how speech is essentially performative; that is, although words are often assumed in everyday life to be separate from actions, speech act theorists assume the opposite—that by saying words, we are really performing certain actions, such as vowing, promising, or nominating. Representative theorist: Searle.

spiral of silence theory explains how public opinion can minimize social expression of minority opinion while exaggerating the power of the majority. Representative theorist: Noelle-Neumann.

standpoint theory, feminist "traces the ways in which the locations of distinct social groups... shape members' experience, knowledge, and ways of interacting" (Wood, 1999, p. 219). Representative theorist: Wood.

stranger in cross-cultural adaptation theory, the person who comes into a new and immersive cultural situation without much background for understanding that culture.

structural-functional tradition an approach in sociology and management studies that emphasizes how systems can be analyzed in terms of their structures, the functions performed by those structures, and the holistic ways in which subsystems depend upon each other. Structural-functionalism is often said to depend upon biological analogies of the ecological interdependence of living systems.

structuration/structuration theory describes how structures are more dynamic and fluid than has usually been thought in organizational theory. Structuration is the process by which structures define what actions are appropriate, but the acts themselves—as performed within organizations—constitute the structures. Structures are constituted by action, but it's equally true that "action is constituted structurally" (Giddens, 1993, p. 169). Representative theorist: Giddens. See *duality of structure.*

subjective knowledge in the Belenky et al. study of women's learning perspectives, this perspective describes women who elevate subjective or personally developed knowledge while rejecting the answers that external experts provide; this kind of learner claims to understand the world through experience or intuition rather than through rationality, analysis, or argumentation.

super media communication technologies and media that pervade an entire culture.

syllogism a form of logical reasoning that moves from major premise through minor premise to conclusion.

symbol a message that suggests, rather than verifies or mandates, the relations between things. When something symbolizes something else, it does not stand in one-to-one relation in the sense that when we see a symbol we know exactly what is being referred to. Rather, symbols are interpreted socially in different ways by different people.

symbolic convergence theory explains how communicators cooperatively build shared fantasy themes to account for and order their common experience. Representative theorist: Bormann.

symbolic interactionism accounts for the development of self through the processes of social communication and symbolization, and through the relation of self to mind and society. Representative theorists: Blumer; Goffman; Kuhn; Mead.

symmetrical interaction in relational/interactional theory, the attempt to match or mirror another's behavior. For example, someone yelling at you may evoke your symmetrical response of yelling back. See *complementary interaction.*

system See *general systems theory (GST).*

Tao Chinese concept often translated into English as "The Way." Tao is regarded philosophically as the natural flow of the world's processes. See *Taoist ethic.*

Taoist ethic a transactional philosophy that generally advocates allowing processes of communication to develop "naturally," avoiding interference or the artificial manipulation of results. Representative theorists: Lao Tzu; Chuang Tzu.

taxonomy a linguistic category system.

teamwork in impression management, this term refers to how people often cooperate with each other to present a coherent social performance, though not always through careful planning or obvious collusion.

technical dialogue in dialogic theory, interaction that appears to have a give-and-take quality but is actually designed to achieve a specified end through a form of objectifying communication.

teleological ethics/teleology a philosophy that relies on an assessment of consequences and the "greater good" for the greater number of people as a criterion for making ethical decisions; also known as a "consequentialist" position. Representative theorist: Mill.

theory a tentative but usually systematic explanation for a problematic situation; an educated guess open to change. See *formal theory.*

Theory X See *Theory Y.*

Theory Y a management theory that distrusts tactics that attempt to control workers and the assumption that people need to be coerced to work (characteristics of what McGregor calls an outmoded "Theory X"). Instead, proponents claim that people desire to work actively and in a self-directed way, and will do so enthusiastically if they are treated with respect. Representative theorist: McGregor.

third-culture perspective in cross-cultural adaptation theory, an "inclusive viewpoint" that combines home culture and host culture but, "at the same time, transcends both groups" (Kim, 1988, pp. 144–145).

threshold in action assembly theory, the level a record or memory must reach in order to be activated.

tightness syndrome categorization of cultures by their greater or lesser reliance on strict norms and roles for regulating behavior.

time-binding messages integrate issues and understandings of past and present.

transaction a relationship in which each party simultaneously defines, and is defined by, the other. Representative theorists: Dewey and Bentley.

trustworthiness a factor of credibility based on a communicator's honesty, accuracy, and lack of bias.

two-step flow theory asserts that media effects on audiences are not direct but are influenced by the interpersonal communication of opinion leaders. An extension of this theory, the multi-step flow theory, emphasizes the many complex levels of the process. Representative theorists: Katz and Lazarsfeld.

two-valued orientation the belief that a complex process can be reduced to one of two causes or explanations, usually a "good" explanation and a "bad" one. See *dogmatism*.

typology a category system; a set of conceptual labels that help us understand how a phenomenon can be organized.

uncertainty principle researchers studying phenomena directly can influence, through their presence or their methods, the processes they study. This renders the result of their observations "uncertain" to some extent, because it creates a paradox: If they weren't there, these same processes might have happened in different ways; but if they weren't there, they could have no knowledge of these differences. Representative theorist: Heisenberg.

uncertainty reduction theory assumes that a basic motivation for communicators is to use interpersonal information to predict communication outcomes more accurately. Representative theorist: Berger.

unfolding in dialogic ethical theory, an attitude that offers ("unfolds") one's own commitment or perspective to others without attempting to change or manipulate them. See *imposing*.

uses and gratifications theory explains how media audiences use media content for their own gratifications and purposes. Major theorists: Blumler and Katz.

utilitarianism a teleological position in which the most ethical choice is presumed to be the one that produces good consequences for the greatest number of people. Representative theorist: Mill. See *teleological ethics*.

valence in coordinated management of meaning (CMM) theory, the extent to which the actors like or dislike the episode that develops.

variable an object of study that can be present in varying degrees and therefore can be measured quantitatively.

veil of ignorance Rawls's ethical concept of justice and egalitarian fairness: Ethical evaluation and decision making should take place on one side of an imagined metaphorical "veil," while on the other side (unseen) are all the people and relations the decision could conceivably affect, regardless of race, class, gender, power, or other distinctions. The evaluator should assume that affected people are as likely to be friends as enemies, as likely to be rich as poor, and so on. This reminder—of not knowing the specific positive or negative outcomes for individual people—operates as a mental check on biases.

verbing describing processes by verbs, stressing their "changingness," rather than using a noun-label that turns a fluid process into a "thing." For example, some theorists would rather avoid reference to "communication" in many contexts, in favor of "communicating." Representative theorist: Dervin.

verification research contributes to theory by checking/testing the accuracy or truth of hypotheses and tentative answers.

virtual reality a computer-mediated method of generating seemingly immediate experiences that can be digitally packaged for later experience by communicators.

virtue ethics a philosophy that encourages communicators to adhere to the moral qualities that presumably enhance public life (e.g., justice, courage, gentleness, and wisdom). Representative theorist: Aristotle. See *golden mean, principle of*.

vocalics the study of how voice can create context for understanding words.

voice a metaphor for people's willingness to speak and be heard in social situations.

workplace democracy theorizing analyzes organizations as sites, or places, for democratic decision making in which workers can have a voice in the processes and criteria that govern the organization. See *learning organization*.

wu-wei Taoist idea, suggesting "effortless effort" or "not forcing" as ethical guidelines.

yang Taoist concept: the basically assertive, active, and strong forces of the world. See *yin*.

yin Taoist concept: the basically receptive, passive, and weak forces of the world. See *yang*.

References

Abelson, R. P. (1967). Modes of resolution of belief dilemmas. In M. Fishbein (Ed.), *Readings in attitude theory and measurement* (pp. 349–356). New York: Wiley.

Achebe, C. (1959/1969). *Things fall apart*. New York: Fawcett.

Acker, S. R. (1989). Designing communication systems for human systems: Values and assumptions of "social open architecture." In J. A. Anderson (Ed.), *Communication yearbook 12* (pp. 498–532). Newbury Park, CA: Sage.

Agar, M. (1994). *Language shock: Understanding the culture of conversation*. New York: William Morrow.

Allen, M. W., Gotcher, J. M., & Seibert, J. H. (1993). A decade of organizational communication research: Journal articles 1980–1991. In S. A. Deetz (Ed.), *Communication yearbook 16* (pp. 252–330). Newbury Park, CA: Sage.

Ames, A., Jr. (1951). Visual perception and the rotating trapezoidal window. *Psychological Monographs, 65,* 1–31.

Andersen, K., & Clevenger, T., Jr. (1963). A summary of experimental research in ethos. *Speech Monographs, 30,* 59–78.

Andersen, K. E. (1991). A history of communication ethics. In K. J. Greenberg (Ed.), *Conversations on communication ethics* (pp. 3–19). Norwood, NJ: Ablex.

Andersen, P. (1999). *Nonverbal communication: Forms and functions*. Mountain View, CA: Mayfield.

Anderson, R. (1982). Phenomenological dialogue, humanistic psychology, and pseudo-walls: A response and extension. *Western Journal of Speech Communication, 46,* 344–357.

Anderson, R. (1994). Anonymity, presence, and the dialogic self in a technological culture. In R. Anderson, K. N. Cissna, & R. C. Arnett (Eds.), *The reach of dialogue: Confirmation, voice, and community* (pp. 91–110). Cresskill, NJ: Hampton Press.

Anderson, R. (1997). The new digital presence: Listening, access, and computer-mediated life. In M. Purdy & D. Borisoff (Eds.), *Listening in everyday life: A personal and professional approach* (2nd ed., pp. 139–161). Lanham, MD: University Press of America.

Anderson, R. (2000). Public journalism as public dialogue. *Southern Communication Journal, 65,* 259–261.

Anderson, R., Cissna, K. N., & Arnett, R. C. (Eds.). (1994). *The reach of dialogue: Confirmation, voice, and community*. Cresskill, NJ: Hampton Press.

Anderson, R., & McClearey, K. (1984). Pointing toward a poetic of personal growth. *ReVision: A Journal of Consciousness and Change, 7,* 35–48.

Anzaldúa, G. (1987). *Borderlands/La frontera: The new mestiza*. San Francisco: Spinsters/Aunt Lute.

Anzaldúa, G. (1988). Tlilli, tlapalli: The path of the red and black ink. In R. Simonson & S. Walker (Eds.), *The Graywolf annual five: Multi-cultural literacy* (pp. 29–40). Saint Paul, MN: Graywolf.

Appiah, K. A. (1992). *In my father's house: Africa in the philosophy of culture*. New York: Oxford University Press.

Ardener, S. (1978). *Defining females: The nature of women in society*. New York: Wiley.

Aristotle. (1947). *Introduction to Aristotle* (R. McKeon, Ed.). New York: Modern Library.

Aristotle. (1954). *Rhetoric and poetics* (W. R. Roberts & I. Bywater, Trans.). New York: Modern Library.

Arnett, R. C. (1981). Toward a phenomenological dialogue. *Western Journal of Speech Communication, 45,* 201–212.

Arnett, R. C. (1991). The status of communication ethics scholarship in speech communication journals from 1915 to 1985. In K. J. Greenberg (Ed.), *Conversations on communication ethics* (pp. 55–72). Norwood, NJ: Ablex.

Arnett, R. C., & Nakagawa, G. (1983). The assumptive roots of empathic listening. *Communication Education, 32,* 368–378.

Asante, M. K. (1980). *Afrocentricity: The theory of social change.* Buffalo, NY: Amulefi.

Asante, M. K. (1987). *The Afrocentric idea.* Philadelphia: Temple University Press.

Ayer, A. J. (1955). What is communication? In A. Ayer et al., *Studies in communication.* London: Secker & Warburg.

Ayres, J. (1984). Four approaches to interpersonal communication. *Western Journal of Speech Communication, 48,* 408–440.

Bakhtin, M. M. (1981). *The dialogic imagination: Four essays* (C. Emerson & M. Holquist, Trans.). Austin: University of Texas Press.

Bakhtin, M. M. (1986). *Speech genres and other late essays* (C. Emerson & M. Holquist, Eds.; V. McGee, Trans.). Austin: University of Texas Press.

Barker, R. G. (1968). *Ecological psychology.* Stanford, CA: Stanford University Press.

Barnlund, D. C. (1970). A transactional model of communication. In K. K. Sereno & C. D. Mortensen (Eds.), *Foundations of communication theory* (pp. 83–102). New York: Harper.

Barnlund, D. C. (1989). *Communicative styles of Japanese and Americans: Images and realities.* Belmont, CA: Wadsworth.

Bateson, G. (1980). *Mind and nature: A necessary unity.* New York: Bantam.

Bateson, G. (1991). *A sacred unity: Further steps to an ecology of mind* (R. E. Donaldson, Ed.). New York: HarperCollins.

Bateson, G., & Jackson, D. (1964). Some varieties of pathogenic organization. In D. McRoach (Ed.), *Disorders of communication* (pp. 270–283). N.P.: Association for Research in Nervous and Mental Disease.

Bateson, M. C. (1984). *With a daughter's eye: A memoir of Margaret Mead and Gregory Bateson.* New York: Washington Square.

Bateson, M. C. (1990). *Composing a life.* New York: Plume.

Bauer, R. (1964). The obstinate audience. *American Psychologist, 19,* 319–328.

Baughman, R. G. (1989). Organizational communication. In S. S. King (Ed.), *Human communication as a field of study: Selected contemporary views* (pp. 135–150). Albany: State University of New York Press.

Bavelas, J. B. (1995). Quantitative versus qualitative? In W. Leeds-Hurwitz (Ed.), *Social approaches to communication* (pp. 49–62). New York: Guilford.

Baxter, L. A. (1988). A dialectical perspective on communication strategies in relationship development. In S. W. Duck (Ed.), *Handbook of personal relationships* (pp. 257–273). New York: Wiley.

Baxter, L. A. (1990). Dialectical contradictions in relationship development. *Journal of Social and Personal Relationships, 7,* 69–88.

Baxter, L. A., & Montgomery, B. M. (1996). *Relating: Dialogues and dialectics.* New York: Guilford.

Beatty, M. J., & McCroskey, J. C. (2000a). A few comments about communibiology and the nature/nurture question. *Communication Education, 49,* 25–28.

Beatty, M. J., & McCroskey, J. C. (2000b). Theory, scientific evidence, and the communibiological paradigm: Reflections of misguided criticism. *Communication Education, 49,* 36–44.

Becker, C. S. (1992). *Living and relating: An introduction to phenomenology.* Newbury Park, CA: Sage.

Belenky, M. F., Clinchy, B. M., Goldberger, N. R., & Tarule, J. M. (1986). *Women's ways of knowing: The development of self, voice, and mind.* New York: Basic Books.

Bellah, R. N., Madsen, R., Sullivan, W. M., Swidler, A., & Tipton, S. M. (1986). *Habits of the heart: Individualism and commitment in American life.* New York: Harper.

Benhabib, S. (1990). Models of public space: Hannah Arendt, the liberal tradition, and Jurgen Habermas. In C. Calhoun (Ed.), *Habermas and the public sphere* (pp. 73–98). Cambridge, MA: MIT Press.

Benhabib, S. (1992). *Situating the self: Gender, community, and postmodernism in contemporary ethics.* New York: Routledge.

Beniger, J. R. (1990). Who are the most important theorists of communication? *Communication Research, 17,* 698–715.

Berelson, B., & Steiner, G. A. (1964). *Human behavior: An inventory of scientific findings.* New York: Harcourt.

Berger, A. A. (1982). *Media analysis techniques.* Beverly Hills, CA: Sage.

Berger, C. R. (1977). The covering law perspective as a theoretical basis for the study of human communication. *Communication Quarterly, 25,* 7–18.

Berger, C. R. (1998). Big questions and communication theory: Finding the cure for communication. In J. S. Trent (Ed.), *Communication: Views from the helm for the 21st century* (pp. 13–17). Boston: Allyn & Bacon.

Berger, C. R., & Bradac, J. J. (1982). *Language and social knowledge: Uncertainty in interpersonal relations.* London: Edward Arnold.

Berger, C. R., & Calabrese, R. J. (1975). Some explorations in initial interaction and beyond: Toward a developmental theory of interpersonal communication. *Human Communication Research, 1,* 99–112.

Berger, P., Berger, B., & Kellner, H. (1974). *The homeless mind: Modernization and consciousness.* New York: Vintage.

Berger, P., & Luckmann, T. (1966). *The social construction of reality: A treatise in the sociology of knowledge.* New York: Doubleday.

Bergmann, G. (1957). *Philosophy of science.* Madison: University of Wisconsin Press.

Berlo, D. K. (1960). *The process of communication: An introduction to theory and practice.* New York: Holt.

Bernstein, B. (1960). Language and social class. *British Journal of Sociology, 11,* 271–276.

Bertalanffy, L. von (1968). *General systems theory: Foundations, development, applications.* New York: George Braziller.

Birdwhistell, R. L. (1970). *Kinesics and context: Essays on body motion communication.* Philadelphia: University of Pennsylvania Press.

Blair, C., Jeppeson, M. S., & Pucci, E., Jr. (1994). Public memorializing in postmodernity: The Vietnam Veterans Memorial as prototype. In W. L. Nothstine, C. Blair, & G. A. Copeland (Eds.), *Critical questions: Invention, creativity, and the criticism of discourse and media* (pp. 350–382). New York: St. Martin's Press.

Blakemore, C., & Greenfield, S. (Eds.) (1987). *Mindwaves: Thoughts on intelligence, identity and consciousness.* Oxford, UK: Basil Blackwell.

Blau, P. M. (1956). *Bureaucracy in modern society.* New York: Random House.

Blau, P. M. (1963). *The dynamics of bureaucracy: A study of interpersonal relationships in two government agencies* (Rev. ed.). Chicago: University of Chicago Press.

Blau, P. M. (1964). *Exchange and power in social life.* New York: Wiley.

Blum, A., & McHugh, P. (1984). *Self-reflection in the arts and sciences.* Atlantic Highlands, NJ: Humanities.

Blumer, H. (1969). *Symbolic interactionism: Perspective and method.* Englewood Cliffs, NJ: Prentice-Hall.

Blumler, J. G. (1985). The social character of media gratifications. In K. E. Rosengren, L. A. Wenner, & P. Palmgreen (Eds.), *Media gratifications research: Current perspectives* (pp. 41–59). Beverly Hills, CA: Sage.

Blumler, J. G., & Katz, E. (Eds.) (1974). *The uses of mass communications: Current perspectives on gratifications research.* Beverly Hills, CA: Sage.

Bohm, D. (1980). *Wholeness and the implicate order.* London: Routledge & Kegan Paul.

Bok, S. (1979). *Lying: Moral choice in public and private life.* New York: Vintage.

Bok, S. (1983). *Secrets: On the ethics of concealment and revelation.* New York: Random House.

Bolles, E. B. (1991). *A second way of knowing: The riddle of human perception.* Englewood Cliffs, NJ: Prentice-Hall.

Booth, W. C. (1974). *Modern dogma and the rhetoric of assent.* Chicago: University of Chicago Press.

Booth, W. C. (1990). *The vocation of a teacher. Rhetorical occasions, 1967–1988.* Chicago: University of Chicago Press.

Bormann, E. G. (1972). Fantasy and rhetorical vision: The rhetorical criticism of social reality. *Quarterly Journal of Speech, 58,* 396–407.

Bormann, E. G. (1983). The symbolic convergence theory of communication and the creation, raising, and sustaining of public consciousness. In J. I. Sisco (Ed.), *The Jensen lectures: Contemporary communiration studies* (pp. 71–90). Tampa: University of South Florida.

Bormann, E. G. (1989). *Communication theory.* Salem, WI: Sheffield.

Bormann, E. G., Knutson, R. L., & Musoff, K. (1997). Why do people share fantasies? An empirical investigation of a basic tenet of the symbolic convergence communication theory. *Communication Studies, 48,* 254–276.

Borton, T. (1970). *Reach, touch, and teach: Student concerns and process education.* New York: McGraw-Hill.

Boulding, K. E. (1956). *The image: Knowledge in life and society.* Ann Arbor: University of Michigan Press.

Bozarth, J. D., & Brodley, B. T. (1986). Client-centered psychotherapy: A statement. *Person-Centered Review, 3,* 262–271.

Brand, S. (1988). *The media lab: Inventing the future at MIT.* New York: Penguin.

Brehm, J. W. (1966). *A theory of psychological reactance.* New York: Academic.

Bross, I. D. J. (1970). Models. In J. H. Campbell & H. W. Hepler (Eds.), *Dimensions in communication: Readings* (2nd ed., pp. 11–27). Belmont, CA: Wadsworth.

Brown, C. T., & Keller, P. W. (1979). *Monologue to dialogue: An exploration of interpersonal communication* (2nd ed.). Englewood Cliffs, NJ: Prentice-Hall.

Brown, J. A. C. (1963). *Techniques of persuasion: From propaganda to brainwashing.* Baltimore: Penguin.

Brown, R. (1973). *Rules and laws in sociology.* Chicago: Aldine.

Brown, R. H. (1977). *A poetic for sociology: Toward a logic of discovery for the human sciences.* Cambridge: Cambridge University Press.

Brown, R. H. (1987). *Society as text: Essays on rhetoric, reason, and reality.* Chicago: University of Chicago Press.

Bruner, J. (1979). *On knowing: Essays for the left hand* (Expanded ed.). Cambridge, MA: Belknap.

Bruner, J. (1983). *In search of mind: Essays in autobiography.* New York: Harper.

Bruner, J. (1986). *Actual minds, possible worlds.* Cambridge, MA: Harvard University Press.

Bruner, J. (1990). *Acts of meaning.* Cambridge, MA: Harvard University Press.

Bruner, J. S. (1960). *The process of education.* New York: Vintage.

Bruner, J. S., & Goodman, C. D. (1947). Value and need as organizing factors in perception. *Journal of Abnormal and Social Psychology, 42,* 33–44.

Buber, M. (1957). *Pointing the way* (M. S. Friedman, Trans.). New York: Harper Torchbooks.

Buber, M. (1958). *I and thou* (R. G. Smith, Trans.). New York: Scribner.

Buber, M. (1965a). *Between man and man* (R. G. Smith, Trans.). New York: Macmillan.

Buber, M. (1965b). *The knowledge of man: A philosophy of the interhuman* (M. Friedman, Trans.). New York: Harper.

Burgoon, J. K. (1983). Nonverbal violations of expectations. In J. M. Wiemann & R. B. Harrison (Eds.), *Nonverbal interaction* (pp. 77–111). Beverly Hills, CA: Sage.

Burgoon, J. K., Buller, D. B., & Woodall, W. G. (1989). *Nonverbal communication: The unspoken dialogue.* New York: Harper.

Burgoon, J. K., & Dillman, L. (1995). Gender, immediacy, and nonverbal communication. In P. J. Kalbfleisch & M. J. Cody (Eds.), *Gender, power, and communication in human relationships* (pp. 63–82). Hillsdale, NJ: Lawrence Erlbaum.

Burgoon, J. K., & Hale, J. L. (1984). The fundamental topoi of relational communication. *Communication Monographs, 51,* 193–214.

Burgoon, J. K., & Jones, S. B. (1976). Toward a theory of personal space expectations and their violations. *Human Communication Research, 2,* 131–146.

Burgoon, J. K., & Walther, J. (1990). Nonverbal expectancies and the evaluative consequences of violations. *Human Communication Research, 17,* 232–265.

Burgoon, M., & Miller, G. R. (1990). Paths. *Communication Monographs, 57,* 152–160.

Burke, K. (1967). Rhetoric—Old and new. In M. Steinmann, Jr. (Ed.), *New rhetorics* (pp. 60–76). New York: Scribner.

Burke, K. (1969). *A rhetoric of motives.* Berkeley: University of California Press.

Burns, E. (1972). *Theatricality: A study of convention in the theatre and in social life.* New York: Harper Torchbooks.

Burrell, G., & Morgan, G. (1979). *Sociological paradigms and organizational analysis: Elements of the sociology of corporate life.* London: Heinemann.

Bynner, W. (1962). *The way of life according to Laotzu: An American version.* New York: Capricorn. (Original work published 1944)

Campbell, D. T. (1969). Ethnocentrism of disciplines and the fish-scale model of omniscience. In M. Sherif & C. W. Sherif (Eds.),

Interdisciplinary relationships in the social sciences (pp. 328–348). Chicago: Aldine.

Campbell, D. T. (1986). Science's social system of validity-enhancing collective belief change and the problems of the social sciences. In D. W. Fiske & R. A. Schweder (Eds.), *Metatheory in social science: Pluralisms and subjectivities* (pp. 108–135). Chicago: University of Chicago Press.

Carbaugh, D. (1989). *Talking American: Cultural discourses on "Donahue."* Norwood, NJ: Ablex.

Carey, J. W. (1989). *Communication as culture: Essays on media and society.* Boston: Unwin Hyman.

Carpenter, E. (1960). The new languages. In E. Carpenter & M. McLuhan (Eds.), *Explorations in communication* (pp. 162–179). Boston: Beacon.

Chaffee, S. H., & Rogers, E. M. (1997). *The beginnings of communication study in America: A personal memoir by Wilbur Schramm.* Thousand Oaks, CA: Sage.

Charity, A. (1995). *Doing public journalism.* New York: Guilford.

Chen, G.-M., & Starosta, W. J. (1996). Intercultural communication competence: A synthesis. In B. Burleson (Ed.), *Communication yearbook 19* (pp. 353–383). Thousand Oaks, CA: Sage.

Cheney, G. (1995). Democracy in the workplace: Theory and practice from the communication perspective. *Journal of Applied Communication Research, 23,* 167–200.

Cheney, G., Straub, J., Speirs-Glebe, L., Stohl, C., DeGooyer, D., Jr., Whalen, S., Garvin-Doxas, K., & Carlone, D. (1998). Democracy, participation, and communication at work: A multidisciplinary review. In M. E. Roloff (Ed.), *Communication yearbook 21* (pp. 35–91). Thousand Oaks, CA: Sage.

Cheng, C.-Y. (1987). Chinese philosophy and contemporary human communication theory. In D. L. Kincaid (Ed.), *Communication theory: Eastern and Western perspectives* (pp. 23–43). San Diego: Academic.

Chesebro, J. W., & Bonsall, D. G. (1989). *Computer-mediated communication: Human relationships in a computerized world.* Tuscaloosa, AL: University of Alabama Press.

Christians, C. G., Ferré, J. P., & Fackler, P. M. (1993). *Good news: Social ethics and the press.* New York: Oxford University Press.

Christians, C. G., Rotzoll, K. B., & Fackler, M. (1991). *Media ethics: Cases and moral reasoning* (3rd ed.). New York: Longman.

Cissna, K. N., & Anderson, R. (1990). The contributions of Carl R. Rogers to a philosophical praxis of dialogue. *Western Journal of Speech Communication, 54,* 125–147.

Cissna, K. N., Cox, D. E., & Bochner, A. P. (1990). The dialectic of marital and parental relationships within the stepfamily. *Communication Monographs, 57,* 4–61.

Cissna, K. N. L., & Sieburg, E. (1981). Patterns of interactional confirmation and disconfirmation. In C. Wilder-Mott & J. Weaklind (Eds.), *Rigor and imagination* (pp. 230–239). New York: Praeger.

Clark, G. (1990). *Dialogue, dialectic, and conversation: A social perspective on the function of writing.* Carbondale: Southern Illinois University Press.

Clark, K., & Holquist, M. (1984). *Mikhail Bakhtin.* Cambridge, MA: Harvard University Press.

Cody, M. J., & McLaughlin, M. L. (1985). The situation as a construct in interpersonal communication research. In M. L. Knapp & G. R. Miller (Eds.), *Handbook of interpersonal communication* (pp. 273–312). Beverly Hills, CA: Sage.

Cohen, H. (1994). *The history of speech communication: The emergence of a discipline, 1914–1945.* Annandale, VA: Speech Communication Association.

Coles, R. (1989). *The call of stories: Teaching and the moral imagination.* Boston: Houghton Mifflin.

Collins, P. H. (1991). *Black feminist thought: Knowledge, consciousness, and the politics of empowerment.* New York: Routledge.

Condit, C. (1993). The critic as empath: Moving away from totalizing theory. *Western Journal of Communication, 57,* 178–190.

Condit, C. M. (1989). The rhetorical limits of polysemy. *Critical Studies in Mass Communication, 6,* 103–122.

Condit, C. M. (2000a). Culture and biology in human communication: Toward a multi-causal model. *Communication Education, 49,* 7–24.

Condit, C. M. (2000b). Toward new "sciences" of human behavior. *Communication Education, 49,* 29–35.

Cooper, J. C. (1972). *Taoism: The way of the mystic.* New York: Samuel Weiser.

Corsini, R. J. (Ed.). (1984). *Encyclopedia of psychology* (Vol. 1). New York: Wiley.

Cottone, R. R. (1992). *Theories and paradigms of counseling and psychotherapy.* Boston: Allyn & Bacon.

Coughlin, E. K. (1996, February 16). Not out of Africa. *Chronicle of Higher Education,* pp. A6, A7.

Cragan, J., & Shields, D. (1981). *Applied communication research: A dramatistic approach.* Prospect Heights, IL: Waveland.

Craig, R. T. (1995). Review of E. V. Rogers, *A history of communication study: A biographical approach,* and H. Cohen, *The history of speech communication: The emergence of a discipline, 1914–1945. Communication Theory, 5,* 178–184.

Craig, R. T., & Carlone, D. A. (1998). Growth and transformation of communication studies in U.S. higher education: Towards reinterpretation. *Communication Education, 47,* 67–81.

Crawford, L. (1996). Everyday Tao: Conversation and contemplation. *Communication Studies, 47,* 25–34.

Cronen, V. E. (1991). Coordinated management of meaning theory and post enlightenment ethics. In K. G. Greenberg (Ed.), *Conversations on communication ethics* (pp. 21–53). Albany: State University of New York Press.

Cronen, V. E. (1998). Communication theory for the twenty-first century: Cleaning up the wreckage of the psychology project. In J. S. Trent (Ed.), *Communication: Views from the helm for the 21st century* (pp. 18–38). Boston: Allyn & Bacon.

Cronen, V. E., Pearce, W. B., & Harris, L. M. (1982). The coordinated management of meaning: A theory of communication. In F. E. X. Dance (Ed.), *Human communication theory* (pp. 61–89). New York: Harper.

Cushman, D. P. (1977). The rules perspective as a theoretical basis for the study of human communication. *Communication Quarterly, 25,* 30–45.

Cushman, D. P., & Cahn, D. D., Jr. (1985). *Communication in interpersonal relationships.* Albany: State University of New York Press.

Cuzzort, R. P., & King, E. W. (1989). *Twentieth-century social thought* (4th ed.). Fort Worth: Holt.

Czarniawska, B. (1997). *Narrating the organization: Dramas of institutional identity.* Chicago: University of Chicago Press.

Daly, M. (1973). *Beyond God the father.* Boston: Beacon.

Dance, F. E. X. (1967). Toward a theory of human communication. In F. E. X. Dance (Ed.), *Human communication theory: Original essays* (pp. 288–309). New York: Holt.

Dance, F. E. X. (1982). A speech theory of human communication. In F. E. X. Dance (Ed.), *Human communication theory* (pp. 120–146). New York: Harper.

Dance, F. E. X. (1989). Ong's voice: "I," the oral intellect, you, and we. *Text and Performance Quarterly, 9,* 185–198.

Dance, F. E. X., & Larson, C. E. (1976). *The functions of human communication: A theoretical approach.* New York: Holt.

Darnell, D. K. (1984, October). Communication. *Spectra, 20,* 11.

Davidson, M. (1983). *Uncommon sense: The life and thought of Ludwig von Bertalanffy, father of general systems theory.* Los Angeles: Tarcher.

Davis, O. (1969). The English language is my enemy. In N. Postman, C. Weingartner, & T. P. Moran (Eds.), *Language in America* (pp. 73–79). New York: Pegasus.

Dayan, D., & Katz, E. (1992). *Media events: The live broadcasting of history.* Cambridge, MA: Harvard University Press.

Deal, T. E., & Kennedy, A. A. (1982). *Corporate cultures: The rites and rituals of corporate life.* Reading, MA: Addison-Wesley.

Deetz, S. (1982). Hermeneutics and research in interpersonal communication. In J. J. Pilotta (Ed.), *Interpersonal communication: Essays in phenomenology and hermeneutics* (pp. 1–14). Washington, DC: University Press of America.

Deetz, S. A. (1992). *Democracy in an age of corporate colonization.* Albany: State University of New York Press.

Deetz, S. A. (1995). *Transforming communication, transforming business: Building responsive and responsible workplaces.* Creskill, NJ: Hampton Press.

Delia, J. G. (1976). A constructivist analysis of the concept of credibility. *Quarterly Journal of Speech, 62,* 361–375.

Delia, J. G. (1977). Constructivism and the study of human communication. *Quarterly Journal of Speech, 63,* 66–83.

Delia, J. G. (1987). Communication research: A history. In C. R. Berger & S. H. Chaffee (Eds.), *Handbook of communication science* (pp. 20–98). Newbury Park, CA: Sage.

Delia, J. G., O'Keefe, B. J., & O'Keefe, D. J. (1982). The constructivist approach to communication. In F. E. X. Dance (Ed.), *Human communication theory* (pp. 147–191). New York: Harper.

Denzin, N. K. (1992). *Symbolic interactionism and cultural studies: The politics of interpretation.* Oxford, UK: Basil Blackwell.

Derber, C. (1979). *The pursuit of attention: Power and individualism in everyday life.* Oxford: Oxford University Press.

Derrida, J. (1982). *Margins of philosophy.* Chicago: University of Chicago Press.

Dervin, B. (1993). Verbing communication: Mandate for disciplinary invention. *Journal of Communication, 43*(3), 45–54.

Deutscher, I. (1973). *What we say/what we do: Sentiments and acts.* Glenview, IL: Scott, Foresman.

DeVito, J. A. (1986). *The communication handbook: A dictionary.* New York: Harper.

Dewey, J. (1927). *The public and its problems.* Denver: Alan Swallow.

Dewey, J. (1933). *How we think.* Boston: Heath.

Dewey, J. (1934). *Art as experience.* New York: Putnam.

Dewey, J., & Bentley, A. F. (1949). *Knowing and the known.* Boston: Beacon.

Dillard, A. (1975). *Pilgrim at Tinker Creek.* New York: Bantam.

Dillon, J. T. (1990). *The practice of questioning.* London: Routledge.

Douglas, M. (1975). *Implicit meanings: Essays in anthropology.* London: Routledge & Kegan Paul.

Druckman, D., Rozelle, R. M., & Baxter, J. C. (1982). *Nonverbal communication: Survey, theory, and research.* Beverly Hills, CA: Sage.

Dubin, R. (1969). *Theory building: A practical guide to the construction and testing of theoretical models.* New York: Free Press.

Duncan, H. D. (1962). *Communication and social order.* London: Oxford University Press.

Eco, U. (1976). *A theory of semiotics.* Bloomington: Indiana University Press.

Edelman, M. (1964). *The symbolic uses of politics.* Urbana: University of Illinois Press.

Eisenberg, E. M. (1994). Dialogue as democratic discourse: Affirming Harrison. In S. A. Deetz (Ed.), *Communication yearbook 17* (pp. 275–284). Thousand Oaks, CA: Sage.

Eisenberg, E. M., & Goodall, H. L. Jr. (1997). *Organizational communication: Balancing creativity and constraint* (2nd ed.). New York: St. Martin's Press.

Elbow, P. (1973). *Writing without teachers.* London: Oxford University Press.

Ellul, J. (1964). *The technological society.* (J. Wilkinson, Trans.). New York: Vintage.

Ellul, J. (1985). *The humiliation of the word.* (J. M. Hanks, Trans.). Grand Rapids, MI: William B. Eerdmans.

Ethics of young decried. (1992, November 26). *St. Louis Post-Dispatch,* p. 8D.

Etzioni, A. (1993). *The spirit of community: Rights, responsibilities, and the communitarian agenda.* New York: Crown.

Farrell, T. B. (1987). Beyond science: Humanities contributions to communication theory. In C. R. Berger & S. H. Chaffee (Eds.), *Handbook of communication science* (pp. 123–142). Newbury Park, CA: Sage.

Farrell, T. J. (2000). *Walter Ong's contributions to cultural studies: The phenomenology of the word and I-Thou communication.* Creskill, NJ: Hampton Press.

Fay, B. (1996). *Contemporary philosophy of social science: A multicultural approach.* Oxford, UK: Basil Blackwell.

Ferguson, M., & Golding, P. (Eds.). (1997). *Cultural studies in question.* Thousand Oaks, CA: Sage.

Ferrarotti, F. (1988). *The end of conversation: The impact of mass media on modern society.* New York: Greenwood.

Festinger, L. (1957). *A theory of cognitive dissonance.* Stanford, CA: Stanford University Press.

Fischler, A. (1989, August 2). From the inferno: Reflections on a sojourn in a communication program. *Chronicle of Higher Education,* p. A28.

Fisher, B. A. (1978). *Perspectives on human communication.* New York: Macmillan.

Fisher, B. A. (1982). The pragmatic perspective of human communication: A view from system theory. In F. E. X. Dance (Ed.), *Human communication theory* (pp. 192–219). New York: Harper.

Fisher, W. R. (1987). *Human communication as narration: Toward a philosophy of reason, value, and action.* Columbia: University of South Carolina Press.

Flew, A. (1984). *A dictionary of philosophy* (Rev. 2nd ed.). New York: St. Martin's.

Frank, F., & Anshen, F. (1983). *Language and the sexes.* Albany: State University of New York Press.

Friedman, M. (1974). *Touchstones of reality: Existential trust and the community of peace.* New York: Dutton.

Friedman, M. S. (1960). *Martin Buber: The life of dialogue* (2nd ed.). New York: Harper Torchbooks.

Friedman, M. S. (1981–1983). *Martin Buber's life and work* (Vols. 1–3). New York: Dutton.

Friedrich, G. W., & Boileau, D. M. (1999). The communication discipline. In A. Vangelisti, J. A. Daly, & G. W. Friedrich (Eds.), *Teaching communication: Theory, research, and methods* (2nd ed., pp. 3–13). Mahwah, NJ: Lawrence Erlbaum.

Fry, D. (1977). *Homo loquens: Man as a talking animal.* Cambridge, UK: Cambridge University Press.

Gadamer, H.-G. (1982). *Truth and method* (2nd ed., G. Barden & J. Cumming, Trans.). New York: Crossroad.

Garfinkel, H. (1967). *Studies in ethnomethodology.* Cambridge: Polity Press.

Garko, M. G. (1990). Perspectives on and conceptualizations of compliance and compliance-gaining. *Communication Quarterly, 38,* 138–157.

Gates, H. L., Jr. (1992). *Loose canons: Notes on the culture wars.* New York: Oxford University Press.

Geertz, C. (1983). *Local knowledge: Further essays on interpretive anthropology.* New York: Basic Books.

Geist, P., & Dreyer, J. (1993). The demise of dialogue: A critique of medical encounter ideology. *Western Journal of Communication, 57,* 233–246.

Geller, L. (1982). The failure of self-actualization theory: A critique of Carl Rogers and Abraham Maslow. *Journal of Humanistic Psychology, 22,* 56–73.

Gerbner, G. (1970). Cultural indicators: The case of violence in television drama. *Annals of the American Association of Political and Social Science, 338,* 69–81.

Gerbner, G. (1990). Epilogue: Advancing on the path of righteousness (maybe). In N. Signorielli & M. Morgan (Eds.), *Cultivation analysis: New directions in media effects research.* Newbury Park, CA: Sage.

Gerbner, G., Gross, L. P., Morgan, M., & Signorielli, N. (1980). The "mainstreaming" of America: Violence profile no. 11. *Journal of Communication, 30,* 10–29.

Gergen, K. G. (1969). *The psychology of behavior exchange.* Reading, MA: Addison-Wesley.

Giddens, A. (1984). *The constitution of society: Outline of the theory of structuration.* Berkeley, CA: University of California Press.

Giddens, A. (1993). *New rules of sociological method* (2nd ed.). Stanford, CA: Stanford University Press.

Gilligan, C. (1982). *In a different voice: Psychological theory and women's development.* Cambridge, MA: Harvard University Press.

Glatzer, N. N. (1966). Preface. In M. Buber, *The way of response: Martin Buber* (N. N. Glatzer, Ed.). New York: Schocken.

Glendon, M. A. (1991). *Rights talk: The impoverishment of political discourse.* New York: Free Press.

Goffman, E. (1959). *The presentation of self in everyday life.* New York: Doubleday Anchor.

Goffman, E. (1974). *Frame analysis: An essay on the organization of experience.* New York: Harper Colophon.

Goffman, E. (1981). *Forms of talk.* Philadelphia: University of Pennsylvania Press.

Goldenson, R. M. (Ed.). (1984). *Longman dictionary of psychology and psychiatry.* New York: Longman.

Goldner, V., Penn, P., Sheinberg, M., & Walker, G. (1990). Love and violence: Gender paradoxes in volatile attachments. *Family Process, 29,* 343–364.

Goodall, H. L., Jr. (1991). *Living in the rock 'n' roll mystery: Reading context, self, and others as clues.* Carbondale: Southern Illinois University Press.

Gordon, W. T. (1997). *Marshall McLuhan: Escape into understanding: A biography.* New York: Basic Books.

Goss, B. (1989). *The psychology of human communication.* Prospect Heights, IL: Waveland.

Gouran, D. S. (1990). Speech communication after seventy-five years: Issues and prospects. In G. M. Phillips & J. T. Wood (Eds.), *Speech communication: Essays to commemorate the 75th anniversary of the Speech Communication Association* (pp. 1–32). Carbondale: Southern Illinois University Press.

Gozzi, R., Jr. (1999). *The power of metaphor in the age of electronic media.* Cresskill, NJ: Hampton Press.

Gozzi, R., Jr., & Haynes, W. L. (1992). Electric media and electric epistemology: Empathy at a distance. *Critical Studies in Mass Communication, 9,* 217–228.

Gray, J. (1992). *Men are from Mars, women are from Venus.* New York: HarperCollins.

Greene, J. O. (1984). A cognitive approach to human communication: An action assembly theory. *Communication Monographs, 51,* 289–306.

Greene, J. O. (1989). Action assembly theory: Metatheoretical commitments, theoretical propositions, and empirical applications. In B. Dervin, L. Grossberg, B. J. O'Keefe, & E. Wartella (Eds.), *Rethinking communication: Vol. 2. Paradigm exemplars* (pp. 117–128). Newbury Park, CA: Sage.

Greene, J. O. (1997). A second generation action assembly theory. In J. O. Greene (Ed.), *Message production: Advances in communication theory* (pp. 151–170). Mahwah, NJ: Lawrence Erlbaum.

Gregory, R., & Miller, J. (1983). Visual perception and illusions: A dialogue with Richard Gregory. In J. Miller, *States of mind* (pp. 42–64). New York: Pantheon.

Griffin, S. (1992). *A chorus of stones: The private life of war.* New York: Anchor.

Gronbeck, B., Farrell, T. J., & Soukup, P. A. (Eds.). (1991). *Media, consciousness, and culture: Explorations of Walter Ong's thought.* Newbury Park, CA: Sage.

Grossberg, L. (1984). Strategies of Marxist cultural interpretation. *Critical Studies in Mass Communication, 1,* 392–421.

Grossberg, L. (1993). Can cultural studies find true happiness in communication? *Journal of Communication, 43*(4), 89–97.

Grossberg, L., Nelson, C., & Treichler, P. (Eds.). (1992). *Cultural studies.* New York: Routledge.

Gudykunst, W. B. (1997). Cultural variability in communication: An introduction. *Communication Research, 24,* 327–348.

Gudykunst, W. B., & Kim, Y. Y. (1984). *Communicating with strangers: An approach to intercultural communication.* Reading, MA: Addison-Wesley.

Gunaratne, S. A. (1998). Old wine in a new bottle: Public journalism, developmental journalism, and social responsibility. In M. E. Roloff (Ed.), *Communication yearbook 21.* Thousand Oaks, CA: Sage.

Gurwitsch, A. (1974). *Phenomenology and the theory of science.* Evanston, IL: Northwestern University Press.

Habermas, J. (1979). *Communication and the evolution of society* (T. McCarthy, Trans.). Boston: Beacon.

Habermas, J. (1990). *Moral consciousness and communicative action* (C. Lenhardt & S. W. Nicholsen, Trans.). Cambridge, MA: MIT Press.

Habermas, J. (1992). *Autonomy and solidarity: Interviews with Jurgen Habermas* (Rev. ed., P. Dews, Ed.). London: Verso.

Haiman, F. S. (1981). *Speech and law in a free society.* Chicago: University of Chicago Press.

Haiman, F. S. (1991). Majorities versus the First Amendment: Rationality on trial. *Communication Monographs, 58,* 327–335.

Hall, B. J. (1997). Culture, ethics, and communication. In F. L. Casmir (Ed.), *Ethics in intercultural and international communication* (pp. 11–41). Mahwah, NJ: Lawrence Erlbaum.

Hall, E. T. (1959). *The silent language.* New York: Doubleday.

Hall, E. T. (1966). *The hidden dimension.* Garden City, NY: Anchor.

Hall, E. T. (1977). *Beyond culture.* Garden City, NY: Anchor.

Hall, E. T. (1992). *An anthropology of everyday life: An autobiography.* New York: Doubleday.

Hall, E. T., & Hall, M. R. (1987). *Hidden differences: Doing business with the Japanese.* New York: Anchor.

Hall, S. (1989). Ideology and communication theory. In B. Dervin, L. Grossberg, B. J. O'Keefe, & E. Wartella (Eds.), *Rethinking communication: Vol. 1. Paradigm issues* (pp. 40–52). Newbury Park, CA: Sage.

Hall, S. (1992). Cultural studies and its theoretical legacies. In L. Grossberg, C. Nelson, & P. Treichler (Eds.), *Cultural studies* (pp. 277–294). New York: Routledge.

Hall, S. (1996). On postmodernism and articulation. (An interview with Stuart Hall; edited by L. Grossberg). In D. Morley & K.-H. Chen (Eds.), *Stuart Hall: Critical dialogues in cultural studies* (pp. 131–150). New York: Routledge.

Haney, W. V. (1973). *Communication and organizational behavior: Text and cases* (3rd ed.). Homewood, IL: Irwin.

Hanson, N. (1958). *Patterns of discovery.* Cambridge, MA: Harvard University Press.

Hardison, O. B., Jr. (1972). *Toward freedom and dignity: The humanities and the idea of humanity.* Baltimore: Johns Hopkins University Press.

Hardt, H. (1992). *Critical communication studies: Communication, history, and theory in America.* London: Routledge.

Hardt, H. (1997). The quest for public journalism. *Journal of Communication, 47*(3), 102–109.

Harper, N. (1978). *Human communication theory: The history of a paradigm.* Rochelle Park, NJ: Hayden.

Harré, R., & Gillett, G. (1994). *The discursive mind.* Thousand Oaks, CA: Sage.

Harrison, T. M. (1994). Communication and interdependence in democratic organizations. In S. A. Deetz (Ed.), *Communication yearbook 17* (pp. 247–274). Thousand Oaks, CA: Sage.

Hart, R. P., & Burks, D. M. (1972). Rhetorical sensitivity and social interaction. *Speech Monographs, 39,* 75–91.

Hasnain, I. (1988). Communication: An Islamic approach. In W. Dissanayake (Ed.), *Communication theory: The Asian perspective* (pp. 183–189). Singapore: Asian Mass Communication Research and Information Centre.

Hauerwas, S. (1981). *A community of character: Toward a constructive Christian social ethic.* Notre Dame, IN: University of Notre Dame Press.

Hauser, G. A. (1986). *Introduction to rhetorical theory.* New York: Harper.

Havelock, E. A. (1986). *The muse learns to write: Reflections on orality and literacy from antiquity to the present.* New Haven, CT: Yale University Press.

Hawkins, R. P., Wicmann, J. M., & Pingree, S. (Eds.). (1988). *Advancing communication science: Merging mass and interpersonal processes.* Newbury Park, CA: Sage.

Hawley, A. H. (1986). *Human ecology: A theoretical essay.* Chicago: University of Chicago Press.

Hayakawa, S. I. (1941). *Language in action.* New York: Harcourt.

Heider, F. (1958). *The psychology of interpersonal relations.* New York: Wiley.

Heim, M. (1987). *Electric language: A philosophical study of word processing.* New Haven, CT: Yale University Press.

Heim, M. (1993). *The metaphysics of virtual reality.* New York: Oxford University Press.

Heisel, A. D., McCroskey, J. C., & Richmond, V.P. (1999). Testing theoretical relationships and nonrelationships of genetically-based predictors: Getting started with communibiology. *Communication Research Reports, 16,* 1–9.

Heisenberg, W. (1958). *Physics and philosophy.* New York: Harper.

Henley, N. M. (1977). *Body politics: Power, sex, and nonverbal communication.* Englewood Cliffs, NJ: Prentice-Hall.

Henley, N. M. (1995). Body politics revisited: What do we know today? In P. J. Kalbfleisch & M. J. Cody (Eds.), *Gender, power, and communication in human relationships* (pp. 27–62). Hillsdale, NJ: Lawrence Erlbaum.

Hickman, C. A., & Kuhn, M. H. (1956). *Individuals, groups, and economic behavior.* New York: Dryden.

Hoggart, R. (1972). *On culture and communication.* New York: Oxford University Press.

Hollinger, R. (Ed.). (1985). *Hermeneutics and praxis.* Notre Dame, IN: University of Notre Dame Press.

Holquist, M. (1990). *Dialogism: Bakhtin and his world.* London: Routledge.

Homans, G. C. (1961). *Social behavior: Its elementary forms.* New York: Harcourt.

Horton, D., & Wohl, R. R. (1956). Mass communication and para-social interaction: Observations on intimacy at a distance. *Psychiatry, 19,* 215–229.

Hovland, C. I., Janis, I. L., & Kelley, H. H. (1953). *Communication and persuasion.* New Haven, CT: Yale University Press.

Hurt, H. T., Scott, M. D., & McCroskey, J. C. (1978). *Communication in the classroom.* Reading, MA: Addison-Wesley.

Infante, D. A. (1980). Verbal plans: A conceptualization and investigation. *Communication Quarterly, 28,* 3–10.

Infante, D. A., Parker, K. R., Clarke, C. H., Wilson, L., & Nathu, I. A. (1983). A comparison of factor and functional approaches to source credibility. *Communication Quarterly, 31,* 43–48.

Infante, D. A., Rancer, A. S., & Womack, D. F. (1990). *Building communication theory.* Prospect Heights, IL: Waveland.

Innis, H. A. (1951). *The bias of communication.* Toronto: University of Toronto Press.

James, W. (1896). *Principles of psychology.* New York: Henry Holt.

James, W. (1982). An interview: Pragmatism—What it is. In H. S. Thayer (Ed.), *Pragmatism: The classic writings* (pp. 131–134). Indianapolis, IN: Hackett.

Janis, I. (1982). *Groupthink.* Boston: Houghton Mifflin.

Jensen, J. V. (1987). Rhetorical emphases of Taoism. *Rhetorica, 5,* 219–229.

Johannesen, R. L. (1990). *Ethics in human communication* (3rd ed.). Prospect Heights, IL: Waveland.

Johannesen, R. L. (2000). Nel Noddings's uses of Martin Buber's philosophy of dialogue. *Southern Communication Journal, 65,* 151–160.

Johnson, J. R. (1984). The role of inner speech in human communication. *Communication Education, 33,* 211–222.

Johnson, K. G., Senatore, J. J., Liebig, M. C., & Minor, G. (1974). *Nothing never happens.* Beverly Hills, CA: Glencoe.

Johnson, W. (1946). *People in quandaries.* New York: Harper.

Jones, S. (Ed.). (1994). *Cybersociety: Computer-mediated communication and community.* Thousand Oaks, CA: Sage.

Kalbfleisch, P. J., & Cody, M. J. (Eds.). (1995). *Gender, power, and communication in human relationships.* Hillsdale, NJ: Lawrence Erlbaum.

Kaplan, A. (1961). *The new world of philosophy.* New York: Vintage.

Kaplan, A. (1964). *The conduct of inquiry: Methodology for behavioral science.* San Francisco: Chandler.

Kaplan, S. J. (1990). Communication technology and society. In G. M. Phillips & J. T. Wood (Eds.), *Speech communication: Essays to commemorate the 75th anniversary of the Speech Communication Association* (pp. 205–234). Carbondale, IL: Southern Illinois University Press.

Katz, E., & Lazarsfeld, P. F. (1955). *Personal influence: The part played by people in the flow of mass communications.* New York: Free Press.

Katz, R. L. (1963). *Empathy: Its nature and uses.* New York: Free Press.

Keen, S. (1970). *To a dancing god.* New York: Harper.

Keller, E. F. (1985). *Reflections on gender and science.* New Haven, CT: Yale University Press.

Keller, P. W., & Brown, C. T. (1968). An interpersonal ethic for communication. *Journal of Communication, 18,* 73–81.

Kellner, D. (1995). *Media culture: Cultural studies, identity, and politics between the modern and the postmodern.* London: Routledge.

Kelly, G. A. (1963). *A theory of personality: The psychology of personal constructs.* New York: Norton.

Kelman, H. C. (1966). Three processes of social influence. In M. Jahoda & N. Warren (Eds.), *Attitudes* (pp. 151–162). Baltimore: Penguin.

Kennedy, G. (1963). *The art of persuasion in Greece.* Princeton, NJ: Princeton University Press.

Key, M. R. (1980). Preface. In M. R. Key (Ed.), *The relationship of verbal and nonverbal communication* (pp. vii–viii). The Hague: Mouton.

Kiesler, C., Collins, B., & Miller, N. (1969). *Attitude change: A critical analysis of theoretical approaches.* New York: Wiley.

Killenberg, G. M., & Anderson, R. (1989). *Before the story: Interviewing and communication skills for journalists.* New York: St. Martin's.

Kim, Y. Y. (1984). Searching for creative integration. In W. B. Gudykunst & Y. Y. Kim (Eds.), *Methods for intercultural communication research* (pp. 13–30). Newbury Park, CA: Sage.

Kim, Y. Y. (1988). *Communication and cross-cultural adaptation: An integrative theory.* Clevedon, UK: Multilingual Matters.

Kim, Y. Y. (1991). Intercultural communication competence. In S. Ting-Toomey & F. Korzenny (Eds.), *Cross-cultural interpersonal communication* (pp. 259–275). Newbury Park, CA: Sage.

Kincaid, D. L. (Ed.). (1987a). *Communication theory: Eastern and western perspectives.* San Diego: Academic.

Kincaid, D. L. (1987b). Communication east and west: Points of departure. In D. L. Kincaid (Ed.), *Communication theory: Eastern and western perspectives* (pp. 331–353). San Diego: Academic.

Kinneavy, J. L. (1980). *A theory of discourse.* New York: Norton. (Original work published 1971)

Klapp, O. E. (1962). *Heroes, villains, and fools: The changing American character.* Englewood Cliffs, NJ: Prentice-Hall.

Klapp, O. E. (1969). *Collective search for identity.* New York: Holt.

Klapp, O. E. (1978). *Opening and closing: Strategies of information adaptation in society.* Cambridge: Cambridge University Press.

Koestler, A. (1967). *The ghost in the machine.* New York: Macmillan.

Koffka, K. (1935). *Principles of gestalt psychology.* New York: Harcourt.

Kohn, L., & LaFargue, M. (Eds.) (1998). *Lao-tzu and the Tao-te-Ching.* Albany: State University of New York Press.

Koman, K. (1990, March 30). Oh, that mayor's mouth! *St. Louis Post-Dispatch,* pp. 1, 4.

Kramerae, C. (1981). *Women and men speaking: Frameworks for analysis.* Rowley, MA: Newbury.

Kramerae, C., & Treichler, P. A. (1990). Power relationships in the classroom. In S. L. Gabriel & I. Smithson (Eds.), *Gender in the classroom: Power and pedagogy* (pp. 41–59). Urbana: University of Illinois Press.

Kress, P. F. (1970). *Social science and the idea of process: The ambiguous legacy of Arthur F. Bentley.* Urbana: University of Illinois Press.

Krippendorf, K. (1989). On the ethics of constructing communication. In B. Dervin, L. Grossberg, B. J. O'Keefe, & E. Wartella (Eds.),

Rethinking communication: Vol. 1. Paradigm issues (pp. 66–96). Newbury Park, CA: Sage.

Kubie, L. S. (1961). *Neurotic distortion of the creative process.* New York: Noonday.

Kuhn, M. H., & McPartland, T. S. (1954). An empirical investigation of self-attitudes. *American Sociological Review, 19,* 68–76.

Kuhn, T. S. (1970). *The structure of scientific revolutions* (2nd ed.). Chicago: University of Chicago Press.

Laing, R. D. (1969). *Self and others* (2nd ed.). New York: Penguin.

Laing, R. D., Phillipson, H., & Lee, A. R. (1966). *Interpersonal perception: A theory and a method of research.* New York: Perennial Library.

Lakoff, G. (1987). *Women, fire, and dangerous things: What categories reveal about the mind.* Chicago: University of Chicago Press.

Lakoff, G., & Johnson, M. (1980). *Metaphors we live by.* Chicago: University of Chicago Press.

Lakoff, R. (1975). *Language and women's place.* New York: Harper.

Lakoff, R. T. (1990). *Talking power: The politics of language.* New York: Basic Books.

Lambeth, E. B. (1998). Public journalism as a democratic practice. In E. B. Lambeth, P. E. Meyer, & E. Thorson (Eds.), *Assessing public journalism* (pp. 15–35). Columbia, MO: University of Missouri Press.

Landow, G. P. (1992). *Hypertext: The convergence of contemporary critical theory and technology.* Baltimore: The Johns Hopkins University Press.

Langer, E. J. (1978). Rethinking the role of thought in social interaction. In J. H. Harvey, W. Ikes, & R. F. Kidd (Eds.), *New directions in attribution research* (Vol. 2). Hillsdale, NJ: Lawrence Erlbaum.

Langer, E. J. (1989). *Mindfulness.* Reading, MA: Addison-Wesley.

Langer, S. (1951). *Philosophy in a new key* (2nd ed.). New York: New American Library.

Lanham, R. A. (1993). *The electronic word: Democracy, technology, and the arts.* Chicago: University of Chicago Press Expanded Book (hypercard version).

Lasch, C. (1979). *The culture of narcissism: American life in an age of diminishing expectations.* New York: Warner.

Lawson, H. (1985). *Reflexivity: The post-modern predicament*. London: Hutchinson.

Lazarsfeld, P. F., Berelson, B., & Gaudet, H. (1948). *The people's choice*. New York: Columbia University Press.

Leary, T. (1957). *Interpersonal diagnosis of personality: A functional theory and methodology for personality evaluation*. New York: Ronald.

Leeds-Hurwitz, W. (1990). Notes on the history of intercultural communication: The Foreign Service Institute and the mandate for intercultural training. *Quarterly Journal of Speech, 76*, 262–281.

Leeds-Hurwitz, W. (1993). *Semiotics and communication: Signs, codes, cultures*. Hillsdale, NJ: Lawrence Erlbaum.

Legge, J. (Ed.). (1962). *The texts of Taoism* (Vol. 1). New York: Dover. (Original work published 1891)

Levant, R. F., & Shlien, J. M. (1984). *Client-centered therapy and the person-centered approach: New directions in theory, research, and practice*. New York: Praeger.

Lewin, K. (1951). *Field theory in social science: Selected theoretical papers*. New York: Harper.

Lievrouw, L. A., & Finn, T. A. (1990). Identifying the common dimensions of communication: The communication systems model. In B. D. Ruben & L. A. Lievrouw (Eds.), *Mediation, information, and behavior* (pp. 37–65). New Brunswick, NJ: Transaction.

Lincoln, Y. S., & Guba, E. G. (1985). *Naturalistic inquiry*. Beverly Hills, CA: Sage.

Lippmann, W. (1922). *Public opinion*. New York: Free Press.

Littlejohn, S. W. (1982). An overview of contributions to human communication theory from other disciplines. In F. E. X. Dance (Ed.), *Human communication theory* (pp. 243–285). New York: Harper.

Littlejohn, S. W. (1996). *Theories of human communication* (5th ed.). Belmont, CA: Wadsworth.

Llinas, R. (1987). "Mindness" as a functional state of the brain. In C. Blakemore & S. Greenfield (Eds.), *Mindwaves* (pp. 339–358). Oxford, UK: Basil Blackwell.

Logue, C. M., & Miller, E. F. (1996). Gap-bridging, interaction, and the province of mass communication. *Critical Studies in Mass Communication, 13*, 364–373.

Luft, J. (1970). *Group processes: An introduction to group dynamics* (2nd ed.). Palo Alto, CA: National Press Books.

Luria, A. R. (1961). *The role of speech in the regulation of normal and abnormal behavior*. New York: Liveright.

Lynch, J. J. (1977). *The broken heart: The medical consequences of loneliness*. New York: Basic Books.

Lynch, J. J. (1985). *The language of the heart: The human body in dialogue*. New York: Basic Books.

Lynn, S. (1990). A passage into critical theory. *College English, 52*, 258–271.

Lyotard, J.-F. (1984). *The postmodern condition: A report on knowledge* (G. Bennington & B. Massumi, Trans.). Minneapolis: University of Minnesota Press.

MacIntyre, A. (1984). *After virtue: A study in moral theory* (2nd ed.). Notre Dame, IN: University of Notre Dame Press.

Marshall, J. (1993). Viewing organizational communication from a feminist perspective: A critique and some offerings. In S. A. Deetz (Ed.), *Communication yearbook 16* (pp. 122–143). Newbury Park, CA: Sage.

Marvin, C. (1988). *When old technologies were new: Thinking about electric communication in the late nineteenth century*. New York: Oxford University Press.

Marwell, G., & Schmitt, D. R. (1967). Dimensions of compliance-gaining behavior: An empirical analysis. *Sociometry, 30*, 350–364.

Maslow, A. (1965). *Eupsychian management*. Homewood, IL: Irwin.

Mathison, M. (1997). Complicity in epistemology: Reinscribing the historical categories of "woman" through standpoint feminism. *Communication Theory, 7*, 149–161.

Matlon, R. J. (1992). *Index to journals in communication studies through 1990* (Vols. 1–2). Annandale, VA: Speech Communication Association.

McCarthy, T. (1990). Introduction. In J. Habermas, *Moral consciousness and communicative action* (C. Lenhardt & S. W. Nicholsen, Trans., pp. vii–xiv). Cambridge, MA: MIT Press.

McCombs, M. E., & Shaw, D. L. (1972). The agenda-setting function of the press. *Public Opinion Quarterly, 36*, 176–187.

McCroskey, J. C. (1998). *Why we communicate*

the ways we do: A communibiological perspective (Carroll C. Arnold distinguished lecture, NCA). Boston: Allyn & Bacon.

McCroskey, J. C., & Burgoon, M. (1974). Establishing predictors of latitude of acceptance-rejection and attitudinal intensity: A comparison of assumptions of social judgment and authoritarian personality theories. *Speech Monographs, 41,* 421–426.

McFarlane, R. W. (1992, January 5). The art of asking questions. *New York Times Book Review,* p. 31.

McHugh, P. (1968). *Defining the situation.* Indianapolis, IN: Bobbs-Merrill.

McLaughlin, M. L. (1984). *Conversation: How talk is organized.* Beverly Hills, CA: Sage.

McLuhan, M. (1962). *The Gutenberg galaxy.* Toronto: University of Toronto Press.

McLuhan, M. (1964). *Understanding media: The extensions of man.* New York: Signet.

McLuhan, M., & Fiore, Q. (1968). *War and peace in the global village.* New York: McGraw-Hill.

McPhail, M. L. (1994). *The rhetoric of racism.* Lanham, MD: University Press of America.

McQuail, D. (1997). Policy help wanted: Willing and able media culturalists please apply. In M. Ferguson & P. Golding (Eds.), *Cultural studies in question* (pp. 39–55). Thousand Oaks, CA: Sage.

McQuail, D., & Windahl, S. (1993). *Communication models for the study of mass communication* (2nd ed.). London: Longman.

Mead, G. H. (1934). *Mind, self and society: From the standpoint of a social behaviorist.* Chicago: University of Chicago Press.

Mead, G. H. (1956). *The social psychology of George Herbert Mead.* Chicago: University of Chicago Press.

Mehrabian, A. (1981). *Silent messages: Implicit communication of emotions and attitudes* (2nd ed.). Belmont, CA: Wadsworth.

Merritt, D. (1995). *Public journalism and public life: Why telling the news is not enough.* Hillsdale, NJ: Lawrence Erlbaum.

Meyrowitz, J. (1985). *No sense of place: The impact of electronic media on social behavior.* New York: Oxford University Press.

Meyrowitz, J. (1994) Medium theory. In D. Crowley & D. Mitchell (Eds.), *Communication theory today* (pp. 50–77). Stanford, CA: Stanford University Press.

Miller, G. A. (1967). *The psychology of communication: Seven essays.* Baltimore: Penguin.

Miller, G. R., & Boster, F. (1988). Persuasion in personal relationships. In S. W. Duck (Ed.), *Handbook of personal relationships* (pp. 275–288). New York: Wiley.

Mitchell, J. N. (1978). *Social exchange, dramaturgy and ethnomethodology: Toward a paradigmatic synthesis.* New York: Elsevier.

Moerman, M. (1988). *Talking culture: Ethnography and conversation analysis.* Philadelphia: University of Pennsylvania Press.

Moffitt, M. A. (1993). Articulating meaning: Reconceptions of the meaning process, fantasy/reality, and identity in leisure activities. *Communication Theory, 3,* 231–251.

Montagu, A. (1962). *The humanization of man: Our changing conception of human nature.* New York: Grove Press.

Montagu, A., & Matson, F. (1979). *The human connection.* New York: McGraw-Hill.

Montgomery, B. M., & Baxter, L. A. (Eds.). (1998). *Dialectical approaches in studying personal relationships.* Mahwah, NJ: Lawrenace Erlbaum.

Moon, D. G. (1996). Concepts of "culture": Implications for intercultural communication research. *Communication Quarterly, 44,* 70–84.

Mori, K. (1997). *Polite lies: On being a woman caught between cultures.* New York: Fawcett Books.

Morris, M., & Ogan, C. (1996). The Internet as mass medium. *Journal of Communication, 46*(1), 39–50.

Mortensen, C. D. (1972). *Communication: The study of human interaction.* New York: McGraw-Hill.

Motley, M. T. (1990). On whether one can(not) communicate: An examination via traditional communication postulates. *Western Journal of Speech Communication, 54,* 1–20.

Moyers, B. (1989). *A world of ideas.* New York: Doubleday.

Mulac, A., & Bradac, J. J. (1995). Women's styles in problem-solving interaction: Powerless, or simply feminine? In P. J. Kalbfleisch & M. J. Cody (Eds.) *Gender, power, and communication in human relationships* (pp. 83–104). Hillsdale, NJ: Lawrence Erlbaum.

Mumby, D. K. (1996). Feminism, postmodernism, and organizational communication studies: A critical reading. *Management Communication Quarterly, 9,* 259–295.

Murray, A. (1970). *The Omni-Americans.* New York: Vintage.

Negroponte, N. (1995). *Being digital.* New York: Vintage.

Noddings, N. (1984). *Caring: A feminine approach to ethics and moral education.* Berkeley: University of California Press.

Noelle-Neumann, E. (1984). *The spiral of silence: Public opinion—Our social skin.* Chicago: University of Chicago Press.

Nofsinger, R. E. (1989). Collaborating on context: Invoking alluded-to shared knowledge. *Western Journal of Speech Communication, 53,* 227–241.

Nofsinger, R. E. (1991). *Everyday conversation.* Newbury Park, CA: Sage.

O'Hair, D., Friedrich, G. W., Wiemann J. M., & Wiemann, M. O. (1994). *Competent communication.* New York: St. Martin's Press.

O'Keefe, D. J. (1975). Logical empiricism and the study of human communication. *Speech Monographs, 42,* 169–183.

O'Keefe, D. J. (1990). *Persuasion: Theory and research.* Newbury Park, CA: Sage.

Oliver, R. T. (1962). *Culture and communication.* Springfield, IL: Charles C Thomas.

Olson, S. R. (1994). Renewed alchemy: Science and humanism in communication epistemology. In F. L. Casmir (Ed.), *Building communication theories: A sociocultural approach* (pp. 49–85). Hillsdale, NJ: Lawrence Erlbaum.

O'Neill, D. (1990, March 30). Happy talk: Phils' Leyva stresses communication. *St. Louis Post-Dispatch,* p. 3D.

Ong, W. J. (1967). *The presence of the word: Some prolegomena for cultural and religious history.* New Haven, CT: Yale University Press.

Ong, W. J. (1982). *Orality and literacy: The technologizing of the word.* New York: Methuen.

Ong, W. J. (1983). *Ramus, method, and the decay of dialogue.* Cambridge, MA: Harvard University Press.

Orbe, M. P. (1996). Laying the foundation for co-cultural theory: An inductive approach to studying "non-dominant" communication strategies and the factors that influence them. *Communication Studies, 47,* 157–176.

Osgood, C. E., & Tannenbaum, P. H. (1955). The principle of congruity in the prediction of attitude change. *Psychological Review, 62,* 42–55.

O'Sullivan, T., Hartley, J., Saunders, D., Montgomery, M., & Fiske, J. (1994). *Key concepts in communication and cultural studies* (2nd ed.). New York: Routledge.

Pacanowsky, M. (1989). Creating and narrating organizational realities. In B. Dervin, L. Grossberg, B. O'Keefe, & E. Wartella (Eds.), *Rethinking communication: vol. 2. Paradigm exemplars* (pp. 250–257). Newbury Park, CA: Sage.

Pacanowsky, M., & O'Donnell-Trujillo, N. (1982). Communication and organizational cultures. *Western Journal of Speech Communication, 46,* 115–130.

Pacanowsky, M., & O'Donnell-Trujillo, N. (1983). Organizational communication as cultural performance. *Communication Monographs, 50,* 126–147.

Palmer, R. E. (1969). *Hermeneutics.* Evanston, IL: Northwestern University Press.

Palmgreen, P. (1984). Uses and gratifications: A theoretical perspective. In R. N. Bostrom (Ed.), *Communication yearbook 8* (pp. 20–55). Beverly Hills, CA: Sage.

Palmgreen, P., Wenner, L. A., & Rosengren, K. E. (1985). Uses and gratifications research: The past ten years. In K. E. Rosengren, L. A. Wenner, & P. Palmgreen (Eds.), *Media gratifications research: Current perspectives* (pp. 11–37). Beverly Hills, CA: Sage.

Pauly, J. (1999). Public journalism in international perspective. *Communication Research Trends, 19,* 4–17.

Pearce, W. B. (1989). *Communication and the human condition.* Carbondale: Southern Illinois University Press.

Pearce, W. B. (1994). *Interpersonal communication: Making social worlds.* New York: HarperCollins.

Pearce, W. B. (1998). On putting social justice in the discipline of communication and putting enriched concepts of communication in social justice research and practice. *Journal of Applied Communication Research, 26,* 272–278.

Pearce, W. B., & Cronen, V. E. (1980). *Communication, action and meaning: The creation of social realities.* New York: Praeger.

Pearce, W. B., & Foss, K. A. (1990). The historical context of communication as a science. In

G. L. Dahnke & G. W. Clatterbuck (Eds.), *Human communication: Theory and research*. Belmont, CA: Wadsworth.

Pearce, W. B., & Littlejohn, S. (1997). *Moral conflict: When social worlds collide*. Thousand Oaks, CA: Sage.

Pearce, W. B., & Pearce, K. (2000). Extending the theory of coordinated management of meaning (CMM) through a community dialogue process. *Communication Theory, 10,* 405–423.

Pearson, J. C., & Cooks, L. (1995). Gender and power. In Kalbfleisch, P. J., & Cody, M. J. (Eds.), *Gender, power, and communication in human relationships* (pp. 332–349). Hillsdale, NJ: Lawrence Erlbaum.

Pearson, J. C., Turner, L. H., & Todd-Mancillas, W. (1991). *Gender and communication* (2nd ed.). Dubuque, IA: Brown.

Peirce, C. S. (1931–1958). *Collected papers of Charles Sanders Peirce* (Vols. 1–6, C. Hartshorne & P. Weiss, Eds.; Vols. 7–8, A. W. Burks, Ed.). Cambridge, MA: Harvard University Press.

Perry, W. G., Jr. (1970). *Forms of intellectual and ethical development in the college years: A scheme*. New York: Holt.

Philipsen, G. (1995). The coordinated management of meaning theory of Pearce, Cronen, and associates. In D. P. Cushman & B. Kovačić (Eds.), *Watershed research traditions in human communication theory* (pp. 13–43). Albany: State University of New York Press.

Phillips, D. C. (1976). *Holistic thought in social science*. Stanford, CA: Stanford University Press.

Pilotta, J. J. (Ed.). (1982). *Interpersonal communication: Essays in phenomenology and hermeneutics*. Washington, DC: University Press of America.

Plato. (1927). *Plato: Selections* (R. Demos, Ed.). New York: Scribner.

Polanyi, M. (1962). *Personal knowledge: Towards a post-critical philosophy*. Chicago: University of Chicago Press.

Polanyi, M. (1967). *The tacit dimension*. Garden City, NY: Anchor.

Poole, M. S. (1990). Do we have any theories of group communication? *Communication Studies, 41,* 237–247.

Popper, K. (1980). Science: Conjectures and refutations. In E. D. Klemke, R. Holliger, & A. D. Kline (Eds.), *Introductory readings in the philosophy of science* (pp. 19–34). Buffalo, NY: Prometheus.

Popper, K. R. (1968). *The logic of scientific discovery* (2nd ed.). New York: Harper.

Poster, M. (1990). *The mode of information: Poststructuralism and social context*. Chicago: University of Chicago Press.

Poster, M. (1995). *The second media age*. Cambridge, UK: Polity Press.

Postman, N. (1985). *Amusing ourselves to death: Public discourse in the age of show business*. New York: Penguin.

Powers, J. H. (1995). On the intellectual structure of the human communication discipline. *Communication Education, 44,* 191–222.

Press, L. (1995). McLuhan meets the net. *Communications of the ACM, 38,* 15–20.

Putnam. L. L. (1989). Perspectives for research on group embeddedness in organizations. In S. S. King (Ed.), *Human communication as a field of study: Selected contemporary views* (pp. 163–182). Albany: State University of New York Press.

Putnam, L. L., & Pacanowsky, M. E. (Eds.). (1983). *Communication and organizations: An interpretive approach*. Beverly Hills, CA: Sage.

Putnam, R. D. (1995). Bowling alone: America's declining social capital. *Journal of Democracy, 6,* 65–76.

Putnam, R. D. (2000). *Bowling alone: The collapse and revival of American community*. New York: Simon & Schuster.

Rasmussen, K. (1976). A transactional perspective. In D. K. Darnell & W. Brockriede (Eds.), *Persons communicating* (pp. 29–35). Englewood Cliffs, NJ: Prentice-Hall.

Rawlins, W. K. (1992). *Friendship matters: Communication, dialectics, and the life course*. New York: Aldine de Gruyter.

Rawls, J. (1971). *A theory of justice*. Cambridge, MA: Harvard University Press.

Real, M. R. (1989). *Super media*. Newbury Park, CA: Sage.

Reardon, K. K. (1987). *Interpersonal communication: Where minds meet*. Belmont, CA: Wadsworth.

Redding, W. C. (1968). Human communication behavior in complex organizations: Some fallacies revisited. In C. E. Larson & F. E. X. Dance (Eds.), *Perspectives on communication*.

Milwaukee: University of Wisconsin Speech Communication Center.

Reddy, M. (1979). The conduit metaphor. In A. Ortony (Ed.), *Metaphor and thought*. Cambridge: Cambridge University Press.

Reid, L. (1990). *Speech teacher: A random narrative*. Annandale, VA: Speech Communication Association.

Rice, R. E., & Williams, F. (1984). Theories old and new: The study of new media. In R. E. Rice & Associates (Eds.), *The new media: Communication, research and technology* (pp. 55–80). Beverly Hills, CA: Sage.

Richards, M. C. (1973). *The crossing point: Selected talks and writings*. Middletown, CT: Wesleyan University Press.

Ricoeur, P. (1981). *Hermeneutics and the human sciences* (J. B. Thompson, Trans.). Cambridge: Cambridge University Press.

Roberts, C. V., & Watson, K. W. (Eds.). (1989). *Intrapersonal communication processes: Original essays*. New Orleans: SPECTRA.

Rogers, C. R. (1959). A theory of therapy, personality, and interpersonal relationships, as developed in the client-centered framework. In S. Koch (Ed.), *Psychology: A study of a science: Vol. 3. Formulations of the person and social context* (pp. 184–256). New York: McGraw-Hill.

Rogers, C. R. (1961). *On becoming a person: A therapist's view of psychotherapy*. Boston: Houghton-Mifflin.

Rogers, C. R. (1980). *A way of being*. Boston: Houghton-Mifflin.

Rogers, E. M. (1994). *A history of communication study: A biographical approach*. New York: Free Press.

Rogers, E. M. (1995). *Diffusion of innovations* (4th ed.). New York: Free Press.

Rogers, E. M., & Chaffee, S. H. (1993). The past and the future of communication study: Convergence or divergence? *Journal of Communication, 43*(4), 125–131.

Rogers, M. F. (1983). *Sociology, ethnomethodology, and experience: A phenomenological critique*. Cambridge: Cambridge University Press.

Rokeach, M. (1960). *The open and closed mind: Investigations into the nature of belief systems and personality systems*. New York: Basic Books.

Roloff, M. (1981). *Interpersonal communication: A social exchange approach*. Beverly Hills, CA: Sage.

Rommetveit, R. (1987). Meaning, context, and control: Convergent trends and controversial issues in current social-scientific research on human cognition and communication. *Inquiry, 30,* 77–99.

Rosaldo, R. (1989). *Culture and truth: The remaking of social analysis*. Boston: Beacon.

Rosen, J. (1994). Making things more public: On the political responsibility of the media intellectual. *Critical Studies in Mass Communication, 11,* 363–388.

Rosen, J. (1999). *What are journalists for?* New Haven, CT: Yale University Press.

Rosenau, P. M. (1992). *Post-modernism and the social sciences: Insights, inroads, and intrusions*. Princeton, NJ: Princeton University Press.

Rosenblatt, L. M. (1978). *The reader, the text, the poem: The transactional theory of the literary work*. Carbondale: Southern Illinois University Press.

Rosenthal, R., & Jacobson, L. (1968). *Pygmalion in the classroom: Teacher expectation and pupils' intellectual development*. New York: Holt.

Ross, S. (1996, November 11). More multinational firms sending execs abroad. *St. Louis Post-Dispatch,* p. 18BP.

Ruben, B. D., & Kim, J. Y. (Eds.). (1975). *General systems theory and human communication*. Rochelle Park, NJ: Hayden.

Rudner, R. S. (1966). *Philosophy of social science*. Englewood Cliffs, NJ: Prentice-Hall.

Ruesch, J., & Bateson, G. (1968). *Communication: The social matrix of psychiatry* (2nd ed.). New York: Norton.

Rybacki, K., & Rybacki, D. (1991). *Communication criticism: Approaches and genres*. Belmont, CA: Wadsworth.

Sackmann, S. A. (1990). Managing organizational culture: Dreams and possibilities. In J. A. Anderson (Ed.), *Communication yearbook 13* (pp. 114–148). Newbury Park, CA: Sage.

Said, E. W. (1978). *Orientalism*. New York: Pantheon.

Said, E. W. (1981). *Covering Islam*. New York: Pantheon.

Said, E. W. (1993). *Culture and imperialism*. New York: Vintage.

Sanchez-Tranquilino, M., & Tagg, J. (1992). The pachuco's flayed hide: Mobility, identity, and buenas garras. In L. Grossberg, C. Nelson, & P. Treichler (Eds.), *Cultural studies* (pp. 556–566). New York: Routledge.

Saussure, F. de (1966). *Course in general linguistics* (W. Baskin, Trans.). New York: McGraw-Hill.

Schauer, F. (1982). *Free speech: A philosophical enquiry*. Cambridge: Cambridge University Press.

Scheflen, A. E. (1974). *How behavior means*. Garden City, NY: Anchor Books.

Schneider, D. E., & Beaubien, R. A. (1996). A naturalistic investigation of compliance-gaining strategies employed by doctors in medical interviews. *Southern Communication Journal, 61,* 332–341.

Schön, D. A. (1983). *The reflective practitioner: How professionals think in action*. New York: Basic Books.

Schroll, C. J. (1999). Theorizing the flip side of civic journalism: Democratic citizenship and ethical readership. *Communication Theory, 9,* 321–345.

Schultz, D. (1977). *Growth psychology: Models of the healthy personality*. New York: Van Nostrand Reinhold.

Schultz, E. A. (1990). *Dialogue at the margins: Whorf, Bakhtin, and linguistic relativity*. Madison: University of Wisconsin Press.

Schumacher, E. F. (1979). *A guide for the perplexed*. New York: Perennial Library.

Schutz, A. (1967). *The phenomenology of the social world*. Evanston, IL: Northwestern University Press.

Schutz, W. C. (1966). *The interpersonal underworld*. Palo Alto, CA: Science and Behavior Books.

Scott, R. L. (1977). Communication as an intentional, social system. *Human Communication Research, 3,* 258–268.

Searle, J. R. (1969). *Speech acts: An essay in the philosophy of language*. Cambridge: Cambridge University Press.

Seibold, D. R. (1998). Groups and organizations: Premises and perspectives. In J. S. Trent (Ed.), *Communication: Views from the helm for the 21st century* (pp. 162–168). Boston: Allyn & Bacon.

Shannon, C., & Weaver, W. (1949). *The mathematical theory of communication*. Urbana: University of Illinois Press.

Shimanoff, S. B. (1980). *Communication rules: Theory and research*. Beverly Hills, CA: Sage.

Shotter, J. (1993). *Conversational realities*. London: Sage.

Signorielli, N., & Morgan, M. (1990). Preface. In N. Signorielli & M. Morgan (Eds.), *Cultivation analysis: New directions in media effects research*. Newbury Park, CA: Sage.

Simons, H. W. (1976). *Persuasion: Understanding, practice, and analysis*. Reading, MA: Addison-Wesley.

Simpson, C. (1996). Elisabeth Noelle-Neumann's "spiral of silence" and the historical context of communication theory. *Journal of Communication, 46*(3), 149–173.

Singer, P. (1986). Morality, egoism and the prisoner's dilemma. In C. H. Sommers (Ed.), *Right and wrong: Basic readings in ethics* (pp. 192–199). New York: Harcourt.

Skinner, B. F. (1953). *Science and human behavior*. New York: Free Press.

Slack, J. D. (1989). Contextualizing technology. In B. Dervin, L. Grossberg, B. J. O'Keefe, & E. Wartella (Eds.), *Rethinking communication: Vol. 2. Paradigm exemplars* (pp. 329–345), Newbury Park, CA: Sage.

Slack, J. D. (1996). The theory and method of articulation in cultural studies. In D. Morley & K.-H. Chen (Eds.), *Stuart Hall: Critical dialogues in cultural studies* (pp. 112–127). New York: Routledge.

Smith, A. L. [M. K. Asante] (1973). *Transracial communication*. Englewood Cliffs, NJ: Prentice-Hall.

Smith, D. H., & Pettegrew, L. S. (1986). Mutual persuasion as a model for doctor–patient communication. *Theoretical Medicine, 7,* 127–146.

Smith, M. J. (1988). *Contemporary communication research methods*. Belmont, CA: Wadsworth.

Snyder, I. (1996). *Hypertext*. Melbourne, Australia: University of Melbourne Press.

Sokolov, A. N. (1972). *Inner speech and thought* (G. T. Onischenko, Trans.). New York: Plenum Press.

Solmsen, F. (1954). Introduction. In Aristotle, *Rhetoric and poetics* (W. R. Roberts & I. Bywater, Trans., pp. v–xxii). New York: Modern Library.

Sommer, R. (1969). *Personal space: The behavioral basis of design*. Englewood Cliffs, NJ: Prentice-Hall.

Sommer, R. (1974). *Tight spaces: Hard architecture and how to humanize it.* Englewood Cliffs, NJ: Prentice-Hall.

Speech Communication Association. (1995). *Pathways to careers in communication* (4th ed.). Annandale, VA: Author.

Spitzberg, B. H., & Cupach, W. R. (1984). *Interpersonal communication competence.* Beverly Hills, CA: Sage.

Stamp, G. H., & Knapp, M. L. (1990). The construct of intent in interpersonal communication. *Quarterly Journal of Speech, 76,* 282–299.

Stamp, G. H., Vangelisti, A. L., & Knapp, M. L. (1994). Criteria for developing and assessing theories of interpersonal communication. In F. L. Casmir (Ed.), *Building communication theories: A socio/cultural approach* (pp. 167–208). Hillsdale, NJ: Lawrence Erlbaum.

Stephenson, W. (1967). *The play theory of mass communication.* Chicago: University of Chicago Press.

Stewart, J. (1983). Interpretive listening: An alternative to empathy. *Communication Education, 32,* 379–391.

Stewart, J. (1990). *Bridges not walls* (5th ed.). New York: McGraw-Hill.

Strate, L. (1999). The varieties of cyberspace: Problems in definition and delimitation. *Western Journal of Communication, 63,* 382–412.

Strate, L., Jacobson, R., & Gibson, S. B. (Eds.) (1996). *Communication and cyberspace: Social interaction in an electronic environment.* Cresskill, NJ: Hampton Press.

Strauss, A. (1956). Introduction. In G. H. Mead, *The social psychology of George Herbert Mead* (A. Strauss, Ed., pp. iv–xvi). Chicago: University of Chicago Press.

Streff, C. R. (1984). The concept of inner speech and its implications for an integrated language arts curriculum. *Communication Education, 33,* 223–230.

Strine, M. S. (1997). Cultural diversity and the politics of inquiry: Response to Mathison and McPhail. *Communication Theory, 7,* 178–185.

Stubbs, M. (1983). *Discourse analysis: The sociolinguistic analysis of natural language.* Chicago: University of Chicago Press.

Sudnow, D. (1978). *Ways of the hand: The organization of improvised conduct.* Cambridge, MA: Harvard University Press.

Tannen, D. (1989). *Talking voices: Repetition, dialogue, and imagery in conversational discourse.* Cambridge: Cambridge University Press.

Tannen, D. (1990). *You just don't understand: Women and men in conversation.* New York: Morrow.

Taylor, J. R. (1993). *Rethinking the theory of organizational communication: How to read an organization.* Norwood, NJ: Ablex.

Taylor, J. R. (1995). Shifting from a heteronomous to an autonomous worldview of organizational communication: Communication theory on the cusp. *Communication Theory, 5,* 1–35.

Taylor, J. R., Cooren, F., Giroux, N., & Robichaud, D. (1996). The communicational basis of organization: Between the conversation and the text. *Communication Theory, 6,* 1–39.

Taylor, M. C., & Saarinen, E. (1994). *Imagologies: Media philosophy.* London: Routledge.

Tehranian, M. (1988). Communication theory and Islamic perspectives. In W. Dissanayake (Ed.), *Communication theory: The Asian perspective* (pp. 190–203). Singapore: Asian Mass Communication Research and Information Centre.

Terkel, S. (1981). *American dreams: Lost and found.* New York: Ballantine.

Thayer, L. (1968). *Communication and communication systems.* Homewood, IL: Richard D. Irwin.

Theodorson, G. A., & Theodorson, A. G. (1969). *Modern dictionary of sociology.* New York: Thomas Y. Crowell.

Thibaut, J. W., & Kelley, H. H. (1959). *The social psychology of groups.* New York: Wiley.

Thomas, L. (1974). *The lives of a cell.* New York: Viking.

Thomas, L. (1983). *Late night thoughts on listening to Mahler's ninth symphony.* New York: Viking.

Toch, H., & MacLean, M. S., Jr. (1962). Perception, communication, and educational research: A transactional view. *Communication Review, 10,* 55–77.

Toch, H. & Smith, H. C. (Eds.). (1968). *Social perception.* Princeton, NJ: Van Nostrand.

Todorov, T. (1984). *Mikhail Bakhtin: The dialogical principle* (W. Godzich, Trans.). Minneapolis: University of Minnesota Press.

Triandis, H. C. (1994). *Culture and social behavior*. New York: McGraw-Hill.

Turkle, S. (1995). *Life on the screen: Identity in the age of the Internet*. New York: Simon & Schuster.

Turner, V. W. (1986). Dewey, Dilthey, and drama: An essay in the anthropology of experience. In V. W. Turner & E. M. Bruner (Eds.), *The anthropology of experience* (pp. 33–44). Urbana: University of Illinois Press.

Ullmann, S. (1966). Semantic universals. In J. H. Greenberg (Ed.), *Universals of language* (2nd ed., pp. 217–262). Cambridge, MA: MIT Press.

Vangelisti, A. L., Knapp, M. L., & Daly, J. A. (1990). Conversational narcissism. *Communication Monographs, 57,* 251–274.

Vivian, B. G., & Wilcox, J. R. (2000). Compliance communication in home health care: A mutually reciprocal process. *Qualitative Health Research, 10,* 103–116.

Vygotsky, L. S. (1962). *Thought and language* (E. Hanfmann & G. Vakar, Trans.). Cambridge, MA: MIT Press.

Wallace, K. R. (1955). An ethical basis of communication. *The Speech Teacher, 4,* 1–9.

Wallace, K. R. (1963). The substance of rhetoric: Good reasons. *Quarterly Journal of Speech, 49,* 239–249.

Walters, M., Carter, E., Papp, P., & Silverstein, O. (1988). *The invisible web*. New York: Guilford.

Walther, J. B. (1992). Interpersonal effects in computer-mediated interaction: A relational perspective. *Communication Research, 19*(1), 52–90.

Walther, J. B. (1993). Impression development in computer-mediated interaction. *Western Journal of Communication, 57,* 381–398.

Walther, J. B. (1996). Computer-mediated communication: Impersonal, interpersonal, and hyperpersonal interaction. *Communication Research, 23,* 3–43.

Wann, T. W. (Ed.). (1964). *Behaviorism and phenomenology: Contrasting bases for modern psychology*. Chicago: University of Chicago Press.

Warnke, G. (1987). *Gadamer: Hermeneutics, tradition, and reason*. Stanford, CA: Stanford University Press.

Wartella, E. (1997). *The context of television violence (SCA Carroll C. Arnold distinguished lecture)*. Boston: Allyn & Bacon.

Watts, A. (1975). *Tao: The watercourse way*. New York: Pantheon.

Watzlawick, P. (1984). Self-fulfilling prophecies. In P. Watzlawick (Ed.), *The invented reality: How do we know what we believe we know? (Contributions to constructivism)* (pp. 95–116). New York: Norton.

Watzlawick, P., Beavin, J. H., & Jackson, D. D. (1967). *Pragmatics of human communication: A study of interactional patterns, pathologies, and paradoxes*. New York: Norton.

Watzlawick, P., & Weakland, J. H. (Eds.). (1977). *The interactional view: Studies at the Mental Research Institute, Palo Alto 1965–74*. New York: Norton.

Watzlawick, P., Weakland, J., & Fisch, R. (1974). *Change: Principles of problem formation and problem resolution*. New York: Norton.

Weaver, R. M. (1971). Language is sermonic. In R. Johannesen (Ed.), *Contemporary theories of rhetoric: Selected readings* (pp. 163–179). New York: Harper.

Weber, M. (1946). *From Max Weber: Essays in sociology* (H. Gerth & C. Wright Mills, Eds.). New York: Oxford University Press.

Weick, K. E. (1983). Organizational communication: Toward a research agenda. In L. L. Putnam & M. E. Pacanowsky (Eds.), *Communication and organizations: An interpretive approach* (pp. 13–29). Beverly Hills, CA: Sage.

Weick, K. (1995). *Sensemaking in organizations*. Newbury Park, CA: Sage.

Weitz, S. (Ed.). (1974). *Nonverbal communication: Readings with commentary*. New York: Oxford University Press.

Wenner, L. A. (1985). Transaction and media gratifications research. In K. E. Rosengren, L. A. Wenner, & P. Palmgreen (Eds.), *Media gratifications research: Current perspectives* (pp. 73–94). Beverly Hills, CA: Sage.

Wertsch, J. V. (1991). *Voices of the mind: A sociocultural approach to mediated action*. Cambridge, MA: Harvard University Press.

West, C. (1993). *Keeping faith: Philosophy and race in America*. New York: Routledge.

Westley, B. H., & MacLean, M. S., Jr. (1957). A conceptual model for mass communication research. *Journalism Quarterly, 34,* 31–38.

Wheelis, A. (1976). *How people change*. New York: Perennial Library. (Original work published 1973)

Whitehead, A. N. (1930). *Process and reality: An essay in cosmology.* New York: Macmillan.

Wilson, S. R. (1998). Introduction to the special issue on seeking and resisting compliance: The vitality of compliance-gaining research. *Communication Studies, 49,* 273–275.

Whorf, B. L. (1956). *Language, thought, and reality* (J. B. Carroll, Ed.). Cambridge, MA: MIT Press.

Wiemann, J. M., Takai, J., Ota, H., & Wiemann, M. O. (1997). A relational model of communication competence. In B. Kovačić (Ed.), *Emerging theories of human communication* (pp. 25–44). Albany: State University of New York Press.

Williams, R. (1976). *Keywords: A vocabulary of culture and society.* New York: Oxford University Press.

Williams, R. (1981). *The sociology of culture.* New York: Schocken Books.

Wilmot, W. W. (1971). Ego-involvement: A confusing variable in speech communication research. *Quarterly Journal of Speech, 57,* 429–436.

Windahl, S., & Signitzer, B., with Olson, J. T. (1992). *Using communication theory: An introduction to planned communication.* London: Sage.

Wittgenstein, L. (1953). *Philosophical investigations* (Trans. G. E. M. Anscombe). Oxford, UK: Basil Blackwell.

Wolf, G. (1996, January). The wisdom of Saint Marshall, the holy fool. *Wired,* 121–125, 182, 184.

Wolman, B. B. (Ed.). (1973). *Dictionary of behavioral science.* New York: Van Nostrand Reinhold.

Wood, J. T. (1982). Communication and relational culture: Bases for the study of human relationships. *Communication Quarterly, 30,* 75–83.

Wood, J. T. (1995). *Relational communication.* Belmont, CA: Wadsworth.

Wood, J. T. (Ed.). (1996). *Gendered relationships.* Mountain View, CA: Mayfield.

Wood, J. T. (1999). *Communication theories in action* (2nd ed.). Belmont, CA: Wadsworth.

Wood, J. T., & Cox, R. (1993). Rethinking critical voice: Materiality and situated knowledges. *Western Journal of Communication, 57,* 278–287.

Work, W., & Jeffrey, R. C. (Eds.). (1989). *The past is prologue.* Annandale, VA: Speech Communication Association.

Yancey, W. L. (1977). Architecture, interaction, and social control: The case of a large-scale public housing project. In W. E. Arnold & J. L. Buley (Eds.), *Urban communication: Survival in the city* (pp. 65–81). Cambridge, MA: Winthrop.

Young, I. M. (1990). *Justice and the politics of difference.* Princeton, NJ: Princeton University Press.

Young, J. Z. (1978). *Programs of the brain.* Oxford: Oxford University Press.

Zhang, L. (1988). The myth of the other: China in the eyes of the west. *Critical Inquiry, 15,* 108–131.

Zukav, G. (1979). *The dancing wu li masters: An overview of the new physics.* New York: Morrow.

Index

389

Acknowledgments

H. L. Goodall, Jr. Excerpt from page 29 in *Living in the Rock 'n Roll Mystery*. Copyright © 1991 by Board of Trustees, Southern Illinois University.

R. Llinas. Excerpt from pp. 351–352 in *Mindwaves* by C. Blakemore and S. Greenfield, eds. Copyright © 1987 Blackwell Publishers. Reprinted with permission.

G. H. Mead. Excerpts from pp. 71, 90, and 364 in *Mind, Self & Society*. Copyright © 1934 University of Chicago Press. Reprinted with permission.

Theory Extension: "The Cultural Impact of Contexting." Adapted material from pp. 8, 11 in *Hidden Differences* by Edward T. Hall and Mildred Reed Hall. Copyright © 1987 by Edward T. Hall and Mildred Reed Hall. Reviewing Key Ideas: "Hall's Context Distinctions for Cultures." Adapted material from *Beyond Culture* by Edward T. Hall. Copyright © 1976, 1981 by Edward T. Hall. Used by permission of Doubleday, a division of Random House, Inc.